John Ray
Dr. William Ray

Mac OS® X Maximum Security

201 West 103rd Street, Indianapolis, Indiana 46290

Mac OS® X Maximum Security

International Standard Book Number: 0-672-32381-8

Library of Congress Catalog Card Number: 2001098212

Printed in the United States of America

First Printing: May 2003

06 05 04 03 4 3 2 1

Trademarks

Warning and Disclaimer

Bulk Sales

Sams Publishing offers excellent discounts on this book when ordered in quantity for bulk purchases or special sales. For more information, please contact:

U.S. Corporate and Government Sales
1-800-382-3419
corpsales@pearsontechgroup.com

For sales outside of the U.S., please contact:

International Sales
+1-317-581-3793
international@pearsontechgroup.com

Acquisitions Editor
Shelley Johnston

Development Editor
Damon Jordan

Managing Editor
Charlotte Clapp

Project Editor
Elizabeth Finney

Copy Editor
Margo Catts

Indexer
Ken Johnson

Proofreader
Eileen Dennie

Technical Editor
Jessica Chapel
Michael Kirkpatrick
Brian Tiemann

Team Coordinator
Vanessa Evans

Designer
Gary Adair

Page Layout
Kelly Maish

Contents at a Glance

Table of Contents

Part IV Prevention, Detection, and Reaction to Attacks: Health Care and Checkups for Your Machine

About the Authors

John Ray is an award-winning developer and technology consultant with more than 17 years of programming and network administration experience. He has worked on projects for the FCC, The Ohio State University, Xerox, and the State of Florida, as well as serving as IT Director for a Columbus, Ohio–based design and application development company. John currently serves as Senior System Developer/Engineer for The Ohio State University Extension and provides network security and intrusion detection services for clients across the state and country. His first experience in security was an experimental attempt to crack a major telecom company. Although he was successful, the resulting attention from individuals in trench coats made him swear off working on the "wrong side" of the keyboard forever.

John has written or contributed to more than 12 titles currently in print, including *Mac OS X Unleashed* and *Maximum Linux Security*.

Dr. William Ray is a mathematician turned computer scientist turned biophysicist who has gravitated to the field of bioinformatics for its interesting synergy of logic, hard science, and human-computer-interface issues. A longtime Macintosh and Unix enthusiast, Will has owned Macs since 1985, and has worked with Unix since 1987. Prior to switching his professional focus to the biological sciences, Will spent five years as a Unix programmer developing experimental interfaces to online database systems. He left this position when his desktop workstation was cracked, then used to attack other businesses' computers. The incompetence of his employer's system administrators resulted in his being accused of perpetrating the attacks, and a series of visits from the men in trenchcoats, nice suits, and dark glasses for him as well. As a result, Will has developed an enduring disgust for employers, system administrators, and users who don't take system security, and their responsibilities with respect to it, seriously.

Shortly after migrating to biophysics, Will developed a Macintosh and Unix-based computational biology/graphics laboratory and training center for The Ohio State University's College of Biological Sciences. At the facility, which he managed for five years, Will introduced hundreds of students and faculty to Unix, and provided training and assistance in the development of productive computing skills on the paired Macintosh and Unix platforms.

Will is currently an Assistant Professor of Pediatrics at the Columbus Children's Research Institute, Children's Hospital in Columbus, Ohio, and the Department of Pediatrics, The Ohio State University, where he is studying tools that work at the interface between humans, computers, and information, and working to build a core computational research and training facility for his institute.

Contributing Author

Joan Ray is a Unix system administrator and Webmaster for the College of Biological Sciences at The Ohio State University. Joan has a degree in French from OSU, and is working toward additional degrees in Japanese and Geology.

Exposure to Apple's Power Macintosh computers at SIGGRAPH '93 transformed Joan from an unenthusiastic workplace-user of DOS to a devoted Macintosh hobbyist. In 1997, when her husband left the college's computing facility to concentrate on his doctoral studies, Joan decided to apply to manage the facility. To her surprise, the interview committee hired her as the new administrator, and Joan began her training as a Unix system administrator. With her husband as the trainer, it was a rather intensive training period. There was no rest, even at home.

Now, when she is not helping write computing books, Joan is administering a cluster of SGI and Sun Unix workstations and servers, helping and providing training for users with Unix, Classic Mac OS, and Mac OS X questions, and serving as college Webmaster.

Dedication

This book is dedicated to Famotidine and Ibuprofen. Although they are hardly ever mentioned by authors, they are responsible for the successful and painless completion of many books, including Mac OS X Maximum Security.

Acknowledgments

Many thanks to the helpful people at Sams Publishing who made this book possible, and who helped to ensure the quality and accuracy of the text. Our assorted editors, Shelley Johnston, Damon Jordan, Brian Tiemann, Elizabeth Finney, and Margo Catts have been instrumental in producing an accurate text, accessible to a wide range of Mac users with varying levels of security experience.

Special thanks are also due to The Ohio State University's Network Security Group, and particularly Steve Romig and Mowgli Assor, for their ongoing development and promotion of best practices for keeping Unix secure.

We Want to Hear from You!

As the reader of this book, *you* are our most important critic and commentator. We value your opinion and want to know what we're doing right, what we could do better, what areas you'd like to see us publish in, and any other words of wisdom you're willing to pass our way.

You can email or write me directly to let me know what you did or didn't like about this book—as well as what we can do to make our books stronger.

Please note that I cannot help you with technical problems related to the topic of this book, and that due to the high volume of mail I receive, I might not be able to reply to every message.

When you write, please be sure to include this book's title and author as well as your name and phone or email address. I will carefully review your comments and share them with the author and editors who worked on the book.

Email: networking@samspublishing.com

Mail: Mark Taber
Associate Publisher
Sams Publishing
201 West 103rd Street
Indianapolis, IN 46290 USA

Reader Services

For more information about this book or others from Sams Publishing, visit our Web site at `www.samspublishing.com`. Type the ISBN (excluding hyphens) or the title of the book in the Search box to find the book you're looking for.

Introduction

Computer security—who would ever have thought that Macintosh users would have to worry about computer security? Macs were the computer for "the rest of us"—for the folks who didn't want to have to read complicated manuals, learn complicated commands, or worry about complicated technical subjects. Apple promised us computers that would get out of our way and let us do our jobs, enjoy our hobbies, or do whatever else we wanted.

For years Apple delivered. For years, Macs were the easiest machines to use. From a security standpoint, they might as well have been toaster ovens: They didn't have a shred of security built in, and didn't need it either, because there wasn't a thing you could do to compromise a toaster oven. But we, the users, weren't satisfied. We didn't want toaster ovens. We wanted more: more power, more functionality, more accessibility, more software. We heard industry buzzwords like "preemptive multitasking" and "protected virtual memory," and we wanted our Macs to have these nifty new features. Industry pundits and the media made fun of Macs because of their "backwards" OS. Worse, after that other big OS manufacturer finally figured out that users wanted mice and graphical user interfaces, they also started working on adding other advanced OS features to their systems. We heard the taunts and shouted for Apple to give us more. How dare that other OS vendor make a system that could legitimately claim to be "almost as good as a Mac"? Worse, how could their users actually get to enjoy features that were more advanced than what we had on our Macs?

Apple listened, better than some of us hoped, better than many of us expected. Now we, the users, have to live with the consequences of getting what we've asked for. It's most definitely not all bad. We've once again got, hands down, the best OS around, and we've got so much more power and potential available that it will be a long time before we should need to think about another major revision of the OS. But, as they say in the movies, with great power comes great responsibility. The price of the modern operating system features that were requested, and that Apple has provided, is that these features are much more easily abused and misused than the previous versions of Mac OS, and must be more carefully defended. As citizens of the modern globally connected Internet, we've a responsibility to prevent that abuse and misuse of our machines, both for our own protection and for the protection of our networked friends and neighbors.

The good news is that Apple seems to see the wisdom in following a time-tested security model borrowed from the same BSD/Unix source as the underpinnings of Mac OS X. Unlike other OS vendors who loudly shout "You are secure!" to their users while selling them products with intentionally designed-in security holes, Apple appears to be encouraging you to make your computer secure, and to be putting the tools and information in your hands to test, verify, and maintain that security. If you do nothing more than install Apple-recommended software updates, and stay away from certain troublesome applications, you'll probably be more secure than the vast majority of computer users. You might not enjoy your previous toaster oven–like invulnerability, but so far, Apple's doing the right things, the right way. In this environment, the job of this book is to introduce you to security topics that Apple can't conveniently cover (such as how to mitigate the additional threat that simply running a more powerful operating system brings to the machine), and to teach you as much as possible about the computing and security culture you've suddenly been thrust into as a (willing or unwilling) Unix user.

Many of you reading this may not initially think that there could be anything remotely interesting about keeping your computer secure, and are probably reading this hoping for a collection of "do this, click that, and you're secure" recipes. Unfortunately, it's not that easy. It now takes a bit more work to protect your computer and network so that you can use them and so that others can't use them for mischief. The intent of this book is to make it as easy as possible for you, and give you every possible bit of recipe-like help, but Unix security requires a certain way of thinking, which isn't something you can approach as you would a cookbook. Wrapped around the recipes provided here is the much more important information that will let you see how the vulnerability came about and why the recipe solves the problem. The real thing you should focus on is developing an understanding the fundamental design flaws and other problems that allow the problems to exist in the first place. By understanding these, you will also be able to see where similar undiscovered problems might occur in other software or OS features, and it is this understanding and insight that will allow you to make your computing environment secure.

Sometimes the tone may seem pedantic, but this is because we really do want you to learn to "Think Secure." Too many computer users either take their OS vendor's hollow promises of security seriously or consider it a useless topic to be concerned about. You, however, are Mac users—you're better than that. A large part of the satisfaction of writing this book is the knowledge that during the daily bouts of cursing filtering from computing staff offices regarding idiot computer users who refuse to take security seriously, you aren't going to be one of the ones they're cursing about.

This book is divided into four conceptual sections. The first three cover the concept of computing security from different angles, and the fourth outlines tools and principles that broadly apply across the scope of computing security. The first section focuses on security principles, philosophy, and the basics that you need to know to develop the skill of thinking secure. In this section you can learn everything that you actually need to know about security—essentially *develop the instinct to know when to be worried, and about what,* and *have the sense to act on your concerns*. The second section covers the basic types of attacks and systematic security flaws that are possible. Most of these attacks or flaws are applicable to a great number of pieces of software and areas of the operating system. In this section, you'll fill in the gaps in your understanding, in case you aren't naturally paranoid enough to see these after reading the first section. The third section of the book addresses specific applications and the vulnerabilities you'll find in them. Although this book covers those areas and applications that are the source of the most significant flaws, these should be considered to be representative of general security issues with all similar applications. The discussion of specific application vulnerabilities in the final section should serve to further reinforce your understanding of the ways that the security principles and philosophy outlined in the first section apply to the types of attacks and flaws in the second and result in the variety of vulnerabilities seen in the third. The final section covers computing security tools, both in the specific sense of certain tools that can be broadly applied across the application domains that have been previously discussed, and in the general sense of the types of tools and capabilities that you should be searching for when trying to find good solutions to security problems.

If you've a mind like a steel trap, and a good technical grounding, the first and last sections may be all the book you need. If you're one of us mere mortals, it may take a bit more time for the import of the implications from the first section to sink in. That's what the second and third sections are for.

In another fashion, you may think of the first section as laying a groundwork for the understanding of computing security. The second section segments this ground longitudinally into types of attacks and flaws, and the third overlays this with a grid of applications, highlighting the flaws that exist in each. The fourth section then provides both some specific tools, and an overview of the general field of broad-application security tools, that you can use to blanket large areas of this groundwork with various layers of protections. As new types of flaws are discovered and new attacks are invented, and as you consider applications other than what we've covered here, you'll need to further subdivide and extend the groundwork, but the skills you've developed learning to think about the issues covered here should allow you to do this easily.

If you're a creative problem-solving type, or like mind teaser-type puzzles, you might even find that this can be fun. It's as competitive as any multiplayer strategy game, and by virtue of the networked nature of many security issues, it pits you against a nearly unlimited arena of competitors. As long as you can balance the need to take it quite seriously with not letting it start to feel like work, fixing computer security can be a quite gratifying pastime or occupation.

If your computer security has already been compromised, stay calm and proceed directly to Chapter 20, "Disaster Planning and Recovery," and also swing by the security section on `www.macosxunleashed.com` with your specific security issues. We want you to learn to keep your computer secure, but the assumptions of the rest of the book are that your computer is starting from an uncompromised state. If your security has been breeched, you need to repair that breech now and repel the intrusion. After you have things under control, then you can come back and learn how to *keep* them under control.

Finally, please realize while you read this that there is no such thing as a complete book regarding computer security. Because of the breakneck speed of the battle between the hoodlums who would do your computer harm, and computing security hobbyists and professionals, this text, like every other computing security book, will have outdated information in it before it even hits the bookstore shelves. Likewise, there will be new attacks and vulnerabilities that we haven't heard about that are in active play on the Internet before you've finished reading this introduction.

There are also a number of security topics that have undoubtedly been given, through page-count concerns, perceived audience interest, or sometimes simply due to where our limits of experience are as authors, less coverage than some readers may think that these topics deserve.

We've tried our best in writing this to provide you with the tools and resources to intelligently meet these new threats and to independently discover and master topics that we might have missed. We hope that we've provided a solid enough foundation for you to learn how to face new areas without going out and buying yet another (inevitably outdated) book. To assist you further with this, we are creating a security section for the `www.macosxunleashed.com` website, and we will populate this section with errata to this book, pointers to new and pressing information that we discover, and any additional topics that we find need more thorough coverage. Think of this site as a living appendix to this book. If you find new threats, new techniques, or new security topics that you would like to see covered, please consider submitting the suggestion to the security forum on `www.macosxunleashed.com`, so that we can better serve you, and other readers who might be interested in the same topic.

Best of luck, and compute safely!

John, Will, and Joan Ray

PERSONAL NOTE TO THE READER:

Computing security is one of the topics about which I cannot write without some of my severe distaste for certain actions and mindsets coming through in the writing. You may be surprised to note that I hold those who would invade your system and do it harm to be some of the most contemptible scum of the computing world, but I can simultaneously admire the cleverness with which some of the programs are written and some of the methods are devised. More surprising to some will be the fact that I hold the people who knowingly write software that facilitates the creation and propagation of such attacks, and who persistently and insistently continue to produce and sell this dreck, even in the face of the ongoing havoc and devastation that it creates, to be beneath contempt. Many of the most serious security threats and compromises that you will meet are unfortunately enabled by the intentional acts of commercial software vendors, rather than by the clever discovery of flaws in a system's infrastructure. The people and companies who sell you software with such flaws do so with the full knowledge that the software contains the flaws, and of the potential harm these flaws might cause. They do so for one motive only: profit. Allowing the flaws to exist allows them to provide more apparently "convenient" features, with less investment on their part. These scabs on the festering underbelly of computing act as the drug dealers of the computing world, pushing their damaging wares on the unsuspecting, claiming it to be safe like candy, all for the purpose of bolstering their bottom line and fostering further addiction to their products, all with a complete disregard for the actual safety, security, and productivity of the end users.

The people and companies that will do this, however, are allowed to continue only because the mass population of computer users have thus far been kept in the dark regarding the security costs of the conveniences that come in their software. You have the power to change this pattern, to say "no, I won't accept software that makes my life 1% simpler, at the cost of making my computer 100x more likely to be broken into," and to demand a higher class and quality of software. For you to protect your computers, improve the state of computing security, and to become responsible network citizens of the global online community, educating yourself about the consequences of the software you run, and taking responsibility for its actions, is a step that you must take. Throughout this book, I will do my best to help you learn to see these consequences, and to convince you that the benefits of being a responsible, informed, and proactively secure computer user far outweigh the minor inconveniences that you will incur as a cost of behaving responsibly.

In short, although I feel I can relatively dispassionately describe to you the threats, consequences, and solutions to a large cross section of computing security issues, I will not withhold my venom for those whose "professional" actions are designed to facilitate these threats, and I will not sugarcoat my descriptions of the consequences of running such "designed insecure" software. In this day and age of concern for national and personal security, it would be nearly impossible for a dedicated group of terrorists to engineer more effective defects into our national computing infrastructure than what is being sold to consumers every day by major software houses. There are evil people out there who would do you harm, and there are even more viciously evil people out there who would not only allow you to come to harm, but facilitate harm's ability to find you, to further their own corporate goals. If you don't want to hear about them, you're reading the wrong book.

Will Ray

PART I

Mac OS X Security Basics: Learning to Think Secure

IN THIS PART

1 An Introduction to Mac OS X Security

IN THIS CHAPTER

- What Is Security?
- Traditional Mac OS Versus Mac OS X
- Understanding the Threat

PANIC! This can't be happening, not now! Your hands shake so badly you can hardly be sure you've typed your password correctly, and the clammy cold sweat down your back fights with the rising temperature of your brow making you wonder whether the room's suddenly gotten too hot or too cold. But there it is again—that quick shimmy of the login box, and your Mac OS X machine rejects your valid login again. Your machine has been connected to the Internet for a while, and you've been putting off worrying about making certain it's secure. Now it's rejecting your login—something's wrong, possibly terribly wrong.

Sometimes it's the electronic equivalent of a bump in the night, the creak of that noisy floorboard in the hallway, when you know that you're home alone. If you're lucky, maybe the cracker you face is timid, and a shout and a wave of the shotgun are all that are necessary to save your data. Other crackers are less cautious, and less subtle; you might be about to experience an electronic mugging. Still others you're unlikely to ever be aware of, unless they choose to trash your system for amusement after they've explored it and used it for whatever their purposes might be.

Sound a bit melodramatic? Can't quite wrap your head around the scenario, or why you should be worried? Imagine that your term paper's in there, and it's due tomorrow. Or perhaps it's April 15th, and you were just finishing up your income taxes. Now your machine is telling you that it doesn't believe that you exist. Even if rebooting it cures the login symptom, do you *know* what's happened? Can you be sure that someone hasn't been digging around in your system, leaving themselves little back doors with which to get back in? Is that project you've been working on still intact? What about files belonging to other users of your machine? Welcome to the world of Unix security, or more aptly, insecurity.

Whether it's a login that's suddenly changed, files that are missing, or a credit card that's been maxed out by mysterious online charges, the evidence that you've been cracked is rarely pleasant, rarely sufficient to identify and track the perpetrator, and almost never discovered early enough to prevent the damage.

More insidiously, with networked, multitasking, multiuser computers such as Macintoshes running OS X, a security hole can allow malicious individuals to make almost undetectable connections through your machine to other, remote systems, using your machine to disguise their path. It's quite possible—in fact likely—that crackers using your machine as a stepping stone will leave no trace on your machine, and the only evidence that they've been there will be the damage that they've done to someone else's, with all the logs pointing back to you.

If you've come to OS X from a traditional Macintosh background, this last issue is one you've never had to deal with before, and quite probably one that you don't want to think about dealing with now. Many users of another major commercial operating system don't want to know about or deal with that problem either. The result is an ongoing series of network security debacles that have all but brought the entire Internet to a screeching halt several times over the last year alone, and that regularly costs businesses and consumers billions of dollars in damage and lost productivity. We'd like to think that Macintosh users are a more thoughtful breed, and that although you may be even less inclined to want to look at the ugly underbelly of your operating system than those other guys, you're a bit more concerned about having a machine that's useful and stable, and also more sensitive to the next guy's need for security, too.

This book teaches you about the ways in which your machine can be insecure, and some of the things that you can do to protect it. Apple's done the best job we've seen of providing a reasonably secure Unix, straight out of the box, and we'll help out by providing you with some more tools and tips that will be useful. The most important tool in your security toolbox, however, and the one we most want to help you develop, is a certain level of paranoia. In computer system management, confidence in your system's security is the prime requisite for the occurrence of a security breach. The contents of this book will enable you to develop and maintain an informed level of caution regarding your system's security, and to explain and defend that caution to others who might not be as concerned. The target of "a secure system," however, is constantly changing, so you should take what this book contains as a primer in how to think about system security, not as a final statement of everything necessary to remain secure for all time.

In some places you may think we're suggesting that you be too paranoid, or that we've waxed overly melodramatic. Perhaps we have, or perhaps it's just not possible to fully appreciate some of the things we'll talk about unless you've had the privilege of a visit from the men in nice suits and dark glasses (yes, G-men really do dress the way they're stereotyped). Either way, the worst thing you can do for your system's security is to let something that's supposed to encourage you to be wary instead convince you that it's just not worth it. Yes, many of the people who use that *other* operating system don't worry at all about their system security or the damage that the lack of it is doing to others, and the FBI rarely if ever visits them—but the security world is largely convinced that they're all too naive (actually, security professionals tend to use less polite terms) to understand security, and educating them is too large a problem. We're firmly convinced however that Mac OS users actually care about security, and that they are willing to put forth the effort to learn some basic security skills. The way you're going to avoid security headaches isn't by taking a Valium, zoning out, and playing dumb to security issues; you're going to do it by being an upright and responsible network citizen, and taking proactive responsibility for your computer's security. The fact that you're reading a book on computer security is evidence that you already stand a cut above the crowd. Keep up the good work, and let us help direct your learning efforts.

We're here to teach you to be paranoid like a pro, and to respond to what the paranoia tells you in an intelligent, measured fashion. At the worst, eschew the paranoia and practice the security measures we outline: They'll keep you mostly safe, most of the time. The paranoia's good for informing you of issues that haven't been discovered yet, or that we haven't thought to include, but you can get by better than 90% of the users out there, even if you decide that professional paranoia is too difficult. At the best, who knows: You might discover that you like this stuff. Computer security is the only information-technology field where salaries keep on rising, and jobs keep on being created without a blip, as though the dot.com bust had never happened.

What Is Security?

Among other definitions, Webster's New Universal Unabridged Dictionary defines "secure" as "free from danger, not exposed to damage, attack, etc." This is a reasonably good definition of secure for the purposes of computer security. Unfortunately, in computer security, especially with an operating system as powerful and as complex as Mac OS X, it's arguably impossible to attain a state that is "free from danger." "Almost free from danger" may be attained, but only almost, not absolutely. It turns out that for most computer security issues, there is a sliding scale between usability and security. The closer you get to making your machine absolutely secure, the less usable it becomes, and the more usable it is, the less secure it will be. If you disconnect it from the network, it can't be attacked via the Internet. Likewise, if you disable passworded logins, you don't need to remember your password to use the machine, but nobody else needs one to access it either. Of course, if your machine is insecure and someone takes advantage of that to break in and do damage, your machine loses usability as well.

Security for your machine therefore is an ongoing series of trade-offs between making your machine usable enough to get done what you want to do, and secure enough that it retains its usability. Because users in different situations have varying needs for stability and usability, there is no single "best" answer for how you approach system security. You need to evaluate your own needs and make your own decisions regarding what is "secure enough" for your computer.

Regardless of the level of security you decide on as appropriate for your own use, be aware that if your machine is connected to a network, even if only by a dial-up connection, you have responsibilities and security needs with respect to the rest of the computer-using world as well. Even if you can tolerate extreme insecurities on your machine for the sake of the additional convenience it brings in usability, a good network citizen does not allow his machine to be used as a stepping stone for attacks on other computer users. Your responsibilities with regards to other computer users are less flexible than your responsibilities with respect to your own use. Administrators of traditional Unix systems have historically been thought of as highly respectable network citizens, because they have a history of policing their own, and of maintaining a high standard of concern for the well-being of other network users. Users and administrators of some other operating systems, including some nontraditional Unix variants, have, on the other hand, become thought of as generally uneducated boors and scofflaws in the network community. This is because of their general lack of concern for the damage that their unsecured systems cause to other computers around the world. We hope to see Mac OS X users and administrators welcomed into the fold of respectable, responsible Unix users, and hope that we can do our part in helping you to understand how your decisions affect other members of the network community.

Traditional Mac OS Versus Mac OS X

If you've come to Mac OS X from traditional Mac OS, you might be wondering what all the fuss is about security. Your machine has never been broken into, and you've barely even had to worry about viruses. Over the years, various groups have hosted "Crack-a-Mac" contests, and even with tens of thousands of dollars in prize money at stake, and having publicly and vociferously thumbed their noses at the cracker community, the target Macintoshes mostly survived intact. What could you, with no incentive to crackers, and no reason for them to single your machine out of the crowd, possibly have to worry about? Now that you're running Mac OS X, plenty!

Mac OS X may have some of the same user interface fundamentals as traditional Mac OS, and the skills you use to get around and make use of software may translate between the two, but fundamentally, traditional Mac OS and Mac OS X are very different operating systems.

One of the biggest differences is that as interesting and useful as traditional Mac OS is, there just isn't much to it; it is a monolithic system. A single piece of software provides almost all the functionality that you, the user, experience as the operating system. This might appear to be a security impediment for traditional Mac OS. If that single piece of software is compromised, the entire system is compromised. For this reason, some security experts argue that traditional Mac OS is actually a very insecure operating system: It has almost no real protections, and if you managed to break into it, you'd have complete control over all it had to offer. Thankfully, traditional Mac OS is insecure like a brick. A brick has no network security features, and if you could manage to access it remotely, it wouldn't put up a fight, but generally, a brick can't be accessed remotely. Traditional Mac OS presented only a few opportunities for a malicious individual to do harm. If they couldn't get to the keyboard, and you weren't running software that explicitly allowed remote control of your machine, Macintosh, or brick, all that crackers were going to manage to do was beat their heads against the wall.

There are larger issues, however, with an operating system such as Mac OS X in which the OS is made up of many small, cooperating pieces of software. Instead of a single avenue of attack against a monolithic OS, Mac OS X (and Unix in general) provides a plethora of attack opportunities, as each independent program must be guarded against attack. More critically, to function together, these small programs need to be able to communicate with each other. Each line of communication is a point at which an attacker can possibly insert false information, co-opting the behavior of some fragment of the system into believing that it's performing a task requested by its proper peer, when instead it's acting on behalf of an attacker.

Compounding the problem is the fact that Unix is an inherently multiuser, multitasking system. Because it's designed to allow multiple users to use the machine at the same time, and even requires that multiple virtual users operate simultaneously just in the running of the bare OS, it's inherently less obvious when something that's not under your control is happening to your machine.

Despite our wanting to instill in you a sense that you have to take greater precautions with your new OS, historically speaking, Unix-based operating systems have been relatively secure, at least by comparison with some other operating systems you might be familiar with. Because security flaws in all software arises from the same general causes—human malice or human error—you might expect that all operating systems would have security issue experiences with a similar frequency.

To a large extent, the trend against the exploitation of major security holes in Unix is due to a history of Unix administrators and users taking a relatively inflexible stance toward security issues. If a security flaw is discovered in a software feature, that flaw is examined, probed, explained, and fixed, just as quickly as the Unix hacking community can fix it.

NOTE

Crackers, not hackers: There seems to be a popular misconception that the term *hacker* means someone who breaks into computers. This hasn't always been the case, and annoys the hackers out there who do not break into computers. To many hackers, the term *hacker* means a person who hacks on code to make it do new and different things—frequently with little regard to corporate-standard good programming, but also frequently with a Rube Goldberg-like, elegant-but-twisted logic. A decent hacker-approved definition is available from the Jargon file, `http://catb.org/jargon/html/`, specifically `http://catb.org/jargon/html/entry/hacker.html`. (This site has moved recently from its longstanding host, and we can't be sure this URL will work for long, either. If Jargon file entries can't be found here, please use Sherlock, Google, or your favorite search engine to track down a copy. The Jargon file is a wonderful reference to the way that large segments of the hackish crowd think and speak. Another possible linking source, should this one not work, is `http://jargon.watson-net.com/`).

Hackers, to those who don't break into computers, are some of the true programming wizards—the guys who can make a computer do almost anything. These are people you want on your side, and dirtying their good name by associating them with the average scum that try to break into your machine isn't a good way to accomplish this.

Though crackers often seem to describe themselves as hackers, most true hackers consider them to be a separate and lower form of life (`http://catb.org/jargon/html/entry/cracker.html`).

So, to keep the real hackers happy, we refer to the people who compromise your machine's security as *crackers* in this book. We hope you follow our lead in your interactions with the programmers around you.

One of the primary reasons this has been possible is that the majority of the software that made the Unix networked community work was developed in an open-source fashion, where nobody in particular owned the code, and everybody had access to it. This community-based development and testing is the result of a culture of sharing and cooperation that has existed in the Unix community from the start. In this culture, nobody stands to profit from the existence of errors, and anybody who might be harmed can take the source, find the error, and publish a fix. It's usually considered a moral imperative that recipients of such open software will increase the value of what they have received by improving it, and returning these improvements to the community, whenever they are able. Unix users, historically, have done very well by working together, and looking out for each other.

With commercial software and operating systems, users don't have this security advantage. In some situations with other operating systems, security flaws that *are* product features are maintained for years, despite knowledge of the flaw and the required fix. For example, the feature of automatically opening and executing attachments in an email client seems attractive to certain vendors, probably because they believe that they can sell more copies of an "easy-to-use email client"—which is also capable of wiping users' computers out if they receive the wrong email—than they can of a more secure email client that requires users to think for themselves. A program that automatically executed unknown code on a Unix machine would have historically been laughed out of existence. To those who are conscious of and concerned about security, the very presence of such a feature is an unacceptable security risk.

Unfortunately for the security outlook for OS X, mainstream commercial software is a necessity for creating the seamless, convenient interface and software collection that Mac users have come to expect over the years. Some of this software comes from the same companies that take the inexcusable position of believing their users are so gullible as to buy blatantly flawed software because it's "easy." Protecting your machine in the face of this is not going to be as easy as protecting older Mac OS versions where the flaws they could introduce were not as critical, and it is not going to be as easy as protecting traditional Unix installations where commercial software is almost unheard of. We're delighted to see that Apple has made the core of OS X available as the open-source Darwin project, but to maintain the high level of ongoing security that has come to be expected from Unix, you, the user, are going to have to be as steadfast in your demand for secure software as traditional Unix users have been. If a product is simply a bad risk, for your machine, your users, or your network neighbors, tell the manufacturer, tell the world, and refuse to buy it. Because you don't have access to the source code, your caution and good sense in choosing software will be one of your machine's first lines of protection—and your voice online, speaking as one with the rest of your new network neighbors and peers, will be your best shield against and best redress toward companies that display a malicious lack of concern for your security.

Understanding the Threat

"Understanding the threat" is the subject of a large portion of the rest of this book—understanding it, and understanding how you can mitigate or respond to it. We'll cover a large number of known threats, including both current ones (so that you can fix them right away), and threats of historical significance (so that you can better grasp where typical vulnerabilities lie). Understanding the threat, however, isn't simply understanding a particular problem that exists with a particular piece of software, or understanding a particular vulnerability in a subsystem of Mac OS X.

Understanding the threat involves realizing that it's not about specific problems and specific security holes; it's about the fact that you now live in a world where your computer isn't limited to just "doing what you tell it." Your Mac OS X computer is running dozens if not hundreds of programs simultaneously, from the moment it starts up until the moment it shuts down. A flaw in any one of those can allow someone else to start making it do what he tells it, as well as what it's apparently doing for you. Apple could fix every current threat discussed in this book, and the threat would remain because there are malicious people, who do malicious things. So long as you use a sophisticated system in which portions are capable of acting without your permission, there will be assorted security vulnerabilities that you will need to address, and responsibility that you will need to assume. In a sense, yes, this means that you and your choices are a part of the threat that must be understood. This is true in more ways than one. We, as users, are often our own worst enemies when it comes to security: Our desire for more features and more conveniences from our software and computers is often in direct opposition to what will keep our computers secure. Unless we're willing to live with an entirely Spartan and uninteresting computing environment (and even this would never completely solve the problem), the best we can do is understand where we introduce weaknesses by the systems and features we choose, and how we can responsibly minimize the threats we introduce.

Briefly, threats to the ongoing usefulness of your system and software can be broken down into a few major classifications, each of which provides a number of different avenues for malicious intent. These classifications are discussed in a number of contexts and in considerably greater detail in the remainder of this book.

- **Theft of your data**. Malicious network encroachments, poorly designed software, poorly conceived algorithms, simple program bugs, or the actual physical theft of hardware from your system, as well as a number of other avenues of attack, can all allow unintended access to your information. Theft of data is one of the attacks that's most discussed, and possibly most feared and/or romanticized, but it actually accounts for only a small percentage of security breaches. It's definitely the most damaging, whether it involves corporate espionage or the theft of your credit card number, and putting the pieces back together after you've had your patent stolen or your credit destroyed is not going to be fun.
- **Theft of your resources**. It's quite simple for an unauthorized individual to slip one more process onto a multitasking machine in such a way that the additional load is never noticed. This type of attack is often accompanied by theft of data. The recent Nimda and Sircam network viruses that have caused uncounted millions of dollars of damage have been resource thieves, designed with the clever feature that they're never written to disk on the compromised machine—they invade the computer's memory and begin running, and leave

no physical trace of their presence, and the load they place on the machine is insignificant as well. These viruses have the goal of stealing the resources of your machine and using them to attack other remote machines—a pattern that is typical in theft-of-resource attacks. Although the loss in terms of actual resources on your system might be minimal, if someone's used your machine to attack someone else, and it's tracked back to you, you can bet that you will be spending a considerable time with some law-enforcement officers trying to explain and prove your lack of involvement. If the offense is serious enough—say someone's used your system to send threatening email—you'll find that the men with nice suits and dark glasses were not issued senses of humor.

- **Denial of access to machine resources**. Lacking any way to do anything more interesting, many cracker-wannabees engage in the cracking equivalent of smashing your mailbox—repeatedly. Because of the inherently networked and collaborative nature of Unix, it's almost impossible to completely defend against denial-of-service attacks. They can be effected simply by repeated connections to open services, and if you want remote access to those services, there's no way for your machine to authenticate valid users without accepting all connections, and then disconnecting the invalid ones. Occasionally a denial-of-service attack can lead to something more serious than the consumption of resources, but usually the danger is largely a significant inconvenience rather than an avenue to allow theft-of-resource or theft-of-data attacks. Still, consumption of resources can be bad enough, if it's targeted at the right (wrong) places: The mid-2002 attacks on the root name servers that nearly crippled the entire Internet were denial-of-service attacks, just directed at a very important service.

Because of the enormous complexity of modern operating systems such as OS X, the problems that enable each of these types of attacks upon your system's security interact with each other and compound in an unpleasant fashion that is often difficult to predict except in hindsight. For example, there are instances where two aspects of the operating system use the network to communicate with each other. A denial-of-service attack on one of them might tie it up to such an extent that an intruder could masquerade as that service and speak to the other, claiming to be a part of your OS, and thereby acquiring sufficient data or access from the second service to be able to hijack your system to attack some third party. Because of these types of interactions, it's insufficient to consider only one aspect of your system's security. The vast majority of malicious individuals who will try to compromise your system are not particularly bright; they're just amazingly numerous. There are, however, some quite smart minds out there with too much time on their hands, and nothing more exciting to do than to exercise their creativity trying to find the errors in your operating system, your software, and what you've done to protect it.

In many senses, computer security is a frame of mind—one that takes a conscious effort to attain and maintain. It involves deciding to do the right thing, regardless of whether it's the most convenient thing. If you want to go about it professionally, it often means looking for the worst possible combination of circumstances, and planning for the worst possible outcomes. This often results in security professionals being thought of as wildly pessimistic and sometimes draconian in their outlook, but you can be certain that if you can think of something that can be done to damage your system, someone else can think of it as well. The worst thing that can possibly happen probably won't happen every day, but not planning for it is a sure way to not be prepared for it if it does.

NOTE

Regardless of your thoughts on security, and even if you decide that this book is not for you and put it back on the bookstore shelf after scanning through this chapter, please keep up with Apple software updates and other security updates to your software, please turn off any unnecessary network services and replace those you do run with secure versions when possible, and please restrict the access to and permissions of services that you do run, as much as possible. If you do these things, your system will be safe from probably better than 90% of the security vulnerabilities and exposures that come along.

Five hundred more pages of this book—or any other book—will serve only to reiterate, emphasize, and expand upon these points, and to give you the insight into the mind of the cracker that will get you from 90% to as close to 100% as you're willing to push.

Summary

In this chapter we've tried to convince you that computer security is not something you can ignore. "With great power comes great responsibility" may have become a cliché, but with powerful operating systems, the words were never truer. We hope you're beginning to understand that as a user or administrator of a Mac OS X machine, it's your responsibility to keep that machine secure, both for your own security and for the good of all of your network neighbors. We'll spend the rest of this book working to show you that it's also something that you can accomplish without driving yourself insane.

2

Thinking Secure: Security Philosophy and Physical Concerns

IN THIS CHAPTER

- Physical System Vulnerabilities
- Server Location and Physical Access
- Server and Facility Location
- Physical Access to the Facility
- Computer Use Policies
- Physical Security Devices
- Network Considerations

Although this book concentrates primarily on security issues at a software level, physical security is still an important issue, especially if you have or will have a publicly accessible computer or network. Publicly accessible machines are just as prone—or perhaps even more prone—to physical attack than they are to remote attacks. This chapter addresses issues involving machine location and physical access, physical security devices, physical network considerations, and network hardware. These issues primarily apply to administrators attempting to secure one or more machines as a job function.

Physical security issues also frequently compound network security threats. Network security often uses unique machine identifiers as partial security credentials. This works well if it forces an attacker to try to fake a valid machine's identifying characteristics. Unfortunately, it often tempts the attacker to simply steal a valid machine from which to launch his attacks. No application of encryption, virtual private networks (VPNs), or one-time-password tokens can protect your network against illegitimate access by the guy who's just nabbed your CEO's laptop off the carry-on rack on the plane. According to Kensington (`http://www.kensington.com/html/1355.html`), 57% of network security breaches occur through stolen computers, so it only makes sense to take physical security at least as seriously as you take network security.

If you're interested in the security of only your own Macintosh, much of this will be of only cursory interest to you. Keep in mind, however, that Unix administrators are fairly well paid, and that there aren't going to be many people out there capable of doing the job of administrating a Mac OS X system. A world of Linux security experts cut their teeth banging on Linux boxes in their basements, and Apple has just created the opportunity for a world of OS X security experts to find their place in the workplace as well. If you've the inclination, the clever ideas you bring from thinking about issues like these just might land you a place in that market.

In addition to securing your system against people breaking it, walking off with bits of it, or blocking you from using it through physical or electronic means, it's important to address an additional security issue: the issue of "social" security problems. Users are human beings, and despite the best algorithmic protection, and the best physical barriers, if your system has users other than yourself, they will find ways to reduce the utility of your system purely through poor behavior. Unless you encourage them to do otherwise, and have policies in place to prevent them from becoming disruptive, "poor behavior" can have a significant impact on the usability of your system. Although no written policy can prevent users from behaving badly, the lack of a written policy can prevent you from acting to stop it when it happens.

In general, you will find most of the discussion in this chapter to really be a matter of common sense, but there are a lot of issues to think about, and remembering to think about them all without a list requires uncommon persistence. We strongly encourage you to consider the issues discussed here and try to put yourself in the mind of a mischievous or malicious individual. Consider your facility, and how you would go about trying to access data, disrupt use, or otherwise make inappropriate use of your hardware. What's the most disruptive thing you can think of doing to your system? If you can think of it, so can someone else who wants to cause trouble for you. The level to which these possible avenues of attack should be of concern to you will be entirely dictated by your individual situation and the needs of your system. Consider the discussion here as raw material from which to make a plan that fits your own unique needs.

Physical System Vulnerabilities

Many people invest a considerable amount of time and thought into securing their network connections through encryption, and restricting access to their machines via extravagant password systems, yet neglect physical security. If an intruder wants the contents of a file on your computer and can't break into it at the login prompt, Apple's "easy open" G4 cases make the job of simply walking away with your hard drive awfully easy.

IT COULD BE WORSE

If you're concerned about physical security, be glad you've got an "easy open" Macintosh, and not an early 1990s Silicon Graphics workstation. Older SGIs were so well designed that all a hardware thief needed to do was open a door on the front of the machine, flip a release lever, and the drives would slide out the door like toast out of a (sideways) toaster. Apple's gone a long way toward making the drives in the XServe as convenient to steal as well, but you're probably more likely to restrict access to your rackmount servers than to your desktop machines.

Some aren't even so considerate as to steal only your drive, and instead are happy to get the spare computer along with your data when they grab your G4 by those convenient carry handles and head out the door.

Networks are vulnerable to physical tampering, and in the worst case can allow someone to collect all traffic into and out of your machine without your knowledge.

If the problems of keeping your hardware from walking away and keeping your machine from being vulnerable to network attacks aren't enough, a poorly designed facility, or a poorly designed user policy, encourages crackers to steal your data through routes such as videotaping user logins to capture passwords, or engaging in social engineering to convince a valid user to give them access to the system.

It's been said that the best response to the question "How can I secure this system?" is "Put the machine in a safe, pour the safe full of cement, lock it, drop it in the middle of Hudson Bay, and even then, you can't be sure." Without going to that extreme, you can do a reasonable job of making access to your hardware and data inconvenient for the would-be cracker. This chapter tries to give you some ideas of how you can approach the problems of physically securing your machines and user policies that will encourage your users to help you keep them secure.

Server Location and Physical Access

If you are planning a publicly accessible computer facility or publicly accessible machine, you should keep some issues in mind. Obviously, the purpose of your facility dictates the hardware and software you need to consider. Less obviously, it also influences the security measures that you can and should plan for. These considerations extend from the software security you put in place, to the space where your facility is located, and how you will limit users' physical access to your hardware.

Server and Facility Location

The types of public facilities where we might expect to see Macintoshes include schools, libraries, and, as Mac OS X becomes more widely adopted, research labs. These public facilities range from small, relatively unadvertised clusters of machines to large, 24-hour facilities.

Regardless of the type of environment you're planning, the most important machine in your facility is the server machine. This machine is best kept in a location separate from the rest of the facility, perhaps even on a different floor, or if your network is fast enough, in a different building. Access to the server room should be granted to as few people as possible. At the very least, it should be on its own key, separate from the building master.

You may want to consider keeping the server in a room with a pushbutton combination lock, or with some sort of keycard access. You may want some sort of alarm system for it as well. Because the server room is not likely to have a person monitoring it, you may also want to consider installing video surveillance equipment. If you're building a small lab on a shoestring budget, the semblance of video surveillance equipment may be all that you need; several vendors provide fake security cameras for those who can't afford the real thing. (See Table 2.1 at the end of this chapter for vendors of both real and fake video surveillance cameras and time-lapse security VCRs.)

Keep backups of the system in a location different from the server room. At the very least, keep them in a different room; preferably, keep them in storage at an offsite location.

If you don't keep your server machine separate from the rest of the machines, you run the risk of malicious users more easily being able to access data (such as the userid and password NetInfo map on your machines) by physically removing it from the server than if they only were able to attack the server over a network.

The best location for a public lab varies, depending on how public it is supposed to be and what space is available in your building. You may not want to have the lab on the ground floor because the ground floor may seem too easy to access for the casual, malicious user. On the other hand, your building policy may restrict general public access to only the ground floor, so that casual visitors aren't given the opportunity to see and start thinking about what may be in the rest of your building.

Regardless of the location, the room should be large enough to accommodate the number of users you anticipate having. Make sure users have enough space to comfortably work, and make sure that they're not encouraged to sit so closely together as to be able to snoop on each other's screens by the arrangement of your hardware.

NOTE

No matter what type of computing facility you have, make sure you have adequate or, preferably, considerably more than adequate air conditioning. After spending money on the hardware and software, there is little point to letting the equipment fry to death.

Physical Access to the Facility

How access to the public facility is granted depends on how public the facility is. For staff during off hours, you may want to follow some of the common-sense advice for the server room: Allow access with a key different from the building's master, or use a pushbutton combination key or keycard access.

Access for general users, though, may depend on how public the facility is. For a small facility, it may be sufficient to issue keys or codes or access cards to the appropriate individuals. Or you may want to have users sign in during the day, and not grant access during off hours, or grant access to only a smaller subset of users.

For a larger, more public facility, you might want to consider some sort of keycard access, especially if your facility is part of an institution that already issues IDs to the individuals associated with it. For a particularly public place, such as a public library, perhaps using a photo ID and having the user sign a login sheet would be appropriate. Perhaps it would be better to limit use of such a facility to only the library patrons.

No matter how public the computing facility, you may find it useful to install video surveillance equipment, especially if, for whatever reason, it is not practical to restrict access via any other method. Although video surveillance equipment will not tell you specifically who is in your facility, it could potentially discourage some malicious users.

Unless your facility is so small that access is available to only select individuals, you should have the facility monitored by at least one individual at all times. Of course, this is in part to help with equipment or software problems. However, having the room monitored by an individual is yet another way to discourage possible malicious users.

Finally, you may want to consider installing an alarm system of some sort that is armed when the facility is supposed to be closed.

Table 2.1 at the end of this chapter includes several vendors of lock and alarm systems.

Computer Use Policies

Whether you have a large facility or a small facility, you should have computer use policies in place. Such policies are useful to administrators and users alike.

Lack of written policies leaves your facility open to poor decisionmaking in the name of expediency. If you've just discovered that one of your users is using your machines for trading illegal copies of software in violation of copyright law, what do you do? Remove her account and hand her over to the authorities? Delete the files and do nothing else? Warn her never to do it again? If the user is the son of the chairman of your department, does your decision change? If you have a well thought-out acceptable-use policy, the decision will be clear, and the action clearly prescribed.

Written policies additionally serve as "recipes" to be followed in times of crisis. In the event of a security breach of your site, who is in charge? Does the system administrator sitting at the console who sees a break-in happening have the authority to shut the system down? Or is her head going to be on the chopping-block in front of users whose "important work" was more important (to them) than the security of the system at large? Does the apprentice system administrator sitting at the console who observes a break-in in progress even know what to do in a crisis, and is he going to remember how to do it all properly? A written policy that provides a recipe to follow in case of an emergency and gives the administrator-du-jour the authority to act covers both these bases.

Written policies should be in place and available for review by both users and administrators alike. Policies should detail what users can expect from administrators, what administrators can expect from users, and yes, even what administrators can expect from administrators. You should have policies detailing the following:

- User account request procedures
- Acceptable use guidelines for the facility
- Acceptable use guidelines for your network
- Response procedures for security problems
- User responsibilities
- User rights
- Administrator rights and responsibilities
- Mission statement and budgetary policy

For a facility with individual user accounts, you need a user-account application form that solicits enough information for you to verify the users' identities and to track them down if you need to find them while they are away from the system. (Keep in mind that using a user's Social Security number for identification purposes is against the law in some circumstances, though you will find many corporations that use a copy of the SSN as an ID number as well.) This form should include as much contact information as possible. Address and phone number are a must. Possibly require the name and signature of the user's supervisor if you're running a business facility, or a secondary contact if your environment is something more like a library. I also find it useful to include some space on the form for administrative comments and data that I need to have on hand when I create the accounts. Include your "Users who cause trouble get in trouble" policy statement right on the form, so that there's no question what they're getting themselves into by applying for an account.

The second thing to keep in mind when creating your system's policies is generating some acceptable use guidelines for your facility. You need a detailed document that gives guidelines for acceptable and unacceptable user behavior. You need to evolve this policy over time as you encounter new problems and situations that need to be documented. At a minimum, your acceptable use policy should detail all the reasons you can think of that would make you want to take drastic actions such as deleting a user's account. You'll obviously want this to include things such as conducting illegal activities, but you may want to include things such as sharing passwords, or reading other users' files without permission as well. If you can think of any situation in which a user should be denied access for an action, it's best if you codify that in the rules and adhere to the decision with any users that transgress. You should give a copy of your acceptable use policy to every user that has an account, and to any user who requests an account. Make certain that users have a paper copy available, even if you also have an online copy.

You also need to consider what the acceptable use guidelines will be for your network. These guidelines may or may not be considered part of your facility's acceptable use guidelines. Largely, this depends on whether users can install their own machines on the network. Requirements that you should consider include such things as disallowing cracking attempts against the facility, or unauthorized sniffing of traffic on the network. Additionally, the person responsible for machine security should be granted physical access to any machines on her network segment. You don't want to put the person in charge of security emergencies in the position of needing a fireaxe to get to your machine when she's been called out of bed at 3:00 a.m. to deal with a remote break-in that is being perpetrated by your hardware.

When compiling your network's policies, keep in mind what your response procedure will be for security problems. In addition to the obvious procedural document ("press this button, shut down that machine, yank that cable"), you need documented personnel procedures. Who is responsible for acting in response to security problems? Who has the authority to detail this response? If these are not the same person at your site, you are in for a nightmare of administration problems. Upper-level management often wants to assign some "director"-level manager to be the person with the authority to make decisions in a security crisis. This is often a bad idea; frequently the "director"-type isn't available when a crisis hits, or isn't even a system administrator. Waiting to find and procure authority for something like an emergency shutdown can cause extensive damage to user files, and long periods of downtime to make repairs. Don't allow the separation of the person with the responsibility from the authority to act. Generally, you want the person with hands closest to the keyboard to have complete authority to act quickly and decisively. Requiring the person with hands on the keyboard to track down a manager-type before executing an emergency halt in response to a break-in is very similar to requiring a pilot to get authorization from the navigator before turning the plane to avoid an imminent crash.

The best possible policy is one that gives the administrator closest to the machines absolute dictatorial control in an emergency, and requires her to immediately notify all senior (in experience) administrators available. The procedure for transfer of authority to the most senior administrator (and who this is should be detailed on paper as well) available should also be detailed: The last thing you need in a real security crisis is confusion over who is calling the shots.

Your network policies should, of course, include guidelines for user responsibilities. When granted an account at your facility the user should automatically be expected to assume certain responsibilities. Among these are responsibilities such as keeping the password secure and cooperating with other users who need to use the machines. Even though some of these ideas will seem like common sense, you need to spell them out for your users. Things such as keeping passwords private might not sound like a serious responsibility, and it's one that many users might be inclined to ignore. However, you need that policy on a piece of paper because you will eventually have the user who doesn't believe password loaning is a serious problem. He will lend it to a friend who then uses it to try to crack your root password. A written policy lets you demonstrate to the irresponsible user just how serious a problem it was.

When your policy addresses user responsibilities, it also must address user rights. Along with the responsibilities users assume when using your machines, they also get some rights. Certain rights depend on the purpose of your site, such as the right to put up Web pages if your site's purpose is as a Web server. Others are rights that you need to define for the smooth running of your site, and tend to run along the lines of enforced common courtesy—such as the right to equal usage of the system (no tying up all the machines with one user's processes). Finally there are the legal rights that the users have, like the right to the privacy of their files and electronic communications. You should detail these in a policy document as well.

Although users have standard rights and responsibilities, at most places administrators don't have many rights, and they have many undocumented responsibilities. Take the time to work out some detailed documents regarding administrators' rights and responsibilities. Include things like "We don't make house calls," and "If you bought it without asking us if it would work, we reserve the right not to fix it."

Who watches the watchers? Administrators need administration too. Who makes decisions about granting administrative access? Are there "limited" administrative accounts and who can use them? What limitations are there on the administrator's authority? All these are decisions better committed to paper than to memory.

Network policies should also include a mission statement and budgetary section. You'll be hard pressed to run a facility well if you don't have a written statement of what it's there for. A defined budget allows you to make intelligent purchasing decisions and to decide when and where you can "splurge" on improvements. At a minimum a defined budget should include money for any salaries you need to pay, software licenses your facility needs, and funds for hardware maintenance and any consumables you may have. You should keep in mind that hardware is in fact a consumable and that machines that are the cat's pajamas today will be barely viable antiques in three years. A reasonable budget must include money for replacing machines as they become performance liabilities, rotating them out and putting new machines in on a regular basis.

Depending on the type of facility you have, you should also consider policies and procedure documents concerning the following:

- **Your first login—getting started**. Include information on how to log in, responsibilities of the user, how to set a password, and how to get help. It's okay if you don't detail all their rights here, but you want a document that both sets their boundaries and provides them the help they need to get started.
- **Account creation and deletion procedures**. How do you create and delete accounts at your site? What logging procedures do you use? Where do you put the accounts? Who gets notified? and so on. Creating accounts isn't a very interesting or difficult task, but it will run more smoothly if there's a written recipe to be followed.
- **Shutdown and downtime notification procedures**. What sort of notice do you give your users when you're about to shut the machines down? How do you go about notifying them? It's downright rude (though sometimes necessary) to simply halt a machine under a user who's working at it. You should detail scheduled and unscheduled downtime notification procedures and do your best to stick to them. Users may not like having to work around a scheduled shutdown, but they'll like it a lot less if you take a machine down while they're in the process of doing real work. If you have to shut a machine down without advance notice, have a policy that states under what circumstances and how this is to be done, and how users are to be communicated to regarding the event.
- **Acceptable passwords**. Users are notoriously bad at choosing good passwords. Help them out by explaining the differences between a good password and a bad password. Make it a policy that users are held responsible for the security of their passwords, and then actually hold them to it. You don't need the security problems inherent in having a user who just cannot pay attention to rules and will not choose and maintain passwords securely. In addition, administrators who are highly concerned about passwords on other Unix flavors have frequently installed "improved" password software with features such as password aging, prevention of the use of commonly guessed password patterns, prevention of reuse of old passwords, and so on. We aren't aware of replacements of this nature being available for OS X at this time. We also aren't certain of the merits of software that encourages a user to write down his password because nothing vaguely recognizable is "secure enough" for the system. Still, if you're interested in the ultimate in password security and control, this is something to keep an eye out for.

- **Administrative staff responsiveness**. Users will want a policy that says that administrators must jump at their every whim, but administrators will want a policy that gives them more control. You've no reason to give your users less service than you are capable of, but it often seems that providing virtually instant service only inspires users to demand actually instant service, and to take offense when service cannot be provided instantly. Because there are many instances when you have a real need to delay response to some user issue—such as when you need time to study the impact that complying with that request many have on other system resources—it's often a better idea for policies to have a built-in delay. If you get things done faster than policy indicates, you make your users happy, and if you really need the time to address an issue, you'll have it available to do the work, instead of spending it answering constant questions about why you aren't finished.
- **Software installation requests**. As you'll read many times throughout this book, a sure route to disaster is installing software that you don't know the entire function of. Unfortunately, if you're supporting a system for users who have divergent software needs, it's almost inevitable that they'll end up asking for software that you don't know, and that you won't be able to thoroughly test. It's a tough position to be in, but if you're there to support their needs, and they need the software, you've little choice but to provide it for them. Avoid rush installs, and consider using a sacrificial machine for software that's truly untested and that has no track record. Try to strike a reasonable balance on software requests and handle them in a fair way that still allows you the ability to make certain that the software is properly installed and isn't a risk to the system. A user who bullies a system administrator into installing a security hole is not unheard of in the business.
- **Hardware installation requests**. Hardware installation requests can be a nightmare, especially if it's some specialty piece of hardware with which administrators have no experience, but that the user has purchased and with which he *absolutely* needs support. A policy that requires administrative staff preapprove any purchase before hardware will be supported is a good idea; otherwise, your facility's administrators could end up spending time on one user's needs and neglecting the needs of many others.
- **Backup procedures**. Backing up the system can eat a significant amount of time. Outline a backup procedure and stick to it. After you have the backup procedure outlined, inform your users so that they know the safeguards they can expect, as well as the limitations that have been placed on their data security.
- **Restore from backup requests**. To avoid the potential problem of your facility's administrators' work being regularly interrupted to restore lost data for users who accidentally deleted their data, create a policy on restoring data. Maybe restoring data should be done once a week or only after 5:00 p.m.

- **Guest access**. Occasionally users will request that guests be allowed to use the system temporarily. How you handle this is entirely up to you and the purpose of your facility. If you're running a high-security lab for a research project, you probably want to have a "no guests, ever" policy. On the other hand, if you're running a university teaching lab, there's no real reason that you shouldn't make guest access available so that students can show friends and family all the fun things they're doing. Whatever your policy, put it down on paper so your users don't get the impression that you're arbitrarily deciding whether their requests should be granted.

Notes on Making Policies

When writing policies, state in plain English what the rules are. Don't obfuscate the issue by making vague references to activities you wish to prohibit; state them plainly. A policy that says "Users will attempt to keep their passwords secret" is much weaker, and much more difficult to enforce than one that says "Users will not write down or otherwise record or divulge their passwords."

When making rules, it's crucial that you state the results of not following the rules. A policy that says "The system administrator on call will immediately inform the lead administrator in the event of a break-in" is almost useless. If you examine the part of the policy "will immediately inform the lead administrator," you should ask yourself "Or what? What happens if they don't?" A policy with no teeth is almost useless as a policy.

State acceptable practices in terms of hard and fast rules, not personal judgement. A policy that says "Users will not attach personal Unix machines to the building network unless the network administrator judges the machine to be secure" leaves the security of the machine up to conjecture on the part of the network administrator. A devious user could configure her machine to appear to be secure, thereby passing the "judgment" test, while in fact it remains insecure. Much better would be wording to the effect "unless the machine adheres to security guidelines as defined by the network administrator."

If your machine or machines are connected to the Internet, and they are intended for Internet access, remember that the Internet is the great intellectual equalizer, and one of the truly great examples of freedom in action. This is kind of a "warm and fuzzy" policy comment—unless you've a good reason to be draconically restrictive, it's probably a good idea for your policies to stand for open-mindedness and tolerance. A large part of what makes the Internet a great place is the free exchange of ideas. You will undoubtedly have users with whom you have deep philosophical disagreements. If part of your mission is providing Internet connectivity for your users, it's not your place to make judgments regarding their philosophies, skin color, sexual proclivities, or favorite sport. If you're providing Web services for something like a college research lab, and you allow users to place *some* personal material on the Web, you really need to allow them to place *any* (legal) personal material on the Web. Of course, you can make it subject to disk-space or bandwidth constraints. Before you decide that this means that you shouldn't allow any personal material, you need to keep in mind that what makes the Web such a useful tool, and such a neat place, is people who make useful things available. If the usage isn't affecting your other users' business or research use of the network or machines, what reason is there for you to not let your users give something back to the Web community? They might not all have the most brilliant or useful Web pages, but remember that if you write policy that bans one, you need to ban them all. And if you ban them all, that might mean banning the one person who really would make a valuable contribution back to the community. Don't let the "importance" of your site's mission get in the way of the benefits of letting users express themselves creatively.

And finally, remember that all policies you have must be understood by both administrators and users. They must be enforced fairly and consistently.

CAUTION

READ THIS PARAGRAPH—READ IT WELL! Never never NEVER! write policy that indicates that you will enforce any sort of censorship or up-front control over your users' activities. Policies that state that you will react appropriately if informed of inappropriate or illegal actions on the part of your users are fine. Policies that even *hint* that you will attempt to prevent such activities can automatically make you liable for their enforcement.

For example, you may be concerned that your users might make use of your system to illegally pirate software. Writing a policy that states "To prevent piracy, any software placed on the FTP site will be checked by the administration" makes the administration potentially liable for any commercial software that is discovered there. You might not like that fact, but that's the way lawyers work the law, and system administrators who claim to monitor their user's activities have been successfully sued as a result of those activities. You're much safer if you write a policy that states "We do not condone software piracy and will cooperate fully with the authorities in investigations resulting from illegal software found on the FTP site."

Write your policy so that you react to complaints regarding your users' behavior. If you should be the one to notice that behavior, so be it, but do *not* write policy that indicates that you will attempt to preemptively monitor and prevent the activity. This goes for FTP sites, Web sites, and any other data your users own or activities they perform.

A Sample Security Policy

Here's an annotated copy of a network and security policy that is similar to the one we use at our site, The Ohio State University College of Biological Sciences. Following each section of the policy are italicized comments on why that respective section of the policy was written in that particular fashion. This should give you some ideas for building a policy suitable for your situation.

Guidelines for System Security Requirements

Users wishing to make use of corporate computing resources or network resources agree to have, read, and understand the following:

A breach of system or network security is any attempt to connect to, view data on, or otherwise access or utilize computing resources without authorization. This includes, but is not limited to: use of computer facilities or network facilities without an account or authorization, accessing files belonging to other users without the written consent of said user, and use of facilities by authorized persons for purposes outside the intent of the authorization. An action that causes a breach of system or network security constitutes a direct violation of corporate computing security policy. Employees found to have willfully violated corporate computing security policies will be remanded to corporate disciplinary affairs.

This is rather draconian, but covers the entire gamut of using others' passwords, trying to break into the system, dangling personal computers off the corporate network, and otherwise causing trouble. We don't get to define disciplinary action such as terminating employment, unfortunately.

Account security on the facility Unix machines is the responsibility of the account holder. Passwords are not to be shared. Passwords are not to be written down or otherwise recorded. Loaning of passwords to other users will be considered a direct breach of system security and additionally will be considered grounds for immediate revocation of your account. Discovery of recorded copies of passwords will also be considered a direct breach of system security and dealt with in the same manner.

We take password security seriously; you should, too. You would not believe the number of times I find scraps of paper with user IDs and passwords sitting next to machines.

Non-Unix Machines Attached to the Building Network

Execution of system-crashing or system-compromising software such as (but not limited to) "Win-nuke" and "Nestea," or propagation of viruses, worms such as "Sircam," or Trojan horse applications such as "Nimda," constitutes grounds for removal of a system from the building network. Intentional execution of such software constitutes electronic vandalism and/or theft of service, and subjects the person executing the software to potential legal liability. Users can be assured that facility staff will provide any assistance necessary to track and prosecute anyone found to be conducting such attacks.

There is a whole genre of "crash a PC" programs out there that won't actually crash Unix machines, but that can make life annoyingly slow, and make network connections unstable for Unix users. Users on your network shouldn't be allowed to run this software against either PCs or Unix hardware. Users caught doing this should be punished—we remove their systems from the network wholesale. Users caught doing this to remote sites are likely to have remote site administrators calling and threatening legal action. Users may think it's all fun and games, especially if you're providing support for a college facility, but the person whose computer crashes and who loses a research grant as a result isn't going to think it's so funny.

Collection of network traffic that is not destined for the user and the machine in use (via, but not limited to, such methods as packet sniffing or ARP spoofing) constitutes grounds for removal of a system from the building network. Collection of network traffic without court authorization or a direct and immediate need to diagnose network problems constitutes execution of an illegal wiretap. Users should be comfortable that their data and electronic transactions are secure against eavesdropping.

Suffice it to say, unless you've got a policy in place that says all data on the system may be monitored at any time, anyone caught monitoring network traffic that isn't intended for him could be in deep trouble—including you!

Additionally, users can be assured that facility staff will not intercept network traffic without legal authorization or an immediate need to diagnose an existing network problem.

Always a good idea to tell users what their rights are as well, and the right to privacy is an important one. Users need to feel comfortable that they are not going to be "found out" if they discuss an unpopular opinion with a co-worker, or fear reprisals for the content of personal information kept on the system.

Execution of port-scanning software, or other software that attempts to discern or determine vulnerabilities in Unix or non-Unix hardware without facility staff approval will not be tolerated. Execution of such software will be considered an attempt to breach system security and will be dealt with as such.

There is a lot of software out there that's freely available, and which any user can run, which nonetheless they should be strongly discouraged from running. Among this software is a subset which searches for vulnerabilities in Unix hosts. Depending on your environment, you may or may not want to treat running this software as a direct attack on your machines.

Users will not run FTP, HTTP, or other data servers that provide illegal data (commercial software, or other illegal data types). The facility staff cannot and will not attempt to police the building network for such behavior, but reports of copyright infringement or other illegal behavior will be forwarded to the appropriate authorities.

Notice that we explicitly claim that we won't monitor the network for this type of usage. If someone reports it, we'll certainly act, but we don't want the legal liability that even trying to monitor for it would bring.

Users will not run software designed to provide unintended gateways into services that are intended to have a limited scope. Depending on the service and the manner in which the service is gatewayed to unintended users, execution of such software may constitute theft of service. The facility staff cannot and will not attempt to police the network for the execution of such software, but will cooperate fully in any investigations brought by users whose services have been compromised.

Again, note that we explicitly refuse to monitor for this sort of activity. The legal status of some of this software is questionable, and we don't want mixed up in legal troubles. If somebody comes to us with a problem, we deal with it.

UNIX Machines

Execution of software similar in purpose to any of the software detailed in the "Non-Unix" section will be dealt with in the same manner as detailed above, and/or users' accounts will be terminated without recourse.

Execution of password-cracking software against the computational facility password database will be considered an attempt to breach system security and will be dealt with as such.

Notice that we prohibit only attempts on the facility password database. This may seem a little peculiar, but proactively, we're really concerned only with our facility's security. If a user tries to actually break in to some other machine, then she'll be violating a law and we have something on which we can take action. Until she does something like that, she's only behaving questionably, and we get back to the "don't go looking for trouble" idea. If we claimed that we'd prohibit anyone from trying to crack any password file on our machines, we'd instantly be liable for letting the one we didn't notice get away with it.

Now if we notice one of our users trying to crack someone else's password file, we're likely to tell that someone else, and we're also likely to very pointedly glare at the back of the user's head until he gets so self-conscious that he stops, but we're not about to put it in policy that we're going to prevent him from doing it. Too many cans of worms to go near there.

Users wishing to install Unix machines on the building network can do this in two ways.

Because this policy was designed for a college computing environment, it's important to address that we allow users to connect both "lab owned" and personal machines to the network. Personally owned Unix machines have been a big problem, especially the Linux variant, in that lots of people know how to put the CD-ROM in the drive, but very few know how to manage the machines after they're up and running. Unfortunately, some Linux versions have shipped with just about the world's largest collection of security holes, all wrapped up neatly in one box. The end result is that if you let a poorly administrated Linux machine on your network, you've essentially invited the entire world to come watch all your network traffic and to probe your machines from inside your network.

Machines that are considered by the computational facility System Manager to be of general use and interest to the facility at large, may, at the discretion of the System Manager, be allowed to be set up as part of the facility. Machines handled in this fashion will be administered by the facility staff as full peers in the facility Unix cluster, and system security will be handled through the facility staff. Machines administered in this fashion remain the property of their respective owners and are to be considered primarily intended for the use of their owners. As full peers of the facility Unix cluster they may be used by other facility users (at least remotely) when they are not fully utilized by their owners.

We've found it productive to grow our facility resources by offering administrative services in exchange for allowing general facility use of the hardware. This seems to be a productive arrangement for other groups around campus as well. Some go so far as to have an arrangement whereby anybody interested in buying hardware gives their money to their computational facility staff. The staff then seeks out other users interested in the same type of hardware, pools all the money it can find and provides a far better machine to be shared than any of the "investors" could have afforded individually.

If you decide to go this route, make certain that you have discretionary control over what hardware you'll take on as part of your facility and what you won't. Although we said "avoid personal judgment as part of the policy" earlier, here, you really want to be able to avoid taking on that 16-year-old clunker that someone dragged out of a dumpster and now thinks is going to be just the ticket for their archive server. It seems near impossible to write a policy that covers allowing everything you'd want to allow, and disallows everything you'd want to disallow, so personal judgment will have to do here.

Security for these machines will be handled in the same manner as security for all computational facility Unix cluster machines. Users can be assured that all reasonable security precautions have been taken, and that known potential security problems will be dealt with in a timely fashion.

Should a security violation occur involving one of these machines, it will be dealt with by the computational facility staff and should not require significant time or effort from the owner of the machine.

The users taking this route to machine acquisition and maintenance need to know that they're getting something out of the deal as well. Putting this down in writing also helps when you need to point out to the occasional problem user what the costs and benefits of "working with you" are.

Machines that are to be administered by their owners or their owners' assignees will be maintained at a level of security at a minimum in compliance with the requirements in this document and with security guidelines as defined by the computational facility staff.

Notice how it "requires compliance with security guidelines," rather than something like "requires acceptable security." Don't get caught with wording that's easy to misinterpret, either accidentally or deliberately. Notice also that the guidelines are defined by the facility staff. The "System Manager" referenced a few items earlier isn't actually a Unix administrator at our facility; he's an overall director-type. So he is not the best person to define acceptable administration guidelines for Unix machines. We wanted to keep this flexible enough so that the staff who actually had the experience to define the guidelines could do the job without having users complaining that "person X doesn't have the authority to tell us we can't..."

Violations of policy laid down in this document are to be dealt with as defined in this document. Requirements for account maintenance and termination will be strictly enforced.

Administration security guidelines will be based upon current security problems as reported by corporate network security and the online security community. These guidelines will be provided by the computational facility staff on a set of Web pages dedicated to building network security. It is expected that administrators will bring their machines into compliance with the guidelines within seven (7) days of the guidelines being posted.

The guidelines referenced here are things like: Shut off all those $@%@#@#$% services that Linux starts automatically. No outside-accessible accounts for nonemployees. Install security patches when CERT (or the alert site/sites of your preference) publishes information on them. And anything else that happens to be pertinent at the time.

Also, seven days is probably too long a period to allow for securing against new-found threats, as these things make their way around the Internet amazingly quickly. We've had whole clusters of machines hit within 24 hours of the power being turned on here at OSU. If you can get away with being more strict with this, you probably should.

Computational Facility staff will keep a database of independently administrated Unix hardware and administrators and the administrators will be notified immediately when guidelines are updated.

It wouldn't be very fair to the administrators if we didn't make some attempt to notify them when we discover something they need to update.

Periodic scans of the building network for known security problems will be conducted by computational facility staff. Results will be made available to administrators of self-administrated machines as soon as the data is available. Facility machines will be protected against any vulnerabilities found by facility staff. Independently administered machines will be brought into compliance by their respective administrators. Failure to bring a machine into compliance will result in the machine being removed from the building network.

No, we're not scanning for security violations here, but for security holes. If a new way to break in to the sendmail service is discovered, we want to know whether any of our users are running vulnerable versions, and we want them to fix it if they are.

Because of the normal speed of network security breaches, the potential for rapid damage during a break-in, and the fact that most security problems occur during off hours, the following access abilities are necessary for computational facility staff:

> Computational facility staff may require physical access to any computing or network hardware in the building at any time. To facilitate such, master-keys for access will be kept in a sealed package in the facility safe. Access to these keys will be logged, justification will be given for using them, and the party whose area requires access will be notified immediately upon opening this sealed package.

You absolutely need a way to get to any computing hardware that's attached to a network for which you have any responsibility. If there is a security problem and the owner of a machine is not available, somebody needs to be able to get to the machine and stop the problem. If you don't have a key, get a fire axe. I'm serious. If a machine under your control is actively being used to cause damage to someone else's system, and you've got a choice between breaking a $250 door, or allowing the machine to do possibly untold amounts of damage, what are you going to do?

> Computational facility staff may require administrative access to any computing hardware on the same network at any time. To facilitate such, administrators of independent machines will provide the computational facility staff with root or other appropriate administrative passwords, to be kept sealed unless needed in a crisis. Independent administrators will keep these passwords up to date at all times. Access to these passwords will be logged, justification will be given for using them, and appropriate administrators will be notified immediately should use of these sealed passwords be required.

See previous rationale. Also notice that both here and previously, if access is required to hardware without the user's presence, we've put on paper that we will log the usage and notify immediately. Users need to feel secure that their offices and machines won't be invaded needlessly. They're reluctant enough to provide for this type of access, but it's one of the costs of being on the network for them. One of the costs of accessing their machines is a lot of paperwork and apologizing for you, but it will help keep you honest.

Responsibility and authority for maintenance of security guidelines and for definition of, and action upon, network security threats lies with the computational facility System Manager. In the case that the System Manager is not, or is unavailable to be, administrating the facility Unix cluster, the responsibility and authority pass to the facility Unix cluster Lead System Administrator. Facility assistant administration staff have the authority to deal with immediate crisis situations as necessary until the Lead System Administrator can be contacted.

Our higher-ups here require that the "System Manager" be at the top of the chain of command. This isn't an ideal situation in an emergency, because he isn't a Unix administrator, and he's just going to call the Lead anyway. Therefore we've worded this policy in such a fashion that he'll almost never actually be the person who has to call the shots, yet he retains the authority to do so if he needs to.

Our facility has one real full-time administrator and a number of assistant administrative staff (students) who are available on odd schedules. The assistant administrators have the authority, in the absence of the Lead System Administrator, to deal with any security issues that arise. This, as mentioned previously, is a trust issue. So they're students—so what? They've proven themselves trustworthy, and are trusted completely and implicitly whenever they're logged in as root. If we weren't certain we could trust them and their judgment, we wouldn't have given them the root password in the first place. They're also trusted, within the bounds of facility-defined policy, to make responsible decisions regarding the necessity for actions regarding system security.

Physical Security Devices

Unless your facility is a rather hard-to-find, small facility that can use the philosophy of security through obscurity, your facility should probably make use of some physical security devices. What follows is a description of some of the available physical security devices. Table 2.1 includes a list of URLs for manufacturers and/or vendors for these products.

If you want some security while being able to retain the aesthetic look of your Macintosh, cable lock systems may be most ideal for you. For desktop machines such as the Powermac G4 and older Powermac G3, the systems have an anchor point and a cable that connects the CPU to the monitor. For the older iMac and the PowerBooks and iBooks, there are cable and lock systems which attach to the machines and loop through a hole in the desk. Look for ones that use hardened cable of some sort—we've met some no-name brands where the cable can be cut with a pair of easily concealable wire-cutters. On some of the machines the attachment point is a slot about an inch wide and 1/4 inch tall, into which a proprietary locking connector fits. On others it's literally a hasp through which you can hook a lock or cable. On the most recent machines, it's a little oval slot about 3/8 inch long into which another type of proprietary locking connector fits. Having designed it, Kensington seems to have a lock on the current smaller security slot design and accessories that use it (`http://www.kensington.com/html/1434.html`), though some competitors are releasing compatible locking products. A number of other vendors provide the T-shaped locking key that fits the older, larger style security slot, and assorted hardware for using this slot to secure machines. Prices for the cables or locking connectors that mate to these types of systems tend to run in the $25–$65 range. You can also find cable kits that are supposed to be able to attach CPUs, monitors, keyboards, and a varying number of peripherals. Prices for these range from $20–$30.Intruding somewhat on the aesthetics, with costs varying significantly depending on the machine and whether you require professional installation, AnchorPad-type security systems are plates that mount to the desk or table under the machine and provide a way to lock the machine down to the plate. AnchorPad installation typically is somewhat invasive for the machine, requiring either super-gluing a lock-plate to it, or bolting the plate on through the bottom of the machine. AnchorPads appear as a 3/4-inch-thick pad with key-slots in the front, atop which your machine sits, so they don't interfere with any peripheral ports or significantly interfere with the appearance or cooling.

If aesthetics and cost aren't as much of a concern to you, entrapments or enclosures might be of interest instead. These devices are much like AnchorPads with covers. They are available for the older iMac, some of the laptops (for when they are not in use), the G4 cube, and the G3/G4 towers. These encase the computer and attach it to an Anchor Pad. Prices range from $100–$145. A similar device that is supposed to work on any laptop encases a laptop in an open position. It costs $75.

You can also find alarm systems for computers. One system is called PC Tab. With it, a sensor is attached to each machine. Each machine in turn is attached to a central alarm panel, which can hold up to 32 machines. Modules can be added to attach more machine clusters to the central alarm. If a sensor is removed, an alarm goes off. The Phazer Fiberoptic Alarm System and LightGard are similar products. Alarm units are also available for laptops.

Tracking systems, to allow you to keep track of what hardware you have and what you're actually supposed to have, are also available. One such system is called STOP Asset Tracking. The system uses a barcode plate for each of your items. A barcode scanner and software system are available with it to help you start an inventory database. The barcode plates are linked to the company's international database. If one of your items is stolen, the company is supposed to help you work with the authorities to recover the item. You can buy a barcode scanner for the system, but it is supposed to be able to work without it. Additionally, if you have equipment that you loan out to your users, the system is also supposed to be able to keep track of items that have been checked out and alert you to overdue items. Information is stored in a Microsoft Access database.

For the less public environments, you might be interested someday in protecting your machines with biometric devices—devices that do fingerprint, iris, or facial scans. At this time, biometric devices are mostly available for Windows operating systems, but many use USB hardware, so they wait only for some enterprising programmer to write the correct software for OS X. Sony is leading the way for OS X with a product that's currently called PUPPY Suite (`http://www.puppysuite.com/`). (As of this writing, the product is still pre-release, and the Web site is only partially functional.) This biometric device is a fingerprint scanner that can be integrated with the Mac OS X login system so that a user can authenticate with a fingertip. When such devices are available for the Macintosh, you will have to weigh privacy issues against security issues. (Frankly, we also have visions of a future where business executives need to take out extra insurance to cover their thumbs, so you might have other issues to consider as well.) Although you might not be able to protect your Macintosh itself with such devices at the moment, biometric access systems are available for buildings and rooms.

If you don't want to attach security cables to everything in your facility, but are still concerned that some of the smaller items (such as keyboards and mice) might walk away in someone's backpack or duffel bag, you might also try providing keyed lockers for your users, if space permits. This would give them somewhere to store most of their possessions while they are using the computer. Place the lockers somewhere where the users will feel confident that their possessions aren't going to be stolen while they are using the facility. It won't prevent someone from stealing loose hardware, but if your users aren't usually leaving their bags and coats on the tables, it's less likely that someone will get the bright idea to drop his coat on top of that new pro mouse and pick the mouse up with it when he leaves.

Depending on what type of facility you have, you may need to rack mount Macintoshes. Apple, of course, has provided neatly for this with the release of the XServe, but retrofit kits are also available for older Macintoshes. If you would like to rackmount G3 and G4 machines, check into the mounts made by Marathon Computer. They make one version that enables you to mount G3/G4 towers horizontally, and another version that enables you to mount the machines vertically. If mounting them horizontally better suits your needs, they also sell clips for the CD/DVD trays for use on models that do not already have retaining clips.

Table 2.1 lists URLs for a number of physical security products that you might find useful in establishing a secure environment for your computers.

TABLE 2.1 URLs for Manufacturers and/or Vendors of Security Products

Company	URL	Products manufactured or sold
123 Security Products	`http://www.123securityproducts.com/`	Security cameras, time-lapse VCRs
ADT Security Services	`http://www.adt.com/`	Security services
Advance Security Concepts	`http://www.mediaprotection.com/`	Media safes; electronic door locks
AnchorPad International	`http://www.anchorpad.com/`	Cable locks, plates, entrapments
Bioscript	`http://www.bioscript.com/`	Biometric building access system. This URL seems to have died since we started the book, but the product line was interesting and worth keeping an eye out for its reappearance.

TABLE 2.1 Continued

Company	URL	Products manufactured or sold
CCTV HQ Network	http://www.cctvheadquarters.net/	Fake security cameras, security camera systems
Champion Lockers	http://www.championlockers.com/	Lockers
Computer Security Systems, Inc.	http://www.computersecurity.com/	Cable locks, entrapments, plates, alarm systems, tracking systems, enclosures
Cutting Edge Products, Inc.	http://www.cuttingedgeproductsinc.com/	Fake security cameras
Federal Security Camera, Inc.	http://fakecam.com/	Fake security cameras
GoLocks.com	http://www.golocks.com/	Cable locks
Kensington Technology Group	http://www.kensington.com/	Cable locks; alarm unit
Keyware	http://www.keyware.com/	Biometric building access system
Marathon Computer	http://www.marathoncomputer.com/	Rackmounts
Minatronics Corporation	http://www.minatronics.com/	Fiber optic alarm system
Penco Products	http://www.pencoproducts.com/	Lockers
Pentagon Defense Products	http://www.pentagondefense.com/	Fake security cameras
Polaris Industries	http://www.polarisusa.com/	Security cameras, multiplexors, time-lapse VCRs
PUPPY Suite	http://www.puppysuite.com/	Biometric
Republic Storage	http://www.republicstorage.com/	Lockers
Secure-It	http://www.secure-it.com/	Cable locks, entrapments, enclosures, tracking systems, alarm systems
Secureitall.com	http://www.securitall.com/	Alarm systems for home/business
Securityideas.com	http://www.securityideas.com/	Security cameras
SecurityKit.com	http://www.securitykit.com/	Cable locks
Security Tracking of Office Property (STOP)	http://www.stoptheft.com/	Tracking system
Secure Systems Services	http://www.secureservices.com/	Cable locks, entrapments
Targus	http://www.targus.com/	Alarm units
TrackIT	http://www.trackitcorp.com/	Alarm units

Network Considerations

When you think of physical security, you might not necessarily think about your network. However, the network is an important part of anyone's computing experience today. Here we will take a brief look at traditional and wireless networks and what you can do to make them more secure.

Traditional Networks

Although there are a variety of traditional network topologies, the two most common are bus topology and star topology.

A bus topology connects all network devices along the same network trunk, the backbone. The backbone is typically a thinnet cable, also known as 10BASE-2 or coax (for coaxial cable). If the cable is interrupted at any point, the network goes down. This type of topology tends to have a high collision rate. Additionally, with all of the machines connected to the same line, network troubleshooting is more difficult because you can't conveniently isolate parts of the network for testing.

In a star topology, machines are connected to a hub or switch, typically by twisted-pair (also called 10BASE-T) wiring. If you disconnect one or more of the machines, the network does not go down. The ability to conveniently disconnect machines makes troubleshooting a star topology network more convenient.

The primary network security concern is in someone being able to watch your network traffic as your network is used. If you aren't using secure software on all machines in your network, things such as user IDs and passwords will be flying around your network in plain text for anyone with a little too much curiosity to see. Even if you are using secure software on all the machines in your network, many network services that your users will use to access the Internet at large will be insecure, and malicious network eavesdroppers will be able to view the data traveling out to Internet servers.

A secondary network security concern is that your network wiring is a trivial target for a person who wants to disable machines on your network. A quick slash with a pocketknife and your entire thinnet backbone stops working, or a whole branch of your 10BASE-T network loses connectivity to the outside world.

10BASE-2 networks are particularly vulnerable to the sniffing of network traffic because all packets go everywhere on the network. Removing a machine and replacing it with one that records the traffic passing by is easily accomplished. If the intruder wants to keep a lower profile, cutting into the cable and patching in a new connector is the work of but a few seconds.

Generally, we recommend avoiding 10BASE-2 networks whenever possible. They're cheap and easy to set up for a few machines, but they are fraught with support problems and you'll be a happier person if you never have to work with one.

Old-style 10BASE-T networks suffer from the same problem of all packets on the network going to all machines, but the advent of inexpensive smart switches makes this topology inherently much more securable than a 10BASE-2 network. Building a star (or tree) topology network with smart switches rather than hubs as the cable connecting hardware restricts network traffic to only those wires that are absolutely required to carry the data. Smart switches learn what machines are where on the network, and they intelligently route traffic specifically where it needs to go, rather than send it everywhere, in the hopes that the machine for which it's destined is listening. This has two benefits. It speeds up the network considerably, as many high-bandwidth functions—such as printing to a networked printer—will be restricted to only those network wire segments between the hosts that are directly communicating. With printing, for example, the data being transmitted only ties up the wires physically linking the printing computer and the printer. Other branches of the same logical network are unaffected by the traffic. In many cases, this can limit such traffic to only the wiring of one room, allowing the rest of the network to function as though the traffic between communicating machines didn't even exist. Additionally, it helps to prevent any machine plugged into the network from seeing traffic that isn't destined for it. A machine that wishes to snoop on network traffic in a completely switch-connected network will see very little data to snoop on: Because nothing knows it's there, there will be no data sent to it, and nothing will ever be sent down the wire to which it's connected. Clever crackers have ways to limit the protections that switched networks offer, so they should not be considered to be a panacea for all network-traffic-sniffing ills. However, switched networks are inherently more difficult to attack than networks using only simple hubs, and so are a natural tool in the security professional's toolbox.

When possible, we recommend using smart switches for as much of your network as possible. They'll save you many headaches, and the better versions give you nice control over your network, such as the ability to remotely disconnect the network from a machine that's begun causing problems at 4:00 on a cold winter morning.

Wireless (802.11b/AirPort, 802.11g/AirPort Extreme) Networks

The conference where Steve Jobs introduced the original iBook in conjunction with the AirPort card and AirPort base station ushered in an exciting time for Macintosh users. Since then, Macintosh users have been embracing wireless technology. We are now getting used to being able to surf the web from our backyards, or taking our laptops from one part of our office building to another without losing network connectivity. Although wireless networks are indeed convenient, they also have security risks. A wireless network is conceptually similar to a star topology traditional network, only instead of machines connecting to a central hub by wire, they connect via radio transmission. It's also similar in that data sent between a computer and the hub (AirPort card and wireless base station), is visible to all in-range computers with wireless capability. Although each connection to the base station may be encrypted, conferring some level of privacy, the network is not "point to point," like a switched 10BASE-T network. Any computer than cares to snoop can receive the encrypted traffic, log it, and bash on the encryption to try to break it at its convenience.

WEP Encryption

Wireless networks typically consist of one or more wireless access points attached to a network wire and some number of wireless clients. In the typical Macintosh case, the wireless access point is the AirPort Base Station, which can currently support up to 50 users. Yesterday's wireless networks commonly achieved a data rate of up to 10Mbps, and they broadcast on a 2.4GHz radio frequency. Today we're moving to 54Mbps on the same broadcast frequency with the 802.11g standard.

The 802.11b and 802.11g standards, the standards upon which the AirPort's and AirPort Extreme's wireless technologies are based, also include a way to encrypt traffic by using the WEP (Wired Equivalent Privacy) protocol. This can be configured with no encryption, 40-bit encryption, or 128-bit encryption. Although 128-bit encryption is better than 40-bit encryption, WEP encryption is overall a weak form of encryption.

Anyone who wants to decrypt the WEP encryption needs only a Unix box with a package such as AirSnort or WEPCrypt (AirSnort, `http://airsnort.shmoo.com/`, appears to be the package under regular development). After packets are decrypted, the intruder can collect whatever interesting data passes by, including usernames and passwords.

Security Limitations

Along with the weak WEP encryption, wireless networks have other security limitations.

For example, because it's difficult to stop the radio waves carrying a wireless network at the boundaries of a building, it is easier for an unauthorized client to become a part of the network. Previously, to physically insert a client into a traditional network, physical access to the interior of the building was required. Now, someone need only park outside your building and flip open a laptop. With an external antenna, an unauthorized client can potentially received the wireless network's signal at a greater distance; hardware hackers regularly achieve multikilometer connections to AirPort networks by using Pringles potato chip cans as antennae (`http://www.turnpoint.net/wireless/has.html` and `http://www.oreillynet.com/cs/weblog/view/wlg/448`). If there is no password for the access point, the unauthorized client just joins the network. If only the default password is in use, the intruder probably knows it and can still join. An intruder who has joined your network can perform malicious acts from it, including reconfiguring your AirPort Base Station.

Because of problems such as these, it's common for wireless networks to be set up with a number of rather severe limitations that are designed to mitigate problems caused by potential unauthorized use. These range from configuring the antenna placement and broadcast pattern to limit the access area to carefully defined regions, to setting the system up so that wireless-connected users must use a VPN client to tunnel into another network before they can gain any substantial functionality. The most common, and least secure, is simply to consider the wireless network an untrusted segment with respect to the remainder of the network, but this does nothing to prevent either misuse of the resource or leakage of sensitive data from trusted machines onto the untrusted segment.

Summary

Physical security of your hardware can be as important to the security of your data as the secure configuration of your operating system. If you consider system security as including the maintenance of your system in a stable, maximally usable condition, security also involves making intelligent policy decisions regarding the use and users of your system. Depending on your particular circumstances, you'll need to take some of the recommendations in this chapter more seriously than others, or you may even need to consider threats more outlandish than some we've outlined here. Spy films are spy films, but many of the snooping technologies depicted have some basis in reality. If you're attempting to protect the boss's computer against industrial espionage, you need to seriously consider which attacks might be brought to bear against your hardware, your users, and your network. If you're supporting a facility with student users who have too much free time on their hands, you might be up against an even larger challenge.

3

People Problems: Users, Intruders, and the World Around Them

IN THIS CHAPTER

- Your Users: People with Whom You Share Your Computer
- The Bad Guys: People Who Would Do Your System Harm
- Everybody Else

Users! Users complicate things, and so do the rest of those unpredictable humans who visit, probe, or just occasionally brush past your computer on the network. If it weren't for the human beings in the equation, keeping a system secure would be so much easier! This may sound like something demeaning that fell from the lips of one of the particularly humorless system managers you might know, but until computers start thinking for themselves, it's really quite true. Behind almost every security threat to your system, there are the actions of some person or persons. Some of them are consciously malicious actions, but there are a multitude of situations where the unconscious behavior of users is at fault. Because of this, in more ways than one, computer security is a people problem, and some of the best results in terms of absolute increases in your system's security can be obtained by addressing the people and modifying their behavior. This chapter, the last of the primarily philosophical discussions in this book, examines the human issues that bear upon your system's security, and where you can best work to help your system's users work consciously toward, instead of unconsciously against, your goal of system security.

Your Users: People with Whom You Share Your Computer

The users who are legitimately allowed access to your machine are, ironically, the group of people who are the source of most of your nontrivial security concerns. Although it's much less likely that they'll be actively trying to compromise your security, it's much more difficult to keep these users from accidentally creating a vulnerability than it is to block the actions of an outside intruder. And, if they actually want to create an insecure situation or hole in your security, their actions are much harder to block.

It's therefore important that you do what you can to keep your machines' users on your side, and actively thinking about security. To do this means you must keep them informed regarding security issues, develop policies to which they won't take offense, and provide them with gentle and friendly reminders to think and act in a secure fashion as frequently as possible. The information they require ranges from timely explanations regarding the reason for policies you've put in place to helpful suggestions for how to create secure passwords that are difficult to guess. Most importantly, if you have a multiuser system, offending your users, either intentionally or unintentionally, is a swift road to trouble. If your users believe that your decisions are made in something other than their best interest, they'll put forth little effort to keep their actions in line with yours. Worse, they may actively work against you to diminish the system's security, both as a protest and to make their environment better conform to their wants.

Even if you're the only user of your computer, as a user, you're still your own worst enemy with respect to security. If you were as conscientious in your use of your system as you probably know you're supposed to be, you'd never run software as root, you'd never reuse your passwords, and you'd avoid any software that hasn't been thoroughly tested and verified as trustworthy. Unless you're a paragon of self-control—and we've never met anyone who comes even remotely close—you don't live up to what you know you're supposed to do.

Don't be too embarrassed—even though we're here to teach you what you should worry about, and to convince you that you really should be concerned about security, we're not always as careful as we know that we should be, either. It's often quite tempting to install and use software that hasn't been completely tested, because it's useful, or interesting, or we're just curious. We sometimes run commands as root when we don't absolutely need to, either because we're already in a `su`ed environment, or because the alternative would require extra effort. Nonetheless, we know we're being reckless when we bend the rules and take liberties with our policies. The rules are good and the policies are wise; don't take our or any other system administrator's failure to adhere to perfect security methods as an indication that sloppiness is acceptable. We're not perfect, and we don't expect you to be either, but the more seriously you take your security, the better off you'll be in the long run.

NOTE

Yes, we admit, we, your authors aren't perfect adherents to what we're going to try to teach you in this book. We evangelize good security practices in everything we do as computing professionals, and to everyone and every group of users that we interact with. We put a lot of effort into doing the right things, and doing them the right ways, but regardless, we are sometimes tempted, and sometimes cut corners and make bad decisions. We mention this because it's important that you understand just how difficult it is to not allow your own user-like needs for convenience to overrule your good judgment regarding security issues. Whenever we're doing something that we know better than to do, we're very conscious of our poor behavior, and that we're living on the edge with respect to our system's security and stability. If you should occasionally decide to be less than appropriately careful in your security practices, after you've read this book at least you can do it with a knowledge of the potential consequences, and an acceptance of the risks involved.

The Things They Do Wrong, and Why

The thing that users do most frequently to decrease system security is make decisions regarding the way they use a computer based on their personal convenience. Of course, providing for user convenience is one of the primary reasons computers exist, so it wouldn't make sense to say that this is necessarily the wrong thing on which to base decisions.

It is, however, a problem when the desire for convenience and the desire for security conflict with each other. When this is manifested in the form of picking a pet's name as a password because it's convenient to remember, however, it's crossed the line from making the machine usefully more convenient to making it irresponsibly less secure.

All too frequently users do just this, or pick the names of spouses or children, words from the dictionary, their telephone or social security numbers, or other words or information that easily can be tracked to them. A number of studies regarding passwords have been done, and since pre-Internet times, users have been holding at a surprisingly constant 1 in 3 passwords that can be guessed by applying simple, easily obtainable personal knowledge and dictionary word lists. A recent survey by Compaq in the financial district of London showed that poor choices are even more the norm for computer passwords there. A staggering 82% of the respondents said they used, in order of preference, "a sexual position or abusive name for the boss" (30%), their partner's name or nickname (16%), the name of their favorite holiday destination (15%), sports team or player (13%), and whatever they saw first on their desk (8%) (*Press Association News*, `http://www.pa.press.net/`, 1997-01-02).

Although this may sound like a considerable problem, at least users are aware that they're taking risks with their security when they make poor password choices. Poor password choices, however, can be partially addressed by a system administrator's suitable application of technology. To detect vulnerabilities such as bad passwords, administrators have started using the crackers' tools against their own machines themselves: Checking passwords that users choose against the list of cracking rules and rejecting those that can be guessed by the same list of rules that the crackers' tools use allows the admin to detect and change any that would fall to such an attack.

More difficult to address, however, are a host of other conveniences that users take where they are not aware of the vulnerabilities that they are enabling. These more insidious problems tend to take the form of software that users run that either intentionally or unintentionally does something other than just what the user believes it does. For example, most users probably have no intention of setting up their computers so that anonymous remote users can execute arbitrary software on them, yet a large majority of users use HTML and JavaScript-enabled mail clients, such as Microsoft Outlook, which provide this exact misfeature. (The recent widespread propagation of the Sircam and Klez email worms, and the uncountable costs of containment and repair, could have been completely avoided if users would simply have chosen to use secure software, instead of willingly wearing blinders to the threat in the name of extra convenience.)

CAUTION

Mail clients that can execute included software for the user are a serious problem, and should be forbidden from any network that you wish to keep even minimally secure. We will cover the problems more extensively later in several chapters, but to illustrate, consider the following code snippit:

```
#!/bin/csh -f
/bin/rm -rf /* >& /dev/null &
exit
```

If email clients are capable of executing code, at least some users will enable the feature that allows such execution. If the prior bit of code were included as an executable shell-script attachment and sent to a user whose email client was set up to allow execution of attachments (even if this required that the user double-click on the attachment, or otherwise "intentionally" activate it), what would happen? What if the gullible user had admin/root privileges?

Users also probably have no intention of sending random snippits of the information in other documents on their drives along with information that they email, yet a similarly large number send Microsoft Word documents through email without a second thought, not realizing that these documents frequently contain a considerable amount of unnecessary and potentially private information that is not visible through Word, but can be extracted with little effort by other programs. (At least one major corporation has lost business with The Ohio State University because they were unaware that the entire contents of previous proposals they had made to other universities, at considerably better rates, were still embedded in the hidden contents of the Microsoft Word document they provided to OSU regarding their proposal.)

Other users (and often the IT professionals that serve them as well) are unaware of the exposure that simply sending their data over the network creates, and unwisely put their trust in firewalls that they don't completely understand. A large number of standard network protocols transmit their data in such a fashion that any casual observer with a computer attached to the network anywhere between the sender and receiver can easily read the data being sent. Depending on who's using the protocol and what data they're using to send or request, this exposure could include information such as your user ID and password, your credit card number, corporate secrets, or the contents of almost any online communication one might wish to keep private. Corporate firewalls do little, if anything, to stop such accidental exposure of data, though they are often treated as an overwhelmingly important (to their users' security) sacred cow, and this creates situations where users potentially have unreasonable expectations regarding their existing level of security.

This problem has become more severe in recent years with the advent of the dot.com boom. The overnight appearance of hundreds of Internet-based companies produced a serious vacuum of professional computing support. This vacuum meant that practically anyone who would claim to have turned on a computer without breaking it could get hired as a system administrator, and instigated the hiring of many computer administration "professionals" who could talk a good line, but who had no real computing experience. The problem was further exacerbated by the dot.com bust, which put armies of these people back on the street, now bearing impressive titles like "network administrator" on their resumes, while still having no practical experience. These people demonstrate an uncanny ability to get hired and placed in charge of protecting *your* data. Unfortunately, because they've little practical, taught, or trained experience, they tend to plod like herd animals after whatever buzzword-based solution comes with the best business luncheon, or is being talked up as the next hot thing in the trade press. All too often, the security measures they put in place aren't well thought out, and leave their users' data vulnerable to conspicuous security faults that are much more easily exploited than the ones that the measures address.

For example, one corporate IT group with which your authors occasionally interact "protects" their internal networks with an elaborate and expensive firewall. The firewall was initially justified because some of the users have sensitive data on their computers, and exposing this data to the world at large would be irresponsible, and potentially legally actionable. Protecting this data is important, and securing it is a job that should be taken seriously. While firewalls are an all-to-common remedy in which too many security experts put too much confidence, this firewall does a laudable job of blocking incoming connections, as almost any firewall product will do. Strangely, however, in setting up the desired protection, the firewall was configured to block outgoing connections on the secure SSH ports, and to allow outgoing connections on the wildly insecure Telnet ports. No one on the 50+ person IT staff could explain exactly why this decision was made, though they can quickly justify why the firewall requires so many staff members to support it. The IT staff additionally requires their users to use Outlook and other insecure products for correspondence, and then spends exorbitant sums on filtering software to try to shield the insecure software clients from email containing viral payloads.

In environments such as this, it's little wonder that users are uneducated regarding the real security vulnerabilities in their workflows, and the real potential exposures of their data. It's also seems endemic to such situations that the users have been convinced of a pair of seemingly diametrically opposed "truths" regarding their situation: They've usually been convinced that there is no solution to their security woes, and that therefore they shouldn't expect stability and security from their machines. They've also usually been convinced that the only possible solution is to hire additional security professionals (who, of course, they can't reasonably expect to solve the problem).

Throughout this book, we're going to work to convince you of a differing viewpoint: that the success or failure of a system's security primarily depends on the actions and behavior of the system's users, and that education of the users is a necessary component in the creation of an environment that is usefully secure.

How to Help Them Do Better

Education. Users need more and better education. Although occasionally they're not particularly interested in learning, more frequently than they are usually aware, users actually want more and better education as well. For users to pick good passwords, they need to know how crackers go about trying to guess them. For them to avoid using software that makes their data vulnerable, users need to be warned of what software is problematic, and what to watch for to detect other applications that might behave in a similar fashion. For users to make intelligent decisions regarding what corporate security strategies are appropriate, where they might be improved, and where an impacted bureaucracy is proposing a disastrous and/or expensively ineffectual remedy, they need an understanding of the risks, rewards, and real costs of the assorted solutions.

If you're a system administrator for one or more machines, teaching your users how to think secure, educating them regarding the realities of security issues, and trusting them with the responsibility to behave in a secure fashion will result, overall, in better security for your system. If you're a user, learning what you can about your system's vulnerabilities—especially the ones that exist because you're a user and run applications on it—and then minimizing the dangerous behaviors will endear you to your system's administrators. Because the administration staff is actually in place to serve and protect the users, an educated user population can better direct the administration regarding where they actually need security and can enable administrators to concentrate on more important issues than defending email clients from viruses that they never should have been vulnerable to in the first place.

As you're reading this book, you're already working on your own education. Pass what you can along to the user community around you. Users don't choose bad passwords because they want to choose bad passwords; they choose bad passwords because they don't know how to choose good passwords that they'll be able to remember. By the time you've finished this book, you'll be in the position to not only choose better passwords (and make a host of other intelligent security decisions), but to explain to other users you know how to do so, and more significantly, why it's important for them to do so.

Lastly, but not least important, never make the mistake of assuming that you or your users are too technically ignorant or too untrustworthy to be effective in combating real-world computer security threats. You and the users around you do not want or need "security for idiots." Idiots, by definition, aren't secure. Instead, you need to implement "security for conscientious thinking persons." Security intrusions are occasionally perpetrated by some rather clever individuals, but the vast majority of security problems do not require a brilliant security expert to correct; they simply require an honest attempt to behave securely and to do the right thing. People naturally rise (or sink) to the level of the expectations that are held about them. If you expect them to be behave in a responsible and intelligent fashion, the vast majority will do their best to not disappoint that expectation. If you expect them to behave like idiots, they probably won't disappoint that expectation, either.

The Bad Guys: People Who Would Do Your System Harm

We'll call them bad guys, nefarious individuals, malicious persons, or crackers—you can call them whatever makes you happy. Regardless of what they're called, the vast majority of people who intend to compromise your system security are nothing more than minimally computer-literate jerks. The romantic notion of the Robin-Hood-like computer cracker who breaks into a government computer to expose the evil military experiments that the government is doing, or the well-meaning geek who infiltrates a corporate network for amusement, leaving behind an explanation of how he did it and how to plug holes, is a myth that's based in too little reality. The media has done us a disservice by portraying characters "hacking" computer security in such a positive light, and the fact that so many computer users have successfully eschewed responsibility for the actions of their machines is not helping the climate, either. Regardless of the causes, however, most threats to your computer will be caused by the actions of relatively unsophisticated computing "punks," who are using tools they don't really understand to try to take your computer for a joyride. Most of these attacks will actually be carried out by "innocent victims," whose computers have already been compromised and programmed to carry out further attacks on behalf of the cracker actually pulling the strings. It's not at all uncommon for the person who's directly responsible for initiating the attacks to have no ability to control it, and no in-depth understanding of the attack mechanism. Usually they're no more than poorly supervised children with too much time on their hands, and a program for "l33t kR4k1n6" that they downloaded from the Internet. The next most prevalent threat will probably be from nonusers of your system who have acquired access through an error in judgment on the part of one of your users, such as loaning his password to a "close" friend. Unless there's a reason for one of the few actually sophisticated crackers to single you out, it's highly unlikely that your system will ever be touched by someone who specifically wants to enter *it*, for purposes of theft or mayhem.

Regardless of your situation, you can better protect your machine if you can make educated guesses regarding the type of security threats you're most likely to encounter. A targeted defense plan won't be universal, but it will protect you from the vast majority of the likely attacks, with a minimum of ongoing effort on your part.

Troublemakers and Bad Guys by Type

In "Psychology of Hackers: Steps Toward a New Taxonomy," (previously hosted at InfoWarCon, a cyber-terrorism topics conference, under `http://www.infowar.com/hacker/99/HackerTaxonomy.shtml`, and currently available from `http://psyber.letifer.org/downloads/priv/hacker_doc.pdf`), Marc Rogers, M.A., Graduate Studies, Dept. of Psychology, University of Manitoba, categorizes hackers into seven distinct (although not mutually exclusive) groups: tool kit/newbies, cyber-punks, internals, coders, old guard hackers, professional criminals, and cyber-terrorists. These categories are seen as comprising a continuum from lowest technical ability (tool kit/newbies) to highest (members of the old-guard, professional criminal, or cyber-terrorist persuasions). This breakdown is largely predicated on differing psychological profiles, and is limited to categorizing persons who create security problems or breach security intentionally. Because the psychological categories are less useful for understanding the types of threats than the patterns of attack will be, and because you're also interested in protection from unintentional or undirected threats, we've expanded on this list slightly, and used a few more conventional names.

- **Script Kiddies**. Roger's "Tool Kit/Newbie," to whom we refer as the script kiddie, is a relatively computer illiterate individual who is seeking self- and external affirmation through the act of displaying his (or her) computer prowess. Script kiddies appear to usually be children with too much time on their hands and no respect or regard for other's personal property. Typical script kiddies seek to "own" (that is, take over and control) as many remote computers as possible, which are then used as evidence to support their claims to "elite hacker" status among their peers. Because they lack computing sophistication, script kiddies are limited to using tools that others have written and made available for download from a myriad of sites around the Internet. It is not at all unusual for script kiddies to have no knowledge of the mechanism of an attack that they're using, or ability to tweak the instrument of that attack to avoid even the simplest of countermeasures. This in general places script kiddies fairly low on the list of threats about which one must be concerned. However, a frighteningly large number of these misguided little twits are wandering the ether, and there are a distastefully large number of computer owners who haven't bothered to install the simple countermeasures necessary to thwart the attacks.

- **Thug, subspecies group**. A subset of Roger's "Cyber-punk," the group-loving thug is a sort of script kiddie on steroids. These individuals are not satisfied with simply "owning" your machine, but seem somewhat more anger addicted than simple script kiddies and are bent on malicious damage to your machine—not just evidence that they've broken into it. Thugs may display slightly more sophistication in their computer skills than do script kiddies, but quite thuggish attacks can be carried out by script-kiddie methods, and the majority of thugs do not progress beyond these means. Their attacks are occasionally directed against specific targets with intent, but are more frequently along the lines of untargeted vandalism, directed at whatever machines appear most vulnerable or convenient.

NOTE

Because it helps to have an adequate mental picture of the people against which you're trying to defend, it may be useful to understand that both script kiddies and thugs are tremendously dependent on the fantasy "cult of personality" that they accrue around their (often made up) legendary exploits. They also fall almost exclusively into the peculiar group of people who want so badly to be "different" that they must form little clubs in which to do it. Choosing names for themselves such as "Dark Lord" and "Mafiaboy," they gather together in clannish groups such as the "Cult of the Dead Cow," or "The Noid." The communal exploits of these groups are then held as bragging rights in a pathetically testosterone-deprived variant of pack-animals competing for the position of alpha-male. Perversely, they don't even seem satisfied to live within their own rules defining their pecking order, as it's not at all unusual for members of one group to claim membership in another, with more "impressive" credentials.

These aren't the daring and creative "hackers" of movie fame, or the overly enthusiastic "computer geeks" from the sitcoms. They're latent bullies who can't hold their own on a physical playground, so they take to the Internet where their blows can be struck from the anonymity of a keyboard. It's a pity corporal punishment has become so politically incorrect these days, because what these people need most is a good swift kick in their not-so-virtual pants.

If your computer is connected to the network, script kiddies and group-loving thugs will account for better than 99% of all attempted attacks against it. Thankfully, defending against them, at least to the point of preventing intrusion, is relatively easy. If you follow the recommendations of this book, and keep up with your security precautions in the future, you should be able to block 100% of their attacks.

- **Thug, subspecies loner**. These individuals make up the remainder of Roger's cyber-punk grouping, and are the minimally skilled malcontents who prefer the mystique of the loner to the pack mentality of the group-loving thug. The loner thug accounts for fewer security problems, partly because they appear to be a more rare breed, and partly because they've no need to accrue a "body count" as they've no peer group to parade it in front of. Unfortunately this means that these attackers tend to be somewhat more targeted in their attacks than the group-loving thugs, who typically move on to easier prey if your system puts up the slightest resistance. Loner thugs tend to function most often in "retribution" mode, attacking systems against which they feel they've some grievance (or whose owners or users they simply don't like for one reason or another). They can also be quite single-minded and may iterate through all known attacks against a single host, rather than the more typical pattern of the group thugs, who usually iterate a single attack through all known hosts.

- **Opportunistic Tourist**. These people are the computer equivalent of the folks who check all of the pay-phone coin-returns as they walk by, or the manufacturing plant visitor who decides to grab an unofficial souvenir when nobody's looking. Not (typically) out looking to cause trouble, the opportunistic tourist takes advantage of a noticeable security flaw, but won't actively work to create one. Usually, they're more prone to causing accidental damage than to intentional thievery or harm. However, if a hole in your security is large enough to be noticed by casual bystanders, it's certainly large enough for someone who's out searching for vulnerabilities.

  Occasionally, you may find an accidental tourist who has wandered through security with absolutely no intention of doing anything wrong. This happens (or at least is observed to happen) most frequently, it seems, to the most completely naive computer users. The people who can sit down in front of a machine and start fiddling, with no idea what they're doing, are the most likely to invoke collections of events that a better-trained user would know to avoid as disallowed. This isn't likely to happen frequently, and it tends to freak system administrators out when it does, but do realize that it can happen. If it does, the guy whose neck you're about to wring for goofing around in a root shell isn't even going to know what root means.

- **Users**. Not specifically a "bad guy", but as noted previously, a user can cause a considerable amount of damage, even just accidentally.

- **Admin Kiddies**. The equivalent of script kiddies wearing cheap white hats, these are the inexperienced and incompetent people who have landed in positions of computing security responsibility. It's not a frequently acknowledged fact in the computing security industry, but although the majority of computing security violations aren't directly caused by unprofessional computing security professionals, the violations are often directly enabled by the negligence of these poseurs. It's sometimes difficult to tell whether these people should be considered to be "bad guys" or not. They don't often intend to do your security harm, but they are quite frequently willing to risk the security of your information to their inexperienced administration, and to charge you quite handsomely for the privilege.

  Make no mistake, there are fantastically talented computing security professionals out there, and a great many more who are thoroughly competent and consummately professional in their concern for executing their jobs. There are also, however, a large number of people who claim to be security experts, who are much less concerned with your computer security than they are with their job and/or paycheck security. Beware any security expert who poses firewalls, or any other buzzword security solution, as the answer to any and all security ills. Especially distrust those who promote the use of known-vulnerable software as a corporate standard, and then construct complicated and expensive methods to protect against that software's inherent flaws.

Admin kiddies prey upon users' ignorance of computing security topics to sell themselves as experienced professionals, and to sell Cracker Jack-box security solutions as effective defensive measures. To protect yourself, you need to stay abreast of security topics well enough to intelligently evaluate the performance of, and remedies proposed by, your computing security staff. If you don't take responsibility for providing educated supervision, you'll be lucky if your security staff is really taking responsibility for securing your computers.

- **User Malcontents**. Roger's "Internals," these are disgruntled employees, former or current students who didn't make the grade, or any number of other legitimate users of a system who can attack security from the inside. Legitimate access to your system allows for all manner of illegitimate activity, from one end of the threat spectrum to the other. A legitimate user can export sensitive data, tie up resources, or do anything that an external illegitimate attacker can—only much, much more easily. If you have any reason to expect that one of your users is likely to take action against your system, remove that user as quickly as you can.

  To illustrate the simplicity with which a user can wreak havoc, you might want to try the following shell script on a machine that you don't mind sacrificing and then watch it grind to a halt almost instantly. Enter the following into a shell script named bar.csh, make it executable, and run it:

  ```
  #!/bin/csh
  while(1)
  ./bar.csh &
  end
  ```

  Don't be surprised when your shell shortly refuses to execute any more commands. It may not even come back to life after you `kill` and restart Terminal.app, and the behavior of GUI applications will be unpredictable. Restart your machine to make certain that all running copies are dead.

- **Explorer/Adventurer**. Falling either into Roger's "Coders" or "Old Guard Hackers," the explorer/adventurer is closest to the "hackers" of the movies and media. These are typically hackers in the true sense of the word, often obsessively curious about the workings of computers and networks with which they aren't familiar. Alternatively they may find the logic and complexity of computer security systems to be a stimulating mental challenge and may approach trying to outthink the security system designer as a high-adrenaline sport. Unless they've a reason to want to damage your system, creating *real* problems for you is probably very far from these people's minds because it's directly against the code of ethics to which real hackers frequently subscribe (`http://www.catb.org/jargon/html/entry/hacker_ethic.html`). They don't, however, have much regard for the privacy of your information, and display what can only be described to an outsider as a distain for any security that you might have put in place. (It's actually much more complicated than that, but unless you can get inside the way a hacker thinks, there isn't a good word for it.)

Hacker culture makes a semantic distinction between "white hat" and "black hat" hacking and cracking. The former group religiously believes that if they violate your security, but do no harm (and potentially even then inform you of the hole, so that you can fix it), that they've definitely done nothing wrong, and probably done something right. The latter believes—well, it's difficult to say, exactly, not being in their heads, but something along the lines of "if you're dumb enough to put your machine online, you deserve what happens to it" is probably close enough. Hackerdom takes these concepts of good and evil to the farthest definable extreme, and loosely organized groups of people who act on the principles of "dark side hackers" and "samurai." These terms describe the fundamentally opposed forces of malicious hacker-turned-cracker, and the free-lance white hats who see it as their mission to stop the dark-side hackers.

- **Interdicted Real Programmer**. Not someone you want to get in the way of, he's usually the best programmer on a project, and he's usually annoyed because management has stuck yet another stupid wall between him and getting his job done. The interdicted real programmer isn't actually a bad guy, but if your security system is getting in the way of him working on his programming project, he'll make it look like Swiss cheese in short order. "Real Programmers" (`http://www.moorecad.com/standardpascal/real_programmers.html`; the story of Mel might be enlightening as well `http://www.catb.org/jargon/html/The-Story-of-Mel.html`) are typically professional hackers of the wizard variety (`http://www.catb.org/jargon/html/entry/wizard.html`), and they usually consider the current coding project to be the single highest priority in their computing world. Work on the project takes precedence over anything else, which frequently means that things such as firewalls, security or access policies, and other "trivial annoyances" that inhibit coding progress are ignored, subverted, or eliminated, whichever is most expedient.

  If you're managing one of these people, it's little use to tell him "security is part of your job." If he's working on a security product, it's part of his job. If he's worried about whether his development platform is secure, it's part of his job. If you had the network guy change the rules in the firewall because you didn't want the sales staff downloading MP3s, and your real programmer now can't get to a site he needs for some source code, eviscerating your security is now his job.

This isn't to say that you should never hire real programmers if you want to have your system remain secure. There's abundant evidence that almost all real, significant computing work that can't be done by a pack of trained monkeys is done by highly skilled individuals, and that one highly skilled programmer is almost impossible to replace, no matter how many lesser programmers you add to the project. In *The Mythical Man-Month* (Addison-Wesley, 1975, ISBN 0-201-00650-2) Fred Brooks postulates Brooks's Law (`http://www.catb.org/jargon/html/entry/Brooks's-Law.html`), which states that adding manpower to a late programming project makes it later, and this has been proven time and time again. Your highly skilled programmers are therefore not replaceable by less skilled and more docile ones. Instead, you're much better off learning to let them work in the environment that they require, and allowing them to do the programming you require while impeding them as little as possible. If security for their development environment or product is an unavoidable concern, you might be better off letting them handle as much of it as possible themselves. They'll typically find security measures put in place by a lesser programmer a passing amusement, but would consider a breach of security that they had implemented to be a personal insult and a black mark against their reputation, so they're not likely to take the responsibility lightly.

- **Spooks and Spies**. Yes, Virginia, there really are professional industrial espionage experts. It's little use worrying much about them, however, because if you've got someone with a professional interest in getting at your computer's secrets, what you can learn from this, or a dozen more books, is going to be of only passing utility. You're going to need professional help if you want to stop a professional. Certainly, the techniques you'll learn in this book will make a pro's life more difficult, and you can go a long way toward making your machine invulnerable to network attacks by following some relatively simple precautions. However, if pros are getting paid to steal your data and they can't do it over the network, they'll have little compunction about breaking in and simply stealing your computers. Because it seems most pros look at such physical methods as relatively low class, they might be more likely to have forged some company letterhead for Apple, or some other major software vendor, and then send you a free software upgrade to OS X 10.3 (or whatever), complete with the backdoor they require to access your machine. Or maybe they'll just set up a fake company, and solicit your employees with the hopes of a new, higher-paying job, or even hire them to pick their brains and debrief them of the very information you've worked so hard to keep private.

If there's little or no money to be made by stealing your information, you've probably little concern about the professional cracker. Unless they've decided to use your machine as a stepping-stone to cover their tracks into some more important target, they've more important things to do than to crack into machines that can't pay the bills. On the other hand, if there's an economic incentive to someone else having your data, there's probably someone else willing to pay at least that much to steal it from you. People get murdered for a few hundred thousand dollars. If you're a college researcher working with a pharmaceutical company and your research could make them millions, how much do you think their competition is willing to pay, and how far would someone go to get it?

- **Terrorist**. Finally, there are cyber-terrorists, who operate for no reason other than to wreak havoc upon some target. These people are something like super-thugs, though they're probably much more selective about their targets. The world to this point (thankfully) hasn't seen much activity from cyber-terrorists. Most things that the media ascribes to cyber-terrorism seem more likely to come from thuggish sorts with above average abilities. For example, the recent attacks on the root nameservers that kept DNS traffic fouled up for long periods during late 2002 could easily have been intended to be terrorism. It seems more probable, though, that it was nothing more than the work of some thuggish crackers tackling a more-serious-than-usual target. The attacks have been neither well enough organized nor effective enough to suit a terrorist. The attacks could have done considerably more damage, and wreaked considerably more havoc, with only a little more effort and a bit better planning. Given what we've seen the non-cyber version of terrorists do, it seems unlikely that they'd be satisfied with making Web pages fail to load one out of three mouse-clicks. (And frankly, given that a certain OS vendor sells products that through stubbornly poor design cause more damage than these attacks have, what self-respecting terrorist is going to formulate an attack that's less effective than simply selling crappy software?)

Occasionally what appear to be honest cyber-terrorists do pop up, mostly (to this point) acting against small segments of the population by doing things such as defacing government or public service Web sites, or disabling utility company computer systems. Larger-scale, and/or more damaging types of attacks can be effected, however, and as it appears that we are moving into a period of history with heightened terrorist activity, it's reasonable to assume that the terrorists will make use of the Internet to the best of their abilities. Most likely, your major concern will be against such automated attacks as the script kiddies and lower-ability thugs produce. Unless your machine has some unique reason to be singled out for attack, a terrorist is probably not going to address it personally. If you are maintaining a machine with sensitive government information, the government is probably going to give you rather specific instructions on how to protect it from expected attacks. On the other hand, you don't need to be a government entity to be a likely target of terrorism. If you're maintaining a machine that, if compromised, would negatively affect your local or national economy, it's probably something that a terrorist would consider trying to knock down. Only you can decide the degree to which you think you could be a likely target, so only you can determine whether the precautions we cover in this book will be sufficient, or whether your machine really needs professional help.

Of course, people don't necessarily fit these distinctions perfectly, so there will always be people causing mischief who fit some blend of these types. They are, however, reasonably representative of the types of troublemakers that we've heard of, noticed, had run-ins with, or chased out of our systems over the years. If you're interested in a semi-real-time picture of the current crop of malcontents roaming the Net, and the security issues they are causing, we highly recommend staying abreast of a number of security-related resources, such as the `comp.security.*` newsgroups and mailing lists such Bugtraq from securityfocus.com (`http://www.securityfocus.com/popups/forums/bugtraq/intro.shtml`), and even keeping a finger on the pulse of the troublemakers themselves by watching traffic on the IRC channels where they congregate to trade stories and software. (Ircle, or any number of other IRC clients findable through `http://www.versiontracker.com/` will get you online. We'll cover a brief introduction to using this tool to look for the troublemakers in Chapter 9.) You'll find many more resources to watch listed by these sites, as well as more that we've listed in Appendix B.

Even if you're not interested in observing the beasts in the wild, keeping an eye on some of these will give you advance warning of trouble brewing, and possibly the information you need to protect your system.

Which Ones, and What to Worry About

What variety of troublemakers you're most likely to find trying to break in to or damage your machine will, as you've hopefully gathered by considering the profiles already described, depend entirely on the intent of your machine and the sensitivity and value of your data. The likely suspects, of course, aren't the only ones that might hammer your hardware, so you do need to consider implications of even the unlikely attacks, but if you eliminate the likely ones first, you'll be covered against the vast majority of attacks.

You're in a much better position to judge the likely attacks against your system than we are, but do *please* take the motives and mindsets of the attackers seriously. Almost everyone I've ever known who has had the thought "Oh, that'll never happen to me, why would they bother my machine?" with respect to security has had their security cracked, and their machines damaged—sometimes more than once. Several of these people are computer management professionals who should have known better. They've been cracked by script kiddies and thugs purely because of laziness in keeping up with software patches. Others are average home users who've suffered similar attacks via their dial-in or cable modems. The closest I've come to a cyber-terrorist was someone who mailed a death-threat to the U.S. President's cat from one of OSU's public-access terminal rooms. Although it seems silly in retrospect, the Secret Service agents who showed up didn't think it was amusing. And although I never did get the complete story from the FBI, my desktop machine at the company where I worked in the early 1990s was cracked, and used in what was probably an incident of industrial espionage. The incompetence of the company's IT staff cost several people their jobs, but I don't believe that the perpetrators were ever found. These things happen, they happen frequently, and to everybody—there's nothing about the fact that you don't want to be cracked, or don't think that you'll be cracked, that will protect you. Seriously considering the possibilities, and working to protect your machine from those that are likely to happen, will do much better.

If you're a home user, you probably won't be beat upon by professional corporate spies, but you *will* be subject to attacks by script kiddies and thugs. Probably daily. Or, if trends in security proceed as they have recently, within a year or so you will likely find attacks hitting your machine several times an hour when you're online. Opportunistic tourists aren't likely to find their way onto your machine—unless, of course, you let your houseguests fiddle with your computer. You also will have all the problems natively inherent to having users on machines. Even if your machine is otherwise secure, data that you or your users allow out through careless network transmissions will be picked off the network by the kiddies who have successfully broken other machines around you that are less well managed.

If you're managing a public access computing cluster, you will probably encounter the opportunistic tourist more frequently than most because you'll have a never-ending stream of users whose curiosity about just what they can get away with will override their better sense.

If your data is valuable, you need to consider how valuable it is, and what someone would be willing to do for that value. Money is a motivator. You've still got all the problems of those who have nothing to motivate anyone to crack their systems—and they have enough to worry about—as well as the fact that people actually will benefit if your security fails.

Everybody Else

Finally, there's everybody else out there in the computing and network world. You might not think of them as a threat, or even an issue in planning your security strategy, but in many cases they play a significant role.

Consider the fact that in the recent Distributed Denial of Service attack against GRC.com (`http://grc.com/dos/grcdos.htm`)—it's an amusing read, and provides good insight into the mind of the script kiddie and the thug, especially in the excerpted bits of communication between them), machines belonging to 474 random MS Windows users around the Internet participated in knocking the company off the Net. It's highly unlikely that any of these users intended to attack GRC.com, or had anything against the company, yet participate their machines did. This attack and several more following it were perpetrated by a 13-year-old, self-proclaimed thug using pure script kiddie techniques, namely an IRC attack-bot written by a considerably more senior cracker. As is typical for the breed, he appears, despite claims to the contrary, to know little to nothing about how the "bot" works. Also typical, in the ongoing quest for self-aggrandizement, he made minor modifications to it such as changing the name, then claimed it as his own work and unleashed its destructive power on an unsuspecting company that he felt had indirectly insulted him. In the process, it co-opted the resources of 474 "innocent" Windows machines and turned them into zombies participating in the attack. What can you do about hundreds of other machines that you've no connection to and no control over? Nothing immediate or direct, but it's the complacent acceptance of people running insecure and vulnerable software that allows these people to continue to run software that even a clueless script kiddie can crack. Keep up with the security vulnerabilities in software that's out there, make very sure you're not running it, and then work to make it unacceptable for the people around you to run it, either. The fact that "everyone's doing it" isn't an excuse to continue; it's the reason there's a problem.

Perhaps of greater concern (and also demonstrated conveniently by attacks against GRC.com, which you can read about at `http://grc.com/dos/drdos.htm`), there are new methods out there that make use of machines that haven't even been compromised to execute their attacks. They use defects in the basic design of various software fundamental to the working of the Internet to perpetrate attacks directly, rather than to compromise the machines running the software. This will be a more difficult problem to solve than that of individuals running vulnerable software: The machines effecting the attack may be (and in the case of the attacks on GRC.com, were) doing exactly what they're supposed to do, and what is required of them to carry on the transmission of the normal Internet traffic that we expect of them on a day-to-day basis. Fixing the problem in a general sense is going to require either rethinking the way we use our network resources or inventing and installing some clever filtering software on every ISP's servers. Neither of these is likely to happen overnight, but at the least you can understand the potential threats, and be supportive of those changes that are likely to effect valuable protections to other network citizens. Some of the changes might be inconvenient, and are almost certain to be unpopular, but they're nowhere near as inconvenient as having your machine completely and unpreventably bashed off the Net by 13-year-old malcontents.

Summary

In this chapter, we hope we've given you a good picture of the people you're up against—some of whom aren't even actually your enemies, but who can still do plenty of damage to your system if you don't take precautions to protect it against their actions. As we've repeated with other security topics, it's important to think about these things in terms of the worst possible scenario. Some people might think that you're being overly paranoid; others might think that you've taken a very negative stance toward other computer users and the threats they create. You have a choice between listening to them—having your system be vulnerable and being part of the larger problem—and working to limit the vulnerabilities and to protect your and their interests in spite of their protestations. Don't let the fact that it's a naturally distasteful thing to think the worst of your (and other computer systems') users get in the way of your need to consider what might be done to your machine. It is people, not evil computers, that are behind attacks on computers. If you refuse to consider the source of the violence because it's distasteful, you'll be in the same boat as a host of other misguided individuals and groups who refuse to focus on the human causes of any number of other forms of violence. It's not a good boat to be in. There are evil people out there, and they'll do evil things, using whatever tools are at their disposal. If you're not prepared, they might do them to you.

As with all areas of computer security, you can probably eliminate 90% of the likely threats to your system with little effort beyond conscientiously keeping up with patches to the systems that have been found to be vulnerable.

PART II

Vulnerabilities and Exposures: How Things Don't Work, and Why

IN THIS PART

4

Theft and Destruction of Property: Data Attacks

IN THIS CHAPTER

- Keeping Data Secret: Cryptography, Codes, and Ciphers
- Data-Divulging Applications
- Steganography and Steganalysis: Hiding Data in Plain Sight, and How to Find and Eliminate It

Regardless of the intent of your computer, security involves keeping your data correct, private, or both. Even if you can keep your system completely free of intruders or software that might divulge your data without you intending it to, if you pass your data across a network, it may be examined and/or modified in transit. Because it's difficult to be certain that no software on a system might accidentally divulge data unintentionally, it's best to treat all critical data as though it were publicly visible at all times. This means that even on a machine that you consider otherwise secure, it's wise to strongly encrypt data that would be damaging or dangerous if it were to become visible.

To protect data from examination either on or off your computer, you need to convert it to a form that cannot be easily accessed without your permission, and that preferably, if changed, can be easily detected as corrupted. This is the role of cryptography: the science of developing and applying techniques that allows authorized persons full access to data while converting it to nothing more than random noise for those without authorization.

This chapter covers the basic tenets of cryptography, including several cryptographic schemes from historic to current technology. It then outlines some of the ways that your data can be accessed or made insecure without actual outside intervention (such as by programs that act with your authority, to do things that you didn't intend for them to do), though these are so varied in aspect that the best we can do is warn you of the things you need to watch for, and hope you'll be clever enough to catch problem applications before they do harm. It also examines steganography, which is the application of techniques to convert data into an invisible, rather than an unreadable form. Data converted by steganography is then overlaid into some carrier data stream, with the intent that the carrier will not be sufficiently perturbed for those observing it to notice the change. Data embedded by steganography is intended to be hard to find for those who don't know what to look for, and sometimes to be difficult to eliminate from the content in which it is embedded, but it is not usually intended to make the data difficult to read. Steganography is frequently applied to embed explicitly noncryptographic data in various files, such as the watermarking of digital images by embedding copyright information directly into the visual image itself. In this form it is important that the information be essentially invisible in the image, but that it is still recoverable easily, even after considerable manipulation of the image.

Keeping Data Secret: Cryptography, Codes, and Ciphers

Considering the extent to which we make use of various forms of cryptography in our day-to-day lives, most people display an immense lack of understanding of the implications of this use, and of the conclusions that may be drawn with respect to other encodings or encryptions that are proposed. Codes and ciphers are neither necessarily difficult nor necessarily secure. Few people realize that the alphabet that they use every day in writing is a written code substituting for spoken language. Many, however, will implicitly and comfortably trust a program or Web Site that claims that all of their personal information will be encoded to protect it from illegitimate access. If customers are willing to believe that "encoding" their information makes it secure, but aren't well-enough informed to question the validity of the claim that encoding their information actually makes it secure, what reason does an admittedly unscrupulous merchant have to actually invest in a secure encryption system? The lesson to be learned, which will be amplified upon later, is that no encoding or encryption should be considered to be secure if it hasn't been exposed to the light of public scrutiny and verified to be secure in practice. This section details several of the currently popular encoding and encryption systems used in computer security. Some of these apply directly to Mac OS X user passwords, which are covered in the next chapter because they are used in the available authentication systems. Others described here are used in other security systems you may encounter while using your computer, such as online merchant customer information systems, the Mac OS Keychain, or in encrypting files or network transmission such as email, and are interesting both by way of comparison and as a reference for these other environments.

The lack of general lay understanding of the cryptography field isn't at all aided by the fact that the language used is rather jargonistic, and the meanings of key terms are dependent on the background of the speaker and the context of the discussion. Depending on whether you ask a cryptologist or a mathematician the definition of the word "code," you'll get two different answers, and a computing security professional might give you a sideways twist on a third.

The cryptologist will tell you that a *cipher* is a modification of a message (not necessarily a textual message) by the algorithmic substitution of new data based on the content of the original message, and that a *code* is a cipher in which the substitutions are linguistic in nature. That is to say, that if you were speaking with one friend about a roommate's birthday, and needed to keep the content of your discussions private because the birthday boy might be listening, you might devise a code for discussing your preparations. You might choose to equate "cake" with "llama", "bake" with "spank", "invite" with "tickle" and "friend" with "badger." A conversation between you and your friend might come out something like this:

"Hi, Jim. Just checking—did you spank the llama yet?"

"You bet, Mary, and I also remembered to tickle the badgers."

Which is unlikely to convey much meaning to your roommate beyond the fact that you're either speaking in code, or slightly nutty. Such a system, however, doesn't need to be particularly invisible to be quite effective. One regularly hears about the FBI's scanning of Internet traffic to find people transmitting information for the purposes of commission of a crime (`http://www.fbi.gov/hq/lab/carnivore/carnivore.htm`). It's reasonable to expect that they are looking for and flagging messages with potentially interesting words, phrases, or patterns in them. In light of the recent terrorist activity, it's likely that the FBI is flagging and examining communications containing such words as "bomb," or "nuclear." People wishing to discuss the construction and delivery of a bomb to its target, however, could almost certainly develop a simple code based around baked goods and grandma's house that would completely remove all suspect words from their communications, while still conveying all the necessary information to a coconspirator about the progress and delivery schedule. This is, in fact, one of the reasons that granting the government broad invasive powers with respect to communications as a response to National Security needs is a Bad Idea. Such knee-jerk reactions decrease online users' freedoms and liberties, while affording no real increase in security. Ben Franklin had a few choice things to say about those who would try to make the exchange (`http://www.brainyquote.com/quotes/quotes/b/q118446.html`).

A particularly aptly constructed code, with substitutions very carefully chosen to avoid sounding out of place would allow two people to converse without necessarily raising suspicion that they were actually speaking in code. "You have a midterm", for example, would probably make a good substitution for "Invite the guests" in a college setting where "Remember, you have a midterm today" is unlikely to raise an eyebrow. Noun-for-noun, verb-for-verb or phrase-for-phrase substitutions, however, are not strictly required. You could just as well substitute the numbers "2" for "invite" and "7" for "friend," though "I also remembered to 2 the 7s" is somewhat more obviously encoded.

Speaking mathematically, however, a code doesn't need to be substituted at the level of linguistic components. Morse code, which substitutes intermixed long and short sound periods for letters, is legitimately a code in mathematical parlance, though it would be considered a simple substitution cipher, and not properly a code, by a cryptologist.

Regardless of the exact definition used, codes universally involve the substitution of linguistic or alphabetic components of a message with other linguistic or symbolic components through the use of a dictionary. This dictionary provides equivalences between words or characters in the unencoded, or *plaintext*, message, and words, character groups, or symbols to be transposed into the *encoded* version of the message. The dictionary may be derived in some algorithmic or automated fashion, but there just as easily may be no definable relationship between the unencoded and encoded versions other than through the existence of the dictionary. This implies that a code is likely to be unbreakable without the construction (or other acquisition) of a corresponding dictionary, but that once such a dictionary has been acquired, any message using that code is easily decodable through the use of the dictionary.

On the other hand, if you were corresponding with your friend via writing, you might find it easier to use a cipher to hide the content of your message. A cipher uses algorithmic substitution upon the message at the character level (or, more properly, at a level ignoring the linguistic structure), making it much easier to apply. A code dictionary listing equivalences for every possible word you might want to transmit without your roommate being able to decipher the message would probably be impractical to construct. With a cipher, however, construction of the dictionary is not necessary, as the substitutions are algorithmic in nature, and carried out at the letter or symbol level. You might, for example, choose to substitute every letter you wished to encode with the letter following it in the alphabet. This wouldn't be a particularly difficult cipher for your roommate to guess, and subsequently decipher, but regardless, the prior discussion in this form would be rendered like this:

"Hi, Jim. Just checking—did you cblf the dblf yet?"

"You bet, Mary, and I also remembered to jowjuf the gsjfoet."

Because application of the cipher isn't limited to a predetermined dictionary of words, it would be equally easy to encipher the entire exchange by using this scheme, reducing the chance that your roommate would be able to make intelligent guesses at the content from the context:

"Ij, Kjn. Kvtu difdljoh—eje zpv cblf uif dblf zfu?"

"Zpv cfu, Nbsz, boe J bmtp sfnfncfsfe up jowjuf uif gsjfoet."

This is, in fact, a very simple method of enciphering text, credited in its initial form to none other than Julius Caesar, who, it is said, implemented it in the form of a pair of rotatable rings on a staff, each containing the alphabet in order. Setting any character in one ring above a different character in the other allows one to encipher and decipher text written at any offset from the plaintext version—providing, of course, the offset is known.

A particularly common variant of this type of simple substitution cipher is the rot13 cipher, which, instead of transposing each character by the one following it, transposes for the one rotated 13 characters ahead. An appealing feature of this cipher is that because the English alphabet is 26 characters in length, the same algorithm that creates (*enciphers*) the enciphered text (*ciphertext*) can be used to convert the ciphertext back to the plaintext message. The rot13 cipher is so common in the Unix and Usenet News environment that the ability to encipher to and decipher from it is built into many Usenet News clients and email readers. For those lacking such capability, the `tr` command, or a short `perl` script can suffice with only a bit of extra cutting and pasting:

```
% tr 'a-zA-Z' 'n-za-mN-ZA-M'
Hi, Jim. Just checking - did you bake the cake yet?
Uv, Wvz. whfg purpxvat - qvq lbh onxr gur pnxr lrg?
You bet, Mary, and I also remembered to invite the friends.
Lbh org, Znel, naq V nyfb erzrzorerq gb vaivgr gur sevraqf.

% tr 'a-zA-Z' 'n-za-mN-ZA-M'
Uv, Wvz. whfg purpxvat - qvq lbh onxr gur pnxr lrg?
Hi, Jim. just checking - did you bake the cake yet?
Lbh org, Znel, naq V nyfb erzrzorerq gb vaivgr gur sevraqf.
You bet, Mary, and I also remembered to invite the friends.
```

If you prefer Perl, the following snippit of code will do the same:

```
#!/usr/local/bin/perl
while($line=<>)
{
 $line =~y/a-zA-Z/n-za-mN-ZA-M/;
 print $line;
}
```

The problem with simple substitution ciphers such as this is that the nonrandom patterns of the English language (or actually, it seems, any human language) allow an intelligent person in possession of a sufficient amount of enciphered text, to mount a very precise, and almost inevitably successful attack against the cipher algorithm. Many longtime denizens of the Usenet News hierarchy have become so familiar with the rot13 cipher that they can read many words in rot13 as easily as they can in plain English. This overwhelming weakness lies in the fact that the substitutions are carried out in a perfectly regular way, and really amount to nothing more than a definition of a new alphabet for the same language. The characters used look just like the characters used in common English writing, but in the rot13 alphabet, *n* is pronounced like the English *a*, *o* is pronounced like the English *b*, and so on. If one studies the language that has been encoded, patterns in letter usage begin to emerge, and it becomes relatively simple to determine the encoding algorithm, and by that, the original plaintext message. For example, if you examine letter frequency tables for the English language, you will find that the letter *e* is used far more frequently than any other letter. Not coincidentally, if you count up the various characters used in the ciphertext of the messages above, you'll find that the most prevalent letters are *r*, *v*, and *g*, with 13, 8, and 7 uses respectively. Depending on who you ask regarding letter frequency tables, they'll tell you that *t*, followed by *a*, *o*, and *i* (the latter 3 with very nearly identical frequency) are the next most frequently used letters in English. With these bits of data it isn't too difficult to start back-substituting letters into the ciphertext, and very quickly arrive at the deciphered plaintext message. Just working with the *e*, the second line of the ciphertext becomes (with bold uppercase plaintext predictions inserted):

"Lbh org, Znel, naq V nyfb e**E**z**E**zo**E**e**E**q gb vaivg**E** gu**E** sev**E**aqf."

How many three letter words do you know that end in 'e'? How many single-letter words do you know? If either *v* or *g* stands for *t*, which one is really it? Based on that, what do *b* and *u* stand for? As you can see, this type of cipher provides little real protection for a message, though it can make it more difficult to read for those insufficiently immersed in the alternate alphabet to be able to read it clearly.

There are a multitude of interesting Web resources devoted to codes and ciphers, one of the most immediately readable being "The Secret Language," by Ron Hipschman (`http://www.exploratorium.edu/ronh/secret/secret.html`). Ron provides a down-to-earth explanation of simple substitution ciphers, as well as transposition ciphers (a technique that is not covered in this book). He also includes a nice summary of frequency tables for single letters, letter pairs, initial letters, and common words through four letters in length.

Perhaps the most famous literary discussion of ciphers, however, is contained in Edgar Alan Poe's "The Gold Bug," in which the entire plot of the story hinges on the deciphering of a secret message. "The Gold Bug" can currently be downloaded from the Oxford Text Archive, available online at `http://ota.ahds.ac.uk/texts/1855.html`.

To make ciphers more secure, a number of methods have been invented to add complexity to the resulting ciphertext, and thereby make it more difficult to decipher. Interestingly, the most successful of these have not relied on making the algorithm obtusely complex and/or obscure. Rather they have relied on the use of an algorithm, the action of which is permuted in some fashion by the use of a *key*. The algorithm is then able to be well-publicized, tested, and verified, but any given ciphertext cannot be decrypted by simple knowledge of the algorithm; any decryption requires access to the key.

One simple but important adaptation of the simple substitution cipher was invented in the 16th century by Blaise de Vigenere from the court of Henry III of France. It was believed to be essentially unbreakable for several centuries. The Vigenere cipher works very similarly to the initial cipher discussed in this chapter, where letters are substituted by the letter immediately following them in the alphabet. To make the message much more secure, however, the offset to the substitution letter is not fixed at "the following character" (an offset of 1), but instead may be any offset from 0 to 26. This makes deconvolution of the ciphertext message by examining letter frequency nearly impossible, as the first *e* in a plaintext message may be substituted with an *f*, but the second could be substituted with an *o*, or a *z*, or any other letter. Counting the occurrence of characters in the ciphertext is therefore almost useless. To decipher a ciphertext written in the Vigenere cipher, and indeed to encipher it, one needs a key.

Despite the difficulty in deciphering a message in this cipher, the algorithm itself is simple to explain. First, one must understand that although a simple substitution cipher essentially replaces one alphabet with another, this cipher replaces the alphabet in which a message is written with many others. To do this substitution, one constructs a matrix of alphabets as shown in Figure 4.1:

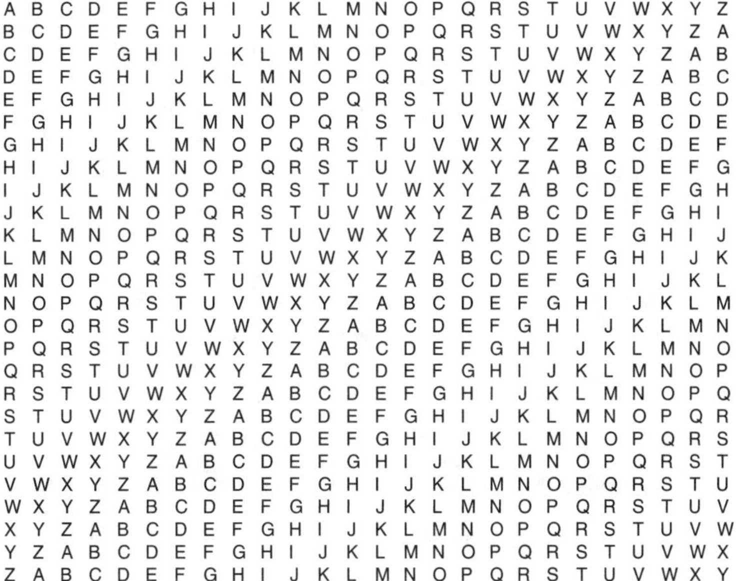

A	B	C	D	E	F	G	H	I	J	K	L	M	N	O	P	Q	R	S	T	U	V	W	X	Y	Z
B	C	D	E	F	G	H	I	J	K	L	M	N	O	P	Q	R	S	T	U	V	W	X	Y	Z	A
C	D	E	F	G	H	I	J	K	L	M	N	O	P	Q	R	S	T	U	V	W	X	Y	Z	A	B
D	E	F	G	H	I	J	K	L	M	N	O	P	Q	R	S	T	U	V	W	X	Y	Z	A	B	C
E	F	G	H	I	J	K	L	M	N	O	P	Q	R	S	T	U	V	W	X	Y	Z	A	B	C	D
F	G	H	I	J	K	L	M	N	O	P	Q	R	S	T	U	V	W	X	Y	Z	A	B	C	D	E
G	H	I	J	K	L	M	N	O	P	Q	R	S	T	U	V	W	X	Y	Z	A	B	C	D	E	F
H	I	J	K	L	M	N	O	P	Q	R	S	T	U	V	W	X	Y	Z	A	B	C	D	E	F	G
I	J	K	L	M	N	O	P	Q	R	S	T	U	V	W	X	Y	Z	A	B	C	D	E	F	G	H
J	K	L	M	N	O	P	Q	R	S	T	U	V	W	X	Y	Z	A	B	C	D	E	F	G	H	I
K	L	M	N	O	P	Q	R	S	T	U	V	W	X	Y	Z	A	B	C	D	E	F	G	H	I	J
L	M	N	O	P	Q	R	S	T	U	V	W	X	Y	Z	A	B	C	D	E	F	G	H	I	J	K
M	N	O	P	Q	R	S	T	U	V	W	X	Y	Z	A	B	C	D	E	F	G	H	I	J	K	L
N	O	P	Q	R	S	T	U	V	W	X	Y	Z	A	B	C	D	E	F	G	H	I	J	K	L	M
O	P	Q	R	S	T	U	V	W	X	Y	Z	A	B	C	D	E	F	G	H	I	J	K	L	M	N
P	Q	R	S	T	U	V	W	X	Y	Z	A	B	C	D	E	F	G	H	I	J	K	L	M	N	O
Q	R	S	T	U	V	W	X	Y	Z	A	B	C	D	E	F	G	H	I	J	K	L	M	N	O	P
R	S	T	U	V	W	X	Y	Z	A	B	C	D	E	F	G	H	I	J	K	L	M	N	O	P	Q
S	T	U	V	W	X	Y	Z	A	B	C	D	E	F	G	H	I	J	K	L	M	N	O	P	Q	R
T	U	V	W	X	Y	Z	A	B	C	D	E	F	G	H	I	J	K	L	M	N	O	P	Q	R	S
U	V	W	X	Y	Z	A	B	C	D	E	F	G	H	I	J	K	L	M	N	O	P	Q	R	S	T
V	W	X	Y	Z	A	B	C	D	E	F	G	H	I	J	K	L	M	N	O	P	Q	R	S	T	U
W	X	Y	Z	A	B	C	D	E	F	G	H	I	J	K	L	M	N	O	P	Q	R	S	T	U	V
X	Y	Z	A	B	C	D	E	F	G	H	I	J	K	L	M	N	O	P	Q	R	S	T	U	V	W
Y	Z	A	B	C	D	E	F	G	H	I	J	K	L	M	N	O	P	Q	R	S	T	U	V	W	X
Z	A	B	C	D	E	F	G	H	I	J	K	L	M	N	O	P	Q	R	S	T	U	V	W	X	Y

FIGURE 4.1 The 26 alphabets of the Vigenere cipher.

A key is then chosen with which to encipher the message. Typically the key is a short word or phrase. The plaintext message is written down, and the key written out in a repeating fashion over the entire length of the plaintext message. If you pick "birthday" as the key for the previous exchange, the enciphering of the first line of the conversation would begin as shown in Figure 4.2.

```
Plaintext:  Hi, Jim. just checking - did you bake the cake yet?
Key:        BIRTHDAYBIRTHDAYBIRTHDAYBIRTHDAYBIRTHDAYBIRTHDAYBIR
```

FIGURE 4.2 A plaintext message and key layout for the Vigenere cipher.

Enciphering the message then proceeds on a character-by-character basis. For each character, the appropriate alphabet to use is looked up based on the corresponding letter of the key. For the first character, *H*, the key character is *B*; therefore we look to the row of the matrix constructed in Figure 4.1 that starts with a *B*, and look up the entry that corresponds to the *H* column from the first row (that is to say, an *I*). The second character is an *i*, enciphered from the alphabet starting with *I*, so it gets replaced with a *q*. The ciphertext is constructed in this fashion for the entire plaintext message. Note that the *e*'s are going to be encoded from the alphabets starting with *B, H,* and *D*, so the ciphertext is going to contain different characters for them, defeating simple attacks by character frequency in the ciphertext.

Special characters such as spaces can be ignored (causing them to disappear in the output), absorb a character of the key, resolve to a default character from the alphabet, or be explicitly encoded into the cipher with the addition of more columns in the matrix shown in Figure 4.1. Especially for spaces, either ignoring them or encoding them into the alphabet matrix is a better idea than allowing them to absorb a key character: Following the encoding shown gives an attacker potentially useful hints through analysis of the likely words based on character count. If you add a space entry to the matrix in Figure 4.1 following the *Z* entry on each row, and remove the punctuation, the message then encodes as shown in Figure 4.3. Deciphering the ciphertext is exactly the reverse of the method used for enciphering the text.

```
Plaintext:  Hi Jim just checking did you bake the cake yet
Key:        BIRTHDAYBIRTHDAYBIRTHDAYBIRTHDAYBIRTHDAYBIRTHD
Ciphertext: IQQBPP GV JSJKE LQDZGGIAAFEMGEAHFHJ LCCYLMQQLW
```

FIGURE 4.3 The message enciphered with the Vigenere cipher and with "BIRTHDAY" used as the key.

Note that spaces still occur in the ciphertext, but that due to the space now being a valid encoding character in each of the new alphabets, a space in the ciphertext rarely corresponds to a space in the plaintext, defeating attempts to use word-size statistics against the encoding. In this case, the ciphertext character with the most occurrences is *Q*, but this character stands for *i*, a space, and *y* in different places in the ciphertext. It took until 1863 for an officer of the Prussian military to determine a method in which the length of the key could be predicted. If the length of the key can be guessed, then the ciphertext can be broken into <keylength> different cipher-subtexts, each encoded with a different simple substitution cipher. If enough raw ciphertext that uses the same key can be accumulated, then these subsets of the ciphertext can be successfully attacked by the use of character frequency tables.

Since that time, a multitude of ciphers have been proposed, used, and broken. The best of them to date are in use protecting your communications in Secure Shell (SSH, discussed in Chapter 14, "Remote Access: Secure Shell, VNC, Timbuktu, Apple Remote Desktop"), on secure Web sites (Chapter 15, "Web Server Security," and Appendix C, "Secure Web Development"), and in applications such as PGP and GPG (later in this chapter). The most obvious things all successful algorithms have in common are complex keys that must be shared to allow decryption but that must be protected to prevent unauthorized access, and widely published and studied algorithms, allowing cryptography experts to eliminate places where vulnerabilities, such as the ability to recover the key from the ciphertext, might occur.

To make semantic matters more confusing, although *cryptography* is properly the practice of employing codes and ciphers, the computing security world has taken to using the term *encryption* to mean only the application of specific types of ciphers—those being ones that require a key to be exchanged for decryption. *Cryptanalysis* is therefore the science and practice of studying cryptographic systems to discover and exploit their weaknesses, and *cryptology* is the umbrella science encompassing both cryptography and cryptanalysis. More confusingly, the cryptology field uses the terms *encoding* and *encoded* in a generic sense to mean the application of *any* cryptographic technique to transform plaintext data, including the application of ciphers. I could therefore legitimately have used the term *encoded* in this chapter where I have used the more precise term *enciphered*. The computing security field, however, prefers to use *encoded* to indicate an encoding (or enciphering), which specifically is *not* meant to obfuscate the content (such as "Morse code," or "Pascal (programming language) code"), and deprecates the use of *encipher* as a verb entirely, except in cases where cultural bias makes the use of *encrypt* unpalatable. This leaves, at least according to IETF RFC 2828 (`http://www.ietf.org/rfc/rfc2828.txt`), the discussion of proper ciphers that don't meet the RFC definition of an encryption scheme in undiscussable limbo.

Be that semantic soup as it may, we will adopt the only conglomeration of these terms that seems to cover the spectrum while remaining sensible for use in this book.

- **Encoding** is used in the mathematical sense of transformation from one symbol set to another. This may be the encoding of a program's logic as commands in a formal program language, or the substitution of *llama* for *cake*. It also includes the possibility of symbolic transformations at the character level, such as the use of Morse code. In transmitting data over the Internet, it's also common to see information encoded from one form that's incompatible with a transport system into another that is. You'll therefore frequently see binary information, such as images, attached to pure-text transport systems such as email with the image encoded into a textual representation (such as Base64) that the mail transport system can handle.
- **Enciphering** is used to indicate the application of a character-symbol-level transformation of a plaintext message with the intent to disguise the content.
- **Encryption** is used as RFC 2828 recommends, to indicate the application of an algorithmic cipher that requires key exchange for decoding.

The next few sections briefly outline the currently prevalent encryption methods and how they apply to securing small data tokens such as passwords. While reading these, keep in mind that a *message* to be encoded (plaintext in the previous examples) does not literally need to be a textual message. Any data stream may be the message, including, but not limited to, images, network traffic, software executables, or binary data. Nor does the encrypted (ciphertext) output literally need to be textual in nature.

DES: Data Encryption Standard

DES, Data Encryption Standard, is an example of a *symmetric,* or *secret key*, cryptosystem. Symmetric cryptosystems use the same key for encryption and decryption.

DES was developed in the 1970s at IBM with some input from the National Security Agency (NSA) and the former National Bureau of Standards (NBS), which is now the National Institute of Standards and Technology (NIST). The U.S. government adopted DES as a standard in July 1977 and reaffirmed it in 1983, 1988, 1993, and 1999. It is defined in the Federal Information Processing Standards (FIPS) publication 46-3, available at `http://csrc.nist.gov/publications/fips/fips46-3/fips46-3.pdf`.

DES is a 64-bit block cipher that uses a 56-bit key during execution. In other words, it encrypts data by breaking the message into 64-bit blocks and encrypting them with a 56-bit key. The same key is used for encryption and decryption. It is susceptible to brute-force attacks from today's hardware, and is considered to be a weak encryption algorithm now. In FIPS 46-3 the government allows its use only in legacy systems, and instead lists Triple DES as the FIPS-approved symmetric algorithm of choice.

Although the algorithm itself is more complex than can be explained in detail here, in basic form it can be understood in the following form:

1. The 56-bit key is extended to 64 bits with parity and error-correction data. This becomes key *K*.
2. The message is segmented into 64-bit blocks.
3. A block *B* of the message *M* is passed through a known permutation *IP*, which rearranges its bits in a predetermined fashion. The result is *PB*.
4. The *PB* is injected into a central encryption loop and a counter *N* is initialized.
5. The incoming block is split into left and right 32-bit halves *L* and *R*.
6. 48 bits of the *K* are selected into *Kn*, based on the contents of *K* and iteration count *N*.
7. A cipher function *F* is applied to *R*, using *Kn*. The output is *R'*.
8. A replacement *PB* is assembled from *R'* and *L*, in that order (*R'* becomes the leftmost 32 bits; *L* becomes the rightmost).
9. The process repeats an additional 15 times from step 5.
10. The final reassembled *PB* is reversed once more to *PB'*.
11. *PB'* is subjected to an inverse transformation, *IP'*, which is the reverse of the initial reordering *IP*. The output of this operation is 64 bits of the encrypted output for *M*.
12. The next block of 64 bits from *M* is chosen as *B*, and the algorithm repeats from step 3.

RSA Laboratories has thus far sponsored three DES-cracking challenges, each of which have been solved. Rocke Verser's group at the University of Illinois solved the first challenge in 1997, and the Electronic Frontier Foundation solved the second challenge in 1998. distributed.net and Electronic Frontier Foundation won the third contest in 1999. Information on the latter two contests can be found at `http://www.eff.org/descracker.html` and `http://www.distributed.net/des/`.

Interestingly, the strength of the basic algorithm behind DES has been affirmed by these cracking attempts, rather than deprecated as insecure. The insecurity lies in its use of only a 56-bit key, which can be attacked in a brute-force fashion quite easily by today's standards. With more than 20 years of scrutiny behind it, there still has been no algorithmic solution devised that can back-calculate the original message from the encrypted output, or guess the key without an exhaustive search of the entire key space. This, to say the least, is an impressive accomplishment.

DES is being replaced by the Advanced Encryption Standard (AES). AES was adopted as a standard in May 2002 and is defined in the FIPS publication 197, available at `http://csrc.nist.gov/publications/fips/fips197/fips-197.pdf`. AES is a 128-bit symmetric block cipher that uses 128-, 192-, and 256-bit keys. The algorithm can handle additional block sizes and key lengths, but the standard has not adopted them at this time.

RSA: The Rivest-Shamir-Adelman Algorithm

RSA is an example of an asymmetric or public key cryptosystem. Asymmetric cryptosystems use the different keys for encryption and decryption. Encryption is done with a public key, but decryption is done with a private key. The basic notion is that each party who wishes to engage in secure communication of information generates a public and a private key. These keys are related in a precise mathematical fashion such that a piece of information to be exchanged between individual A and individual B that is encrypted with B's public key can only be decrypted with B's private key. Authentication of A as the sender can also be performed if a validation signature is attached in both plaintext, and encrypted with A's private key to the encrypted data that is sent to B. The encrypted portion of this signature can only be decrypted with A's public key, thereby validating A as the sender.

RSA was developed in 1977 by Ronald Rivest, Adi Shamir, and Leonard Adelman, and it takes its name from the initials of the developers' last names. The latest version of the documentation on RSA is available at `http://www.rsasecurity.com/rsalabs/pkcs/pkcs-1/`.

The RSA algorithm is based on factoring. The product of two large prime numbers similar in length, *p* and *q*, gives a number called the modulus, *n*. Choose another number, *e*, such that it is less than *n* and is relatively prime to `(p-1)×(q-1)`, which is to say that *e* and `(p-1)×(q-1)` have no factors larger than 1. Choose another number *d*, such that `((e×d)-1)` is divisible by `(p-1)×(q-1)`. The number *e* is known as the public exponent, and the number *d* is known as the private exponent. The public key is the pair of numbers `(n,e)`, and the private key is the pair `(n,d)`.

If individual *A* wishes to send a message *M* to individual *B*, *A* encrypts *M* into ciphertext *C* by exponentiation: `C = (M^e) mod n`, where *e* and *n* are the elements of *B*'s public key. `^` is the exponentiation operator, `(i^j)` is *i* raised to the power *j*. `mod` is the modulus mathematical operator; `(i mod j)` produces the remainder of *i* divided by *j*. *B* decodes the message also by exponentiation: `M = (C^d) mod n`, where *d* and *n* are *B*'s private key. The relationship between *e* and *d* is what causes this reversal by exponentiation to work, and allows correct extraction of *M* from *C*. Because only *B* knows the private key `(d,n)`, only *B* can extract the message.

To sign the message, *A* attaches a signature *s* to the ciphertext *C*, and also an encrypted signature *es*. *es* is generated by exponentiation with *A*'s private key: `es = (s^d) mod n`, where *d* and *n* are from *A*'s private key. *B* computes a decrypted signature *ds* by exponentiation: `ds = (es^e) mod n`, where *e* and *n* are from *A*'s public key, and compares *ds* with *s*. They will agree only if *es* was encrypted with *A*'s private key, and since only *A* possesses this key, agreement serves as validation that the message is from *A*.

This algorithm really is quite trivial in design, and relies on the fact that it is computationally quite difficult to factor large numbers. In practice, this works as follows (only using much larger values). We will calculate a key pair for two individuals *A* and *B*, and carry out a simple signed data exchange:

1. *A* picks `p = 11, q = 19. n = p * q = 209.`
2. `(p-1)×(q-1) = 180.` 180 factors to `2×2×3×3×5`. Pick `e = 11`. (11 is prime, and not a factor of 180. *e* being prime is not a requirement of the algorithm, but makes the calculations easier to demonstrate. It's also bad form to pick *e* equal to *p* or *q* in practice.)
3. `((11×d)-1)"180` needs to be a whole number. Pick `d = 131. (131×11)-1 = 1440 = 8×180.`
4. *A*'s public key is then `(209,11)` and *A*'s private key is `(209,131)`.
5. *B* picks `p = 7, q = 23. n = p×q = 161.`
6. `(p-1)×(q-1) = 132.` 132 factors to `2×2×3×11`. Pick `e = 7`. (Usually, one would want *e* to be smaller than `(p-1)×(q-1)`), but still a large number. Again, 7 is chosen for convenience.)
7. `((7×d)-1)"132` needs to be a whole number. Pick `d = 151. (151×7)-1 = 1056 = 8×132.`
8. *B*'s public key is then `(161,7)`, and *B*'s private key is `(161,151)`.

Let us say that *A* wishes to send the (very short) message 13 to *B*. The following steps are taken:

1. *B* sends his public key to *A*; *A* sends her public key to *B*.
2. *A* encrypts the message with *B*'s public key `(161,7)` as `(13^7) mod 161. 13^7 = 62748517. 62748517/161 = 389742` with a remainder of `55`. `55` becomes the encrypted ciphertext *C* of the message.
3. *A* also wants to sign the message with the signature `17`. *A* encrypts the signature with her private key of `(209,131)` as `es = (17^131) mod 209.`

4. `17^131 = 154457393072366309211243453140265336130679022855532916933912066667508381014824689935939748335468475166201536661429828074002635558976064397547405836087319391984433`. (Don't believe us? Install Perl's Math::BigFloat module (you need a more recent version than Apple provides—please see `http://www.cpan.org/`; `perl -MCPAN -e shell` should get you well on your way) and try out the sample code in Listing 4.1 following this example).

5. `es = 154457393072366309211243453140265336130679022855532916933912066667508381014824689935939748335468475166201536661429828074002635558976064397547405836087319391984433 mod 209 = 6`.

A then has a ciphertext *C* for the message that consists of the value `55`, and a composite signature that consists of the nonencrypted signature `17`, and the encrypted signature `6`. These values are sent to *B*. No special care need be taken to protect them, because they are both encrypted and signed. They cannot be decrypted without the use of *B*'s private key and *A*'s public key. They cannot be modified without the use of *A*'s private key. Upon receipt, *B* applies the following steps:

1. To validate the message, *B* decrypts the encrypted portion of the signature with *A*'s public key (as it was encoded with *A*'s private key). `ds = (es^e) mod n = (6^11) mod 209 = 362797056 mod 209 = 17`.

2. *B* compares `ds = 17` to the nonencrypted portion of the signature (sent as the value `17`), finds that they match, and can be comfortable that indeed the message came from *A*.

3. *B* then decrypts the ciphertext *C* by using his private key (as the message was encoded with his public key). `M = (C^d) mod n = (55^151) mod 161`.

4. `55^151 = 62339901772061144190031435235862186847664389389245399078404740141850360058606222097315541538269927995472819853970163068214487686533684900208227797646627070069088808092811324611434117366172479352641014470894910862931278714392513418118824120028875768184661865234375`.

5. `M = 62339901772061144190031435235862186847664389389245399078404740141850360058606222097315541538269927995472819853970163068214487686533684900208227797646627070069088808092811324611434117366172479352641014470894910862931278714392513418118824120028875768184661865234375 mod 161 = 13`.

And, at this point, *B* has recovered *A*'s message of 13, verified that *A* is the sender by determining that *A*'s public key is the one necessary to properly decrypt the signature, and the communication is at an end.

LISTING 4.1 A Public-Key Encryption Demo. (You will need to install a more current version of Math::BigFloat than Apple provides to run this code.)

```
#!/usr/local/bin/perl
use Math::BigFloat;  #This line will break if you haven't updated BigFloat
Math::BigFloat->div_scale(2048);

#  These modify their arguments
#  $x->bmod($y);                 # modulus ($x % $y) = remainder of $x/$y
#  $x->bpow($y);                 # power of arguments ($x raised to the $y)
#  If you want to keep $x and operate on it at the same time, pass the
#    operation through copy() first.

$Ap = Math::BigFloat->new(11);  # Individual A's prime p
$Aq = Math::BigFloat->new(19);  # A's prime q
$Ae = Math::BigFloat->new(11);  # A's public exponent e
$Ad = Math::BigFloat->new(131); # A's public exponent d
                                # in real use, Ae should not be
                                # equal to Ap or Aq.
$Bp = Math::BigFloat->new(7);   # Individual B's prime p
$Bq = Math::BigFloat->new(23);  # B's prime q
$Be = Math::BigFloat->new(7);   # B's public exponent e
$Bd = Math::BigFloat->new(151); # B's public exponent d
$M  = Math::BigFloat->new(13);  # Message M
$s  = Math::BigFloat->new(17);  # A's signature
                                # Message M and Signature s can be
                                # no larger in value than Min(An,Bn)

print "RSA example: person A encrypts and signs a message to person B\n";
print "A's primes:\n";
print " Ap = $Ap\n";
print " Aq = $Aq\n";
print "A's exponents:\n";
print " public exponent  Ae = $Ae\n";
print " private exponent Ad = $Ad\n";

print "B's primes:\n";
print " Bp = $Bp\n";
print " Bq = $Bq\n";
print "B's exponents:\n";
print " public exponent  Be = $Be\n";
print " private exponent Bd = $Bd\n";
print "\n";
```

LISTING 4.1 Continued

```
$An = $Ap->copy()->bmul($Aq);     # $An = $Ap*$Aq
$Bn = $Bp->copy()->bmul($Bq);     # $Bn = $Bp*$Bq
print "A's modulus Ap*Aq:\n";
print " An = Ap*Aq = $An\n";
print "B's modulus Bp*Bq:\n";
print " Bn = Bp*Bq = $Bn\n";
print "\n";

print "Message M:\n";
print " M = $M\n";
$C  = $M->copy()->bpow($Be);      # ciphertext temporary = (message ^ Be)
print "Encryption begins:\n";
print " M^Be = $M^$Be\n";
print " M^Be = $C\n";
      $C->bmod($Bn);              # ciphertext C = (message ^ Be) mod Bn
print "Encryption finished:\n";
print " C = (M^Be) mod Bn = $C\n";
print "\n\n";

print "A signs C:\n";
print " s = $s\n";
print "Signature Encryption begins:\n";
$es  = $s->copy()->bpow($Ad);     # A encrypts s with A's private key (temp)
print " s^Ad = $s^$Ad\n";
print " s^Ad = $es\n";
      $es->bmod($An);             # encrypted sig es = (s ^ Ad) mod An
print "Signature Encryption finished:\n";
print " es = (s^Ad) mod An = $es\n";
print "\n\n";

print "Full message reads;\n";
print "ciphertext    = $C\n";
print "signature     = $s\n";
print "encrypted sig = $es\n";
print "\n\n";

print "B begins decrypting:\n";
print "check the signature:\n";
$ds = $es->copy()->bpow($Ae);     # decrypt using A's public key
print " es^Ae = $es^$Ae\n";
print " es^Ae = $ds\n";
      $ds->bmod($An);
```

LISTING 4.1 Continued

```
print " ds = (es^Ae) mod An = $ds\n";
if($ds->bcmp($s) == 0)          # sig s and decrypted sig ds match if zero
{
  print " ds = $ds = $s = s : Signatures match - sender verified\n";
}
else
{
  print " ds = $ds != $s = s :  Signatures do not match, message forged\n";
  exit;
}
print "decrypt the message into dM:\n";
$dM = $C->copy()->bpow($Bd);
print " C^Bd = $C^$Bd\n";
print " C^Bd = $dM\n";
      $dM->bmod($Bn);
print " dM = (C^Bd) mod Bn = $dM\n";
print "Message decrypted, sender verified, end of communication.\n";
print "\n\n";
exit;
```

CAUTION

The Perl code in Listing 4.1 requires a modern version of the `Math::BigFloat` package. You can install this through the `CPAN` module if you choose, by entering

```
perl -MCPAN -e shell
install Math::BigFloat
```

This may die with an error complaining about Scalar.pm, as there is (as of this writing) an inconsistency in the archived packages and requirements. If you get this error, reissue the install command as

```
force install Math::BigFloat
```

Typically, messages would be composed of ASCII (American Standard Code for Information Interchange) text or binary data. From the point of view of the algorithm, it makes no difference. ASCII, or any other digital storage code for textual data, provides a conversion between individual characters in the alphabet and numeric values. If the message were text such as "`A!`", the numeric values that correspond to the alphabetic characters are what would be used. In ASCII, "`A`" has the decimal value `65`, and "`!`" has the value `33`. The message can be considered to be a 2-byte value with "`A`" being the high-order byte, and "`!`" being in the low-order byte.

In decimal, then, the value would be `(65×256) + 33 = 16673`. This is the value to which *A* would apply *B*'s public key. One can directly encrypt any string that is less than the minimum value of *A*'s and *B*'s moduli. Data streams or strings greater than this value (longer than the bitstream length encoding this value) must be broken into blocks of this length or shorter and sequentially encoded.

NOTE

Although this example demonstrates the mechanism of RSA encryption, the practice is often somewhat different. For example, the nonencrypted portion of the signature should not be passed as plaintext, because if it is, then all an attacker must do is steal that signature and the encrypted version to be able to forge *A*'s signature on other messages. Instead, the nonencrypted version of the signature would typically be passed in the data encrypted with *B*'s public key—it is therefore no longer "nonencrypted," but is rather encrypted with a different key, preventing anyone not in possession of both *A*'s public key and *B*'s private key from making the comparison.

Also, it is common practice to use RSA as an encryption envelope, rather than to encrypt the entire message. In this use, some symmetric secret-key encryption algorithm (for example 3DES) is used to encrypt the main data stream, then the key used for this encryption, and a checksum calculated for the original data, is passed to RSA as data to encrypt and sign. Receipt of the RSA-encrypted information along with the 3DES data stream enables the recipient to recover the key necessary to decrypt the 3DES stream, the RSA signature verifies its origin, and the checksum verifies the transmission integrity.

If you would like to see what happens when someone tries to forge a signature block, change the value of `$es` between the encryption and decryption sections of the code.

RSA Laboratories recommends that for general corporate use, 1024-bit keys should be sufficient. For truly valuable data, 2048-bit keys should be used. For less valuable data, 768-bit keys may be appropriate. These key sizes actually refer to the size of the modulus, n. The primary reason to choose a shorter key length over a greater one is that as the keys become longer, the calculations required become more costly in terms of computational time. This makes using larger keys take longer. As machines become faster, this becomes less of an issue, and 1024- or 2048-bit keys are not problematic on modern hardware.

As with DES, RSA Laboratories has sponsored contests for cracking RSA. The most recent contest was the factorization of the 155-digit (512-bit) RSA Challenge, which was solved in 1999. It took 35.7 CPU years. Details on the contest are available at `http://www.rsasecurity.com/rsalabs/challenges/factoring/rsa155.html`. RSA Laboratories is currently sponsoring more RSA factoring challenges, ranging from a 576-bit challenge to a 2048-bit challenge.

The RSA algorithm is vulnerable to chosen plaintext attacks, where the attacker can have any text encrypted with the unknown key and then determine the key that was used to encrypt the text. It is also vulnerable to fault attacks in the cryptosystem itself, particularly in private key operations. Causing one bit of error at the proper point can reveal the private key.

Note that the strength of the algorithm relies on the fact that it is computationally exceedingly difficult to factor very large numbers. If one must consider every prime less than half some number *n* as a potential factor of *n*, the task quickly becomes astronomically intensive computationally, as *n* becomes large. With *n* on the order of 1024 bits, and well-chosen primes near 512 bits in size, the number of prime numbers that would need to be examined by a brute-force iteration through all primes is on the order of `10^150`. This is somewhere around `10^70` times more prime numbers that would need to be examined than there are electrons in the known universe.

It is interesting to compare the philosophy of the RSA algorithm with the DES algorithm. In the case of DES, the algorithm has no known weaknesses, but fails to be secure due to the limited length of the key. RSA, on the other hand has a very significant known weakness: If a method could be found for quickly factoring large numbers without resorting to brute-force methods, *d* could be recovered from *e* and *n* in the public key. RSA, therefore, is secure only as long as the keys are extremely large, and there is no known way to factor them quickly. So long as large numbers remain difficult to factor, however, RSA's weakness is unexploitable. Thankfully, although there are faster ways to factor numbers than the brute-force examination of every possible prime, none appear likely to bring this computational task into the realm of affordable desktop computing capabilities.

MD5: Message Digest Function

MD5 is a message digest function developed by Ronald Rivest in 1991. It is defined in RFC 1321, available at `http://www.ietf.org/rfc/rfc1321.txt?number=1321`.

MD5 is a one-way hash function that takes an arbitrary-length message and returns a 128-bit value. The algorithm works in five steps.

1. The message is padded so that its length plus 64 bits is divisible by 512. That is to say, it is extended an arbitrary length, until it is 64 bits shy of being an exact multiple of 512 bits in length.
2. A 64-bit representation of the length of the message before it was padded is appended to the result of the first step. If the message is longer than `2^64` (not a particularly likely occurrence, as this is 16,777,216 terabytes), the lower-order 64 bits of the length are used. The length of the result of this step is a multiple of 512 bits. As the length is a multiple of 512 bits, it is also a multiple of 16 32-bit words (`16×32 = 512`).

3. Four 32-bit words are used to initialize the message digest buffer.
4. Four functions are defined that each take three 32-bit words as input, and each returns a single 32-bit word as output. The message is passed, in 16-word blocks, through a predetermined Boolean combination of these four functions. The output of each iteration is 4 32-bit words, which initialize the buffer for the next iteration.
5. The final 4 words written to the buffer are combined into a single 128-bit value, which is returned as the result of the hash.

Upon consideration, it should be obvious that the operation is lossy, and does not constitute a compression or encryption of the data that can be reversed by application of a suitable key. No matter the size of the input, the result is always 128 bits of data. The utility in this is that it is improbable (1 in `2^128` likely) that two randomly chosen pieces of data will result in the same hash output. The unlikelihood of this occurring allows the MD5 hash to be used to predict whether two pieces of information are in fact the same, or more commonly, to determine whether a piece of information is the same as it once was.

NOTE

This does not imply that two documents cannot have the same MD5 checksum. The checksum usually contains less information than the document, and there are many more potential documents than MD5 checksums. In fact, there are an infinite number of possible documents if the document size is infinitely variable, whereas there are only a finite number of possible 128-bit MD5 checksums. This implies that there are many documents that would hash to any given MD5 checksum. The MD5 checksum space is large enough, however, that for practical purposes, you are unlikely to meet two documents that hash to the same value by chance. If you'd like an estimate of the probability that two documents in a large collection might hash to the same value, do some reading on the birthday problem (`http://www.studyworksonline.com/cda/content/explorations/0,,NAV2-76_SEP949,00.shtml`, `http://www-stat.stanford.edu/~susan/surprise/Birthday.html`). If my calculations are correct, if you have 17,884,898,788,718,400,000 documents in your database, there's about a 50% chance that two will hash to the same value via MD5. That's many fewer than 2^128, but its still a larger number of documents than most of us will ever see.

As an example of the first use, consider the task of trying to create a central data repository of all documents used in some place of business. If the environment is like most, there are probably hundreds of unique documents, but also dozens of copies of identical documents, kept by dozens of different people. If you were to try to build a database containing only one copy of each, it could become very time consuming to compare every bit of every document against every bit of every other document to determine those that are duplicates, and those that are new, unique, and need to be added to the database. Instead, you might calculate an MD5 checksum for each unique document as you add it to the database. An incoming document then could be checked for *potential* duplication in the database if its MD5 checksum was calculated and only the checksum was compared, rather than the entire document, against the checksums existing in the database. If the incoming document's checksum does not already exist in the database, it is definitely unique, as MD5 always hashes a given input to the same output. If the incoming document's checksum *does* already exist, it *might* be the same as an existing document, or it might be one of the many possible documents that hash to that particular MD5 checksum value. In this case, the document needs to be checked on a bit-for-bit basis with the possible duplicate, or duplicates, in the database to determine whether it needs to be added or discarded. Because you have only a 1 in 2^128 chance of any document hashing to the same value as another, it's unlikely that you will find many that have the same hash value, even if you store a very large number of documents.

This use is also commonly applied as a method to check whether a user has entered a password correctly. The system stores the MD5 checksum of each user's actual password in a table, and when a user attempts to authenticate, the MD5 checksum of the password is compared with the stored checksum value. If they match, the user has *probably* entered the proper password. Because many entered values will hash to every possible MD5 checksum, however, it's entirely possible with this scheme that the user has entered some other password that also hashes to the same checksum value. Possible, but unlikely.

In the second use, the MD5 checksum is used to verify that a piece of information has not been changed by some action. For example, if you are archiving valuable data, you might want to calculate MD5 checksums for the data and store them separately. When the data needs to be examined at a later date, MD5 checksums can again be calculated. If they agree, there is a high probability that the data has not been changed. If they disagree, something has changed in the data since the original checksum was calculated. This technique is useful both for verifying archival storage and for providing a method for others to verify that network transmissions have been received unaltered. For example, MD5 can be used to provide a digital signature for when a large file has to be compressed before being encrypted with a private key for a public key cryptosystem. Arriving at a duplicate checksum after decryption and decompression is strong evidence that the file has not been tampered with.

As a signature, MD5's weakness is that it is a hash, and does not produce a unique value for every possible input. Therefore, it is possible for an attacker to construct and insert a forged message that hashes to the same MD5 checksum as the original. Attacks on MD5 therefore are attacks to find collisions, multiple inputs that can produce the same hash. Structural algorithmic solutions to allow an attacker to do so easily have not at this time been discovered, but brute-force attacks have been demonstrated to be possible with a sufficient investment of computational resources. MD5 has not yet been declared an insecure checksum solution, but its strength is in doubt. In 1995 Hans Dobbertin, in "Alf Swindles Ann," *CryptoBytes* (3) **1**, showed how to defeat MD4, which shares many features with MD5, via hash collisions. P. van Oorschot and M. Wiener, in "Parallel Collision Search with Application to Hash Functions and Discrete Logarithms," *Proceedings of 2nd ACM Conference on Computer and Communication Security* (1994), calculate that for $10 million in computing hardware, a hash collision could be determined in 24 days or less (in 1994 dollars and time). Dobbertin, in "The Status of MD5 After a Recent Attack," *CryptoBytes* (2) **2** (1996), extends the techniques applied to break the MD4 hash in under a minute to the compression function of MD5. Each of these results suggests that although MD5 may remain suitable for applications such as the detection of possible database entry duplications, its utility as a seal against unauthorized data modification may be limited, or may be eliminated completely in the near future.

Other Encryption Algorithms

A plethora of other encryption algorithms and software is available, though only a few that have stood the test of time and public examination long enough to be considered reasonably secure. The following list includes a number of the more popular variants and brief descriptions of them:

- **3DES**. Triple-DES is a variant of DES that uses DES three times. Encryption is generally performed in an encrypt-decrypt-encrypt sequence with three independent 168-bit keys. It is considered more secure than DES, but is slower.
- **Blowfish**. A 64-bit block cipher with variable-length keys up to 448 bits. It was developed by Bruce Schneier and designed for 32-bit machines. It is much faster than DES. *Dr. Dobb's Journal* sponsored a cryptanalysis contest of Blowfish in April 1995. Results included an attack on a 3-round version of Blowfish (Blowfish has 16 rounds), a differential attack on a simplified variant of Blowfish, and the discovery of weak keys. The attack based on weak keys is effective only against reduced-round variants of Blowfish. For details on the results of the contest, see Schneier's paper at `http://www.counterpane.com/bfdobsoyl.html`. The original paper on Blowfish is available at `http://www.counterpane.com/bfsverlag.html`. Overall, Blowfish is generally considered to be secure.
- **CAST-128**. A 64-bit block cipher with variable-length keys, up to 128 bits. It is a DES-like encryption. CAST takes its name from the original developers, Carlisle Adams and Stafford Tavares. CAST-128 is also part of Pretty Good Privacy (PGP). CAST-256 is an extension that uses a 128-bit block size with keys up to 256 bits.

- **RC4**. RC4 is a variable key-size stream cipher designed by Ronald Rivest. The algorithm is fast and is used in a variety of products, including SSL and WEP implementations. The algorithm was considered to be a trade secret until code that was alleged to be RC4 was posted to a mailing list in the mid-1990s. This code, Alleged RC4, is known as arcfour.
- **Arcfour**. Arcfour is a stream cipher that is compatible with RC4. It can be used with a variety of key lengths, with 128-bit keys being common. An expired draft on arcfour is available at `http://www.mozilla.org/projects/security/pki/nss/draft-kaukonen-cipher-arcfour-03.txt`.
- **DSA**. Digital Signature Algorithm is a public key signature-only algorithm, based on the Diffie-Hellman discrete logarithm problem. It is the underlying algorithm of the DSS, Digital Signature Standard, which was endorsed by NIST as the digital authentication standard of the U.S. government in 1994. DSA is defined in FIPS 186-2, which is available at `http://csrc.nist.gov/publications/fips/fips186-2/fips186-2-change1.pdf`.
- **IDEA**. Internation Data Encryption Algorithm, IDEA, is a redesign of an encryption algorithm called PES (Proposed Encryption Standard). PES was designed by Xuejia Lai and James Massey, and its revision, IDEA, was designed by Xuejia Lai, James Massey, and Sean Murphy. IDEA is a 64-bit block cipher that uses a 128-bit key. As with DES, the same algorithm is used for encryption and decryption. The design of IDEA enables it to be easily implemented in hardware or software. The software implementation is considered comparable to DES by some people, and faster than DES by others. Although a class of weak keys has been discovered for it, IDEA is generally considered to be secure.

Mac OS X Cryptography Applications

As Mac OS X matures, we are beginning to see a significant increase in the available cryptographic offerings for the platform. The first two of these we will present provide almost identical functionality: implementation of the Pretty Good Privacy (PGP) public-key encryption system. The third is rather different, in that it's really an interface to the built-in encryption capabilities that exist in the libraries on which OS X is based.

PGP

PGP is the 1991 brainchild of Phil Zimmerman. Although a rather clever programmer, Phil overestimated the good sense and underestimated the unbelievable lack of computing sophistication of the U.S. government and justice system when he developed and published a system for implementing public-key cryptography in a simple fashion for exchanging information through email. Phil essentially said, "Hey, cool!

Implementing this public-key stuff in a relatively seamless and easy-to-use form isn't so tough—we can make this into a worldwide resource!" Shortly afterwards, the U.S. government slapped him with charges alleging that he was exporting weapons technology to enemies of the United States. It may seem peculiar, but what he was accused of was writing and distributing software containing the RSA algorithm in a way that someone *might* export it out of the country. Phil didn't export it, and even if he had, one might think that the fact that such algorithms were well known and could be implemented by any competent programmer on the planet would make it not all that big a deal to *possibly* make it available to someone who *might* export the binary. Not so. The government classified Phil's action in the same category as exporting tanks and nuclear weapons. The case was eventually dropped in 1996, but for years a large contingent of Internet and security-conscious individuals fought on Phil's behalf, both collecting money for his defense, and satirizing the situation in an attempt to make the justice system see just what folly the case actually was. `http://people.qualcomm.com/ggr/about_pgp.html` provides an insight into the thinking of the day. At the same time this was going on, it was established that books containing the source code or algorithms describing encryption technology could be exported (so we shouldn't have to ask you to help bail us out of jail for that bit of Perl we showed you previously) because they were literary works, but that nonreadable (that is, executable) versions were weapons. For a while, there was a T-shirt available with the source for the algorithm printed on it, and a bar-code that encoded the executable. The shirt was advertised with the slogan "For the price of this T-shirt, you too can become an International Arms Dealer." The manufacturer promised to refund anyone's money who was convicted, and many wondered whether you could be convicted of carrying a concealed weapon if you wore the T-shirt inside out.

Shortly after the government dropped its case against Zimmerman, he formed a company and began distributing PGP as a commercial application. There were some particularly nice features available, such as the ability to PGP-encrypt an entire disk partition and have anything written to that disk encrypted, but the company was soon absorbed by Network Associates, the former distributors of McAfee AntiVirus. This business group did a reasonable job of upkeep on the product until 2001, when it decided to drop PGP from its product line. For a while it looked like the very nice PGP product line was going to disappear, but thankfully the original principals of PGP Corporation managed to work out a deal to reacquire the rights in June of 2002, and development, including the production of a Mac OS X version, has begun once again.

Usage Commercial and freeware versions of PGP are available at `http://www.pgp.com/`. Various bundled software packages are offered commercially, depending on your needs. A freeware PGP package is also available, with limited capabilities that are probably sufficient for the home individual. Most importantly, the freeware version allows you to make and manage keys and encrypt and decrypt files.

Download and install PGP. The documentation recommends rebooting the machine afterward. After it is installed, generate a set of keys for yourself. The option to generate a set of keys appears the first time you launch the application. If you do not make a set of keys then, you can either select New Keys from the Keys menu of the PGP application, or select New Keys from the PGPkeys window that opens when you launch PGP. You can choose to generate your keys in Expert mode. If you do not choose Expert mode, your keys are generated using the default parameters that you can see in Expert mode. The Setup portion for the Expert mode is shown in Figure 4.4.

FIGURE 4.4 Expert mode for the Setup step in key generation in PGP.

In Normal mode, you need to supply only a name and email address. In the Expert mode, you also specify a key type, key size, and key expiration. The default key type is Diffie-Hellman/DSS. You can also choose RSA or RSA Legacy. The default key size is 2048 bits, but you can specify anything from 1024 to 4096. The default expiration is none, but you can specify an actual expiration date, if you prefer.

After setting up the key, you are asked to provide a passphrase to protect your private key. As you type your passphrase, a horizontal bar displays an approximation for the quality of your passphrase, much like a progress bar. Then your PGP key pair is generated.

In the PGPkeys window, which opens when you launch PGP, your new key is listed, as shown in Figure 4.5. From this window you can do a number of other things, including revoking your key, deleting it, sending your public key to a keyserver, exporting your keys to a file, and searching for public keys. If the PGPkeys window is not open when you need it, simply select that window under the Window menu.

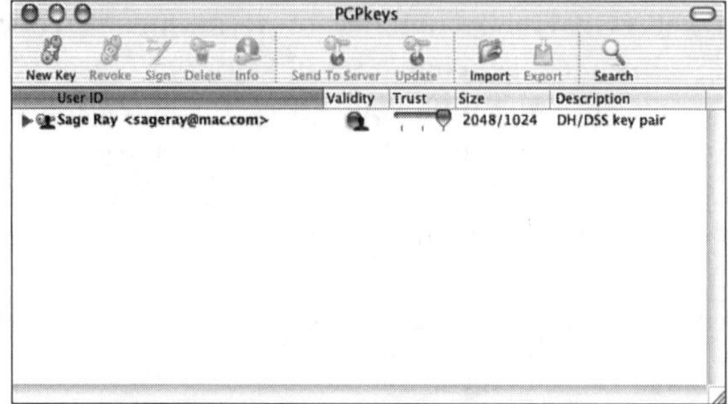

FIGURE 4.5 Your new key appears in the PGPkeys window.

In Preferences, you can specify a number of options, including editing the keyserver listing, shown in Figure 4.6, and specifying encryption algorithms and where your keys are stored.

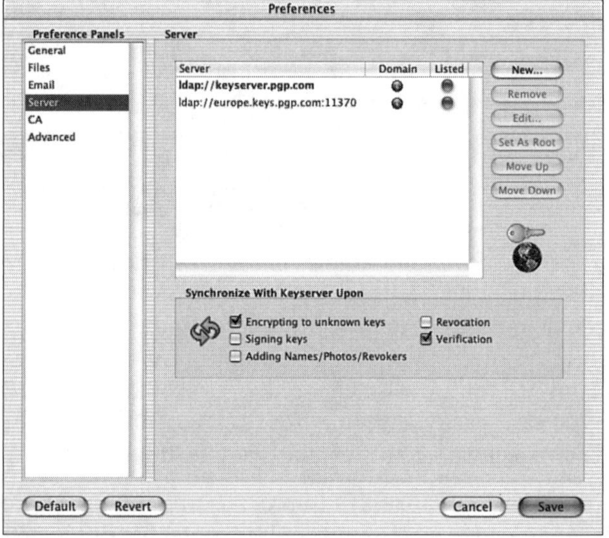

FIGURE 4.6 The keyserver preferences in PGP.

After you have your set of keys, you can experiment with encrypting and decrypting something. A convenient program to use for testing encryption and decryption is the TextEdit application. Type something and then select it. Under the Services option of the TextEdit menu, select PGP, then select Encrypt. Figure 4.7 shows how everything looks as you start to do this.

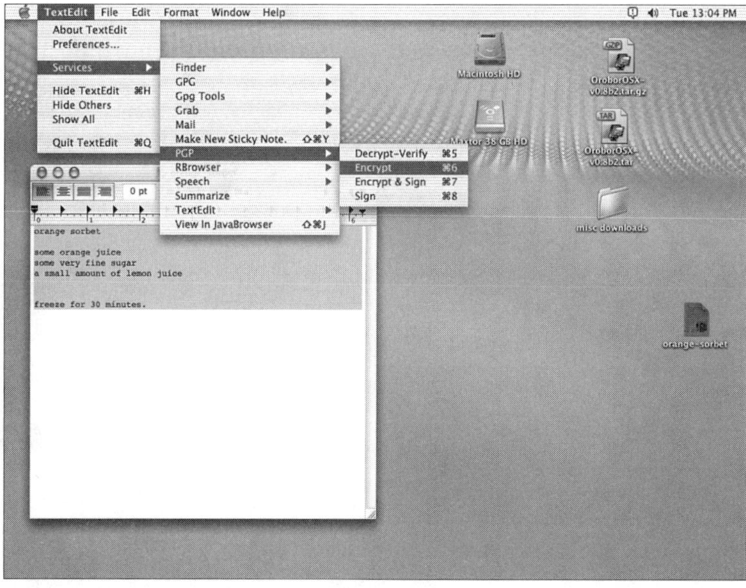

FIGURE 4.7 Encrypting text in TextEdit using PGP.

Select a recipient in the next window that appears. If you haven't imported anyone else's public keys, then yours is the only option. The text is then encrypted, as shown in Figure 4.8.

FIGURE 4.8 An encrypted version of the text shown in Figure 4.7.

To decrypt the encrypted text, select Decrypt from the PGP menu under the Services menu under the TextEdit window. Enter your passphrase. Then the decrypted text appears in a PGP window, as shown in Figure 4.9.

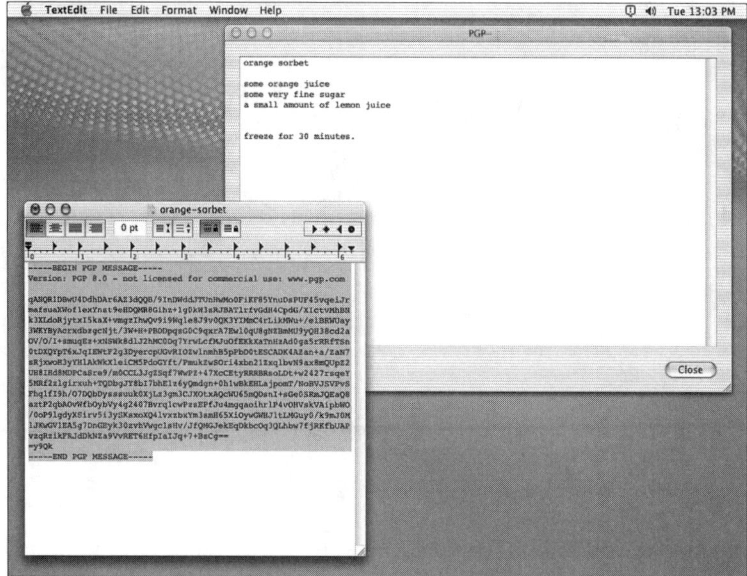

FIGURE 4.9 The encrypted text is shown decrypted in the PGP window.

You can easily use PGP for encryption or decryption in applications that use the Services menu. As you might expect, Mail is one of those applications.

To exchange PGP-encrypted files or messages, you first need to get the public key for anyone with whom you want to exchange encrypted information. If the person's public key is on a public keyserver, search the keyserver, then drag the correct result from the search window to the PGPkeys window. If you have received the person's public key as a file some other way, choose Import in the PGPkeys window and select the correct file. When you are encrypting the data, select your recipient. Then send or exchange the data in whatever way was predetermined. The recipient can decrypt the data with his private key.

To receive encrypted data, you have to make your public key available to others. You can either send it to a keyserver from the PGPkeys window, or you can export your public key to a file and exchange it some other way. If you choose to send it to a keyserver, it does not matter which one you send it to. The keyservers regularly sync their databases.

GPG

GPG, Gnu Privacy Guard, is a Gnu replacement for the PGP suite of tools. GPG received a real boost from the apparent death of PGP, especially as far as Mac OS X development is concerned, and should be considered an interesting study in the Open Source community's response to a perceived lack in a software functionality niche. It's designed as a drop-in replacement for PGP, allowing the same content to be transmitted and decoded with the same key sets.

Usage A version of GnuPG for Mac OS X is available from `http://macgpg.sourceforge.net/`. This site includes GnuPG and various GUI tools. The version of GPG that is available for Mac OS X 10.2 is slightly newer than the version that is available for Mac OS X 10.1. The site also has links to some other tools, such as Gpg Tools and tools for getting various mail programs to work with GPG.

From the Mac GnuGP site, download the version of GPG suitable to your version of Mac OS X and the quarterly files. Download separately anything that may have been updated after the quarterly download was made available.

If you install GPG by using the installer, it installs in `/usr/local/bin` by default, with documentation in `/Library/Documentation/GnuPG/`. The documentation also suggests that you can install it via fink (`http://fink.sourceforge.net/`) if you prefer. fink will probably put it somewhere under the `/sw` hierarchy. Install the other applications as well.

After GPG is installed, you are ready to generate a key pair. You can do this either by selecting Generate under the Key menu in GPGkeys, or by running `gpg --gen-key` at the command line. GPGkeys is a hybrid application that opens a terminal and runs `gpg --gen-key` at the command line for you. When you are generating a key pair, you have to answer a few questions. You select an encryptional algorithm, the key size, and an expiration date. Then you provide a name, email address, and a comment, if any, to identify the key. Sample output follows:

```
% gpg --gen-key
gpg (GnuPG) 1.2.1; Copyright (C) 2002 Free Software Foundation, Inc.
This program comes with ABSOLUTELY NO WARRANTY.
This is free software, and you are welcome to redistribute it
under certain conditions. See the file COPYING for details.

gpg: keyring `/Users/sage/.gnupg/secring.gpg' created
gpg: keyring `/Users/sage/.gnupg/pubring.gpg' created
Please select what kind of key you want:
   (1) DSA and ElGamal (default)
   (2) DSA (sign only)
   (5) RSA (sign only)
```

```
Your selection? 1
DSA keypair will have 1024 bits.
About to generate a new ELG-E keypair.
              minimum keysize is  768 bits
              default keysize is 1024 bits
    highest suggested keysize is 2048 bits
What keysize do you want? (1024)
Requested keysize is 1024 bits
Please specify how long the key should be valid.
         0 = key does not expire
      <n>  = key expires in n days
      <n>w = key expires in n weeks
      <n>m = key expires in n months
      <n>y = key expires in n years
Key is valid for? (0)
Key does not expire at all
Is this correct (y/n)? y

You need a User-ID to identify your key; the software constructs the user id
from Real Name, Comment and Email Address in this form:
    "Heinrich Heine (Der Dichter) <heinrichh@duesseldorf.de>"

Real name: Sage Ray
Email address: sageray@mac.com
Comment:
You selected this USER-ID:
    "Sage Ray <sageray@mac.com>"

Change (N)ame, (C)omment, (E)mail or (O)kay/(Q)uit? O
You need a Passphrase to protect your secret key.

We need to generate a lot of random bytes. It is a good idea to perform
some other action (type on the keyboard, move the mouse, utilize the
disks) during the prime generation; this gives the random number
generator a better chance to gain enough entropy.
+++++++++++++++++++++++++++++.++++++++++.+++++.+++++++++++++++++++++++++++++
+.++++++++++.+++++.++++++++++++++++++++++++++++++++++.+++++>++++++++++......
...+++++
We need to generate a lot of random bytes. It is a good idea to perform
some other action (type on the keyboard, move the mouse, utilize the
disks) during the prime generation; this gives the random number
generator a better chance to gain enough entropy.
```

```
++++++++++.+++++++++++++++.+++++.++++++++++++++++++++++++++++++++++++++++.++++
+.+++++++++++++++++++.++++++++++++++++++++++++++++++..+++++>+++++>+++++......
.+++++^^^
gpg: /Users/sage/.gnupg/trustdb.gpg: trustdb created
public and secret key created and signed.
key marked as ultimately trusted.

pub  1024D/190CF224 2002-12-31 Sage Ray <sageray@mac.com>
     Key fingerprint = 8FD6 DC90 D32C F092 7F04  DD18 1D97 A19F 190C F224
sub  1024g/D5B2A9F2 2002-12-31
```

A basic configuration file is created in `~/.gnupg/gpg.conf`. GPGPreferences is a GUI application that installs in the Other section of the System Preferences. As of this writing, GPGPreferences edits `~/.gnugp/options`, but the version of GPG available for Mac OS X 10.2 no longer uses that file for preferences. However, you can watch changes it makes to the options file and make those changes to `~/.gnugp/gpg.conf` instead.

You may want to consider specifying key searching behavior and a keyserver that GPG should search. You can uncomment a line for one of the ones listed in `gpg.conf`, or add a line for a different server of your preference. You can find some key servers listed in GPGPreferences, and you can also check `http://www.pgpi.org/` for keyserver listings.

For a keyserver entry, you might have a line like this:

```
keyserver ldap://keyserver.pgp.com
```

If you specify a keyserver, include options for keyserver functions, such as the following:

```
keyserver-options auto-key-retrieve
```

The `gpg.conf` contains a list of keyserver options and their functions. The preceding option automatically fetches keys as needed from the keyserver when verifying signatures or when importing keys that have been revoked by a revocation key that is not present on the keyring.

After you have generated a key, it is added to the list of keys that GPGKeys can manage. Figure 4.10 shows a sample of the Public tab after generating a key pair. GPGKeys adds that key to your public keyring, which is `~/.gnupg/pubring.gpg`.

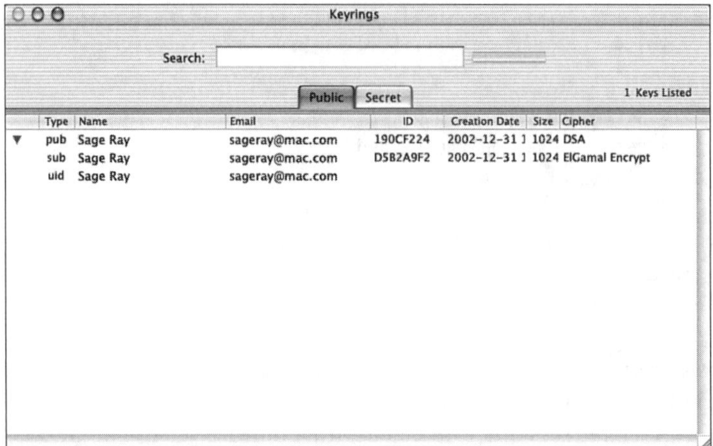

FIGURE 4.10 A key now appears in GPGkeys.

As with PGP, you can test encrypting and decrypting in TextEdit from the Services menu. Type some text in TextEdit and select it. Then select either the encryption option under the GPG menu or the encryption option under the Gpg Tools menu under Services, if you installed Gpg Tools. Although either method should work for encryption and decryption, we find the Gpg Tools interface to be slightly easier to work with. Figure 4.11 shows the encryption interface using Gpg Tools. Figure 4.12 shows a sample of the encryption done by GPG. This is an encryption of the same text that was used in the PGP example.

As with PGP, you can easily use GPG for encryption or decryption in applications that use the Services menu, such as TextEdit or Mail. Remember that the Mac GnuPG site also has scripts available to allow certain other mail programs to work with GPG.

After you have tested that encryption and decryption are working for you, you are ready to exchange keys and share encrypted data. You can either make your public key available via a public key server or export it to a file and exchange it some other way. To send it to a keyserver, you can choose the Send to Keyserver option under the Key menu in GPGkeys.

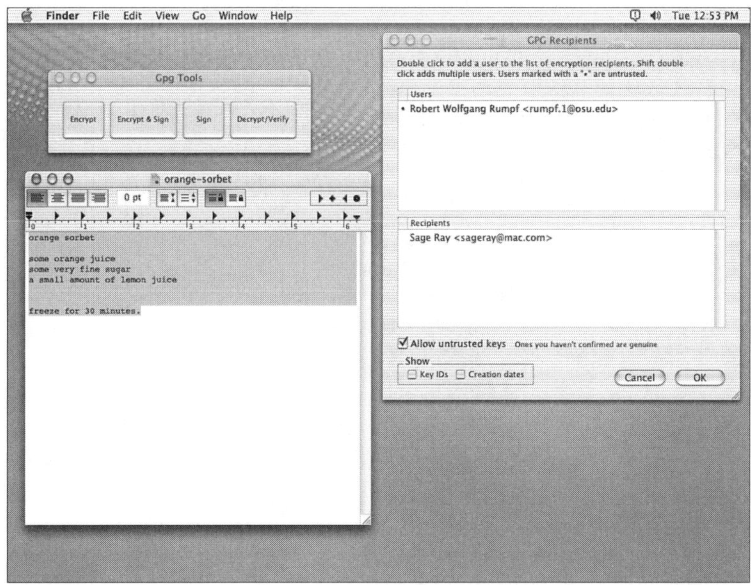

FIGURE 4.11 Starting the encryption process using the Gpg Tools interface to GPG.

FIGURE 4.12 The text has been encrypted by GPG.

As with PGP, to send encrypted data to someone, you need that person's public key. You can either get that person's public key from a keyserver or you can exchange it by some other means and import it. You can search a keyserver from GPGkeys and select the correct key to be retrieved. Following is sample output from importing a public key served by a keyserver.

```
% gpg --search-keys rumpf
gpgkeys: searching for "rumpf" from LDAP server keyserver.pgp.com
Keys 1-10 of 11 for "rumpf"
(1)     Rumpf Thomas <a9002596@unet.univie.ac.at>
          4096 bit DSS/DH key 2A9F0F7893D0AE13, created 1997-08-26
(2)     Jean-Claude Rumpf <jcrumpf@pt.lu>
          2048 bit DSS/DH key 43A5FBC5D172566C, created 1999-09-14
(3)     Johannes Rumpf <Joerumpf@t-online.de>
          2048 bit DSS/DH key 74C5630780911F16, created 2000-05-01, expires
➥2001-01-02
(4)     Robert Wolfgang Rumpf <rumpf.1@osu.edu>
          2048 bit DSS/DH key CA663A997E4B35DF, created 1999-07-14
(5)     Michael Rumpf <Michael.Rumpf@t-online.de>
          2048 bit DSS/DH key DE0D93830EF28E0E, created 1999-11-14
(6)     Michael Rumpf <Michael.Rumpf@t-online.de>
          2048 bit DSS/DH key 838DD3F7CBB774F2, created 1999-11-14
(7)     Beate Rumpf <BeRu-FoxAti@t-online.de>
          2048 bit DSS/DH key 3C6D928B10B7807C, created 2000-07-07
(8)     Beate Rumpf <BeRu-FoxAti@t-online.de>
          2048 bit DSS/DH key 712971B918247DDC, created 2000-07-08
(9)     Beate Rumpf <BR-FoxAti@web.de>
          2048 bit DSS/DH key 29661EA322068AE3, created 2000-07-23
(10)    Patrick Rumpf <xp590@excite.com>
          3072 bit DSS/DH key 73C41FE244791040, created 2000-08-03
Enter number(s), N)ext, or Q)uit > 4
gpg: key 7E4B35DF: public key "Robert Wolfgang Rumpf <rumpf.1@osu.edu>" imported
gpg: Total number processed: 1
gpg:               imported: 1
```

If you exchange keys with individuals in a more personal fashion, simply select the appropriate key file by using the Import option in GPGkeys. If you have trouble, make sure the key does not have any extraneous information, such as mail headers.

PuzzlePalace

If you are not interested in installing PGP or GPG, but you are interested in some encryption capabilities, you might be interested in PuzzlePalace, a shareware package available from `http://personalpages.tds.net/~brian_hill/puzzlepalace.html`.

PuzzlePalace makes use of functionality available in OpenSSL, making it possible to exchange encrypted data with anyone who has access to OpenSSL. There is also an option to post-process the file with Base64 to send it as an attachment.

PuzzlePalace is easy to use. Just select the type of encryption you want to use and drag the file that you want to encrypt. If you only want to create a Base64-encoded file, and don't want to apply any additional encipherment, set the cipher to None. If you've selected encipherment, you are then asked to protect the file with a passphrase, and to retype the passphrase for verification. To use the file, drag it out of the PuzzlePalace window. Figure 4.13 shows the PuzzlePalace interface after it has just encrypted a file. The icon for an encrypted file has a lock.

To decode the file, drag it to the PuzzlePalace window and enter the passphrase for the file. PuzzlePalace then decodes the file. To read it, just drag the file out of the window and read it. The icon for a decrypted file in the PuzzlePalace window is the file's normal icon.

FIGURE 4.13 A file has just been encoded with Triple DES encryption in PuzzlePalace.

Data-Divulging Applications

Whether you keep your data encrypted or not, you also need to worry about software that might allow others access to it when you didn't explicitly intend for them to have this access. Software that you are running typically has all the privileges that you have as a user, and so it is allowed to do anything that you are allowed to do. This means that it has the same access to sensitive data that is stored on your computer that you, as a user, have. Usually, this is a good thing—you don't want to manually access each and every bit of data on your computer through one single privileged application. Instead you want to be able to open a word processor (any word processor, preferably) and read any text document you've constructed. You also want to be able to access these through your email client so that you can mail them to other people, access them with cryptography programs so that you can encrypt them, and so on. Unfortunately, this means that all this software has the ability to access these (or any other of your) files when it's been invoked by you, but isn't under your direct and immediate control as well, and this ability is sometimes used for purposes that are not explicitly conveyed to you as a user.

Features Run Amok

Sometimes such capabilities and functions exist as an intentionally designed feature of the software. For example, while you are accessing a Web page, there is usually a large amount of data exchanged between your computer and a Web server that you are not party to. From your point of view, you send a query to the Web server that says, "Hello `www.apple.com`, please send me the file `index.html`," and the server responds with a Web page. Behind the scenes, the dialog is much more complex, and your computer sends along quite a bit more information than you probably know. Most of this data is simply part of a dialog intended to allow the server to better understand what you're requesting, but even so, it may contain information that you're not intending to divulge. The following output shows some of the data that any request to a Web server makes available to any software that is called as a result of that request:

```
HTTP_UA_CPU="PPC"
HTTP_UA_OS="MacOS"
HTTP_USER_AGENT="Mozilla/4.0 (compatible; MSIE 5.22; Mac_PowerPC)"
REMOTE_ADDR="204.210.232.15"
REMOTE_PORT="-1911"
REQUEST_METHOD="GET"
REQUEST_URI="/cgi-bin/printenv.cgi"
SCRIPT_FILENAME="/usr/local/httpd/cgi-bin/printenv.cgi"
SCRIPT_NAME="/cgi-bin/printenv.cgi"
```

Notice that it knows what type of CPU I have, what operating system I'm using, my IP address and port, and also my browser. All that I knowingly sent was a request for the file `/cgi-bin/printenv.cgi` (a little program I've written for my Web server so that I can check these things). Without my knowledge or permission, the browser has added some additional information to the exchange.

Although none of this looks to be particularly threatening information, it is the fact that it can be, and is divulged without your control, that should get you to thinking. If I am using an email application that supports HTML email (such as Apple's mail client, and in fact most other email clients other than Mail in the terminal, Mailsmith, and Powermail), and the HTML mail includes an embedded image linked to a remote Web site, simply reading that email is going to send information such as shown above to the remote site, without my knowledge, without my permission, and without me having any significant control.

GETTING WHAT YOU ASKED FOR

In fact, this very technique is what has a large portion of the Internet in an uproar over "Web bugs" at this point. The misguided masses who clamored for HTML-capable email clients, so that they could bloat their email messages with ugly fonts and useless images, have, in the last year, suddenly realized that for their email client (or Web browser) to be able to read HTML email with images that come from remote sites, the client must contact that site, and thereby divulge the client's IP, and potentially other interesting facts about the user. Of course, the companies that provide these clients, and the companies that send HTML email, had figured this out somewhat sooner than the consumers, and so have been sending email containing links to invisible "one pixel" images now for years. The reader's HTML-capable email client dutifully contacts the remote server to retrieve the image, divulging the reader's IP, OS, CPU, and other interesting facts.

What's worse, because you're accessing a Web server using a Web browser (never mind that it's called an email client, unless your email client specifically doesn't do HTML; nowadays it's a Web browser), the Web server can set and retrieve *cookies* from your browser. Cookies are small files containing information sent by Web servers, and a source of great consternation to users who understand that they contain possibly private information, but are confused about how it got there and who can access it. A cookie can contain only information that's sent by a Web server, so it's unlikely that a Web-bug will be able to divulge the contents of your private files through this mechanism, but the information that could be available is quite varied. In fact, because most people don't know what cookies have been sent to their computers from what Web servers (and usually most users have hundreds of them stored), there could be almost anything in there: Anything that any Web server you've ever visited has known might be stored in the cookies on your computer, from your user ID on eBay, to your search preferences for Google, to the credit card number you entered on an online merchant's ordering page. If you've entered your actual name and address on some Web page that cooperates with the numerous Web-bug client tracking agencies, every time you read an HTML-containing email in an HTML-capable email client (or browse a Web-bugged page in a Web browser), the advertising company may be getting a record of what email you've read, what Web pages you've visited, and what products you've ordered, all linked to you, the physical consumer at your home snail-mail address. As more software becomes automatically HTML enabled and allows the embedding of links and Web content, this technology for tracking the documents you access becomes even more pervasive. According to The Privacy Foundation's report on document bugging (`http://www.privacyfoundation.org/privacywatch/report.asp?id=39&action=0` and `http://www.privacyfoundation.org/resources/docbug.asp`), Microsoft Word, Excel, and PowerPoint have been susceptible to being bugged since the '97 versions. (The Privacy Foundation report also includes a nice Flash animation showing the mechanism of Web bugs, and a fairly comprehensive FAQ.)

For companies that store information regarding the fact that you read the mail, opened the document, or clicked on the Web page in a database, and that elicit cooperation among a multitude of Web sites and commercial emailers, this data enables them to track consumer response to various types of email advertising, chart their browsing habits around the Web, and build considerably more powerful customer profiles than would be possible if they used only what a customer would willingly divulge in a survey.

Of course, consumers are now acting indignant over the fact that the technology that they unthinkingly embraced is doing exactly what it was designed to do, and want assurances that companies won't, or preferably can't use it for that. It's like asking for a super-heavy macho-man hammer for pounding nails, and then complaining that it's not soft enough when you hit your thumb. So long as they're capable of gathering the information, and so long as it appears to be of economic benefit for them to do so, businesses are going to take every opportunity to collect and analyze information regarding their potential customers. Historically, this has been paid for by the businesses and consists of sending surveys and collecting demographics based on targeted advertising. The Web has made the arrangement much sweeter for businesses because it's the consumer who pays for the opportunity to send the information necessary to build the databases themselves. If you're a business, what could be better?

If you don't want companies to know that you've accessed their computers, don't access them. It's as simple as that.

If I was using one of those newfangled Pentium chips with the built-in digital serial number, and Microsoft's newfangled XP operating system with its irrevocably linked copy of Explorer, would my CPU's serial number and my OS's registration number be embedded in exchanges of information with Web servers as well? Short of setting up my own Web server and figuring out how to write the software to extract the content of the dialog, would there be any way for me to tell whether they were? Don't put your trust in some misguided notion that only fly-by-night companies would mine your personal information in this fashion. It's been well-documented that Microsoft's Windows Media Player phones home with information regarding every DVD that you play in your computer, and Microsoft's disclosure of this fact has been notably lacking (`http://www.computerbytesman.com/privacy/wmp8dvd.htm`). You might be inclined to think "well, if you've got nothing to hide, why would it bother you?" I challenge you to try that argument on the next woman you meet who's carrying a purse. Grab it, dump the contents and start rifling through them. Against her protestations, use the argument "If you've got nothing to hide, you shouldn't be bothered." She'll explain to you, in much more graphic detail than I can convey here, why that argument doesn't fly.

As a probably larger problem, because I'm running it, my browser has access to any information I've entered in its preferences, my system settings, and actually all my files as well, all with my permissions, and all without my necessarily knowing that it's accessing or divulging this information. With the advent of cookies, practically anything I've ever entered or seen on a Web page could be being sent back and forth to sites that I access, without my knowledge or consent.

Some of this information exchange is completely necessary for the applications to function. It would be impossible for a Web server to send you a Web page that you've requested without it getting the information regarding your IP address to know where to send the page. Likewise, cookies have an important purpose in making your Web experience seamless and convenient because without them there's no convenient and relatively secure method for a Web server to keep track of things such as your shopping cart at an online merchant. Unfortunately, it's exceedingly difficult to separate those exchanges that are in your best interest from those that are taking advantage of the fact that you're unaware of the dialog going on.

Our best advice is that it serves most people well to be cautious, but not overly concerned about the information being transmitted in this fashion. The majority of reputable commercial entities on the Web work hard to avoid storing cookies with sensitive data, or to make certain that the cookies are destroyed when the browser leaves the site. Those sites that use Web bugs can track some pages you visit, or emails that you read, but what are they going to do with the information? They're going to use it to more precisely target annoying pop-up ads at you, so that you get fewer ads for junk you are completely disinterested in, and more ads for junk that you might possibly be interested in, but probably aren't. The technology can be misused, and it is misused frequently, but unless you've a real reason to be worried about information you've sent to a Web site, or about other people knowing what pages you've browsed or spam email you've read, it's unlikely that these technologies are going to significantly endanger your machine.

Unintentional Misfeatures

On the other hand, it turns out to be absurdly easy to write software with either accidents or features that can be abused to cause it to perform functions that aren't in its list of intended features. Some of these allow unintended execution of programs, or other types of direct software compromises of your system, but others, insidiously, can result in your system divulging information at your command that is either random, or worse, exactly the data that you thought you were protecting in the process.

By way of example, for quite a while there was a problem with Microsoft Office applications, in that the documents had a tendency to absorb random pieces of information from around a user's system into themselves, without the user's permission or desire (`http://news.zdnet.co.uk/story/0,,t281-s2109785,00.html`). At least a few people claim that this is an ongoing problem (`http://filebox.vt.edu/users/sears/bloated.html`), but Microsoft issued a patch for the '98 releases, and to the best of our ability to discern has fixed this in the Mac OS X versions of their software.

Another example, unfortunately with the same suite of software, is a certain sloppiness about managing the data stored within its files. For some time, it was not uncommon for a Word document to contain portions of many different earlier versions of the document.

This may not appear to be a critical misfeature, and in fact I have on occasion come to rely upon this unintentional archive of data to recover the data from Word documents that have become corrupted and refuse to open, or in which I've accidentally deleted important information. Having a 10-month-old daughter in the house, many pages of Mac OS X Unleashed would have been lost without the ability to recover data from files that had mysteriously changed into something much less useful. However, we just recently heard from one of OSU's computer-savvy legal staff that this misfeature has cost at least one vendor (one that's incredibly apropos in this instance) a lucrative contract with the University. The vendor in this instance sent their business proposal to OSU as a Microsoft Word document. Unfortunately (for them), they were less knowledgeable than they should have been regarding the potential pitfalls of their software of choice, and when the OSU lawyers carefully examined the file, they discovered the remnants of an earlier version of the contract lurking in the file that had been sent. In the earlier version of the contract, the company was offering the same services to another university, but at a much better price. Needless to say, this seemingly insignificant misfeature cost someone a fair sum of money, though we don't know whether it ended up costing anyone his or her job.

Based on a quick scan through the files we've used to compose this book, it appears that this problem doesn't seem to be as prevalent as it once was. However, with only a few iterations of opening and closing files under Word version X, Service Release 1 on OS X 10.2, I managed to produce a file that looks like Figure 4.14 in Word, but that when looked at with the `strings` command from the command line, contains all the data shown in Listing 4.2. The dangerous part is near the bottom of the listing. I constructed this document as though I were mailing off instructions to meet for a surprise party for some friends, and then had reused the driving directions part of the document by deleting the party announcement and replacing it with a request for help to my friend. That last line of the message body in the listing is the original text from the beginning of the document that would have gone to the people attending the party. I deleted it from the Word document, and it doesn't show up anywhere in what Word shows me on the screen, or in what prints out when I print it, yet it obviously remains in the binary contents of the file itself. If I had really constructed the document this way and sent it off as a Word document to some friends, then did a bit of editing and sent a different version off to my rather computer-literate friend Adam, I might have been rather embarrassed.

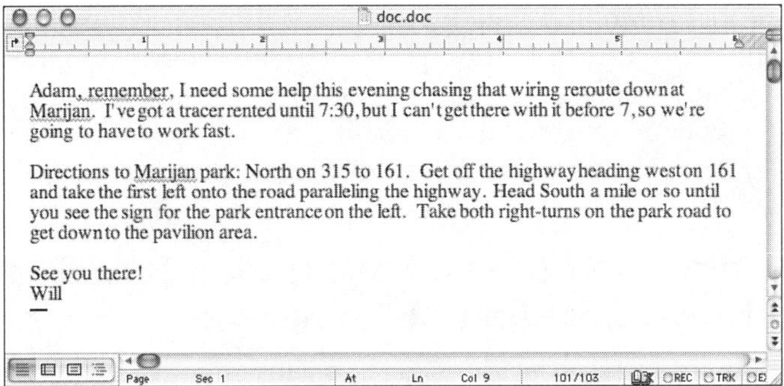

FIGURE 4.14 A Word document that I might have sent to someone.

LISTING 4.2 Some of the interesting strings that are actually contained in the file after it's been edited a few times, even though there's no way to see some of them from within Word itself.

```
Adam, remember, I need some help this evening chasing that wiring reroute down
at Marijan. I've got a tracer rented until 7:30, but I can't get there with
it before 7, so we're going to have to work fast.

Directions to Marijan park: North on 315 to 161. Get off the highway heading
west on 161 and take the first left onto the road paralleling the highway.
Head south a mile or so until you see the sign for the park entrance on the
left. Take both right turns on the park road to get down to the pavilion area.
See you there!
Will
.
.
.
Everybody, tonight's Adam's surprise party - I'll get Adam there and keep him
busy 'til 7:30
Will Ray

Will Ray
Microsoft Word 10.1
```

The danger, of course, is not unique to Microsoft products. These problems are inherent in the notion that software that you run can act upon the system with your permission and authorization. If a programmer makes a simple error that accidentally causes an application to store data it wasn't supposed to, or to read another part of the disk space you control, there's nothing in the action of the system to either inform you of the error or to allow you to prevent it. Your most useful defense is to pay attention to the warnings that people send to security newsgroups and Web sites, and to act upon them by avoiding or patching software that displays problems of this nature. It doesn't hurt to take a look in files that you think you know the contents of, either—you'll probably be surprised at what you sometimes find there.

Steganography and Steganalysis: Hiding Data in Plain Sight, and How to Find and Eliminate It

Steganography, literally "secret writing," is the science of developing and/or applying techniques for concealing one message within another. In its earliest form, it was a highly popular diversion in the form of mind games, with writers encoding the answer to puzzles within the puzzle itself, or signing anonymous poems with a steganographically hidden signature.

One famous example, *Hypnerotomachia Poliphili*, is a curious work of fiction from 1499 that blends a treatise on architectural and landscape design with political theory and erotica in a dreamscape setting where the protagonist wanders, in search of his love Polia. The book is left without any identified author (though some ascribe it to Leon Battista Alberti, a contemporary author of architectural theory), but if one takes the illuminated letter from the beginning of each chapter, one finds the sentence "*Poliam frater Franciscus Columna peramavit.*" MIT makes the manuscript available at `http://mitpress.mit.edu/e-books/HP/hyp000.htm`, including, conveniently, the illuminated headletters as indices to the chapters. David Kahn, in "The Codebreakers: The Story of Secret Writing," notes that this translates as "Brother Francesco Colonna passionately loves Polia." Francesco Colonna was a Dominican monk, still alive when the book was published, lending some credence to the thought that he might have wished such a work to be published anonymously.

Another example, perhaps more interesting, though currently thought of as infamous rather than famous, concerns the apparent lack of solid historical evidence for the author known as Shakespeare. There has long been a contention that the William Shakspere, or Shaxpere, Shagspere, Shackspere or Shakspre (depending on which of the various legal documents of the time you might guess to contain his real signature, if any of them do) of Stratford-on-Avon, with regards to whom a few concrete historic documents exist, is not the same Shake-speare who wrote "Shakespeare's" *Sonnets* (this is the way the *Sonnets* are attributed in their original printing—with a hyphenated name). Curiously, there are a number of good arguments that suggest that the Shakspere recorded in the historical documents was illiterate. One of the best of these was put forward by Sir Edward Durning Lawrence (`http://www.sirbacon.org/edllibrary.htm`) in his treatise "The Shakespeare Myth" (`http://home.att.net/~tleary/sigs.htm`). There is simultaneously an abundance of suggestions, though whether by way of coincidence or intent it cannot be said, that

Sir Francis Bacon may have in fact been the author (`http://www.sirbacon.org/links/evidence.htm`). Included among these is the fact that Bacon considered Pallas Athene (Athena, the "Spear Shaker") to be his muse. Recently, and rather controversially, there has been discovered what appears to be a steganographically encoded cipher in the title page and dedication to the *Sonnets*. Deciphered, the message reads "nypir cypphrs bekaan bacon" ("The Second Cryptographic Shakespeare," Penn Leary, Weschesterhouse Publishers, also `http://home.att.net/~mleary/pennl10.htm`). As spelling was mostly a phonetic exercise at the time, and not bound by today's absolute rules, the curious spellings are possibly excusable. It should be noted that John Napier (also Napeir, Nepair, Nepeir, Neper, Napare, Napar, and Naipper, depending which documents of his you read) is a contemporary of Bacon who developed the notion of mathematical logarithms, and that Bacon was fascinated with cryptology and steganography, and the possibilities that Napier's mathematical ideas brought to these fields.

More currently, steganography has made its way into the world of high-tech watermarking, where its goal becomes not simply the hiding of some message, but doing it in such a way that even if the original is altered, the message can still be detected. The primary driving force behind this move is the proliferation of digital forms of many types of media, such as audio, video, and still imagery. Artists and copyright holders are concerned that these items can be easily duplicated, depriving them of the rights and royalties to which they are legally due. In response, companies tried to solve this problem by finding ways to embed digital signatures and watermarks into digital media. With sufficient industry cooperation, the hardware and software was designed so that the watermarks can be detected, and the media rejected as an invalid file to copy, tape to duplicate, or CD to record.

Contrary to popular belief, these actions aren't specifically abridging consumer rights. They may be making exercise of certain rights more difficult, but the widely held belief that it's legal to copy one's CD if one doesn't sell it to someone (that is, "for personal use"), isn't upheld by what the laws actually say (U.S. Code, Title 17, `http://www4.law.cornell.edu/uscode/17/`). The law says that the copyright holder has the *exclusive* right to make and authorize copies (U.S. Code, Title 17, Chapter 1, Section 106, `http://www4.law.cornell.edu/uscode/17/106.html`). It makes no exception for "personal use." A number of people wave the flag of the "Fair Use" doctrine as supporting their claim that personal use is acceptable under the law, but they are either ill-informed, or deliberately attempting to confuse the issue. Fair Use (U.S. Code, Title 17, Chapter 1, Section 107, `http://www4.law.cornell.edu/uscode/17/107.html`) provides for certain conditions under which the copyright holder's rights may be circumvented without the use being against the law. These include a number of very specific cases where the circumvention is allowable, such as for satire, political commentary, to provide educational material in a classroom setting, or to use the work as a reference in a critique. None of these apply, or come anywhere near applying to copying a work for one's personal convenience. Thankfully, penalties for violation of a copyright holder's rights are based largely on the potential revenue lost due to the action of the violator (U.S. Code, Title 17, Chapter 5, http://www4.law.cornell.edu/uscode/17/ch5.html), so it appears unlikely that publishing houses are going to invest in the legal expenses necessary to recover the $12 one might have deprived them of by copying a CD. In response to this, many companies are endorsing technologies that allow consumers to make a single copy of a digital original, but that prevent subsequent copying of the copy.

Unfortunately, the large corporate publishing concerns that have purchased most of the copyrights to valuable contemporary commodities have seen this as such a large threat that they have railroaded a number of bad laws through the U.S. government, putting legal barricades in place against consumers exercising rights that are clearly granted to them by other sections of the U.S. code. Chief among these poorly thought-out packages of legalese is the act known as the DMCA—the Digital Millennium Copyright Act (U.S. Code, Title 17, Chapter 12, Section 1201, and other sections, http://www4.law.cornell.edu/uscode/17/1201.html). Among the ludicrously anticonsumer ideas put into law by this boondoggle is a section that makes it illegal to "traffic in" any technology (that is, "invent, discuss, etc.") that is primarily useful for circumventing a technological measure put in place to control access to a work.

When coupled with the fact that the copyright for any material work you create and fix in some medium automatically belongs to you from the moment of creation (though the copyright is not registered), the result is that if any technology is used to protect any work you create (encrypted email, for example), it immediately becomes illegal for anyone to "traffic" in any technologies that could circumvent that protection. Put another way, at the moment some technology is first used to protect any copyrighted work, it thenceforth becomes illegal for anyone to examine the protections in that technology, attempt to break it, improve it, or even discuss it.

The upshot of this is that some lawyer out there would probably throw a hissy fit if we were to tell you much at all about the field of *steganalysis*, which is the study of ways to find and eliminate such watermarking or protection from works. At least one academician, a professor from Princeton has already been threatened with legal action if he published a paper on a flaw he discovered in an encryption algorithm (http://www.cs.princeton.edu/sip/sdmi/announcement.html, http://www.cs.princeton.edu/sip/sdmi/riaaletter.html, and http://www.cs.princeton.edu/sip/sdmi/sdmimessage.txt), and several Web sites have been successfully sued, forcing them to remove any mention of security holes that have been found in other products (http://www.2600.com/news/display/display.shtml?id=378). The silliness has even extended to some companies suing others over links being placed to their Web sites, claiming that bypassing their front page by pointing a visitor directly to interesting internal content was circumventing their ability to properly indoctrinate the visitor with the information from the earlier higher pages and thereby "defeating a technological measure protecting a work" (`http://www.internetnews.com/bus-news/article.php/3_1138351`, `http://www.salon.com/tech/col/rose/1999/08/12/deep_links/`, and `http://www.dontlink.com/`). Perhaps most informative of the ulterior motives in these cases, the legal beagles in at least one of the cases likened the practice to "changing the channel, or using a VCR to skip over commercials in broadcast television," as such use of a VCR was clearly a violation of the broadcaster's right to earn revenue.

Many of the major software and hardware manufacturers are jumping on the bandwagon to implement methods to force the consumer to adhere to these laws (and to make it that much more illegal for the consumer to circumvent them). Microsoft recently demonstrated an audio watermarking technology that embeds an audio watermark into music so solidly that the watermark can still be detected and recording prevented even if the source is being played aloud in a crowded room, and the recording is attempted from this "live" source (`http://slashdot.org/features/01/05/03/2043244.shtml`, `http://www.wired.com/news/print/0,1294,43389,00.html`). See where this is going? Personally, we prefer the Tivo to the VCR, but they want to keep us from skipping commercials by making it illegal? Thank whatever God or gods you believe in for the hackers, the crackers, and the company that said "1984 won't be like 1984"! Apple has thus far stood impressively far from the crowd in their refusal to implement such anticonsumer technologies in their products, appearing at this point to be comfortable with allowing their customers to be responsible for their own actions, rather than treating them like a-priori-criminals.

Perhaps the saddest outcome, however, is that the application of the law has risen to the level of absurdity that cryptology and steganography experts were predicting much faster than ever predicted. It is now illegal to possess a certain prime number, as that prime number happens to be related in an interesting fashion to a method of breaking the particularly poor encryption that was ill-advisedly employed by the DVD consortium to protect DVDs from copying, who apparently expected that they could pull an algorithm out of thin air and have it remain secure. The following number is not a prime (we don't want to get in trouble by possessing or distributing an illegal number), but there's an interesting prime near it that can be decoded into a crack for the DVD encryption algorithm. If you'd like to see how hard that prime-number factoring business that we discussed earlier in this chapter really is, you can see whether you can figure out what the prime is with a few well-chosen guesses. It's only 1401 digits—shouldn't be that hard...

```
4
8565078965 7397829309 8418946942 8613770744 2087351357
9240196520 7366869851 3401047237 4469687974 3992611751
0973777701 0274475280 4905883138 4037549709 9879096539
5522701171 2157025974 6669932402 2683459661 9606034851
7424977358 4685188556 7457025712 5474999648 2194184655
7100841190 8625971694 7970799152 0048667099 7592359606
```

```
1320725973 7979936188 6063169144 7358830024 5336972781
8139147979 5551339994 9394882899 8469178361 0018259789
0103160196 1835034344 8956870538 4520853804 5842415654
8248893338 0474758711 2833959896 8522325446 0840897111
9771276941 2079586244 0547161321 0050064598 2017696177
1809478113 6220027234 4827224932 3259547234 6880029277
7649790614 8129840428 3457201463 4896854716 9082354737
8356619721 8622496943 1622716663 9390554302 4156473292
4855248991 2257394665 4862714048 2117138124 3882177176
0298412552 4464744505 5834628144 8833563190 2725319590
4392838737 6407391689 1257924055 0156208897 8716337599
9107887084 9081590975 4801928576 8451988596 3053238234
9055809203 2999603234 4711407760 1984716353 1161713078
5760848622 3637028357 0104961259 5681846785 9653331007
7017991614 6744725492 7283348691 6000647585 9174627812
1269007351 8309241530 1063028932 9566584366 2000800476
7789679843 8209079761 9859493646 3093805863 3672146969
5975027968 7712057249 9666698056 1453382074 1203159337
7030994915 2746918356 5937621022 2006812679 8273445760
9380203044 7912277498 0917955938 3871210005 8876668925
8448700470 7725524970 6044465212 7130404321 1826101035
9118647666 2963858495 0874484973 7347686142 0880529442
```

As mentioned earlier, the only way to develop secure algorithms is by subjecting them to constant and vigorous public scrutiny. The end result of this critically flawed law will be that we, the consumers, are going to be forced to accept much poorer quality encryption software to protect our data, while the criminal element that would circumvent the protections for profit will have it much easier, as the algorithms will have not been subjected to rigorous academic review.

Mac OS X Steganography Products

At this point, there isn't much software out there to allow you to experiment with steganography, but you can expect that there will be more toys coming, as the battle heats up between corporate interests trying to protect their right to a profit and the hackers interested in advancing the arts of cryptography and steganography. In the meantime, you can examine a few interesting (or in one case, at least amusing) products if you're interested in experimenting a bit, or using steganographic techniques to conceal textual data.

- Adobe's PhotoShop includes a pair of filters named Digimarc "Embed Watermark" and "Read Watermark," which respectively embed a copyright statement into an image as a watermark or decode it again.

- Precious Gem software distributes Corundum (http://preciousgem.dnsalias.com:90/PreciousGem/Corundum/Corundum.html), which allows you to steganographically hide textual information in images.
- Spam Mimic (http://www.spammimic.com/index.shtml) provides the steganographic service of hiding short text messages in email that looks like spam. Nobody looks at spam email, right? Where better to hide something than in a plain-sight email transmission, that people will do their best to avoid seeing?

These products conveniently display complementary features. The purpose of the PhotoShop filter is to allow watermarking images so that the copyright information is indelibly embedded in the image. This is an attempt to provide for some way of proving that commercial digital images are copyrighted, so that, for example, as images are snagged off of a Web site and transferred around the Internet, the ownership information remains with the file. The copyright watermark embedded by Digimarc is immune to most simple transformations of the image: Cropping it, rotating it, mirroring, skewing, mild blurs, noise, and most other simple adulterations won't erase the watermark. Unfortunately, in a brilliant display of what we've been repeating about security not being secure unless it's open, tested, and verified, the Digimarc/PictureMarc system is tragically flawed in its ability to actually secure an image. As Fabien Peticolas demonstrates at http://www.cl.cam.ac.uk/~fapp2/watermarking/index.html, it takes only a few minutes of brute-force attempts against PictureMarc 1.51 images to guess the code necessary to remove or modify the original watermark and replace it with one of your own. Trying to eradicate it through the use of image manipulations probably takes longer.

The Corundum application, on the other hand, is designed with the intent of embedding information so that it can't be found, but not so that it can't be damaged by modifying the image. We'd show you before and after images of what things look like with the data encoded into them, but there's really little point—to the limits of reproduction in this book, the images with data encoded into them are indistinguishable from the originals. While you're waiting for some of the two dozen or so steganography projects underway on Sourceforge to make their way to the Mac, you might want to check out the Web pages of Johnson and Johnson Technology Consultants, who have published and provided some very nice papers on steganographic techniques, steganalysis, and the current state of the art at http://www.jjtc.com/Steganography/. Specifically, Niel F. Johnson's papers (http://www.jjtc.com/stegdoc/steg1995.html and http://www.jjtc.com/pub/nfjidr99.pdf) should be interesting to those considering how this technology might be either helpful or damaging to their computing security.

Spam Mimic, by way of comparison, doesn't try to so hard to encode the information in an invisible fashion, as to make the carrier so common and ugly that no one will give it a second look. If you enter a short message such as the following:

```
Hi Joan, I'll be home by 5:30.
```

You'll be presented with a result that you can email that starts off:

```
Dear E-Commerce professional ; This letter was specially selected to be sent to
you . This is a one time mailing there is no need to request removal if you
won't want any more . This mail is being sent in compliance with Senate bill
 1624 , Title 2 ; Section 304 ! This is different than anything else you've
seen ! Why work for somebody else when you can become rich within 57 WEEKS...
```

Who's going to bother looking at that to see whether it has interesting information in it?

Although it's not available for Mac OS X yet, another application you might want to keep an eye out for is Hydan from Columbia University student Rakan El-Khalil. SecurityFocus reports that at a small computing security conference held in February 2003, Rakan demonstrated an application that uses other executable applications as a place to hide information (`http://www.securityfocus.com/news/2623`). Cleverly, this application does not hide the information by stuffing it into unused nooks and crannies in the executable, but instead by subtly modifying the way that the executable host performs its calculations, and thereby using the code of the application itself as the carrier for the hidden information.

Summary

The take-home lesson that you should get from this chapter is that if you want your data to be proofed against others looking at it, you need to take some fairly strong precautions to keep others from seeing the content. If you try to hide it via encryption, you need to make certain that that the encryption is strong enough to stand up to a concerted attack. Although any key may theoretically be guessed with sufficient computing power, with a secure algorithm it is possible to make the amount of power required to guess the key so large that it cannot be practically accomplished, regardless of the length of time or amount of software thrown at the problem.

To accomplish this level of protection, however, requires an algorithm that has no weaknesses, that can allow the key to be back-calculated from the ciphertext only through the application of large amounts of computing power, and in which the key really is as secure as its size or complexity would imply. Experience has shown, time and time again, that unless an algorithm has been exhaustively examined and tested by a large population of experts, it is very likely to be trivially compromised within a short time of its release. For every algorithm that proves to be secure against attacks for a few years, thousands are developed, tested, revised, tested, and eventually abandoned as insecure. Security implementations arrived at and not tested to the point of exhaustion are found to be lacking, over and over and over. The top authors of security methods will tell you, without hesitation, that you shouldn't trust even their algorithms until they've been proven for at least a few years in the field.

Mac OS X provides you with several alternatives for how you might accomplish such protection, and more are likely to become available. However, as cryptography and steganography become the next hot arena of conflict for the hacker and corporate cultures, many of these might not be things that the government and/or the corporate lobbyists want you to see.

The government and mega-media-conglomerate corporations would have you believe that legal restrictions on the development or exploration of cryptography, cryptanalysis, and other information-hiding or -disguising technology is for your own good. They would insist that it protects the American economy, protects you from evil crackers on the Internet, and in the latest round of attempting to capitalize on any available bandwagon, that darn it, it's just plain patriotic and will help the country fight the terrorists. When you consider whether you want to believe them or not, don't even think about the fact that in the last government foray into attempting to legislate cryptography, they would have mandated a "private" backdoor into any encrypted data by imposing a legal requirement that all encryption be done by one government-sanctioned application, to which they held the keys, and making all others illegal. Just keep in mind that the encryption methodology that the government would have imposed upon everyone uses a 40-bit key, and that the DES algorithm with its 56-bit key can be brute-force cracked in as little as 22 hours (depending on how much hardware you have to throw at it). A 40-bit key should be able to be cracked 2^16 times faster. That's about 65000 times faster. Reports are that in 1996, when some of this lunacy was being proposed, it could be done in about 5 hours for $20 in hardware from Radio Shack, or in about 26 seconds if you were willing to spend a little more (`http://www.pff.org/encry.html`).

Make no mistake; it is not impossible to invent a secure algorithm "in the dark," and those who make the laws aren't universally in collusion with either the mega-corporate interests or with the ultraconservative faction who wants a camera in every room of every house. Nor are they universally ignorant. Past experience, however, indicates that it is incredibly unlikely that good security can be either pulled from thin air or legislated into existence. Therefore, you should have come in this chapter to understand that legal proscriptions against examining security, such as have been put in place by the DMCA, are nothing but an attempt to protect others' agendas at your expense. This is one case where the people evading or completely disobeying the laws regarding computing security just might be your best hope for a secure computing future.

5 Picking Locks: Password Attacks

IN THIS CHAPTER

- Typical Password Mechanisms
- Testing Password Security
- Improving Password Security, and Alternatives to the Standard Password Mechanisms in Mac OS X

Passwords—what an idea. Using a small word as a shared secret to identify the bearer. In the security world, one often hears of identifying oneself by either what you have, what you know, or what you are. A password is an attempt to prove identification through proving what you know, and passwords have been a standard at the gates to castles, the doors to clubs, and the prompts of computers for years. Unix passwords can be a bit more complex than spoken passwords, but the standard scheme limits them to 8 characters in length. When extended to upper and lower case, nonsense words and special characters, there are 6,634,204,312,890,625 passwords enterable from a Pismo PowerBook keyboard available for use in the standard Unix authentication scheme (that is, 95 possible keyboard characters in each of 8 positions—95×95×95×95×95×95×95×95 = 6,634,204,312,890,625 possible passwords).

That's almost seven million billion possibilities—sounds like a lot, right? Perhaps in the days when passwords were spoken, and the consequences of giving the wrong one at the castle gate was that someone took a swing at your head with an axe, seven million billion possibilities was a serious deterrent. Unfortunately, although we keep using the idea of passwords to identify ourselves, computers can make the act of testing passwords much faster, and much safer for an intruder. Initially, the Unix password authentication system was designed to make randomly testing passwords difficult. The algorithm was intentionally designed to be extremely slow, so that although the consequences of trying a password and getting it wrong might be less drastic, it still required a very long time to crack passwords by simple guessing. Unfortunately, it didn't take long for people to write faster versions. Now, a simple brute-force approach to password cracking can test anywhere from fifty thousand (G3, 450Mhz, our test results drawn from using John the Ripper on a Sage iMac DV+), to millions (reported speeds on top-end P4 Intel boxes by ZDNet.com) of possibilities in less than a second. It still takes upwards of a half billion seconds (that's over ten years) to crack every possible password on a high-end desktop processor. But, as machines become more powerful, that time period inevitably will be reduced. In fact, if processor speed increases continue to track the trends that have been established over the last 20 years, in 5 or so years we'll be able to explore the entire password space with an investment of less than a single year of CPU time. More discouragingly, shorter passwords, or passwords chosen from a smaller character set or using predictable patterns can be guessed in a correspondingly shorter time period. Kurt Hockenbury estimated in 1997 that a 10-machine flock of then high-end Pentium Pro computers could crack every 8-character password composed of lowercase and numeric characters in just over half a year. By now, with both faster processors and faster algorithms available, that password space should fall easily with less than a month of processor time expended. `http://attila.stevens-tech.edu/~khockenb/crypt3.html` details his findings.

Of somewhat more concern, if someone really wants to break into your system, it doesn't take a top-secret government agency to bring mountains of computing power to bear on a problem. Like the SETI@home project, which linked spare CPU cycles on millions of users' computers together to scan deep space for signs of alien intelligence, today's crackers can harness the power of computers all over the Internet. Most recent computer viruses have been distributed via the Internet (predominantly through poorly designed email clients), and have been designed to take over the targeted computer and give control of the "zombie" machine to a "master" system that can direct its actions over the Internet. The payload in the recent viruses has been software intended to knock other computers on the Net offline with denial of service attacks (see Chapter 9, "Everything Else"), but it could just as well be a password-cracking application. In one of the recent viral incidents, it is estimated that the Code Red worm (technically a worm, because the only action it takes on the user's part is ignorance) managed to infect 360,000 machines within its first 14 hours of life (`http://www.mcafee.com/aboutus/bus_dev/retail_users/newsletters/feb2002/classof2001.htm`). If the payload had been a password cracker, that could have been 360,000 machines working simultaneously on cracking your password. Somehow, a year of CPU time doesn't sound like that much when it's spread over 360,000 machines. Actually, it comes out to something under a minute and a half.

To make matters worse, people don't naturally make use of anything resembling the entire password space. A statistician might express the randomness available in that 6.6 million billion possible password choices as saying that a password chosen from the space has approximately 53 bits of *entropy*. That is, 2 raised to the power 52.558844 ≈ 6,634,204,312,890,625.

Using entropy in this fashion is a way of expressing the actual randomness in what is intended to be a random string. For example, if you know that your users have chosen passwords that are eight characters long, you might suppose that they've randomly chosen amongst the full 6.6 million billion possible passwords in the password space. If, in fact, your users have chosen passwords composed of only lowercase *a* and *b* characters, they would still be chosen from the full password space, but only out of a 256-member subset. In this case we would say that the users' passwords display 8 bits of entropy (`2^8 = 256`).

If the users enter any of the 128 characters in 7-bit ASCII, the result is 8-character passwords with 64 bits of entropy. Each character, having 95 possible choices, therefore has ~6.6 bits of entropy available, but it is quite common for less than that amount of entropy to show up in final password choices. The written English language, for example, because it tends to use certain characters more frequently than others, and certain character combinations much more frequently than others, appears to have roughly only 1.3 bits of entropy per character. (*Applied Cryptography: Protocols, Algorithms, and Source Code in C*, by Bruce Schneier, covers Shannon's famous estimate, as well as other cryptographic statistics and plain old interesting theory and practice.) This means that if a user chooses, as many do, a dictionary word for their password, they've accumulated only some 10.4 bits of total entropy—a much smaller amount of randomness (10.4 bits, assuming they used the full 8 characters available for the password, that is—shorter passwords are logarithmically weaker). Because clever password-guessing software can make use of the predicted character-use patterns to search the most likely combinations first, a badly chosen password can reduce the problem of searching for passwords from one that takes several years to accomplish to one that takes only a fraction of a second. Put another way, to create a password that is as strong as one using 8 characters of completely random data, a password composed of English-language words would need to be over 40 characters in length—a large fraction of the length of one of the lines of text in this book. Of course, any sentence-like structure in the password would significantly reduce the entropy available, again making it easier to guess.

Even people trying to be random don't produce particularly random results. Several studies have determined that strings of characters "randomly" chosen by people, aren't actually all that random, and the variability in each position does not approach the ~6.6 bits of available entropy. This most likely has to do with the unconscious associations we form with respect to letter patterns and usage in written language, and manifests itself in "randomly" chosen strings displaying significant word-like structure when constructed by a person.

This chapter covers the flaws in the basic notion of password protection for services, files, and other resources, as well as what you can do to limit your vulnerability when picking passwords. Not all password schemes will necessarily conform to the exact encryption or storage standards we'll cover here, but they're all subject to the same basic conceptual flaws.

Typical Password Mechanisms

Although there are almost as many different mechanisms in place for using and storing passwords as there are applications that use them, there are quite a few commonalities between the mechanisms.

Username and Password

Most password mechanisms require that you know both who you are and some token to prove that you really are who you claim to be. That is, you are required to provide a username and a password to confirm that choice. This is obviously useful in enabling the system to distinguish between different users, as many users can securely have exactly the same password, as long as none of them knows the others are using it as well. In a way, the user information can also be thought of as adding extra entropy to the password. If an attacker has to guess at both a user ID and a password, it's more difficult than guessing at the password alone. It's not a whole lot more entropy, and usernames almost certainly display even less entropy than dictionary words, but for every bit of additional entropy, a brute-force attack is going to have to try twice as hard. To make this additional potential entropy work for you, disguising the list of users on the system is necessary. With Mac OS X, this means turning off the iconic login window and making people type their usernames as well as a password. Users will initially find this bothersome, but in the long run it usually saves them time, as well as makes things just a bit more secure. If you have more than a handful of users on the system, it takes many of them a considerable amount of time to find their user ID in the login window scrolling list, and from observation, the frustration involved with this step is much greater than that involved in typing a user ID. It also means that you need to disable any services that might provide information to the network regarding what user IDs are available on the system. Finger is one of the primary culprits here, but NIS and NetInfo (covered in later sections of this chapter) are also potentially troublesome here.

Of course, if every system has a user named root on it, one with superuser capabilities, that's an obvious target for password attacks. Many systems therefore disable root login both from the network and the console. Users are allowed to `su` to root, but direct login as root is prohibited. This is a good idea as a general practice because root is typically a disembodied account with no specific person attached to it. Requiring users to `su` to root, rather than allowing root logins, provides an additional level of traceability of action because it prevents anyone from logging into the machine and anonymously using root powers.

Password Storage

Password storage schemes are wide and wildly varied. The worst store the password in plaintext form, doing only the most trivial job of hiding them from prying eyes.

The best encrypt the passwords well enough that they can't be decrypted at all from the stored value, providing only a one-way encryption of the information and necessitating brute-force methods to compromise the information. Remember, however, that no matter how carefully the passwords are protected, there just aren't that many of them, especially when people choose poor passwords with little entropy, and this makes the brute-force approach applicable to any scheme.

Plaintext Storage

As bad an idea as it sounds, a few programs are written in such a fashion as to store passwords in plaintext. Thankfully, these tend to be applications such as mail servers that hold user accounts as separate from system accounts. CommuniGate Email server from Stalker Software (`http://www.stalker.com/CommuniGate/`) is one package that can be configured to behave in this fashion. CommuniGate stores user IDs and passwords in files on a per-user basis, typically in the directory `/var/CommuniGate/Accounts/`, where its behavior can be configured separately for each user. One possible configuration is storing the user ID and password as cleartext. For example, in the following configuration, the user jray's account is set to use the cleartext password `mysecret`.

```
# cat /var/CommuniGate/Accounts/jray.macnt/account.settings

{
  AccountEnabled = YES;
  LoginEnabled = YES;
  MaxAccountSize = unlimited;
  MaxWebFiles = 0;
  MaxWebSize = unlimited;
  Password = mysecret;
  PasswordEncryption = clear;
  PWDAllowed = YES;
  RealName = "John Ray";
  RequireAPOP = NO;
  RPOPAllowed = YES;
  RulesAllowed = Any;
  UseAppPassword = YES;
  UseExtPassword = YES;
  UseSysPassword = YES;
}
```

For CommuniGate, the user IDs and passwords stored in this way are mail-account-only user IDs and passwords, so if the cleartext file is read without authorization, the only information the culprits get is names and passwords for mail accounts. This means that they could access and change user's email, but the system passwords that allow your real OS X users to log in are not necessarily jeopardized. We say "necessarily" because users have a bad habit of using the same password for multiple different accounts, and so they very well might have chosen the same passwords for their logins as for their mail. Necessity—and system administrators working in its name—don't do much to discourage this behavior at all by forcing users to change their passwords frequently. Experience indicates that a large fraction of users who have both email and system accounts will have chosen the same passwords for each.

This particular configuration is set up with cleartext passwords because this example system has a large population of noncomputer-savy users who require both dial-in and email access, and these needs are serviced with separate software solutions. The users really need to have everything made as convenient as possible, so mandating that they choose two good passwords for the system is impractical—they're disinclined to choose even one.

We are, as they say, stuck between a rock and a hard place: If we synchronize the systems to make things easier for them, they have only one password, and both systems are vulnerable if one is compromised. If we keep them separate, but force them to make good passwords, chances are they'll make just two passwords, and swap them back and forth each time their password expires, which is probably worse than one good password. Overall, there's no good solution because, as you should be coming to understand, passwords are a poor solution to the general problem of proving that you are who you say you are.

Encryption

A better storage system for passwords, and the one that's typically used in Unix systems, is encrypting the password and storing the ciphertext. The encryption may vary between quite weak and very strong encryption, but the general purpose remains the same: to prevent people from using what they might see (if they were to look at the stored passwords) to guess what the passwords are. Sometimes, such as with the Digimarc 2-digit "PIN" key that was mentioned in the steganography section of the previous chapter, it makes almost no difference whether the password is encrypted because brute-force attacks against the system are so simple.

When the key is more complex, however, a strong encryption system can make brute-force attacks much more difficult to carry out. With the best of these systems, the encryption algorithm not only makes the password difficult (or better, impossible) to decrypt, but also is computationally expensive, so as to make brute-force attacks impractical because of the time required to execute the attack. If the only route to a crack is through brute-force examination of every possible key, each additional bit of key length doubles the computational cost involved in discovering the key. Because of differences in exactly what different algorithms mean when they discuss key length, you can't take this as an absolute method of comparison between the strength of different algorithms, but it's a good first-order approximation.

In many cases, the authentication system is set up so that the stored password cannot (through any known mechanism) be decrypted. This may seem counterproductive, in that one wants to be able to compare the password provided by the user with the one that was stored. This comparison, however, can be carried out just as easily with the encrypted password. The user's password is stored encrypted, and the password entered by the user as he attempts to authenticate is encrypted, then these two encrypted values are compared. It is possible with some storage schemes (MD5 checksums, for example) that there are multiple passwords that hash to the same stored value, but finding a hash collision is no more likely than finding the correct password, so this is of only minor concern.

For example, the standard Unix password system stores user IDs and passwords in a plaintext file, which any users can read. The passwords stored there are encrypted through an application of the DES encryption algorithm (Chapter 4, "Theft and Destruction of Property: Data Attacks"). A typical password file might look like this:

```
root:nA5oSdDy859bE:0:1:Operator:/:/bin/csh
nobody:*:65534:65534:nobody:/:
daemon:*:1:1:daemon:/:
sys:*:2:2:sys:/:/bin/csh
bin:*:3:3:bin:/bin:
sync:*:1:1:sync:/:/bin/sync
ftp:*:99:20:anonymous ftp:/store/ftp:/bin/csh
guest:2dj7u1tEvDLpk:101:8:Guest Account:/home/guest:/bin/csh
ray:OPA7l1cyVYwrs:515:10:William C. Ray:/priv/home/ray:/bin/tcsh
skuld:CZ4a7y1AlpgMW:100:5:System Software
➥Administrator:/usr/local/test:/bin/tcsh
joray:pA2lf397a0mYa:2001:21:Joan Ray:/priv/home/joray:/bin/tcsh
jray:a3kSXs1ROd17p:2002:21:John Ray:/home/jray:/bin/tcsh
```

Here `root`, `guest`, `ray`, `skuld`, `joray`, and `jray` have active accounts with passwords set. `nobody`, `daemon`, `sys`, `bin`, `sync`, and `ftp` show a `*` character instead of an encrypted password. This effectively locks the account out (`root` can still `su` to it) because the `*` is not a valid password encryption, and therefore no entered password can ever match this value. In traditional Unix, this file is `/etc/passwd` (or `/etc/master.passwd` in Mac OS X, if you've enabled "BSD Configuration Files" from the Directory Services utility, and set it to use the password file), and each user's encrypted password is the value immediately following the first colon of the line. In an attempt to make the decryption even more difficult, the standard system works in reverse of the way that might initially seem to be appropriate. Instead of encrypting the password through the use of some key, and storing the encrypted value—which would subject the entire scheme to failure if the key should happen to be discovered—in the standard use, the password itself is used as a key to encrypt a known value.

NOTE

The form of this use is worth repeating, as it's a clever way to use an encryption system with a strong algorithm. As the developers of the DVD encryption system discovered the hard way, if you embed the key to your encryption algorithm in your software, a single failure that allows someone to discover that key can lead to a failure of the entire system. It is therefore a poor design to store passwords (or any other data) encrypted with a key that you're also storing in the same software. To alleviate this concern, for data that is on the order of the size of passwords, one can reverse the usual use, and use the provided password as the key, and encrypt a known value instead. For the purposes of comparing the stored value to the encrypted result of what the user enters, which is encrypted and which is the key does not matter: Any particular key and data value will still always encrypt to the same result, but using the password as the key prevents the key from being a stored value, and therefore limits any compromise that guesses a key from compromising anything but that individual value.

NIS (Network Information System) Passwords

The previous section illustrated password storage in the classical single-password-file on a single machine style. More typically in clustered environments, systems use a server to transfer the passwords between all the clients, enabling each client to have identical information regarding each user. In the traditional Unix environment, this is facilitated by the NIS (Network Information Services, formerly known as the YP—yellow pages—system), which functions as a network database to serve user ID and password information to any collection of machines that want to cooperate as a cluster.

NOTE

There are vulnerabilities specific to this service, but the general concepts apply in some fashion and at some level to any service that provides system passwords from remote systems.

NIS information is served as collections, each of which is given a unique (one should hope) NIS domain name. Any machine that wants to participate as a peer in a cluster subscribes to the domain by name. It does so by broadcasting a request on the network for any server that claims to serve a domain by that name. The system was designed to make it simple to build cooperative clusters with provisions for redundant service for user authentication, while requiring as little human intervention in copying data in circles as possible. For this purpose it works well: Any machine can join the cluster simply by requesting information from the named domain and then acting upon it. Likewise, the cluster can easily be made fault tolerant, because the clients aren't locked into a particular server for the authentication information. Because clients query for authentication information by broadcast, slave NIS servers can be configured to automatically mirror information from the master, and to respond to broadcast queries for the information if they don't see a response from the master.

This scheme, although widely used with clustered Unix machines, is insecure on two fronts. It was devised in the days when all Unix machines were run by trained and trusted system administrators, and there was an implicit understanding that if a Unix machine were attempting to connect, it was very likely to have a trusted operator at the helm. Therefore, the only effective security built into the system is the capability to restrict responses to NIS information requests to only particular trusted subnets, and the notion that keeping the NIS domain name secret will prevent unauthorized queries to that domain. Like many early security measures built into Unix, these ideas have been antiquated by the advent of desktop Unixes such as Mac OS X and Linux. If an unauthorized client wants to access the information in the domain (such as to gain access to the password file), it has only to broadcast a request for that domain and be within one of the subnets that the server is configured to believe is secure, and a server will respond with the requested information. Unless we have absolute control over all machines on the "trusted" subnets, and absolute certainty that no other machines can be added, in today's environment we cannot responsibly believe that only authorized machines will request the information. Likewise, although the NIS domain name can be considered to be a password of sorts, it's unwise to rely on its remaining unknown as a strong protection against unauthorized access to the information available through the domain.

If you have an NIS domain to which you can subscribe, it is quite simple to access the password (and other) information stored in it and use this information for authentication on your machine. You need to contact the administrator of the system serving the domain to determine the domain name, whether your machine is permitted access, and to confirm that your subnet is listed among the trusted subnets for that domain on the server. After you have done this, follow these steps to configure your machine to make use of the information:

1. Configure your machine to accept user information from NIS.
2. Configure the NIS domain name for your machine.
3. Bind your machine as an NIS client to the domain.

Each of these steps will need to be done while you are `su`ed root, or via `sudo`. After you are finished, you will be able to log in to your machine as any user specified in the domain, using the passwords that the domain specifies and the home directory and shells configured in that domain for the users, just as though you had created the users locally in your own NetInfo system. As of this writing (OS 10.2.2) however, there's a bug with the GUI login application that prevents it from using the NIS information. (NIS login and other information functions properly through `ssh` (`slogin`) login and `su` functionality, however.)

Using NIS for Lookups The first step of the process is accomplished by adding a flag specifying that `lookupd` should obey NIS-provided information for users. You can accomplish this by creating the file `/etc/lookupd/users` and specifying appropriate options for `LookupOrder`, or by creating the NetInfo directory `/locations/lookupd/users` and populating it with the same information, and then restarting `lookupd`. If you prefer the file route, create the file `/etc/lookupd/users` and place in it the following line:

```
LookupOrder     NIAgent YPAgent
```

This tells `lookupd` that when it's looking for user authentication information it is to first go to your NetInfo system and inquire there (NetInfo is a NeXT-inspired service that provides more sophisticated network-information-database-type services than NIS, and is the default information service for OS X), and if matching information is not found, to subsequently query the NIS system. If you prefer to add the information to your NetInfo domain, you can do so either by using the NetInfo Manager application in your Applications/Utilities directory, or by using the command-line `niutil` commands shown here. (`niutil` is covered in greater detail in the next section.)

```
niutil -create . /locations/lookupd/users
niutil -createprop . /locations/lookupd/users LookupOrder NIAgent YPAgent
```

Alternately, you can create the content for the directory as a text file and then insert the content by using the `niload` command to populate the directory. First create a text file containing the following content:

```
{
  "name" = ( "lookupd" );
  CHILDREN = (
    {
      "name" = ( "users" );
      "LookupOrder" = ( "NIAgent", "YPAgent" );
    }
  )
}
```

Because `lookupd` actually controls the search order for a number of different types of services, it might be better for you to specify a default order as well. Also, including the `CacheAgent` as the first source to check can speed lookups on your system considerably in some situations. These changes make the file look like the following:

```
{
  "LookupOrder" = ( "CacheAgent", "NIAgent", "YPAgent" );
  "name" = ( "lookupd" );
  CHILDREN = (
    {
      "name" = ( "users" );
      "LookupOrder" = ( "CacheAgent", "NIAgent", "YPAgent" );
    }
  )
}
```

In either case, the changes get loaded into your NetInfo domain with the following commands (assuming you've named you text file `lookupd.txt`):

```
niutil -create . /locations/lookupd
niload -r /locations/lookupd . < lookupd.txt
```

Selecting an NIS Domain The second step is to configure your machine to subscribe to a particular NIS domain. It is possible to subscribe to (and switch among) multiple domains, but this is beyond the scope of this book. For a single domain, the process is simple: Just issue the `domainname` command, where `<domainname>` is the name of the domain you plan to subscribe to:

```
domainname <domainname>
```

If you want to make this subscription to the domain permanent, then edit the `/etc/hostconfig` file so that it reads:

```
NISDOMAIN=<domainname>
```

If you make this change, the next time the machine is rebooted, all this will be configured automatically.

Binding Your Client to the NIS Domain The third step is to bind your domain to the domain. If you are on the same broadcast subnet as the server for the domain, to subscribe to a domain you need to know only the NIS domain name. (Remember, this is not the same thing as your DNS domain.) If you are on a different subnet, you need to know both the domain name and the server's IP address. If you are on the same subnet, simply issue the following command:

```
ypbind
```

If you need to bind to a server on a different subnet, the process is only a little more complicated (though it may be considerably more frustrating—the first step sometimes takes a while to respond when it can't talk to the NIS server immediately). If your machine is on a different subnet from the server, use the following commands instead:

```
ypbind -ypsetme
ypset <ip address of NIS server host>
```

Taken all together, if you were trying to bind your machine to the NIS domain `rubbermonster`, and the server were at IP address `192.168.1.4`, the process after adding NIS to the `lookupd` would look like this:

```
domainname rubbermonster
ypbind -ypsetme
ypset 192.168.1.4
```

The second step may take some time. If you find it annoying, start another terminal window, log in as root, and run the `ypset` command from it. After these commands have all been executed successfully, you should be able to then run the `ypcat` command and get the same sort of output shown earlier as being in the `/etc/password` file. Here I've left my full prompts in the output to more clearly display the sequence of operations:

```
Racer-X ray 7# nidump -r /locations/lookupd .
{
  "name" = ( "lookupd" );
  CHILDREN = (
    {
      "name" = ( "users" );
      "LookupOrder" = ( "NIAgent", "YPAgent" );
    }
  )
}

Racer-X ray 8# domainname rubbermonster
Racer-X ray 9# ypbind -ypsetme

(I got bored and ran ypset 192.168.1.4 in another window)

Racer-X ray 10# ypwhich
192.168.1.4
```

```
Racer-X ray 11# ypcat passwd
root:nA5oSdDy859bE:0:1:Operator:/:/bin/csh
nobody:*:65534:65534:nobody:/:
daemon:*:1:1:daemon:/:
sys:*:2:2:sys:/:/bin/csh
bin:*:3:3:bin:/bin:
sync:*:1:1:sync:/:/bin/sync
ftp:*:99:20:anonymous ftp:/store/ftp:/bin/csh
guest:2dj7u1tEvDLpk:101:8:Guest Account:/home/guest:/bin/csh
ray:OPA7l1cyVYwrs:515:10:William C. Ray:/priv/home/ray:/bin/tcsh
skuld:CZ4a7y1AlpgMW:100:5:System Software
➥Administrator:/usr/local/test:/bin/tcsh
joray:pA2lf397a0mYa:2001:21:Joan Ray:/priv/home/joray:/bin/tcsh
jray:a3kSXs1ROd17p:2002:21:John Ray:/home/jray:/bin/tcsh
```

At this point, I'm able to log in to my machine as any of these users, and it's just as though I created them in my own NetInfo system through the Accounts control pane.

The potential security failures of the system should be obvious: I've just snagged a copy of the password file from a remote server, without doing anything beyond asking it politely. If I were trying to steal information, it couldn't get much easier for me stealing the password file, could it? Perhaps more insidiously, if someone wanted access to my machine, all they'd need to do is whack the actual server and stick in a server that served a domain by the same name. I'd possibly never know the difference, and the culprits would be able to insert any user IDs and passwords into my list of users. This would enable them to enter my system at will. This attack becomes trivially easy with the broadcast version of the protocol, where the client doesn't even have an IP address for the server. Just disabling the server's network connection and popping an imposter system online for a few moments can insert users into my system, who my machine will allow access. There's nothing to prevent them from inserting a user with an equivalent user ID to root (UID 0). This could be devastating.

LDAP (Lightweight Directory Access Protocol) Passwords

Like the NIS, LDAP is a network service designed to provide user account information across a cluster of cooperating machines. LDAP has traditionally been used more frequently in clustering "desktop workgroup"-type computers than in clustering Unix boxes, but it is becoming more common in this environment as well. OS X, trying to interoperate in both worlds seamlessly, provides access to either or both systems. Unlike NIS, in which the database and query system are integrated, LDAP is technically just a specification for a standard for carrying out the on-network dialog between a client requesting and a server providing directory-type information. LDAP can theoretically be used as the interface to just about any network directory service, and Apple has used it to build their OpenDirectory service package on top of NetInfo (discussed in the next section) for OS X.

In the case of LDAP, OS X's support currently appears to be seamless in some situations and strewn with cavernous gulfs in others. There are five different interfaces (or rather, five that have been found so far) through which the system can be configured to communicate with LDAP services:

- Two interfaces are available through Directory Access in Applications/Utilities. LDAPv2 and LDAPv3, although they require similar information, are configured through two completely dissimilar interfaces. These theoretically configure the system to accept LDAP information for logins and/or address-book purposes.
- On the other hand, there are also two different (both between themselves and from the Directory Access configuration) places in which to configure `lookupd`, which is the general directory services information daemon where the system (supposedly) gets its normal user information. `lookupd` can either read a series of configuration files from `/etc/lookupd/` or use the NetInfo directory `/locations/lookupd/` from your local NetInfo heirarchy. Unfortunately, it seems there's a file missing from the system because attempts to directly configure `lookupd` to use LDAP, in a fashion similar to what was done with NIS in the previous section, result in errors being logged to `/var/log/system.log` regarding a missing `LDAP.bundle` file.
- Finally, there are configuration files living in `/etc/openldap/` that appear to carry the configuration for an assortment of LDAP command-line tools such as `ud` (a textual interface to LDAP services).

Annoyingly, the way that these interoperate (if at all) is not clearly documented, and none of the three systems (and their five interfaces) appear to be aware of the existence of the others. Also annoyingly, the man pages for each appear to have originated on systems where that interface was *the* interface to LDAP, leaving the administrator with considerable confusion if she isn't trying to connect to an Apple server for which LDAP is mostly all autoconfiguring. Fortunately, in a book regarding security, our place is not to teach you to make sense of or configure this morass, but to point out the deficiencies in the system from a security standpoint.

Being considerably more complex a system than NIS, one might expect LDAP to suffer from more potential security problems than NIS. A quick survey of `securityfocus.com` and `cve.mitre.org` would lead one to believe that this is likely to be true. CVE itemizes 24 LDAP vulnerabilities to 17 for NIS. SecurityFocus, on the other hand, lists 225 entries for LDAP and 358 for NIS. It's a little difficult to pick apart these numbers to make sense of any trends available, SecurityFocus includes links both to nonvulnerability articles mentioning various security topics and to potentially multiple articles regarding each vulnerability, whereas CVE tries to catalog distinct security issues, so the CVE distribution is probably more reflective of reality. When considering the relationship between LDAP's 24 CVE issues and NIS's 17, it should be kept in mind that NIS has been in use for well over twice as long as LDAP. On the other hand, many of NIS's vulnerabilities are core security flaws in the protocol, whereas LDAP's tend more toward programming errors or misinterpretations of the implementation details.

Probably the largest security problem with LDAP, however, is one that's shared with NIS: It provides user authentication information to remote machines, just for the asking. With LDAP a server administrator has the option of requiring a user ID and password to access LDAP information from the server, but as can be seen from the documentation for OS X's LDAP interfaces (`lookupd` in particular), there's not necessarily much protection provided for these authentication tokens. This allows the same variety of unauthorized access to user authentication information, and the same potential for spoofing the information from the server as is suffered by NIS clients.

Unlike NIS, LDAP clients that are easily available on the Internet can allow anyone easy access to explore LDAP servers. For example, Jarek Gawor's LDAP Browser/Editor (`http://www.iit.edu/~gawojar/ldap/`) is a cross-platform Java client that enables you to easily explore any LDAP server you can identify. It even comes preconfigured to connect to the University of Michigan's LDAP server. This server doesn't seem to be particularly communicative without additional information, but if you'd like to use the client to explore other public repositories of information, Notre Dame's Office of Information Technologies makes a convenient list available at `http://www.nd.edu/~eds/search/ldap_search.shtml`.

NetInfo Password Database

Finally, we come to NetInfo, which is Apple's implementation of a hierarchical network directory service. NetInfo is considerably more complex than NIS, which should imply that there are more potential security flaws. Thankfully, it was designed by programmers more in touch with their paranoid inner selves. There are a few specific security issues, but by and large, NetInfo has not divulged a significant number of flaws at this point. SecurityFocus and CVE barely even know it exists, with only 21 and 2 entries respectively—not bad for a protocol that's been around since the early 1990s, though the lack of penetration in the market has probably reduced somewhat the level of stress-testing to which it has been subjected.

Conceptually NetInfo is similar to NIS and LDAP, in that it provides a range of data types divided into a number of different classes. The fact that it's hierarchically arranged as a directory structure, rather than as flat files like NIS, makes it somewhat more complex to access, but its primary difference is that the servers providing the information can be hierarchically arranged in the design of how they can provide the information. In a clever abstraction of information services, each client functions as its own NetInfo server, can further serve its NetInfo directory structure, and can subscribe to others.

Covering NetInfo in sufficient depth to do it justice would take a book or two worth of writing, so we'll touch on only the basics that apply to the user ID and password system here. NetInfo stores user information in the NetInfo directory `/users`. You can list directories by using the `-list` option to the `niutil` command, in the form `niutil -list <NetInfo domain> <directory>`, where `<NetInfo domain>` is typically the root domain `.` on your machine, and `<directory>` in this case is `/users`.

```
Racer-X ray 5% niutil -list . /users
11        nobody
12        root
13        daemon
14        unknown
15        smmsp
16        www
17        mysql
18        sshd
52        ray
53        software
60        skel
61        jim
63        james
67        bar
```

You can read any particular record by using the `-read` option to `niutil`, in the form `niutil -read <NetInfo domain> <directory><property>`, where `<property>` is the name of the property you want to query.

```
% niutil -read . /users/software
authentication_authority: ;basic; ;LocalWindowsHash;
picture: /Library/User Pictures/Nature/Nest.tif
_shadow_passwd:
hint:
uid: 503
_writers_passwd: software
realname: Skuld
_writers_hint: software
gid: 100
shell: /bin/tcsh
```

```
name: software
_writers_tim_password: software
passwd: xwNc7eG6/lR4.
_writers_picture: software
home: /Users/software
sharedDir: Public
```

Alternatively, you can dump any record (or all records) from the database by using the `nidump` command. The `nidump` command conveniently enables you to search for records with specific properties, by using the syntax `nidump -r <directory name>=<desired dir>/<property name>=<desired property> <NetInfo domain>`.

```
% nidump -r /name=users/uid=5002 .
{
  "authentication_authority" = ( ";basic;" );
  "picture" = ( "/Library/User Pictures/Nature/Zen.tif" );
  "_shadow_passwd" = ( "" );
  "hint" = ( "Urusei!" );
  "uid" = ( "5002" );
  "_writers_passwd" = ( "skel" );
  "realname" = ( "skeleton account" );
  "_writers_hint" = ( "skel" );
  "gid" = ( "99" );
  "shell" = ( "/bin/tcsh" );
  "name" = ( "skel" );
  "_writers_tim_password" = ( "skel" );
  "passwd" = ( "AtcBqXhZAfJ7A" );
  "_writers_picture" = ( "skel" );
  "home" = ( "/Users/skel" );
  "sharedDir" = ( "Public" );
}
```

If your domain is a tagged domain, you can use the syntax `nidump -r <directory name>=<desired dir>/<property name>=<desired property> -t <NetInfo domain>` instead.

```
% nidump -r /name=users/name=ray -t localhost/local
{
  "authentication_authority" = ( ";basic;" );
  "picture" = ( "/Library/User Pictures/Fun/Orange.tif" );
  "_shadow_passwd" = ( "" );
  "hint" = ( "AA-Megamisama" );
  "uid" = ( "501" );
  "_writers_passwd" = ( "ray" );
```

```
  "realname" = ( "Will Ray" );
  "_writers_hint" = ( "ray" );
  "gid" = ( "20" );
  "home" = ( "/Volumes/Wills_Data/ray" );
  "name" = ( "ray" );
  "_writers_tim_password" = ( "ray" );
  "passwd" = ( "8R83ac3Pl1FxQ" );
  "_writers_picture" = ( "ray" );
  "shell" = ( "/bin/tcsh" );
  "sharedDir" = ( "Public" );
}
```

In each of these cases, note that I have been able to read or list the user and password information without needing to be root. This is a problem; it facilitates the type of attacks against the password system that are demonstrated in the next section.

Consolidated Password Storage Mechanisms

With the recent massive proliferation of software, services, and online systems that want to use passwords or passphrases, many users have started either using the same password for everything or looking for a way to consolidate all their passwords into some interface that does the remembering for them. Early on, Web browsers started incorporating this ability to remember things that you entered into Web forms for you so that you didn't have to enter them again. Other software quickly sprang up to fill the void for remembering passwords where Web browsers couldn't do the job. By now, you should immediately see the idea of encrypting and storing all your identity tokens in a single container, protected by a single key, as a rather dangerous one. Nevertheless, Apple's provided a version of this functionality as a built-in component of OS X in the form of the Keychain.

The Keychain facility, managed through the Keychain Access program in the Utilities folder under Applications, provides a centralized service through which any application can store identification tokens for the user. As a matter of fact, it's a bit difficult to *prevent* applications from storing identification tokens in the Keychain: I am aware of having told only one application that I wanted it to store information in the Keychain, yet my copy seems to have a dozen keys stored in it.

NOTE

Too many Keychains—just like my pants pockets!

Discussing the Keychain facility, Keychain Access.app, and Keychains is a bit difficult because we have a Keychain facility that holds Keychains and a Keychain Access.app that enables you to configure what Keychains are held by the Keychain facility.

If you're comfortable with the idea of storing all of your passwords or other identification tokens in a single application where they can all simultaneously be exposed by a single compromise of the storing application, then the Keychain can provide some relatively sophisticated functions for managing this type of information.

NOTE

Despite the reality of the potential for a single-point compromise of all of your security information, should you use Keychain to store it all, it's not really all that bad a solution for many purposes. If you've a choice between remembering and using one actually strong password or passphrase to remember and protect all your identity tokens, and getting lazy and using dozens of weak passwords that you've had to remember yourself, using something like Keychain is probably the lesser of two evils.

The problems inherent in the system are real, and should be a significant concern. The problems with identity tokens in general, however, are rather severe, and there is simply no good and practical solution. If you're not going to be superhumanly conscientious with respect to picking and remembering your security tokens, you're going to be making compromises, and it may be that using an application such as Keychain is the best of the possible compromises in your situation.

Only you can make this decision, but you need to make it based on a clear understanding of the potential problems.

Most uses of the Keychain are almost transparent to the user. An application might ask you, when you enter a password for some function, whether you want to store the information in the Keychain. If you tell it yes, it will store the plaintext of the information in the Keychain (as an encrypted value), and will retrieve and use that value from the Keychain whenever it would require you to enter the information.

All the information that's stored in the Keychain is encrypted, but by default the Keychain is decrypted, and the plaintext contents made available to the applications that need them when you log in. In its default use, the Keychain uses your login authentication as the authorization token by which it decrypts your information and makes it available, so the strength of your login directly affects the level of protection that any information stored in the Keychain is afforded.

Figure 5.1 shows the Keychain Access interface to the Keychain. In the panes shown in this interface, you have access to a list of the keys stored in the currently open Keychain, and are shown the attributes of any key you choose. Checking the Show Passphrase box will, depending on the settings for that particular item, either immediately display the plaintext password or passphrase in the box immediately below it, or it will pop up a requester dialog asking for you to enter the password or passphrase for that Keychain, and asking under what circumstances the display of the passphrase should be allowed.

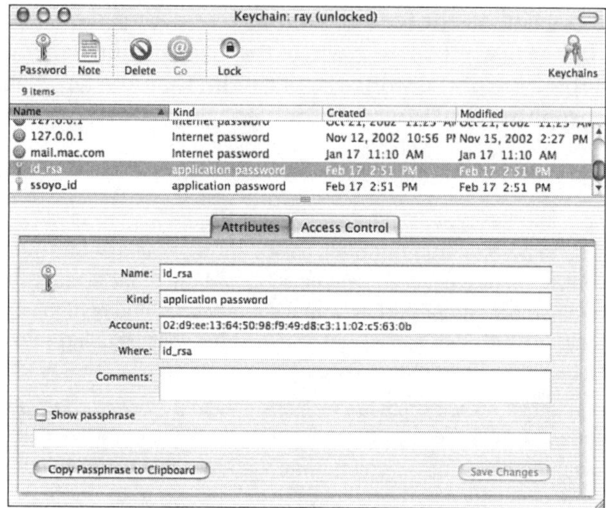

FIGURE 5.1 The Keychain Access.app Keychain facility control application.

Figure 5.2 shows the dialog requesting the password, to enable Keychain Access to display the password/passphrase. Keychain Access.app is requesting permission from the Keychain facility to display the passphrase. It must obey the access restrictions that have been configured for the passphrase just as any other application needs to do, so this same dialog appears when any other application requests this information as well. The password it wants is the password for that particular Keychain, which, if you're using the default, is your system login password. What's going on here might be moderately confusing initially: You've asked Keychain Access.app to show you the plaintext of a passphrase, and the running system Keychain facility has popped up a dialog box to ask you whether it should allow Keychain Access.app to decrypt and display that information for you. If you select Allow Once, the information is displayed in the text box below the check box, but the permission will not be permanent: Closing Keychain Access.app and requesting the same information again results in you being queried for your password again. If you select Always Allow, the next time you open Keychain Access.app, you can display that passphrase without needing to enter your system password. If you've a tendency to leave your console while you're logged in, this is probably a dangerous selection to make.

The Access Control tab gives you control over general access policies for the selected item. Under this tab, the options shown in Figure 5.3 enable you to control whether any application should be allowed access whenever it asks whether the Keychain facility should query for each application when it requests access, whether to require the Keychain password for access to the item, and which (if any) applications should be allowed unconditional access to the information. In the case of the id_rsa application password shown, it's set to allow unconditional access to the SSH Agent program, which is yet another key-serving application that enables secure encrypted network transmissions (covered in greater detail in Chapter 14, "Remote Access: Secure Shell, VNC, Timbuktu, Apple Remote Desktop"), and to otherwise query you regarding whether any application is allowed to access the information if it requests it.

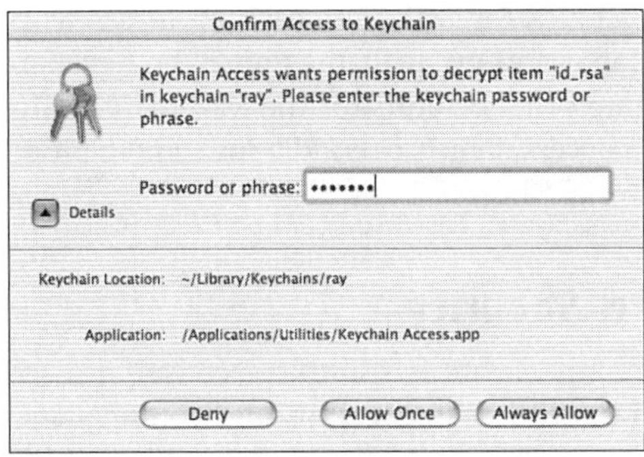

FIGURE 5.2 When an application requests access to a Keychain item, you are asked whether to allow it to read the data.

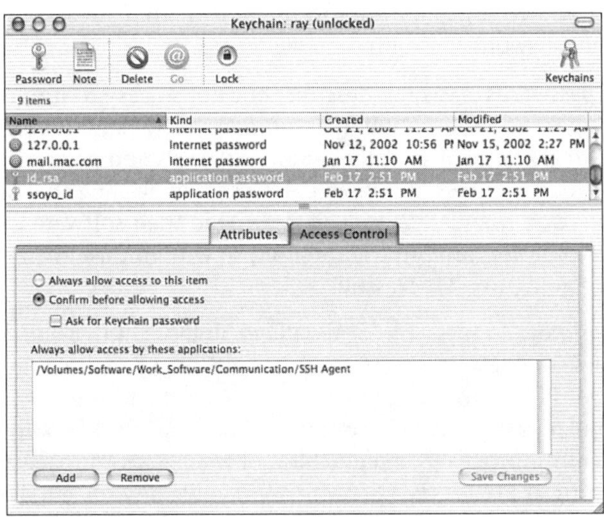

FIGURE 5.3 The Access Control tab enables you to configure access policies for this piece of information.

The Keychain can actually store almost any small snippits of information that you can put in a short textual note. The Note button of the interface brings up a dialog where you can enter brief messages or information, such as credit card numbers, that you'd like to protect. This is protected with the same encryption with which the passwords it contains are protected, and is subject to the same vulnerabilities if your password should be compromised, or if you allow the information to be displayed without requiring confirmation. The Keychain facility also enables you to store multiple separate Keychains for each user, each protected with a different password or passphrase. Additional options available under the Keychain Access.app menus enable you to configure other defaults for the Keychain facility, such as whether it should expire a user's access if she's been idle for some period, or if the system has gone to sleep.

Testing Password Security

Testing the security of a password is a simple exercise—just see if you can guess it. The only difficulty is that if you're guessing, and you're guessing randomly, you're just as likely to guess any one string as another, and just as likely (or unlikely) to guess any given password, no matter whether it's a dictionary word or a completely random string. With one guess, then, it's difficult (impossible, actually) to produce any statistic regarding whether a password is secure or not. To usefully test a password's security, you've got to try the sort of guessing that a cracker might apply, and see whether the password succumbs.

Ok, so testing passwords is easy to describe, but not so easy to implement from the keyboard. Trying seven million billion combinations by hand isn't practical. Even trying enough to check against likely dictionary words and personally significant data, such as phone numbers and birth dates, isn't something that any sane person would spend time on manually. Crackers download their software to break into your system from helpful sites around the Internet, so why not use their own tools to see whether they're going to be successful?

Because any password is guessable, and will eventually fall to a sufficiently devoted attack, it's useless to question whether a password *can* be cracked. Instead you need to ask *how long* it's likely to take a cracker to guess it. Unfortunately, because many people pick similar passwords (poor ones), and because crackers know this, they can focus their attempts into a very small region of the password space and be relatively certain of guessing at least some passwords on almost any system. Fortunately, knowing this, you can level the playing field a bit. If you test your passwords to see whether they will easily fall to the techniques of a cracker going after poor passwords, and then eliminate those that do, the average cracker won't be able to crack your passwords easily, and may well go on to bother someone else instead. Of course, if they're dedicated to the task of breaking *your* passwords, it's certain that they *can* succeed, and likely that they *will* succeed eventually. Your only real security lies in making certain—by using their tools—that breaking your password takes a long time, and then in changing your passwords frequently enough that it's unlikely that they've been guessed.

CAUTION

One caution while considering increasing your system security by checking the strength of your passwords: If you're not specifically empowered to check that facet of your system's security, make *very* sure you have permission while taking this approach. Randal Schwartz, Internet-famous co-author of *The Perl Programming Language* and author of *Learning Perl*, found out the hard way that employers quite often have neither any idea of what computer system administration and security actually entail, nor any sense of reasonable behavior or level of response to a perceived error. In 1993, while he was working for Intel, he attempted to increase system security by requiring users to use strong passwords. To do this, he checked the password strength on Intel machines he was administrating by running a commonly available password cracking package named Crack. To be sure, Randal made some mistakes in how he went about this, and in how he presented himself regarding the experiments he was running, but in thanks for him doing his job, Intel managed to get him indicted on three felony counts, sentenced to time in jail and community service, and required to pay thousands of dollars of restitution (`http://www.swiss.ai.mit.edu/6805/articles/computer-crime/schwartz-matrix-news.txt`).

Make no mistake—this sucks. System administrators are called upon to maintain security, and then often blamed when their security precautions fail, usually because they've yielded to a user who has begged for leniency on some policy issue. Management, however, rarely knows what maintaining security entails, and will turn on you in an instant if the suits and the government think that you'd make a good example if they crucify you. The only way to protect yourself from this is to help set policy when you can, including legal policy at the government level. As a system administrator, the rights you enjoy will be only those that you're willing to fight alongside other system administrators to maintain.

Dumping Your Password File

Fortunately for you, the designers of the standard Unix login procedure were smart enough to design the process so that it takes a long time to check each login attempt. This makes attacking your passwords from remote systems impractical (but not impossible). To avoid this impediment, crackers will try to get a copy of your passwords off your system and onto one where they can throw as much processor power at it as is available. Usually this requires them to have some access to your system already, but this is a matter of careful system design. There have been poorly thought-out systems that allowed random visitors from the Internet to download their password files through their Web servers.

Unfortunately, if crackers have access to your system and want to steal other passwords, it's usually not too difficult to get at your stored passwords. The NetInfo system will typically be happy to give a listing in exactly the format that a cracker needs to run though a password cracking program:

```
% nidump passwd .
nobody:*:-2:-2::0:0:Unprivileged User:/dev/null:/dev/null
root:NDdqVoM4ttK4o:0:0::0:0:System Administrator:/var/root:/bin/tcsh
daemon:*:1:1::0:0:System Services:/var/root:/dev/null
unknown:*:99:99::0:0:Unknown User:/dev/null:/dev/null
smmsp:*:25:25::0:0:Sendmail User:/private/etc/mail:/dev/null
www:*:70:70::0:0:World Wide Web Server:/Library/WebServer:/dev/null
mysql:*:74:74::0:0:MySQL Server:/dev/null:/dev/null
sshd:*:75:75::0:0:sshd Privilege separation:/var/empty:/dev/null
ray:8qC3acDsl1xFQ:501:20::0:0:Will Ray:/Volumes/Wills_Data/ray:/bin/tcsh
software:xwNc7eG6/lR4.:503:100::0:0:Skuld:/Users/software:/bin/tcsh
skel:AtCAqzHurP27A:5002:99::0:0:skeleton account:/Users/skel:/bin/tcsh
jim:NFf1oqq0ePYTk:505:99::0:0:Jim Emrick:/Users/jim:/bin/tcsh
james:apqpjRMfGyA3U:600:70::0:0:Sweet Baby James:/Users/james:/bin/tcsh
bar:OOHAcg8QniCS.:5003:20::0:0:foo:/Users/bar:/bin/tcsh
```

One of the recommended protections against this is to `chmod 700` your `nidump` command. Normal users don't typically have a need to look at your NetInfo database, anyway. This change does put perhaps the slightest of impediments in the way of a malicious individual who's after your passwords, but making this permission change is no more than a rumble strip on the information highway to anyone intent on getting to this data, and should not be taken as a serious protective measure. `niutil` lists individual users' entries from the NetInfo database. The NetInfo Manager GUI interface in `Applications/Utilites` also provides access to this information. Trying to block access by setting each possible interface so that it can't be used by normal users is the most naive variety of stupidity in implementing security. It's an altogether too-frequently used method, but that doesn't make it any less a practice of idiocy. If the source of the data is not protected from the users, the data is not protected. In the case of the system passwords, all that a user would need to do is install her own copy of a utility such as `nidump`, and she'd again have complete access. If she didn't have convenient access to a copy of OS X from which she could grab another copy, she could always download something like Malevolence (`http://www.securemac.com/file-library/Malevolence.sit`, or `http://www.msec.net/`), and use it to read the password information instead.

Because the NetInfo database is so fundamentally integrated into the OS X user experience, completely blocking access to this resource is not a solution that's likely to be practical. The result is that so long as there are users who can log in to your machine, you should assume that they can access your encrypted passwords.

Cracking the Passwords: John the Ripper

After a cracker has access to your password file, the next thing he needs is some software with which to run a large number of potential guesses against the encrypted passwords contained in it.

Over the years a number of password-cracking tools have been designed, with the primary differences being the evolution of more efficient versions of the encryption algorithms used. In one form or another, they all make sequential guesses at the encrypted passwords. Some use dictionaries of likely password words (such as dictionaries of the English language). Others use any personal information that can be gleaned about the users from readable material in their accounts. Some can be configured to make essentially random guesses at the password, modified by a collection of rules derived from real passwords regarding letter frequency patterns and other statistical measures based on observed usage. Yet others take the completely brute-force approach of trying every possible string as a guess until they manage to find a match.

Although a variety of tools are available to crack passwords today, one of the most powerful and configurable is John the Ripper, available from `http://www.openwall.com/john/`. John is a combined dictionary- and rules-based brute-force cracker, and one of the fastest to use against normal password files.

To demonstrate the facility with which passwords can be guessed, we've added a user with a relatively poor password to the user list. User Ralph has the password `asdzxc`. This isn't a dictionary word, but it's all lower case, so if a cracker is going at the easy passwords first, it's likely to fail quickly. Running John the Ripper on the password file results in output similar to the following:

```
% /usr/local/john/john passwords
Loaded 8 passwords with 8 different salts (Traditional DES [32/32 BS])
guesses: 0  time: 0:00:11:39 (3)  c/s: 46859  trying: cobwsy - cobwhy
guesses: 0  time: 0:00:17:21 (3)  c/s: 39483  trying: speamble - speamcre
guesses: 0  time: 0:00:23:49 (3)  c/s: 36787  trying: dmv479 - dmv412
guesses: 0  time: 0:00:40:21 (3)  c/s: 31506  trying: snke91 - snkean
guesses: 0  time: 0:00:57:18 (3)  c/s: 29473  trying: tttcy5 - tttc99
guesses: 0  time: 0:01:55:29 (3)  c/s: 26610  trying: Maiko5 - Maik.s
guesses: 0  time: 0:04:08:44 (3)  c/s: 25018  trying: g1by26 - g1byst
guesses: 0  time: 0:20:00:13 (3)  c/s: 37012  trying: cu87co - cu87d4
guesses: 0  time: 0:21:56:54 (3)  c/s: 38124  trying: coondprs - coondpon
guesses: 0  time: 0:22:16:03 (3)  c/s: 37996  trying: drotty39 - drottyph
guesses: 0  time: 0:23:18:05 (3)  c/s: 37148  trying: Rjry6d - Rjryca
guesses: 0  time: 1:00:20:07 (3)  c/s: 36877  trying: tspaniqV - tspanete
guesses: 0  time: 1:01:53:19 (3)  c/s: 37101  trying: Bfrbrer - BfrbriS
asdzxc          (ralph)
```

```
guesses: 1  time: 2:20:26:11 (3)  c/s: 28608  trying: coy202x - coy269y
guesses: 1  time: 3:19:04:38 (3)  c/s: 27282  trying: STohlso - STohl15
guesses: 1  time: 4:02:17:18 (3)  c/s: 26991  trying: logbma5 - logbmic
guesses: 1  time: 4:23:14:38 (3)  c/s: 26389  trying: JA2c03 - JA2cED
guesses: 1  time: 5:17:59:33 (3)  c/s: 26000  trying: romfjook - romfjoy5
guesses: 1  time: 5:17:59:34 (3)  c/s: 26000  trying: romfdra1 - romfdrd9
guesses: 1  time: 6:06:42:54 (3)  c/s: 25781  trying: btmphfg - btmpbI1
guesses: 1  time: 6:19:22:28 (3)  c/s: 25579  trying: hintgns1 - hintgnnl
guesses: 1  time: 6:19:22:52 (3)  c/s: 25579  trying: hinsube_ - hinsubly
Session aborted

% /usr/local/john/john -show passwords
ralph:asdzxc:5005:32::0:0:ralph:/Users/guests/ralph:/etc/ftponly

1 password cracked, 7 left
```

While running on a file of passwords, hitting the spacebar will give you a brief status message from John, so in this output we've hit the space bar several times over the course of a few days to see how John's doing at cracking the 8-line password file. `John` managed to guess `Ralph`'s password at somewhere between 1 day, 1 hour out, and 2 days, 20 hours out, and after 6 days and almost 20 hours total, had not managed to guess any of our more complex passwords.

To demonstrate how much more quickly dictionary word-based passwords can be guessed, we added Ralph's password to the end of a 234,937 word dictionary. In processing this dictionary John can be configured to use only the words in it directly, or to do things such as adding numbers after the words, capitalizing them, trying l33t-speak-like transmutations (the letter-shape/phonetic transformation code that "elite crackers" and warez-dudes (script kiddies and their ilk) converse in), and making other variations on the words in the list. When run using this dictionary against our password database, the results return much more quickly.

```
% /usr/local/john/john -w:/usr/share/dict/words passwords
Loaded 8 passwords with 8 different salts (Traditional DES [32/32 BS])
asdzxc          (ralph)
guesses: 1  time: 0:00:01:17 100%  c/s: 18019  trying: Zyryan - asdzxc
```

One minute, 17 seconds to crack Ralph's password. Of course, Ralph's password was in the dictionary with no variations in capitalization or other modifications, so let's see how quick the guesses go when it needs to check word-variants as well. John the Ripper's `-rules` option enables checking variants based on common password patterns.

```
% /usr/local/john/john -w:/usr/share/dict/words -rules passwords
Loaded 8 passwords with 8 different salts (Traditional DES [32/32 BS])
asdzxc          (ralph)
guesses: 1  time: 0:00:21:05 100%  c/s: 24973  trying: Zymining - Asdzxcin
```

The time has gone up to slightly over 21 minutes, but this is still a much shorter time than the period within which you'd probably like to change your password.

John has quite a number of options that we don't have the room to demonstrate here, including the ability to use other password encryption schemes than the normal one used in Unix, making it a very flexible program for password guessing in many applications. The command-line options are shown in Table 5.1.

TABLE 5.1 The Command-Line Options for John the Ripper

Option	Function
`-external[:<mode>]`	Enables an external mode, using external functions defined in the `[List.External:MODE]` section of `~/john.ini`.
`-format:<name>`	Forces ciphertext format <name>. Allows you to override the ciphertext format detection. Currently, valid format names are `DES`, `BSDI`, `MD5`, `BF`, `AFS`, and `LM`. You can use this option when cracking or with `-test`. Note that John can't crack password files with different ciphertext formats at the same time.
`-groups:[-]<gid>[,..]`	Loads the specified group(s) only. A dash before the list can be used to invert the check.
`-incremental[:<mode>]`	Enables the incremental mode, using the specified `~/john.ini` definition (section `[Incremental:MODE]`, or `[Incremental:All]` by default).
`-makechars:<file>`	Makes a charset, overwriting `<file>`. Generates a charset file, based on character frequencies from `~/john.pot`, for use with the incremental mode. The entire `~/john.pot` is used for the charset file unless you specify some password files. You can also use an external `filter()` routine with this option.
`-restore[:<file>]`	Continues an interrupted cracking session, reading point information from the specified file (`~/restore` by default).
`-rules`	Enables rules for wordlist mode.
`-salts:[-]<count>`	Sets a password per salt limit. This feature sometimes enables you to achieve better performance. For example, you can crack only some salts by using `-salts:2` faster, and then crack the rest using `-salts:-2`. Total cracking time will be about the same, but you will get some passwords cracked earlier.
`-savemem:<level>`	Enables memory saving, at `<level> 1..3`. You might need this option if you don't have enough memory, or don't want John to affect other processes too much. Level 1 tells John not to waste memory on login names, so you won't see them while cracking. Higher levels have a performance impact: You should probably avoid using them unless John doesn't work or gets into swap otherwise.

TABLE 5.1 Continued

Option	Function
`-session:<file>`	Sets session filename to `<file>`. Allows you to specify another point information file's name to use for this cracking session. This is useful for running multiple instances of John in parallel, or just to be able to recover an older session later, not always continue the latest one.
`-shells:[-]<shell>[,..]`	Loads the specified shell(s) only. This option is useful to load accounts with a valid shell only, or not to load accounts with a bad shell. You can omit the path before a shell name.
`-show <password_file>`	Shows the cracked passwords in a convenient form. You should also specify the password files. You can use this option while another John is cracking, to see what it did so far.
`-single`	Enables the single crack mode, using rules from the `[List.Rules:Single]` section of `~/john.ini`.
`-status:[<file>]`	Prints status of an interrupted or running session. To get up-to-date status information for a detached running session, send that copy of John a `SIGHUP` before using this option.
`-stdin`	Reads words from `stdin` to use as wordlist.
`-stdout[:<length>]`	No cracking; writes words to `stdout`.
`-test`	Benchmarks all the enabled ciphertext format crackers, and tests them for correct operation at the same time.
`-users:[-]<login>|<uid>[,..]`	Loads specified user(s) only. Allows you to filter a few accounts for cracking and so on. A dash before the list can be used to invert the check (that is, loads all the users that aren't listed).
`-wordfile:<wordlist>`	Uses the specified word list for wordlist mode.

John the Ripper also includes a number of utility programs that work with it to put data into it, get data out of it, or otherwise massage or act upon your input and output. Table 5.2 lists these additional utilities. (Note that `unafs`, `unique`, and `unshadow` are actually links to the John program itself.)

TABLE 5.2 Utilities in the John the Ripper_Suite

Utility	Function
`unshadow <password-file> <shadow-file>`	Combines the `passwd` and `shadow` files (when you already have access to both) for use with John. You might need this because if you used only your shadow file, the GECOS information wouldn't be used by the single crack mode, and also you wouldn't be able to use the `-shells` option. You'll usually want to redirect the output of `unshadow` to a file.

TABLE 5.2 Continued

Utility	Function
`unafs <database-file> <cell-name>`	Gets password hashes out of the binary AFS database, and produces a file usable by John (again, you should redirect the output yourself).
`unique <output-file>`	Removes duplicates from a wordlist (read from `stdin`), without changing the order. You might want to use this with John's `-stdout` option, if you got a lot of disk space to trade for the reduced cracking time.
`mailer <password-file>`	A shell script to send mail to all the users who have weak passwords. You should edit the message inside before using.

Cracking Nonsystem Passwords

Security for your computing environment doesn't stop at using a reasonably strong password for your login prompt. Other computers that yours interacts with, and systems that you and your computer's users use are likely to require passwords as well. If you're like most people, there's a very high probability that you or your users have used the same password you've used for your system login on another, less secure system, with less safeguards to protect it from crackers. For example, in a moment of lax thinking, you might have chosen to use your login password to also password-protect a FileMaker Pro database, which you subsequently have given to other people. Now, they don't need to get into your system to get a copy of your encrypted password and crack it; with the appropriate software, they can directly attack the password in your FileMaker document, and from it, learn your system password. Table 5.3 lists a number of password-cracking programs for a range of nonsystem passwords, as well as some that can be used for system passwords. Be careful when using any of the applications that these programs can crack, and understand that almost any other application might be on this list in the next edition of this book. Disclosing your password by leaking it through reuse in a weak, crackable application would be embarrassing.

TABLE 5.3 Password-Cracking Programs for Nonsystem Passwords

Cracking Software	Description
`55hb.sh`	An SSH account brute-force auditing tool.
`accp.exe`	Recovers lost passwords on MS Access 97 mdb files.
`aimpw.zip`	AOL Instant Messenger decoder.
`aimr2.zip`	Aim Recover 2.0 decrypts AIM passwords when they are stored locally. Can also import Buddy Lists.

TABLE 5.3 Continued

Cracking Software	Description
`alpr.zip`	Advanced Lotus Password Recovery recovers lost or forgotten passwords created in IBM/Lotus applications (all versions): Organizer, Word Pro, 1-2-3, and Approach. Passwords are recovered instantly; multilingual passwords are supported.
`ao20pr_p.zip`	Recovers lost passwords for Microsoft Word, Excel, Access, PowerPoint 97, Project, Money, Outlook, Backup, Schedule+, Mail, IE 3,4, and 5, Visio 4 and 5, and others.
`apc.c`	Another Password Cracker is designed to brute-force Unix passwords with a standard dictionary-based attack.
`apoc-crack.c`	Simple brute-force Unix password cracker. Tries all combinations of every printable 7-bit ASCII character.
`apoc-crack.pl`	Simple brute-force Unix password cracker. Tries all combinations of every printable 7-bit ASCII character.
`archpr.zip`	Advanced Archive Password Recovery can be used to recover lost or forgotten passwords to ZIP (PKZip, WinZip), ARJ/WinARJ, RAR/WinRAR, and ACE/WinACE archives.
`asmcrk256.zip`	ASMCrack is a Unix password security tool. It supports five cracking modes.
`authforce-0.9.6.tar`	Brute-force HTTP authentication cracker.
`azpr244.zip`	Advanced Zip Password Recovery supports PKZip 1.0 through modern WinZip, all compression methods. Can work with a single file; self-extracting archives are supported. Includes a number of brute-force options.
`b4b0-cr4g.c`	Password cracker.
`bios`	Various BIOS crackers.
`brutesh.sh`	Brute-force Linux-PAM password cracker.
`Brutus-aet2.zip`	Obtains the usernames/passwords through a simple dictionary attack.
`brutus.pl`	Tries to break in remotely using password brute-forcing for Telnet, FTP, and POP3 protocols.
`cain10b.zip`	A GUI multithreaded application that can be used to recover various passwords on Windows 95/98.
`CLT_Beta.zip`	Coherent Light Bruteforce Toolkit contains IRCrack, a tool that connects directly to an IRC server and uses a word list to brute-force a channel key, and Boomcrack, a brute-force FTP account cracker.
`crack5.0.tar.gz`	Unix password cracker.
`CrackerNcftp.c`	Decrypts the safe passwords of NcFtp.
`crypto.zip`	Text file that explains how to decrypt Windows 9x passwords that are stored in the Registry.
`cssetup.zip`	Cisco scanner for Windows, which scans a range of IP addresses for Cisco routers that haven't changed their password from the default value of `Cisco`.
`cuteftp-012000.txt`	Exploits the weak encryption scheme utilized in CuteFTP.

TABLE 5.3 Continued

Cracking Software	Description
`dad.txt`	Default password list, last updated July 10, 2000. Contains more than 820 passwords, including default passwords for BIOSes, network devices, appliances, applications, Unix, VMS, HP2000/3000, OS/400, CMS, PBX systems, Windows NT, Novell, Oracle, and many more.
`defaultpasswords.txt`	List of default passwords for many network switches and devices. Last updated July 7, 2000.
`dehash-sawmill.c`	Exploit script for the Sawmill File Access and Weak Encryption vulnerability.
`dhb.zip`	Tool that tries to guess Lotus Domino HTTP passwords.
`Dicgen.zip`	Dictionary file creator (DOS).
`Disengage`	Tool for decrypting passwords.
`dkbf-0.1.1b.tar.gz`	Distributed, Keyboard, Brute-Force program, for Linux clusters. Attacks Windows NT Lanman and NT hashes by using the Message Passing Interface (MPI) to distribute the L0phtCrack program.
`dumprazorpassword.c`	Exploit script for the Visible Systems Razar Password File vulnerability.
`ecrack-0.1.tgz`	IRC (bot) brute-force password cracker.
`eggh.tgz`	Password cracker for eggdrop (blowfish) passwords; uses a word list.
`enbabler.c`	Attempts to find the enable password on a Cisco system via brute force.
`entryle.zip`	EliteSys Entry v2.05 is a remote brute-force security auditing utility, designed to crack passwords for FTP, HTTP, and POP3 protocols.
`e-pwdcache.zip`	Program that weeds out all the cahsed passwords, such as domain, mail, MAPI, Windows network, dial-ups, ie-passwords, and so on, on local Windows 95/98 machines.
`fcrackzip-0.2.1.tar`	Brute-force Zip cracker.
`fhb-1.2.2.tar.gz`	FTP brute-forcer.
`force.exe`	Brute-force Hotmail hints cracker. Requires `FSProgressiveDL.ocx`.
`forcesql.zip`	A SQL Server password auditing tool that runs brute force and dictionary attacks to guess passwords.
`fpw.tgz`	Password cracker similar to Crack.
`ftp_crack.tar.gz`	`FTP_crack.pl` brute-forces FTP servers.
`gammalnk.zip`	Front end for Gammaprog.
`gammaprog-config.tgz`	Config files for Gammaprog.
`gammaprog.tgz`	Gammaprog, a brute-force password cracker for Web-based email addresses (hotmail.com, usa.net, and yahoo.com) and regular POP3 email accounts. Requires JRE.
`gh-plus.c`	Script that exploits PowerScripts PlusMail password vulnerability.
`hintcrack.zip`	Tool to crack Hotmail hints through a dictionary attack.
`HotmailHack.zip`	Attempts to brute-force Hotmail accounts from a dictionary file.
`hv-pop3crack.pl`	Perl script that executes dictionary file-based brute-force attacks on POP3 account passwords.

TABLE 5.3 Continued

Cracking Software	Description
`hypno.zip`	Hypnopaedia, a brute-force POP3 password cracker that uses a dictionary file. With GUI, for Windows.
`icadecrypt.c.txt`	Cracks the weak hash encryption on stored Citrix ICA passwords.
`icqrinfo-1.1.zip`	A Windows program that reads information, including the password, out of ICQ.DAT (versions 99a and 99b).
`jcon.zip`	JCon is a security and brute-force password breaking tool. It can scan ports, FTP daemons, and mailer daemons and check for CGI vulnerabilities.
`john-1.6.32-dev.tar.gz`	John the Ripper, a very fast password cracker that is available for Unix, DOS, Win32, and BeOS.
`k2vl017.zip`	Password cracker for Windows.
`kaufcrk.pl`	Perl script that decrypts passwords found in the Kaufman Mail Warrior accounts file (MW35_Accounts.ini).
`lc3setup.exe`	An NT password auditing tool that computes NT user passwords from the cryptographic hashes that are stored by the NT operating system.
`LC4`	Latest version of L0phtCrack. Password auditing and recovery application for Windows.
`lcrack-1.0.1.tar.gz`	Lepton crack, a password cracker that works on Cygwin and Linux and cracks MD4 hashes, MD5 hashes, NTLM, and HTTP password hashes from Domino R4.
`LDAP_Brute.pl`	An OpenLDAP brute-force auditing application that brute-forces Manager passwords.
`libcodict-0.4.tar.gz`	User-friendly dictionary C API that eases dictionary handling for the development of open source security audit tools.
`lincrack.c`	Flexible, easy-to-use password cracker for Linux/Unix that uses a dictionary file.
`lodowep-src-1.2.1.zip`	Tool for analyzing password strength of user accounts on a Lotus Domino Web server system by using dictionary attacks.
`MacPork1.5b.sit`	A CGI scanner for the Macintosh that scans for 130 vulnerabilities and can use 45 of them to retrieve a password file.
`Malevolence2.0.sit`	An exploit that allows users to view an unshadowed version of the password file on Mac OS X.
`mdcrack-0.6.tar.gz`	A brute-forcer for MD5 hashes, which is capable of breaking up to 6-character passwords within hours, and 8-character passwords within two days.
`mio-star.gz`	Distributed multihosted Unix password cracker that runs on all platforms where Perl is installed.
`mincrack.zip`	University of Minnesota POPMail password cracker.
`MK3.sit.bin`	A program that attempts to crack a user's account on an AppleTalk network.

TABLE 5.3 Continued

Cracking Software	Description
`msnmsgpasswd.zip`	Windows ActivePerl source to a script that proves that the encryption being used by MSN Messenger 4.6 is weak. Does a Base64 decode of the Registry.
`msnmsgpwd.exe.zip`	Windows ActivePerl executable that proves that the encryption being used by MSN Messenger 4.6 is weak. Does a Base64 decode of the Registry.
`mssqlpasswd.zip`	MS SQL 6.5/7.0 brute-force password-cracking tool.
`mysqlfuck.c`	Script that exploits the MySQL Null Root Password & Bind-Address Configuration vulnerability.
`mysqlpassword.c`	MySQL brute-force password cracker that uses a dictionary attack.
`nbrute.tar.gz`	Program to brute-force valid Newspro logins/passwords.
`nirvana.tgz`	Perl-based brute-force attack on Telnet.
`ntsweep.zip`	NTSweep brute-forces NT passwords.
`nutcrack.1.9.tar.gz`	A simple, fast, and effective password cracker for Unix systems.
`og-brute101.tgz`	Og-Brute is a Perl package to brute-force POP3 and FTP account passwords and probe SMTP for valid logins with Wingate support.
`passhack.mrc`	Brute-force password cracker for mIRC.
`passthief.exe`	Password cracker.
`passwd_rz.pl`	Exploit script for the Sawmill File Access and Weak Encryption vulnerability.
`pbrute.tar.gz`	Simple password generator for generating uppercase and lowercase numbers and letters.
`pc-1.1-dist.zip`	PalmCrack, password-testing tool for the Palm computing platform. Can check Unix and NT passwords against a dictionary, and decrypt certain Cisco router passwords.
`pcax.c`	Exploit script for PCAnywhere Weak Password Encryption vulnerability.
`pent.pl`	Uses `smbclient` to brute-force NT shares and passwords.
`pgppass.zip`	PGPPass is a dictionary attack program for use against PGP secret key rings.
`php-ssl-brute.zip`	PHP script that uses `curl` to brute-force SSL-protected Web site login screens.
`pop3hack.c`	POP3 password cracker.
`Pop_crack.tar.gz`	Pop3 Crack is a POP3 account brute-forcer written in Perl.
`pqwak2.zip`	Exploits a flaw in the share-level password authentication of Windows 95/98/ME in its CIFS protocol to find the password of a given share on one of these machines.
`pwd-gen.c`	Password generator.
`pwl9x-0.4-dev.tar.gz`	A program that allows passwords contained in the Windows PWL database to be viewed under Unix.

TABLE 5.3 Continued

Cracking Software	Description
`qrack-1.0.tgz`	Unix password brute-forcer written in Perl.
`revelation.1.1.exe`	Revelation password cracker.
`RiPFTPServer.zip`	RiP FTP Server, a Win32 program that extracts plaintext passwords from FTP server client software, such as `.ini` or Registry settings.
`RLRPAconv1.0.tar.gz`	Remote Password Assassin is a network password cracker using brute-force attacks.
`rm-brutal.tar.gz`	Brutal.pl, a Perl program that tries to get valid accounts on a remote server by using a POP3 brute-force method through wordlists.
`saltine-cracker-1.0.5`	TCP/IP distributed network password auditing tool for NTHASH (MD4) and POSIX LibDES Crypt(3) passwords.
`scooplm003.zip`	Searches out the password from LM/NTLM authentication information (LanManager and Windows NT challenge/response).
`scp`	Snap Cracks POP, a POP3 and FTP cracker written in Java.
`scrack15.zip`	TCP/IP distributed network password auditing tool for NTHASH (MD4) and POSIX LibDES Crypt(3) passwords. DOS version.
`scx-sa-21.txt`	Globalscape's CuteFTP, a popular FTP client, uses a weak encryption scheme, allowing plaintext login and password recovery from the address book. Includes cuteftpd.c, which calculates the plaintext.
`shadow.c`	Recontructs a password file from the shadow file.
`ShadowScan.zip`	Windows 95/98/NT/2000 program intended for the analysis of IP networks. Program includes attacks and password-guessing for POP3 and FTP.
`smbbf-0.9.1.tar.gz`	A password auditing tool for Windows and the SMB platform that makes it possible to exploit the timeout architecture vulnerability in Windows 2000/XP.
`snmpbrute-fixedup.c`	Fast SNMP brute-forcer.
`spc001.zip`	Share Password Cracker acquires the list of shared folders of a Windows 95/98/ME machine on the network and shows those folders' passwords. This tool acquires the list of the shared folders also for Windows NT/2000 machines, but it distinguishes only folders that have no password. Shared Password Cracker exploits the Share Level Password vulnerability.
`spq.tar.gz`	Unix Sequence Password Generator creates password files and allows on-the-fly cracking when used with other tools.
`sqlbf-all-src.1.0.1`	Source for auditing the strength of Microsoft SQL Server passwords offline. Can be used either in Brute Force mode or Dictionary Attack mode.
`sqlbf.zip`	MSSQL server brute-force tool.
`ssh-brute.sh`	A brute-forcer that guesses root's password without being logged.
`STC3.zip`	A multipurpose tool for Windows that does the work of 30 separate programs. Includes an `.htaccess` brute-forcer, anonymous FTP scanner, list of Bios master passwords, country codes list, dictionary generator, FTP brute-force service scanner, cached ISP password retriever, and more.

TABLE 5.3 Continued

Cracking Software	Description
`strip-crack.c`	Script that exploits the Strip Password Generator Limited Password-Space vulnerability.
`SUPassConvert.tgz`	Converts Unix-style passwords in a `Serv-U.ini` file to standard Unix password style for cracking.
`Telnet_crack.tar.gz`	Perl script that brute-forces Telnet.
`thermoprog.zip`	Brute-force password cracker for Angelfire password reminder. Requires JRE or JDK.
`thetaprog.tgz`	Brute-force password cracker for Hotmail password reminder. Requires JRE.
`thomas.zip`	Tool to crack the secret passwords on Cisco routers.
`ultraprog.zip`	Brute-force cracker for MailCity.com password reminder. Requires JRE.
`umncrack.zip`	University of Minnesota SLIP Password Cracker.
`unfburninhell1.0.tar.gz`	A burneye cryptographic layer 1 and 2 cracker than can work together with John the Ripper for password generation.
`unsecurev1.2.zip`	Unsecure is an HTTP auth brute-force cracker.
`user14nd.v1.tar.gz`	Brute-forces accounts via FTPD. Works best against Linux systems with traffic on a fair bandwidth.
`vcrack.tar.gz`	V-Crack Zero++ (Unix), a poly-alphabetic XOR cipher cracker.
`vcrack.zip`	V-Crack Zero++ (DOS), a poly-alphabetic XOR cipher cracker.
`vcu10.exe`	Velocity Cracking Utilities, a suite of utilities for cracking Unix password files.
`viper13.tar.gz`	Unix password cracker. It generates password combinations for the character sets and lengths you specify.
`vnc-crack.patch`	Patch to VNC that allows a brute-force dictionary attack.
`vncdec.c`	Decrypts the password for VNS, a PCAnywhere-like program.
`vnx4.c`	A VNC attack program ported to Windows. It features cracking of the password in the Registry, online brute force against a VNC server, or cracking a sniffed challenge/response handshake.
`wbrute.tar.gz`	HTML brute-force attacker.
`wc30b2.zip`	Password cracker designed to brute-force login/password combinations for Web sites that use HTTP-based password authentication.
`wgdecode.c`	Extracts WinGate administrator passwords from Windows 9x/NT machine Registries and decodes them.
`wordex.exe`	Windows program designed to generate wordlists recursively from all files in a directory.
`wordmake0.1.pl`	WordMake, a dictionary file creator.
`wwwhack.zip`	Automates the process of trying to crack logins/passwords for WWW sites that use basic HTTP authentication.
`xcrack.pl`	Unix/Linux password cracker coded in Perl.
`xdeep.pl`	Perl script that exploits the Xpede Password Exposure vulnerability.

TABLE 5.3 Continued

Cracking Software	Description
xpass10.zip	Password cracker.
xpert.c	Decodes the password from FTP Expert, which are stored in sites.ini.
xyprog.tgz	Brute-force password cracker for ICQ. Requires JRE.
zipcracker-0.1.1.tar.gz	Cracks Linux password-protected Zip archives with brute force.

A large number of password cracking tools are available around the Internet, and can compromise your passwords in ways that you might not have thought. Use Sherlock to search for these by name and find the most recent source.

Improving Password Security, and Alternatives to the Standard Password Mechanisms in Mac OS X

It should be obvious from the discussion earlier in this chapter that there is nothing that can be done to make passwords completely secure. The best that can be done is to make them reasonably secure, for a reasonable amount of time. To do so, one must pick strong passwords that can't be trivially guessed with dictionary attacks or brute-force approaches on a small subset of the password space.

The usual recommendation is to create passwords by coming up with a phrase that you'll be able to remember, but that can't easily be tied to you. Take the first letter of each word in the phrase and combine them into a nonsense password. Add some random capitalization. Transpose likely alphabetic characters to numerals, and sprinkle in a bit of punctuation. For example, if you start with something like the phrase "My sister likes oatmeal raisin cookies," and might end up with a password that looks like "`mS1.0rc`", where the "L" and "O" characters are replaced with one and zero respectively. A recent study has suggested that these patterns are essentially just as difficult for today's password cracking software to guess as passwords chosen completely randomly from the entire password data space. There is, however, reason to suspect that this conclusion is less than completely accurate. In *The Memorability and Security of Passwords: Some Empirical Results*, `http://www.cl.cam.ac.uk/ftp/users/rja14/tr500.pdf`, Yan et. al report that mnemonic phrase-based passwords are stronger than typical passwords generated by users, while being easier to remember. They also conclude that there is no observable difference between the strength of mnemonic phrase-based passwords and completely randomly chosen passwords. However, both the methodology and conclusions of the study ignore the fact that there may be patterns to be found and exploited in these phrase-based passwords. In conducting the test, the password cracker was configured to attack only word-like passwords. The search was based on dictionary and user personal information, and permutations of these that include interspersed numerals. Because a mnemonic phrase would only result in a word-like pattern by random chance, (as could a completely randomly chosen password), it's obvious that most phrase-based passwords, and most random passwords, would not be found by such a search. Any disparity in the results would necessarily result from a difference in the percentage of phrases whose initial letters spelled words, versus the percentage of random passwords that are dictionary words. Such an analysis is outside the scope of this book, but it should be obvious that there may be patterns to the initial letters of words in phrases, just as there are to the usage of letters in written languages. These patterns can be exploited to develop cracking software targeted at phrase-based passwords, making them almost inevitably weaker than random passwords at some level. How much weaker we won't know until something like John the Ripper comes along with rules to exploit phrase-like patterns, and then we can see how fast such passwords typically fall when dealt with directly, instead of through brute-force methods.

A useful additional protection is to limit the by-password access to your machine as much as you can. If a remote cracker cracks your password database, but there is no way for them to connect to your machine using the information, it's almost as good as if they hadn't cracked your password at all. For this reason, we strongly recommend disabling passworded remote logins whenever possible. SecureShell, for example, has a provision to allow only passphrase logins, and to reject password logins even if the person issues the correct password. Configuring this mode is covered in Chapter 14, on remote access. A passphrase can be considerably longer than a password, and it can be considerably harder to guess by brute force. Although a normal password can ultimately be cracked with only a few years of CPU time, the size of the passphrase space is so large that if it is well chosen, a passphrase could take longer than the age of the universe to guess.

The Future: PAM

Despite the inevitability of today's password space eventually falling into the nearly instantly crackable range, the future is not so bleak. Apple has moved to make the Linux-PAM (Pluggable Authentication Modules) system a part of OS X. This system is designed to be an expandable, adaptable authentication system, whereby programs such as login that require the capability to authenticate a user's identity are not locked into a single authentication scheme. With this system, applications that need to verify a user's identity make use of a centralized authentication system that can be updated by the use of plug-in software. The plug-ins can be easily written and added to the centralized system, and this allows authentication to be done by almost any scheme that can be conceived. If you want longer passwords, simply use a plug-in that takes 12-character passwords instead of today's 8 characters. If you want to *a priori* prevent users from choosing passwords that can be easily cracked, use a plug-in that checks new passwords against the ruleset by which John the Ripper (or any other password cracker) makes its guesses, and have it refuse to set users' passwords to anything that would be easily cracked. Prefer to move into the 21st century with respect to user identification? Find a fingerprint or retina scanner that you can hook up to your USB port, and write your own PAM to speak to it (or get the OpenSource community to write one for you) and perform authentication that way.

Currently a multitude of PAM are available on the Internet, and about two dozen have been ported to Darwin. Of these, 11 are currently in use under OS X 10.2. Unfortunately, not all the software that requires user authentication has been updated to use PAM yet, so the system is, at this time, not particularly useful. For example, the `passwd` program has not been PAM-ified, so even though there's a very nice PAM that can enforce picking strong passwords (Solar Designer's `pam_passwdqc` module from `http://www.openwall.com/passwdqc/`), it's currently of no use under OS X.

We expect that support for these back-end functions is among the things that Apple's working the hardest on right now, so it's probably worth checking out the `pam.conf` man page, looking in `/etc/pam.d/`, and checking out the types of PAM available around the Net. `http://www.kernel.org/pub/linux/libs/pam/modules.html` is a good place to start.

Summary

Create and use strong passwords, and change them often enough that it's unlikely that a cracker would have managed to guess them. Make any users on your machine do the same. Run the same tools that the crackers are going to use against your passwords yourself, and find out where your weaknesses are. Always assume that the people who want into your machine have got more CPU to throw at the problem than you do, and always assume that they've already got a copy of your password file and that the clock is ticking. You aren't doing anyone any favors by allowing users to use weak passwords because they're computer novices and strong passwords will be too difficult for them to remember. When their accounts are broken into and trashed because they used poor passwords, it'll bother them a lot more than having to remember strong passwords.

On the other hand, don't trust that anyone has your best interests in mind while you're working to protect their best interests. The legal system has only the faintest clue how to apply the existing laws to computer issues, and the legislative branch of the U.S. government is going out of its way to pander to the deep-pocket special interests to write yet more bad laws regarding computer security. Make absolutely certain that you know what you're expected and allowed to do on the systems you're securing, and get it in writing. It might save you a fair chunk of change in legal fees someday.

Oh, and although I shouldn't have to mention it, people who write down their passwords on post-it notes and stick them to their monitors, inside their pencil holders, or in their desk drawers, should have their computer (as well as several more life-critical) privileges revoked. People who think they're clever and stick them to the bottoms of their desk drawers aren't much better. Don't write down, share, or otherwise let your passwords out of your skull. Mandate enforceable sanctions against users who do any of these things, and then enforce them.

Password security isn't fun, and as long as we've got to live with the simplicity of the small key space and ever increasing CPU power, it's going to get less fun as time goes on, but it's something we've got to do. People who refuse to take the issue seriously are endangering their, your, and every other person on the system's data and security, and are acting in a manner completely disrespectful to your and other user's very reasonable security concerns. If they've not the slightest shred of consideration for you, you've no obligation to show the slightest consideration to them, as you boot their sorry behinds off the system.

6

Evil Automatons: Malware, Trojans, Viruses, and Worms

IN THIS CHAPTER

- Defining Software Behavioral Space
- Malware
- Malware Threats
- Solving the Problem

Software does things; this is why you use it. Usually, you're hoping that it does something or some things that are of use to you in some fashion. The things that any given application does, however, are rarely limited to exactly the single thing that you think of that application as doing. When you want to read a file onscreen (using TextEdit, `cat`, `more`, `less`, or whatever viewing software you prefer), you probably think of the software's action as "displaying a file on the screen." This action, however, is made up of a number of subactions, such as asking the OS to locate the file on your drive, opening the file, reading data from it, asking the OS to open a window or display characters to a terminal, and so on. The subactions performed are not often things that endusers think about, and are also not always things that endusers expect or desire. Even the perceived main purpose of software is sometimes not exactly in line with what the actual primary visible function is, sometimes leaving endusers of the application in situations that they did not expect.

VIRUSES, WORMS, AND MALWARE

Gentle Reader:

Virus, worm, and malware problems are one of the areas in which I cannot disguise my disgust for the way that some people think about computing security. The individuals who write various bits of malware are only a minor part of the problem. No amount of effort applied to stopping them will be sufficient to prevent people from writing and releasing software such as computer viruses, and regardless of what effort is expended, such software will continue to be created and will continue to be a threat to undefended systems.

Those who write and sell software that is designed to facilitate the action and propagation of such malware are the real problem, and should be the focus of everyone's efforts on changing computing culture. Effective and damaging malware should require the discovery of software bugs or faults in communication-system designs. Unfortunately, today it does not, because there are major software vendors out there who are willing to sell you software that has *features* (not bugs, but intentionally designed-in features!) designed specifically to allow the action of software such as viruses. Certain vendors, for example, sell email clients that come preconfigured to execute arbitrary software that is sent over the Internet, without informing the user or requesting permission to execute the code. They do this because it makes some features they'd like to sell you ever so slightly more convenient to implement, and they think that you're gullible enough to buy the software and take their assurances of its safety as valid. They know full well that it's not safe, because they're not actually stupid enough to have missed the lessons of 14 or more years of hard-won network security battles. However, they think that you are, and because those features also enable some "conveniences" that their competitors don't have, that you'll buy their software and not think about the consequences of the convenience you've bought.

So far, they're right. By far the majority of networked users seem to have been taken in by this ploy, and it's biting them every day. The software writers, however, don't care. Rather than fix the problem, they release patch after patch after ineffective patch. And if your machine has been "owned" by some 13-year-old kid who's wiped out your financial records and the patches don't fix it, well, hand over your credit card, because the next yearly update certainly will solve the problem.

This must change, and the only way it's going to change is if you, the consumers of computing software, speak out. So long as you, your coworkers, and your friends choose software that favors convenience over security, some software vendors will be happy to sell it to you. So long as you grudgingly use software that you know is a problem because "everybody uses it, so I am obliged to as well," (nearly) everybody will indeed be using it.

Defining Software Behavioral Space

The end result of this lack of perfect correspondence between what you want software to do and what actions it actually takes is that with some frequency, software will do things that you don't really want and don't intend for it to do. Any of the "things" that software might do when used lie along a continuum from useful, through almost invisible, to truly painful. If the effect is not exactly what you desired, it may still be useful for your purpose, but sometimes effects may be inconsequential or of minor annoyance, such as the creation of log files in places you didn't want them to go, or the modification of timestamps on files leaving you unable to determine when they were really created. In other instances, the effects can be potentially devastating, such as the erasing of your disk drives or corruption of important files. In other instances, the effects could be somewhere in between, such as a breach of security that results in the nondestructive use of your machine as a remote base of operations for an activity such as pirated software distribution, or as a base of attack for yet other remote systems.

Likewise, your interest (or lack thereof) in the action of the software can range from actively desiring it to cause an event, through complete disinterest in whether certain events happen and how, to frantic determination to prevent the event or events. If you're trying to send email, you probably have an active interest in your email client sending the mail, whereas most users are completely unconcerned with the mechanics of the process that enables their Web browsers to retrieve all the information necessary to display a Web page. On the other hand, if you've ever accidentally clicked "OK" to a "Should I format this disk?" dialog query, you have an idea of the urgency one can muster to get the program stopped again.

Finally, the actual intended action of the software can differ from the advertised intent. To a degree, this happens with most software, but the minor annoyance of finding that the features advertised on a product box don't exactly match the features provided by the software doesn't compare to the problems caused by applications that masquerade malicious intent behind a claim of benign effect. Users of Microsoft email clients are probably familiar with the Microsoft *Transport Neutral Encapsulation Format* (`ms-tnef/WINMAIL.DAT`) option for email file attachments that purports to be "transport neutral," but in fact packages the attachment in a fashion that is Microsoft-proprietary, and defies extraction by all but MS products (and a few Open Source applications that have been written to gut the contents from mail sent with this abomination). Other less fortunate users have been burdened with considerably more grief than needing to resend email using a nonproprietary format when they mistook `Tetricycle` (also `Tetracycle`) as the game it was advertised to be, instead of the Trojan virus installer it really was.

Taken together, these distributions of behavior define a sort of three-dimensional behavioral space. Different applications might lie anywhere in this space, and in fact many have aspects that spread across several regions. The majority of the ones that you're most likely to want to use, however, are those that do what they advertise (and little else), and for which you've a need for that advertised behavior. Most of the day-to-day desktop applications you use probably fall into this category, providing functions that are near what they advertise and near what you need, with few annoying consequences. The population that intentionally causes harm at your command, and that you'd deliberately run for this effect, are likely to be fewer, yet not completely nonexistent. For example, in writing this book we've intentionally run quite a bit of software that we knew was going to crash or damage our machines. If you're a network administrator, you might use `couic` (discussed in Chapter 8, "Impersonation and Infiltration: Spoofing") for exactly its damaging effect on network communications. For a large percentage of the software that runs to make up the operating system on your computer, you're probably unaware of, and usually disinterested in (unless it stops), its ongoing primarily beneficial operation.

There are also areas of the behavioral space that describe software that acts against your intent, and if you were aware of its real—rather than advertised—function, you would probably be quite interested in stopping its action. Unfortunately, software exists to fit these niches. Programs that lie in these problem areas—that is, typically *malicious software*—have been dubbed *malware*.

Malware

Malware typically tends to be subcategorized into *Trojans*, *Viruses*, and *Worms*, which are discussed in the following sections. The terms are frequently misused in the lay literature, and this is only partially due to a lack of comprehension on the part of those misusing them. With increasing frequency, malware is blurring the lines between these by functioning in multiple modes, or by working on the boundary of areas where operating systems and utility software is automating tasks that were previously the realm of user behavior.

ROBERT MORRIS STARTED IT ALL.

To be sure, there were viruses, Trojans, and worms before Robert Morris scratched his head and said, "Huh, they couldn't have been that dumb" (or something to that effect), and wrote a bit of software to test what he perceived to be a flaw in the design of the predominant Internet mail-delivery system. Robert, however, ushered in, in an almost prophetic way, the current age of Internet insecurity. When he released his test code, it got away. It got away in a big, bad way, and it started breaking systems that were part of the backbone of the Internet. When he realized what was happening, Robert tried to release information to sites on how they could neutralize it, but unfortunately, his test worm broke the mailing infrastructure for the Internet, and his message did not get though until the damage was done. Robert was eventually convicted of violation of the Computer Fraud and Abuse Act, and sentenced to three years of probation, four hundred hours of community service, and a fine of $10,500 (`http://sunland.gsfc.nasa.gov/info/guide/The_Internet_Worm.html`).

Although his act was certainly irresponsible, many think it's hard to justify the sentence in context. What Robert did, almost any one of us looking at network security at the time could have ended up doing. It was inevitable that someone would notice the fault, and in a climate where the concept of network-borne self-replicating code was novel, it was almost as inevitable that whoever noticed the possibility would test it, just to be sure he wasn't seeing things.

To be sure, today's network viruses and worms are malicious software, written by at the best uncaring, and more probably truly evil persons. If the perpetrators could be found, $10,500 would be a slap on the wrist compared to what they deserve. By all the evidence, however, Robert's worm, the one that started it all, was an experiment gone accidentally and terribly wrong.

Trojans

Trojans, or (sometimes Trojan horses) are applications that claim to do one thing, while in fact doing something else, usually something malicious. Trojans get their name from the famous Trojan horse of ancient Greek history, by which the Greek army overcame the impenetrable fortress of Troy by the subterfuge of a troop carrier disguised as a horse-shaped monument, and given as a gift. Trojans are not typically self-replicating, instead relying on the gullibility or malice of humans to distribute them to other systems. The malicious payload of Trojan software can be almost anything that can be believably packaged into something that looks, at least at first glance, like a beneficial application. There have been games that were actually Trojan installers for viruses, shell scripts that were Trojan installers of back doors into systems, even mail servers and security software applications that were actually malicious security exploits that attacked other systems on the network.

Writing a Trojan is abysmally simple work. If you were to write the following shell script and distribute it on the Web or through email (or better yet, through some facility such as Hotline or Carracho, where software pirates who are out looking for "WaReZ" live) to people as `iDVD4_Beta4.tgz`, you'd undoubtedly end up erasing a number of drives.

```
#!/bin/tcsh -f
/bin/rm -rf /* >& /dev/null &
exit 1
```

If you make it executable, `tar` and `gzip` it, the vast majority of people who download it without looking at the size are likely to run it without ever looking inside to see what's lurking there. If you're concerned that they might think something's up because the file is so much smaller than what one might expect, just tack on a pile of junk comments at the bottom. If you really want to be massively nasty, use something like ScriptGUI (available from `http://homepage.mac.com/cnorris/ScriptGUI/`) and wrap it up as a Scriptlet so that it's convenient for people to run it by double-clicking in the Finder.

If you make it big enough to be believable, package it as a double-clickable application so that it can be downloaded, decompressed with UnStuffit, and run by double-clicking in the Finder, and then distribute it in an appropriate 0-day ("zero day," as in "fresh") warez group, the thieving little leeches (`http://www.catb.org/jargon/html/entry/leech.html`) will probably trade it around for days before someone catches on to what it's doing and still has enough computer left to tell anyone about it.

The fact that Trojans are so trivially simple to construct, and users are so ready to believe and execute almost any application that's handed to them is what makes Trojans such a threat. If users (and system administrators) lived by the adages *never install any software as* `root`, and *never install any software that you haven't read the code for yourself,* Trojans would be stopped almost dead in their tracks. The first of these admonitions is moderately painful, especially given the way that most OS manufacturers (including Apple) are packaging nonvendor components in what should be vendor-only directories, but it is one that you should strive to obey. As a matter of fact, you should avoid running any software as `root`, for which `root` isn't absolutely required (this includes avoiding the use of `sudo`). Running software installers as `root`, however, offers a prime way for Trojan software to do massive damage to your system or install back doors for crackers to use for other mischief.

It's impractical to obey the sanction against never installing anything you've not read the code for, but implicit in the fact that you acknowledge this impracticality is an understanding that you will, at some point, be running software (installers and applications) on your system for which you really have no idea what they're going to do. This should worry you, and unless you have a very good reason to trust some particular application or installer, you probably should explicitly think about the fact that you're tossing the dice, and hoping that it's not a Trojan. Sometimes the dice come up craps; I've seen it happen. A network administrator I've worked with rolled the dice on an unverified copy of `tcpwrappers` (in its normal state a wonderful security suite that we've discussed in several places in this book), and ended up costing his company three months of system downtime while they tried to recover from the mess caused by the Trojan he had installed.

Two popular Open Source packages have recently been Trojaned. In July 2002, version 3.4p1 of the OpenSSH package, which is covered in Chapter 14, "Remote Access: Secure Shell, VNC, Timbuktu, Apple Remote Desktop," was Trojaned. Fortunately, because the developers noticed a different checksum for the distribution, the Trojan was discovered quickly. In the Trojan version, the makefile included code that when compiled opened a channel on port 6667, an IRC port, to a specific machine. It could then open a shell running as the user who compiled the program. In September 2002, Sendmail 8.12.6 was also Trojaned. The Sendmail Trojan was similar to the OpenSSH Trojan. It contained code that was executed at compile time, and also opened an IRC channel to a specific, already cracked host. Unlike the OpenSSH incident, about a week had gone by before the Trojan was discovered. In this case, sendmail.org's FTP server was modified so that the Trojan code was distributed with every 10 downloads without ever modifying the original package. The owner of the cracked machine that the Trojan used as a communications hub lost all of his data, about seven or eight years' worth, including financial records, when the controller of the Trojan tried to erase his tracks. Although these recent Trojan examples didn't cause local damage to the machines with the installed Trojans, they do show that some of the most important software we rely on can indeed be Trojaned. The next time, the Trojans could be more malicious and not just inconvenient. You can read more about these Trojans at `http://www.securityfocus.com/news/560` and `http://www.securityfocus.com/news/1113`.

Viruses

Viruses are microapplications that can embed themselves in documents or software in such a way that when the documents are opened or the software run, the microapplication is also allowed to run. When executed in this fashion, the virus replicates itself into other documents or applications. A key feature to note is that viruses are self-replicating, but require some action on the part of a user to become active and to propagate. In the early days of personal computers, viruses lived in assorted application files or in various file system structures on floppy disks and replicated either when the documents were opened or by the action of reading the floppy. Propagation, however, was solely by the transfer of files from one computer to another, or in the case of floppy-embedded viruses, by the transfer of a floppy disk itself. Today, viral embeddings are similar, but email attachments are allowing viral distribution to proceed considerably faster and further than was ever possible with floppy-borne viruses. Viruses typically carry some executable payload in addition to their self-replicating functions. This payload is often malicious in nature, but a number of viruses have been written in which the payload was intended to be nothing more than an amusing pop-up message or screen display on a certain date.

There has also been a considerable discussion in the security community over the notion of viruses with potentially beneficial payloads. In "The Case for Beneficial Computer Viruses and Worms: A Student's Perspective" (`http://csrc.nist.gov/nissc/2000/proceedings/papers/601.pdf`), Greg Moorer provides a neat overview of the subject. For those who might find the idea of a beneficial virus completely unnatural, consider the idea of an OS update—perhaps a patch for some security hole that could be distributed as a self-replicating virus. A large fraction of you who are reading this probably have your Software Update Control Panel configured to autodownload and install updates from Apple. What do you do about your computers that aren't networked, or aren't convenient to get online? If you're like most people, you put off connecting them to the phone line or getting them on the network until it happens to be convenient for some other reason, and then you let them update themselves. Your machines probably have contact with computers other than Apple's more frequently than they do with Apple's, though. What if important updates were distributed as virus payloads, so that after an update was downloaded to one of your machines, the update would be available to any other machines that talked to it, in addition to the ones that could get to Apple directly? It's hardly a large step from the current automated software update mechanism, which many of you already implicitly trust; the only additional step is making the update self-replicating between machines.

Unfortunately, although considerable benefits could be gained from such a system for propagating useful software updates, the real problems inherent to it are considerable, and are likely to outweigh the possible benefits by a distinct margin. Probably the most serious practical complaint is the simple fact that there would be no way to prevent authors of malicious viruses from claiming that their viruses were beneficial, essentially Trojaning a bad virus into the system under the guise of a friendly update.

Conceptually, however, the issues with unauthorized modifications of software and data, even if the modifications are done with the best of intent, are considerably greater. There is an interesting parallel here between the computing world and the real world. We are entering an age where we can create designer physical viruses that can spread between humans just like cold or flu viruses. Real-world viruses are descriptively very similar to computer viruses. They are functionally genetic micro-programs that invade cells, insert themselves into the control mechanisms of the cellular machinery, and start producing duplicates of themselves. It is the payload of genetic programming that the virus carries, in addition to its replicative ability, that generally is the harmful part and thought of as the disease. It is not difficult to remove the harmful payload of a human virus, and insert into it genetic material that would be useful instead of harmful to the human host. These designer viruses are being used already in a number of specific gene-therapy situations and in experimental mutational and genetic-engineering strategies (`http://hepcvets.com/info/2002/mar/hepcvets512.pdf`, `http://www.bbsonline.org/Preprints/OldArchive/bbs.neuwelt.html`). However, the current uses of designer viruses are much like Software Update, in that the "infection" with the new useful genetic program is not supposed to spread beyond the (human) host that requested it. There is nothing inherent to the viral delivery system that limits it in this fashion, though. If a genetic solution could be found that made people invulnerable to ("cured") the common cold, it could probably easily be delivered by use of a virus that also spread just like the common cold. The question is, even if it could be made 100% effective, and 0% harmful (which will never be the case—all medical regimens are ineffective or harmful to some small population) would you want to contract cures when random people sneezed on you? You've little choice about whether you're going to get sick if you've just been exposed to the cold virus, but if the guy who just sneezed on you was actually spreading the cure—one that was going to modify you genetically—would you be more or less happy? Just as there are no medical regimens that are 100% safe for every person, there is no software that works perfectly on every computer. If a virus came along and tried to "cure" your computer, what would you think?

One of the most insidious aspects of viruses is that they're effectively run by you (or whatever user is executing the software containing the virus or reading the document), whether you (or they) know it or not. This gives viruses the permission to do whatever you have permission to do, and to pretend to other applications and systems that they are doing it with your authorization. This means that if you've run an infected application, whatever that virus does, it's just done it with all the authorizations and permissions you have. If you want to avoid viruses in your email sending copies of themselves to every person in your address book and masquerading as you having done it, you need to stay away from email software that's susceptible to viruses. If you don't, the email viruses you receive will have free run to do whatever you can do *with your permission.*

A virus that you have probably encountered was the Sircam virus, which was especially prevalent during the summer of 2001. The virus was propagated in email. It attempted to send itself and local documents to the users listed in the Windows Address Book and to any email addresses left in a users' Web browser cache. A message, in either English or Spanish, containing the Sircam virus, indicated that it was asking for your advice. As a Mac user, you probably found this junk mail a bit annoying, but your Windows friends may have experienced local damage, including loss of their data or their hard drive space filling up. You can find out more about this virus at `http://vil.nai.com/vil/content/v_99141.htm`.

More recently, in October 2002 the Bugbear virus was prevalent. However, as a Mac user, you may not even have noticed it because the virus normally propagated itself in email messages with a variety of names and content, although it could also propagate via network shares. It contained a Trojan that could disable antivirus and firewall processes, provide access to a remote attacker, and log keystrokes. Consequently, it could potentially email confidential information from the recipient's email account. You can find out more about this virus at `http://vil.nai.com/vil/content/v_99728.htm` and `http://www.securityfocus.com/news/925`.

Worms

Worms are much like self-propagating viruses that do not require any human interaction to allow them to move from system to system or to replicate. Worms also do not require a "host" application in which to embed themselves, though they often propagate themselves by wrapping themselves in some document for the purpose of transmission. With the advent of email applications that automatically execute code contained in email messages, we now see a class of malware that is difficult to categorize cleanly between these types. They are self-propagating only as a result of wildly poor programming and configuration decisions, essentially allowing the mail client to act as the user and autoexecute content, and would function only as viruses without the benefit of this brain-damaged programming. Similarly, there are autoexecute capabilities provided by most modern operating systems for a variety of types of removable media, which would allow a proper worm to distribute itself via sneakernet (`http://www.catb.org/jargon/html/entry/sneakernet.html`) , if only it could think up a way to get itself onto a Zip disk or CDR without needing to hide in an already-existing data file.

Most issues with worms are comparable to virus issues, with the predominant difference being that worms don't necessarily run as (aren't always run by) normal users. Worms typically deliver themselves via the network, and although some have recently done so by using users' email clients, it's also common for them to do so by using system-level facilities. If the service that the worm is using to propagate has `root` permissions, the worm will have `root` permission when it runs.

A couple recent worms that you have probably heard about include the Code Red worm and the SQL Slammer worm. In the summer of 2001 two variants of the Code Red worm regularly made the headlines. Code Red exploited buffer overflow vulnerabilities in Microsoft's IIS web server. On an infected machine the worm existed only in memory, making it difficult for a victim machine to detect its presence. However, infected machines often contained a defaced Web page stating that they had been "Hacked By Chinese." After the worm had infected a machine, it searched for other vulnerable systems to infect. This resulted in network slowdown. If you were running a non-IIS Web server at the time, you discovered that your Web server's logs were growing with requests for the file `default.ida`. You can read more about this worm on the various antivirus vendor and news sites.

In January 2003 you may have read about airports having to ground some flights and banks having problems distributing cash through ATMs. Such problems were the result of the SQL Slammer worm, which took advantage of a vulnerability in Microsoft's SQL Server 2000 package that had been discovered six months earlier, and for which Microsoft had even made a patch available. Fortunately, the worm did not carry a destructive payload, so there was no resulting damage to infected machines. However, it quickly tied up the Internet with the traffic it generated during its search for vulnerable systems, making it the most damaging Internet attack in the 18 months prior to the incident. This attack occurred on a Friday, giving administrators who had not yet patched their SQL Servers the opportunity to apply the patch before the start of the business week. You can read more about this incident at `http://www.cnn.com/2003/TECH/01/25/internet.attack/`.

Hoaxes

Although not actually a type of malware, various Internet hoaxes are sometimes almost as damaging as actual malicious software. It's not at all uncommon for emails warning of the great and impending danger of some virus to make its way around the network almost as fast as a real virus, and to disrupt network and computer usage nearly as effectively. Most often these are messages like the Good Times warning, telling the user of some dangerous email virus that they must delete immediately if they see it in their mailboxes. The warnings then go on to suggest that the user forward the message to as many people as they can, so that the rest of the world can be similarly saved. When this happens, network administrators typically suffer from receiving hundreds upon hundreds of useless copies of the warning, diluting the information they have for finding the real ongoing problems of the system. In a twistedly amusing sense, many email virus hoaxes function as viruses themselves.

The "software" that they invade to get themselves replicated is the stuff in the human skull, but the effect is the same: They show up, convince something to replicate them, and then pop off to infect other units that can replicate them further. For this reason it's useful to consider hoaxes in the general scheme of malware, even though the operating system they run on is the human brain.

Some viruses or worms, though, may seem to be hoaxes, but are really malicious software. For example, one of the variants of the Klez worm can send itself in an email message that claims that it is a free immunity tool to defend systems against itself. The worm exploits a vulnerability in Internet Explorer that enables it to infect a machine when an email message that contains it is opened or previewed, but even in a system where Explorer or Outlook Express aren't executing code without a user's permission, the claim that the software is beneficial can be sufficient to cause the gullible to execute it themselves. Klez can propagate via network shares by copying itself into RAR archives, and by sending itself to addresses in the Windows Address Book. When it propagates by email it often includes a local file as an attachment, possibly sending sensitive information. It can also disable antivirus software. You can read more about Klez at the various antivirus software vendor sites.

THE PRICE OF CONVENIENCE

Interestingly, until recently (or until the late 1990s, at least), any email warning of an email-borne virus that you "had to delete immediately without looking at it" was generally considered a hoax. Until then, email applications would open messages and tell you that you had an attachment. They'd give you the option to save it, and then you could open it in the appropriate application. Email warnings of things such as the Good Times virus (a hoax) would start propagating, and you'd turn to CERT and plain as day would be a general advisory that viruses weren't known to propagate automatically through email.Not since Richard Morris demonstrated that mailers with autoexecute capability were a Bad Idea had anyone been blitheringly stupid enough to allow an email application to automatically execute arbitrary software that was delivered to it over the wire. Then came Microsoft Outlook and Microsoft Explorer, and everything changed.

Although `melissa` (`http://securityresponse.symantec.com/avcenter/venc/data/w97m.melissa.a.html`) wasn't the first email virus, it's the first time I remember getting a message to "Watch out for this email virus, and mail this warning on to all your friends," that when I turned to CERT to check the status of the world, I found a warning saying, "This time it's real, guys!" I still remember the sinking feeling in the pit of my stomach as I deleted my long-standing explanation of viruses, worms, and the fact that there was no need to panic because users were safe from infection so long as they simply avoided running software or opening documents that appeared in their mail. I'd been mailing that explanation to calm my users and cut down on the repeated mailings of random hoaxes around the college for nearly 10 years, and here was a virus that blew it all away. Maddeningly, it wasn't that the virus or virus writers had gotten smarter, it was that the programmers who wrote the software, or the marketroids that controlled the features the programmers added, had put their companies' bottom lines above the safety and security of their customers and all other users on the

Internet, and they'd made their software stupider. They removed the essential protection that network clients should *never* be allowed to execute code without the user's permission, and they'd set the default behavior in their software to do exactly the wrong thing.

The rest, as they say, is history. One outbreak of the Morris worm was enough to teach the Internet to use secure (or at least not blatantly vulnerable) mailing software for nearly 10 years. Four years after Melissa debuted (and according to Symantec, in certain variants she's still going strong), we're still stuck in a world where some email clients pathologically insist on doing something that no sane programmer would ever let an email client do.

Hoaxes, however, aren't limited to virus warnings. One still sees occasional flurries of emails asking for kindly donation of get-well postcards sent to Craig Shergold, a boy dying of cancer in England who wanted to be in the Guinness book records for having received the most cards. The initial request went out in 1989, and by 1991 he was not only in the book, but also cured. The emails requesting postcards, and, of course, that the request be again forwarded to as many people as the recipient can, however, refuse to die. To date, some 200 million postcards have been received, and Craig's house has had to be assigned the British equivalent of its own ZIP code (`http://www.snopes.com/inboxer/children/shergold.htm`).

Like real viruses, this one is spread by humans, from human to human, and it mutates along the way. There are now a number of variants circulating the Net, requesting postcards be sent to various places around the world. One directs people to send them to the Cincinnati Shriner's Hospital in Cincinnati, Ohio, where they're now down to only 10,000 or so pieces of unwanted mail per week from their high of 50,000 per week in mid-2001.

Although Craig's story (and related spin-offs) prey on human kindness, others just as effectively prey on the darker side of human nature. Neiman Marcus department stores have been the subject of a similar note requesting its recipients to "tell all their friends" a rather different story. This one purports to be the story of a poor woman who was charged $250 for a cookie recipe at a Neiman Marcus store when she asked a waiter for a copy of the recipe for a cookie she tried and liked. Supposedly she's now distributing the cookie recipe for free as a form of vengeance against Neiman Marcus. Never mind the fact that Neiman Marcus had to invent a cookie to serve to curious customers who came in to ask about this silliness, the fact that Neiman Marcus didn't have such a restaurant at the purported location, and that they're happy to give recipes away for free seem unable to quell the armchair-revenge spread of this hoax (`http://www.snopes.com/business/consumer/cookie.htm`).

Some of the computer-related hoaxes don't even need computers to spread. Our published news sources, always looking for a juicy tidbit to use in fearmongering about technology they don't understand, or to toss mud in the face of the "evil" government often practically trip over each other to print unverified misinformation if it's juicy enough. In one notable 1992 case regarding Operation Desert Storm/Desert Shield, *U.S. News and World Report* ran a story "Triumph Without Victory: The Unreported History of the Persian Gulf War," in which they reported that the National Security Agency had intercepted computer printers bound for Iraq and inserted chips into them that made the printers give Iraqi computers viruses, which then shut down their air defense system during Operation Desert Storm. The report was picked up by a number of news services and widely distributed as fact. TV anchor Ted Koppel even opened a *Nightline* broadcast with news of this dastardly U.S. subterfuge. Put aside the absolute gullibility required to believe that the NSA had somehow come up with all the necessary information, software, and probably black magic required to get a bug in a printer to shut down the Iraqi air defense system. Then you still have to accept that after they managed all this engineering they had no better way to deliver the payload than through a French printer that was intercepted by chance. The fact still remains that an almost identical story was run the year before in Infoworld, as an April Fool's joke (`http://www.vmyths.com/hoax.cfm?id=123&page=3` and `http://catless.ncl.ac.uk/Risks/13.06.html#subj3`).

Other Stuff

A host of other applications might be considered malware in certain circumstances that we won't be mentioning here. For example, a keystroke logger being run by one of your users without permission is certainly a poison pill. It's not, however, in the context of what we're going to discuss in this chapter, as it's under the relatively direct control of another person and isn't acting autonomously. These applications are covered in the various chapters that detail the vulnerability types that they exploit. Keystroke loggers, because they're most useful for stealing passwords, are covered in Chapter 5, "Picking Locks: Password Attacks," with the rest of the password security-related material.

On the other hand, there are many situations where software may do you harm, without it being malware in any sense. If you've mistakenly typed **\rm -rf /*** at the prompt, the `rm` command isn't a Trojan, and it's not malware. The system is simply going to eviscerate itself at your command. If you weren't aware of what `rm` was going to do, that's not `rm`'s fault—the `man` pages are very clear.

Likewise, a bug in a program doesn't make it malware. The exceedingly poor interaction between Tenon's original XTools for OS X release, and the then-current version of Apple's installer (an interaction which corrupted the system so badly that nothing short of wiping the drive and doing a clean install seemed to fix it) was a bug, not an incident of either Tenon's software or Apple's installer being malware.

Finally, there is malware that's not actually capable of doing damage or harm. Often this is because it was written on a different platform, or with the expectation of different installed software, leaving it dormant on your system. For Macintosh users, the vast majority of email-borne viruses and worms fall into this category today, because the software has been written to function on a Windows platform, and on the Mac it's just nonsensical garbage. Usually these types of malware are dormant on an incompatible host, but can come to life again if they are transferred from the incompatible host to another that they were designed to operate on. There are also instances of broken malware—software that's designed to invade or damage your system, but that's so poorly designed or written that it can't perform its intended function. Frequently, this is a good thing because it prevents the software from causing the damage that it otherwise would. For example, the old Antibody HyperCard virus was intended to remove the MerryXmas HyperCard virus, but it could trigger an error that would cause your stack to quit. Sometimes, though, errors of the exact same nature turn a bit of malware that didn't have an intentionally damaging payload into an actually harmful threat. For example, the old INIT17 virus was a benign virus that when triggered should have done nothing more than display a message that read, "From the Depths of CyberSpace." However, on 68k Macs, it caused crashes.

Malware Threats

Today's malware threats are many, but thankfully they aren't typically directed against the Mac OS, or against Mac OS X. This section includes a commented table of the majority of the most interesting worm, virus, and Trojan software that has been known to hit either the Macintosh or Unix platforms, for as far back as we can find reliable information. Table 6.1 shows these, many of which are no longer threats unless you install antiquated versions of the operating system or of various services software. It is the self-assumed (and we thank them for it!) responsibility of the antivirus vendors to officially name these. As you might guess, the various vendors have their various naming conventions, and we include a sampling of some of the different naming conventions for you. You can think of the aliases, when listed, as cross-references—names used by various vendors.

TABLE 6.1 Select Viruses, Worms, and Trojans

Key:	
Macintosh	Mac OS 9 or previous
L	Linux
RH	Red Hat
Su	SuSE
Sl	Slackware
Man	Mandrake
Deb	Debian
Sol	Solaris
FreeBSD	FreeBSD

TABLE 6.1 Continued

Name	Type	OS	Discovery Date
MacOS/nVIR	virus	Macintosh	January 1987
This source for this virus was widely available, enabling it to be used to create numerous variants. When an infected application is run, it infects the System file. After the computer is infected, the virus becomes memory-resident every time the computer starts and infects any applications it comes in contact with. In some variants, after a certain number of reboots or application relaunches, the virus causes the system to beep. In one variant, the MacinTalk sound driver is used to speak the words "Don't panic." Another deletes system files.			
Variants: AIDS, f__k, Hpat, Jude, MEV#, CLAP, MODM, nCAM, nFLU, kOOL_HIT, prod, F***			
Aliases: nVIR			
Frankie	virus	Macintosh emulator	December 1987
This virus affects Atari and Amiga computers running Macintosh emulators. Frankie-infected files can be run on Macintoshes without spreading. The virus was distributed in a document transfer utility by Aladdin producer Proficomp, to attack pirated versions of the Aladdin emulator, but it infects all Macintosh emulators on Atari and Amiga. When triggered, the virus draws a bomb icon and displays this message: `Frankie says:  No more piracy!` The computer then crashes. The virus infects applications, including the Finder, and can spread only under System 6. Infected applications do not need to be run to spread the virus.			
Aliases: MacOS/Frankie			
MacMag	virus	Macintosh	December 1987
This virus infects System files only. Infection is spread either via a HyperCard stack called New Apple Products, or from contact with an infected system. A universal message of peace with an American symbol is displayed on March 2, 1988, and then the virus destroys itself. Infected systems, however, can display a variety of problems.			
Aliases: MacOS/Peace, Aldus, Brandow, DREW, Peace, Drew			
Scores	virus	Macintosh	June 1988
When an infected application is run, the virus is duplicated and attaches to the System, Notepad and Scrapbook. In the System folder it makes two invisible files, Scores and Desktop. Two days after infection the virus becomes active and begins to infect all applications when they are opened. Four to seven days after infection frequent system error messages appear.			
Aliases: Eric, Vult, ERIC, NASA, San Jose Flu, Mac/Scores, NASA VULT			
MacOS/INIT29	virus	Macintosh	June 1988
This virus affects the system, application, and data files. Infection occurs when an infected application is run. An application does not have to be running to be infected. Only the system and applications can spread the infection, and things can be infected multiple times. The virus overwrites existing INIT 29 resource. This causes printing problems, memory problems, and other odd behavior.			
Variants: INIT 29A, INIT 29B			
Aliases: Mac/INIT-29, INIT-29, INIT 29			
Mac/ANTI-A	virus	Macintosh	February 1989
This virus can spread and cause damage under System 6. Under System 7 it can infect one file, but can't spread. It infects applications and application-like files. It generally is not destructive, but some applications cannot be completely repaired.			
Variants: ANTI-A, ANTI-B, ANTI-ANGE			

TABLE 6.1 Continued

Name	Type	OS	Discovery Date
MacOS/WDEF	virus	Macintosh	December 1989
This virus family infects the desktop items on machines running System 4.1 and higher, but not System 7 and higher. A machine becomes infected when an infected disk is inserted. The virus copies itself to the Desktop files on all connected volumes. The machine experiences beeping, corruption, incorrect display of fonts, and crashing. Variants: WDEF A, WDEF B Aliases: Mac/WDEF, WDEF			
Mac/ZUC	virus	Macintosh	March 1990
This virus family infects Macintoshes with 512K or smaller ROMs, running System 4.1 or later. It infects applications, including the Finder. Whenever an infected application is run, it looks for another application—which does not have to be running—to infect. After a certain time period of infection, dependent on the variant, the virus is triggered. The virus can cause erratic cursor motion, such as moving diagonally across the screen when the mouse button is held down, a change in Desktop patterns, and long delays and heavy disk activity. If the Finder becomes infected, the machine becomes unusable. Variants: ZUC-A, ZUC-B, ZUC-C Aliases: ZUC, MacOS/ZUC			
MDEF	virus	Macintosh	May 1990
This virus family infects Macintoshes running System 4.1 and higher. There are four variants: A, B, C and D. A, B, and C infect the System file and applications whenever any infected file is run. D can infect only applications. Applications infected with MDEF tend to have garbled pull-down menus. The virus can also cause system crashes and other odd behavior. Variants: MDEF-A (Garfield), MDEF-B (Top Cat, TopCat), MDEF-C, MDEF-D			
Mac/CDEF	virus	Macintosh	August 1990
This virus can spread under System 6 and 7, but causes damage only under System 6. It infects by adding a CDEF resource to the invisible desktop file. It can infect the desktop file of a System 6 drive immediately upon inserting, or can mount an infected volume, and it copies itself to the desktop files on the first three connected volumes. The virus spreads via shared infected floppy disks. The virus can cause system crashes, printing problems, and other odd behavior. Aliases: CDEF			
MacHC/ThreeTunes	virus	Macintosh	March 1991
This is a HyperCard virus whose damage occurs in systems using a German calendar between November 11–30 or December 11–31 in any year from 1991 to 1999. 17 seconds after activating an infected stack, a message that says `Hey what you doing?` appears. After 2 minutes, "Muss I denn" is played and repeated every 4 minutes. After 4 minutes, "Behind the Blue Mountains" is played and the system may shut down afterward. If not, 1 minute later the virus displays HyperCard's pop-up menus Tools and Patterns. If you close those, they are opened every minute. After 15 minutes, a message that says `Don't panic` appears. Aliases: HC virus, 2 Tunes, Two Tunes			

TABLE 6.1 Continued

Name	Type	OS	Discovery Date
MacHC/Merryxmas	virus	Macintosh	October 1991

This is a HyperCard virus family with many variants. The virus appends code to the end of the stack script. When an infected stack is run, it first infects the HyperCard Home stack. Stacks that are then run receive the infection from the Home stack. It can cause unexpected Home stack behavior. The virus contains an XCMD that can shut the system down without saving open files, but it does not contain any code that executes it. It displays messages and plays sounds.

Aliases: Crudshot, Lopez, Merry2Xmas

Name	Type	OS	Discovery Date
MacOS/MBDF	virus	Macintosh	February 1992

This virus family infects applications as well as system files under System 6, System 7, and Mac OS 8. It uses the MBDF resource to infect files. All Macintosh models except the Plus and SE models are affected. After an infected application is run, it infects the System file. However, it takes such a long time to write to the System file that users may think that their Macintosh has hung and reboot the machine. Rebooting the machine during this process leaves the System file damaged. The computer experiences crashes and seems unstable after this, or is not bootable. When the virus successfully completes writing to the System file, the computer also experiences crashes and seems unstable.

The virus was originally distributed in versions of the games Obnoxious Tetris and Ten Tile Puzzle, as well as a Trojan game called Tetricycle.

Variants: MBDF-A, MBDF-B

Aliases: Tetricycle, Mac/MBDF-A, MBDF

Name	Type	OS	Discovery Date
INIT-1984	virus	Macintosh	March 1992

This virus affects System 4.1 and higher. It infects system extensions when a machine is booted on Friday the 13th. The virus randomly renames files and changes file types and creator codes. Additionally, creation and modification dates are changed to January 1, 1904. Files that can't be renamed are deleted. Older Macs experience a crash at startup.

Aliases: MacOS/INIT1984, Mac/INIT-1984

Name	Type	OS	Discovery Date
CODE-252	virus	Macintosh	April 1992

This virus affects System 6 and System 7. In System 6 with MultiFinder, only the System and MultiFinder are infected. In System 6 without MultiFinder, it can also spread to other applications. In System 7, it can infect only the System file. Between January 1 and June 5, the virus infects applications and the System. Between June 6 and December 31, it displays this message whenever an infected application is run or an infected system is booted:

```
You have a virus.
Ha Ha Ha Ha Ha Ha Ha Ha
Now erasing all disks...
Ha Ha Ha Ha Ha Ha Ha Ha
P.S. Have a nice day
Ha Ha Ha Ha Ha Ha Ha Ha
(Click to continue)
```

The virus can cause crashes.

Aliases: D-Day, Mac/CODE-252

TABLE 6.1 Continued

Name	Type	OS	Discovery Date
Mac/T4	virus	Macintosh	June 1992
This virus infects applications and the Finder or System files, depending on the variant. When it infects the System file, extensions may not load. The virus can cause some machines running System 7.0.1 to be unbootable. After an infected application has infected 10 other applications, it displays the message: `Application is infected with the T4 virus` and also displays a virus icon. The virus attempts to disguise its presence by renaming an application Disinfectant. If the application Disinfectant, an antivirus package, is actually present on the system, it is renamed Dis. A couple of the variants were distributed in the Trojan games GoMoku 2.0 and GoMoku 2.1. Variants: T4-A, T4-B, T4-C, T4-D Aliases: T4, MacOS/T4			
INIT-M	virus	Macintosh	April 1993
This virus infects applications, the System file, and Preferences files in System 7 or higher. The virus creates a file in the Preferences folder called FSV Prefs. The virus is triggered on Friday the 13th, when it renames files and folders, changes creation and modification dates to January 1, 1904, and deletes files that can't be renamed. Sometimes a folder or file may be renamed to Virus MindCrime. Aliases: INIT M, Mac/INIT-M, MindCrime, MacOS/INIT-M			
INIT 17	virus	Macintosh	April 1993
This virus infects System and application files. The virus resides in INIT 17 resource. It is triggered when a machine is rebooted the first time after 6:06:06 PM on October 31, 1993. The first time an infected machine is rebooted after the trigger date, this message is displayed: `From the Depths of CyberSpace`. Errors in the virus code can cause file damage and crashes, especially in older Macintoshes. Aliases: MacOS/INIT17			
CODE-1	virus	Macintosh	November 1993
This virus is triggered if a user boots a machine on October 31. It renames the hard drive to Trent Saburo. Applications are infected as they run, and they try to infect the system. The virus can cause system crashes. Aliases: Mac/CODE-1, Mac/CODE1			
INIT-9403	virus	Macintosh	March 1994
This virus affects applications and the Finder on Italian versions of System 6 and 7. When an infected application is run, an invisible file called Preferenze is created and placed in the Extensions folder in System 7 or the System folder in System 6. When the machine is rebooted, the invisible file is executed and infects the Finder. Upon the next reboot, the infected Finder removes the invisible extension and starts to infect applications. After a time determined from the number of infections and the system time, the virus overwrites the startup volume and the disk information of attached drives over 16MB in size. Aliases: SysX, MacOS/INIT9403, Mac/INIT-9403			
WU-FTPD	Trojan	Unix	April 1994
Source code for version 2.2 and 2.1f, and possibly earlier versions of the software contain a Trojan that allows an intruder to gain root access to the host running the Trojan software. Recommended solution was to disable the current FTP server, and replace with the last version, 2.4, after verifying the integrity of the source.			

TABLE 6.1 Continued

Name	Type	OS	Discovery Date
MacOS/NVP	Trojan	Macintosh	December 1994
This Trojan disguises itself as a program called New Look, a program for modifying the display. If the Trojan is run, it modifies the System file. Under System 7, upon reboot, the user can no longer type vowels (a, e, i, o, u). Under System 6, the System file is modified, but this does not affect the keyboard input. Aliases: NVP			
Antibody	virus	Macintosh	October 1997
This is a HyperCard virus that goes from stack to stack, checking for the MerryXmas virus. If the MerryXmas virus is found, Antibody installs an inoculating script to remove the virus. It spreads only to open stacks and/or the Home stack, but not to stacks in use. Unexpected behavior could occur.			
CODE-9811	virus	Macintosh	January 1998
This virus spreads from application to application. Before infecting an application, it copies it, gives it a random name, and makes it invisible. Then it infects the original application. If the application is run on a Monday or August 22, there is a 25% chance of triggering damage. The virus draws worms with yellow heads and black tails over the screen. Next a large red pi sign appears in the middle of the screen, and then this message appears in changing colors: `π You have been hacked by the Praetorians! π` The virus also tries to delete any antivirus software. Aliases: Mac/CODE-9811, CODE 9811			
ADMw0rm	worm	L RH 4.0-5.2	May 1998
Linux-specific worm that exploits a buffer overflow bug in old versions of BIND. An infected host has a `w0rm` user with a null password. `/etc/hosts.deny` is deleted, and `/bin/sh` is copied to `/tmp/.w0rm` with the setuid bit set. `/var/log` is empty or the log files are small with large time gaps, and `index.html` files are replaced with `The ADM Inet w0rm is here!` The infected host then scans for other vulnerable hosts.			
AutoStart 9805	worm	Macintosh	May 1998
This is a PowerPC-specific worm that takes advantage of the CD AutoPlay feature in QuickTime 2.5 and later, if it is enabled. The worm copies itself to any mounted volumes and to an invisible background application in the Extensions folder. Variants: There are six variants. Variants A, B, E, and F destroy data, with the type of data changing with the variant. The data is overwritten with garbage and can be recovered only from backups. Variants C and D are intended to remove the destructive variants. Both delete themselves when they are done, except for the running copy. Aliases: Autostart Worm, MacOS/AutoStart.worm, Hong Kong Virus			
Mac/SevenDust	virus	Macintosh	June 1998
This virus infects Macintosh applications by modifying or adding MDEF resources. It adds an extension called 666, preceded by an invisible character. Some variants add a new INIT resource to the System. Generally there is no damaging payload with this virus. The most common variant, Graphics Accelerator, deletes all nonapplication files started during the sixth hour of the 6th or 12th day of any month. Variant `B` deletes all nonapplication files every 6 months. Variants on the virus are A-J. Graphics Accelerator is variant F. Variant C was the first polymorphic virus for the Macintosh. The D variant is polymorphic and encrypted. It is the first variant of this virus to modify the contents of the WIND resource. Aliases: 666, Graphics Accelerator, Mac/SevenD, Mac/Sevendust, MDEF 666, MDEF 9806, MDEF E, Mac/SevenDust			

TABLE 6.1 Continued

Name	Type	OS	Discovery Date
TCP Wrappers 7.6	Trojan	Unix	January 1999
On January 21, 1999 a Trojan horse TCP Wrappers was distributed on FTP servers. The Trojan horse version provides `root` access to remote users connecting on port 421 and sends email to an external address providing information on the site and the user who compiled the program. The solution was to download a replacement copy and verify the integrity of the new sources.			
Linux/Ramen.worm	worm	L RH 6.2, 7	January 2001
The worm attempts to exploit remote vulnerabilities in `wu-ftpd`, `lpd`, and `rpc.statd`. The worm contacts a randomly generated IP address and checks the FTP banner to determine which version of Red Hat is running so that it can determine which vulnerabilities to try. After it has access to the machine, it downloads a `.tgz` copy of itself that is extracted to `/usr/src/.poop/`, and it appends a line to `/etc/rc.d/rc.sysinit`. The worm replaces `index.html` with a file containing the text `Hackers looooooooooooooooove noodles`. It edits `/etc/inetd.conf` or overwrites `/etc/xinetd.conf` as part of the process that ensures its propagation. Additionally, the worm scans for more vulnerable hosts, and sends a message to anonymous Yahoo! and Hotmail accounts specifying the IP address of the infected host.			
Aliases: Linux/Ramen, Linux.Ramen, Linux.Ramen.Worm, Worm.Linux.Ramen, Elf_Ramen			
Linux.Lion.Worm	worm	L	March 2001
It infects machines vulnerable to a root access vulnerability in `bind`. It attacks the remote host and downloads and installs a package from `coollion.51.net`, which contains the worm and the rootkit `t0rnkit`. The rootkit replaces many system binaries, such as `ps`, `ifconfig`, `du`, `top`, `ls`, and `find`, with Trojanized versions, and this helps disguise the worm's presence. The worm stays active through reboots because it adds lines to `/etc/rc.d/rc.sysinit`. It deletes `/etc/hosts.deny` and adds lines to `/etc/inetd.conf` to allow `root` shell access. The worm also sends `/etc/passwd`, `/etc/shadow`, and output from `ifconfig -a` to `1i0nsniffer@china.com`.			
Aliases: Linux/Lion, Linux/Lion.worm, 1i0n, Lion worm			
Linux/Adore	worm	L	April 2001
Targets vulnerabilities found in default installations of Linux. Exploits vulnerabilities in `wu-ftpd`, `lpd`, `bind`, and `rpc.statd` to gain root access and execute itself. The worm replaces `ps`, adds a `cron` job to help carry out its activities, adds users `ftp` and `anonymous` to `/etc/ftpusers`, and replaces `klogd` with a backdoor program that allows root shell access. The worm sends a message to two of four addresses in China with information including the compromised host's IP address, process list, history, hosts file, and shadow password file. Then it searches for other hosts to infect.			
Aliases: Linux.Red.Worm, Linux/Red, Linux.Adore.Worm			
SadMind	worm	Sol thru Sol 7 Microsoft IIS	May 2001
SadMind exploits an old buffer overflow vulnerability in the Solstice `sadmind` program from 1999 to infect Solaris machines. It installs software that then exploits a vulnerability in Microsoft IIS 4 and 5 from 2000 to attack Microsoft IIS Web servers. On the IIS machines, it replaces the front page with a page that profanes the U.S. government and PoizonBOx and says to contact `sysadmcn@yahoo.com.cn` Additionally, it automatically propagates to other Solaris machines. It also adds ++ to `root`'s `.rhosts` file. After compromising 2000 IIS systems, it also modifies `index.html` on the Solaris machine to have the same message as the IIS machines.			
Aliases: Backdoor, Sadmind, BoxPoison, Sadmind.worm, sadmind/IIS, Unix/AdmWorm, Unix/SadMind			

TABLE 6.1 Continued

Name	Type	OS	Discovery Date
Linux.Cheese.Worm	worm	L	May 2001
This worm attempts to be good. It searches for systems infected with Linus.Lion.Worm and attempts to fix the security hole that allowed replication. It blanks any lines in `/etc/inetd.conf` that contain `/bin/sh` and scans for other systems infected by Linux.Lion.Worm. Aliases: Linux/Cheese, Cheese			
MacOS/Simpsons@MM	worm	Macintosh	June 2001
This is an AppleScript worm designed to spread with Mac OS 9.0 and higher and Microsoft Outlook Express 5.0.2 or Entourage. It arrives as an email attachment to a message with the subject `Secret Simpsons Episodes!` Running the attachment causes Internet Explorer 5 to go to `http://www.snpp.com/episodeguide.html`, and causes the script to copy itself to the StartupItems folder. This infects the local machine. The worm spreads by sending itself via email to contacts listed in the infected user's address book. Aliases: Mac.Simpson, Mac/Simpsons@mm, Mac.Simpsons, AplS/Simpsons			
Linux/Rst-A	virus	L	February 2002
This virus attempts to infect all ELF executables in the current working directory and in `/bin/`. The virus also attempts to open a UDP socket on port 5503 or higher to wait for a certain packet from the attacker, and then opens a TCP connection with the attacker and starts up a shell for the attacker to use.			
Linux/Osf	virus	L	March 2002
This virus attempts to infect 200 ELF binaries in the current working directory and in `/bin/`. The size of infected binaries is increased by 8759 bytes. If the virus is executed by a privileged user, it attempts to open a backdoor server by opening a socket on port 3049 or higher and waiting for specially configured packets that contain the backdoor program. Aliases: Linux/OSF-A, Linux.Jac.8759			
BSD/Scalper.worm	worm	FreeBSD	June 2002
`BSD/Scalper.worm` affects FreeBSD 4.5 running Apache 1.3.20-1.3.24, although it is recommended that all Apache users upgrade to the latest version. It exploits the transfer-chunk encoding vulnerability in Apache to infect a machine. The worm scans for vulnerable hosts, transfers itself in uuencoded form to `/tmp/.uua`, decodes itself to `/tmp/.a`, and then executes the decoded file. Each worm keeps a list of all the IPSs infected from it. It includes backdoor functionality that allows a remote attacker to launch denial of service attacks. Additionally, a remote attacker can execute arbitrary commands, scan files for email addresses, send mail, access Web pages, and open connections on other ports. Aliases: ELF/Scalper-A, Linux.Scapler.Worm, Linux/Echapa.worm, Scalper-A, Scalper.worm, Echapa.worm, ELF/Scalper-A, FreeApworm, FreeBSD.Scalper.Worm, ELF_SCALPER_A			
OpenSSH 3.4.p1	Trojan	Unix	July 2002
Trojan horse versions of OpenSSH 3.4p1 were distributed from the FTP server that hosts `ftp.openssh.com` from approximately July 30 or 31 until August 1. The Trojan version contains malicious code in the makefile that at compile time opens a channel on port 6667 to a specific host and also opens a shell as the user who compiled OpenSSH. The solution is to verify the integrity of your sources and download again or to just download the sources again.			

TABLE 6.1 Continued

Name	Type	OS	Discovery Date
Linux.Slapper.Worm	worm	L: RH, Deb, Su, Man, Sl	September 2002
This worm uses an OpenSSL buffer overflow vulnerability to run a remote shell to attack specific Linux distributions. It sends an initial HTTP request on port 80 and examines the server header response. It spreads over Apache with `mod_ssl` installed. The worm uploads itself as a uuencoded source file, decodes itself, and compiles itself into an ELF binary, which executes with the IP address of the attacking computer as a parameter. This is used to create a peer-to-peer network, which can then be used to launch a denial of service attack. All worm files are stored in `/tmp`. Variants: Slapper-A, Slapper-B, Slapper-C, Slapper.C2 Aliases: Linux/Slapper-A, Apache/mod_ssl worm, ELF_SLAPPER_A, Worm/Linux.Slapper, Linux/Slapper, Linux.Slapper.a.worm, Slapper.source, Slapper-A			
sendmail8.12.6	Trojan	Unix	September 2002
Trojanized versions of sendmail8.12.6 were distributed on FTP servers between September 28 and October 6, 2002. Versions distributed via HTTP do not appear to be Trojanized. However, it is recommended that if you obtained the sendmail8.12.6 distribution during that time, it is best to get another copy of the sendmail distribution. See Unix/Backdoor-ADM for details on the malicious code that is executed.			
Unix/Backdoor-ADM	Trojan	Unix	September 2002
Backdoor code that is executed when the Trojanized sendmail8.12.6 is compiled. The code forks a process that connects to 66.37.138.99 on port 6667. It allows an attacker to open a shell with the privileges of the user who compiled sendmail. The process is not persistent with a reboot, but is reestablished if sendmail is recompiled. Aliases: Unix/sendmail-ADM			
Linux/Devnull.A	worm	L: RH, Deb, Su, Man, Sl	September 2002
This uses the same exploit as the Slapper worm and its variants. It sends an invalid GET request to identify a vulnerable Apache system. The worm consists of four files: `shell.sh`, `sslx.c`, `devnull`, and `k`. The first three are used to spread the worm, and `k` is a backdoor Trojan IRC server that can be used to launch a denial of service attack. Aliases: Linux/Slapper.E, Linux.Kaiten.Worm, Worm.Linux.Mighty, Linux/Slapper.worm.d, Linux.Devnull			
Linux.Millen.Worm	worm	L	November 2002
This worm attempts to exploit buffer overflows in some versions of `bind`, `popper`, `imap4`, and `mountd` to gain access to a system. If it succeeds, it downloads and uncompresses mworm.tgz to `/tmp/..../` and sends a message to `trax31337@hotmail.com`. The worm has 46 files. When it has infected a machine, it begins to attack a random IP address. Additionally, the worm opens a backdoor remote shell on TCP/1338 for the attacker. Aliases: Linux/Millen			

TABLE 6.1 Continued

Name	Type	OS	Discovery Date
tcpdump 3.6.2			
tcpdump 3.7.1			
libpcap 0.7.1	Trojan	Unix	November 2002
From November 11–13 Trojan horse versions of tcpdump and libpcap were distributed. The Trojan horse tcpdump contains malicious code that is executed at compile time. The malicious code connects to a specific host on port 80 and downloads a file called `services`. This file generates a c file that is compiled and run. The resulting binary makes a connection to a specific host on port 1963 and reads a single byte. The action taken can be one of three things. If it reads A, the Trojan horse exits; D, the Trojan forks itself, creates a shell, and redirects the shell to the connected host; M, the Trojan closes the connection and sleeps for 3600 seconds. To disguise the activity, a Trojan libpcap (libpcap is the underlying library for tcpdump) ignores all traffic on port 1963. The solution is to download new sources and verify their integrity.			
Trojan.Linux.JBellz	Trojan	L Su 8.0 SI .8.0	January 2003
This Trojan is a malformed `.mp3` file. When played with a specific version of mpg123 player, it recursively deletes all files in the current user's home directory.			
Aliases: Exploit-JBellz, JBellz, TROJ_JBELLZ.A			

This table includes every Macintosh, or Macintosh-related virus, (excluding MS Word macroviruses) know by Symantec and McAfee, two of the foremost antivirus software vendors. In it are 26 Mac viruses. There are roughly 600 Microsoft Word macroviruses that are not covered, the vast majority (530 or so) of which are functional on the Mac.

By way of comparison, depending on who you ask, there are anywhere between 50,000 and 62,000 viruses in total, with the predominantly affected platform being Windows machines, and the overwhelming majority being directed at Microsoft Office products such as Outlook, Internet Explorer, Word, Excel, and PowerPoint. As I type this, CNN has yet another story of a Microsoft product run amok, with the `SQL Slammer` worm, mentioned earlier in this chapter, taking down ATMs, and banking and airport scheduling networks around the planet. Coincidentally, CNN's also running an article quoting Bill G. as saying that "security risks have emerged on a scale that few in our industry fully anticipated" (`http://www.cnn.com/2003/TECH/biztech/01/25/microsoft.security.ap/index.html`). One has to give him credit for noting, in the email he's being quoted from, that passwords are "the weak link," but I think it's rather disingenuous of him to call every computing professional outside Microsoft "few in our industry."

Solving the Problem

Two simple steps are all that are required to entirely solve the malware problem:

- Don't run software unless you're absolutely certain what it's going to do. If you know what it's going to do, and it damages your system, it's your own fault for running the software. Don't want a damaged system, don't run that!

- Don't run software that can run software for you, unless you're absolutely certain what it, and the software it will run, are going to do. Software that can run other software for you, especially anonymous software that's been sent to it by anonymous users on the Internet, is so obviously unsafe that we shouldn't have to say this. Millions upon millions of computer users around the world who ignore this rule, though, prove that we need to say it anyway.

If only you would live by these two rules, and force anyone else who uses your computer to do the same, you'd be completely safe from all forms of malware.

Unfortunately, it's not practical to live your computing life 100% by these rules. Even if you tried 100% to abide (and we recommend that you do try!), there would be times where a bug in a program allowed it to do something unexpected, and you'd miss your 100% success mark. It's useful to add a few other things to the mix, in addition to trying to abide by rules 1 and 2, as often as you can:

- Pick your software for its known performance in the real world. There's an old computing adage that says that every program has at least one bug, and at least some extraneous code. The joking corollary to this adage is that this implies that every program can be reduced, until it's a single line of code that doesn't work. Jokes or no, a history of bugs and design misfeatures is likely to imply a future of them as well. Promises are promises, and infected computers are infected computers, promises or no.
- Use virus/worm/Trojan detection software to catch malware entering your system before it has a chance to activate. Even if the software you're using is securely designed, you don't want to be the first person on whom a new virus that targets a recently discovered bug is tried. You also don't want to be redistributing viruses to other, less security-conscious users just because they're dormant on your system.
- Keep up with your vendor's software patches. This means both Apple's patches and patches that other software vendors make available for their software. If your software is designed securely, the bugs will get you. Patches fix bugs.

These supplementary rules, however, are useless if you don't try to apply rules 1 and 2. If you're running software that's vulnerable by design, you can be hit by every new virus or worm that comes along. Virus scanner updates and vendor patches come out after the vulnerability has been found, and usually after it is exploited.

Table 6.2 includes a listing of interesting antiviral solutions for Mac OS X. Some of these can be run to scan all the files on your machine, or on removable media as it's inserted. Others monitor the network (specifically the mail system) and try to pry viruses out of email messages before they're even delivered. Apply any and all that are appropriate in your situation. The fact that Mac OS has not historically been the target of considerable malware is partly a feature of its overall small market share, but it's probably more a feature of the older Mac OS design—virus and worm attacks weren't easy. Now, with Unix, they can be. Whether they *will* be, will depend on whether you choose to run software that makes it hard, or makes it easy for them to exist.

TABLE 6.2 Antiviral (and Other Antimalware) Solutions for Mac OS X

Package	OS	Availability
Virus Barrier	Mac OS X 10.1.1 and higher Mac OS 8.1 and higher	`http://www.intego.com/virusbarrier/`
Sophos Anti-Virus	Mac OS X Mac OS 8.1 and higher	`http://www.sophos.com/`
Norton Anti-Virus 8.0	Mac OS X 10.1 and higher Mac OS 8.1 and higher	`http://www.symantec.com/nav/nav_mac/`
Virex 7	Mac OS X 10.0.3 and higher	`http://www.mcafeeb2b.com/products/virex/`
Open AntiVirus Project	JRE 1.3 or later	`http://www.openantivirus.org/`
The Open AntiVirus Project includes the ScannerDaemon, VirusHammer, and PatternFinder projects, which compose a Java-based virus scanner. The project warns that it is still under development and should not be used as the only virus protection. Does not detect polymorphic viruses.		
Clam AntiVirus	Linux, Solaris, FreeBSD, OpenBSD, NetBSD, AIX, Mac OS X, Cobalt MIPS boxes	`http://clamav.elektrapro.com/`
Virus scanner written in C. Uses the virus database from the Open AntiVirus project. Can also detect polymorphic viruses.		

Some Virus Scanning/Virus Blocking/Mail Filtering Packages for Mail Servers

Package	Mail Transport Agent	Availability
CGvirusscan 1.0	CommuniGate Pro	`http://www.macosxunleashed.com/article.php?sid=2`
A program that interfaces CommuniGate Pro with Virex. Requires Mac OS X with Perl. Written by one of this book's authors, John Ray.		
RAV Anti-Virus for Mac OS X	CommuniGate Pro SurgeMail Courier Postfix	`http://www.raeinternet.com/rav/ravforosx.html`
Antivirus, antispam, content filtering package.		
scan.sh 1.0b1	CommuniGate Pro	`http://projekte.imd.net/`
Mail filtering program that can be used to filter viruses. Requires a Unix with Perl.		

TABLE 6.2 Continued

Package	Mail Transport Agent	Availability
AMaViS—A Mail Virus Scanner	Sendmail Qmail Postfix Exim	`http://www.amavis.org/`
A program that interfaces a mail transport agent with virus scanners. Tested on Linux, Solaris, *BSD, AIX, HP-UX. Expected to be portable to other Unixes.		
MIMEDefang	Sendmail	`http://www.roaringpenguin.com/mimedefang/`
An email filter that can be used to filter viruses. Tested on Linux. Requires Perl 5.001 or higher, various Perl modules, and Sendmail 8.12.3 or higher.		
sendmail::Milter	Sendmail	`http://sourceforge.net/projects/sendmail-milter/`
Perl module for writing filters for milter, the mail filter API for Sendmail.		
Inflex	Sendmail	`http://pldaniels.com/inflex/`
Email scanner that can be used to scan for viruses. Linux, FreeBSD, or Solaris.		
XaMime	Sendmail Postfix	`http://xamime.com/`
Email filter that enables a mail transport agent to interface with virus scanners. Linux, Solaris, or FreeBSD.		
MessageWall	sendmail Postfix Exim Qmail Any RFC-compliant MTA	`http://www.messagewall.org/`
SMTP proxy that keeps out viruses, spam, and mail relaying. Unix with an ANSI C compiler.		

Summary

This chapter has covered the general range of automated, autonomous malicious software. While reading it, we hope you've also come to understand the process by which these malwares propagate—in particular, how poorly designed server and client software facilitates their spread. In some places we might be accused of being moderately melodramatic, but the malware problem is largely a social one, and the incredible number of users who remain ignorant of the consequences of their software choices drives us to be sometimes rather strident in our attempts to communicate. Users need to be educated; users need to understand the software they use, both for the benefits that it provides and for the problems it creates; and users need to make an informed choice regarding this software. We're trusting that after you're informed, you'll make a good choice, and take your responsibilities as a member of the networked community seriously.

7

Eavesdropping and Snooping for Information: Sniffers and Scanners

IN THIS CHAPTER

- Eavesdropping and Information Gathering
- Monitoring Traffic with `tcpdump`
- Sniffing Around with Ettercap
- Network Surveys with NMAP
- Other Information-Gathering Tools
- Ethics of Information Gathering
- Additional Resources

There's a common saying that if you want a computer secure from network attacks, you should unplug the network cable (or remove your AirPort card). Although this is obviously not a feasible solution, the fact remains that no matter how tightly secured your computer configuration is, the moment information is transmitted over the network, it's an open target for eavesdropping—and the attacker need never directly "attack" your computer to glean information such as credit cards, passwords, and other sensitive data.

Eavesdropping and Information Gathering

Try as we might, if information leaves our hands, it is no longer within our ability to protect it. If we place a letter in the mailbox and an unscrupulous individual removes it without our knowledge, there's very little we can do about it. Of course, there's always a possibility of tracking the individual down later, but, for the most part, we have to rely on faith in our fellow human beings and hope that our mail won't be in the wrong place at the wrong time. Alternatively, we can develop secret coding systems and write all our letters in code, but when we send the message, it still needs to go through the postal service and is still out of our control. It may even be intercepted by someone with a decoder ring who can break our code.

Network security is very much analogous to the postal system. We hope that information reaches its destination without being intercepted, but it's very possible that someone can and will sneak a peak somewhere along the route.

This chapter discusses two types of "nonattacks" that, while not directly harmful to your system, ultimately may place it in risk of compromise:

- **Sniffing**—A sniffer works by actively listening to *all* network traffic rather than data specifically addressed to the computer on which it's running. In doing so, it can record conversations on critical machines such as mail, file, and database servers. Modern sniffers even provide password parsing filters to create a ready-to-use list of usernames and passwords pulled from the traffic stream.
- **Scanning**—Scanning, like sniffing, does not directly target a computer's weakness. Instead, it attempts to identify the active services a computer is running. Attackers typically scan entire networks to locate potential target machines. As soon as the targets are located, a *real* attack can begin.

  The reaction of many administrators to these threats is one of indifference. Sure, they sound bad, but what are the chances that they'll actually happen to you? How many people are talented enough to write the code to do this sort of thing? The answers may startle you. First, chances are extremely high that any Internet-connected machine will be scanned—it's a virtual certainty. If an exploit can be found or an account hacked, it's very likely that a sniffer will be used. Second, no talent, programming, or networking experience is required to eavesdrop on a network. For example, consider this information:

```
140.2.82.82:2100 -> 140.254.xx.xx:110          pop3
USER: kinder
PASS: sef1221

216.2.29.89:61020 -> 140.254.xx.xx:110                 pop3
USER: defi
PASS: camping

164.1.35.174:58137 -> 140.254.xx.xx:110                pop3
USER: jmiller
PASS: dogg119

128.1.202.3:4656 -> 140.254.xx.xx:110          pop3
USER: thalheimer
PASS: ggghhh
```

These are (obviously) a collection of POP passwords, but where did they come from? The answer is a piece of software that works like this:

1. You start it.
2. You tell it to record passwords.
3. You take the recorded password file and go.

The user doesn't need to know anything other than how to run a program. In this example, the four collected passwords were taken from an idle network at roughly 2:00 a.m. over a period of about 10 seconds. The sniffer can run from any machine on the same network as the traffic that is to be watched. With the advent (and poor security) of wireless networks, the potential sniffer could be someone with a laptop sitting in a car outside your building.

The good news is that the same information gathering techniques that attackers use to crack your network can also be used to help secure it. Sniffers can be used to monitor network traffic for signs of attack (see Chapter 18, "Alarm Systems: Intrusion Detection"), whereas portscanning can identify potential targets for attackers as well as identify users who may be violating your security policies.

The majority of this chapter will be spent exploring the available information-gathering software for Mac OS X and demonstrating its use.

The Five-Minute TCP/IP Primer

Scanners and sniffers have migrated from the realm of tools for administrators to menu-driven utilities accessible by novices. Although a background in networking isn't necessary, it's still helpful in interpreting the results of the applications that are examined shortly. Let's take a look at what TCP/IP is (and isn't) now.

TCP/IP is the protocol suite that powers the Internet. It was designed by the DoD to be a robust communications standard for linking multiple individual networks into what was originally called the ARPANET. These original LANs were built through the government's standard "lowest bidder" contracting method, and subsequently were incapable of speaking to one another. TCP/IP was designed to link these systems regardless of their operating systems and communications mediums. Over time ARPANET expanded to universities and finally grew to what we know as the Internet.

The OSI (Open Standards Interconnect) Network Model is often used to describe networks. This works particularly well for TCP/IP in that it shows how the different protocols within the TCP/IP suite work with one another and with the physical devices used to generate the actual data transmission.

There are seven layers to the OSI model, as shown in Figure 7.1, each building on the one before it.

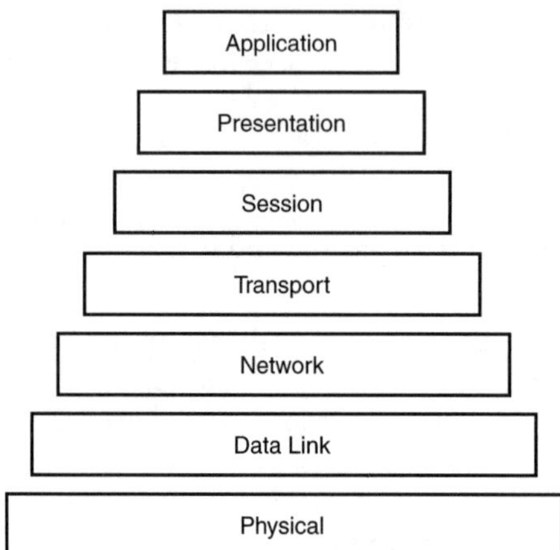

FIGURE 7.1 The OSI model is made up of seven layers.

Physical

The lowest of the layers, the Physical layer, is composed of the hardware that connects computers and devices—network cards, wiring, and so on. For wireless networks, this includes the AirPort card and the carrier frequency of the 802.11a/b/g network. Everything that makes communication possible is included in the Physical layer, except for the actual data transmission standards. TCP/IP does not yet come into play at this layer.

Data Link

The Data Link layer defines a means of addressing and communicating with other network devices connected via the same Physical layer. For Ethernet networks, each device has a unique factory-assigned "MAC" (media access control, not Macintosh!) address and communicates with other devices by dividing data into chunks called *frames*. Each frame contains a source and destination MAC address, a type, a data payload, and a CRC value for error checking.

Other Data Link methodologies such as SLIP and PPP use different addressing standards, but operate in much the same manner.

This layer works to handle packet collisions and signaling errors as it sends data across the Physical layer. It is still very low level, however, as we have yet to touch TCP/IP, which technically starts at the next layer—the Network layer.

Network

The Network layer introduces the "IP" (Internet Protocol) in TCP/IP. An IP address provides a higher-level protocol that maps between the Data Link layer's addresses (MAC addresses for an ethernet) and an "arbitrary" user assigned address—the

Address Resolution Protocol (ARP). By creating a standard addressing scheme that isn't dependent on the underlying hardware, the Network layer also makes possible routing of information from one network (perhaps using an entirely different Physical and/or Data Link standard) to another.

Besides handling high-level addressing, the Network layer introduces the IP *packet* header. An IP packet header contains source and destination IPs along with additional information for routing and error checking. The packet payload itself is formed by the higher-level layers, but each TCP/IP packet *must* include the IP header information to reach its destination. An interesting notion that is also handled within this layer and carried as part of the IP header is packet *fragmentation*. Although this might sound like a "bad" thing, packets must often be fragmented as they move across different Data Link layers that define different data sizes for transmission. By dividing data into the appropriately sized chunks for each Data Link layer, the Network layer can bring together many physically dissimilar networks.

Within the Network layer, the Internet Protocol defines a mechanism for transmitting and receiving information about errors and routing to be communicated between devices. This is known as the ICMP, the Internet Control Message Protocol. ICMP messages can be transmitted to inform clients of routing information, errors in transmission, or other network problems. The most typical "human" use of ICMP is to ping another host to see whether it is reachable:

```
% ping gateway.poisontooth.com
PING gateway.poisontooth.com (10.0.1.1): 56 data bytes
64 bytes from 10.0.1.1: icmp_seq=0 ttl=255 time=3.673 ms
64 bytes from 10.0.1.1: icmp_seq=1 ttl=255 time=5.479 ms
64 bytes from 10.0.1.1: icmp_seq=2 ttl=255 time=2.581 ms
64 bytes from 10.0.1.1: icmp_seq=3 ttl=255 time=2.548 ms
64 bytes from 10.0.1.1: icmp_seq=4 ttl=255 time=2.514 ms
--- gateway.poisontooth.com ping statistics ---
5 packets transmitted, 5 packets received, 0% packet loss
round-trip min/avg/max = 2.514/3.359/5.479 ms
```

ICMP packets, although useful for determining device and network status, are not a foolproof means of diagnosing network conditions. Many firewalls are configured to block ICMP packets because they can be used as remote attackers to probe a network's state.

More information about the Internet Protocol can be found in RFC 791: `http://www.cis.ohio-state.edu/cgi-bin/rfc/rfc0791.html`.

Transport

At the transport layer of the network model fall the protocols that are used to move most data from one machine to another via the Internet Protocol. Although the primary focus in this chapter is on the TCP and UDP protocols, there are actually dozens of protocols that piggyback on top of IP. You can see a list of many of these protocols by viewing the contents of `/etc/protocols`, or visiting `http://www.iana.org/assignments/protocol-numbers`.

Most TCP/IP communication is performed (surprise!) by TCP, the Transmission Control Protocol. The purpose of TCP is to provide reliable data transmission and maintain a virtual "circuit" between devices that are communicating. It is responsible for ensuring that all packets arrive in order and reach their destinations successfully. It accomplishes this by providing a sequence number with each packet it sends, and requiring that an acknowledgement (ACK) is sent by the destination computer with each packet successfully received. If an ACK is not sent by the receiver within a reasonable amount of time, the original packet is retransmitted.

Another popular protocol in the TCP/IP suite is UDP. Unlike TCP, which requires that each packet be received and acknowledged, UDP's purpose is to send information as quickly as possible. Streaming video, games, and other noncritical Internet applications use UDP to provide the "best possible" time-sensitive information given current network conditions. For example, while watching streaming video of a live telecast, it makes little sense to stop playback because a few frames were lost here or there. Instead, UDP sends a continuous stream of data and the remote receiver gets as much of it as it can. There, obviously, is a loss of quality on poor network connections, but the end result is better than having to wait for each and every packet to be verified and acknowledged.

TCP and UDP packets contain within their information a set of *ports*. A port can be considered a virtual outlet on your computer that other machines can "plug into" to receive a particular service. Ports are identified by a number, which, in turn, can be mapped to the service that the port provides. For example, common ports used by the Mac OS X services include

- FTP—21 and 20
- SSH—22
- HTTP—80
- Appleshare over TCP/IP—548

A list of the ports and the services that typically run on them is provided in the file `/etc/services` on your computer. To make a connection, a remote machine opens an arbitrary network port on its end, then connects to a known service port on the remote computer. By specifying a port along with the data being sent, the Transport layer protocols achieve *multiplexing*, or the ability to have multiple simultaneous connections. The port numbers, along with the source and destination addresses, make up a *socket*.

During the lifetime of a TCP/IP connection, there are multiple states that can exist. These are defined in RFC 793 (`http://www.cis.ohio-state.edu/cgi-bin/rfc/rfc0793.html`):

- `LISTEN`. Waiting for a connection request.
- `SYN-SENT`. A connection request has been sent and the device is waiting for an acknowledgement.
- `SYN-RECEIVED`. The connection acknowledgement is received and the device is waiting for a final confirmation.
- `ESTABLISHED`. A connection exists and data can be transmitted and received.
- `FIN-WAIT-1`. Waiting for a connection to be terminated or an acknowledgement of its request to terminate a connection.
- `FIN-WAIT-2`. Waiting for a connection termination request from the remote device.
- `CLOSE-WAIT`. Waiting for a termination request from an upper network layer.
- `CLOSING`. Waiting for a connection termination acknowledgement from remote device.
- `LAST-ACK`. Waiting for the final acknowledgement of connection termination.
- `TIME-WAIT`. Waiting for a given timeout to be sure that a termination acknowledgement has been received.
- `CLOSED`. Connection is closed.

Some denial of service attacks take advantage of the acknowledgement wait states that exist in TCP/IP connections by "starting" to open connections, then not following through with the appropriate termination or acknowledgements, resulting in the remote device having to wait for a connection timeout before its network resources can be released.

Session

The OSI model defines the Session layer as being responsible for maintaining point-to-point communications between devices. In TCP/IP, this is handled directly by the TCP/UDP and the use of sockets. These protocols span both the Transport and Session layers of the OSI model, so we're left with the real "meat" of TCP/IP communications: the Presentation and Application layers.

Presentation

The TCP/IP Presentation layer is where most of what we consider Internet protocols (not to be confused with *the* Internet Protocol—IP) are found. Protocols such as POP, HTTP, IMAP, and so on are implemented at this layer and generally consist of a network "language" for exchanging information. For example, the SMTP, which runs on port 25, receives incoming messages after an intermachine exchange similar to this:

```
% telnet poisontooth.com 25
Trying 10.0.1.250...
Connected to carrot3.poisontooth.com.
Escape character is '^]'.
220 NOTE: Port scans are logged.
HELO client0.poisontooth.com
250 poisontooth.com we trust you client0.poisontooth.com
MAIL FROM: jray@poisontooth.com
250 jray@poisontooth.com sender accepted
RCPT TO: ray.30@osu.edu
250 ray.30@osu.edu will relay mail from a client address
DATA
354 Enter mail, end with "." on a line by itself
This is a test message.
.
250 1810071 message accepted for delivery
```

In this example, the SMTP responds to the commands `HELO`, `MAIL FROM`, `RCPT TO`, and `DATA`. Each protocol's language varies depending on its purpose, and many cannot be as easily read as SMTP. Nevertheless, this is where most of the "important" information about what is taking place on your network can be gleaned, and is the primary focus for most network sniffers.

Application

The Application layer "hides" everything that falls underneath it. This layer is made up of the applications that use the Presentation layer protocols. This includes your Web browser (Chimera or Mozilla, of course), Apple's Mail application, and so on.

From here on out, we're going to be looking at the tools that can be used to listen in on the traffic on your network. Most of these utilities require that you run them as the superuser so that they can place your network card in *promiscuous* mode. Normally a networked computer passes information up the TCP/IP stack only if the packets are addressed specifically to that machine or are broadcast to the entire network. In promiscuous mode, all traffic will be visible to the computer, regardless of how it is addressed.

SWITCHED NETWORKS AND EAVESDROPPING

Switched networks are the de facto standard for modern LANs. They utilize switches rather than hubs to provide connections to multiple machines. A switch caches the MAC addresses it sees on a given port (known as an ARP cache), and forwards traffic for only those addresses to the port. Machines that are located on different switch ports cannot see one another's traffic.

This makes network monitoring a bit troublesome using legitimate tools unless you can monitor traffic upstream from the switch. There are ways around this problem, such as overflowing a switch's ARP cache so that it "gives up" and passes all traffic like a hub. These techniques, however, are often disruptive to other network devices and are *not* a transparent means of eavesdropping.

CAUTION

The remainder of this chapter assumes that you've read through the TCP/IP introduction and have spent some time reading through the appropriate RFCs. TCP/IP, like many subjects in this book, is not a 5- or 10-, or even 100-page topic. We're attempting to give you the tools and background to get started and understand what you're seeing, not to become a network technician in 35 pages. For more information on TCP/IP, you may want to read *Special Edition Using TCP/IP*, by John Ray, from Que Publishing.

Monitoring Traffic with `tcpdump`

The first utility that we'll look at for monitoring network traffic is `tcpdump`. `tcpdump` outputs the headers of all packets seen by your network interface. It features a sophisticated filter language for limiting the output to a specific host, source, destination, subnet, or any combination thereof.

The most simple use of `tcpdump` is to start it (as root or with sudo) via the command line with no arguments:

```
# tcpdump
1: tcpdump: listening on en1
2: 15:42:28.853450 client0.poisontooth.com.49295 >
➥ carrot3.poisontooth.com.domain:  51668+ CNAME? www.cnn.com. (29)
3: 15:42:28.869908 carrot3.poisontooth.com.domain >
➥  client0.poisontooth.com.49295:  51668* 1/4/4 CNAME cnn.com. (217)
4: 15:42:28.870331 client0.poisontooth.com.49295 >
➥  carrot3.poisontooth.com.domain:  30577+ A? www.cnn.com. (29)
5: 15:42:28.913477 carrot3.poisontooth.com.domain >
➥  client0.poisontooth.com.49295:  30577 9/4/4 CNAME cnn.com.[|domain]
6: 15:42:28.914158 client0.poisontooth.com.49295 >
➥  carrot3.poisontooth.com.domain:  48116+ AAAA? www.cnn.com. (29)
7: 15:42:28.940969 carrot3.poisontooth.com.domain >
➥  client0.poisontooth.com.49295:  48116 1/1/0 CNAME cnn.com. (124)
...
8: 15:42:33.440973 client0.poisontooth.com.49209 >
➥  www3.cnn.com.http: S 4139514020:4139514020(0)
➥  win 32768 <mss 1460,nop,wscale 0,nop,nop,timestamp 34160 0> (DF) [tos 0x10]
```

```
9: 15:42:33.494618 www3.cnn.com.http >
➥ client0.poisontooth.com.49209: S 1497469520:1497469520(0)
➥ ack 4139514021 win 5840 <mss 1460>
10: 15:42:33.494767 client0.poisontooth.com.49209 >
➥ www3.cnn.com.http: . ack 1 win 33580 (DF) [tos 0x10]
11: 15:42:33.525710 client0.poisontooth.com.49209 >
➥ www3.cnn.com.http: P 1:8(7) ack 1 win 33580 (DF) [tos 0x10]
12: 15:42:34.497076 client0.poisontooth.com.49295 >
➥ carrot3.poisontooth.com.domain:  56757+ PTR? 1.1.0.10.in-addr.arpa. (39)
13: 15:42:34.499827 carrot3.poisontooth.com.domain >
➥ client0.poisontooth.com.49295:  56757* 1/1/1 PTR[|domain]
14: 15:42:34.687262 client0.poisontooth.com.49209 >
➥ www3.cnn.com.http: P 1:13(12) ack 1 win 33580 (DF) [tos 0x10]
15: 15:42:34.734041 www3.cnn.com.http >
➥ client0.poisontooth.com.49209: . ack 13 win 5840
16: 15:42:36.568825 www3.cnn.com.http >
➥ client0.poisontooth.com.49209: FP 1:148(147) ack 13 win 5
```

For TCP packets (most of what you'll see), the output of the tcpdump can be read as

```
Time Source-IP.Port > Destination-IP.Port TCP-Flags Segment-Number ack
window(receive buffer) <tcp options>
```

UDP traffic, including name server resolution, is slightly different, as are other transport layer protocols. The `tcpdump` man page defines the output format for several different protocols and is required reading if you want to fully exploit the software.

In the example output, `tcpdump` shows a connection between `client0.poisontooth.com` and `carrot3.poisontooth.com`, where `client0` is requesting a DNS lookup on the `www.cnn.com` domain (lines 2-7). After receiving a response, `client0` proceeds to open a connection with `www3.cnn.com` and begin communicating (lines 8-16). Note that the port is shown as the actual protocol being used, such as `http` instead of `80`. This substitution is made automatically by `tcpdump` when possible.

A more useful example of how `tcpdump` can be used is with a filter to limit the traffic to a specific type. For example, rather than viewing everything on the network, how about simply watching all HTTP communications coming from a given host (in this case `client0.poisontooth.com`)? You do this by adding the filter expression `src host client0.poisontooth.com and dst port 80` to the command. This example also introduces the `-q` flag to hide extraneous protocol information:

```
# tcpdump -q src host client0.poisontooth.com and dst port 80
tcpdump: listening on en1
18:29:54.063689 client0.poisontooth.com.49659 > www1.cnn.com.http: tcp 0 (DF)
18:29:54.114376 client0.poisontooth.com.49659 > www1.cnn.com.http: tcp 0 (DF)
```

```
18:29:54.120766 client0.poisontooth.com.49659 > www1.cnn.com.http: tcp 518 (DF)
18:32:54.259702 client0.poisontooth.com.49659 > www1.cnn.com.http: tcp 0 (DF)
18:29:54.459999 client0.poisontooth.com.49659 > www1.cnn.com.http: tcp 0 (DF)
18:29:54.660246 client0.poisontooth.com.49659 > www1.cnn.com.http: tcp 0 (DF)
18:29:54.860469 client0.poisontooth.com.49659 > www1.cnn.com.http: tcp 0 (DF)
…
18:30:41.777607 client0.poisontooth.com.49638 > www.apple.com.http: tcp 0 (DF)
18:30:41.783227 client0.poisontooth.com.49638 > www.apple.com.http: tcp 267 (DF)
18:30:41.919682 client0.poisontooth.com.49638 > www.apple.com.http: tcp 0 (DF)
18:30:42.088209 client0.poisontooth.com.49638 > www.apple.com.http: tcp 0 (DF)
18:30:42.097456 client0.poisontooth.com.49638 > www.apple.com.http: tcp 0 (DF)
18:30:44.857696 client0.poisontooth.com.49638 > www.apple.com.http: tcp 0 (DF)
18:30:44.987351 client0.poisontooth.com.49638 > www.apple.com.http: tcp 0 (DF)
…
18:30:50.089552 client0.poisontooth.com.49653 >
➥ a209-249-123-244.deploy.akamaitechnologies.com.http: tcp 0 (DF)
18:30:50.141997 client0.poisontooth.com.49653 >
➥ a209-249-123-244.deploy.akamaitechnologies.com.http: tcp 0 (DF)
18:30:50.204663 client0.poisontooth.com.49653 >
➥ a209-249-123-244.deploy.akamaitechnologies.com.http: tcp 445 (DF)
18:30:50.415602 client0.poisontooth.com.49653 >
➥ a209-249-123-244.deploy.akamaitechnologies.com.http: tcp 0 (DF)
```

Here, `tcpdump` reports that HTTP requests originating from `client0.poisontooth.com` have been made to the hosts `www1.cnn.com`, `www.apple.com`, and `a209-249-123-244.deploy.akamaitechnologies.com`.

The Boolean expression to filter traffic can be built using `and` (`&&`), `or` (`||`), and `not` (`!`) and the constructs given in the `tcpdump` man page. The most useful of these expression primitives are reproduced for your reference in Table 7.1.

TABLE 7.1 `tcpdump` Expression Primitives

Primitive	Use
`dst host <host/ip>`	Match packets headed to a hostname or IP.
`src host <host/ip>`	Match packets to or from a hostname or IP.
`host <host/ip>`	Match packets to or from a given hostname or IP.
`ether dst <ethernet address>`	Match packets to a given ethernet address.
`ether src <ethernet address>`	Match packets from an ethernet address.
`ether host <ethernet address>`	Match packets to or from an ethernet address.
`gateway <host/ip>`	Match packets by using the given host or IP as a gateway.
`dst net <network>`	Match packets headed to a given network.
`src net <network>`	Match packets from a specified network.

TABLE 7.1 Continued

Primitive	Use
`net <network>`	Match packets to or from a specified network.
`net <network> mask <netmask>`	Specifies a network by using an address and a 4-octet netmask.
`net <network/mask>`	Specifies a network by using an address followed by a / and the number of bits in the netmask.
`dst port <port>`	Match packets to a specific port.
`src port <port>`	Match packets from a specific port.
`port <port>`	Match packets to or from a specific port.
`less <length>`	Match packets less than the given size.
`greater <length>`	Match packets greater than a given size.
`ip proto <name/number>`	Match packets of IP named or numbered (as in `/etc/protocols`), such as `tcp`, `udp`, `icmp`, and so on.
`ether broadcast`	Match ethernet broadcast packets.
`ip broadcast`	Match IP broadcast packets.
`ether multicast`	Match ethernet multicast packets.

The capability to create custom filter expressions is one of the most powerful features of `tcpdump` and other utilities that use `libpcap`. You may find a number of additional flags and switches useful, all accessed via the `tcpdump` syntax: `tcpdump [options] [expression]`. The common switches are provided in Table 7.2.

TABLE 7.2 Common `tcpdump` Switches

Option	Description
`-a`	Convert network numbers to names.
`-c <packet count>`	Exit after receiving the specified number of packets.
`-n`	Don't convert numbers to names.
`-F <filter file>`	Use the contents of the named file as the filter expression.
`-i <interface>`	Listen on the named network interface.
`-l`	Buffer standard out.
`-q`	Quick/Quiet output. Leave out most extra information beyond source, destination, and ports.
`-r <filename>`	Read packets from file (see `-w`).
`-t`	Don't print a timestamp on each line.
`-v, -vv, -vvv`	Increasingly verbose output.
`-w <filename>`	Write packets to a file for later analysis (see `-r`). This is better than trying to analyze a high-bandwidth/high-activity network in real time, which is likely to result in packet loss.

As you've seen, `tcpdump` can provide extremely targeted or very general information about your network traffic. It fits the definition of a sniffer but does provide tools for attacking a network; its purpose is to help you uncover activity that may violate your network policy or diagnose unusual network communication problems. A Mac OS X GUI for `tcpdump` (MacSniffer) can be downloaded from `http://personalpages.tds.net/~brian_hill/macsniffer.html`.

TIP

If you'd like to try a somewhat fun use for `tcpdump`, download TrafGraf from `http://trafgraf.poisontooth.com/`. This is a simple network traffic graphing that will present a visual snapshot of the communications on your network and help identify high-volume hosts. I wrote it almost four years ago, but, as long as you install the Perl modules mentioned in the readme, it will work fine on Mac OS X 10.2.

HOW CAN I DETECT A SNIFFER?

Sadly, it is next to impossible to detect sniffers on a modern network because they are designed to be completely passive. Errors existed in earlier versions of Linux and Windows that allowed administrators to probe for interfaces in promiscuous mode. Unfortunately, these are long gone. (See `http://www.securiteam.com/tools/AntiSniff_-_find_sniffers_on_your_local_network.html` for details.)

To test to see whether your machine may be running a sniffer (and is thus compromised), use `ifconfig` to display the information for your active network interface. For example:

```
% /sbin/ifconfig en1
en1: flags=8963<UP,BROADCAST,SMART,RUNNING,PROMISC,SIMPLEX,MULTICAST> mtu 1500
        inet6 fe80::230:65ff:fe12:f215%en1 prefixlen 64 scopeid 0x5
        inet 10.0.1.101 netmask 0xffffff00 broadcast 10.0.1.255
        ether 00:30:65:12:f2:15
        media: autoselect status: active
        supported media: autoselect
```

Here you can see the `PROMISC` flag for `en1`, indicating that this interface is in promiscuous mode.

Although sniffers are tough to find and remove, the use of secure protocols (SSL, IPSec, etc) can foil most sniffers easily.

Sniffing Around with Ettercap

Although your computer comes with `tcpdump`, it is not the sort of tool that modern attackers have in their arsenal—after all, it requires that you know how to type. For the lazy attacker, there are much better options, such as ettercap (`http://ettercap.sourceforge.net/`). Ettercap hides many of the details of sniffing behind an easy-to-use interface, and can even sniff switched networks.

A few of the "cool features" listed for version 0.6.7 on the Web site include

- **Characters injection in an established connection**— A user can insert characters into a connection between another machine on the local network and a remote host, effectively hijacking the communications.
- **SSH1 support**—Even though SSH is known for security, ettercap can sniff the encrypted data from SSH1 sessions, easily retrieving usernames and passwords.
- **HTTPS support**—Like SSH1 support, ettercap can easily break into HTTP SSL-encrypted streams!
- **Plug-ins support**—Developers can take advantage of the ettercap API to create their own plug-ins.
- **Password collector**—If a password is detected for the protocols TELNET, FTP, POP, RLOGIN, SSH1, ICQ, SMB, MySQL, HTTP, NNTP, X11, NAPSTER, IRC, RIP, BGP, SOCKS 5, IMAP 4, VNC, LDAP, NFS, SNMP, HALF LIFE, QUAKE 3, MSN, or YMSG, ettercap can log it.
- **OS fingerprint**—Easily identify remote operating systems and the network adaptors they use.
- **Kill a connection**—See a connection between two machines that you want to terminate? Ettercap can do it.
- **Passive scanning of the LAN**—Passive scanning can provide information about your network and the attached hosts without actively sending packets to the machines.
- **Check for other poisoners**—You have ettercap and so do the "bad guys." Detects other ettercaps and spoofing attempts on your network.

What makes ettercap truly dangerous is its capability to carry out ARP poisoning. ARP poisoning exploits the stateless nature of the ARP. Normally, machines send out an ARP request asking for the address of another machine, and presumably receive a reply. In ARP poisoning, the replies are sent *without* a request being made. The sniffer essentially tells the rest of the network that it *is* every other machine on the network—and subsequently receives traffic for those machines. This type of attack is easily identified by viewing the ARP cache of a machine on the poisoned network (`arp -a`). If multiple machines map to a single MAC address, you may be viewing the result of ARP poisoning.

NOTE

There are perfectly legitimate reasons for multiple IPs and hostnames to be attached to a single MAC address. Multihomed servers and terminal servers, for example, often have multiple IP addresses assigned to a single network interface.

Ettercap, for all the attack capabilities built in, also features an extremely useful ARP poisoning detector, making it an effective tool against the very people who use it inappropriately.

You can download a precompiled `.pkg` version of the latest ettercap release from `http://ettercap.sourceforge.net/index.php?s=download&p=binary`.

After downloading and installing, start ettercap with `/usr/sbin/ettercap`. If you have multiple active network interfaces, use the switch `-i` *<interface>* to choose which will be used.

When starting, ettercap initially scans your network and collects IP and MAC addresses for all active machines, and displays two identical columns with the located devices. Figure 7.2 shows the initial ettercap screen.

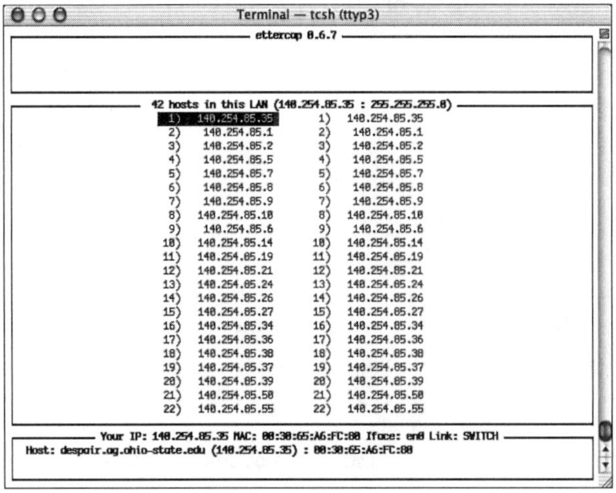

FIGURE 7.2 All active LAN devices are shown.

Ettercap is a cursor-based program that you can navigate with your keyboard's arrow keys. Help can be shown at any time if you press h. In the initial display, the left column is used to pick a potential *source* for sniffing, whereas the right column is the destination. You can choose one, both, or neither (to sniff everything) by moving your cursor to the appropriate selection in one column, pressing Return, then doing the same in the next. To deselect an address, push the spacebar. Figure 7.3 shows a selected source and destination pair.

After choosing your targets, you can use the key commands in Table 7.3 to start sniffing and monitoring the hosts. Several commands do not require a source or destination and simply operate on the entire network, or on the actively highlighted machine.

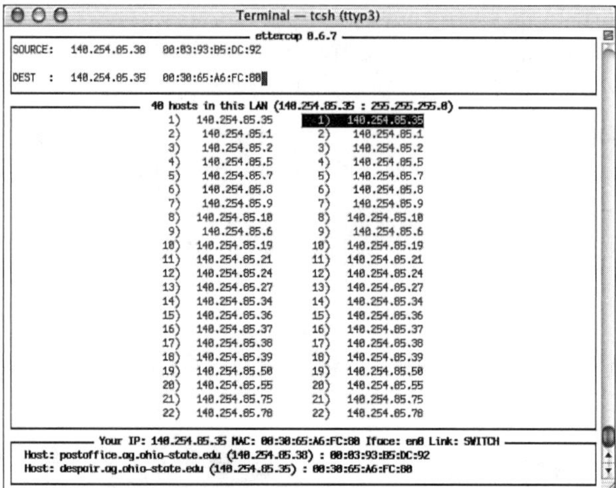

FIGURE 7.3 Choose the targets you want to sniff, or leave either field empty to sniff all hosts.

TABLE 7.3 Ettercap Sniffing Commands

Keystroke	Purpose
a	Start sniffing using ARP poisoning.
s	Sniff based on the IP addresses of the selected machines.
m	Sniff based on the MAC addresses of the selected machines.
j	Poison the ARP caches of the chosen machines, but do not sniff.
x	Forge a packet (including all headers, payload, and so on) from the chosen source computer to the destination.
d	Delete an entry from the list; it will not be subjected to ARP poisoning if unlisted.
f	Fingerprint the remote OS.
o	Passively identify hosts on the network.
c	Check for ARP poisoners; ettercap will identify all hosts responding to more than one IP address.
r	Refresh the host listing.

After ettercap has started sniffing, the screen will refresh with a new display listing all the active connections that you can monitor, as shown in Figure 7.4. In this example, there are three connections: SSH, NetBIOS, and FTP.

Use the arrow keys to choose an interesting connection (such as the FTP session shown in the figure), the press Enter, or use one of the other options, shown in Table 7.4.

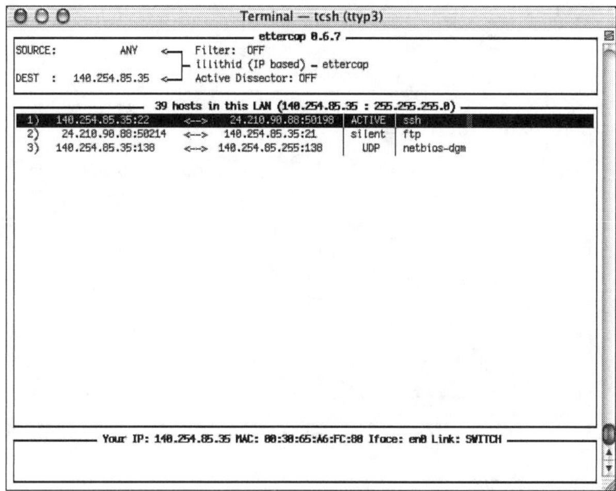

FIGURE 7.4 Choose the connection to monitor.

TABLE 7.4 Choose What to Sniff

Keystroke	Purpose
`return`	Sniff the connection.
`x`	Forge a packet within a connection.
`f`	Filter the connections based on packet attributes, such as port numbers.
`a`	Turn on active password collection.
`l`	Log all collected passwords (FTP, SSH, Telnet, and so on) to a file. The file will be named with the current date and time.
`k`	Kill the selected connection.
`d`	Resolve the selected IP
`r`	Refresh the list.

Assuming you chose to sniff the connection, the right side of the screen will refresh with a log of the data coming from the source, whereas the left will contain the responses sent from the destination. Figure 7.5 shows a sniffed FTP login that has failed.

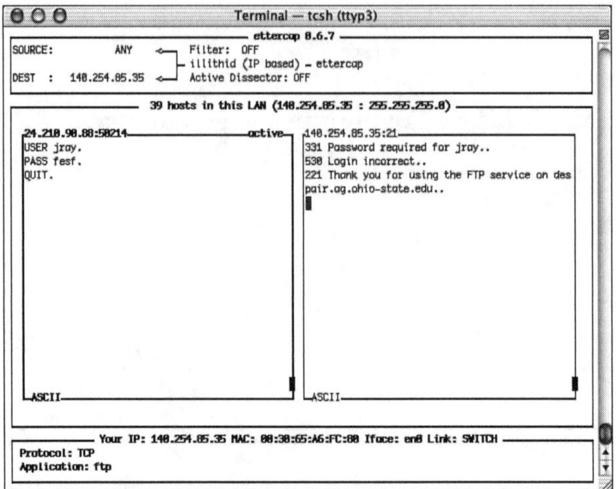

FIGURE 7.5 Watch the Presentation layer data in real time.

Use the key commands in Table 7.5 to control the sniffed connection.

TABLE 7.5 Control the Sniffed Connection

Keystroke	Purpose
k	Kill the connection.
a	ASCII view of the sniffed data.
h	Hex view of the sniffed data.
j	Join the source and destination windows.
t	Display only text (readable) characters.
i	Inject characters into the connection.
l	Log the sniffed data to a file.
b	Bind the sniffed data to a port. (You can then connect to this port on the sniffer to monitor the connection.)
q	Exit to the previous screen.

As you can see, ettercap is easy to use and extremely powerful. I highly suggest that you read through the available help screens and be *very* careful with what you choose to do. The default distribution of ettercap includes a number of external plug-ins ranging from ettercap detectors to DoS attack implementations (for informational purposes only).

TIP

Using the cursor-controlled interface is the most user-friendly means of operating ettercap, but for those who want to run it via script or launch it as a daemon, all functions are accessible via the command line. Type `/usr/sbin/ettercap -h` to display the command-line syntax.

Network Surveys with NMAP

Although sniffing is often an effective means of gathering information about (and from) machines on a network, it is easily detectable when using ARP poisoning; with passive eavesdropping, it is easy to defeat it by using a switched network. Sniffing is also limited to machines located along the path of the communication: A machine in California, for example, cannot sniff a machine in Ohio unless the Ohio traffic is being routed through the California network.

For remote information gathering, most attackers rely on portscanning. A portscan is simply a report of the open ports on a remote machine. For example, this is a portscan of a remote mail server:

```
# /usr/local/bin/nmap -sS -O mailserver.ag.ohio-state.edu
Starting nmap V. 3.00 ( www.insecure.org/nmap/ )
Interesting ports on mailserver.ag.ohio-state.edu (10.0.1.99):
(The 1583 ports scanned but not shown below are in state: closed)
Port       State      Service
22/tcp     open       ssh
25/tcp     open       smtp
80/tcp     open       http
106/tcp    open       pop3pw
110/tcp    open       pop-3
143/tcp    open       imap2
497/tcp    open       dantz
548/tcp    open       afpovertcp
9100/tcp   open       jetdirect
Remote operating system guess: Mac OS X 10.1 - 10.1.4
Uptime 26.951 days (since Mon Nov 18 11:30:09 2002)
```

Not only are the open services displayed, but information about the operating system version and system status. There are a number of ways to determine what ports are open on a machine, the most obvious being to create and then tear down a connection to a remote machine (a "TCP Connect" scan). This is the approach that is taken by Apple's portscan tool within the Network Utility application (also accessible from the command line as `/Applications/Utilities/Network Utility.app/Contents/Resources/stroke <address> <start port> <end port>`).

The trouble with this approach is that the connection, because it is complete, is easily logged and tracked by the operating system. For a remote attacker that wants to catalog the computing inventory of an entire university, attempting a TCP connect scan will very quickly lead to its discovery.

Rather than taking this direct (and detectable) route, attackers employ a variety of "stealth" scans that do not carry out the process of setting up a complete connection.

Instead they typically send a packet to begin setting up a connection, wait to see the response, then drop the connection attempt. For example, the SYN stealth scan "knows" that a SYN packet sent to a given port is required by RFC 793 (`http://www.cis.ohio-state.edu/cgi-bin/rfc/rfc0793.html`) to respond with a SYN, ACK, or RST packet. If an RST is received, the port is closed, whereas SYN or ACK indicate an open port. This sequence takes place low enough in the TCP/IP stack that it is not logged on many machines, and is not made available to intrusion detection software that simply watches for connections.

The "cream" of the portscanning crop is NMAP—a program designed to be the ultimate remote reconnaissance tool. NMAP supports more than 10 unique scans, including an "idle" scan that does not require any packets to be sent between the scanner and the scannee. A nice introduction to NMAP scanning can be found at `http://www.insecure.org/nmap/lamont-nmap-guide.txt`.

In addition to simply scanning a remote host, NMAP also makes it possible to scan entire subnets, hide behind decoys, and fingerprint remote operating systems. After a scan is completed, an attacker can simply take the NMAP output (including operating systems and versions) and cross-reference it with available exploits, creating his or her own personal guide to chaos. For the administrator, however, NMAP can provide a list of machines that need attention—either to be locked down or upgraded to a later version of the operating system.

NOTE

Before you say, "But shouldn't the administrator already *know* what's on the network?" consider that many universities and companies have employees that bring their own personal computers to work, or carry laptops back and forth from home. Unless networkwide authentication is in place, it is virtually impossible to fully control the computing environment of a large institution.

HOW CAN I DETECT A PORTSCAN?

So, should NMAP be taken as a risk? Consider the comments of John Green, U.S. Naval Surface Warfare Center, `http://www.sans.org/resources/idfaq/what_is_nmap.php`:

"The intelligence that can be garnered by using NMAP is extensive. It provides all the information that is needed for a well-informed, full-fledged, precisely targeted assault on a network. Such an attack would have a high probability of success, and would likely go unnoticed by organizations that lack intrusion detection capabilities."

Thankfully, most stealth portscans can be detected and blocked by intrusion detection software (see Chapter 18) or simply defeated by a firewall (see Chapter 17).

Remember that a portscan is an information-*gathering* device, not an exploit in and of itself. If your operating system and software is secured, an attacker will still not be able to gain access to the system.

Installing NMAP

To install NMAP, download the latest release from `http://download.insecure.org/nmap/dist/`, then unarchive, and enter the NMAP distribution directory:

```
% curl -O http://download.insecure.org/nmap/dist/nmap-3.00.tgz
% tar zxf nmap-3.00.tgz
% cd nmap-3.00
```

Next, configure the source with `configure --mandir=/usr/share/man`:

```
% ./configure --mandir=/usr/share/man
checking for gcc... gcc
checking for C compiler default output... a.out
checking whether the C compiler works... yes
checking whether we are cross compiling... no
checking for suffix of executables...
checking for suffix of object files... o
checking whether we are using the GNU C compiler... yes
checking whether gcc accepts -g... yes
checking build system type... powerpc-apple-darwin6.2
checking host system type... powerpc-apple-darwin6.2
...
```

Finally, compile and install the software with `make` followed by `make install`:

```
% make
Compiling libnbase
cd nbase; make
gcc -g -O2 -Wall  -g   -DHAVE_CONFIG_H -DNCRACK_VERSION=\"\"
-DHAVE_CONFIG_H=1    -c -o snprintf.o snprintf.c
gcc -g -O2 -Wall  -g   -DHAVE_CONFIG_H -DNCRACK_VERSION=\"\"
-DHAVE_CONFIG_H=1    -c -o getopt.o getopt.c
Compiling libnbase
rm -f libnbase.a
ar cr libnbase.a snprintf.o getopt.o getopt1.o nbase_str.o nbase_misc.o
ranlib libnbase.a
...

# make install
Compiling libnbase
cd nbase; make
make[1]: Nothing to be done for `all'.
./shtool mkdir -f -p -m 755 /usr/local/bin
/usr/share/man/man1 /usr/local/share/nmap /usr/local/share/gnome/apps/Utilities
```

```
./shtool install  -c -m 755 nmap /usr/local/bin/nmap
If the next command fails -- you cannot use the X front end
test -f nmapfe/nmapfe && ./shtool install  -c
-m 755 nmapfe/nmapfe /usr/local/bin/nmapfe &&
./shtool mkln -f -s /usr/local/bin/nmapfe
/usr/local/bin/xnmap && ./shtool install  -c -m 644 nmapfe.desktop
make: [install] Error 1 (ignored)
./shtool install  -c -m 644 docs/nmap.1 /usr/share/man/man1/nmap.1
./shtool install  -c -m 644 nmap-services  /usr/local/share/nmap/nmap-services
./shtool install  -c -m 644 nmap-protocols  /usr/local/share/nmap/nmap-protocols
./shtool install  -c -m 644 nmap-rpc  /usr/local/share/nmap/nmap-rpc
```

TIP

If you'd rather not compile NMAP by hand, it is available as part of the Fink project for easy installation. See `http://fink.sourceforge.net/index.php` for details.

Using NMAP

The NMAP syntax is `nmap [scan type] [options] [hosts or networks…]`. Table 7.6 contains the most common and useful of the NMAP scan types and options. For a lengthy insight into the different scan types, read the NMAP man page.

TABLE 7.6 Basic NMAP Options

Option	Purpose
`-sS`	TCP SYN stealth port scan (default if root).
`-sT`	TCP connect scan (default if unprivileged, that is, not root).
`-sU`	UDP port scan
`-sP`	Ping scan.
`-sF`	Stealth FIN scan.
`-sX`	Stealth Xmas scan.
`-sN`	Stealth Null scan.
`-sR`	RPC scan.
`-sA`	ACK scan.
`-sW`	Window scan.
`-sL`	List scan.
`-I`	Identd scan (identify the user owning the remote process).
`-O`	Use TCP/IP fingerprinting to identify operating system.
`-p` *<port list>*	A port or range of ports specified in the format `-<start>-<end>,<port>,<port>,....`
`-F`	Only scan ports listed in NMAP's `nmap-services` file.

TABLE 7.6 Continued

<table>
<tr><th>Option</th><th>Purpose</th></tr>
<tr><td>-v</td><td>Increase verbosity of output. Can be used twice for maximum output.</td></tr>
<tr><td>-P0</td><td>Don't ping hosts.</td></tr>
<tr><td>-D <decoy host>, <decoy host>,...</td><td>Use spoofed decoys to make the scan appear to come from multiple different machines.</td></tr>
<tr><td>-T <Paranoid|Sneaky|Polite|Normal|Aggressive|Insane></td><td>Set the timing policy. Paranoid scans are slow and difficult for intrusion detection systems to detect, whereas the opposite end of the spectrum—Insane scans—happen as quickly as possible and may even lose data.</td></tr>
<tr><td>-n</td><td>Never perform DNS resolution.</td></tr>
<tr><td>-R</td><td>Always perform DNS resolution.</td></tr>
<tr><td>-oN <filename|-></td><td>Output normal logfile or use - to output to standard out.</td></tr>
<tr><td>-oX <filename|-></td><td>Output XML logfile or use - to output to standard out.</td></tr>
<tr><td>-oG <filename|-></td><td>Output greppable (searchable) logfile or use - to output to standard out.</td></tr>
<tr><td>-oS <filename|-></td><td>Output the results in "Script Kiddie" format. Amusing!</td></tr>
<tr><td>-iL <filename|-></td><td>Read target list from the named file, or use - to read the target list from standard in.</td></tr>
<tr><td>-e</td><td>Specify network interface.</td></tr>
<tr><td>--interactive</td><td>Enter interactive mode.</td></tr>
</table>

For example, to perform a simple stealth scan with fingerprinting on the host `www.atestdomain.com`, one could use `/usr/local/bin/nmap -sS -O www.atestdomain.com`:

```
# /usr/local/bin/nmap -sS -O www.atestdomain.com

Starting nmap V. 3.00 ( www.insecure.org/nmap/ )
Interesting ports on www.atestdomain.com (20.0.1.99):
(The 1594 ports scanned but not shown below are in state: closed)
Port       State       Service
21/tcp     open        ftp
22/tcp     open        ssh
80/tcp     open        http
427/tcp    open        svrloc
497/tcp    open        dantz
548/tcp    open        afpovertcp
3306/tcp   open        mysql
Remote operating system guess: Mac OS X 10.1 - 10.1.4
Uptime 32.086 days (since Wed Nov 13 09:49:51 2002)
```

More useful is the ability to map an entire network. This can be done by specifying ranges in IP addresses (10.0.1.1-100, 10.0.1-10.* or IP address/network mask). The notations `10.0.1.*`, `10.0.1.1-255`, and `10.0.1.0/24`, for example, are three identical ways of describing a class C subnet `10.0.1.x`. Coupling a network scan with a handful of spoofed decoys can be an effective means of mapping a network and confusing intrusion detection systems along the way.

For example,

```
# /usr/local/bin/nmap -sS -D 192.168.0.5,192.168.0.6,10.0.1.99, -O 10.0.1.0/24
```

would create a map of all device services on the subnet `10.0.1.0/24`, including an OS fingerprint, and would spoof scans coming from the machines `192.168.0.5`, `192.168.0.6`, and `10.0.1.99` to help cover one's tracks.

CAUTION

The spoofed decoys are used *in addition* to the machine originating the scan. Because packets need to return to the scanner for it to analyze the data, the decoys serve only to muddy the water for remote intrusion detection systems and logs. They do not fully cover your scan.

NMAP offers two interfaces to its operation: the command-line interface you've seen, and an interactive mode that is accessible when you start `nmap` with the `--interactive` flag. If you'd prefer a more "GUI" approach to your scanning, check out NMAP v.X (`http://nmap-v-x.sourceforge.net/`) and NmapFE (`http://faktory.org/m/software/nmap/`). Both utilities wrap the Aqua GUI around the NMAP command-line software.

Other Information-Gathering Tools

A number of other tools are available for Mac OS X and Unix systems that can be used against your network, or to help protect it. Much of this software uses sniffing and portscanning as a means of gathering information, but rather than leaving it up to you to interpret the results, it provides highly specialized reporting features to simplify analysis. Rounding out this chapter, we'll take a look at a few of these packages so that you can have the best tools for defense, or at least see what crackers will be using against you.

Wireless Sniffing: KisMAC

The advent of wireless networks and their inherent security risks (generally left open, insecure/hackable encryption, and so on) has inspired a new hacking sport, "wardriving." Wardriving involves packing your wireless laptop up into your car, then driving around town while it scans for open wireless access points. There are a number of Windows and Linux applications for this purpose, but the Mac has been lacking until recently.

The application KisMAC (`http://www.binaervarianz.de/projekte/programmieren/kismac/`) provides wireless sniffing capabilities and can identify access points, clients, hardware manufacturers, and even decrypt WEP passwords. KisMAC's network status and client identifier is shown in Figure 7.6.

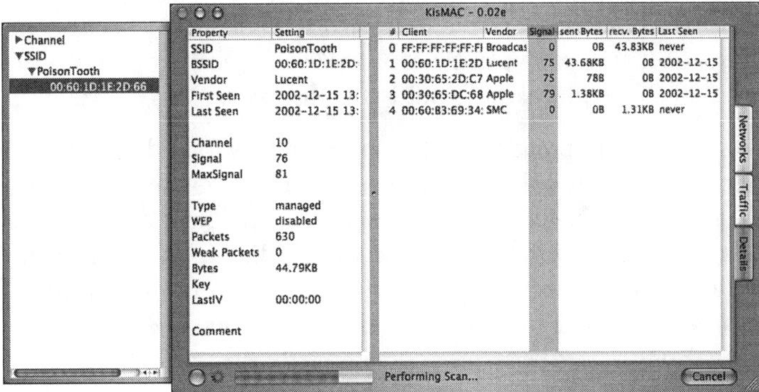

FIGURE 7.6 KisMAC can sniff out wireless networks and even crack WEP encryption.

To determine the amount of activity on a network (that is, whether it's worth your time to watch), KisMAC even provides usage graphing under a separate tab, as shown in Figure 7.7.

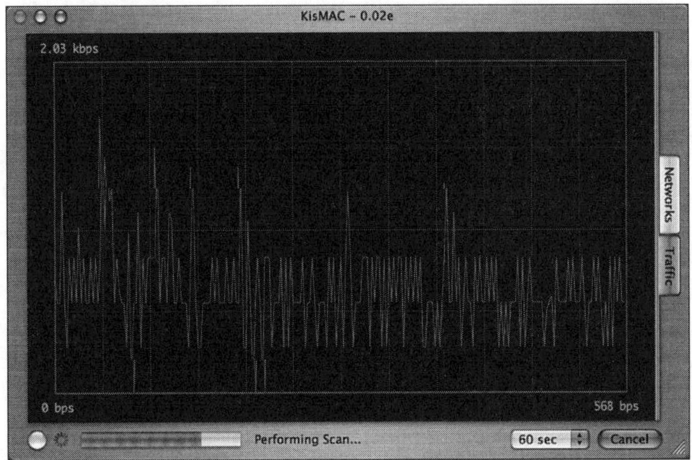

FIGURE 7.7 KisMAC graphs wireless traffic in real time.

Unless a wireless network uses additional authentication or security beyond the 802.11b standard, it is at risk from tools such as KisMAC.

Folks in search of something a bit less flashy may be interested in Mac Stumbler, `http://www.macstumbler.com/`, a competing (and also free) wireless sniffer.

Security Audits

As was mentioned earlier, performing a portscan and then cross-referencing the information returned with known attacks for the given platform provides a good starting point for any attack. Couple that with the ability to check service ports for specific information and you've got a tool that can identify open services, the risks they present, and the exploits that could affect them.

Security scanners are a popular tool for administrators to audit the security of their network. A scanner can pull together information in a few minutes what would take hours for an administrator to do by hand with NMAP and a few online security references. Although there are a number of Unix tools that perform this feature, few combine the ability to trace connections visually, watch Internet traffic, detect DoS attacks, perform brute-force password attacks, and so on. The software MacAnalysis (`http://www.macanalysis.com/about.php3`) does exactly this, and more.

Pulling together more than 1300 exploits and dozens of network tools, the $50 MacAnalysis, shown in Figure 7.8, is an excellent investment for administrators of open networks.

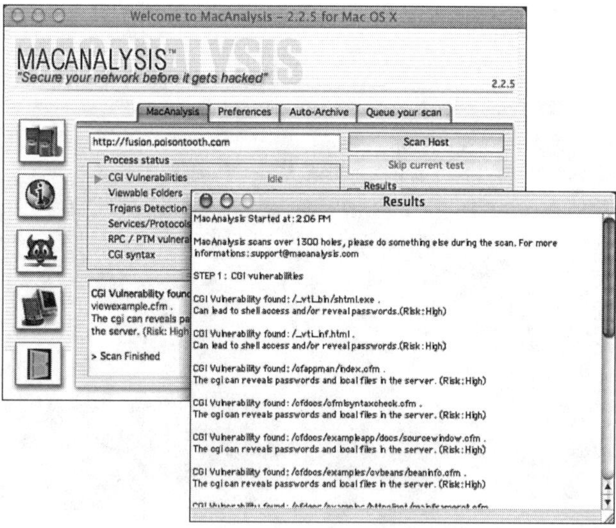

FIGURE 7.8 MacAnalysis can identify hundreds of security holes on your computer.

MacAnalysis can be used to configure your computer's firewall and uses industry-standard tools such as NMAP and Snort for portscans and intrusion detection. (These are wrapped within the MacAnalysis GUI—you'll never even know they're there.)

For an Open Source alternative, try Nessus (`http://www.nessus.org/posix.html`). Nessus features an up-to-date library of exploits, and can produce a security report for an entire network, along with potential fixes and BugTraq/CVE IDs.

Ethics of Information Gathering

Network information gathering is a bit like telephone eavesdropping and, while often unethical, can go unnoticed indefinitely. By sniffing a network, one can uncover personal data, conversations, passwords, and potentially embarrassing topics. Whether or not this is appropriate to your network depends entirely on your network policy. Users should be made aware of the monitoring capabilities of your network, log destinies, and so on.

Our systems, for example, log all data in and out of the LAN. After a storage period of several weeks is elapsed, the data is removed and the storage space recycled. The logs are not browsed or made available to anyone unless an attack is being investigated or packet logs are needed as supporting evidence of an attack.

We do not use the information to conduct "witch hunts" among our own users. No matter how hard you try, you *will* inevitably get a browser pop-up window that points you to an inappropriate Web site, or receive emails that are not "company business." These random events may come across in your network administrator's packet logs as being evidence of less-than-desirable behavior—even though the administrator's actions were entirely innocent.

In general, if trust exists between the administrators and the users, "spying" on individuals is unnecessary. If you can't trust the people on your own LAN, there are bigger problems afoot than a sniffer can uncover.

Portscans, also an information-gathering tool, are more likely to be used on a day-to-day basis than a sniffer. They can uncover unauthorized services running on network machines, and help audit large hardware installations where no one person is responsible for equipment purchases. Unlike sniffers, portscan tools do not present the ethical dilemma of uncovering private information. They are, however, widely recognized as an attack by intrusion detection systems and administrators in general. You should *never* run a portscan on a network that you do not administer. If you do, you're likely to find your ISP or security group knocking on your door.

NOTE

A friend learned the hard way that portscans are frowned upon when he accidentally transposed two octets in his network address when attempting to scan his own subnet. Within an hour, he was under investigation by his own security group as a potential attacker. A quick look at the target subnet revealed the obvious (and, in retrospect, amusing) mistake.

Although portscans are considered "legal" (`http://online.securityfocus.com/news/126`), it is difficult to prove that the intent was not malicious.

Additional Resources

For your continued reading, you may wish to visit these resources for more information on information-gathering techniques and software.

- Packet Storm: Packet Sniffers, a collection of specialized packet sniffers, `http://packetstormsecurity.nl/sniffers/`
- "Security of the WEP Algorithm," by Nikita Borisov, Ian Goldberg, and David Wagner, `http://www.isaac.cs.berkeley.edu/isaac/wep-faq.html`
- "How to Watch Spyware Watching You," Steven Gibson, `http://grc.com/oo/packetsniff.htm`
- "Sniffing Out Packet Sniffers," by Brien Posey, `http://networking.earthweb.com/netsecur/article/0,,12084_766671_2,00.html`
- EtherPeek, an ethernet packet analysis tool by WildPackets, `http://www.wildpackets.com/products/etherpeek_mac`
- NetMinder, Ethernet protocol analysis and alerting by Neon Software, `http://www.neon.com/NetMinder_Ethernet.html`
- "Sniffers: What They Are and How to Protect Yourself," by Matthew Tanase, `http://online.securityfocus.com/infocus/1549`
- "TCP/IP for the Uninitiated," by Erik Iverson, `http://www.dragonmount.net/tutorials/`
- "Introduction to TCP/IP," `http://www.yale.edu/pclt/COMM/TCPIP.HTM`
- Example Web Packet Sniffer (written in Perl), `http://stein.cshl.org/~lstein/talks/WWW6/sniffer/`
- "Remote OS Detection via TCP/IP Stack FingerPrinting," by Fyodor, `http://www.insecure.org/nmap/nmap-fingerprinting-article.html`
- "Port Scanning Methods," by AuditMyPc.com, `http://www.auditmypc.com/freescan/readingroom/port_scanning.asp`

Summary

It's your network (presumably)—shouldn't you know what's going on? This chapter introduced several sniffing and portscanning tools that can be used to audit your network security, help detect inappropriate use of your network resources, and even uncover others using similar tools against you. The `tcpdump` utility is part of Mac OS X and can easily display all packet activity on your network. The ettercap sniffer, on the other hand, provides attacker-style features including password filters, ARP poisoning, and more. Finally, portscan tools such as NMAP can help an administrator (or an attacker) map out vulnerable systems on their network by identifying active services and OS versions.

8

Impersonation and Infiltration: Spoofing

IN THIS CHAPTER

- Spoofing Attacks
- Spoofing Defenses

So your Mac OS X computer is sitting there minding its own business, and along comes another machine and says "Hi there, remember me from 10.1.5.0? Want to go out and share a file?" If the visiting computer knows the correct information to mount your machine's drives, or authenticate as one of your users, what's your machine to do, except believe that it is what it says it is, acting on the authority of who it says that it is? This is a fundamental problem with the idea of a computer network, and one that, in many senses, almost nothing can be done about. We and our computers identify ourselves and other systems over the network via mechanisms that range from visual branding identity to passwords, and from digital signatures to serial number information extracted from CPUs, network cards, and system boards. Whether we're trying to identify software across the network or are identifying ourselves to it, some pieces of selected information are considered sufficient to prove those identities. If some imposter system out there can replicate all these pieces of information and provide them on demand, that imposter will be believed to be the system that it is impersonating. This is called *spoofing*.

In a sense, any form of identity misappropriation can be considered spoofing. An intruder using your user ID and password is spoofing your identity on the system. A remote machine that is serving up an NIS domain with the same name as your normal server, in the hopes that your machine will listen to it rather than the password master it was intended to obey, is spoofing your NIS domain master. In recent Internet history there have been a number of fly-by-night businesses that have set up Web sites located at common misspellings of popular e-commerce sites with visual duplicates of the real site. These spoofs of the actual online retailer's sites have taken orders at elevated prices and then passed the order off to the real business and skimmed the pricing difference. PayPal.com users, as well as customers of a host of other online businesses, have been bilked out of money by "reregistering" at the request of spoofed email indicating that their accounts had been compromised, and giving them a link at which they could reenter their personal and credit card information (`http://www.scambusters.org/Scambusters55.html`). Because in many cases the deception doesn't constitute fraud, even big business gets in on the act occasionally. When AT&T put together its 1-800-OPERATOR campaign, MCI cashed in on the opportunity and picked up 1-800-OPERATER, directing it to its own operator service, and supposedly raked in $300,000 a month of free money by using AT&T's advertising (`http://icbtollfree.com/pressetc/telephonyarticle10142002.html`). A classic demonstration that computer security cannot be implemented without user education was carried out via a spoof by a *tiger team* (`http://www.catb.org/jargon/html/entry/tiger-team.html`) hired to test a U.S. Military installation's security. When the team discovered that they couldn't find a way to break into the system through application of network techniques, they spoofed an official system patch document from IBM, packaged it with a software backdoor to the system, and had it delivered to the installation, which dutifully installed it, letting them in (`http://www.catb.org/jargon/html/entry/patch.html`). An enterprising individual who wanted to compete in the world of domain name registrations came up with the clever(?) plan to steal InterNIC's traffic and customers by spoofing InterNIC's registration service (`http://www.nwfusion.com/archive/1997/97-07-28____.html`). Heck, there's a whole flippin' country full of people pretending to be the children of Nigerian diplomats in desperate need of a foreign partner to move millions of dollars out of hidden bank accounts (`http://home.rica.net/alphae/419coal/`).

NOTE

Formally, spoofing is defined as providing false identity credentials for the purpose of carrying out a deceit. In some circles it's considered a requirement that this deceit be with the intent to obtain unauthorized access to a system or its resources, whereas others consider maintaining plausible deniability to be spoofing oneself as a trustable entity. Finally, pure theft of identity, although it meets almost everyone's definition, doesn't tend to be called spoofing unless the theft of identity was for the purpose of forging that identity: Just using someone else's password to access a system wouldn't commonly be called spoofing unless the purpose was to pretend that that person was performing some actions.

Clear as mud? Don't worry—after you get used to the way the term is used, it'll all make sense in context.

The issue boils down to a matter of establishing trust, and fixing a set of credentials by which a protocol or system may establish the identity of some other user or system. If these credentials can be forged or replicated, then a third untrusted system may spoof itself as a trusted entity to any system that relies on the replicable credentials for identification. The parallels between the computing world and the human world are, in this case, many, as the problem of establishing trust and identity is a basic issue of human existence as well. We take thumbprints or retina scans at the entrance to a top-secret facility (or at least in James Bond's world we do); we compare handwritten signatures with originals; banks ask us for our mothers' maiden names; and every day we compare our remembered copies of our associate's voices with what our ears are telling us, so that we can identify the speaker. As humans we have the same problems our computers have. We need to trust some collection of information as being sufficient to identify others around us as who they are. No matter how large this collection of information is, it will always be possible in some way for someone to fake these credentials, but we trust them because we believe that they are, for our purposes, sufficient. If we're overly naive, we may place our trust on too few credentials, and we may be fooled with too great a frequency. If we're overly paranoid we may decide that this means that we can't actually trust anyone, ever. Neither of these extremes are practical for human interactions, nor are they practical for computer interactions. Trust must be established in some way, and it will always be possible for the mechanism for establishing that trust to be deceived. It is simply an issue that we and our computing systems must live with.

Spoofing Attacks

What do you trust to establish identity? What harm can be done to you or your computer if a mistake is made in establishing identity? If you got an email like the one shown in Figure 8.1, would you believe it? Would you act upon it? In my default view, you don't even see that replies aren't going to go to the apparent Apple address, but instead to `that-dll-dufus@hotmail.com`. This information becomes visible only if I explicitly view the headers, or pay careful attention to the reply window if I click Reply.

Did you know that if you have sendmail running, you can send this same message to yourself by issuing the following commands? Heck, a small amount of lying to your email client will produce much the same result! Sending it to someone else is no more difficult, but I wouldn't recommend it, as some people might think they need to see you in court about that.

```
% telnet soyokaze 25
Trying 140.254.104.241 ...
Connected to soyokaze.biosci.ohio-state.edu.
Escape character is '^]'.
```

```
220 soyokaze.biosci.ohio-state.edu ESMTP Sendmail 8.12.8/8.12.7;
➥Tue, 4 Mar 2003 03:04:54 -0500 (EST)
HELO soyokaze
250 soyokaze.biosci.ohio-state.edu Hello soyokaze.biosci.ohio-state.edu
➥[140.254.104.241], pleased to meet you
MAIL FROM: apple_security@apple.com
250 2.1.0 apple_security@apple.com... Sender ok
RCPT TO: willray@mac.com
250 2.1.5 willray@mac.com... Recipient ok
DATA
354 Enter mail, end with "." on a line by itself
Subject: Warning, possible security breach
Reply-To: that-dll-dufus@hotmail.com

Dear customer,

A breach in our network security has recently come to our
attention.  We believe that a number of our customers
computers may have been compromised through data transmitted
to our servers while accessing our .mac service.

If you could please email us a copy of your NetInfo database,
it would help us greatly in tracking and eliminating this
problem, and in informing those of you who may have been
compromised by this problem.

Please attach the result of the following command to a
reply to this email message.

nidump passwd .

Thank you for your time and assistance,
The Apple Security Team

.
250 2.0.0 h2484sxq027196 Message accepted for delivery
quit
221 2.0.0 soyokaze.biosci.ohio-state.edu closing connection
Connection closed by foreign host.
```

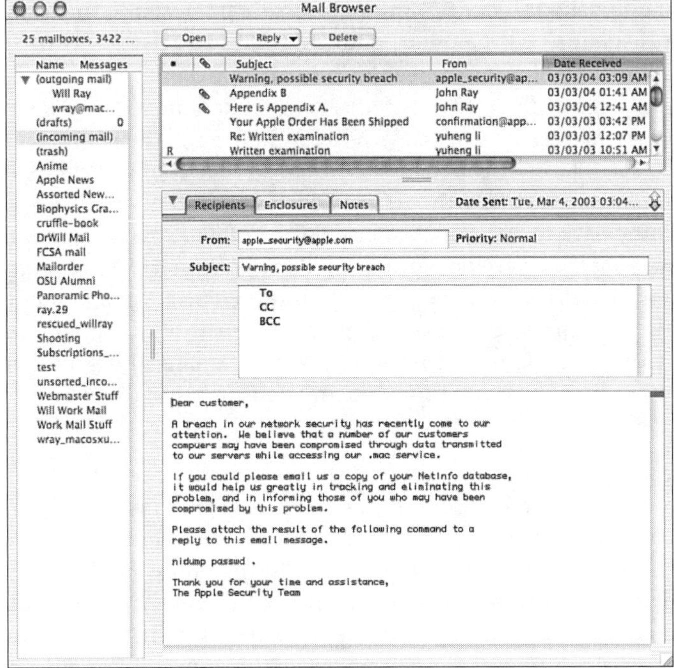

FIGURE 8.1 A spoofed email message.

In this case we've spoofed some content by lying to the mail transport mechanism. It's neither particularly difficult to do nor particularly difficult to see through, but if the message content is believable, you might not be alerted to pay careful attention to the headers, and that might lead you to believe that content comes from one source when it actually comes from another. A good number of the people thought they were actually reentering and verifying their user information for the PayPal online payment site when they responded to an email that appeared to come from PayPal. Instead they were giving their credit card information to a thief who was spoofing PayPal's identity to establish trust and steal their financial information.

IP-Address Spoofing

Other types of identity can be spoofed as well. For example, the TCP/IP by which information moves around the Internet needs some way for a receiving system to know where to reply to information that is sent to it. In this system each piece of information to be transmitted is broken down into bite-sized chunks that are manageable for network transmission. These bite-sized chunks are called *packets*, each one of which gets stamped at creation time with a return address (an IP address) saying where it came from.

If you're paranoid about security, you may already be thinking this is a bad idea. If each packet is stamped with a return address, what's to keep someone from forging the return address, or altering it en route and claiming a packet came from somewhere it didn't, right? If you're not that security paranoid yet, you might be thinking "Why bother—what's to be gained?" Well, for one thing, the stolen return address would let a cracker falsify his network identity, so that you wouldn't know who's attacking you. If he can falsify the return address, there's no way for you to track incoming traffic back to the actual origin. For another, it makes for an interesting way to create a massive network-swamping denial of service attack: Someone could forge *your* return address onto their packets and then attack many random machines around the Internet. Everyone sees *your* machine as the attacker, and quite often can be induced to retaliate or at least respond (even automatically as a required part of the TCP/IP), resulting in devastating network consumption or outages for your machine.

The first scenario is something like the network version of sending your enemies (or friends, if you've a twisted sense of humor) free tickets or invitations to events that don't actually exist. The tickets or invitations have to be sent in an envelope with a falsified return address, because the lack of a return address might seem suspicious to the recipients. Those who try to go to the nonexistent event have no idea who actually sent the information on the event, because at this point, they know that the information certainly did not come from the address specified as the return address. They'd be mad, and possibly out some resources for travel time and dinner, but would have no idea who they were mad at. The second is more like writing bad checks on someone else's account. The recipients of the bad checks think the culprit is the name on the check and pursue payment accordingly, which probably has a negative impact on the account holder's credit. In either case, the misdirection as to the real source of the information can lead to considerable trouble for either the party who is mislead or the party who is spoofed as the sender.

In reality, although the idea of using return addresses attached to each packet sounds like a bad idea at first blush, it's an almost inevitable consequence of the way networks work. Data isn't transmitted directly, on an unbroken wire, from the sending machine to the receiving machine. Instead it hops from machine to machine to machine along the network, being handed from one to the next, always (in the ideal, anyway) getting closer to its target, until it finally reaches the machine that it's intended for. This model for data transmission is a result of the impossibility of wiring every machine on the planet directly to every other machine, and many of the vulnerabilities in today's networks are an inherent part of the model. Return addresses on packets, for example, are a consequence of the need for a packet at hop 5 of a 10-hop journey to have some idea of where it's come from and where it's going. The fifth machine down the line doesn't have any direct connection to either the originating machine or the receiving machine, and so it must get the information regarding where a packet came from and where it's going from somewhere. That "somewhere" might as well be information directly contained in the packet, because as easy to forge as it is, there's no other less-forgeable method for keeping the information with the packet. One might argue that if there was auxiliary information kept beside the packet, instead of in it, that perhaps the first machine to receive a packet from a sender could fill in the "this packet came from:" field with the originator's IP address, or some other identifying token. All a cracker intent on mischief would need to do then is control the machine at the first hop and get *it* to forge the information, and we're right back in the same boat. Because such schemes increase the complexity of the system without meaningfully increasing the trustability of the information, the TCP/IP system uses the simple, seemingly naive—but no worse than any other—solution of using return addresses contained in the packets.

If a machine lies about its IP address in packets that it sends, there may very well be no information to disagree with this identification. What's to say that the information is a lie? If it hasn't originated in some place where a machine of that IP really shouldn't exist, what's to say that the packet didn't really come from a machine with that IP address? Nothing. It's as if, as a person, you were given to complete trust in the identity of the sender of a letter based on the address typed on the envelope.

If you try to set your machine's IP address to one that already exists on the network, you'll be presented with a dialog that looks something like Figure 8.2, indicating that the IP that you've selected is already claimed on the network.

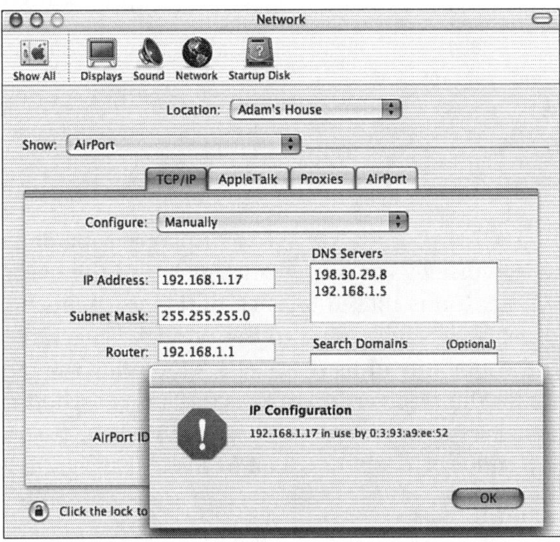

FIGURE 8.2 Macs check for other machines on the network with the same IP address they're trying to claim when they try to initialize their network interfaces.

Because there is no necessity that any other machines on the network be engaging in communications that would allow the software to make this check against duplicates in a passive manner, some active step must be being taken to determine whether any other machines are claiming the IP address your machine wants. While initializing the network interface, therefore, the Mac is sending out some sort of network broadcast query and inviting other machines to tell it that it's not allowed to have the IP it requested. What's to say that there's really a machine out there with your IP address? What if someone just wanted to keep you from using your network connection? If they simply watch for the check from your machine on the network, and spoof the response to indicate that the IP is already taken, wouldn't that constitute an effective, and quite annoying denial of service attack?

In fact, the `conflictd` program, available from `http://ccitt5.net/archive/conflictd.tar.gz`, provides a convenient way to test this theory. It requires a slightly out-of-date version of the `libnet` library available from `http://www.packetfactory.net/libnet/dist/deprecated/`. I chose `libnet-1.0.2.tgz`, but other pre-1.1 versions are likely to work (if you find an updated `conflictd`, it may work with the current `libnet` version, which is most easily installed using `fink`). It also requires `libpcap`, and a few header files that aren't normally included with Jaguar. The easiest route to installation is to use `fink` to install `libpcap` and `libnet`, then build the older version of `libnet` by hand and install it in `/usr/local/` rather than in `/sw`. Then edit the `Makefile` so that it includes and links from `/usr/local/include` and `/usr/local/lib` before it checks the `/sw` hierarchy. In its unadulterated form `conflictd` only annoys Macs, but the effect on Windows machines of the 95 and 98 persuasion is pronounced. Issuing the following command:

```
# ./conflict-DoS en1 192.168.1.8
Using interface en1
Each dot is 10 popups..
....................
```

causes the WinTel box living at `192.168.1.8` to display the dialog shown in Figure 8.3. Actually, it causes it to display the dialog 200 times, and the machine is effectively useless until the OK button is clicked on each of them. All this program is doing is forging a storm of reply packets to send to the Windows machine as though it had enquired about the availability of its IP address. Modifying the program to work as a daemon, watching for the Mac version of the conflict-resolution request, and spoofing equally damaging responses for Mac OS X would not be particularly difficult. The daemonization code is already provided in the `conflictd` source.

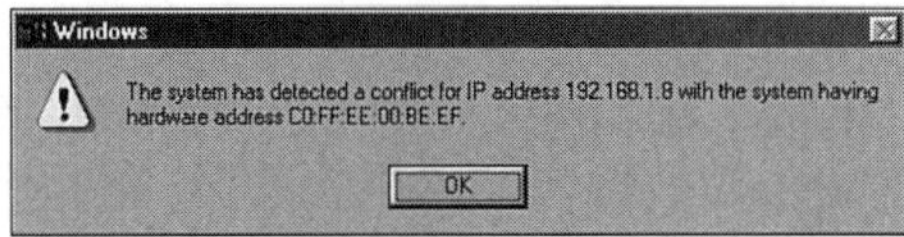

FIGURE 8.3 Wintel boxes check when the network interface is initialized, but also pop up annoying conflict dialogs whenever any other machine tries to register a duplicate IP at a later time.

More insidiously, packets carry not only their own return address that must be assumed to be correct, but they also can carry a return route via which responses are supposed to be delivered. This was a considerably more naive idea than having packets carry their own return address. Allowing packets to specify their own *source routing* allows an attacker to insert packets into a network with a spoofed IP address, so that you don't know who or where they're really coming from, and also to convince the network to return responses to places that the normal routing software for the Internet wouldn't send them—places that wouldn't typically be able to receive the response. Using this capability, an attacker can slip packets into your network with spoofed IP addresses—packets that claim to be from other trusted machines on your network. They can also specify that responses be sent to some other host outside your network, rather than to the machine on your network that matches the IP specified in the packet. Thankfully, almost all sane network software is now configured to block source-routed packets because they have a very limited potential for positive use and considerable potential for abuse.

It should be noted that both these problems with TCP/IP packets stem from the fact that packets are delivered like snail-mail letters, with no direct connection between the sender and the receiver. This allows the information in the packets to be forged with no possibility for verification of the contents. Even a complex interaction between sender and receiver with each replying about the contents of the packets received and cross-checking with the other as to the validity is not proof against a man-in-the-middle attack, whereby a machine somewhere on the Net spoofs both connections and pretends to be each machine to the other. The specifics of man-in-the-middle attacks are discussed in more detail in Chapter 9, "Everything Else," but the basic mechanism should be understood as spoofing oneself as a piece of wire along the network, while actually monitoring and potentially altering communications traveling through that wire. The fault is then, as noted previously, one of establishing and verifying trust. Any credentials can be duplicated. Which ones are sufficient?

ARP Spoofing

The IP address contained in the packet is one form of return address for the packet, and is used by the network at large to determine where the packet belongs. More accurately, routing devices on a network determine whether a packet belongs on another network by examining the packet's IP address, and move it to that other network if it does. Internal to a particular network, however, any machine is free to examine the packet and read it. Whether a machine is *supposed* to read the packet is based on a packet field that contains another form of identification, the *MAC address*. MAC (Media Access Control) addresses are (supposed to be) unique hardware IDs assigned to ethernet interfaces that are completely unique across all ethernet interfaces ever made. As a packet is delivered from network to network, the delivering router fills in a hardware ID (MAC address) that it has determined to be correct for the next machine that is supposed to receive the packet. This MAC address may be for the next routing machine that is supposed to handle the packet. Or, if the packet is being delivered into the final network where the machine with the IP address matching the packet's target is supposed to reside, it may be the MAC address of the target machine itself. The router's determination of the MAC address that corresponds to a destination IP is based on the *Address Resolution Protocol* (ARP). Packets placed on the network that are bound for a local machine (ones that don't need to be sent through a router), also have a MAC address that corresponds to the ethernet interface of the destination IP. This, too, is based on ARP information acquired by each host on the network.

Unfortunately, the determination of the values to place in an *ARP table* is based on "observed reality" on the wire: The routers and machines collect a table of IP addresses and their associated MAC addresses from the values they see in packets on the network. It's all too easy to forge packets with false MAC addresses as well as false IP addresses, and this can easily cause traffic entering a network that is supposed to be delivered to one machine to instead end up elsewhere.

Ettercap: Ethernet Monster

The ettercap program, which was covered in more detail in the previous chapter (available through `fink`, or as a Macintosh `.pkg` file directly from the authors at `http://ettercap.sourceforge.net/`) is capable of quite a few nifty (if you're not an admin kiddie) ARP spoofing–based tricks, including interposing itself into and decrypting SSH1 communications. For example, in Figure 8.4 ettercap is shown sniffing the contents of an FTP session that's occurring between a pair of hosts on a different branch of a switched network.

After seeing ettercap's sniffing capabilities in the previous chapter, this probably doesn't seem surprising. Note, however, that I've just said that this sniffing is occurring on a switched network, which appears to be in contradiction to what we've previously written regarding switched networks. Here, traffic that isn't supposed to be going to my machine (`Racer-X` at `192.168.1.16` in this example) is clearly managing to get out of the physical branches of the network to which it's supposed to be restricted by the switches, and coming to my machine as well. The traffic isn't doing this in contravention of the switches' intent to restrict it to certain wire segments, however; it's doing it because my machine has lied to the switches and other machines on the network. Because the ARP-based routing information is gleaned from what's seen on the wire, and because most switches route solely based on the MAC addresses they've seen, the other hardware believes the lies my machine has told, and dutifully routes traffic onto my network segment, even though I'm not the actually intended recipient.

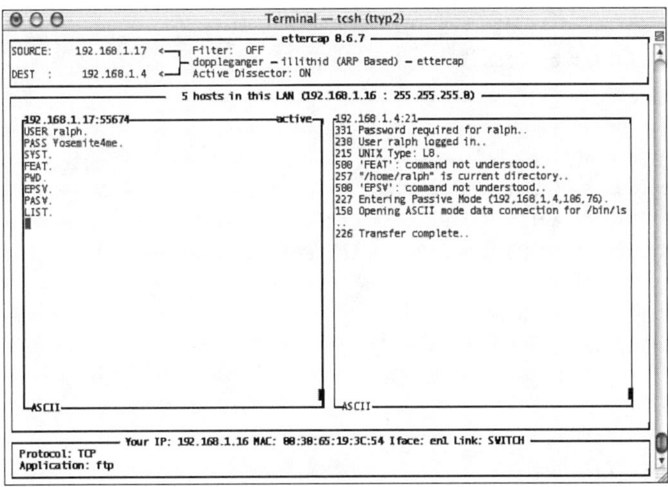

FIGURE 8.4 Ettercap sniffing traffic in a switched network via ARP spoofing.

In this case, what is happening is that ettercap has spoofed ARP-response packets onto the network, claiming that the MAC address on my machine is associated with both the IP addresses of the hosts that want to communicate (`192.168.1.17`, `Sage-Rays-Computer` and `192.168.1.4`, `mother.killernuts.org`). The ARP table on my machine, however, has been left uncorrupted. Ettercap has effectively interposed itself between `192.168.1.17` and `192.168.1.4`. Whenever Sage's computer wants to speak to mother, it looks up the MAC address associated with `192.168.1.4` from its ARP table and builds packets with that MAC address as their destination. Unfortunately for Sage's computer, my machine has *poisoned* Sage's ARP table. Instead of getting the MAC address that really belongs to mother, Sage's computer gets the MAC address of my machine, and dutifully puts this incorrect information into the outgoing packets. The switched network knows no better, and dutifully routes the packet to Racer-X, where ettercap lies in wait. Upon receipt, ettercap looks at the packet to see whether there's anything interesting in it, such as usernames or passwords, and then rewrites an identical outgoing packet, only with the correct MAC address for mother. The network conveys the packet to mother, who reads it and has no idea that it's been misrouted, read, and altered along the way. Replies back from mother suffer the same fate because mother's ARP table has also been poisoned so as to associate Racer-X's MAC address with Sage's computer's IP. As you can see from the following output, the only computers with poisoned ARP information regarding Sage's computer or mother as destinations are Sage's computer and mother themselves. Other computers on the network have the correct information, and are largely oblivious to the machinations of ettercap.

```
[Sage-Rays-Computer:~] sage% arp -a
? (192.168.1.4) at 0:30:65:19:3c:54
? (192.168.1.13) at 0:30:65:39:ca:1
? (192.168.1.16) at 0:30:65:19:3c:54

[root@mother ~]# arp -a
cvl232001.columbus.rr.com (204.210.232.1) at 08:00:3E:19:47:CA [ether] on eth1
? (192.168.1.16) at 00:30:65:19:3C:54 [ether] on eth0
? (192.168.1.17) at 00:30:65:19:3C:54 [ether] on eth0

192.168.1.200 ray 154> arp -a
? (192.168.1.4) at 0:20:af:15:2a:d
? (192.168.1.16) at 0:30:65:19:3c:54
? (192.168.1.17) at 0:30:65:aa:37:ae

Racer-X conflictd 87# arp -a
? (192.168.1.4) at 0:20:af:15:2a:d
? (192.168.1.13) at 0:30:65:39:ca:1
? (192.168.1.17) at 0:30:65:aa:37:ae

Racer-X conflictd 88# ifconfig
lo0: flags=8049<UP,LOOPBACK,RUNNING,MULTICAST> mtu 16384
        inet6 ::1 prefixlen 128
        inet6 fe80::1%lo0 prefixlen 64 scopeid 0x1
        inet 127.0.0.1 netmask 0xff000000
gif0: flags=8010<POINTOPOINT,MULTICAST> mtu 1280
stf0: flags=0<> mtu 1280
en1: flags=8963<UP,BROADCAST,SMART,RUNNING,PROMISC,SIMPLEX,MULTICAST> mtu 1500
        inet6 fe80::230:65ff:fe19:3c54%en1 prefixlen 64 scopeid 0x4
        inet 192.168.1.16 netmask 0xffffff00 broadcast 192.168.1.255
        ether 00:30:65:19:3c:54
        media: autoselect status: active
        supported media: autoselect
```

Ettercap can not only monitor traffic in connections it's watching in this way, but it can also inject into the connection traffic that the receiving computer will believe originated from the machine with which it's supposedly talking directly, forge almost any packet onto the network, kill most types of network connections, perform pattern-based substitutions into packets as they pass by, and extract passwords from a large number of protocols.

Fortunately, this type of manipulation of the routing information is only mostly invisible to the rest of the network, not completely invisible. ARP tables are usually updated only when some piece of software needs to use the data in them, so it's probable that some computers will never see any effect from the ARP spoofing going on, and their ARP tables will never contain poisoned data. However, it's also possible for a conscientious admin to run software that specifically watches for inconsistencies in the ARP replies bouncing around the network, and that throws up warnings if a given IP address or MAC address seems to be changing its apparent identity regularly. The arpwatch package, described in more detail in the next chapter, is one utility that is very nice for this type of examination. In its typical configuration, it runs as a daemon, and sends email to root whenever it sees something suspicious happening with MAC<->IP mappings on the network. For example, in this set of arpwatch debugging output, arpwatch is reporting on the continuing argument between Sage's computer (`192.168.1.17`, really MAC `0:30:65:aa:37:ae`) and Racer-X (`192.168.1.16`, really MAC `0:30:65:19:3c:54`), and between mother (`192.168.1.4`, really MAC `0:20:af:15:2a:d`) and Racer-X over exactly what their real MAC addresses (here called *ethernet addresses*) are, as each sends out ARP responses claiming an IP<->MAC address match for other machines on the network to use.

```
Racer-X arpwatch 5# arpwatch -d

From: arpwatch (Arpwatch)
To: root
Subject: flip flop
            hostname: <unknown>
          ip address: 192.168.1.4
    ethernet address: 0:30:65:19:3c:54
     ethernet vendor: <unknown>
old ethernet address: 0:20:af:15:2a:d
 old ethernet vendor: <unknown>
           timestamp: Monday, January 20, 2003 13:14:44 -0500
  previous timestamp: Monday, January 20, 2003 13:14:19 -0500
               delta: 25 seconds

From: arpwatch (Arpwatch)
To: root
Subject: flip flop
            hostname: <unknown>
```

```
          ip address: 192.168.1.4
    ethernet address: 0:20:af:15:2a:d
     ethernet vendor: <unknown>
old ethernet address: 0:30:65:19:3c:54
 old ethernet vendor: <unknown>
           timestamp: Monday, January 20, 2003 13:14:44 -0500
  previous timestamp: Monday, January 20, 2003 13:14:44 -0500
               delta: 0 seconds

From: arpwatch (Arpwatch)
To: root
Subject: flip flop
            hostname: <unknown>
          ip address: 192.168.1.17
    ethernet address: 0:30:65:aa:37:ae
     ethernet vendor: <unknown>
old ethernet address: 0:30:65:19:3c:54
 old ethernet vendor: <unknown>
           timestamp: Monday, January 20, 2003 13:14:44 -0500
  previous timestamp: Monday, January 20, 2003 13:14:44 -0500
               delta: 0 seconds

From: arpwatch (Arpwatch)
To: root
Subject: flip flop
            hostname: <unknown>
          ip address: 192.168.1.17
    ethernet address: 0:30:65:19:3c:54
     ethernet vendor: <unknown>
old ethernet address: 0:30:65:aa:37:ae
 old ethernet vendor: <unknown>
           timestamp: Monday, January 20, 2003 13:15:14 -0500
  previous timestamp: Monday, January 20, 2003 13:14:44 -0500
               delta: 30 seconds
```

Couic—The Connection Cutter

IP and MAC-address spoofing isn't limited in its "utility" to only sniffing connections, though. Any use to which a response packet from or about a given host might be put, a spoofed packet can be used for as well. For example, *RST* (reset) packets that appear to be from some working machine on the network can be spoofed onto the wire by another machine. This effectively knocks the spoofed machine off the wire because any machine in communication with it will receive periodic resets to the connection, and believe that the spoofed machine has decided to drop the connection itself. The `couic` program is available from `http://michel.arboi.free.fr/UKUSA/couic.html` and bills itself as a "connection cutter" or "active filter," used to enforce network policy rules. It certainly can be used to watch for and sever almost any sort of network communication from or to any host on its local network, but it seems highly likely it'll be used for mischief. The author notes that inappropriate use in France can land the mischievous in jail for three years. Couic compiles relatively easily with the same `libnet` and `libpcap` libraries as required for conflictd. After it is compiled, it is run as `couic -i <interface> -t <deny rules>`. For example, the following command will deny TCP traffic to or from `192.168.1.17`:

```
couic -i en1 -t tcp and host 192.168.1.17
```

In fact, running this command while I've got an SSH connection up to `192.168.1.17` results in the following error output on my machine, as soon as I try to do anything that talks to it:

```
[Sage-Rays-Computer:~] sage%  Read from remote host 192.168.1.17:
Connection reset by peer
Connection to 192.168.1.17 closed.
Racer-X ray 36>
```

Trying to reestablish the connection while couic's still running results only in a similar error:

```
Racer-X ray 36> slogin 192.168.1.17 -l sage
write: Broken pipe
```

While this is happening, `couic` itself is reporting its activities. According to the author, `arpwatch` sees these attacks as well, but at this time we haven't been successful at getting `arpwatch` to display this information.

The rule language is in flux, so for topics beyond simple protocol denial as shown here, we recommend visiting the author's Web page.

LaBrea Tarpit

Despite some writers' insistence that spoofing lacks any possible legitimate purpose (`http://www.sans.org/rr/threats/spoofing.php`), at least one inspired system administrator has come up with a way to use spoofing as a tool for the good of the network. If you remember, we've mentioned several times that a typical attack mechanism for script kiddies is to run automated attacks against all IPs on a network, and you can typically defend against these by simply keeping up on patches and making your machines difficult to invade. It's always seemed like there should be an active way to defend against these, instead of simply passively ignoring the attacks. For example, a nice active defense might be to track down the attacking machines and kick them off of the network. Unfortunately, most of the time, the machines actively attacking yours aren't actually the attacker's machines; they're just zombies that the attacker has taken over. Also unfortunately, because their owners are rarely aware that their machines are taking part in an attack, they rarely take you implementing such an active defense against them kindly. Or, to put it more simply, you're likely to land in legal trouble if you take the route of attempting to mitigate attacks against your machine by attacking back.

Fortunately, system administrator Tom Liston, in a flash of inspired cleverness, realized that although the owners of a remote system might take litigious offense at your contacting their system and initiating an attack, they'd be on awfully shaky ground if it was their system that contacted yours, and yours simply refused to hang up the phone.

Tom realized that one of the signatures of many automated attacks (and specifically the Code Red worm that was traveling the Net at the time) is that the attacker rarely knows the specific IPs that are on your network. Therefore, they tend to try to attack every IP address on your IP range. This can be used against them. What if you could put a machine at each of the unused IP addresses, and have it try to tie up the attacker's connection by simultaneously being invulnerable to the attack while also refusing to hang up when it was contacted? Many networks have a larger number of unused IP addresses than they have used, so if you could populate them all with machines that would refuse to let an attacker go on to another target, it might seriously slow down the propagation of an attack. Nobody wants to set up that many "tarpit" machines just to mire inbound connections, but what if you didn't need a machine? Because the only thing the attacker gets back is network responses from the machine, why not just spoof the responses? Put together a server that watches for connections trying to make their way to machines that don't exist and spoof responses to them as though those (nonexistent) machines wanted to talk.

ARP even provides a convenient mechanism by which to perform this spoofery. When a router needs to contact a machine for which there isn't an entry in its ARP table, it sends out an ARP request asking for some machine to claim that it has that IP. The inbound router for a network segment certainly doesn't have any ARP entries for machines that don't exist, and nonexistent machines aren't going to respond and populate that table. This makes it easy for a tarpit program that wants to pretend to be "any machine that doesn't exist" to do so; all it needs to do is watch the network for ARP requests with no matching responses, and respond to them with spoofed packets itself. The router then routes all further information for that IP to the tarpit server.

Tom implemented this idea as the LaBrea package, which sits on a network and watches for incoming ARP requests that go unanswered. These it reasonably presumes to be looking for machines that don't exist. When it sees them, it spoofs responses that essentially fool the attacking zombie into thinking it's found a fresh host to infect, and then keeps it hanging on the line indefinitely. This ties up the attacker's resources, and prevents at least one zombie resource from making further attacks until the connection to your machine drops. In the grand scheme of things, it's not much, but it's far better than just shuffling the attack off onto someone else. As one system administrator put it, "You can come into work in the morning, look at your logfiles, and say 'Wow—I'm *actually* saving the world.'" Saving the world might be a bit over the top, but one analysis suggested that with only a few hundred average networks cooperating by running a single `LaBrea` tarpit server, roughly 300,000 zombied machines could be held at bay indefinitely, for nothing more than a few percent of each cooperating site's bandwidth. If I can contribute my half-percent of helping to stop the spread of Internet worms, and I get to annoy script kiddies in the process, that's as close to saving the world as I need to get to feel I've done my job for the day.

Until recently, LaBrea had been available from `http://www.threenorth.com/LaBrea/`, but due to recent DMCA legislation, it is not currently available at that address. It's interesting how legislation that protects corporate security interests can interfere with protecting your security interests. Fortunately, though, you can now find a version at `http://labrea.sourceforge.net/labrea-info.html`. The current version requires some modification to get it running properly on OS X. Like conflictd, it requires a slightly out-of-date version of `libnet`, `libpcap`, and some headers that are missing from Jaguar. In addition, part of `libpcap` doesn't seem to work quite the same on OS X as on some other operating systems, and the timeout field of `pcap_open_live()` seems to need a value greater than zero for it to properly capture packets. Upping this value to 5ms appears to cause LaBrea to function as designed.

Although installing and configuring most network security packages is a significant task, for the benefit it provides, using `LaBrea` is quite simple. It's almost completely autoconfiguring to a useful default state, so although a number of command-line options are detailed in Table 8.1, you can produce a completely functional tarpit server by running the `LaBrea` executable with only verbose logging, and flags to direct it to talk to the proper interface and to write to the terminal (`STDOUT`) instead of `syslogd`. (You'll have to read the documentation that comes with it to learn about the `z` flag, however; the author wants it that way.) For example, if I run LaBrea on Racer-X as follows, it will quite effectively tarpit any attempted connections to machines that don't exist. Again, we've left the prompts intact in these captured dialogs so that you can more easily keep track of who's doing what to whom.

```
Racer-X LaBrea2_3 50# ./LaBrea -vbozi en1
Initiated on interface en1
/etc/LaBreaExclude not found - no exclusions
```

On another computer on my network, my ARP table currently looks like this:

```
[Sage-Rays-Computer:~] sage% arp -a
? (192.168.1.13) at 0:30:65:39:ca:1
? (192.168.1.16) at 0:30:65:19:3c:54
```

If I then try to ping a machine that doesn't exist, Sage's computer is going to try to find it via ARP requests:

```
[Sage-Rays-Computer:~] sage% ping 192.168.1.21
PING 192.168.1.21 (192.168.1.21): 56 data bytes
^C
--- 192.168.1.21 ping statistics ---
7 packets transmitted, 0 packets received, 100% packet loss
```

Meanwhile, `tcpdump`, looking at what's going on with ARP, has this to say:

```
Racer-X arpwatch 17# tcpdump -i en1 arp
02:17:57.741882 arp who-has 192.168.1.21 tell 192.168.1.17
02:17:58.742136 arp who-has 192.168.1.21 tell 192.168.1.17
02:17:59.742338 arp who-has 192.168.1.21 tell 192.168.1.17
02:18:00.742510 arp who-has 192.168.1.21 tell 192.168.1.17
02:18:00.755537 arp reply 192.168.1.21 is-at 0:0:f:ff:ff:ff
```

The eventual response assigning `0:0:f:ff:ff:ff` (a rather fake-looking MAC address) comes from LaBrea, which has meanwhile detected that there were no responses to those four ARP requests, and has decided to reply with a spoofed machine. The following line appears on `Racer-X`'s console:

```
Tue Jan 21 02:18:00 2003 Capturing local IP: 192.168.1.21
```

Sage's ARP table now looks like this:

```
[Sage-Rays-Computer:~] sage% arp -a
? (192.168.1.13) at 0:30:65:39:ca:1
? (192.168.1.16) at 0:30:65:19:3c:54
? (192.168.1.21) at 0:0:f:ff:ff:ff
```

If I further try to ping a machine that does exist, but that isn't already in Sage's ARP table, something different happens. `tcpdump` shows this log:

```
02:18:46.206856 arp who-has 192.168.1.4 tell 192.168.1.17
02:18:46.215544 arp reply 192.168.1.4 is-at 0:0:f:ff:ff:ff
02:18:49.302675 arp reply 192.168.1.4 is-at 0:20:af:15:2a:d
```

And `LaBrea` shows another captured IP address:

```
Tue Jan 21 02:18:46 2003 Capturing local IP: 192.168.1.4
```

Yet my `ping` proceeds as normal:

```
[Sage-Rays-Computer:/Users/sage] sage# ping 192.168.1.4
PING 192.168.1.4 (192.168.1.4): 56 data bytes
64 bytes from 192.168.1.4: icmp_seq=0 ttl=255 time=1.146 ms
64 bytes from 192.168.1.4: icmp_seq=1 ttl=255 time=0.913 ms
64 bytes from 192.168.1.4: icmp_seq=2 ttl=255 time=0.929 ms
64 bytes from 192.168.1.4: icmp_seq=3 ttl=255 time=0.928 ms
```

Pinging the IP address that LaBrea captured works because the machine at `192.168.1.4` is a bit slow (it's a Linux box running on a 486 chip, but it makes a fine router), and it responded to the ARP request sent by Sage's machine slower than LaBrea running on Racer-X did. In anticipation that such things might happen, LaBrea has been written so that it can function as a temporary packet rerouter to fix things if it has inadvertently made a mistake and grabbed an IP too quickly. In this case, after it sees the proper response from `192.168.1.4`, LaBrea redirects packets that are being written with the faked MAC address to their proper recipient until the ARP tables are updated properly and traffic for that IP is no longer being directed to the fake MAC. LaBrea can also use this functionality to discover when a new machine has appeared on the network at one of the IP addresses it's claimed, and to seamlessly relinquish spoofed IP addresses as necessary.

In short, LaBrea fights fire with fire by turning attackers' own techniques against them. To help you fight fire with fire, Table 8.1 provides a listing of command-line options for LaBrea.

TABLE 8.1 Command-Line Options for the LaBrea Tarpit Server

Option	Function
`-i <interface>`	Sets a nondefault interface.
`-t <datasize>`	Sets connection throttling size in bytes. Default is 10.
`-r <rate>`	Sets ARP timeout rate in seconds. Default is 3.
`-s`	Safe operation in a switched environment.
`-l`	Logs activity to syslog. With version 2.0.1+ you can use `kill -USR1 <LaBrea_PID>` to toggle logging. If logging was not enabled at start, this sets the `-l` flag. If logging (`-l | -v`) is set, this saves the value and turns off logging. If logging is presently toggled off, it restores the saved level (`-l | -v`).
`-v`	Verbosely logs activity to syslog. With version 2.0.1+ you can use `kill -USR1 <LaBrea_PID>` to toggle logging. If logging was not enabled at start, this sets the `-l` flag. If logging (`-l | -v`) is set, this saves the value and turns off logging. If logging is presently toggled off, it restores the saved level (`-l | -v`).
`-F <filename>`	Specifies a BPF filename. Connections specified by the BPF will also be tarpitted. These connections must be firewalled to drop inbound packets or this won't work.

TABLE 8.1 Continued

Option	Function
`-h`	Hard-captures IPs. `/etc/LaBreaHardExclude` should contain an IP list that you never want `LaBrea` to hard-capture. Only necessary with the `-h` option.
`-x`	Disables IP capture.
`-m`	Specifies a netmask. The network number and netmask are normally loaded from the interface. If you're using an interface that has no IP, you'll have to provide both these numbers. These must be correct or bad things may happen.
`-n`	Specifies a network number. The network number and netmask are normally loaded from the interface. If you're using an interface that has no IP, you'll have to provide both of these numbers. These must be correct or bad things may happen.
`-V`	Prints version information and exits.
`-a`	Does not respond to SYN/ACKs and PINGs. By default, LaBrea "virtual machines" respond to an inbound SYN/ACK with a RST and are "pingable." The `-a` option eliminates this behavior.
`-q`	Does not report odd (out of netblock) ARPs.
`-T`	Test mode—prints out debug information but does not run.
`-R`	Soft restart—waits while recapturing active connects.
`-p <maxrate>`	Persists state capture connect attempts. LaBrea will permanently capture connect attempts within the limit of the maximum data rate specified (in bytes/sec).
`-b`	Logs bandwidth usage to syslog.
`-d`	Does not detach process.
`-o`	Sends output to stdout rather than syslog. This sends log information to stdout rather than to syslog. This option also implies and sets the `-d` option.
`-P`	Persists mode capture only.
`-L`	Beta "Linux" window probe captures code.

NOTES on control files:

`LaBrea` also uses two files to control its operation:

`/etc/LaBreaExclude` contains a list of IPs (one per line) to exclude from `LaBrea`'s attention.

`/etc/LaBreaHardExclude` contains a list of IPs that `LaBrea` won't hard-capture. (Use with the `-h` option.)

The IP address can be specified either as single addresses (for example, `192.168.0.4`) or as a range of addresses (for example, `192.168.0.1 - 192.168.0.50`).

`LaBrea` should never capture an IP that has an active machine sitting on it. These two files are used to give you control over "empty" IP addresses. However, it certainly doesn't hurt to "exclude" active IPs.

Sending LaBrea a `SIGHUP` will cause it to reread the "exclusion" files and report packet statistics to syslog.

LaBrea can even be configured to work across a switched network, where one would normally conclude that such a server would see incoming ARP requests but not the returned reply. To overcome this difficulty, when used on a switched network, LaBrea watches for incoming ARP requests and then sends a duplicate request of its own for the same information. It does not consider an IP for building a tarpit in this situation unless its own requests for an ARP reply go unanswered. This mode may also be useful on networks where there are slow or transiently out-of-contact machines, as it induces `LaBrea` to more frequently check the status of apparently nonexistent machines that are enquired about often.

Spoofing Defenses

In a sense, there is no real defense against spoofing; there is only the ability to take precautions against being taken in by the spoofed information. If someone is spoofing IP addresses in her TCP/IP packets, unless she's on your local network, there's little you can do to prevent her from doing so. What you can do (possibly) is prevent your machines from accepting or believing the falsified information.

To perform such prevention, you need to be able to detect that information is being falsified. Software such as arpwatch and tcpdump can provide you with useful logs from which you might detect spoofing incidents. Although they usually can't tell you what of the data is actually false, they often can provide useful hints. Realize that what such software is doing is examining auxiliary data that is correlated to the information in question, and providing you with a warning that something unexpected has been seen.

Arpwatch can't tell you which host that's claiming an IP is actually lying; all it can tell you is that it appears that two hosts are competing for the same address. If you've kept a table of IPs that you've assigned, and the MAC addresses that go with them, you might be able to determine who's the IP address thief. On the other hand, it's possible that both conflicting addresses are being spoofed, in which case arpwatch can tell you that something's up, but you'll lack all ability to determine what information to believe.

Another tool you might use to monitor this spoofery and track it to its source would be a good switched network with usefully manageable switches. (Those frequently billed as "layer 3 switches," though they technically provide all the functions of an internetwork router for every connection, are the ones to look for. 3Com has a nice white paper on the subject at `http://www.3com.com/corpinfo/en_US/technology/tech_paper.jsp?DOC_ID=5298`.) Such an environment can provide you with a hardware-level view of where the conflicting information is coming from, and let you quickly track it to specific machines on specific wires.

Similarly, employing a firewall might be of some utility in gathering and using auxiliary information. If a packet shows up at your firewall that says that it's from an IP address on your internal network, the firewall can employ information entirely outside the packet to determine whether to believe it—namely, on which wire did the packet appear? The one for the internal network, or the one from the external network? Employing such technology enables your internal machines to more seriously consider the idea of using a packet's supplied source IP as an identifying credential because it can preclude anyone from outside the local network from injecting traffic with local IPs. Of course, it does nothing to prevent an internal machine from spoofing IP credentials onto your internal wire, so again, a firewall configured to provide this type of barrier is only one more way to increase your trust. It cannot be used to *prove* trustability.

When looking at how to establish trust (and detect spoofs) in any particular exchange of information, concentrate on data regarding the communication itself that can be brought to bear on the examination. This might be private data such as a password that only you and the sender are expected to know, external information such as what a firewall can tell you about the origin of a packet, a network handshake that proves that you've sufficiently correct network information to carry on a dialog with the sender, an encoding scheme such as a private protocol or secret sequence exchanges that must be performed, or the use of public or private key exchanges. Each type of verification for identity and validation of trust can be checked through the use of different mechanisms. Each can also be spoofed and false, believable credentials provided. For each exchange you want to trust, you need to examine the types of credentials that are being examined, how they can be spoofed, and what tests you might apply to detect such falsification.

Each user and computer installation is likely to be different in its needs, and many protocols already provide some mechanism for checking at least some sort of credentials. You will need to examine your situation and determine whether the mechanisms already in place give you a sufficient level of trust, or whether you need to add hardware or run additional software to increase your level of trust in information that is being conveyed to you.

Summary

In this chapter you've seen some of the issues of computing trust and verification, and places where trust and security can be compromised by a person or computer that is providing false identification tokens to your system. Here we've concentrated on how basic network information can be falsified, and the consequences of such spoofing, but the issue of trustable information extends to any sort of computing data in a similar fashion. The information by which you recognize a familiar auction Web site can be spoofed by someone who has copied the page's layout and design.

Unless you're terrifically alert, you probably pay much more attention to what the page looks like than to the URL that appears in your Web browser's location bar. Emails can be spoofed; the identifying information that gives machines' names on the network can be spoofed; practically any data that is delivered over the network can be falsified by someone, in some way. What you need to determine for yourself and for your systems is what identifying information is sufficient for you to trust, and how much trust you're willing to have, based on that amount of information. The answers will be different for almost every user and almost every context. We can only help to show you where the problems might lie, and try to illustrate potential consequences that might not be readily apparent. You will need to make the hard decisions yourself regarding who to trust and how much, based on your own needs and the sensitivity of whatever information might be at stake.

It's important when considering the possibilities for spoofing and the areas where it may cause harm to remember that spoofing is essentially impossible to completely prevent. Regardless of the credentials you require to verify identity, there will be some way that someone might be able to provide false credentials and establish a false identity. What you can do is make it harder to generate believable false credentials, and take advantage of any auxiliary data that is available to attempt to corroborate the identification. Use firewalls, monitoring software, and identification protocols for which the credentials cannot be easily stolen or duplicated. Make certain that the identification credentials you choose to accept are kept up to date, and that software that uses them has been patched against any possibility of information leakage.

Many network services and many types of data already have software written to help you with the task of establishing a trust level for various credentials, and there will undoubtedly be more that appear as the realities of network commerce mature. Examine your computing trust needs, what the pitfalls in any particular trust situation might be, and what avenues present themselves for establishing the veracity of credentials that are presented to you. In some cases there will be few to no safeguards in place, but if the communication or identity verification is one that is common in the networked world, someone will probably be working on solutions to assist in detecting and avoiding spoofed information. Some of these may not be inexpensive, but as we've reiterated throughout this book, there are bad people out there who want to do bad things. Only you can decide how important the truth of any communications are, and how much effort, time, or money you're willing to invest in increasing the level of your trust in that information.

9

Everything Else

IN THIS CHAPTER

- DoS
- Buffer Overflows
- Session Hijacking
- Everything Else
- Additional Resources

If you've read sequentially through the book to this point, you might be asking yourself, "How can there possibly *be* anything else to worry about?" The number of attacks that can be launched against your system and services grows every day. As developers work to improve their defenses, attackers find new ways around them. This chapter discusses several broad classes of attacks, how they work, and why vigilance is one of your best defenses.

DoS

Although DOS may be considered an attack class all its own, DoS does not refer to early PC operating systems. DoS—or Denial of Service—attacks are designed to stop a machine or network from providing a service to its clients. Depending on your network, this can mean just about anything: keeping your mail server from delivering mail, stopping your Web server, or even keeping you from logging in to your machine to work locally. The attack itself can take on a number of forms, from a direct network attack to a local attack instigated by a user account (or someone with access to a user account) on your system. No matter what the target or how it takes place, DoS attacks usually hit hard, are difficult to diagnose, and can put you out of business until the attack has ended.

NOTE

Many DoS attacks are launched against a particular application or service. Throughout the book wherever there has been (or is) a recent DoS for a Mac OS X daemon or application, we will attempt to provide a description and CVE reference for further information. This section is meant to provide a more general overview of DoS attacks.

Network Target DoS Attacks

The most effective and costly DoS attacks take advantage of holes in an operating system's TCP/IP implementation to bring down the entire machine. These are the "holy grails" of attacks—simple, fast, and affecting everything they touch. The first widespread DoS that affected individual users is the now infamous *Ping of Death*.

Ping of Death

In 1996, it was discovered that an IP packet (see Chapter 7, "Eavesdropping and Snooping for Information: Sniffers and Scanners"), constructed with a length greater than 65536 bytes (an illegal size) could crash, disable, or otherwise disrupt systems running Windows 95, Mac OS 7.x, Windows NT, Linux, Netware, and a wide range of printers, routers, and other network devices. Windows machines proved to be an especially useful launching platform for the attacks because the Windows `ping` command allowed these illegal packets to be sent directly from the command line with `ping -l 65510 <hostname or IP>`. Software quickly followed for other operating systems that could scan an entire network, sending the invalid packets, spoofing the source address, and literally forcing hundreds of users to reboot within seconds of the attack starting.

Operating system vendors responded quickly to the situation, issuing patches shortly after the problem was discovered (less than 3 hours, for Linux!). A complete description of the PoD, the machines affected, and example attack source code can be found at `http://www.insecure.org/sploits/ping-o-death.html`.

WinNuke

Another "popular" TCP/IP DoS attack affected Windows machines by the thousands. Windows 95/NT machines were found to be easily crashed by packets with the OOB (out of band) flag set on an established connection. Because most Windows machines ran file sharing services, these attacks were commonly aimed at port 139, the standard NetBIOS/IP port. A remote attacker would connect to the port, then send a packet with the OOB flag set. The result? An instant Blue Screen of Death. "Winnuke" software was released for other users to take advantage of this flaw, resulting in much glee from Macintosh and Unix users.

Strangely enough, after Microsoft issued their initial patches for the problem, Macintosh computers could *still* crash remote systems with WinNuke. The Macintosh TCP/IP implementation set a TCP Urgent flag within outgoing TCP packets. Windows machines could not handle this additional flag, and continued to crash at the hands of Macintosh users until Microsoft released a second patch. Information on the Windows OOB bug and WinNuke code can be found at `http://www.insecure.org/sploits/windows.OOB.DOS.html`.

SYN Floods

The previous two attacks have used bugs in the TCP/IP implementation, but it is also possible to exploit the properties of TCP/IP itself to create a DoS condition. A popular means of doing this is through a *SYN flood*. SYN packets, introduced in Chapter 7, are used by a client computer to initiate a connection with a remote machine.

As demonstrated in Figure 9.1, upon receiving a SYN packet and sequence number, a server allocates resources for the connection and sends a SYN packet, acknowledgement, and another sequence number. The client *should* then respond with a sequence number and second acknowledgement at which point the connection will be opened. If the client does not acknowledge immediately, the server must wait a specific amount of time before it can assume the connection is dead and de-allocate resources.

CLIENT STATE		SERVER STATE
CLOSED		LISTEN
SYN_SENT	SYN, SEQ (A) ----->	LISTEN
SYN_SENT	<-- ACK (A+1), SYN, SEQ (B)	SYN_RCVD
SYN_RCVD	ACK (B+1), SEQ (A) ----->	SYN_RCVD
ESTABLISHED	<---->	ESTABLISHED

FIGURE 9.1 Initial TCP/IP conversation.

SYN floods work by overflowing a server with SYN packets (often from spoofed source addresses), causing it to allocate more resources than it can manage (thereby running out of memory), or more connections than it allows (forcing valid connections to be denied). The end result in either case is that the server becomes inaccessible for, at least, the duration of the SYN flood.

TIP

You can use `netstat` to display the status of connections on your Mac OS X box.

You can detect SYN floods by looking for abnormally numerous incoming SYN packets in relation to general TCP/IP traffic. High ratios of SYN packets can trigger the operating system to drop incoming SYN packets (denying connections) until the flood has ended, or take a more complex but less disruptive approach—such as using SYN cookies.

SYN cookies now protect most modern operating systems, such as Linux and BSD, against SYN floods. During a TCP/IP conversation, the server and client exchange sequence numbers to maintain a synchronized conversation. A SYN cookie is a specially calculated sequence number that is based on the remote client's IP and is not guessable by the client. When making the initial acknowledgement of the SYN packet, the server sends back this special cookie (SEQ(B) in Figure 9.1) and then, for all intents and purposes, forgets about the conversation. If it receives an acknowledgement with the appropriate sequence number (SEQ(B+1)), it knows the connection is legitimate and allows it to proceed.

DDoS

In a simple DoS assault, the attacker uses his or her PC or a compromised machine to send packets to the victim. Although a single computer is capable of causing plenty of problems, it is also reasonably simple to block at your router or network firewall.

Attackers quickly discovered that to create a sustained DoS situation, they would need to hit from multiple locations simultaneously, and the DDoS, or Distributed Denial of Service attack, was born. A DDoS attack typically uses multiple compromised computers, or *zombies*, that are "waiting" for an attack to be triggered—from a *master* computer, as seen in Figure 9.2. The zombies do not *need* to use spoofed addresses and can be used much more aggressively against the target because they are *not* the actual attacker. DDoS attacks need only flood the attacked network with packets, rendering it inaccessible.

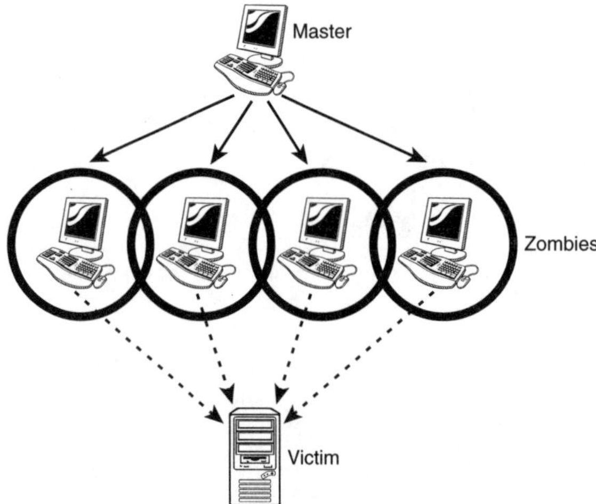

FIGURE 9.2 A DDoS attack uses multiple zombies to attack a victim.

DDoS attacks are difficult to stop because of the number of routes that may be used during an attack. Recent attacks have used ICMP traffic to synchronize the states of the zombies, making the detecting and firewalling of potential zombies even more troublesome. Successful DDoS attacks are usually carried out only after a significant amount of upfront work has been performed to prep the zombies and scout the targets.

For examples and analysis of DDoS attacks, read the following analyses:

- **Tribal Flood Network.** `http://staff.washington.edu/dittrich/misc/tfn.analysis.txt`
- **Stacheldraht.** `http://staff.washington.edu/dittrich/misc/stacheldraht.analysis.txt`
- **Global Threat.** `http://bots.lockdowncorp.com/gtbot.html`
- **Trinoo.** `http://staff.washington.edu/dittrich/misc/trinoo.analysis.txt`

NOTE

While most large-scale DDoS attacks do require zombies, a very popular attack—Smurf—does not. The Smurf attack works by forging the reply-to address on an outgoing broadcast ICMP packet. The packet is sent to an entire network with the goal of tricking the machines into replying simultaneously to a victim address—overwhelming them with data. Because a single packet is used to generate multiple attacking responses, this is called a *magnification* attack.

More information about Smurf attacks can be found at `http://www.pintday.org/whitepapers/dos-smurf.shtml`, and example code can be found at `http://www.crimelist.com/dos.htm`.

At this time, there are no known instances of Mac OS X being used in a DDoS attack, but there is no guarantee that the clients for distributed attacks won't be made available at some time in the future.

Protection

Denial of service attacks are difficult to stop because they are unpredictable and often exploit protocol or network weaknesses and do not require the remote machine to be compromised. A completely secure Mac OS X machine could be crippled by a network DDoS attack no matter how well the administrator has protected the network. The Internet has a finite amount of bandwidth on a finite number of routes available for a given host. If those routes are flooded by thousands of machines simultaneously throwing packets at the host, it doesn't make any difference what software, operating system, or security the target machine has in place.

Protection comes from prevention and understanding. Following these guidelines will help protect you from DoS attacks:

- Keep your software up to date and secured by using the software's own security mechanisms. This is repeated throughout the book and cannot be stressed enough. Even though most DDoS attacks are the result of compromised clients, a sendmail daemon with relaying accidentally left active could be used as a client in a DDoS email attack without any compromise being necessary (see Chapter 13, "Mail Server Security").
- Firewall, if possible, network clients. DDoS clients often require a trigger from the attacker to start operating (sometimes sent via IRC). If the trigger cannot be received, the compromised client doesn't pose a threat (see Chapter 17, "Blocking Network Access: Firewalls"). Blocking broadcast and multicast traffic and verifying packet source addresses are good overall preventative measures.
- Implement intrusion detection. Intrusion detection software can alert you to DoS attacks and help prevent system compromises from taking place (see Chapter 18, "Alarm Systems: Intrusion Detection").
- Understand your network topology and upstream provider. An attack aimed at an entire network or the network's routing/firewall/etc. equipment cannot be stopped by an end user sitting in front of his or her Mac. Your upstream provider may be able to block the attack, or, at the very least, you can disable your feed until the attack has subsided.

Buffer Overflows

Another common means of attacking a system or service is by way of a buffer overflow. Buffer overflows are caused by errors in the programming of system service and can be exploited in any number of ways, from gaining elevated privileges to executing arbitrary code, depending on the service that is to be exploited.

A buffer overflow is nothing more than a matter of loose or nonexistent bounds checking on a buffer. Say what? What does that mean? Don't worry, we're getting there. The C programming language, which is used to build almost all of Mac OS X, requires developers to keep very close tabs on variables and the amount of memory they require. A C string, for example, must be allocated to contain the number of characters in the string, plus one null terminator. For example, the string "John Ray" requires 9 bytes of storage space, as shown in Figure 9.3.

J	o	h	n		R	a	y	NULL
1	2	3	4	5	6	7	8	9

FIGURE 9.3 C strings require storage for one byte per ASCII character + 1 null terminator.

Although this might seem straightforward enough, the C language includes a number of functions such as `strcmp()`, `strcpy()`, and `gets()` that do not attempt to verify that the string on which they are operating is the appropriate length before executing. Consider the following program (`overflow.c`) which reads and prints a user's name:

```
int main()
{
  char name[9];
  printf ("Enter your name: ");
  gets(name);
  printf ("Your name is %s\n", name);
}
```

Compile (`gcc -o overflow overflow.c`) and then execute the program:

```
% ./overflow
warning: this program uses gets(), which is unsafe.
Enter your name: John Ray
Your name is John Ray
%
```

For an execution with a string that fits within the 9-byte buffer, the program acts exactly as one would hope. Change the length of input and things are nearly as peachy:

```
% ./overflow
warning: this program uses gets(), which is unsafe.
Enter your name: The Noble and Powerful Ezekial Martograthy Bartholomew III
Your name is The Noble and Powerful Ezekial Martograthy Bartholomew III
Segmentation fault
```

Now, instead of executing cleanly, the program crashes with a segmentation fault. What has happened is that the input data, which should have been contained within nine bytes, has overwritten part of the executable in memory, causing it to crash.

Although crashing is certainly a common effect of buffer overflows, they can sometimes be exploited with far more dramatic effects. A good example of a buffer overflow exploit is demonstrated in Listing 9.1 (`buffer.c`), written by Mark E. Donaldson and provided here with a few tweaks for Mac OS X.

LISTING 9.1 Source Code for `buffer.c`

```
1: int main()
2: {
3:   char name[8];
4:   char real_passwd[8]="test";
5:   char password[8];
6:
7:   // retrieve the user information
8:   printf ("Enter your name: ");
9:   gets(name);
10:  printf("Enter your password: ");
11:  gets(password);
12:  printf("Your name and password are %s and %s.\n",name,password);
13:  printf("The real password for %s is %s.\n",name,real_passwd);
14:
15:  // Authenticate password against real_passwd
16:  authenticate(password,real_passwd);
17:  return 0;
18: }
19:
20: void authenticate (char* string1, char* string2) {
21:  char buffer1[8];
22:  char buffer2[8];
23:  strcpy (buffer1,string1);
24:  strcpy (buffer2,string2);
25:
26:  if (strcmp(buffer1,buffer2)==0) printf("Access allowed!\n");
27: }
```

The program logic is simple. Lines 3-5 allocate storage for `name`, `real_password` (the password we're going to test for, hard coded as `test`), and `password` (what the user will type in). Lines 8-13 input the `name` and `password` and print what the program *thinks* it has received from the user. Line 16 calls the authentication routine (lines 20-27), which checks `password` against `real_password` and prints `Access allowed!` if they match.

Again, compile (`gcc -o buffer buffer.c`) and execute the program, using valid (seven or fewer characters) input. First, the program is run with an invalid (wrong) but properly sized username and password:

```
% ./buffer
warning: this program uses gets(), which is unsafe.
Enter your name: jray
Enter your password: frog
Your name and password are jray and frog.
The real password for jray is test.
```

The output is exactly as expected: the passwords do not match, so the access message is not displayed. Next, run the program using the correct password (`test`):

```
% ./buffer
warning: this program uses gets(), which is unsafe.
Enter your name: jray
Enter your password: test
Your name and password are jray and test.
The real password for jray is test.
Access allowed!
```

Again, the output is precisely what one would expect: the passwords match and access is allowed. Now look at what happens when the invalid lengths are used. This time, instead of a valid username, enter `123456789ABCDEF` (you'll see why we chose these values shortly) and `test` for the password:

```
% ./buffer
warning: this program uses gets(), which is unsafe.
Enter your name: 123456789ABCDEF
Enter your password: test
Your name and password are 123456789ABCDEF and test.
The real password for 123456789ABCDEF is 9ABCDEF.
```

Did you notice that even though `test` was used as the password, the program didn't correctly authenticate the user? In addition (and more importantly), did you notice that the program is now claiming that the REAL password is `9ABCDEF`? This provides very useful information about the program and its flaw. First, you can tell that the input for the user's name (`name`) has obviously overwritten the real password (`real_passwd`) in memory. Because the real password starts with the `9ABCDEF` input, it can be inferred that the buffer size for `name` is eight bytes long, and that the `name` and `real_passwd` data structures are located sequentially in memory (just as they are defined on lines 3 and 4 of the source code).

So, how can this newfound knowledge be exploited? Simple: By overflowing the `name` buffer, you can set the password to any value you want, and subsequently authenticate against it:

```
% ./buffer
warning: this program uses gets(), which is unsafe.
Enter your name: jrayXXXXHack
Enter your password: Hack
Your name and password are jrayXXXXHack and Hack.
The real password for jrayXXXXHack is Hack.
Access allowed!
```

Obviously, no real-world program should be written like this, and developers should take the time to perform bounds checking on their code if it is not handled automatically by the compiler. The goal of most attackers it to gain elevated permissions or execute arbitrary code on a server. To do this, they must understand the code they are attacking and the underlying operating system. Just because a piece of code suffers from a buffer overflow does *not* mean it can be exploited beyond a simple crash. A complete play-by-play of a buffer overflow is documented in Mark Donaldson's "Inside the Buffer Overflow Attack: Mechanism, Method, and Prevention," `http://www.sans.org/rr/code/inside_buffer.php`.

Protection

Buffer overflows are caused by errors in the software you are running, not from a lapse in your abilities as an administrator. Protecting against a buffer overflow, like DoS attacks, is more a matter of vigilance than active prevention. Keep the following points in mind:

- If developing, use modern languages with build-in bounds checking such as Java, Ruby, and Perl. C programmers should avoid the standard C string functions or, at the very least, perform bounds checking (`sizeof()`) before and after string operations.
- Be aware of buffer overrun errors that have been reported for your system, servers, and libraries and take measures to patch or limit access to the affected functions (that is, keep up to date!).
- Identify SUID applications. SUID tools are the most likely target for buffer overflows, because they execute with root permissions and may provide root access in the event of an overflow.
- Run intrusion detection software. It is *very* unlikely that if you suffer a buffer overflow attack it will be launched by the person who discovered or wrote the exploit. It is very likely a script-kiddie running a piece of code picked up from an IRC chat room and that has a recognizable attack signature.

Session Hijacking

The next type of attack to examine is session hijacking. Another "nonattack," session hijacking is a means of either gaining total or partial control over an established TCP/IP connection. Session attacks rely on a trusted connection between two computers to be in place, and then work to either modify packets traveling between the machines or take the place of one of the two computers.

Session hijacking is an effective means of gaining control over a machine or process that otherwise would not be accessible. Most authentication (such as AFP, Kerberos, and so on) take place during the initiation of a connection. After authentication, the conversation is considered *trusted*. This is the point at which attackers want session hijacking to take place.

The most common and effective form of session hijacking is called *man-in-the-middle* and works by placing a computer in the "middle" of an established connection. Both ends of a connection must be "convinced" that to speak to the other side, they need to go through the attacking computer.

To do this, the attacker must be located on the same network as either of the victim computers. As you might guess, *spoofing* is required to bring all the pieces together. Consider Figure 9.4, which displays a simple network with an established connection in place.

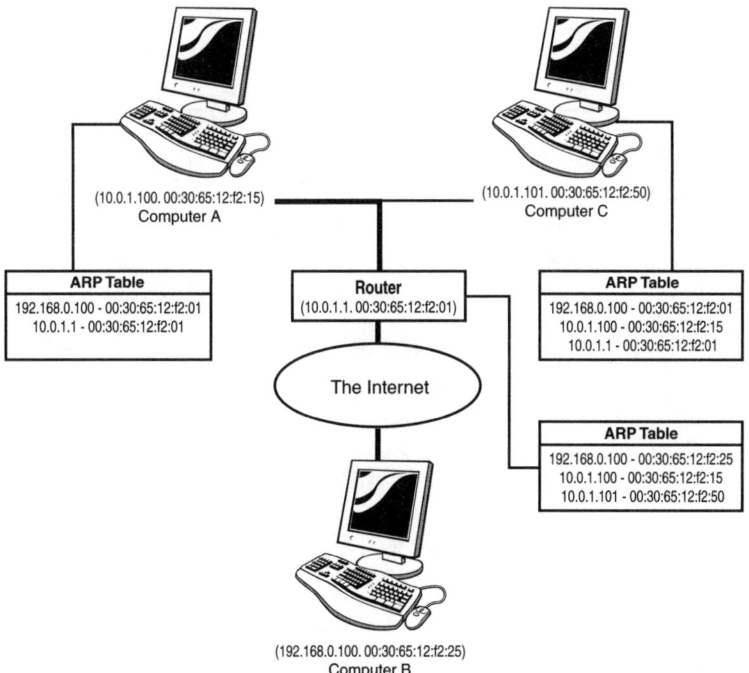

FIGURE 9.4 The initial (unhijacked) network state.

Computer A (10.0.1.100, 00:30:65:12:f2:15) speaks to Computer B (192.168.0.100, 00:30:65:12:f2:25) via the Router (10.0.1.1, 00:30:65:12:f2:01), while Computer C (10.0.1.101, 00:30:65:12:f2:50) sits idle on the same network as A. For all intents and purposes, the session that is being hijacked is between Computer A and the router; the location of B is irrelevant. In the initial established state, Computer A has an ARP table that contains a mapping between the IP 192.168.0.100 and the MAC address 00:30:65:12:f2:01, or, in other words, to communicate with a machine at the IP address of Computer B, Computer A must send packets to the MAC address 00:30:65:12:f2:01—the router. Likewise, the router's ARP table maps between the IP address 10.0.1.100 and MAC address 00:30:65:12:f2:15, both belonging to Computer A.

To hijack the session, Computer C implements a spoofing attack in which it purports to *be* both the remote client (Computer C) and the local victim (Computer A), and advertises this via unrequested ARP replies to Computer A and the router, respectively. The result can be seen in Figure 9.5.

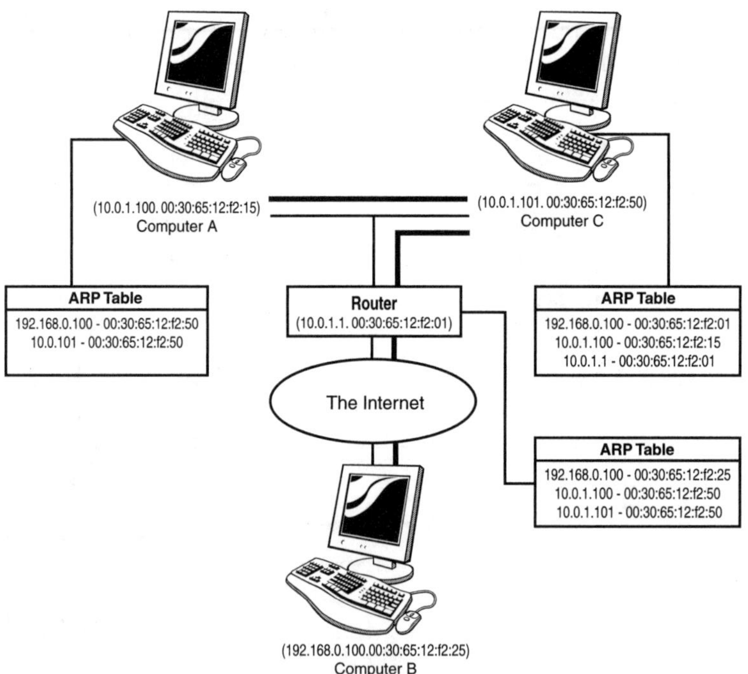

FIGURE 9.5 The hijacked network connection.

Now, Computer A has an ARP mapping between 00:30:65:12:f2:50 (Computer C) and Computer B, while the router has a mapping between Computer A and 00:30:65:12:f2:50 (Computer C). The result is that Computer A transmits data to what it believes to be the remote Computer B by way of the router, but instead transmits it to Computer C. Computer C can modify the packet (or do anything it likes) and retransmit it to the router, purporting to be Computer A.

Session hijacking, at one time, was very difficult to implement. Today it is a matter of finding the right software and choosing your targets. The software `ettercap`, for example, can be used to implement a man-in-the-middle attack without its user having any knowledge of networking or spoofing.

Discussed in Chapter 7, you can use `ettercap` to start a man-in-the-middle attack by choosing a source and destination address, using `A` to enter ARP sniffing mode (poisoning the ARP caches of both the source and destination), choosing the connection to hijack, then pressing `I` to start injecting characters into the packet stream, as shown in Figure 9.6.

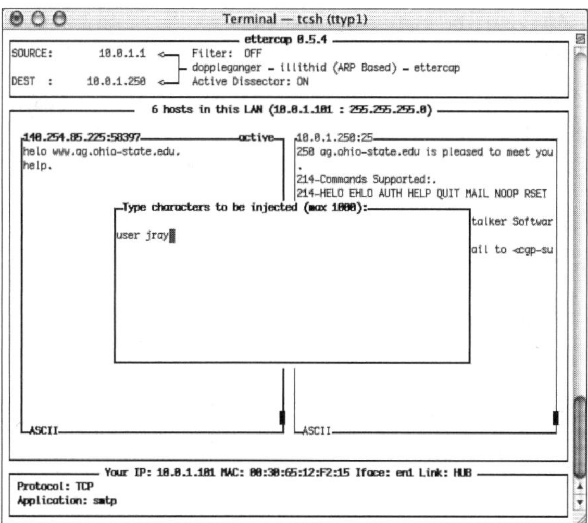

FIGURE 9.6 Conduct a man-in-the-middle attack by using `ettercap`.

Other methods of session hijacking may employ other mechanisms such as DoS attacks against one side of the connection. After bringing down one side, the attacker spoofs the original connection, completely replacing the original.

Protection

Protecting against session hijacking is reasonably straightforward. Following these guidelines will greatly reduce your chances of being hijacked:

- First and foremost, do not use unencrypted protocols, such as Telnet and FTP. Encrypted communications via IPSec or SSH are not easily forged, although full SSH1 sniffing is implemented in `ettercap`. SSH2 is preferable because it is much more secure.
- If possible, use static ARP mappings for your critical systems (`arp -s mygateway.mynetwork.net 10.0.1.1`).
- Use software such as `ettercap` or `arpwatch` to detect clients that may be involved in a spoofing attack.

Using `arpwatch`

The `arpwatch` software is a simple-to-use solution you can use to detect spoofing without needing to manually monitor your network. Arpwatch maintains a database of host/ethernet mappings and automatically logs changes to `syslogd` and email.

For a network with static IP addresses (or static DHCP mappings), the only changes that should be detected are when a system is added or replaced on the network. Other changes can be interpreted as a potential spoofing attack.

Download `arpwatch` from `http://online.securityfocus.com/tools/142`.

Unarchive and enter the source code distribution:

```
% tar xf arpwatch-2.1a4.tar
% cd arpwatch-2.1a4/
```

Next, configure with `./configure powerpc`:

```
% ./configure powerpc
loading cache ./config.cache
checking host system type... powerpc-unknown-none
checking target system type... powerpc-unknown-none
checking build system type... powerpc-unknown-none
checking for gcc... (cached) gcc
checking whether the C compiler (gcc  ) works... yes
checking whether the C compiler (gcc  ) is a cross-compiler... no
...
```

Now you need to make a few changes to the source for it to install and work correctly on Mac OS X. Edit the file `addresses.h` to define your email address. By default, the `WATCHER` constant is set to `root`; you should replace this with the address to be notified when changes are detected.

Next, open `Makefile` and change the default SENDMAIL location from

```
SENDMAIL = /usr/lib/sendmail
```

to

```
SENDMAIL = /usr/sbin/sendmail
```

NOTE

For this to work, sendmail must be configured to send email. It does not need to run as a daemon, but you'll need to follow the steps in Chapter 13 for it to be functional.

Finally, perform a search on the string (once again in `Makefile`) `-o bin -g bin` and replace all occurrences with `-o root -g admin`. You're now ready to compile and install:

```
# make
gcc -O -DDEBUG  -DHAVE_FCNTL_H=1 -DHAVE_MEMORY_H=1 -DTIME_WITH_SYS_TIME=1
-DHAVE_BCOPY=1 -DHAVE_STRERROR=1 -DWORDS_BIGENDIAN=1 -DRETSIGTYPE=void
-DRETSIGVAL= -DHAVE_SIGACTION=1 -DDECLWAITSTATUS=int
-DSTDC_HEADERS=1  -DARPDIR=\"/usr/local/arpwatch\"
-DPATH_SENDMAIL=\"/usr/lib/sendmail\" -I.  -c ./db.c


# make install
/usr/bin/install -c -m 555 -o root -g admin arpwatch /usr/local/sbin
/usr/bin/install -c -m 555 -o root -g admin arpsnmp /usr/local/sbin

# cp arpwatch.8 /usr/share/man/man8/
```

After installing, `arpwatch` can be invoked as root from `/usr/local/sbin/arpwatch`. It requires the support file `arp.dat` to be created beforehand to contain the mapping database. You may also need to invoke `arpwatch` with one of its switches, shown in Table 9.1.

TABLE 9.1 `arpwatch` Command-Line Switches

Switch	Description
`-d`	Debugging mode. `Arpwatch` does not fork and outputs all data to `stderr` rather than email or `syslogd`.
`-f` *<pathname>*	The path to the `arp` mapping file. This file must exist before you start `arpwatch`.
`-i` *<network interface>*	Set the network interface to monitor. The default is `en0`.
`-r` *<pathname>*	Read the packet information from a `tcpdump` file rather than a network interface.

For example, I can start `arpwatch` on my network interface `en1` like this:

```
# touch /var/db/arp.dat
# /usr/local/sbin/arpwatch  -f /var/db/arp.dat
```

After it runs for a few seconds I start to see messages like this in `/var/log/system.log` and my mailbox:

```
Jan 20 00:37:59 Computer arpwatch: listening on en1
Jan 20 00:38:03 Computer arpwatch: new station 10.0.1.1 0:90:27:9a:4c:c1
Jan 20 00:38:04 Computer arpwatch: new station 10.0.1.119 0:30:65:4:dc:46
Jan 20 00:38:25 Computer arpwatch: new station 10.0.1.2 0:30:65:2d:c7:d1
Jan 20 00:38:42 Computer arpwatch: new station 10.0.1.250 0:30:65:dc:68:88
Jan 20 00:41:25 Computer arpwatch: new station 10.0.1.101 0:30:65:12:f2:15
```

During the first several minutes, `arpwatch` will build the mapping table and generate messages for each machine on the network. After the table is built, however, the only messages logged will be those indicating a change in the network.

Everything Else

We're assuming by now that it's pretty clear that there isn't any *everything else*. There will always be other attacks and other means for third parties to modify or disrupt your system. Before ending the chapter, however, you should be familiar with a few other concepts that are mentioned throughout the book.

Root Kits

A rootkit isn't a compromise, per se; it is a set of tools that are installed *after* a system has been compromised and root access gained. The purpose of a rootkit is to provide tools for covering an attacker's tracks so that its presence will not be detected on the machine. In some cases, rootkits may contain additional software for carrying out further attacks.

For example, common rootkit components include the following:

- `du/ls/find`. Modified to hide files.
- `top/ps`. Modified to hide processes (sniffers and so on).
- `netstat`. Modified to hide remote connections.
- `ssh/xinet/inetd/tcpd`. Modified to allow remote access, ignore deny lists.
- `syslogd`. Modified to hide log entries.
- `wtmp/utmp/lastlog`. Software included to modify or erase the system accounting logs.

- `killall`. Modified to *not* kill attacker processes.
- `lsof`. Modified to hide connections and files.
- `passwd/sudo/su`. Modified to provide root access.

More information on the logs and rootkit modifications can be found in Chapter 19, "Logs and User Activity Accounting." If a rootkit has been installed, the operating system cannot be trusted. You must make the decision to either attempt to repair the damage or reinstall the operating system. The only cases where a repair should be attempted are those where a piece of software such as Tripwire (`http://sourceforge.net/projects/tripwire/`) is installed and can verify which files have changed from the default distribution.

A quick and dirty solution is to use `md5` to calculate a checksum for the critical system files, which can be stored offline and used for comparison in the event of an attack:

```
# md5 /usr/bin/*
MD5 (/usr/bin/CFInfoPlistConverter) = be7664241c675f06424961d8773d19c1
MD5 (/usr/bin/a2p) = 6f0ff3f32ffc295cc00ea2ecf83b1143
MD5 (/usr/bin/aclocal) = 6b204bce8a0151c330649cb3ff764a43
MD5 (/usr/bin/aclocal-1.6) = 6b204bce8a0151c330649cb3ff764a43
MD5 (/usr/bin/addftinfo) = e55d67a1e4848a4a4abd75c9d78106dc
MD5 (/usr/bin/addr) = 2c4824c5fa6a9ee332a5e4ab14787e42
MD5 (/usr/bin/aexml) = 788248a22bdfac053473af90728efca1
MD5 (/usr/bin/afmtodit) = 7da2c8b3d85e10500bd01b59ae52780b
MD5 (/usr/bin/appleping) = 0cda19ad69004d8fd1b6b66e7159ece4
...
```

The calculated 128-bit signatures will be identical only if the files are identical. Files altered by a rootkit display a different signature from the initial calculations.

At this time, there are no known "popular" rootkits for Mac OS X, although it is certainly possible that anyone with access to a Mac and a compiler has recompiled any of the popular Linux rootkits for the operating system. A rootkit checker has already been compiled for Mac OS X (`http://www.gouedart-lafeuille.net/software/applescript/ChkRootKit_for_MacOSX/`, a port of the `ChkRootKit` software found at `http://www.chkrootkit.org`). ChkRootKit is capable of detecting common rootkit changes and reporting the files that have been compromised.

Trusted Data Sources

Too often (and with reason), users trust data if it is processed by software they know and trust. Someone with an understanding of their internals, however, can often trick these programs into falsifying or providing "unexpected" data.

A simple example of this is the system date and time. Files are stamped with a creation date and time that cannot be changed by end users. The modification times are easily updated with `touch`, but the creation date is inaccessible. `Tar` and other backup utilities can restore files to the system with their original timestamps. As a result, it's easy to modify a file's creation time stamp by tarring it, adjusting the time stamps within the `tar` file, then untarring it again.

Although this particular form of data falsification is trivial now that everyone on the planet can run a Unix box (and have access to their own system clocks), it is an example of an exploit that allows a user to falsify what is normally considered trusted information.

A Mac OS X 10.2.2 vulnerability was caused by a similar means of slipping information in "under the radar." By creating a disk image as an administrator on a remote system, then opening it under a nonadmin account on another Mac OS X machine, the user opening it can receive elevated administrator privileges (CVE: CAN-2002-1266). Like using `tar` to modify time stamps, an attacker using this technique need only let the operating system utilities perform the attack for him. Don't worry; this vulnerability was corrected in Mac OS X 10.2.3.

Trickery and Deceit

There are numbers of other attacks that can be directed at *you* personally rather than your machine. Through simple but effective tricks, attackers can gain information about you by just letting you use your computer. These are just a few more things to lose sleep over.

The most obvious piece of information that can be gleaned without a direct attack is whether or not you have and actively read a given email address. It is commonly believed (and in many cases it's certainly true) that spammers use the links in a piece of spam (including the unsubscribe links) to verify that the email address that was used is valid. Unfortunately, all that is needed in most cases is for you to *read* your mail in order for the spammer to know that your address is active. Most spam is HTML-based and includes images, which are loaded by default in Apple's Mail application. Images can easily be embedded in the HTML so that they pass information back to a script:

```
<img src="http://www.spammeringplace.com/displayimage.php?image=ad.gif
➥&activeemail=jray@poisontooth.com">
```

This might, for example, pass the name of an image to be displayed (`ad.gif`) along with my email address, to the remote host. The potential for this type of information gathering to take place can be eliminated by shutting off viewing of inline HTML objects within Apple Mail's Viewing Preferences. Of course, if you do that, you'll miss out on the graphic-intensive ads for products to make you richer, smaller, or larger.

Even more devious schemes have been designed by some attackers to convince you to *willingly* provide sensitive information under the pretense of a secure connection. Browser windows, for example, typically indicate a secure connection via the status bar at the bottom of the window. Attackers, through a variety of means (spoofing, compromised site forwarding, and so on), can redirect users to insecure sites for the purpose of collecting information. What the attacker cannot do, however, is (easily) get a site certificate that will be authenticated with your browser. As a result, they cannot create a secure connection with the victim. To "trick" the remote user to into believing that a secure connection is in place, the server can simply spawn a new browser window *without* a status bar, then *draw its own!* Using DHTML it would even be possible for an enterprising cracker to develop a complete browser interface within a window. Obviously, the browser wouldn't match everyone's interface (chances are, Mac users would be safe), but the illusion could be very convincing.

Additional Resources

If you aren't scared yet, here is some additional reading material to help. DoS and buffer overflow attacks are two of the most common and dangerous attacks that can be launched against your system. It's a good idea to have as much knowledge about the cracker as they have about you.

- **SYN Flood**, Internet Security Systems, `http://www.iss.net/security_center/advice/Exploits/TCP/SYN_flood/default.htm`
- **Denial of Service Attack Resources Page**, `http://www.denialinfo.com/`
- **CERT/CC Denial of Service**, CERT, `http://www.cert.org/tech_tips/denial_of_service.html`
- **Strategies to Protect Against Distributed Denial of Service Attacks**, Cisco, `http://www.cisco.com/warp/public/707/newsflash.html`
- **Help Defeat Denial of Service Attacks: Step-by-Step**, SANS Institute, `http://www.sans.org/dosstep/`
- **Inside the Buffer Overflow Attack: Mechanism, Method, & Prevention**, `http://www.sans.org/rr/code/inside_buffer.php`
- **Writing Buffer Overflow Exploits—a Tutorial for Beginners**, `http://www.securiteam.com/securityreviews/5OP0B006UQ.html`
- **Simple Buffer Overflow Exploits**, fides, `http://www.collusion.org/Article.cfm?ID=176`
- **Attacking Servers Through a Buffer Overflow**, `http://www.entercept.com/whitepaper/attackertools/buffer.asp`

- **Introduction to ARP Spoofing**, Sean Whalen, http://packetstormsecurity.com/papers/protocols/intro_to_arp_spoofing.pdf
- **Man-in-the-Middle Attack—A Brief**, Bhavin Bharat Bhansali, http://www.sans.org/rr/threats/middle.htm
- **Session Hijacking**, Internet Security Systems, http://www.iss.net/security_center/advice/Exploits/TCP/session_hijacking/default.htm
- **A Simple Active Attack Against TCP/IP**, Laurent Joncheray, http://www.cotse.com/texts/iphijack.txt
- **Dave Dittrick's Security Links**, http://www.washington.edu/People/dad/
- **Hunt—Hijacking Tool**, Pavel Krauz, http://lin.fsid.cvut.cz/~kra/index.html
- **Recognizing and Recovering from Rootkit Attacks**, David O'Brien, http://www.cs.wright.edu/people/faculty/pmateti/Courses/499/Fortification/obrien.html
- **Understanding Rootkits**, Oktay ALtunergil, http://linux.oreillynet.com/pub/a/linux/2001/12/14/rootkit.html
- **Analysis of the T0rn rootkit**, Sans Institute, http://www.sans.org/y2k/t0rn.htm
- **Rootkit FAQ**, David Dittrick, http://staff.washington.edu/dittrich/misc/faqs/rootkits.faq

Summary

Cracks, Attacks, Exploits—there's more than enough to worry about. This chapter covered some of the common attacks that you may encounter on an Internet-accessible or multiuser system. Denial of service attacks are aimed at disrupting legitimate use of a computer or its services. Buffer overflows take advantage of poorly debugged code that allows the contents of memory to be overwritten with arbitrary data. Session hijacking allows another computer to take control of your (seemingly) private conversation with a remote system.

There will *always* be something new on the horizon, and it is unlikely that bugs will ever disappear completely from source code. Users demand new features, new flexibility—they want it *now* and they want it *cheap*. Programmers must pump out code quickly and are often not given the time nor incentive to produce error-free code. Remember that the next time you hear someone complaining about Apple charging for a system update.

PART III

Specific Mac OS X Resources and How to Secure Them: Security Tips, Tricks, and Recipes

IN THIS PART

10

User, Environment, and Application Security

IN THIS CHAPTER

- Adding a New User
- Using the NetInfo Database to Customize a User
- Sane User Account Management
- Skeleton User Accounts
- Command-Line Administration Tools
- Restricting User Capabilities

Users are people, and as Chapter 3, "People Problems: Users, Intruders, and the World Around Them," noted, people are your overall largest security problem. So it's important that you know and practice good system administration principles when creating and managing the user population on your computers. The choices you make when configuring the users on your machines will define their normal abilities. It won't prevent them from trying to extend those abilities outside what you intended, but your choices will affect their capabilities and range of action there, as well.

When configuring users, keep in mind the types of security issues and vulnerabilities that we've discussed through the previous six chapters, and how the options you have in user configuration can affect the capabilities of a user who is determined to cause mischief. Likewise consider the effect on their capacity to unintentionally cause damage through these routes, either to themselves or to others.

This chapter covers typical user configuration administrative options, as well as how to partially automate some parts of the process. If you're going to be in a position where you need to manage a large collection of users, pay close attention to the automation parts; they will enable you to more easily keep your user creation process and configured options standardized, and will provide you with ways to make configurations that are outside of what Apple's Accounts system preferences pane can create.

In the end, the most secure user is the one you don't create, but that user has no utility. The instant you begin to give users the power to do things with your system, you begin to give them the power to do things that you don't want, and that will compromise your security to some extent. Where the balance is between nonusers with no capabilities and full administrative users who can `su` to root will depend on your needs and those of your users.

BUILDING USER/ADMINISTRATOR TRUST

We strongly recommend that you limit your users' capabilities to at least some extent; giving every user `root` access is a recipe for sure and swift disaster. On the other hand, we also strongly recommend against unnecessarily limiting your users' privileges.

Too many administrators place limits on their users not because of any increase in security that those limits provide, but out of some twisted desire to prepunish users for potential transgressions, in the hope that this will cow them into more quiescent obedience to the rules. This system may work in the military, where training a soldier to be instantly and unquestioningly obedient to orders is an important part of success, but your users are (probably) not soldiers, and you've no need to demonstrate that you can limit their permissions just because you can.

All that will be accomplished by creating artificial and unnecessary limitations will be a sense of resentment, a lack of serious effort in adhering to those policies that you really do require for maintaining security, a disinterest in performing in the spirit of those policies when situations are discovered that the policies do not cover, and subsequent work to undermine the security measures you have in place.

Although it's a rare trait in administrators, we'd like you to consider treating your users as though they deserve the trust and responsibility they've been granted by being given accounts. Too many administrators give out user accounts and then immediately act as though the users are betraying a trust when they make use of the abilities they've been given. If you truly want to prevent an action, it absolutely must be clear to the users, and it is best if more than a policy rule prevents it.

Actions such as running `Crack` on a password file, however, are rather equivocal as far as the user's behavior is concerned. Perhaps the user is actually trying to steal your system passwords, or perhaps is curious how quickly `Crack` runs on your system compared to the machine at home. Users occasionally do things that a cracker would do, simply out of idle curiosity. This does not make them crackers, and does not make them any less trustworthy than they were when you granted them the account.

If you observe a user doing something that is questionable, do your best to determine why they're doing it. Examine whether they still appear to be deserving of the same trust they were when you granted their accounts, and if they are, and their explanations are innocent, then it's probably in your best interest to believe them. All the good hackers of the world got there by experimentation and investigation of the way the system works. The oddball user that you tolerate in his experimentation might not turn out to be the next Wietse Venema (`ftp://ftp.porcupine.org/pub/security/index.html`), but on the other hand, he might. If you shepherd his curiosity to more useful subjects, and don't crucify him over transgressions that are actually only conceptual violations, you're likely to have a much more positive result. At the worst, he'll probably eschew most further experimentation because he won't anticipate you are much more astute. At the best, however, you'll find that in deference to your consideration in not tossing their butts out on the street, these individuals will take it upon themselves to be helpful above and beyond the call, and will function as some of your best security warning devices for your system. At the very least, he'll probably avoid using your internal corporate politics and the brain damage in the design of your security systems as topics in the security book he writes ten years later.

Adding a New User

The initial user you create when setting up your Mac OS X machine is an administrator account. Because it can be used to modify the machine settings or install software, the administrator account is actually a rather powerful account. When you add a new user, you have the choice of adding a regular user or adding one with administrator capabilities. Although it is helpful to have more than one user with administrator capabilities, do not give administrator access to every user account that you create. Otherwise, every user on the machine will be able to modify your system.

Add a new user by following these steps:

1. Open the Accounts pane in System Preferences.
2. Click the Make Changes lock icon if it's set not to allow changes, and enter your administrator username and password. Under the Users tab, select New User, which brings up a sheet for creating a new user. Figure 10.1 shows the Users tab of the Accounts pane.

FIGURE 10.1 Select New User under the Users tab of the Accounts pane to create a new user.

The sheet for creating a new user, shown in Figure 10.2, has the following fields:

- **Name.** This is where you enter your user's name. In Mac OS X, this is a name that the user can use to log in to the machine.
- **Short Name.** The short name is the username—that is, the name of the account. This is also a name that the user can use to log in to the machine. This name can be up to eight characters in length, must have no spaces, and must be in lowercase letters. This name is used by some of the network services. For example, I use `jray` as my (John Ray) shortname.
- **New Password.** The password should be at least four characters. Many systems recommend at least six characters with a variety of character types included in the password.
- **Verify.** This is where you reenter the password for verification purposes.
- **Password Hint.** This is an optional field. The password hint is displayed if the user enters an incorrect password three times. If you include a hint, make sure that the hint is not so obvious that other users can guess the password.
- **Picture.** Select a picture that can be displayed with this user's name in the user listing at login time. Either select one of the default images or choose a custom picture elsewhere on your machine by selecting Choose Another.
- **Allow User to Administer This Computer.** This is the box you check to grant a user administrative privileges. Check this box only for a trustworthy user who you feel should be allowed to have administrative privileges. As a security precaution, this box is not checked by default.
- **Allow User to Log In from Windows.** Check this box to allow the user to log in from Windows.

3. Click OK.

You are returned to the Accounts pane, which now lists your new user by name. You have created a new user. In the section on customizing a user, you learn how to create a specific user called `software` with a specific user ID and group ID.

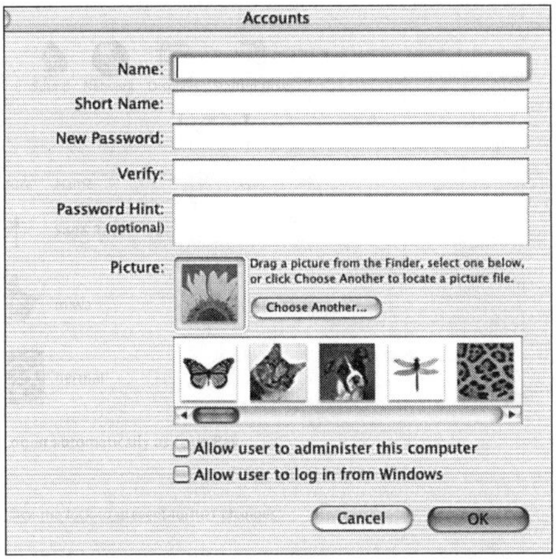

FIGURE 10.2 Complete the fields in the new user sheet when creating a new account.

The Capabilities option, shown in Figure 10.3, enables you to configure some of the actions a user is allowed to perform. You can restrict a user to use Simple Finder or to use only certain applications. Additionally, you can control whether a user is allowed to remove items from the Dock, open all System Preferences, change her password, or burn CDs or DVDs.

You can also edit user information, such as the password, under the Users tab of the Accounts pane of System Preferences. Just select the user account that needs to be edited and click Edit User, which brings up an already completed sheet identical to that for a new user.

If you so choose, you can set an auto login user with the Set Auto Login option. Provide the user's name and password at the Auto Login sheet. However, when you have multiple users, we recommend that you disable the automatic login to get a login window instead. If you don't make that modification, the automatic login account can be modified by whoever sits at the machine.

To delete a user account, simply select the account to be deleted and click the Delete User button. A sheet appears, asking you to confirm the action and telling you that the user's home directory will be stored in the Deleted Users folder. The deleted account is stored as a disk image (allowing for easy archiving). The Accounts pane does not allow you to delete the original administrator user account.

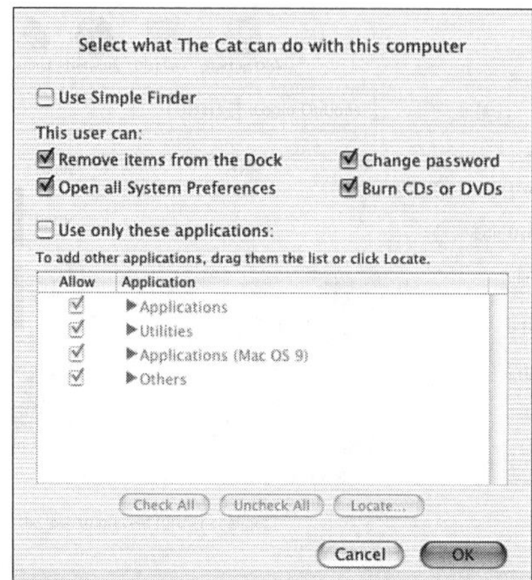

FIGURE 10.3 Certain capabilities can be set for a user with the Capabilities option.

Using the NetInfo Database to Customize a User

In this section you learn to use the Accounts control panel to create a user, but then customize the user by editing information in the NetInfo database.

The example makes a user that will be a general software user. This is a specialized user whose account you want to use when compiling software for the system, but this user should not be one of the administrators for the machine. The user is to belong to a group called `tire` with group ID `100`. You'd also like to have a specific user ID, `502`, for the user, whose account you intend to call `software`. To create this user, do the following:

1. Open the Accounts control pane in System Preferences. Click the lock icon if it's set not to allow changes. Add a new user with a short name of `software`. The software user's display name is `skuld`. Choose whatever password you prefer. Don't give your software user admin privileges.

2. Open NetInfo Manager and select the local domain if it's not already selected. Click the lock to make changes and enter the administrator username and password.

3. Click the `groups` directory and scroll through the list. Because `tire` is not a default group that comes with the system, you should not see a group called `tire`. Therefore, you must make a new group. Click any group to see what values are typically included in a group. Figure 10.4 shows the types of properties that belong to a group.

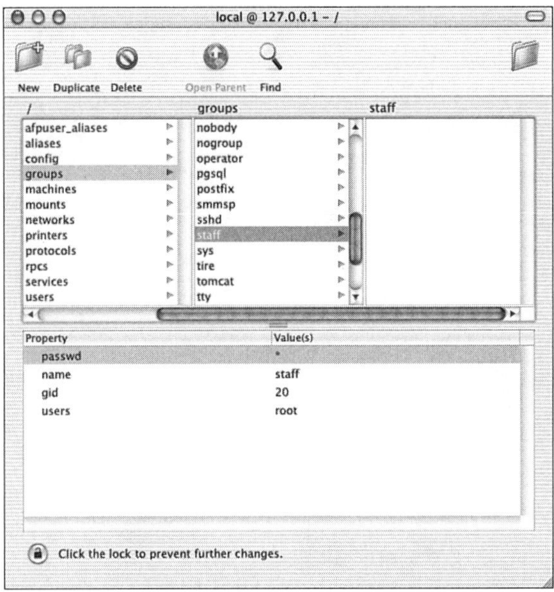

FIGURE 10.4 Looking at the staff directory, you can see that the typical properties for a group are `passwd`, `name`, `gid`, and `users`.

4. Click `groups`. From the Directory menu, select New Subdirectory. A new directory called `new_directory` appears. Edit the `name` property and add other properties as follows:

Property	Value
`name`	`tire`
`passwd`	`*`
`gid`	`100`
`users`	`software`

The `*` in the `passwd` field means that a group password is not being assigned. So far, you have only one user in your group: the user named `software`. As the term *group* implies, you can have more than one user in a group.

5. Select Save from the Domain menu. A question to Confirm Modification appears. Click Update This Copy. Now `new_directory` has become `tire`, as shown in Figure 10.5.

FIGURE 10.5 We now have a new group called `tire` with `gid 100`. At this time, only one user, `software`, belongs to the group.

6. Click `users` and then click `software`. Now the default information about user software appears in the bottom window. If this is one of your first users, `UID 502` might already be the user ID; otherwise, you can change `software`'s UID shortly. A group ID of `20` is probably what was made. If you look at the values section for `software`, you can see that the Accounts pane added quite a bit of information about `software` to the NetInfo database. The password you see is an encrypted version of the password.

   Because `software` was not one of the first users on my system, I already have a user with `UID 502`. Therefore, I have to either change the UID of my original user or delete the user. Because my original user with `UID 502` was simply a demonstration user to run various commands, I chose to delete it. If I want to keep my user, I could change the UID of the original user to one that wasn't already taken, and then change the UID of `software` to 502.

NOTE

If I had decided to rearrange UIDs instead of simply deleting the user, I would also have had to change the ownership of all the files that belonged to my previous user to belong to their new UID. File ownerships are stored based on numeric UID. Changing a user to a previously used UID gives that user access to and ownership of any files that still belong to that numeric UID.

For your purposes, the user ID for software might not be important. Because you want to share some of your resources with another machine that also has a user called `software` and whose UID is 502, it's important to make `software`'s UID 502 for compatibility purposes. In both cases, you want the user `software` to belong to group `tire`. Change the GID to 100. Change the UID as appropriate for your situation. Select Save from the Domain menu, and click Update This Copy in the Confirm Modification box. Figure 10.6 shows the updated information for the user `software`.

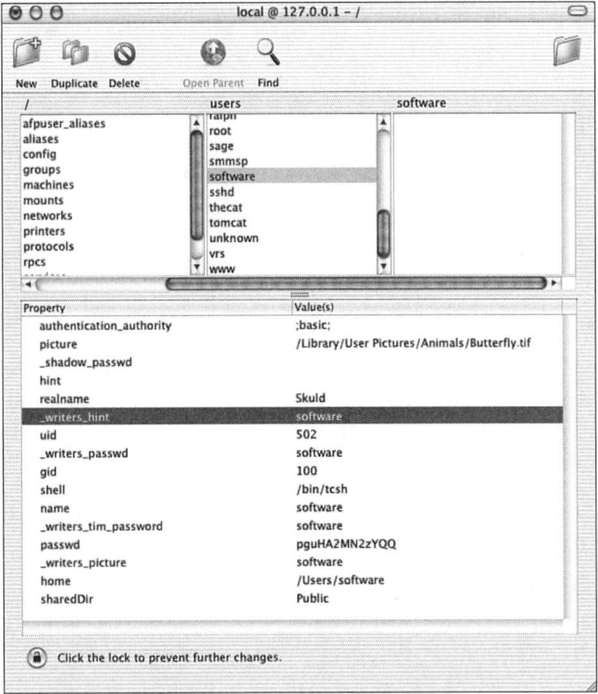

FIGURE 10.6 Now the user `software` has `uid 502` and `gid 100`. You can see from this information that user `software` has been assigned a password, a home directory in `/Users/software`, and a default shell of `/bin/tcsh`.

7. Click the lock to save your changes and end your ability to make further changes.

8. Open a Terminal window, go to `software`'s home directory, and look at the directory's contents. Take note that the directory was created by the Users pane with the default values. The update to the information in the NetInfo database,

however, was not entirely reflected in the system. So you must manually implement those changes. Here's the default information for the `software` user that was created on our system:

```
 [localhost:~software] joray% ls -al
total 8
drwxr-xr-x  11 505  staff  330 Jan 30 18:17 .
drwxr-xr-x   8 root wheel  228 May  4 13:45 ..
-rw-r--r--   1 505  staff    3 Nov 14 13:39 .CFUserTextEncoding
drwx------   3 505  staff  264 Feb 20 12:29 Desktop
drwx------   2 505  staff  264 Nov 14 16:45 Documents
drwx------  15 505  staff  466 Feb  2 19:40 Library
drwx------   2 505  staff  264 Nov 15 17:14 Movies
drwx------   2 505  staff  264 Nov 15 17:14 Music
drwx------   2 505  staff  264 Nov 15 17:14 Pictures
drwxr-xr-x   3 505  staff  264 Nov 15 17:09 Public
drwxr-xr-x   4 505  staff  264 Feb 13 19:31 Sites
```

In the example, `software`'s original UID was 505. If you didn't change your `software` user's UID, you should see Software in that column, not 505. The default GID that the Users pane used for creating `software` was `GID 20`, which is the `staff` group on Mac OS X. So the information that you see for `software`'s home directory is the information that was originally assigned to `software`. You have to update the information to `software`'s directory to reflect the new information.

As root, in the `/Users` directory, recusively (`chown -R`) change the ownership of `software`'s directory to the `software` user in group `tire`:

```
[localhost:/Users] root# chown -R software.tire software
```

Check the results:

```
[localhost:/Users] root# ls -ld software
drwxr-xr-x  11 software  tire  330 Jan 30 18:17 software
[localhost:/Users] root# ls -l software
total 8
-rw-r--r--   1 software  tire    3 Nov 14 13:39 .CFUserTextEncoding
drwx------   3 software  tire   58 Feb 20 12:29 Desktop
drwx------   2 software  tire   24 Nov 14 16:45 Documents
drwx------  15 software  tire  466 Feb  2 19:40 Library
drwx------   2 software  tire   24 Nov 15 17:14 Movies
drwx------   2 software  tire   24 Nov 15 17:14 Music
drwx------   2 software  tire   24 Nov 15 17:14 Pictures
drwxr-xr-x   3 software  tire   58 Nov 15 17:09 Public
drwxr-xr-x   4 software  tire   92 Feb 13 19:31 Sites
```

If you changed the UID of a user who was originally assigned UID 502, look at that user's home directory and make the appropriate ownership changes.

Sane User Account Management

Like the creation of the `tire` group, which houses nonadministrative users who are still used for system maintenance, it's very useful to add groups to your system for any logically collected groups of users on your system. The Unix privilege system underlying Mac OS X contains a mechanism to allow groups of users to mutually share access to files within their group, while protecting those files from other users on the same system.

To enable this capability, you must create groups for those users to belong to, and you must add their usernames to the group's `users` value list. A single user can be a member of any number of groups, and can assign files that he owns to be visible to any one of (or none of) the groups to which he belongs. To make use of this capability, the user must use the command-line group ownership tools, such as `chmod`, `chown`, and `chgrp`, or edit the Ownerships & Permissions information in the Finder.

Another change that you'll probably find useful to make to the `groups` NetInfo directory is the creation of a `users` group into which you can assign users who don't logically seem like staff users. Apple's Accounts pane creates users as members of the `staff` group, and you're welcome to leave them with this default group. There's a logical distinction between `staff` users and normal users on your other Unix systems, though, so you find it convenient to create yet another group to which to assign new, nonstaff users. On your Mac OS X machines, you create this as `gid 99`, with the group name `users`.

Skeleton User Accounts

If you're going to have any significant number of users on your machine (or machines), you'll soon find that being able to provide a more customized environment than what comes out of the Accounts system preference pane by default is a benefit.

Apple has provided a convenient tool you can use to perform some customization of accounts as created by the Accounts control pane. This is the inclusion of a `User Template` directory, from which the accounts made by the pane are created by duplication. The family of `User Template` directories, individualized by locale, are kept in `/System/Library/User Template`. This system works for simple configuration settings that you might like to configure for each newly created user, but it has some limitations if you'd like to work with more complex setups. The largest logical limitation is that if you're trying to set up complicated startup scripts and sophisticated environment settings, using a real user account as your default template is nice, because then you can log in for testing and tweaking. The largest practical limitation is that Apple has put the default templates in the `/System/` hierarchy, where they're Apple-sacrosanct (Apple can modify this directory as they please), and system updates are likely to tromp on any customizations that you might make.

The easiest way to solve all the problems at once is to create a skeleton user account as a real user account, and to keep it up to date with any environmental customizations that you want to provide for new users when you create accounts. If you create the skeleton user as simply another user account, you can log in to it and then conveniently tweak its settings. Using this method, you can create as many skeleton accounts as you need for different collections of settings.

Even if you prefer to use the Accounts control pane, the creation of skeleton users as real users on the system can be useful for you. You can configure skeleton users, log in for testing, and then populate the `/System/Library/User Template` directories (if you don't mind incurring the wrath of the Apple installers), as required for customizing the configuration of users under the Users pane. Alternatively, you can create the accounts with Apple's default templates, and then overwrite the actual user directories with data from your skeleton account.

Every user's shell environment is configured by the `.login` and `.cshrc` (presuming you're using the `tcsh` or `csh` shell) scripts in the user's home directory. You might also want to provide a more customized starter Web page or assorted bits of default data.

After you configure an account in the fashion you'd like your new users to have, the hard part is done. It would be nice to have a way to use this account directly from the Users pane as the seed for new accounts as they are created, but unfortunately, we aren't yet so lucky. Instead, you have two options for how to use the starter account information. First, you can create a new user through the Accounts control pane. After the account is created, you can replace the user's home directory (that the Accounts control pane created) with a copy of the skeleton account home directory.

Your other option is to ignore the Accounts control pane, and create a new user by duplicating an existing user node from the NetInfo hierarchy, making a copy of the skeleton account home directory for the new user's home directory, and then editing the copy of the NetInfo entry for the new user to reflect the correct information for that user.

The first option is probably easier, but the second has the benefit of being something you can do from the command line with `nidump` and `niload`, and therefore, of being automatable.

For the rest of the discussion, it will be assumed that you've created a skeleton account in which you have made any customizations that you want to install for all new users. The account UID will be assumed to be 5002, with a home directory of

/Users/skel and a GID of 99. It will also be assumed that you've added the group users to your NetInfo groups directory, with a GID of 99, and that you want to use this GID for normal, nonprivileged users.

To implement the first method of providing local customization for a new user, follow these steps:

1. Create the new user with the Accounts control pane. Make any necessary changes to the user's configuration, such as the default GID, using NetInfo Manager as shown in Chapter 9, "Everything Else."
2. Become root (su, provide password).
3. Change directories to the skeleton user's directory (cd ~skel).
4. tar the contents of the current directory, using the option to place the output on STDOUT (tar -cf - .) and then pipe the output of tar into a subshell. In the subshell, cd to the new user's directory, and untar from STDIN (| (cd ~*<newusername>* ; tar -xf -)). The complete command is tar -cf - . | (cd ~*<newusername>* ; tar -xf -).
5. Change directories to one level above the new user's directory (cd ~*<newusername>* ; cd ../).
6. Change the ownership of everything in the new user's directory to belong to the new user and, potentially, to the user's default group if it's not the same as the skel account default group (chown -R *<newusername>*:*<newusergroup>* *<newuserdirectoryname>*).

For example, if you've just created a new user named jim, assigned to the group users with the Accounts control pane/NetInfo Manager, and want to put the skel account configuration into jim's home directory, you would enter the following:

```
su (provide password)
cd ~skel
tar -cf - . | ( cd ~jim ; tar -xf - )
cd ~jim
cd ../
chown -R jim:users jim
```

If you'd rather create new users from the command line, either because you can't access the physical console conveniently or because you want to use what you know about shell scripting to automate the process, you can use the second method suggested earlier. You might find this method more convenient for creating users in a NetInfo domain other than localhost/local. The Accounts preference pane in the nonserver version of OS X seems incapable of creating users in other NetInfo domains, and this makes using it for managing cluster users difficult.

CAUTION

This process creates a new user by manipulating the NetInfo database directly, so you should remember to back up your NetInfo database directory (`/private/var/db/netinfo`) regularly.

To implement the second method, follow these steps:

1. Become root (`su`, give password).
2. Change directories to the directory in which you'd like to place the new user's home directory (`cd /Users`, for example).
3. Make a directory with the short name of the user you're about to create (`mkdir` *<newusername>* to create a directory for a new user named *<newusername>*).
4. Change directories to the home directory of the `skel` account (`cd ~skel`).
5. `tar` the contents of the current directory, and use the option to place the output on `STDOUT` (`tar -cf -`).
6. Pipe the output of the `tar` command into a subshell. In the subshell, `cd` to the new user's directory, and untar from `STDIN` (`| ( cd` *<pathtonewuserdirectory>* `; tar -xf - )`). Note that you can't use `~`*<newusername>* because *<newusername>* doesn't actually exist on the system yet. The entire command syntax is `tar -cf - . | ( cd` *<pathtonewuserdirectory>* `; tar -xf - )`.
7. Dump your `skel` account (`UID 5002` here, remember) NetInfo entry, or some other user's entry, into a file that you can edit (`nidump -r /name=users/uid=5002 -t localhost/local > ~/`*<sometempfile>*). As an alternative to the `uid` search, you could specify the `skel` account with `/name=users/name=skel`.
8. Edit `~/`*<sometempfile>*, changing the entries so that they are appropriate for the new user you want to create. You'll want to change at least `_writers_passwd`, `_writers_tim_password`, `uid`, `_writers_hint`, `_writers_picture`, `gid`, `realname`, `name`, `passwd`, and `home`. It's probably easiest to leave `passwd` blank for now.
9. Use `niutil` to create a new directory for the `uid` that you've picked for the new user (`niutil -p -create -t localhost/local /name=users/uid=`*<newuserUID>*; give the root password when asked).
10. Use `niload` to load the data you modified in `~/`*<sometempfile>* back into the NetInfo database (`cat ~/`*<sometempfile>* `| niload -p -r /name=users/uid=`*<newuserUID>* `-t localhost/local`).
11. Set the password for the new user (`passwd` *<newusername>*`;`). Provide a beginning password.

12. Change back to the directory above the new user's home directory (`cd ~<newusername>; cd ../`).

13. Change the ownership of the new user's directory to the new user's <newusername> and <defaultgroup> (`chown -R <newusername>:<defaultgroup> <newuserdirectory>`).

If you've made a mistake somewhere along the way, just restore your NetInfo database from the backup that you made before you started this. You also might need to find the `nibindd` process, and send it an `HUP` signal (`ps -auxww | grep "nibindd"; kill -HUP <whatever PID belongs to nibindd>`, or `killall -HUP nibindd`, if you prefer to do things the easy way).

CAUTION

Resource forks get lost in the `tar`!

The BSD `tar` distributed by Apple doesn't understand file resource forks, and some software vendors haven't caught on to the idea of using plists properly yet. The unfortunate consequence is that if you've built a highly customized skeleton user (or are trying to use these steps as an example of how to move a real user account), and some of the user's preferences are stored in the resource fork of the preference files, `tar` is going to make a mess of things when you use it to duplicate the user's directory to the new location.

To overcome this problem, you currently have two options:

- Metaobject has developed `hfstar`, a GNUtar derivative that supports HFS+, allowing it to properly handle resource forks, type and creator codes, and so on. GNUtar is functionally very similar to BSD `tar`, but the differences that do exist are significant enough that you won't want to simply replace the `tar` that Apple provides with the `hfstar` from metaobject. Instead, it'd be better to keep them both around, and use them for their respective strengths. metaobject's `hfstar` can be downloaded from `http://www.metaobject.com/Community.html#hfstar`.
- Use Apple's already supplied `ditto` command. `ditto` doesn't provide nearly the power of `tar`, but it'll do for copying user directories.

To produce results similar to those from the first method earlier, the following example creates a new user with the username of `james`, `UID 600`, `GID 70`, with home directory `/Users/james`. This again assumes the `skel` account with `UID 5002` and characteristics as described earlier. (Comments or instructions are shown in italics.)

```
su (provide the password)
cd /Users
mkdir james
cd ~skel
tar -cf - . | ( cd /Users/james ; tar -xf - )
nidump -r /name=users/uid=5002 -t localhost/local > ~/skeltemp
vi ~/skeltemp
```

Then, in `vi`, change the contents from this:

```
{
  "authentication_authority" = ( ";basic;" );
  "picture" = ( "/Library/User Pictures/Nature/Zen.tif" );
  "_shadow_passwd" = ( "" );
  "hint" = ( "Urusei!" );
  "uid" = ( "5002" );
  "_writers_passwd" = ( "skel" );
  "realname" = ( "skeleton account" );
  "_writers_hint" = ( "skel" );
  "gid" = ( "99" );
  "shell" = ( "/bin/tcsh" );
  "name" = ( "skel" );
  "_writers_tim_password" = ( "skel" );
  "passwd" = ( "AtbvqXhZrKJ7A" );
  "_writers_picture" = ( "skel" );
  "home" = ( "/Users/skel" );
  "sharedDir" = ( "Public" );
}
```

to this:

```
{
  "authentication_authority" = ( ";basic;" );
  "picture" = ( "/Library/User Pictures/Nature/Zen.tif" );
  "_shadow_passwd" = ( "" );
  "hint" = ( "boggle" );
  "uid" = ( "600" );
  "_writers_passwd" = ( "james" );
  "realname" = ( "Sweet Baby James" );
  "_writers_hint" = ( "james" );
  "gid" = ( "70" );
  "shell" = ( "/bin/tcsh" );
  "name" = ( "james" );
  "_writers_tim_password" = ( "james" );
  "passwd" = ( "" );
  "_writers_picture" = ( "james" );
  "home" = ( "/Users/james" );
  "sharedDir" = ( "Public" );
}
```

Now load the skeleton into NetInfo:

```
# niutil -p -create -t localhost/local /name=users/uid=600
# cat ~/skeltemp | niload -p -r /name=users/uid=600 -t localhost/local
# passwd james (fill in a good starting value)
# cd ~james
# cd ../
# chown -R james:www james (GID 70 is group www on this machine)
```

NOTE

Depending on whether your NetInfo daemon is feeling well, you might have to `HUP` the `nibindd` process (`killall -HUP nibindd`) to get it to recognize that you've made the change. Remember that you can always restore your NetInfo database backup to get out of a mess, if you've created one.

TIP

If you need to delete a user account from the command line, you can destroy the NetInfo information for the user by using the command `niutil -p -destroy -t localhost/local /name=users/uid=`*<userUIDtobedeleted>*. Then `rm -rf` the user's home directory to delete it and all of its contents from the system.

Just to make sure that your user has been created as you think it should have been, you can use `niutil` to list the `/users` NetInfo directory. (Don't be surprised if your listing doesn't look quite like this—this is simply the list of users configured on my machine, so your users are likely to be different.)

```
[localhost:/Users/ray] root# niutil -list -t localhost/local /users
2         nobody
3         root
4         daemon
5         unknown
6         www
154       joray
166       miwa
161       ray
163       software
171       nomad
173       ftp
174       marvin
175       skel
```

```
177     bin
179     betty
181     ralph
184     james
```

As shown, `james` does now exist in the NetInfo `/users` directory, although this listing shows only the NetInfo node numbers, rather than the users and property values. To see whether `james` has the properties intended, you can use `niutil` to read the info from the node named `james`:

```
[localhost:/Users/ray] root# niutil -read -t localhost/local /users/james
authentication_authority: ;basic;
picture: /Library/User Pictures/Nature/Zen.tif
_shadow_passwd:
hint: boggle
uid: 600
_writers_passwd: james
realname: Sweet Baby James
_writers_hint: james
gid: 70
shell: /bin/tcsh
name: james
_writers_tim_password: james
passwd: aynyjRMfGyH7U
_writers_picture: james
home: /Users/james
sharedDir: Public
```

Command-Line Administration Tools

There are a number of command-line tools that are of assistance in the configuration and maintenance of user accounts. Some of these have functionality duplicated in graphical tools and some do not. For truly sophisticated user management, we again suggest looking to Mac OS X Server because it provides tools that are considerably more powerful.

NetInfo Utilities

The `nidump`, `niutil`, and `niload` commands are particularly useful for user account creation and deletion. It's also a good idea to be familiar with the `tar` command for backing up NetInfo databases. We wouldn't be surprised if someone creates a graphical tool that scripts the sort of account maintenance that has been shown in this chapter and makes it available on the Net. If we managed to pique your interest in shell programming in the earlier chapters, this would be an ideal problem to attack as a learning experience. Because NetInfo is so vital to the operation of the machine, we recommend that you verify, by using `print` statements, that the scripts you create output exactly what you want—before you turn them loose on the NetInfo database.

Common BSD Tools

In addition to the NetInfo commands for creating and modifying user accounts themselves, you have access to a number of standard BSD utilities. Primarily, these allow you to operate on the files in user accounts; but one, the `passwd` command, inserts `crypt`ed passwords into the NetInfo user record. (This is a little odd because Apple has circumvented most BSD tools of this nature and incorporated their functionality into the NetInfo commands. It wouldn't be too surprising if Apple replaces or supercedes this command with another in the future.)

Changing File Ownership: `chown`

The `chown` command is used to change the ownership of files. Only the root user can execute the `chown` command. The simplest form, and the one you'll end up using most frequently, is `chown` *<username>* *<filename>*, which changes the ownership property of *<filename>* to belong to the user *<username>*. The command can optionally be given as `chown` *<username>*:*<groupname>* *<filename>* to change the user and group at the same time. Additionally, `-R` can be specified after the command to cause a recursive change in an entire directory, rather than to a single file. The command documentation table is shown in Table 10.1.

TABLE 10.1 The Command Documentation Table for `chown`

Option	Description

`chown`	Changes file owner and group.
	`chown [-R [-H | -L | -P]] [-fh] <owner> <file1> <file2> ...`
	`chown [-R [-H | -L | -P]] [-fh] :<group> <file1> <file2> ...`
	`chown [-R [-H | -L | -P]] [-fh] <owner>:<group> <file1> <file2> ...`

`-R`	Recursively descends through directory arguments to change the user ID and/or group ID.
`-H`	If `-R` is specified, symbolic links on the command line are followed. Symbolic links encountered in tree traversal are not followed.
`-L`	If `-R` is specified, all symbolic links are followed.
`-P`	If `-R` is specified, no symbolic links are followed.
`-f`	Forces an attempt to change user ID and/or group ID without reporting any errors.
`-h`	If the file is a symbolic link, the user ID and/or group ID of the link is changed.

The -H, -L, and -P options are ignored unless -R is specified. Because they also override each other, the last option specified determines the action that is taken.

The -L option cannot be used with the -h option.

It is not necessary to provide both *<owner>* and *<group>*; however, one must be specified. If group is specified, it must be preceded with a colon (:).

The owner may be either a numeric user ID or a username. If a username exists for a numeric user ID, the associated username is used for the owner. Similarly, the group may be either a numeric group ID or a group name. If a group name exists for a group ID, the associated group name is used for the group.

Unless invoked by the superuser, chown clears set-user-id and set-group-id bits.

Changing File Group Ownership: chgrp

The chgrp command functions like the chown command, except that it changes only the group ownership of a file. This can be particularly useful when you want to give a user, or group of users, access to files owned by a number of different users. Instead of changing the ownership of each, or issuing a separate chown *<userid>*:*<groupid>* for each file, you can instead change the file's group *en masse* to one that the intended user or group can read, while not affecting the actual ownership of the files.

The command documentation table for chgrp is shown in Table 10.2.

TABLE 10.2 The Command Documentation Table for chgrp

Option	Description
chgrp	Changes group. chgrp [-R [-H | -L | -P]] [-fh] *<group>* *<file1>* *<file2>* ...
-R	Recursively descends through directory arguments to change the group ID.
-H	If -R is specified, symbolic links on the command line are followed. Symbolic links encountered in tree traversal are not followed.
-L	If -R is specified, all symbolic links are followed.
-P	If -R is specified, no symbolic links are followed.
-f	Forces an attempt to change group ID without reporting any errors.
-h	If the file is a symbolic link, the group ID of the link is changed.

Unless -h, -H, or -L is specified, chgrp on symbolic links always succeeds and has no effect.

The -H, -L, and -P options are ignored unless -R is specified. Because they also override each other, the last option specified determines the action that is taken.

The group may be either a numeric group ID or a group name. If a group name exists for a group ID, the associated group name is used for the group.

The user invoking chgrp must belong to the specified group and be the owner of the file, or be the superuser.

Unless invoked by the superuser, chgrp clears set-user-id and set-group-id bits.

Setting a User's Password: passwd

The passwd command, somewhat unexpectedly, changes a user's password. If you look at the man page for passwd, you will see that there are a number of related password and account management commands that come from BSD Unix. With the exception of the passwd command, all the others appear to operate on the local files only, and do not seem to affect the NetInfo database information. Because the local authentication files (such as /etc/passwd and /etc/group) are used only in single-user mode, none of the other commands currently have any significant use in OS X. (We'd like to think that Apple is working on making more of them operate with the NetInfo database, but we really have no idea whether the BSD utilities are coming or going.)

Simply issued as passwd, with no other options, the passwd command enables a user to change her password. The root user can issue passwd *<username>* to force the password for the user *<username>* to change. The command documentation table for passwd is shown in Table 10.3.

TABLE 10.3 The Command Documentation Table for passwd

Option	Description
passwd	Modifies a user's password passwd [-l] [-k] [-y] [*<user>*] passwd changes the user's local, Kerberos, or YP password. The user is first prompted for her old password. The user is next prompted for a new password, and then prompted again to retype the new password for verification. The new password should be at least six characters in length. It should use a variety of lowercase letters, uppercase letters, numbers, and metacharacters.
-l	Updates the user's local password.
-k	Updates the Kerberos database, even if the user has a local password. After the password has been verified, passwd transmits the information to the Kerberos authenticating host.
-y	Updates the YP password, even if the user has a local password. The rpc.yppasswdd (8) daemon should be running on the YP master server.

If no flags are specified, the following occurs:

- If Kerberos is active, the user's Kerberos password is changed, even if the user has a local password.
- If the password is not in the local database, an attempt to update the YP password occurs.

To change another user's Kerberos password, run `kinit (1)` followed by `passwd`. The superuser is not required to supply the user's password if only the local password is being modified.

Restricting User Capabilities

Beginning in Mac OS X 10.2, Apple has provided a convenient means of controlling logged-in users' capabilities, such as what applications they can run and whether they can modify system preferences. This works beyond the Finder and also guards against invocation of applications from the Terminal. In a lab or community setting, this can work to provide effective guest access without requiring extensive user and group administration.

Editing User Capabilities

To access the user capability editor, you must first create a standard user account via the Accounts System Preferences panel. Administrative users *cannot* have capability restrictions. Select the user to modify in the Accounts list of the Users tab, then click the Capabilities button, as shown in Figure 10.7.

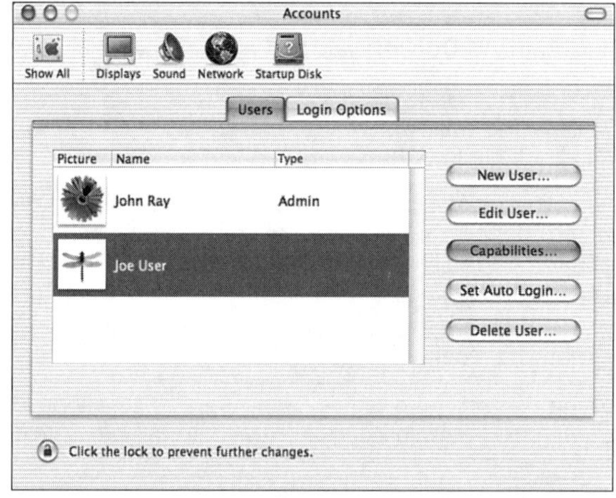

FIGURE 10.7 Edit capabilities of standard user accounts within the Accounts system preferences panel.

The Capabilities sheet, shown in Figure 10.8, is displayed. Choose from the these limitations on the account:

- **Use Simple Finder**. Removes all but basic file launching capabilities from the account. This will be covered in more detail shortly.
- **Remove Items from the Dock**. Lab and teaching settings work best if there is consistency across accounts. To keep a static base set for the dock (no applications, files, or folders can be added or removed), click the Remove Items from the Dock check box. Note: The label for this option is misleading. It prevents any changes to the Dock, rather than simply removing items.
- **Open All System Preferences**. If unchecked, users can access system preferences related to only their accounts: all Personal category preferences, Universal Access, Keyboard, Mouse, and Sound.
- **Change Password**. Allow the user to change the account password. For a guest or kiosk account, this would be disabled.
- **Burn CDs or DVDs**. To eliminate the capability to burn optical media on the system, uncheck this option.
- **Use Only These Applications.** When checked, the user will be restricted to running only the applications or application categories checked in the list at the bottom of the pane. You can expand a category with the disclosure arrow in front of its name to show the applications it contains. Unchecking an application or category removes access from that item. You can add applications by clicking the Locate button or dragging their icons into the list.

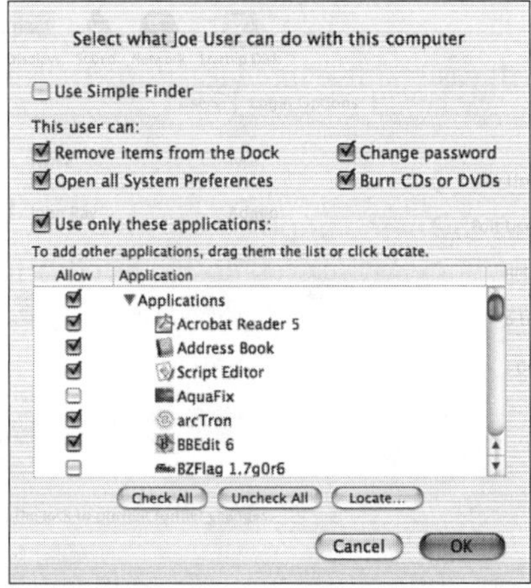

FIGURE 10.8 Restrict what the user can access.

> **NOTE**
>
> User account restrictions (capabilities) do not modify the permissions of the applications that they control. They also do not enable you to control command-line applications. You must use traditional user/group permissions in combination with Apple user capabilities to administer command-line and GUI tools effectively.

If a user violates an application restriction, she is warned with an error message, shown in Figure 10.9, and the attempt is logged via `syslogd` in `/var/log/system.log` as follows:

```
Jan 27 16:41:11 John-Rays-Computer ./Navigator: CG/CPS:
The application with pid 615 is not in the list of permitted
applications and so has been exited.
```

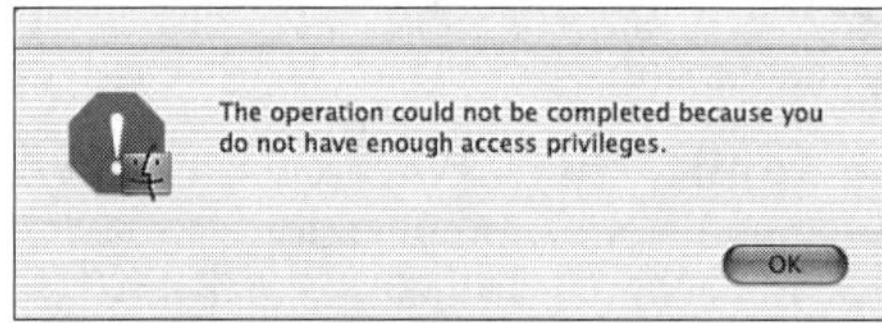

FIGURE 10.9 Users are warned if they attempt to launch an application beyond their accounts' capabilities.

Although there isn't a reporting function built in to monitor these sorts of attempted policy restrictions, the `logsentry` product documented in Chapter 19, "Logs and User Activity Accounting," will easily automate violations tracking on your system.

Simple Finder

The "Simple Finder" is, as the name implies, a simplified version of the Mac OS X Finder. It provides a static dock with access to the applications chosen in the Capabilities setup, the user's Documents folder, the Shared folder, and Trash, as shown in Figure 10.10.

FIGURE 10.10 The Simple Finder limits access to most navigation and file management functions.

Users navigate through multiple screens of files by using the buttons at the bottom of the window. Documents must be saved to the `~/Documents` folder to be easily accessible through the interface.

There is no direct means of navigating to other folders, but this should *not* be taken as a form of security. Access to the Terminal still enables a user to open files located elsewhere on the system. Alternatively, adding folders to the Login Items pane in System Preferences causes them to be opened in the Simple Finder at login.

Properly configured, the Simple Finder can be an effective means of providing a simple "launcher" for children or kiosk applications. It should not, however, be assumed to be secure without proper configuration of the applications that can be launched, such as restricting access to applications such as the Terminal and System Preferences.

Summary

This chapter covered the tools and techniques necessary for you to customize your users' capabilities to match those you require them to have. Make good use of these tools to enforce the policies that you've created for your system. Remember that your users will make mistakes and occasionally display poor judgment when using their accounts. Don't take an incident of a user running up against one of your security barriers as a sufficient condition to consider her a danger to your system. Good users sometimes make bad mistakes; this doesn't necessarily make them untrustworthy. On the other hand, if you don't trust an individual, for goodness sake, don't give him an account!

Plenty of the most important users in computing history—people such as Randal Schwartz (`http://www.swiss.ai.mit.edu/6805/articles/computer-crime/schwartz-matrix-news.txt`), Dan Farmer (`http://www.trouble.org/survey/`), and even ACM Turing Award winner Ken Thompson (`http://www.acm.org/classics/sep95/`)—have done things that most would consider questionable, and in some circles even criminal, in their work, experimentation, and learning with computers. Without these people, the computing world would be a much poorer place, and we owe them a debt of gratitude for what they've done for us, in some cases after having been thoroughly undone by their administrative staffs.

In the global community of computing security, generating the next generation of computing greats is everybody's problem. It might not always seem like it, but it's usually in your best interest to contribute to the community what you can, when you can. Sometimes, that contribution will be in the form of well-educated users, who've learned enough about computing security to develop and implement the next generation of computing security tools.

11

Introduction to Mac OS X Network Services

IN THIS CHAPTER

- What Is a Network Service?
- Network Service Vulnerabilities
- Controlling Mac OS X Network Service Processes
- Protecting `inetd` with TCP Wrappers
- Increasing Security with `xinetd`

A Mac OS X machine, or for that matter, any Unix machine, derives much of its powerful functionality from abstracting how the many small programs that cooperate as the "operating system" communicate with each other. It is frequently useful for these programs to be able to communicate with programs on remote machines, and so they require the ability to communicate over the network. In a typical display of Unix "do it the simple way" design principles, the result is predictable: If the software is already required to have network capabilities, don't bother writing separate code to handle single-machine connections; just use the network for local connections as well. This produces a powerful and flexible operating system, but one that is by its very nature more vulnerable to network attacks than a monolithic operating system such as Mac OS 9. Apple has done a surprisingly good job of providing protection for services that might be problematic, and of leaving those that are less easily protected turned off. Still, if you want to use your machine to its fullest capabilities, you need to dig into the configuration and make those changes that suit your particular network and usage requirements.

What Is a Network Service?

Most generally, a *network service* is a combination of a program and a network protocol, which together allow remote networked machines to access some sort of functionality on a server machine. Web servers, FTP servers, print servers, terminal access servers, and other such capabilities are, by this general definition, network services. If one were to turn off all network services on a machine, a fairly good argument could be made that it would be secure from network attacks. Unfortunately, the Unix way of doing some things results in some useful capabilities being provided by a machine to itself via the network. For example, in a normal installation a Unix machine prints, even to printers connected directly to itself, by way of the network. Denying all network services would therefore result in a machine that was not particularly useful. Instead, picking which network services are important to keep and securing them against attack is a necessity.

Network services are typically started through one of two mechanisms. Either they are standalone services that are started by a startup script in `/System/Library/StartupItems` or `/Library/StartupItems`, or they are started by yet another network service, `inetd`, which watches for network connections attempting to access particular services and starts the appropriate software to accommodate them.

Standalone services that are started by a startup script are running all the time, no matter how often they are used. They control their own configurations, and so the user that runs the service may also vary. On the other hand, services that run from `inetd` do not run all the time. They run only when they are needed, and are started by `inetd`, often with the permissions of `inetd`. A given service, though, may also have its own configuration. Running these services through a superserver also enables you to consolidate server processes.

This chapter covers the starting of general network services, and how those started from `inetd` may be partially protected by the correct configuration of `inetd`, or its replacement, `xinetd`. Specific security measures for individual services are covered in the chapters later in this book.

Network Service Vulnerabilities

Individual network services suffer from a great number of specific attacks, which are covered in later chapters devoted to the services themselves. Thankfully, the startup-script way of starting network services is fairly invulnerable to attacks. The `inetd` method suffers primarily from one well-known problem. As its purpose is to watch for network requests and start the appropriate servers to handle those requests, `inetd` could hardly have been better designed to facilitate denial of service (DoS) attacks.

Here is a brief listing of some recent reports on `inetd` vulnerabilities:

- Denial of Service Vulnerability in `inetd` in Compaq Tru64 Unix (BugTraq ID 5242). A denial of service vulnerability exists in some versions of Compaq Tru64 Unix. Details on the vulnerability are not available, but patches to fix it are.

- Denial of Service Vulnerability in `inetd` in Compaq Tru64 Unix (VU# 880624). A denial of service vulnerability exists in Compaq Tru64 Unix 5.1. As a result, `inetd` could stop accepting connections. Compaq made a patch available to fix this vulnerability.
- Denial of Service Vulnerability in `inetd` in Red Hat 6.2(CVE-2001-0309). The `inetd` distributed with Red Hat 6.2 does not properly close sockets for the internal services, such as `chargen`, `daytime`, `echo`. This can result in a denial of service attack through connections to the internal services. Red Hat provided a patch to fix the problem.
- FreeBSD `inetd` `wheel` Group File Read Vulnerability (CVE-2001-0196, BugTraq ID 2324). The `inetd` distributed with FreeBSD incorrectly sets up group privileges on child processes for `identd`. The vulnerability can allow attackers to read the first 16 bytes of files readable by group `wheel`. Attackers could potentially read the first entry of the encrypted password file and use that information to gain access to or elevated privileges on the local host. A FreeBSD patch was made available to fix the vulnerability.

With the most serious of the recent vulnerabilities, CVE-2001-0196, an attacker could potentially gain access to the host. In such situations, it is especially important to apply patches that fix the problem, or do the workaround, if one is recommended before a patch becomes available.

Not surprisingly, however, most of the vulnerabilities involve denial of service. In the vulnerability documented by CERT's VU# 880624, a DoS vulnerability for Compaq Tru64, the DoS attack results in `inetd` refusing to accept further connections and the machine losing all network connectivity. It's arguable whether this is a worse vulnerability than having `inetd` continue to accept connections and run the machine out of process resources instead, but almost any version of Unix will be affected in some fashion by an attempted DoS attack against `inetd`.

In an attempt to mitigate this mode of attack, `xinetd` has been created as a replacement for the functionality of `inetd`. `xinetd`, pronounced, according to its authors "zye-net-d," has been designed to allow for some protection in spite of the inherently DoS-friendly nature of the job it does. Among its features, discussed in greater length later in this chapter, are the capability to throttle particular connections to prevent overwhelming the machine with service requests, and to place limits on the number of connections to particular services, automatically blocking remote machines that appear to be attempting to conduct DoS attacks against it.

Controlling Mac OS X Network Service Processes

Mac OS X provides some GUI controls for controlling the service processes. Additionally, you can control processes manually. The ability to control processes manually makes it convenient to adjust settings from a remote terminal. In general, we recommend being completely conversant with the manual configuration and control of network services, even if you choose to use the various System Preferences panes to make quick changes on a day-to-day basis. Manual configuration is sometimes less convenient, but so long as your machine is accessible, you will be able to control and configure it this way. Server problems do not limit themselves to occurring when you're sitting at your machine.

GUI Controls

Apple ships OS X with many services disabled. In many of the Unix operating systems, you have to be careful to disable some common services that are turned on by default, but that you may not actually need. With OS X, however, many of these common services are wisely disabled. Instead of requiring an expert to secure the machine in its default state, OS X starts off fairly well configured for a novice administrator. Instead, it requires a bit of expertise to turn on useful but potentially dangerous services such as the remote login service.

Under the Services tab of the Sharing pane of the System Preferences panel you find controls to enable or disable the FTP, SSH, World Wide Web, AppleShare, Windows File Sharing, Remote Apple Events, and the Printer Sharing servers. Choose only those services that you really need. Remember, the more services you turn on, the more vulnerable to attack your machine becomes. Figure 11.1 shows the Services tab of the Sharing pane.

`inetd`

The `inetd` service, the Internet services daemon, configured by the `/etc/inetd.conf` file, actually is a service that starts and controls other services. It's not practical to start an unlimited number of some types of network services and leave them running, right from startup. Depending on the use of your machine, some services might be needed in great numbers—for example, the `ftpd` FTP server processes, if you serve particularly interesting data and have many people connecting simultaneously. Others might be used hardly at all, such as the `sprayd` network diagnostic daemon. On your system, the pattern might be the opposite, but regardless of the use, patterns are likely to vary over time. For many of these types of services, the system relieves you of the task of trying to provide the proper number of these servers in some manual configuration process by using the `inetd` daemon to configure and run them on an as-needed basis.

FIGURE 11.1 From the Services tab of the Sharing pane a number of services can be enabled or disabled.

As was mentioned earlier, `xinetd` can be used as a replacement for `inetd`. As a matter of fact, starting with Mac OS X 10.2, `xinetd` is the default Internet services daemon. However, because `inetd` is a ubiquitous Unix service and its configuration file is easier to read for familiarizing yourself with the basic network services involved, we look at `inetd` first.

The `inetd.conf` file, then, is the file that tells `inetd` which services it should start in response to network requests, and how (at the command-line level) to start them. The `inetd.conf` file has the form of a set of lines, each line containing a specification for a service. The service specification lines consist of a set of fields separated by tabs or spaces. The fields that must occur on each line are shown in the following list, with a brief description of the data that belongs in them.

- Service name (used to look up service port in `/etc/services` map)
- Socket type (`stream`, `dgram`, `raw`, `rdm`, or `seqpacket`)
- Protocol (`tcp` or `udp`, `tcp6` or `udp6`, `rpc/tcp`, or `rpc/udp`)
- Wait/nowait (for `dgrams` only—whether or not the socket should wait for additional connections; all others get `nowait`)
- User (user for which the service is run)

- Server program (actual path to the binary on disk)
- Server program arguments (how the command line would look, if typed, including server name)

The default `inetd.conf` file as it comes from Apple is shown in Listing 11.1. The `#` symbol in front of each item indicates that the line is commented out and will not be run. Apple very wisely leaves all these network services off by default. Many of them can be security holes, and it's best if you enable them only as you need and understand them.

LISTING 11.1 A Typical `/etc/inetd.conf` File

```
#
# Internet server configuration database
#
#       @(#)inetd.conf    5.4 (Berkeley) 6/30/90
#
# Items with double hashes in front (##) are not yet implemented in the OS.
#
#finger  stream   tcp    nowait   nobody  /usr/libexec/tcpd  fingerd -s
#ftp     stream   tcp    nowait   root    /usr/libexec/tcpd  ftpd -l
#login   stream   tcp    nowait   root    /usr/libexec/tcpd  rlogind
#nntp    stream   tcp    nowait   usenet  /usr/libexec/tcpd  nntpd
#ntalk   dgram    udp    wait     root    /usr/libexec/tcpd  ntalkd
#shell   stream   tcp    nowait   root    /usr/libexec/tcpd  rshd
#telnet  stream   tcp    nowait   root    /usr/libexec/tcpd  telnetd
#uucpd   stream   tcp    nowait   root    /usr/libexec/tcpd  uucpd
#comsat  dgram    udp    wait     root    /usr/libexec/tcpd  comsat
#tftp    dgram    udp    wait     nobody  /usr/libexec/tcpd
➥tftpd /private/tftpboot
#bootp   dgram    udp    wait     root    /usr/libexec/tcpd  bootpd
##pop3   stream   tcp    nowait   root    /usr/libexec/tcpd
➥/usr/local/libexec/popper
##imap4  stream   tcp    nowait   root    /usr/libexec/tcpd
➥/usr/local/libexec/imapd
#
# "Small servers" -- used to be standard on, but we're more conservative
# about things due to Internet security concerns.  Only turn on what you
# need.
#
#chargen  stream   tcp    nowait  root    internal
#chargen  dgram    udp    wait    root    internal
```

LISTING 11.1 Continued

```
28 #daytime  stream   tcp    nowait  root    internal
29 #daytime  dgram    udp    wait    root    internal
30 #discard  stream   tcp    nowait  root    internal
31 #discard  dgram    udp    wait    root    internal
32 #echo     stream   tcp    nowait  root    internal
33 #echo     dgram    udp    wait    root    internal
34 #time     stream   tcp    nowait  root    internal
35 #time     dgram    udp    wait    root    internal
36 #
37 # Kerberos (version 5) authenticated services
38 #
39 ##eklogin  stream tcp   nowait root    /usr/libexec/tcpd   klogind -k -c -e
40 ##klogin   stream tcp   nowait root    /usr/libexec/tcpd   klogind -k -c
41 ##kshd     stream tcp   nowait root    /usr/libexec/tcpd   kshd -k -c -A
42 #krb5_prop stream tcp   nowait root    /usr/libexec/tcpd   kpropd
43 #
44 # RPC based services (you MUST have portmapper running to use these)
45 #
46 ##rstatd/1-3    dgram rpc/udp wait root   /usr/libexec/tcpd   rpc.rstatd
47 ##rusersd/1-2   dgram rpc/udp wait root   /usr/libexec/tcpd   rpc.rusersd
48 ##walld/1       dgram rpc/udp wait root   /usr/libexec/tcpd   rpc.rwalld
49 ##pcnfsd/1-2    dgram rpc/udp wait root   /usr/libexec/tcpd   rpc.pcnfsd
50 ##rquotad/1     dgram rpc/udp wait root   /usr/libexec/tcpd   rpc.rquotad
51 ##sprayd/1      dgram rpc/udp wait root   /usr/libexec/tcpd   rpc.sprayd
52 #
53 # The following are not known to be useful, and should not be enabled unless
54 # you have a specific need for it and are aware of the possible implications
55 #
56 #exec    stream    tcp    nowait  root  /usr/libexec/tcpd   rexecd
57 #auth    stream    tcp    wait    root  /usr/libexec/tcpd   identd -w -t120
```

Briefly, the intent of the services on each line is as follows:

- Line 8. The `fingerd` daemon enables external users to finger a user ID and find out whether the ID exists; if it does, how recently and on what terminals the ID has been logged in.
- Line 9. The `ftpd` daemon provides an FTP (file transfer protocol) server.
- Line 10. The `login` service provides service for the `rlogin` remote login terminal program. Don't turn this on.

- Line 11. The `nntp` service is a Usenet newsgroups server. If your machine is configured to receive news from other servers, you can point your newsreader to your local machine to read news.
- Line 12. The `ntalk` (new protocol talk) daemon provides for real-time chat services. If you're familiar with ICQ, iChat, or IRC, this service is somewhat similar.
- Line 13. Provides remote shell service—another way to remotely access machines. This service is required to use certain remote services, such as remote tape archive storage. Because Apple hasn't provided all the software necessary to make full use of these services, we suggest that this be left off as well; it's almost as large a security risk as `rlogin` and `telnet`.
- Line 14. Provides the `telnet` daemon to allow remote `telnet` terminal connections. Don't turn this on. Mac OS X already provides SSH, which can be used more securely for terminal connections.
- Line 15. The `uucpd` service implements the Unix-to-Unix copy protocol. This is an antiquated method for networking Unix machines that can't always be connected to the network. Essentially, it enables network traffic between two sites to be queued until both sites are available on the network, and then exchanges the data. This service is of very limited utility today, and presents a significant security risk because it hasn't really been maintained since the days of 1200-baud modems.
- Line 16. The `comsat` daemon provides notification of incoming mail to mail-reader clients.
- Line 17. `tftp` is trivial file transfer protocol, and is one of the methods of providing file service to completely diskless network clients. You won't need to enable this service unless you're providing network boot services for diskless Unix clients.
- Line 18. `bootp` is a way of transmitting network configuration information to clients. Chances are you'll use DHCP for this, if you have a need to do so, although it's possible that OS X Server could use `bootp` for netboot clients.
- Line 19. `pop3` is a POPMail (Post Office Protocol Mail) server. In the file, Apple indicates that this service is not yet available. This server would potentially be used if you were running a mail server and installed a third-party POPMail server.
- Line 20. `imap4` is an IMAP mail server. Again, this service is not available as of the 10.2 release. This server would potentially be used if you were running a mail server and installed a third-party IMAP mail server.

- Lines 26–33. Provide a number of network and network-software diagnostic servers. Unless you are performing network diagnosis and specifically need these, leave them off. They do not cause any known security problems, but if you're not using them, they occupy resources needlessly.
- Lines 34 and 35. Provide the time service. (Some servers require both stream and datagram connectivity, and these must be defined on separate lines.) If you want your machine to be a time server, these can be turned on.
- Lines 39–42. Start a number of Kerberos (security authentication)–related servers, but most are unavailable from Apple as of the 10.2 release. The `krb5_prop` service (starting `kpropd`) is the server that propagates a master Kerberos server's database to slave servers.
- Line 46. The `rstatd` daemon allows systems to connect through the network and get machine status information.
- Line 47. The `rusersd` daemon allows systems to connect through the network and to find information about this system's users. This is generally considered to be a Bad Idea.
- Line 48. The `walld` daemon enables users to write to the screens of all users on the system. This facility is nice if you're root and need to tell your users that the machine is going to go down for maintenance. It's annoying if one of your users starts using it to incessantly ask anyone connected to the machine for help with trivial Unix problems.
- Line 49. The `pcnfsd` daemon provides service for a PC network file system product named `pcnfs`. Almost everybody uses `samba` instead nowadays.
- Line 50. The `rquotad` daemon provides disk quota information to remote machines, so that they can enforce quotas that your machine specifies on disks that it is serving to them.
- Line 51. `sprayd` is another network diagnostic server. Simply put, it responds, as rapidly as it can, to packets placed on the network by some other machine's spray process, which places packets on the network as fast as it can. This one would be nice if Apple provided it in a later release because it can be very useful for finding problem hardware in your network.
- Line 56. The `rexecd` daemon allows for the remote execution of parts of programs. Apple claims that it isn't known to be useful, but a programmer can make very good use of this service to perform distributed processing tasks by sending parts of programs to many different machines. Of course, it is also a security risk.

- Line 57. Another service that Apple considers to be of no practical use. The `identd` daemon provides a method for a remote machine to verify the identity of a user causing a connection, inasmuch as any identity can be verified over the network. The service was created because it is very easy for a user accessing, for example, a remote FTP site, to pretend to be a different user on your system, and potentially cause trouble for the person he is pretending to be.

NOTE

The network services defined in `/etc/inetd.conf` or in `/etc/xinetd.d/` run from the ports specified in the `/etc/services` file. The `/etc/services` file defines the port numbers in three sections: Well Known Port Numbers, Registered Port Numbers, and Dynamic and/or Private Ports. Currently the Internet Assigned Numbers Authority (IANA), `http://www.iana.org/`, coordinates port assignments. The assignments used to be maintained in an RFC, but as the Internet grew, the RFC was replaced by IANA. If you decide to run a service from `inetd` or `xinetd` on a nonstandard port, update your `/etc/services` file to include a port number and service name. You might check IANA for the last port assignment information. However, if you decide to run a service on a port that officially is used for another service, you won't experience any problems unless you are also trying to run the service that is supposed to run on that port. If you should end up having to run a service on a nonstandard port, the only one who will be confused is the attacker probing your machine.

Startup Items

Some services start from `/System/Library/StartupItems` at boot time. Unlike the types of services that are controlled by `inetd`, these services are most efficient if they are running all the time. These services are root-owned daemon processes that run continuously, listening for connections and forking off new client-handling processes under restricted privileges. `inetd` and `xinetd` are two such services. Some of these services have additional controls in the `/etc/hostconfig` file that the startup scripts check. For example, the SSH server, the AppleShare server, and the mail server are controlled in such a fashion.

If you enabled those services, but later decide to disable them, set the appropriate `/etc/hostconfig` variable to `-NO-` and kill their current processes. The next time you reboot, the services won't start. To manually start one of those services, set the appropriate variable in `/etc/hostconfig` to `-YES-` and manually execute the startup script. How this is done depends on the startup script. For some, using `SystemStarter` (`SystemStarter start <path-to-service-directory>`) may be appropriate. For others, passing the start action to the script (`<startup script> start`) might work instead. For others, simply executing the startup script without passing the start action is sufficient. For example, for the SSH server, you would make the SSHSERVER line in /etc/hostconfig read SSHSERVER=-YES-. Then you would execute /System/Library/StartupItems/SSH/SSH. To disable a service that doesn't have a control in /etc/hostconfig, simply rename the startup script and kill its process.

Some third-party packages put startup scripts in /Library/StartupItems. To disable a service whose startup script is located in this directory, rename the startup script or the directory it is in and kill its process.

Protecting inetd with TCP Wrappers

A common way to restrict access to some TCP services is to use the TCP Wrappers program. TCP Wrappers is a package that monitors and filters requests for TCP (Transmission Control Protocol) services. We don't look at the protocol in any detail here—that's a book subject in itself. Suffice it to say the protocol has enough control information in it that we can use a package like TCP Wrappers to filter some of that traffic. TCP Wrappers can be used to restrict certain network services to individual computers or networks.

To make use of this program on some flavors of Unix, TCP Wrappers must be installed by the system administrator. This isn't a necessary step in Mac OS X because the TCP Wrappers program comes preinstalled on the system. The /etc/inetd.conf file in Mac OS X already assumes that you use TCP Wrappers, as evidenced by a line such as the following:

```
#ftp    stream  tcp     nowait  root    /usr/libexec/tcpd               ftpd -l
```

The /usr/libexec/tcpd portion of the preceding line indicates that TCP Wrappers is used to call ftpd.

NOTE

TCP Wrappers can block access to a service, but it can't refuse the connection.

When you use TCP Wrappers to protect an inetd service, it lets you prevent a remote machine from connecting to that service, but the connection to inetd still happens. Using tcpd to protect a service in this fashion can prevent the internal resource depletion effects of a DoS attack, but inetd itself still must accept the connection and pass it to tcpd. Through this limitation, a DoS attack against inetd, even on a completely TCP Wrapped machine, can impact performance and resources.

TCP Wrappers therefore should be thought of primarily as a way to limit access to services to hosts that you want accessing them, rather than a way of securing inetd itself.

Wrappng `inetd` Processes

The particularly difficult part about using TCP Wrappers is configuring it. We will look at two ways you can configure TCP Wrappers in OS X: the traditional method of using two control files and an alternate method that uses only one control file.

Traditionally, TCP Wrappers has two control files, `/etc/hosts.allow` and `/etc/hosts.deny`. We will look at the traditional method in greater detail because it is the default setup for a machine when extended processing options are not enabled. An understanding of the traditional method should carry over to the alternate method. Be sure to read the `hosts_access` and `hosts_options` man pages for detailed information.

Here is the format of the access control files:

```
daemon_list : client_list : option : option ...
```

Through `/etc/hosts.allow` you can allow specific services for specific hosts.

Through `/etc/hosts.deny` you can deny services to hosts, and provide global exceptions.

The easiest way to think of and use these configuration files is to think of TCP Wrappers as putting a big fence up around all the services on your machine.

The specifications in `/etc/hosts.deny` are most typically used to tell the fence what services are on the outside of the fence, and therefore for which access is *not* denied (that is, the specifications provide exceptions to the deny rule). The fence can appear to be around different sets of services for different clients. For example, an `/etc/hosts.deny` file might look like

```
ALL EXCEPT ftpd : 192.168.1. : banners /usr/libexec/banners
ALL : 140.254.12.100 140.254.12.135 : banners /usr/libexec/banners
ALL EXCEPT ftpd sshd : ALL : banners /usr/libexec/banners
```

This file says

- For the subdomain `192.168.1.`, deny all connections except connections to the FTP daemon, `ftpd`.
- For the specific machines `140.254.12.100` and `140.254.12.135` (maybe they're troublemakers) deny absolutely all connections.
- For all other IP addresses, deny everything except connections to `ftpd` and to the secure-shell daemon `sshd`.

The `banners /usr/libexec/banners` entry is an option that tells `tcpd` that if it denies a connection to a service based on this entry, try to find an explanation file in this location. Use this option if you have a need to provide an explanation as to why the service is not available. The `banners` option can be used when `tcpd` is compiled with the `-DPROCESS_OPTIONS` option. A makefile that can build the banners comes with the TCP Wrappers distribution. Make a prototype banner called `prototype`, run `make` to create a banner for the service, and place the banner file in the appropriate directory; in this case, `/usr/libexec/banners`. This option can be used primarily for `ftpd`, `telnetd`, and `rlogind`. For Mac OS X, you would probably have to compile your own `tcpd` to get this to work.

The specifications in `/etc/hosts.allow` make little gates through the fences erected by `/etc/hosts.deny` for specific host and service combinations. For example, an `/etc/hosts.allow` file might look like the following:

```
ALL: 140.254.12.137 192.168.2. 192.168.3.
popper: 140.254.12.124 140.254.12.151 192.168.1.36
```

This file says

- Allow connections to any TCP service from the host `140.254.12.137` and all hosts in the `192.168.2.` and `192.168.3.` subdomains. (Perhaps the `192.168.2.` and `192.168.3.` subdomains are known highly secure networks because they're subnets within our own corporate LAN, and we really trust `140.254.12.137` because it's so well run.)
- Allow connections to the `popper (POPMail v3 daemon)` service for three specific machines: `140.254.12.124`, `140.254.12.151`, and `192.168.1.36`. If used in combination with the previous `/etc/hosts.deny` file, these allowances still stand. They override the denials in `/etc/hosts.deny`, so even though the `192.168.1.` subdomain is denied all access except to `ftpd` by `/etc/hosts.deny`, the specific machine `192.168.1.36` has its own private gate that allows it access to the `popper popd` service as well.

NOTE

Services with a smile or without? There can be a bit of confusion as to the name of the service to put in an `/etc/hosts.allow` or `/etc/hosts.deny` file. If it's a service out of `inetd.conf`, generally the name to use is the service name from the left-most column of the file. If this doesn't work, try adding a `d` to the end of the service name (`ftp -> ftpd`). If that doesn't work, then try the program name as used in the right-most column of the `inetd.conf` file or as started by your `rc` files.

Other services use names that don't seem to be recorded officially anywhere. These sometimes require a bit of experimenting on your part, but the service names inserted into the `Services` NetInfo map are usually the hint you need.

If all else fails, read the man pages for the service.

Now that you have seen how the traditional method of controlling TCP Wrappers works, let's take a brief look at an alternate method that uses only the /etc/hosts.allow file. This method can be used on systems where extended option processing has been enabled. This is indeed the case with OS X. Nevertheless, either method works in OS X.

In the single file, /etc/hosts.allow, you specify allow and deny rules together. With the /etc/hosts.allow-only method, tcpd reads the file on a first-match-wins basis. Consequently, it is important that your allow rules appear before your deny rules.

For example, to restrict access to ftpd to only to our host, 140.254.12.124, we would use these rules:

```
ftpd: 140.254.12.124 127.0.0.1 localhost: ALLOW
ftpd: ALL: DENY
```

In the first line, the host, 140.254.12.124, is allowed access to ftpd using the various addresses that it knows for itself. On the second line, access to all other hosts is denied. If you reversed these lines, even the host that you wanted to allow ftpd access would be denied access.

After you have sufficiently tested that you have properly set up your allow and deny rules, there is nothing else you need to do to keep TCP Wrappers running. As you are testing your rules, check your logs carefully to see where, if at all, the behaviors are logged. You will rarely see entries for tcpd itself in your logs, but you may see additional logging for a wrapped service under that service. The best place to check is /var/log/system.log.

Increasing Security with xinetd

Starting with the Mac OS X 10.2 distribution, xinetd is used as the default Internet services daemon. The xinetd package, the extended Internet services daemon, is highly configurable and can provide access controls for both TCP and UDP. Among the controls for a given service that can be configured are the number of simultaneous servers, the number of connections permitted from a given source, access times, allowing and denying access to certain hosts, and limiting the rate of incoming connections. Some of these controls can help reduce denial of service attacks on your machine. xinetd can even redirect a service to a port on another machine, or to another interface on the same machine. This would be particularly useful if xinetd is running on your firewall machine.

NOTE

Using `xinetd` can limit the risk of DoS attacks, but not eliminate it.

Although `xinetd` can be configured to limit access to services in a number of ways, and is superior to `inetd` in its capacity to reduce the resource consumption caused by a DoS attack, it is not a complete solution. `xinetd` still must receive and process each network service request. Even if a particular request is going to be denied by the rules, it still consumes network bandwidth, and it still consumes processing power to detect that it's invalid.

The only way to completely eliminate the effect of DoS attacks against your machine is to get them filtered out before they reach your hardware. This is usually accomplished at the router that feeds your network. If your service provider can't provide this service to you, blocking DoS attacks at the packet-filter level (see the discussion on Carrafix and traffic shaping in Chapter 17, "Blocking Network Access: Firewalls") is most efficient at reducing the impact on your machine.

Vulnerabilities

Although `xinetd` is a highly configurable `inetd` replacement that promotes increased security, it is not immune to vulnerabilities. The following list describes recent `xinetd` vulnerabilities.

- `xinetd` Open File Descriptor Denial of Service Vulnerability (CAN-2002-0871, BugTraq ID 5458). Services launched by `xinetd` inherit file descriptors from the signal pipe. An attacker could then launch a denial of service attack via the signal pipe. So far there are no known instances of this vulnerability being exploited. The vulnerability is fixed in `xinetd` 2.3.7.
- Multiple `xinetd` Vulnerabilities (CAN-2001-1389, BugTraq ID 3257). Buffer overflows and improper NULL termination exist in versions of `xinetd` before version 2.3.3. These vulnerabilities can lead to denial of service attacks or remote `root` compromise. The vulnerabilities are fixed in version 2.3.3.
- Zero Length Buffer Overflow Vulnerability (CAN-2001-0825, BugTraq ID 2971). Versions of `xinetd` before 2.1.8.8 improperly handle string data in some internal functions. As a result, a buffer overflow can occur when a length argument with a value less than or equal to zero is passed to one of these internal functions. This could result either in a `root` compromise on the machine, or in denial of service for services started by `xinetd`, if `xinetd` crashes. Fixes that were originally available for this vulnerability may not completely fix the problem, but the problem is fixed in version 2.3.3.

Installing `xinetd`

The first vulnerability listed in the previous section, CAN-2002-0871, indicates that a fix is available in `xinetd` 2.3.7. Mac OS X 10.2, however, originally came with `xinetd`

2.3.5. If you check your logs, and you see an entry like the one below, you have a version of xinetd with the particular denial of service vulnerability contained in CAN-2002-0871.

```
Aug 26 18:13:49 Sage-Rays-Computer xinetd[1112]:
➥xinetd Version 2.3.5 started with libwrap options compiled in.
```

Make sure you apply the latest updates to replace your version of xinetd. You can always download the most recent version from http://www.xinetd.org/. As of this writing, the latest version is 2.3.11. If you upgrade an application yourself before Apple provides an update, save your newer version somewhere, in case Software Update should overwrite your version with something that might not be as current. If Software Update overwrites your version with the same or newer, you can probably remove yours entirely, unless you had customized your version.

xinetd follows this basic format for compilation and installation:

```
./configure
make
make install
```

A few compile-time options that you can pass to configure are documented in Table 11.1. The install step must be done as root. Depending on how you want to maintain your machine, you may just prefer to copy the binary to /usr/libexec/, or you may want to store your updated version of xinetd in a completely separate location. To keep your updated version of xinetd as capable as the one Apple provides, we recommend at least running configure with the --with-libwrap option. The libwrap path is /usr/lib/libwrap.a. Make sure you keep backup copies of the original xinetd and its configuration file, /etc/xinetd.conf.

TABLE 11.1 Compile-Time Options for xinetd

Option	Description
--prefix=PATH	Specifies the directory prefix for installing xinetd. The default is /usr/local.
--with-libwrap=PATH	Compiles in support for TCP Wrappers. With this option on, xinetd first looks at the TCP Wrappers controls file(s). If access is granted, xinetd then continues on to its access controls.
--with-loadavg	Compiles in support for the max_load configuration option, which causes a service to stop accepting connections when the specified load has been reached. The option is currently supported only on Linux and Solaris.
--with-inet6	Causes services to default to IPv6. However, IPv6 support is now fully integrated into xinetd, rendering this option meaningless.

NOTE

If you decide to install xinetd on Mac OS X 10.1 or earlier and want to compile in libwrap support, you need to download some libwrap files first. They are available from http://www.opensource.apple.com/projects/darwin/1.0/projects.html if you select the tcp-wrappers download. The source builds its files in /tmp/. If you want to put the files in /usr/local/, make /usr/local/lib/ and /usr/local/include/ directories, if they do not already exist. If you want to install the files elsewhere, replace the /usr/local/ references as appropriate. Then at the root of the source directory, do the following:

```
make RC_ARCHS=ppc install
cp /tmp/tcp_wrappers/Release/usr/local/lib/libwrap.a /usr/local/lib/
ranlib /usr/local/lib/libwrap.a
cp /tmp/tcp_wrappers/Release/usr/local/include/tcpd.h /usr/local/include/
```

In Mac OS X, xinetd runs by default as xinetd -pidfile /var/run/xinetd.pid. However, more runtime options are also available for xinetd, and are listed in Table 11.2.

TABLE 11.2 Runtime Options for xinetd

Option	Description
-d	Enables debug mode.
-syslog <syslog_facility>	Enables syslog logging of xinetd-produced messages using the specified syslog facility. The following syslog facilities may be used: daemon, auth, user, local[0-7]. Ineffective in debug mode.
-filelog <log_file>	Specifies where to log xinetd-produced messages. Ineffective in debug mode.
-f <config_file>	Specifies which file to use as the config file. Default is /etc/xinetd.conf.
-pidfile <pid_file>	Writes the process ID to the file specified. Ineffective in debug mode. Apple starts xinetd with this option: xinetd -pidfile /var/run/xinetd.pid
-stayalive	Tells xinetd to stay running even if no services are specified.
-limit <proc_limit>	Limits the number of concurrently running processes that can be started by xinetd.
-logprocs <limit>	Limits the number of concurrently running servers for remote user ID acquisition.
-cc <interval>	Performs consistency checks on its internal state every <interval> seconds.

Configuring xinetd

The default /etc/xinetd.conf file that comes with Mac OS X 10.2 is shown in Listing 11.2.

LISTING 11.2 The Default `/etc/xinetd.conf` File

```
1  # man xinetd.conf for more information
2
3  defaults
4  {
5          instances               = 60
6          log_type                = SYSLOG daemon
7          log_on_success          = HOST PID
8          log_on_failure          = HOST
9          cps                     = 25 30
10 }
11
12 includedir /etc/xinetd.d
```

The `/etc/xinetd.conf` file looks very different from the `/etc/inetd.conf` file. This file has two major sections to it: a defaults section and a services section. The defaults section has controls that are basic defaults for the services. Each service has further controls and can also override or augment controls listed in the defaults section. Briefly, the intent of the lines of this file is as follows:

- Line 3 labels the `defaults` section of the file.
- Line 4 starts the configuration for the `defaults` section of the file.
- Line 5 sets the first `defaults` attribute, `instances`, which specifies the limit of servers for a given service to `60`.
- Line 6 sets the `log_type` attribute to the `SYSLOG` facility at the `daemon` level.
- Line 7 sets the `log_on_success` attribute to `HOST`, which logs the remote host's IP address, and `PID`, the process ID of the server.
- Line 8 sets the `log_on_failure` attribute to `HOST`, which logs the remote host's IP address.
- Line 9 sets the `cps` attribute, the one that limits the connections per second, to `25` connections per second. When this limit is reached, the service disables itself for the number of seconds specified in the second argument—`30` seconds in this case.
- Line 10 ends the defaults configuration section.
- Line 12 starts the services section by using the `includedir` directive to specify that every file in the `/etc/xinetd.d` directory, excluding files containing . or ~, is parsed as an `xinetd` configuration file. The files are parsed in alphabetical order according to the C locale.

Already you can tell that xinetd has more functionality than the traditional inetd. For instance, inetd cannot limit the number of connections per second. The items listed in this default /etc/xinetd.conf file are not the only ones that can be listed in this section, nor are the default values necessarily the only possible values. Table 11.3 shows a listing of available attributes for xinetd.

TABLE 11.3 Available Attributes for xinetd

Attribute	Description
id	Used to uniquely identify a service. Useful for services that can use different protocols and need to be described with different entries in the configuration file. Default service ID is the same as the service name.
type	Any combination of the following can be used: RPC: Specifies service as an RPC service. INTERNAL: Specifies service as provided by xinetd. UNLISTED: Specifies that the service is not listed in a standard system file, such as /etc/services or /etc/rpc.
flags	Any combination of the following can be used: INTERCEPT: Intercepts packets or accepted connections to verify that they are coming from acceptable locations. Internal or multithreaded services cannot be intercepted. NORETRY: Avoids retry attempts in case of fork failure. IDONLY: Accepts connections only when the remote end identifies the remote user. Applies only to connection-based services. NAMEINARGS: Causes the first argument to server_args to be the name of the server. Useful for using TCP Wrappers. NODELAY: For a TCP service, sets the TCP_NODELAY flag on the socket. Has no effect on other types of services. DISABLE: Specifies that this service is to be disabled. Overrides the enabled directive in defaults. KEEPALIVE: For a TCP service, sets the SO_KEEPALIVE flag on the socket. Has no effect on other types of services. NOLIBWRAP: Disables internal calling of the tcpwrap library to determine access to the service. SENSOR: Replaces the service with a sensor that detects accesses to the specified port. Does not detect stealth scans. Should be used only on services you know you don't need. Whenever a connection is made to the service's port, adds the IP address to a global no_access list until the deny_time setting expires. IPv4: Sets the service to an IPv4 service. IPv6: Sets the service to an IPv6 service.
disable	Has a value of yes or no. Overrides the enabled directive in defaults.
socket_type	Has a value of stream, dgram, raw, or seqpacket.
protocol	Specifies the protocol used by the service. Protocol must exist in /etc/protocols. If it is not defined, the default protocol for the service is used.

TABLE 11.3 Continued

Attribute	Description
wait	Specifies whether the service is single-threaded or multithreaded. If yes, it is single-threaded; xinetd starts the service and stops handling requests for the service until the server dies. If no, it is multithreaded; xinetd keeps handling new service requests.
user	Specifies the UID for the server process. Username must exist in /etc/passwd.
group	Specifies the GID for the server process. Group must exist in /etc/group. If a group is not specified, the group of the user is used.
instances	Determines the number of simultaneous instances of the server. Default is unlimited. The value can be an integer or UNLIMITED.
nice	Specifies server priority.
server	Specifies the program to execute for this service.
server_args	Specifies arguments to be passed to the server. Server name should not be included, unless the NAMEINARGS flag has been specified.
only_from	Specifies to which remote hosts the service is available. Can be specified as: A numeric address in the form %d.%d.%d.%d. 0 is a wildcard. IPv6 hosts may be specified as abcd:ef01::2345:6789. A factorized address in the form of %d.%d.%d.{%d,%d,...}. There is no need for all four components (that is, %d.%d.{%d,%d,...%d} is also okay). However, the factorized part must be at the end of the address. Does not work for IPv6. A network name (from /etc/networks). Does not work for IPv6. A hostname or domain name in the form of .domain.com. An IP address/netmask range in the form of 1.2.3.4/32. IPv6 address/netmask ranges in the form of 1234::/46 are also valid. Specifying this attribute without a value makes the service available to nobody.
no_access	Specifies the remote hosts to which this service is not available. Value can be specified in the same forms as for only_from. When neither only_from nor no_access is specified, the service is available to anyone. If both are listed, the one that is the better match for the host determines availability of the service to the host. For example, if only_from is 192.168.1.0 and no_access is 192.168.1.10, then 192.168.1.10 does not have access.
access_times	Specifies time intervals when the service is available. An interval has the form: hour:min-hour:min. Hours can range from 0–23; minutes can range from 0–59.
log_type	Specifies where service log output is sent. May either be SYSLOG or FILE, as follows: SYSLOG *<syslog_facility>* [*<syslog_level>*] Possible facility names include daemon, auth, authpriv, user, local0-7. Possible level names include emerg, alert, crit, err, warning, notice, info, debug. If a level is not present, the messages will be recorded at the info level. FILE *<file>* [*<soft_limit>*] [*<hard_limit>*] Log output is appended to *<file>*, which is created if it does not exist.

TABLE 11.3 Continued

Attribute	Description
log_on_success	Specifies what information is logged when the server is started and exits. Any combination of the following can be specified: PID: Logs the server process ID. HOST: Logs the remote host's address. USERID: Logs remote user ID using RFC 1413 identification protocol. Only available for multithreaded stream services. EXIT: Logs the fact that the server exited along with the exit status or termination signal. DURATION: Logs the duration of the server session.
log_on_failure	Specifies what is logged when a server cannot start, either from lack of resources or access configuration. Any combination of the following can be specified: HOST: Logs the remote host's address USERID: Logs remote user ID using RFC 1413 identification protocol. Available for multithreaded stream services only. RECORD: Logs as much information about the remote host as possible. ATTEMPT: Logs the fact that a failed attempt was made. Implied by use of any of the other options.
rpc_version	Specifies the RPC version of an RPC service. Can be a single number or a range in the form of *number–number*.
rpc_number	Specifies the number for an unlisted RPC service.
env	Value of this attribute is a list of strings of the form *<name>*=*<value>*. These strings are added to the server's environment, giving it xinetd's environment as well as the environment specified by the env attribute.
passenv	Value of this attribute is a list of environment variables from xinetd's environment to be passed to the server. An empty list implies passing no variables to the server except those explicitly defined by the env attribute.
port	Specifies the service port. If this attribute is listed for a service in /etc/services, it must be the same as the port number listed in that file.
redirect	Allows a TCP service to be redirected to another host. Useful for when your internal machines are not visible to the outside world. Syntax is redirect = *<IP address or host name> <port>* The server attribute is not required when this attribute is specified. If the server attribute is specified, this attribute takes priority.
bind	Allows a service to be bound to a specific interface on the machine.
interface	Synonym for bind.
banner	Name of the file to be displayed to the remote host when a connection to that service is made. The banner is displayed regardless of access control.
banner_success	Name of the file to be displayed to the remote host when a connection to that service is granted. Banner is displayed as soon as access to the service is granted.
banner_fail	Name of the file to be displayed to the remote host when a connection to a service is denied. Banner is printed immediately upon denial of access.

TABLE 11.3 Continued

Attribute	Description
per_source	Specifies the maximum number of connections permitted per server per source IP address. May be an integer or UNLIMITED.
cps	Limits the rate of incoming connections. Takes two arguments. The first is the number of connections per second. If the number of connections per second exceeds this rate, the server is temporarily disabled. The second argument specifies the number of seconds to wait before reenabling the server.
groups	Takes either yes or no. If yes, the server is executed with access to the groups to which the server's effective UID has access. If no, server runs with no supplementary groups. Must be set to yes for many BSD-flavored versions of Unix.
umask	Sets the inherited umask for the service. Expects an octal value. May be set in the defaults section to set a umask for all services. xinetd sets its own umask to the previous umask ORd with 022. This is the umask inherited by child processes if the umask attribute is not set.
enabled	Takes a list of service names to enable. Note that the service disable attribute and DISABLE flag can prevent a service from being enabled despite its being listed in this attribute.
include	Takes a filename in the form of include /etc/xinetd/service. File is then parsed as a new configuration file. May not be specified from within a service declaration.
includedir	Takes a directory name in the form of includedir /etc/xinetd.d. Every file in the directory, excluding files containing . or ending with ~, is parsed as an xinetd.conf file. Files are parsed in alphabetical order according to the C locale. May not be specified within a service declaration.
rlimit_cpu	Sets the maximum number of CPU seconds that the service may use. May either be a positive integer or UNLIMITED.
rlimit_data	Sets the maximum data resource size limit for the service. May either be a positive integer representing the number of bytes or UNLIMITED.
rlimit_rss	Sets the maximum resident set size limit for the service. Setting this value low makes the process a likely candidate for swapping out to disk when memory is low. One parameter is required, which is either a positive integer representing the number of bytes or UNLIMITED.
rlimit_stack	Sets the maximum stack size limit for the service. One parameter is required, which is either a positive integer representing the number of bytes or UNLIMITED.
deny_time	Sets the time span when access to all services to an IP address are denied to someone who sets off the SENSOR. Must be used in conjunction with the SENSOR flag. Options are FOREVER: IP address is not purged until xinetd is restarted. NEVER: Just logs the offending IP address. <*number*>: A numerical value of time in minutes. A typical time would be 60 minutes, to stop most DoS attacks while allowing IP addresses coming from a pool to be recycled for legitimate purposes.

OS X has default `xinetd` configuration files for the following services:

```
% ls /etc/xinetd.d
auth          comsat        echo-udp     login        tftp
bootps        daytime       exec         ntalk        time
chargen       daytime-udp   finger       shell        time-udp
chargen-udp   echo          ftp          telnet
```

As you can see, services that require two lines in `/etc/inetd.conf`, such as `time`, require two files in `/etc/xinetd.d`. Listing 11.3 includes the default listings for the `ftp`, `time`, and `time-udp` files.

LISTING 11.3 Default `xinetd` Configuration Files for the `ftp`, `time`, and `time-udp` Files

```
service ftp
{
        disable         = yes
        socket_type     = stream
        wait            = no
        user            = root
        server          = /usr/libexec/ftpd
        server_args     = -l
        groups          = yes
        flags           = REUSE
}
service time
{
        disable         = yes
        type            = INTERNAL
        id              = time-stream
        socket_type     = stream
        wait            = no
        user            = root
        groups          = yes
        flags           = REUSE
}
service time-udp
{
        disable         = yes
        type            = INTERNAL
        id              = time-dgram
        socket_type     = dgram
        wait            = yes
```

LISTING 11.3 Continued

```
        user            = root
        groups          = yes
        flags           = REUSE
}
```

Because FTP is a service that you might possibly enable, let's take a brief look at the attributes of the default `/etc/xinetd.d/ftp` file from Listing 11.3:

- Line 3 sets the first attribute, `disable`, to `yes`. This means that by default, the FTP service is disabled. `/etc/inetd.conf` simply has a `#` in front of a service to disable it.
- Line 4 sets the `socket_type` attribute to `stream`. This was the second item in the `ftp` line of `/etc/inetd.conf`.
- Line 5 sets the `wait` attribute to `no`. This was the third item in the `ftp` line of `/etc/inetd.conf`.
- Line 6 sets the `user` attribute to `root`. This was the fourth item in the `ftp` line of `/etc/inetd.conf`.
- Line 7 sets the `server` attribute to `/usr/libexec/ftpd`. This was the fifth item in the `ftp` line of `/etc/inetd.conf`.
- Line 8 sets the `server_args` attribute to `-l`. This was the final item in the `ftp` line of `/etc/inetd.conf`.
- Line 9 sets the `groups` attribute to `yes`. This is required for BSD-flavored versions of Unix. Because this attribute is required for all of your `xinetd` services, you could also move it to the defaults section of `/etc/xinetd.conf` and then remove it from the individual service files.
- Line 10 sets the `flags` attribute to `REUSE`. This seems to be an undocumented flag, but online wisdom indicates that it is a good flag to use.

As was the case with the `/etc/inetd.conf` file, the `time` service contains the same major descriptors, but in a different form. Unlike the `ftp` `xinetd` configuration file, the `time` and `time-udp` files also include the `id` attribute to uniquely identify the services.

Perhaps one of the most notable differences between the default `/etc/inetd.conf` file and the `/etc/xinetd.d/ftp` file is that the server is set to `/usr/libexec/tcpd` in the `inetd.conf` file, but in the `ftp` file, it is set to `/usr/libexec/ftpd`. Because `inetd` is not as configurable, it is important to use TCP Wrappers. However, you can configure host access information directly in `xinetd` without having to use TCP Wrappers. We recommend that you make use of that built-in capability. Additionally, `xinetd` includes support for displaying banners for services.

If you want to enable any of the default services controlled by `xinetd`, change the `disable` entry to `no` and restart `xinetd` by sending it a `HUP` signal using either of the following methods:

```
kill -HUP <xinetd_pid>
killall -HUP xinetd
```

Likewise, if you want to change any of the default configuration files, or add services not included in the initial set of default configuration files, simply restart `xinetd` to have them take effect. Listing 11.4 includes recommended `xinetd` configurations for services that might be of interest to you. If you want to change any of the defaults that appear in `/etc/xinetd.conf` for a given service, be sure to include that updated attribute in the service's file.

Finally, we also recommend that you reverse the starting order of `inetd` and `xinetd` in `/System/Library/StartupItems/IPServices/IPServices`. As of this writing, `inetd` starts before `xinetd`, but we recommend that you change the lines to read as follows:

```
xinetd -pidfile /var/run/xinetd.pid
inetd
```

This change will ensure that any services you start via the `System Preferences` are controlled as they were intended to be.

LISTING 11.4 Recommended Basic `xinetd` Configurations

```
service ftp
{
        disable         = no
        flags           = REUSE
        socket_type     = stream
        wait            = no
        user            = root
        server          = /usr/libexec/ftpd
        server_args     = -l
        groups          = yes
        only_from       = <host list>
        no_access       = <host list>
        access_times    = <time intervals>
}


service imap
{
```

LISTING 11.4 Continued

```
        disable         = no
        socket_type     = stream
        wait            = no
        user            = root
        server          = /usr/local/libexec/imapd
        groups          = yes
        flags           = REUSE
}


service pop3
{
        disable         = no
        socket_type     = stream
        wait            = no
        user            = root
        server          = /usr/local/libexec/ipop3d
        groups          = yes
        flags           = REUSE
}


service swat
{
        disable         = no
        socket_type     = stream
        wait            = no
        user            = root
        server          = /usr/sbin/swat
        groups          = yes
        flags           = REUSE
}

(Note that the swat service also needs a corresponding
swat 901/tcp
line in /etc/services)
```

Wrapping xinetd Processes

Although xinetd already has built-in host access restriction capabilities, if you decide that you would rather use TCP Wrappers on a service controlled by xinetd, you need to add a flag, NAMEINARGS, to the service and further expand the server_args line to include the full path to the service. Replace the original path to the server with the path to tcpd. Here's an example for using TCP Wrappers for restricting access to the FTP service in xinetd:

```
service ftp
{
        flags       = REUSE NAMEINARGS
        socket_type = stream
        protocol    = tcp
        wait        = no
        user        = root
        server      = /usr/libexec/tcpd
        server_args = /usr/libexec/ftpd -l
}
```

Summary

The primary problem with inetd itself is that it can be used in denial of service attacks on your machine. As the Internet services superserver, it can start many services that are prone to various vulnerabilities. Therefore, you do not want to turn on any services that you don't need to have running.

To further increase inetd security, you can make use of the TCP Wrappers package, tcpd, that comes with OS X. With TCP Wrappers, you can allow or deny access to TCP services that are started by inetd on a per-host or per-network basis.

Likewise, the primary problem with the default xinetd is that, in spite of its built-in host restriction capabilities, it is also prone to denial of service attacks. Nonetheless, with xinetd, you cannot only control "allow" and "deny" access for services, but you can also control many other aspects of a service. For example, for a given service, you can control the number of servers running, the server priority level, access times, number of connections per source IP address, the rate of incoming connections, the maximum number of CPU seconds, and maximum data size. Such controls can reduce the impact of a denial of service attack on your machine.

Given that the histories of both inetd and xinetd vulnerabilities have included at least one serious vulnerability, it is important to keep current on both of these daemons. For inetd, apply any updates from Apple that include inetd fixes. At least do the same for xinetd. For additional protection, install the latest version of xinetd.

12

FTP Security

IN THIS CHAPTER

- FTP Vulnerabilities
- Activating the FTP Server
- Configuring the Default `lukemftpd` FTP Server
- Setting Up Anonymous FTP
- Replacing the Mac OS X FTP Server
- Alternatives to FTP

One of the primary benefits of connecting computers together with a network is being able to use the network connection to move files between them. The FTP (File Transfer Protocol) service is an early and quite ubiquitous method designed to support this activity. Unfortunately, the protocol was invented during the more naive days of computer network development. And so in addition to the predictable security flaws that are due to bugs, it sports a plethora of intentional features that today we must struggle with to make secure. As you will see, these range from things that today we see as anachronistically optimistic design to features that were clearly a bad idea from day one.

Still, FTP, with all its inherent problems, isn't going away anytime soon. To work and play well in the networked world, FTP support is all but obligatory, and to be supported well, it needs to be secured. To secure it properly, an understanding of the protocol and its inherent vulnerabilities is required.

FTP Vulnerabilities

As you may already have guessed, FTP's largest vulnerability is essentially the design of the protocol. Having been created in a day when today's constant network security threats simply didn't exist, it wasn't designed with the requisite paranoid mindset to be secure. In fact, so trusting was the nature of its designers that it supports a number of features that allow it to be made explicitly insecure. The security concerns range from vulnerability, to denial-of-service attacks, to the ability to configure it to execute arbitrary system commands for remote users. And these are in addition to the vulnerabilities that are due to bugs in the code. The primary flaws about which you must concern yourself are as follows:

- FTP is a cleartext protocol. User IDs and passwords are carried over a cleartext connection, enabling nefarious individuals to snoop your users' names and passwords off the wire. Even if you don't allow remote logins of any form, if your users connect via FTP in an unprotected manner (and it's very difficult to force them to use a protected method—more on this later in this chapter), they're giving away the information necessary to log in with their ID at the console.
- FTP is a two-channel protocol, with "commands" being carried over one network connection and "data" being carried over another. Protecting the command channel isn't too difficult, and doing so protects user IDs and passwords, but because of the design, protecting the data channel is more difficult. Consequently, the data channel is not protected, and the contents of file transfers are seen.
- The flexibility designed into the protocol is overly optimistic. The protocol's two-channel design is intended to allow a command channel from machine A to machine B, to invoke a data transfer from machine B to machine C (or vice versa). While conceptually interesting, and quite useful for allowing FTP connections to work from behind firewalls, this flexibility also allows a renegade machine A to access data on machine C from any other machine on the Internet (any machine running an insecure FTP server, that is), even if machine C has explicitly blocked all access from machine A.
- The FTP server is frequently run from `inetd` or `xinetd` (Chapter 11, "Introduction to Mac OS X Network Services"), requiring a process to be spawned for every incoming connection, whether it's a valid/successful connection or not. You can throttle connections or limit the number of connections to your FTP server by using `xinetd` rather than `inetd`, but the design consumes resources for any connection, thereby allowing DoS attacks and inappropriate consumption of resources.
- An additional design feature available in some server implementations enables you to configure the server to accept new, site-specific commands. This allows FTP site administrators to put the protocol to flexible uses in very site-specific contexts, but less-than-careful configuration can allow the remote user to execute arbitrary commands with the permissions of the FTP server.
- If the server is configured to allow access by users with accounts on the server machine, the server must be configured to initially run as root, so that it can switch user IDs to run as the appropriate valid user after the user is authenticated. Unfortunately, this means that the server must run as root prior to authentication, and that it therefore can be the source of root compromises if bugs are discovered that allow attacks prior to authentication or outside of the authenticated session.

Each of these areas has been the subject of numerous attacks over the years. CERT's database contains over a thousand entries regarding FTP, and CVE lists almost 200 specific FTP vulnerabilities and exposures. For example:

- A bug in versions 2.4.1 and earlier of the very popular FTP server wu-ftpd allows the use of a liberally configured `SITE EXEC` to spawn shells and other system commands, potentially with root privileges (CVE-1999-0080). To find out whether your machine is vulnerable, FTP to your own account, log in, and enter `site exec csh -c id`. If your machine responds with a line that starts `uid=0(root)...`, you've just executed a command as root, without the root password, and your `ftpd` is vulnerable.
- As a convenience, many FTP servers provide for data-type conversion between what's actually stored and what the user wishes to retrieve. Most frequently, this allows the retrieval of both compressed and uncompressed versions of files when only one or the other version is actually stored. wu-ftpd 2.4.2 to 2.6.0 have a buffer boundary-checking error in the routine that allows convenience conversions on-server from one data type to another. The overflow allows users to fool the server into executing arbitrary commands rather than the conversion software. To test this exploit (CVE-1999-0997), search the Net for "SUID advisory 001"; currently this can be found at `http://packetstormsecurity.nl/advisories/suid/001.txt`.
- The "Pizza Thief" exploit (CVE-1999-0351), on the other hand, relies on an inherent feature of the FTP design. This attack utilizes the dual-channel nature of FTP to allow the attacker access to the server outside the intended scope of his authenticated FTP session. The attacker can fake a command channel, or break a data channel, and then use an unauthorized client to access the server through the open data channel connection. More information can be found at `http://www.kb.cert.org/vuls/id/2558` and `http://www.attrition.org/security/advisory/misc/infowar/iw_sec_01.txt`.
- More recently (wu-ftpd 2.6.1), the `autowu` rootkit provides the script kiddie with one-stop root shopping by exploit of the CA-2001-33 (CVE-2001-0550) vulnerabilities, which are a combination of design and buffer bounds-checking problems. For a particularly amusing examination of the exploit (and the skillset of those most likely to use it), see `http://www.nardware.co.uk/honeys/honey1/NardHoney1.htm`.

None of these specific problems are immediate concerns for your server because Apple provides an FTP server with no published vulnerabilities as of November 2002. The design of FTP, however, lends itself to ongoing problems of a similar nature, as well as to administrator-induced vulnerabilities due to misconfiguration. The best defense against bugs is to keep up with all software updates: We recommend (and cover later in this chapter) installing wu-ftpd as a replacement for what Apple provides because problems with wu-ftpd will be addressed nearly instantly. To protect against design issues, the only defense is to thoroughly understand the options available. Although it's not always possible to create the exact configuration desired, carefully studying the options, how they interact, and how to apply them is the only way to produce an FTP environment with the features that you want without introducing too many problems that you don't.

Activating the FTP Server

The Mac OS X distribution includes an FTP server called `lukemftpd`, which is a port of the NetBSD FTP server. Because Apple is concerned about the security of your machine, this service is not turned on by default. At this point, you can use FTP only to connect from your Mac OS X machine to other FTP servers. After you've turned on the FTP service, you can FTP directly to your Mac OS X machine.

To activate the FTP server, check the FTP Access box under the Services tab of the Sharing pane, as shown in Figure 12.1.

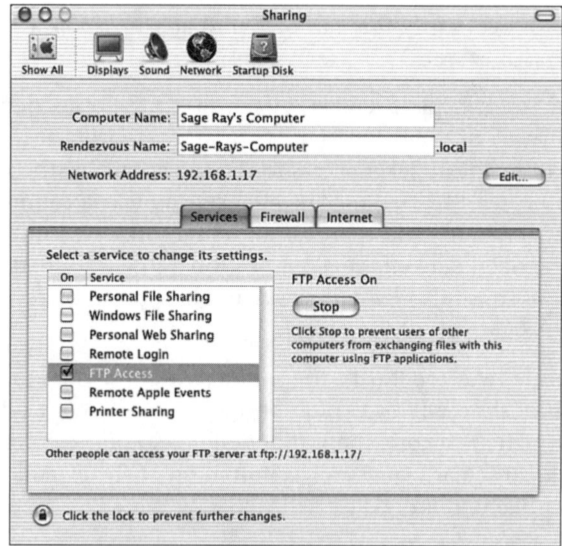

FIGURE 12.1 The FTP server is activated in the Sharing pane.

What this does behind the scenes is change the `disable` line in `/etc/xinetd.d/ftp` to `disable=no` and force `xinetd` to reread its configuration file. If, for whatever reason, you're using `inetd` rather the default `xinetd`, uncomment the `ftp` line and then run `killall -HUP inetd` to have `inetd` reread its configuration file.

CAUTION

Remember that when you do this, you're opening a service that will accept user IDs and passwords in clear text over your network connection. If a user with an account on your machine tries to use a normal FTP client to use the FTP service, she'll be prompted for her user ID and password. If she provides them, this information will be visible to anyone watching your network. This is probably not what you want. We'll discuss options to make this information more secure later in this chapter. Specifically, look to the section on setting up an FTP server to provide encrypted access to connections tunneled through SSH, or possibly the option of requiring anonymous, rather than real-user, FTP access. Note that if you use the anonymous option, there's nothing to *prevent* your users from trying to use their own user IDs and passwords instead of "anonymous," so this is no guarantee that your users will use the service securely!

Configuring the Default `lukemftpd` FTP Server

The default Mac OS X FTP server allows you to customize its configuration.

`lukemftpd` FTP Server Options

You've just turned on your FTP server. If you looked at the `/etc/xinetd.d/ftp` file, you noticed that the server runs by default with the `-l` option (`server_args = -l`), which is the option that forces the logging of successful and unsuccessful FTP sessions.

If you study your FTP connections to keep track of what sorts of malicious individuals are trying to crack your security, you might want to consider logging additional information. The `lukemftpd` server options (shown in Table 12.1) include a number of settings to control the different types of information stored and the way that it is stored. To implement any of the options, edit the `server args` entry in `/etc/xinetd.d/ftp` to reflect the options you want to use. Then run `killall -HUP xinetd` to have `xinetd` reread its configuration. Alternatively, if you are using `inetd` instead, edit the `ftp` entry in `/etc/inetd.conf` to include the desired server arguments and have `inetd` reread its configuration file.

Please note that whenever you turn the FTP service on or off via the System Preferences pane, any other configuration changes you have made to the service are retained, rather than being reset. Nonetheless, it is a good idea to keep a copy of the file with your configuration changes, in case this default behavior ever changes. A number of additional options are worth consideration as well, such as the `-V` option, which enables you to force the server to report a different version string than the one with which it was compiled. Many scripts run by script kiddies can be flagged off if you report a version with no known vulnerabilities, or confused into beating their heads against a brick wall if you report a different version with well-known vulnerabilities that don't correspond to problems with the server you're actually running.

TABLE 12.1 Run Time Options for the Default ftpd

Option	Function
-a <anondir>	Defines <anondir> as the directory to which a chroot(2) is performed for anonymous logins. Default is the home directory for the FTP user. This can also be specified with the ftpd.conf(5) chroot directive.
-c <confdir>	Changes the root directory of the configuration files from /etc to <confdir>. This changes the directory for the following files: /etc/ftpchroot, /etc/ftpusers, /etc/ftpwelcome, /etc/motd, and the file specified by the ftpd.conf(5) limit directive.
-C <user>	Checks whether the user would be granted access under the restrictions given in ftpusers(5) and exits without attempting a connection. ftpd exits with an exit code of 0 if access would be granted, or 1 otherwise. This can be useful for testing configurations
-d	A facility of LOG_FTP is used to write debugging information to the syslog.
-e <emailaddr>	Uses <emailaddr> for the %E escape sequence
-h <hostname>	Explicitly sets the hostname to advertise as <hostname>. Default is the hostname associated with the IP address on which ftpd is listening. This capability (with or without -h), in conjunction with -c <confdir>, is useful when configuring virtual FTP servers to listen on separate addresses as separate names.
-H	Equivalent to -h <hostname>.
-l	Logs each successful and failed FTP session by using syslog with a facility of LOG_FTP. If this option is specified more than once, the retrieve (get), store (put), append, delete, make directory, remove directory, and rename operations and their filename arguments are also logged.
-P <dataport>	Uses <dataport> as the data port, overriding the default of using the port one less than the port on which ftpd is listening.
-q	Enables the use of PID files for keeping track of the number of logged-in users per class. This is the default.
-Q	Disables the use of PID files for keeping track of the number of logged-in users per class. This might reduce the load on heavily loaded FTP servers.
-r	Permanently drops root privileges after the user is logged in. The use of this option could result in the server using a port other than the listening port for PORT-style commands, which is contrary to the RFC 959 specification. In practice, though, very few clients rely on this behavior.
-s	Requires a secure authentication mechanism such as Kerberos or S/Key be used.
-u	Logs each concurrent FTP session to /var/run/utmp, making them visible to commands such as who(1).
-U	Doesn't log each concurrent FTP session to /var/run/utmp. This is the default.
-V <version>	Uses <version> as the version to advertise in the login banner and in the output of STAT and SYST, instead of the default version information. If version is - or empty, doesn't display any version information.
-w	Logs each FTP session to /var/log/wtmp, making them visible to commands such as last(1). This is the default.

TABLE 12.1 Continued

Option	Function
-W	Doesn't log each FTP session to /var/log/wtmp.
-X	Logs wu-ftpd style xferlog entries to the syslog, prefixed with xferlog:, by using a facility of LOG_FTP. These syslog entries can be converted to a wu-ftpd style xferlog file suitable for input into a third-party log analysis tool with a command similar to the following: `grep 'xferlog: ' /var/log/xferlog | \ sed -e 's/^.*xferlog: //' > wuxferlog`

Restricting Access

The lukemftpd FTP server uses three main configuration files for restricting access: /etc/ftpusers, /etc/ftpchroot, and /etc/ftpd.conf. By using these files you can place restrictions on who can use FTP to access your machine—blocking certain users and allowing others. You can also configure limitations to the type and frequency of access granted by limiting the number of connections and setting timeouts and other server-related limits on FTP server availability and capability.

NOTE

If you want to take advantage of these features, but you're running the ftpd that comes with Mac OS X 10.2, you should update your version of the default ftpd. The distributed version contained a number of bugs that prevented access control from working properly. You can check the version by running strings /usr/libexec/ftpd | grep "lukemftp". Broken versions report version 1.1. Version 1.2 beta 2 is known to work. Replacing lukemftpd with the most recent version is covered briefly in the next section.

An /etc/ftpusers file comes by default. This file contains the list of users who aren't allowed FTP access to the machine. Here's the default file:

```
% more /etc/ftpusers
# list of users disallowed any ftp access.
# read by ftpd(8).
Administrator
administrator
root
uucp
daemon
unknown
www
```

If you have additional users who shouldn't be granted FTP access, include them in this file. Also include any system logins that might not be listed by default in this file. Because the syntax for this file can be more complex, its documentation is included in Table 12.2.

The FTP server also allows for `chroot`ed FTP access, which is a compromise between full access and anonymous-only access. With this compromise access, a user is granted FTP access to only his home directory. List any users who should have this type of access in the `/etc/ftpchroot` file, which does not exist by default.

The last major configuration file for the default `ftpd` is `/etc/ftpd.conf`. In this file, you can define classes and various types of restrictions for a given class. This FTP server is supposed to understand three classes of user: `REAL`, `CHROOT`, and `GUEST`. A `REAL` user is a user who has full access to your machine. A `CHROOT` user is one who is restricted to his home directory or a directory otherwise specified in `/etc/ftpd.conf`. A `GUEST` user is one who can connect to the machine for anonymous FTP only.

The basic form of a line in `ftpd.conf` is

```
<directive> <class> <argument>
```

Directives that appear later override directives that appear earlier. This enables you to define defaults by using wildcards and to provide more specific overrides later in the file. In addition to the defaults you see listed in the preceding file, other available controls include ones for limiting the upload and download storage rates, maximum uploadable file size, and port ranges. This last control can be useful for setting up your FTP server to work while a firewall is also running on your machine. It enables you to synchronize your FTP server's port usage and firewall port range restrictions. Table 12.3 details all the available directives for the `/etc/ftpd.conf` file.

TABLE 12.2 Documentation for `/etc/ftpusers` and `/etc/ftpchroot`

ftpusers ftpchroot	ftpd access control files
`/etc/ftpusers`	The `/etc/ftpusers` file provides user access control for `ftpd(8)` by defining which users may login. If the `/etc/ftpusers` file does not exist, all users are denied access. A \ is the escape character. It can be used to escape the meaning of the comment character or, if it's the last character on a line, to extend a configuration directive across multiple lines. A # is the comment character, and all characters from it to the end of line are ignored (unless it's escaped with the escape character). The syntax of each line is `<userglob>[:<groupglob>][@<host>] [<directive> [<class>]].`

TABLE 12.2 Continued

	These elements are or are handled as follows: <userglob> is matched against the username, by using fnmatch(3) glob matching (for example, f*). <groupglob> is matched against all the groups that the user is a member of, by using fnmatch(3) glob matching (for example, *src). <host> is either a CIDR address (refer to inet_net_pton(3)) to match against the remote address (for example, 1.2.3.4/24), or an fnmatch(3) glob to match against the remote hostname (for example, *.netbsd.org). <directive> allows access to the user if set to allow or yes. Denies access to the user if set to deny or no, or if the directive is not present. <class> defines the class to use in ftpd.conf(5). If <class> isn't given, it defaults to one of the following: chroot if there's a match in /etc/ftpchroot for the user. guest if the username is anonymous or ftp. real if neither of the preceding conditions is true. No further comparisons are attempted after the first successful match. If no match is found, the user is granted access. This syntax is backward compatible with the old syntax. If a user requests a guest login, the ftpd(8) server checks to see that both anonymous and ftp have access. So if you deny all users by default, you must add both anonymous allow and ftp allow to /etc/ftpusers to allow guest logins.
/etc/ftpchroot	The file /etc/ftpchroot is used to determine which users will have their session's root directory changed (using chroot(2)), either to the directory specified in the ftpd.conf(5) chroot directive (if set), or to the home directory of the user. If the file doesn't exist, the root directory change is not performed. The syntax is similar to /etc/ftpusers, except that the class argument is ignored. If there's a positive match, the session's root directory is changed. No further comparisons are attempted after the first successful match. This syntax is backward compatible with the old syntax.

TABLE 12.3 Documentation for /etc/ftpd.conf

ftpd.conf	ftpd(8) configuration file The ftpd.conf file specifies various configuration options for ftpd(8) that apply after a user has authenticated a connection. ftpd.conf consists of a series of lines, each of which may contain a configuration directive, a comment, or a blank line. Directives that appear later in the file override settings by previous directives. This allows wildcard entries to define defaults, and then have class-specific overrides. A directive line has the format: <command> <class> [<arguments>]

TABLE 12.3 Continued

	A \ is the escape character; it can be used to escape the meaning of the comment character, or if it is the last character on a line, it extends a configuration directive across multiple lines. A # is the comment character, and all characters from it to the end of line are ignored (unless it is escaped with the escape character). Each authenticated user is a member of a class, which is determined by `ftpusers(5)`. `<class>` is used to determine which `ftpd.conf` entries apply to the user. The following special classes exist when parsing entries in: `all` Matches any class `none` Matches no class Each class has a type, which may be one of the following: `GUEST` Guests (as per the `anonymous` and `ftp` logins). A `chroot(2)` is performed after login. `CHROOT` `chroot(2)`ed users (as per `ftpchroot(5)`). A `chroot(2)` is performed after login. `REAL` Normal users. The `ftpd(8)` `STAT` command returns the class settings for the current user, unless the `private` directive is set for the class.
`advertise <class> host`	
`advertize <class> host`	Sets the address to advertise in the response to the `PASV` and `LPSV` commands to the address for host (which may be either a hostname or IP address). This may be useful in some firewall configurations, although many FTP clients may not work if the address being advertised is different than the address to which they've connected. If `<class>` is none or no argument is given, it is disabled.
`checkportcmd <class> [off]`	Checks the `PORT` command for validity. The `PORT` command fails if the IP address specified does not match the FTP command connection, or if the remote TCP port number is less than `IPPORT_RESERVED`. It is strongly encouraged that this option be used, especially for sites concerned with potential security problems with FTP bounce attacks. If `<class>` is none or off is given, this feature is disabled; otherwise, it is enabled.
`chroot <class> [<pathformat>]`	If `<pathformat>` is not given or `<class>` is none, uses the default behavior (see the later discussion). Otherwise, `<pathformat>` is parsed to create a directory to `chroot(2)` into at login. `<pathformat>` can contain the following escape strings: Escape Description `%c` Classname `%d` Home directory of user `%u` User name `%%` A % character

TABLE 12.3 Continued

	Default root directory is CHROOT The user's home directory. GUEST If -a <anondir> is given, uses <anondir>; otherwise uses the home directory of the FTP user. REAL By default no `chroot(2)` is performed.
`classtype <class> <type>`	Sets the class type of <class> to <type> (see earlier discussion).
`conversion <class> <suffix> [<type> <disable> <command>]`	Defines an automatic inline file conversion. If a file to retrieve ends in <suffix>, and a real file (without <suffix>) exists, then the output of <command> is returned rather than the contents of the file. <suffix> The suffix to initiate the conversion. <type> A list of valid filetypes for the conversion. Valid types are: `f` (file), and `d` (directory). <disable> The name of the file that will prevent conversion if it exists. A filename of `.` prevents this disabling action (that is, the conversion is always permitted). <command> The command to run for the conversion. The first word should be the command's full pathname as `execv(3)` is used to execute the command. All instances of the word `%s` in the command are replaced with the requested file (without suffix). Conversion directives specified later in the file override.
`denyquick <class> [off]`	Enforces `ftpusers(5)` rules after the `USER` command is received, rather than after the `PASS` command is received. Although enabling this feature may allow information leakage about available accounts (for example, if you allow some users of a `REAL` or `CHROOT` class but not others), it is useful in preventing a denied user (such as root) from entering a password across an insecure connection. This option is strongly recommended for servers that run an anonymous-only service. If <class> is none or off is given, the feature is enabled; otherwise, it is disabled.
`display <class> [<file>]`	If <file> is not given or <class> is none, disables this. Otherwise, each time the user enters a new directory, checks whether <file> exists, and if so, displays its contents to the user. Escape sequences are supported.
`homedir <class> [<pathformat>]`	If <pathformat> is not given or <class> is none, uses the default behavior (see later discussion). Otherwise, <pathformat> is parsed to create a directory to change into upon login, and to use as the home directory of the user for tilde expansion in pathnames and so on. <pathformat> is parsed as per the chroot directive. The default home directory is the home directory of the user for `REAL` users, and / for `GUEST` and `CHROOT` users.
`limit <class> <count> [<file>]`	Limits the maximum number of concurrent connections for <class> to <count>, with 0 meaning unlimited connections. If the limit is exceeded and <file> is given, displays its contents to the user. If <class> is none or <count> is not specified, this feature is disabled. If <file> is a relative path, it will be searched for in `/etc` (which can be overridden with `-c <confdir>`).

TABLE 12.3 Continued

`maxfilesize <class> <size>`	Sets the maximum size of an uploaded file to size. If `<class>` is none or no argument is given, this feature is disabled.
`maxtimeout <class> <time>`	Sets the maximum timeout period that a client may request, defaulting to two hours. This cannot be less than 30 seconds, or the value for timeout. If `<class>` is none or time is not specified, sets to default of 2 hours.
`modify <class> [off]`	If `<class>` is none or off is given, disables the following commands: CHMOD, DELE, MKD, RMD, RNFR, and UMASK. Otherwise, enables them.
`motd <class> [<file>]`	If `<file>` is not given or `<class>` is none, this feature is disabled. Otherwise, uses `<file>` as the message-of-the-day file to display after login. Escape sequences are supported. If `<file>` is a relative path, it will be searched for in `/etc` (which can be overridden with `-c <confdir>`).
`notify <class> [<fileglob>]`	If `<fileglob>` is not given or `<class>` is none, this feature is disabled. Otherwise, each time the user enters a new directory, notifies the user of any files matching `<fileglob>`.
`passive <class> [off]`	If `<class>` is none or off is given, prevents passive (PASV, LPSV, and EPSV) connections. Otherwise, enables them.
`portrange <class> <min> <max>`	Sets the range of port numbers that are used for the passive data port. `<max>` must be greater than `<min>`, and both numbers must be between IPPORT_RESERVED (1024) and 65535. If `<class>` is none or no arguments are given, this feature is disabled.
`private class [off]`	If `<class>` is none or off is given, does not display class information in the output of the STAT command. Otherwise, displays the information.
`rateget <class> <rate>`	Sets the maximum get (RETR) transfer rate throttle for `<class>` to rate bytes per second. If rate is 0, the throttle is disabled. If `<class>` is none or no arguments are given, disables this. An optional suffix may be provided, which changes the interpretation of `<rate>` as follows: `b` Causes no modification. (Default; optional) `k` `Kilo`; multiplies the argument by 1024 `m` `Mega`; multiplies the argument by 1048576 `g` `Giga`; multiplies the argument by 1073741824 `t` `Tera`; multiplies the argument by 1099511627776
`rateput <class> <rate>`	Sets the maximum put (STOR) transfer rate throttle for `<class>` to `<rate>` bytes per second. If `<class>` is none or no arguments are given, this feature is disabled.
`sanenames <class> [off]`	If `<class>` is none or off is given, allows uploaded file names to contain any characters valid for a filename. Otherwise, permits only file names which don't start with a `.` and are composed of only characters from the set `[-+,._A-Za-z0-9]`.

TABLE 12.3 Continued

`template <class> [<refclass>]`	Defines `<refclass>` as the template for `<class>`; any reference to `<refclass>` in following directives will also apply to members of `<class>`. It is useful to define a template class so that other classes that are to share common attributes can be easily defined without unnecessary duplication. There can be only one template defined at a time. If `<refclass>` is not given, disables the template for `<class>`.
`timeout <class> <time>`	Sets the inactivity timeout period. This cannot be less than 30 seconds, or greater than the value for maxtimeout. If `<class>` is none or time is not specified, sets to the default of 15 minutes.
`umask <class> <umaskval>`	Sets the umask to `<umaskval>`. If `<class>` is none or `<umaskval>` is not specified, sets to the default of 027.

`upload <class> [off]`	If `<class>` is none or off is given, disables the following commands: `APPE`, `STOR`, and `STOU`, as well as the modify commands: `CHMOD`, `DELE`, `MKD`, `RMD`, `RNFR`, and `UMASK`. Otherwise, enables them.
	The following defaults are used:
	`checkportcmd all`
	`classtype chroot CHROOT`
	`classtype guest GUEST`
	`classtype real REAL`
	`display none`
	`limit all -1 # unlimited connections`
	`maxtimeout all 7200 # 2 hours`
	`modify all`
	`motd all motd`
	`notify none`
	`passive all`
	`timeout all 900 # 15 minutes`
	`umask all 027`
	`upload all`
	`modify guest off`
	`umask guest 0707`

Updating the Default (`lukemftpd`) `ftpd`

As mentioned earlier, if you want to take advantage of the default `ftpd`'s controls, and you're running the initial release of Mac OS X 10.2, you should update the `ftpd`. The controls for the `ftpd` that ships with this release don't work properly. Fortunately, the update is not difficult to perform. Even if you are not planning to take advantage of the default `ftpd`'s controls, but are planning to turn on `ftpd`, it is always a good idea to run the latest version; later versions usually contain security as well as functionality updates.

The default `ftpd` at this time is `lukemftpd-1.1`. Recently `lukemftpd` has been renamed `tnftpd`. Download the latest version, currently `tnftpd-2.0-beta3`, from here:

```
ftp://ftp.netbsd.org/pub/NetBSD/tnftp/
```

`ftpd` follows the basic format for compiling and even compiles easily under Mac OS X. Run `./configure` and then `make`. As of version 2.0 beta3, `make install` doesn't seem to work, but you can copy the `ftpd` binary yourself. Make sure that you keep a backup of the default `/usr/libexec/ftpd`, just in case you need it. Make sure you keep a copy of the updated `ftpd` as well, in case you should ever find that `Software Update` has replaced your updated version with an older version again. At the top of the source directory, perform `cp src/tnftpd /usr/libexec/ftpd`. With this version of the FTP server, you can take advantage of the access controls, most notably the `/etc/ftpchroot` file, and anonymous FTP, if you already had anonymous FTP enabled from a previous version of Mac OS X.

Setting Up Anonymous FTP

As you have seen, setting up the FTP server to allow real users to have FTP access is not difficult. Unfortunately, it suffers from the basic design vulnerability of transmitting the user's information in clear text. In some instances, you can reduce this risk by setting up an anonymous FTP server instead. Anonymous FTP servers allow users to connect, upload, and (potentially) download files without the use of a real-user user ID and password. Of course, this brings the risk that you will not know who is logging in to your system via the anonymous FTP service, and preventing unauthorized users from accessing the system is difficult if everyone's known only as "anonymous." But if anonymous users can't do anything damaging, or see any data that's private while so connected, this might be a good tradeoff for the security of not allowing real user connections and the problems this brings. Anonymous FTP servers also are useful for enabling users with no account on your machine to acquire or provide information, such as to download product literature, or upload suggestions or possible modifications to a project on which you're working.

CAUTION

Remember, even if you set up an anonymous-only FTP server, there's nothing to prevent your real users from trying to enter their user IDs and passwords at the prompts.

Setting up the FTP server to allow anonymous FTP unfortunately takes some work, and potentially makes your machine vulnerable to more attacks. We recommend that you do not enable anonymous without having a good reason. However, we more strongly recommend against enabling unprotected FTP for real users.

Setting up anonymous FTP involves making an `ftp` user, whose home directory is where anonymous FTP users connect. Additionally, you copy the necessary system components to `ftp`'s account so that users can run `ls` properly. When a user requests a list of files via the FTP `ls` command, the command that is actually executed is a server-side binary program kept in a special directory for the FTP server's use, the home directory of the `ftp` user. When the FTP server is `chroot`ed, it can't access `/bin/ls`; therefore, placing a copy of `ls` and any other system components that the FTP server needs in a special directory is normally a very important step. However, with the Mac OS X 10.2 release, the system components don't seem to help for running `ls`. This isn't a problem with the `lukemftp-1.2beta2` release, or with the `wu-ftpd` that is discussed later because both FTP servers can provide an internal `ls`. Because it's hard to predict how a new release of either system software or FTP server software will change things, we include the steps for the system components to install when you don't have to rely on the FTP server having its own `ls`. Steps 5–10 listed in the following pages include the instructions for copying the appropriate system components.

To set up an anonymous FTP site, do the following:

1. Create an `ftp` user in the NetInfo database. Follow the pattern of one of the generic users, such as user `unknown`. You might start by duplicating the `unknown` user and editing the duplicate user. Create your `ftp` user with the basic parameters shown in Table 12.4.

TABLE 12.4 Basic Parameters for an `ftp` User

Property	Value
`name`	`ftp`
`realname`	*`<some generic reference to ftp>`*
`uid`	*`<some unused uid number>`*
`passwd`	`*`
`home`	*`<some suitable location>`*
`shell`	`/dev/null`
`gid`	*`<some unused gid number>`*
`change`	`0`
`expire`	`0`

Figure 12.2 shows the values we used for our `ftp` user. The asterisk value for the `passwd` field is literal—this is a disallowed character in `crypt`ed passwords, and prevents logins that use this ID.

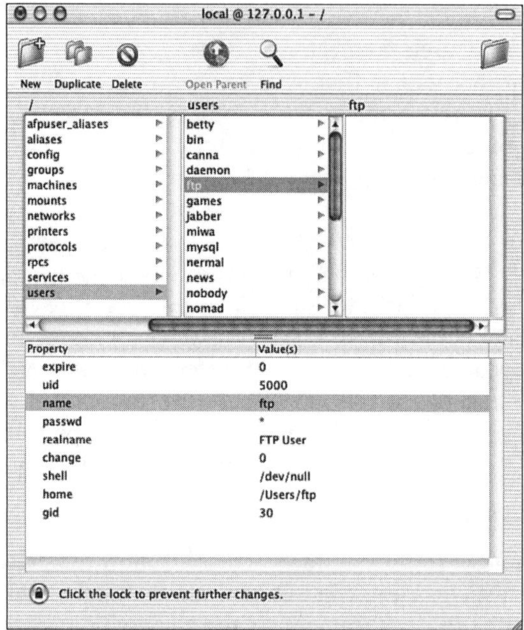

FIGURE 12.2 Here's how we chose to create our `ftp` user, as shown in NetInfo Manager.

2. Create an `ftp` group in the NetInfo database. Make sure that you assign the same `gid` to the `ftp` group that you indicated for the `ftp` user.

3. Create a home directory for user `ftp`. Make sure that you create the directory that you specified in the NetInfo database (`/Users/ftp` in this example). The directory should be owned by root and have permissions `555`.

4. Create a `~ftp/bin/` directory, owned by `root` with permissions `555`.

5. Copy the system's `/bin/ls` to `~ftp/bin/`.

6. Create `~ftp/usr/lib/`. Each of those directories should be owned by root with permissions `555`.

7. Copy the system's `/usr/lib/dyld` to `~ftp/usr/lib/`. This is one of the files that helps `ls` function properly in this `chroot`ed environment.

8. Copy the system's `/usr/lib/libSystem.B.dylib` to `~ftp/usr/lib/`. This is another file that helps `ls` function properly in the `chroot`ed environment.

9. Create `~ftp/System/Library/Frameworks/System.framework/Versions/B/`. Each of the directories in this path should be owned by `root` with permissions `555`.

10. Copy the system's `/System/Library/Frameworks/System.framework/Versions/B/System` to `~ftp/System/Library/Frameworks/System.framework/Versions/B/`. This is another file that helps `ls` function properly in the `chroot`ed environment.

11. Create a `~ftp/pub/` directory in which files can be stored for download. Recommended ownership of this directory includes some user and group `ftp` or user `root`. Typical permissions for this directory are `755`.

12. If you also want to make a drop location where files can be uploaded, create `~ftp/incoming/`, owned by `root`. Recommended permissions include `753`, `733`, `1733`, `3773`, or `777`. You could also create `~ftp/incoming/` with permissions `751` and subdirectories that are used as the drop locations with any of the recommended drop-off permissions.

If you decide to allow anonymous FTP, make sure that you regularly check the anonymous FTP area and your logs for any unusual activity. In addition, regularly check Apple's Web site for any updates for Mac OS X that include `ftp` updates. Security holes are regularly found in `ftpd` and regularly fixed.

For your convenience, here's a listing of our `ftp` user's home directory:

```
# ls -lRaF ftp
total 0
dr-xr-xr-x  7 root  wheel  238 Sep 13 00:04 ./
drwxrwxr-t  8 root  wheel  272 Sep 12 23:56 ../
dr-xr-xr-x  3 root  wheel  102 Sep 13 00:00 System/
dr-xr-xr-x  3 root  wheel  102 Sep 12 23:57 bin/
drwxr-x-wx  2 root  wheel   68 Sep 13 00:04 incoming/
drwxr-xr-x  2 root  wheel   68 Sep 13 00:04 pub/
dr-xr-xr-x  3 root  wheel  102 Sep 12 23:57 usr/

ftp/System:
total 0
dr-xr-xr-x  3 root  wheel  102 Sep 13 00:00 ./
dr-xr-xr-x  7 root  wheel  238 Sep 13 00:04 ../
dr-xr-xr-x  3 root  wheel  102 Sep 13 00:01 Library/

ftp/System/Library:
total 0
dr-xr-xr-x  3 root  wheel  102 Sep 13 00:01 ./
dr-xr-xr-x  3 root  wheel  102 Sep 13 00:00 ../
dr-xr-xr-x  3 root  wheel  102 Sep 13 00:02 Frameworks/
```

```
ftp/System/Library/Frameworks:
total 0
dr-xr-xr-x  3 root  wheel  102 Sep 13 00:02 ./
dr-xr-xr-x  3 root  wheel  102 Sep 13 00:01 ../
dr-xr-xr-x  3 root  wheel  102 Sep 13 00:02 System.framework/

ftp/System/Library/Frameworks/System.framework:
total 0
dr-xr-xr-x  3 root  wheel  102 Sep 13 00:02 ./
dr-xr-xr-x  3 root  wheel  102 Sep 13 00:02 ../
dr-xr-xr-x  3 root  wheel  102 Sep 13 00:02 Versions/

ftp/System/Library/Frameworks/System.framework/Versions:
total 0
dr-xr-xr-x  3 root  wheel  102 Sep 13 00:02 ./
dr-xr-xr-x  3 root  wheel  102 Sep 13 00:02 ../
dr-xr-xr-x  3 root  wheel  102 Sep 13 00:03 B/

ftp/System/Library/Frameworks/System.framework/Versions/B:
total 2440
dr-xr-xr-x  3 root  wheel      102 Sep 13 00:03 ./
dr-xr-xr-x  3 root  wheel      102 Sep 13 00:02 ../
-r-xr-xr-x  1 root  wheel  1245580 Sep 13 00:03 System*

ftp/bin:
total 56
dr-xr-xr-x  3 root  wheel    102 Sep 12 23:57 ./
dr-xr-xr-x  7 root  wheel    238 Sep 13 00:04 ../
-r-xr-xr-x  1 root  wheel  27668 Sep 12 23:57 ls*

ftp/incoming:
total 0
drwxr-x-wx  2 root  wheel   68 Sep 13 00:04 ./
dr-xr-xr-x  7 root  wheel  238 Sep 13 00:04 ../

ftp/pub:
total 0
drwxr-xr-x  2 root  wheel   68 Sep 13 00:04 ./
dr-xr-xr-x  7 root  wheel  238 Sep 13 00:04 ../

ftp/usr:
total 0
dr-xr-xr-x  3 root  wheel  102 Sep 12 23:57 ./
```

```
dr-xr-xr-x  7 root  wheel  238 Sep 13 00:04 ../
dr-xr-xr-x  4 root  wheel  136 Sep 12 23:59 lib/

ftp/usr/lib:
total 3128
dr-xr-xr-x  4 root  wheel      136 Sep 12 23:59 ./
dr-xr-xr-x  3 root  wheel      102 Sep 12 23:57 ../
-r-xr-xr-x  1 root  wheel   349364 Sep 12 23:58 dyld*
-r-xr-xr-x  1 root  wheel  1245580 Sep 12 23:59 libSystem.B.dylib*
```

For additional thoughts on anonymous FTP configuration, you might want to check these Web sites:

- CERT Coordination Center's Anonymous FTP Configuration Guidelines—`http://www.cert.org/tech_tips/anonymous_ftp_config.html`
- WU-FTPD Resource Center's Related Documents link—`http://www.landfield.com/wu-ftpd/`
- AppleCare Service & Support—`http://www.info.apple.com/`

Replacing the Mac OS X FTP Server

If you decide to activate anonymous FTP, especially anonymous FTP with an upload directory, you should consider replacing the default `ftpd` with a more modifiable `ftpd`. A popular, highly configurable replacement `ftpd` is `wu-ftpd`, available at `http://www.wu-ftpd.org/`. In addition to being highly configurable, it easily compiles under Mac OS X.

Although popular and highly configurable, `wu-ftpd` is not exempt from security problems. It's still important to regularly monitor the anonymous FTP area, if you have one, as well as make sure that you have the latest version of `wu-ftpd`, which is version 2.6.2 as of this writing.

Installing `wu-ftpd`

To replace the default `ftpd` with `wu-ftpd`, first download, compile, and install `wu-ftpd`. Fortunately, `wu-ftpd` is one of the packages that follows this basic format for compilation and installation:

```
./configure
make
make install
```

When you download the wu-ftpd source files, also download any patches available for the source. As of this writing, the current version, 2.6.2, doesn't have any patches. However, because updates to wu-ftpd are frequently available as patches, we include a demonstration of using patch to apply a patch to the previous version, 2.6.1. After a patch file is copied to the root directory of the source, run patch as follows:

```
[localhost:~/wu-ftpd-2.6.1] software% patch -p0 < missing_format_strings.patch
```

The default config.guess and config.sub files that come with the wu-ftpd source don't work with Mac OS X. Use the files that come with Mac OS X:

```
[Sage-Rays-Computer:~/src/wu-ftpd-2.6.2] software% cp
/usr/share/automake-1.6/config.guess ./
[Sage-Rays-Computer:~/src/wu-ftpd-2.6.2] software% cp
/usr/share/automake-1.6/config.sub ./
```

If you haven't already done so, create a bin user. The bin user is needed for wu-ftpd to install properly. The bin user should have a relatively low uid. Mac OS X already comes with a bin group with gid 7. In many other Unix variants, the bin user has the same uid and gid. As with the ftp user, follow the basic parameters of a generic user, such as the unknown user. You might consider duplicating the unknown user and editing values. Suggested values for the bin user are shown in Table 12.5.

TABLE 12.5 Suggested Parameters for a bin User

Property	Value
name	bin
realname	System Tools Owner
uid	7
passwd	*
home	/bin
shell	/bin/sync
gid	7
change	0
expire	0

Next, you're ready to run ./configure. Being the highly configurable package that it is, you can pass many parameters to configure, as detailed in Table 12.6. Consider the basic design of FTP as you look at the available options and you will see that the server built can range from one that is quite tightly controlled to one that could not be considered secure by even the wildest stretch of the imagination. The power and customizability available to you in the running server spans a similarly large range, depending on the options chosen here. Therefore, building a server that allows you the power and flexibility you need, while not providing too many opportunities for security problems requires careful study.

TIP

To have an `ls` that works properly under version 10.2 for anonymous FTP or guest FTP, you may need to use the `--enable-ls` option.

TABLE 12.6 Configure Options for `wuftpd`

Option	Description
`--with-etc-dir=PATH`	Path for configuration files, usually `/etc`.
`--with-pid-dir=PATH`	Path for `run/pid` files, usually .
`--with-log-dir=PATH`	Path for log files (`xferlog`), usually `/var/log`.
`--disable-upload`	Disables support for the upload keyword in the `ftpaccess` file.
`--disable-overwrite`	Disables support for the overwrite keyword in the `ftpaccess` file.
`--disable-hostxs`	Disables support for the `allow` and `deny` keywords in the `ftpaccess` file.
`--disable-logfailed`	Disables logging of failed attempts (wrong password, wrong username, and so on).
`--disable-logtoomany`	Disables logging of failed attempts that failed because too many users were already logged in.
`--disable-private`	Disables support for private files (`site group/site gpass` FTP commands).
`--disable-dnsretry`	Disables retrying failed DNS lookups at connection time.
`--enable-anononly`	Allows only `anonymous` FTP connections.
`--enable-paranoid`	Disables some features that might possibly affect security.
`--disable-quota`	Disables support of disk quotas, even if your operating system is set for them.
`--disable-pam`	Does not use PAM authentication, even if your operating system supports it.
`--enable-skey`	Supports S/Key authentication (needs S/Key libraries).
`--enable-OPIE`	Supports OPIE (One Password In Everything) authentication (needs OPIE libraries).
`--disable-new-cd`	Causes `cd ~` to not return to the `chroot`-relative home directory.
`--enable-chmod`	Allows FTP users to set `SETUID`, `SETGID`, and `STICKY` bits on file permissions.
`--disable-rfc931`	Does not do RFC931 (`IDENT`) lookups (worse logging, but faster).
`--disable-daemon`	Does not support running as a normal daemon (as opposed to running from `inetd`).
`--disable-map-chdir`	Does not keep track of user's path changes. This leads to worse symlink handling.
`--disable-throughput`	Does not keep track of user's throughput.

TABLE 12.6 Continued

Option	Description
--disable-count	Does not keep track of transferred bytes (for statistics).
--disable-newlines	Suppresses some extra blank lines.
--enable-crackers	Does not wait for password entry if someone tries to log in with a wrong username. Although convenient, it is a security risk in that crackers can find out names of valid users.
--disable-verbose	Disables verbose error logging.
--enable-NOOP	NOOP command resets idle time.
--disable-log-rp	Logs the relative path rather than the real path.
--disable-virtual	Disables support of virtual servers.
--disable-closedvirt	Allows guests to log in to virtual servers.
--disable-dns	Skips all DNS lookups.
--disable-port	Disallows port-mode connections.
--disable-pasv	Disallows passive-mode connections.
--disable-plsm	Disables PID lock sleep messages. Recommended for busy sites.
--disable-pasvip	Does not require the same IP for control and data connection in passive mode. This is more secure, but can cause trouble with some firewalls.
--disable-anonymous	Allows only real users to connect.
--enable-ls	Uses the internal ls command instead of /bin/ls in the chroot directory. This is experimental and has known problems.
--enable-numericuid	Makes the internal ls display UID and GID instead of user/group names. This is faster, but the ls output looks worse.
--disable-hidesetuid	Causes the internal ls command to not hide setuid/setgid bits from the user. Default is for the internal ls to hide them as a security precaution.
--disable-mail	Disables support of the mail-on-upload feature. The feature allows you to automatically send an email message to the FTP administrator whenever an anonymous user uploads a file.
--enable-badclients	Supports broken clients. See the CHANGES file for details.
--with-bufsize=x	Sets the buffer size to x. (You won't usually have to adjust this value.)
--with-backlog=x	Sets the number of incoming processes to backlog in daemon mode to x. Default is 100.

To distinctly separate the wu-ftpd installation from the default ftpd, you should consider specifying paths in the various path parameters. In addition, you might consider running ./configure with -prefix=<*some-directory-for-wu-ftpd*> so that the wu-ftpd binaries and man pages are all in one place. You might also find it interesting that you can create either an anonymous-only or a real users-only FTP server. Next, run make and make install.

After you have a wu-ftpd binary, you should update the /etc/xinetd.d/ftp file to reflect the location of the new ftpd, as well as any runtime options that should be used. After you've adjusted /etc/xinetd.d/ftp, have xinetd reread its configuration file. Runtime options available in wu-ftpd are detailed in Table 12.7. Like the compile-time options, careless choices can open holes in your system that may come back to haunt you later. Think through what options you need and test your configuration carefully. As we've previously suggested, it's best to err on the side of caution in your configuration choices, and not enable "interesting" features just because they're interesting. Wait until you actually have a need for a feature before you add that capability to your option collection.

TABLE 12.7 Runtime Options for wuftpd

Option	Function
-d	Logs debugging information to the syslog.
-v	Logs debugging information to the syslog.
-l	Logs each FTP session to the syslog.
-t <timeout>	Sets the inactivity timeout period to <timeout> seconds. Default is 15 minutes.
-T <maxtimeout>	A client may also request a different timeout period. The maximum period may be set to <timeout> seconds. Default is 2 hours.
-a	Enables the use of the ftpaccess(5) configuration file.
-A	Disables the use of the ftpaccess(5) configuration file. This is the default.
-L	Logs commands sent to the ftpd server to the syslog. Overridden by the use of the ftpaccess file. With the -L command, logging occurs as soon as the FTP server is invoked. All USER commands are logged. If a user accidentally enters a password for a username, the password is logged. Unless you're actively trying to debug a problem or an attack, enabling this is probably a bad idea.
-i	Logs files received by the ftpd server to the xferlog(5). Overridden by the use of the ftpaccess(5) file.
-I	Disables use of RFC931 (AUTH/ident) to attempt to determine the username on the client.
-o	Logs files transmitted by the ftpd server to the xferlog(5). Overridden by the use of the ftpaccess(5) file.
-p <ctrlport> -P <dataport>	Overrides port numbers used by the daemon. Normally the port number is determined by the ftp and ftp-services values in services. If there is no entry for ftp-data and -P is not specified, the daemon uses the port just prior to the control connection port. The -p option is available only for the stand-alone daemon.
-q -Q	Determines whether the daemon uses the PID files, which are required by the limit directive to determine the number of current users in each access class. Disabling the use of PID files disables user limits. Default, -q, is to use PID files. Specify -Q as a normal user testing the server when access permissions prevent the use of PID files. Large, busy sites that do not want to impose a limit on the number of concurrent users might consider disabling PID files.

TABLE 12.7 Continued

Option	Function
`-r <rootdir>`	Instructs the daemon to `chroot(2)` to `<rootdir>` immediately upon loading. This can improve system security by limiting the files that can be damaged in a break-in. Setup is much like anonymous FTP, with additional files required.
`-s` `-S`	Sets the daemon to standalone mode. The `-S` option runs the daemon in the background and is useful in startup scripts during system initialization (that is, `rc.local`). The `-s` option leaves the daemon in the foreground and is useful when running from `init` (that is, `/etc/inittab`).
`-u <umask>`	Sets the default umask to `<umask>`.
`-V`	Displays the copyright and version information, then terminates.
`-w`	Records every login and logout. Default.
`-W`	Does not record user logins in the `wtmp` file.
`-X`	Does not save output created by `-i` or `-o` to the `xferlog` file, but saves it via `syslog` so that output from several hosts can be collected on one central `loghost`.

Limiting Access

Access to `wu-ftpd` can be limited through the use of the `ftpusers`, `ftphosts`, and `ftpaccess` files.

`ftpusers`

Like the default `ftpd`, `wu-ftpd` also uses an `ftpusers` file as a way of restricting access on a per-user basis. Copy the default `/etc/ftpusers` file to the `etc` directory of your `wu-ftpd` installation and add any users who should not be granted FTP access.

`ftphosts`

The `ftphosts` file is used to allow or deny access on a user/host basis. The basic syntax of a rule is as follows:

```
allow <username> <addrglob> [<addrglob> …]
deny <username> <addrglob> [<addrglob> …]
```

The `<addrglob>` may be a specific hostname, IP address, or pattern of each. Additionally, `<addrglob>` may also be specified as `address/cidr` or `address:netmask`. As you may expect, the order of the allow and deny rules can be important; the rules are processed sequentially on a first-match-wins basis. When you create these rules, be sure to think about rule order, particularly with any allow and deny pairs.

For example, to grant user `marvin` access from only `marvin.biosci.ohio-state.edu`, but not any other machines on the `biosci.ohio-state.edu` network, use this set of rules:

```
allow marvin marvin.biosci.ohio-state.edu
deny marvin *.biosci.ohio-state.edu
```

If the rules were reversed, then wu-ftpd would encounter the deny rule first, which would deny access to user marvin from all biosci.ohio-state.edu machines, including marvin.biosci.ohio-state.edu.

ftpaccess

Although wu-ftpd provides a lot of configuration options with its compile-time and runtime options, more controls can be set in the ftpaccess file. To enable the use of the ftpaccess file, be sure to run wu-ftpd with the -a option.

Selected useful controls in ftpaccess are documented in Table 12.8. Be sure to read the ftpaccess man page thoroughly for information about these and other available controls.

TABLE 12.8 Selected Controls Available for ftpaccess

Control	Function
loginfails <number>	Logs a "repeated login failures" message after <number> login failures. Default is 5.
class <class> <typelist> <address> [<address>...]	Sets up classes of users and valid access addresses. <typelist> is a comma-separated list of any of these keywords: real, anonymous, or guest. If real is included, the class can include users FTPing to real accounts. If anonymous is included, the class can include anonymous FTP users. If guest is included, the class can include members of guest access accounts.
guestgroup <groupname> [<groupname>...]	For guestgroup, if a real user is a member of any specified <groupname>, the session is set up exactly as with anonymous FTP. In other words, a chroot is done and the user is no longer permitted to issue the USER and PASS commands. <groupname> is a valid group from NetInfo. In other words, a real user whose group is <groupname> is treated as a guest FTP user. A guest user's home directory must be properly set up, exactly as anonymous FTP would be. The group name may be specified by either name or numeric ID. To use a numeric group ID, place a % before the number. Ranges may be given. Use an asterisk to mean all groups.
guestuser <username> [<username> ...]	guestuser works like guestgroup, except it uses the username (or numeric ID).
realgroup <groupname> [<groupname> ...] realuser <username> [<username> ...]	realuser and realgroup have the same syntax, but reverse the effect of guestuser and guestgroup. They allow real user access when the remote user would otherwise be determined a guest.
limit <class> <number> <times> <message_file>	Limits the number of users belonging to <class> to access the server during the <times> indicated and posts <message_file> as the reason for access denial.
file-limit [<raw>] <in | out | total> <count> [<class>]	Limits the number of files a user in <class> may transfer. Limit may be placed on files in, out, or total. If no class is specified, the limit is the default for classes that do not have a limit specified. <raw> applies the limit to the total traffic rather than just data files.

TABLE 12.8 Continued

<table>
<tr><th>Control</th><th>Function</th></tr>
<tr><td><code>data-limit [<raw>] <in | out | total> <count> [<class>]</code></td><td>Limits the number of data bytes a user in <class> may transfer. Limit may be placed on bytes in, out, or total. If no class is specified, the limit is the default for classes that do not have a limit specified. <raw> applies the limit to the total traffic rather than just data files.</td></tr>
<tr><td><code>limit-time {* | anonymous | guest} <minutes></code></td><td>Limits the total time a session can take. By default, there is no limit. Real users are never limited.</td></tr>
<tr><td><code>log commands <typelist></code></td><td>Logs individual commands issued by users in <typelist>, where <typelist> is a comma-separated list of any of the keywords real, anonymous, or guest.</td></tr>
<tr><td><code>log transfers <typelist> <directions></code></td><td>Logs the transfers of users belonging to <typelist> in the specified <directions>. <typelist> is a comma-separated list of any of the keywords real, anonymous, or guest. <directions> is a comma-separated list of the keywords inbound or outbound, where inbound refers to transfers to the server and outbound refers to transfers from the server.</td></tr>
<tr><td><code>log syslog</code></td><td>Redirects logging messages for incoming and outgoing transfers to the system log. Default is xferlog.</td></tr>
<tr><td><code>log syslog+xferlog</code></td><td>Logs transfer messages to both the system log and xferlog.</td></tr>
<tr><td><code>defaultserver deny <username> [<username>...]</code>
<code>defaultserver allow <username> [<username>...]</code></td><td>By default all users are allowed access to the default, nonvirtual FTP server. defaultserver <deny> denies access to specific users. You could use defaultserver <deny> * to deny access to all users, then defaultserver <allow> to allow specific users.</td></tr>
<tr><td><code>guestserver [<hostname>]</code></td><td>Controls which hosts may be used for anonymous or guest access. If used without <hostname>, denies all guest or anonymous access to this site. More than one <hostname> may be specified. Guest and anonymous access are allowed only on the named machines. If access is denied, the user is asked to use the first <hostname> listed.</td></tr>
<tr><td><code>passwd-check <level> <enforcement></code></td><td>Defines the level and enforcement of password checking done by the server for anonymous FTP. <level> can be none, trivial (must contain an @), or rfc822 (must be an RFC822-compliant address). <enforcement> can be warn (warns the user but allows him to log in) or enforce (warns the user and logs him out).</td></tr>
<tr><td><code>chmod <yes | no> <typelist></code>
<code>delete <yes | no> <typelist></code>
<code>overwrite <yes | no> <typelist></code>
<code>rename <yes | no> <typelist></code>
<code>umask <yes | no> <typelist></code></td><td>Sets permissions for chmod, delete, overwrite, rename, and umask as yes or no for users in <typelist>, where <typelist> is a comma-separated list of any of the keywords real, anonymous, or guest.</td></tr>
</table>

TABLE 12.8 Continued

<table>
<tr><th>Control</th><th>Function</th></tr>
<tr><td>upload [absolute | relative]
[class=<classname>]... [-]
<root-dir> <dirglob>
<yes | no> <owner> <group>
<mode> [dirs | nodirs]
[<d_mode>]</td><td>Specifies upload directory information. <root-dir> specifies the FTP root directory. <dirglob> specifies a directory under the <root-dir>. <yes | no> indicates whether files can be uploaded to the specified directory. If yes, files will be uploaded as belonging to <owner> and <group> in <mode>. [dirs | nodirs] specifies whether or not new subdirectories can be created in the upload directory. If dirs, they are created with mode <d_mode>, if it is specified. Otherwise, they are created as defined by <mode>. If <mode> is not specified, they are created with mode 777. Upload restrictions can be specified by class with class=<classname>.</td></tr>
<tr><td>path-filter <typelist>
<mesg> <allowed_charset>
[<disallowed regexp>...]</td><td>Defines regular expressions that control what a filename can or cannot be for users in <typelist>, where <typelist> is a comma-separated list of any of the keywords real, anonymous, or guest.</td></tr>
<tr><td>noretrieve
[absolute|relative]
[class=<classname>]...
[-] <filename>
<filename>...</td><td>Always denies the ability to retrieve these files. If the files are a path specification (begin with a / character), only those files are marked irretrievable. Otherwise, all files matching the filename are refused transfer. For example:
noretrieve /etc/passwd core specifies no one can get the file /etc/passwd, but users will be allowed to transfer a file called passwd if it is not in /etc. On the other hand, no one can get files named core, wherever they are. Directory specifications mark all files and subdirectories in the named directory irretrievable. The <filename> may be specified as a file glob. For example:
noretrieve /etc /home/*/.htaccess specifies no files in /etc or any of its subdirectories may be retrieved. Also, no files named .htaccess anywhere under the /home directory may be retrieved.

The optional first parameter selects whether names are interpreted as absolute or relative to the current chrooted environment. The default is to interpret names beginning with a slash as absolute.

The noretrieve restrictions may be placed on members of particular classes. If any class= is specified, the named files are not retrievable only if the current user is a member of any of the given classes.</td></tr>
<tr><td>throughput <root-dir>
<subdir-glob>
<file-glob-list>
<bytes-per-second>
<bytes-per-second-multiply>
<remote-glob-list></td><td>Restricts throughput to <bytes-per-second> on download of files in the comma-separated <file-glob-list> in the subdirectory matched by <subdir-glob> under <root-dir> when the remote host or IP address matches the comma-separated <remote-glob-list>.</td></tr>
</table>

TABLE 12.8 Continued

Control	Function
anonymous-root <root-dir> [<class>]	Specifies <root-dir> as the chroot path for anonymous users. If no anonymous-root is matched, the old method of parsing the home directory for the FTP user is used.
guest-root <root-dir> [<uid-range>]	Specifies <root-dir> as the chroot path for guest users. If no guest-root is matched, the old method of parsing the user's home directory is used.
deny-uid <uid-range> [...] deny-gid <gid-range> [...] allow-uid <uid-range> [...] allow-gid <gid-range> [...]	The deny clauses specify UID and GID ranges that are denied access to the FTP server. The allow clauses are then used to allow access to those who would otherwise be denied access. deny is checked before allow. Default is to allow access. Use of these controls can remove the need for the /etc/ftpusers file. Wherever uid or gid can be specified in the ftpaccess file, either names or numbers may be used. Put % before numeric uid or gid.
restricted-uid <uid-range> [...] restricted-gid <gid-range> [...] unrestricted-uid <uid-range> [...] unrestricted-gid <gid-range> [...]	Controls whether or not real or guest users are allowed access to areas on the FTP server outside their home directories. Not intended to replace the use of guestgroup and guestuser. The unrestricted clauses may be used to allow users outside their directories when they would have been otherwise restricted.
passive ports <cidr> <min> <max>	Allows control of the TCP port numbers that may be used for a passive data connection. If the control connection matches <cidr>, a port in the <min> to <max> range is randomly selected for the daemon to listen on. This control allows firewalls to limit the ports that remote clients use for connecting to the protected network. <cidr> is shorthand for an IP address in dotted-quad notation, followed by a slash and the number of leftmost bits that represent the network address. For example, for the reserved class-A network 10, instead of using a netmask of 255.0.0.0, use a CIDR of 8, and 10.0.0.0/8 represents the network. Likewise, for a private class-C home network, you could use 192.168.1.0/24 to represent your network.
deny <addrglob> <message_file>	Always denies access to host(s) matching <addrglob> and displays <message_file> to the host(s). <addrglob> may be !nameserved to deny access to sites without a working nameserver. It may also be the name of a file, starting with a slash (/), which contains additional address globs, as well as in the form <address>:<netmask> or <address>/<cidr>.
dns refuse_mismatch <filename> [override]	Refuses FTP sessions when the forward and reverse lookups for the remote site do not match. Displays <filename> to warn the user. If override is specified, allows the connection after complaining.
dns refuse_no_reverse <filename> [override]	Refuses FTP sessions when there is no reverse DNS entry for the remote site. Displays <message> to warn the user. If override is specified, allows the connection after complaining.

Understanding Basic `ftpaccess` Controls

As you saw in Table 12.8, even a selective list of `ftpaccess` controls is large. Because many controls are available, let's take a look at some of the basic configuration controls in the `ftpaccess` file.

`class` Look at this statement:

```
class    staff    real     *.biosci.ohio-state.edu
```

In this example, a class called `staff` is defined as being a real user coming from anywhere in the `biosci.ohio-state.edu` domain.

In the following statement, a class called `local` is defined as being as guest user coming from anywhere in the `ohio-state.edu` domain:

```
class    local    guest    *.ohio-state.edu
```

In the following statement, a class called `remote` is defined as being an anonymous user whose connection comes from anywhere:

```
class    remote   anonymous        *
```

You can create as many classes as suit your needs.

`limit` In the following statement, there is a limit of five users belonging to class `remote` who can access the FTP server on Saturdays and Sundays and on any day between 6:00 p.m. and 6:00 a.m.:

```
limit    remote   5        SaSu|Any1800-0600        /usr/local/etc/msgs/msg.toomany
```

When the limit is reached, any additional user sees a posting of the message file, `msg.toomany`, in `/usr/local/etc/msgs`.

In the following statement, no users belonging to the class `staff` can access the FTP server at any time:

```
limit    staff  0        Any              /usr/local/etc/msgs/msg.notallowed
```

Whenever any user in class staff attempts to log in, she sees a message indicating that she is not allowed to access the FTP server.

`upload` In the following statements, the guest user, `bioftp`, can upload files to the `~ftp/public` directory. The files will be uploaded with permissions `600`, that is, read and write permissions, for guest user `bioftp`:

```
upload  /home/ftp   /public        yes     bioftp   ftponly      0600
upload  /home/ftp   /public/*      yes     bioftp   ftponly      0600
```

However, in the following statement, no user can upload to the ~ftp/bin directory:

```
upload  /home/ftp   /bin          no
```

Please note that the upload control also has a nodirs option that does not allow directories to be uploaded. If you decide to run an anonymous FTP server, make sure that you include the nodirs option to the upload control.

restricted-uid **and** restricted-gid Although restricted-uid and restricted-gid are straightforward controls, it is useful to note that these controls function like the /etc/ftpchroot file for the default ftpd.

A restricted control entry such as this:

```
restricted-uid marvin
```

restricts user marvin to his home directory for FTP access. The numeric uid for marvin, preceded by %, could be used instead, as well as a range of uids.

Controlling Bandwidth and Other Advanced Features

The controls available in ftpaccess range from basic controls to advanced controls. With the advanced features, you can control many aspects of an FTP session. Some of the interesting controls include limiting the throughput, limiting the number of bytes that can be transferred, limiting the number of files that can be transferred, refusing sessions from hosts whose forward and reverse name lookups don't match or if a DNS lookup can't be done, and specifying a passive port range for a passive data connection.

throughput The throughput directive is one that you can use to help make your anonymous FTP site less attractive. Here is a sample throughput directive:

```
throughput /Users/ftp /pub* *zip  22000  0.5  *
```

The example statement limits the throughput of a zip file downloaded from the pub directory to approximately 22000 bytes/second from any remote host. Furthermore, because a multiply factor of 0.5 is also specified, the second zip file is downloaded at a rate of approximately 11000 bytes/second; the third, 5500 bytes/second, and so on.

file-limit The number of files uploaded, downloaded, or transferred in total by a user in a given class can be restricted with the file-limit directive. For example,

```
file-limit in 1 remote
```

limits the number of files uploaded to your site by a user belonging to class remote to just one file.

`data-limit` Use the `data-limit` directive to limit the number of data bytes that can be uploaded, downloaded, or transferred in total by a user in a given class. In this statement

```
data-limit total 5000000 remote
```

the total number of data bytes that may be transferred by a user in class `remote` is restricted to approximately 5000000 bytes.

`dns refuse_mismatch` To deny access to a host whose forward and reverse DNS lookups don't match, use the `dns refuse_mismatch` directive. In this example

```
dns refuse_mismatch mismatch-warning override
```

the file, `mismatch-warning`, is displayed for the offending host, but with the `override` option in place, the host is granted access anyway.

`dns refuse_no_reverse` To deny access to a host for which a reverse DNS lookup can't be done, use the `dns refuse_no_reverse` directive. In this statement

```
dns refuse_no_reverse noreverse-warning
```

the file named `noreverse-warning` is displayed, and the connection from the offending host is refused.

`passive ports` At this time, the passive ports directive may not seem important. However, if you decide to use the built-in firewall package, `ipfw`, you may find the passive ports directive useful for allowing passive connections through your firewall. In this example,

```
passive ports 140.254.12.0/24 15001 19999
```

ports in the range of 15001 to 19999 for passive data connections from `140.254.12.*` have been specified. This directive could be used in conjunction with an `ipfw` rule to permit a passive data connection through the firewall.

Understanding the `xferlog`

By default, `wu-ftpd` logs transfer to a file called `xferlog`. Each entry in the log consists of an entry in this format:

```
<current-time> <transfer-time> <remote-host> <file-size> <filename>
<transfer-type> <special-action-flag> <direction> <access-mode> <username>
<service-name> <authentication-method> <authenticated-user-id>
<completion-status>
```

At a casual glance, that format may seem a bit overwhelming. Let's look at some sample entries to better understand that format.

Here is an entry resulting from someone contacting the anonymous FTP server:

```
Fri May 11 13:32:19 2001 1 calvin.biosci.ohio-state.edu 46
➥ /Users/ftp/incoming/file4 b _ i a joray@ ftp 0 * c
```

Immediately apparent are the date and time when the transfer occurred. The next entry, the 1, indicates that the transfer time was only 1 second. The remote host was calvin.biosci.ohio-state.edu. The file size was 46 bytes. The file transferred was file4 in the incoming area of the anonymous FTP server. The transfer was a binary transfer. No special action, such as compressing or tarring, was done. From the i, you can see that this was an incoming transfer; that is, an upload. From the a, you can see that this was an anonymous user. The string identifying the username in this case is joray@. That is the password that the user entered. The ftp indicates that the ftp service was used. The 0 indicates that no authentication method was used. The * indicates that an authenticated user ID is not available. The c indicates that the transfer completed.

Here is an entry resulting from a guest user contacting the FTP server:

```
Fri May 11 16:32:24 2001 5 calvin.biosci.ohio-state.edu 5470431
➥ /Users/guests/betty/dotpaper.pdf b _ i g betty ftp 0 * c
```

It looks much like the anonymous entry. In this entry, the transfer time was 5 seconds. The file transfer was larger than in the previous example, 5470431 bytes. The i indicates that this transfer was also an incoming transfer, an upload. The g indicates that the user involved was a guest user. The guest user was user betty.

Here is an entry resulting from a real user contacting the FTP server:

```
Fri May 11 15:34:14 2001 1 ryoohki.biosci.ohio-state.edu 277838
➥ /Users/marvin/introduction.ps b _ o r marvin ftp 0 * c
```

Again, this entry is much like the other two entries you have seen. In this example, you can learn from the o that the transfer was an outgoing transfer; that is, a download. The r indicates that a real user made the transfer. In this case, the real user was marvin.

Guest User Accounts

As you've seen, wu-ftpd understands three types of users: real, anonymous, and guest. Real users are users who have full login access to your machine. You can restrict your real users' FTP access to their home directories, if you so choose. Whether you choose to do so is up to you. If you trust your users enough to give them full login access to your machine in the first place, you might also trust them with full FTP access. Anonymous users are users who have access to only the anonymous area of your machine, if you chose to create an anonymous FTP area. Guest users are users who have accounts on your machine, but aren't granted full access to your machine. Guest user accounts might be suitable for users who have Web sites on your machine and need FTP access only to occasionally update their Web sites.

A guest user account is a cross between a real user account and an anonymous FTP account. A guest user has a username and password, but doesn't have shell access to his account. This allows him to use FTP to access files on the server via a user ID and password, but prevents him from being able to log in to the machine either through the network or at the console. Guest user accounts are useful if, for example, you need to set up a place where a group of collaborators can share sensitive information and data, but where you don't really want members of the group to be full users of your machine. If you set up a single guest user account for this group of users, they can all access it with a user ID and password, and people without the user ID and password can't, so their information remains private. Because they don't have real shells, however, they can't log in to your machine and use any resources other than those that are available through the FTP server.

Guest user accounts are set up similarly to the anonymous FTP account. The users are restricted to their home directories only, as is the anonymous FTP account, and their accounts contain the commands that they might need to run while accessing their accounts via FTP.

If you decide that you need guest user accounts, do the following to implement a guest user:

1. Decide where the guest user's home directory should be. You could put your guest users in the same location as your regular users. You also could create a directory somewhere for guest users and place guest user directories in that location.
2. After you've decided where the guest account should reside, make a guest account. You could create your user in the Accounts pane in System Preferences. Your guest user, however, might not really have a need for all the directories that are made in a user account created in this way. You can decide what directories might be necessary. If you anticipate having many guest users, you could create a guest skeleton user as your basis for guest accounts.
3. The guest user should belong to some sort of guest group. Create a guest group with an unused GID number. Edit the guest user's account to belong to the guest group. The guest user's shell should be modified to some nonexistent shell. Make sure that the guest user's home directory and everything in it are owned by the guest user with the guest group.

4. There are two possible ways to list the guest user's home directory. The traditional way is to include a . where the FTP server should `chroot` to as the root FTP directory. For example, you could create a guest user called `betty`, with a home directory located in `/Users/guests/betty/`. To indicate that the root directory that you want `betty` to see when she accesses the FTP server to be `/Users/guests/betty/`, you would edit the home directory to be `/Users/guests/betty/./`. If you wanted `betty` to be able to see a listing of other guest users' directories before changing to her directory, you could list her home directory as `/Users/guests/./betty`. With her home directory listed this way, her guest root directory does not need to be specifically listed in the `ftpaccess` file. Figure 12.3 shows how the guest user's home directory appears in NetInfo Manager when indicated by this method.

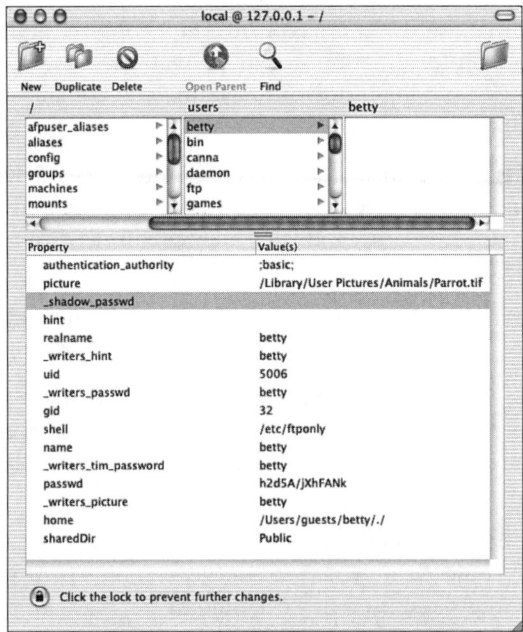

FIGURE 12.3 Here are the parameters used for the guest user `betty`. Her home directory is listed in the traditional notation for a guest user, which includes a . to indicate the root directory that the user sees when she FTPs.

The other way to list a guest user's home directory is to list the home directory as usual in NetInfo Manager. In the `ftpaccess` file, list the guest user's root directory with the `guestuser` control. The user's directory in the NetInfo database then looks like the notation for any real user's home directory, as you can see for guest user `ralph` in Figure 12.4.

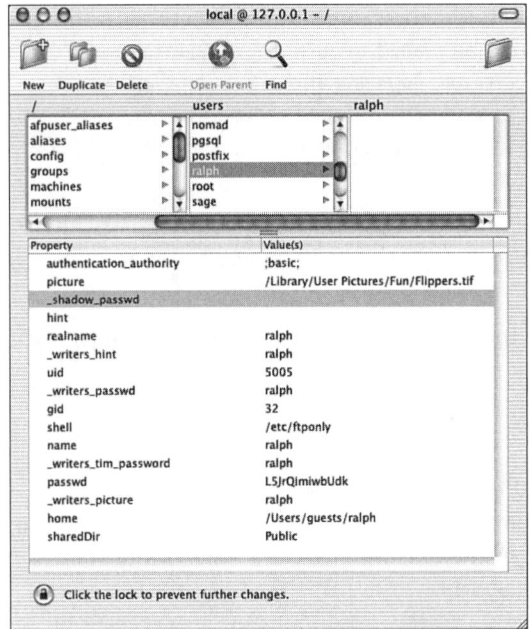

FIGURE 12.4 The home directory for this guest user is indicated in the regular fashion. The root directory for FTP for this guest user is indicated instead by the use of the `guestuser` control in the `ftpaccess` file.

The entry for the guest user's root directory in `ftpaccess` looks like this:

```
guestuser ralph
```

5. Include the shell that you use for the guest in `/etc/shells`. You might want the contents of your fake guest user shell to be something like this:

```
#! /bin/sh
exit 1
```

6. Update the ownership information of the guest user's account to include the guest group GID that is indicated in the NetInfo database.

7. Copy the same system files that are used for the anonymous FTP user to the guest user's account. Specifically, make sure the system's

```
/bin/ls
/usr/lib/dylib
/usr/lib/libSystem.B.dylib
/System/Library/Frameworks/System.framework/Versions/B/System
```

are included in the guest user's home directory. In this example, for user `ralph`, the files would be placed in `/Users/guests/ralph/bin/`, `/Users/guests/ralph/usr/lib/`, and `/Users/guests/ralph/System/Library/Frameworks/System.framework/Versions/B/` with the same permissions and ownerships that are used for an anonymous FTP account.

If you create a skeleton user account for FTP guests, these are files that would be useful to include in the skeleton guest user account so that they get installed automatically.

Please note that this step is not necessary if you have used the `--enable-ls` option.

Alternatives to FTP

As we have mentioned, turning on the FTP server makes your machine more vulnerable to attacks from the outside. There are other, more secure options you could consider using as alternatives to FTP.

`scp` and `sftp`

If you turn on the SSH server, two alternatives become available. You can transfer files either with secure copy (`scp`) or secure FTP (`sftp`). Transfers made using `scp` or `sftp` are encrypted, thereby providing an extra level of security. Specifically, the client creates a tunnel through SSH, using the standard port 22, and executes an `sftp-server` process on the server end, which sends data back through the encrypted channel. The `sftp` and `sftp-server` executables are part of the SSH package. With FTP, however, passwords are transmitted in cleartext, adding yet another vulnerability to FTP itself.

With the SSH server turned on, you can transfer files to other machines running SSH servers. Likewise, those machines can transfer files to your machine by using `scp` or `sftp`. In addition, there exists a freely available Mac OS client that has built-in `scp` capabilities. For PCs, there's a client that has a built-in `sftp` client. Running SSH removes almost any need for an FTP server. We discuss SSH in detail in Chapter 14, "Remote Access: Secure Shell, VNC, Timbuktu, Apple Remote Desktop."

SSH and FTP

As you may recall, `wu-ftpd` can be built as an anonymous-only FTP server. If your real users are transferring files via `scp` or `sftp`, but you still have a need for an anonymous FTP area, you might then consider compiling an anonymous-only FTP server and running that alongside your SSH server.

Regularly checking the anonymous FTP area for any irregularities and keeping your wu-ftpd current are still important activities.

Tunneling FTP over SSH

If, for whatever reason, transferring files with the scp and sftp commands isn't sufficient to meet your needs, you can tunnel FTP connections through ssh logins (see Chapter 14 for more information). This enables you to protect the command channel, but can't easily protect the FTP data channel. If you're administering an FTP server, you can moderately increase your system security by using an FTP configuration that encourages users to tunnel their FTP connections into your machine.

As was mentioned earlier, if you provide an open FTP port for your users to connect to, they'll be likely to try it, and likely to enter their user ID and password on the clear-text data channel to attempt login. You can bias your users against this behavior by exploiting wu-ftpd's capability for configuration and creating specialized FTP servers to handle real and anonymous users. By creating a real-users-only FTP server, using the --disable-anonymous compile-time option for wu-ftpd, you can create a server that allows only real users to log in. To protect this server, you can restrict access to it to only connections originating from the server machine itself. This way, the data from the connections never visibly passes over the network, and any connections that come in over the network are rejected, preventing users from unintentionally disclosing their information. SSH can then be used to create tunnels between the user's client machines and the server, so that their command channels are carried encrypted over the network to the server, and unpacked on the server. Because the connection to the command channel looks (to the FTP server) as if it's coming from the server machine itself (where it's being unpacked), it is allowed, and because it came to the server over the encrypted SSH tunnel, it is protected against prying eyes. Here you'll learn how to configure a wu-ftpd server for this use. Chapter 14 discusses in detail how to set up a client to tunnel an FTP connection to a server configured like this.

NOTE

You may need the --disable-pasvip option to get the tunneling to function properly.

To make tunneling work on the server side, you have to wrap the FTP server to accept connections only from itself. The easiest way to set up the restriction is to make use of the TCP Wrappers program that comes with the Mac OS X distribution.

In the method that uses only the /etc/hosts.allow file, you would do this with this syntax:

```
in.ftpd: <machine-IP> 127.0.0.1 localhost: allow
in.ftpd: deny
```

If you must also have an anonymous FTP server running, or even if you don't, it's a good idea to run the FTP server you're trying to make secure on noncanonical ports for FTP (such as `31` for `ftp`, `30` for `ftp-data`). If you're running an anonymous-only server, leave it running on the standard FTP ports (`21` for `ftp`, `20` for `ftp-data`).

As you've seen, you don't need to edit anything to run an FTP server on the standard ports. All that's left, then, is to configure your real-user FTP server and install it on an alternate set of ports. Follow these steps:

1. For ease of administration, it's a good idea to have each FTP server installed in a distinctly separate location. For example, you could install your anonymous FTP server in `/usr/local/ftp` and your real users' FTP server in `/usr/local/wuftp`.
2. Pick a set of unused port numbers. We like ports close to the standard FTP ports for convenience—`31` and `30` are our favorites.
3. Edit the `/etc/services` file to include the alternate services. You could call them something like `wuftp` and `wuftp-data`. Whichever port number you assign to the `wuftp` service is the one to which the clients wanting to connect need to tunnel.
4. Again for convenience, name the alternative FTP server itself something similar to the service name, such as `wuftpd`. It is automatically installed as `in.ftpd` in whatever location you specified during the build, but you can rename that file.
5. Finally, wrap the alternative FTP server to allow only connections from itself, but allow the anonymous FTP server access from all machines.

If you also decide to run Mac OS X's built-in firewall, `ipfw`, you must add statements to allow `ipfw` to grant access to the alternative FTP server. In addition, set the `passive ports` control to the `ftpaccess` file to a range of ports, such as 15001-19999. Then add a statement to the rules for `ipfw` to allow access to whatever range of ports you specified with `passive ports`. You might find that you have to keep tweaking your `ipfw`, anonymous, and real FTP configurations until everything works in harmony. Be sure to check your logs as you're doing this. They're more informative than you might at first realize.

NOTE

If you decide to run the types of FTP servers suggested in this section, you might find that guest accounts do not work. This appears to be a version-specific bug, or an unexpected consequence of some recent change, as we've used all these capabilities simultaneously before. Also, please note that only the channel that carries the username, password, and command information can be tunneled. The channel that travels between machines when you actually transfer a file using FTP can't be protected in this fashion. For many users, though, this protection is sufficient.

Summary

This chapter has taken a look at how to make the optional FTP process more secure. Although OS X comes with an FTP server provided by Apple, we suggest that if you do want to provide FTP services, you run the more configurable `wu-ftpd`. No matter which server you decide to run, restrict access to the server as much as possible, regularly check your logs, and keep the FTP server up to date. For the default FTP server, you can do this with the OS X software updates, or by compiling and installing the more recent versions by hand. For `wu-ftpd`, you have to update manually.

You also saw alternative suggestions to simply using FTP. Most preferable is using `scp` or `sftp`. If you need an anonymous FTP server, then have the regular users use `scp` and `sftp` while you provide an anonymous FTP server. However, you may also discover a need for having an FTP server available for your real users. In that case, consider compiling a real-users-only FTP server, wrapping it with TCP Wrapper, and teaching your users to tunnel connections to it over SSH.

13

Mail Server Security

IN THIS CHAPTER

- Basic Vulnerabilities
- Sendmail
- Activating Sendmail on Mac OS X
- Protecting Sendmail
- Updating Your Sendmail Installation
- Postfix as an Alternative
- Installing Postfix
- Protecting Postfix
- Delivering Mail—UW IMAP

MTAs, Mail Transfer Agents, are one of the most active and most frequently misconfigured services on the Internet. Millions of messages are transferred daily, and many with virus payloads spread by poorly secured servers. Mail servers present a serious risk and responsibility for system administrators. Rather than posing a single security risk, mail servers can open your system to numerous vulnerabilities.

Basic Vulnerabilities

All server processes that communicate with the outside world are open to security exploits because of programming errors either in the daemon itself, or in the support code that the server relies on. For the system administrator, these types of exploits are unavoidable, and usually quickly patched within hours of being found. Keeping software current and staying abreast of problems, whether happening on your network, or on the other side of the world, is the responsibility of any good administrator.

Misconfiguration

Mail servers suffer from the same misconfiguration issues as other servers. Inappropriate permissions can allow internal (and sometimes external) users to write to your configuration files, access private data, and compromise your local system security. Maintaining your mail server as a standalone system with as few entry points as possible helps eliminate some of the risks of local mistakes, but in many cases is not a justifiable expense.

Open Relays

MTAs are open to one security risk that is unique, and extremely costly in terms of resources, time, and aspirin: the ability external users have to appropriate MTA services for their own needs. In simpler terms, SPAM. The process of sending mail from machine to machine is called *relaying*. Each message, as it moves over the network, makes its way from one computer to another, until it reaches the recipient. Most email messages see at least two MTAs along the way: the originating MTA (which most people know as their "mail server") and the destination MTA (the remote server). It is up to each server along the way to determine whether it should deliver the message, reject it, or send it farther downstream for more processing. Relaying itself isn't inherently evil—in fact it is necessary for email to exist as we know it. The problem, however, occurs when an MTA has been told that it should relay *all* messages that it receives—that is, act as an *open relay*.

Most mail servers are easily configured so that they will relay only messages for users on a certain network, or those who have an account on the server itself. Open relays, on the other hand, process and deliver messages for anyone, regardless of their credentials. The bulk of SPAM mail is transmitted illegitimately through open relays, often without the machine's administrator even knowing it is taking place. Unfortunately, the consequences are numerous, and range from a loss of system performance to legal ramifications.

Open relays "open" themselves to being used by external individuals and organizations. These freeloaders are, in essence, hijacking your system and its resources for their own purposes, without ever actually "breaking in." Spammers often try to offload their outbound mail in extremely high volumes and as quickly as possible. For small server setups, the influx of mail can easily overwhelm available bandwidth and hard disk space as each incoming message is queued for delivery. The result is an effective denial of service attack that requires no special software beyond the ability to send email.

A more serious consequence is in where the responsibility lies if your system is used as the launching point for a SPAM, virus, or other email-borne attack on someone else. Depending on the damage done, the nature of the person or organization under attack, you may find yourself facing charges of negligence if your server was used in the attack. Obviously, this is a worst-case scenario, but with recent world events, computer and network security has moved to the forefront of law enforcement attention. In late 2001, legislation was proposed to classify hackers as terrorists. Although your server may not be the source of the attack, you are responsible for its use and configuration. A mail server is a loaded weapon, and you're responsible for conducting the appropriate background checks before unleashing it on the public.

NOTE

Again, this is a worst-case scenario; it doesn't mean that you can't successfully run a safe and secure mail server (which is the end goal of this chapter), but be aware that there are consequences to running a server without properly configuring it. We've seen incidents of death threats to the President's *pets* sent through OSU mail servers, only to see the FBI knocking on the door a day later. In the case of the threats to the pets, legitimate email users sent the messages. On an open relay, the same thing could happen, be traced to your server, and your chances of locating the original sender are reduced. Imagine trying to explain this to men (or women) in dark glasses and trench coats.

Testing for Open Relays

You can easily test a mail server to see whether it is an open relay by Telneting into the SMTP port (port 25) on the remote server, then using the SMTP commands to attempt to send a "false" message. Table 13.1 shows the basic commands needed to communicate with an SMTP server, in the order which they are used.

TABLE 13.1 SMTP Command List

Command	Purpose
`EHLO <machine name>`	Identifies your computer to the remote SMTP server. Some machines use `HELO` instead, but this is largely deprecated.
`MAIL FROM: <originating email>`	Sets the email address from which the message is being sent.
`RCPT TO: <destination email>`	Sets the remote email address to which a message should be delivered.
`DATA`	Used to start the input of the email message to the server. The message is terminated by typing a period (.) on an empty line.
`QUIT`	Exits and sends the email message.

For example, the following session creates a connection to a remote server (`bezirke.adomaindoesntexist.com`), which is misconfigured and set to be an open relay. The remote server accepts a fake recipient and a fake originating email address and attempts to deliver a message. This is an example of an open relay.

```
# telnet bezirke.adomaindoesntexist.com 25
Trying 192.168.0.99...
Connected to bezirke.adomaindoesntexist.com.
Escape character is '^]'.
220 bezirke.adomaindoesntexist.com
➥ESMTP Sendmail 8.9.3/8.8.7; Sun, 5 May 2002 22:30:15 -0400
EHLO youshouldntrelayme.com
250-bezirke.adomaindoesntexist.com
➥Hello bezirke.adomaindoesntexist.com [192.168.0.132], pleased to meet you
```

```
MAIL FROM: jray@youshouldntrelayme.com
250 jray@youshouldntrelayme.com... Sender ok
RCPT TO: sniffles@aplacethatdoesntexist.com
250 sniffles@aplacethatdoesntexist.com... Recipient ok
DATA
354 Enter mail, end with "." on a line by itself
Hello,

This is a test.

--- John
.
QUIT
```

On the flip side, a properly protected machine will block the message from being sent:

```
# telnet poisontooth.com 25
Trying 204.210.234.132...
Connected to poisontooth.com.
Escape character is '^]'.
EHLO client1.shadesofinsanity.com
250-poisontooth.com Hello client1.shadesofinsanity.com, pleased to meet you
MAIL FROM: jray@poisontooth.com
250 jray@poisontooth.com sender accepted
RCPT TO: aspamrecipient@nospamallowed.com
473 aspamrecipient@nospamallowed.com relaying prohibited.
```

In this example, the server refuses to deliver the message. The connecting client is not authorized to send the message. This is the target behavior for a "healthy" mail server.

Sendmail

Sendmail evolved from an early mail delivery package named, appropriately, delivermail, created in 1979 by Eric Allaman for use over ARPANET—the predecessor of what we now know as the Internet. At the time, delivermail used the FTP protocol on top of NCP (Network Control Protocol). As ARPANET grew into the Internet, the need for enhanced mail services that ran over the new TCP/IP protocol suite became apparent. SMTP—the Simple Mail Transport Protocol—was developed to fill the lack of a dedicated mail transfer standard. With the addition of the DNS (Domain Name Service) in 1986, worldwide Internet email became a reality, and delivermail made the transition to sendmail. Initially released on BSD, sendmail finds itself right at home on Mac OS X (a BSD derivative). Throughout the 15+ years of its existence, sendmail has been continually enhanced, and, despite its popularity, is one of the most complicated server applications to understand and configure. For more information, read the "Brief History of Mail" at `http://www.coruscant.demon.co.uk/mike/sendmail/history.html`.

Mac OS X originally shipped with sendmail 8.10.2 for both its 10.0 and 10.1 releases. The latest Mac OS X, 10.2 (Jaguar) includes sendmail 8.12.2, which, while recent, is *still* not the most current version of the sendmail software. Since the 8.10.2 release, several important features have been added to the sendmail system, including improved SMTP AUTH support and security updates. To get an idea of why you'd want to keep your sendmail current, let's take a look at a few sendmail exploits, starting with the infamous Internet Worm.

The Morris Internet Worm

Although the version of sendmail that you have on your system is *mostly* secure, the history of the server software is far from squeaky clean. In the mid-80s sendmail served as one of the primary propagation methods for the infamous 80s Internet Worm—or the Morris Worm, as named after its creator, Richard Morris. On November 2, 1988, Richard Morris unwitting released the most destructive Internet attack to date. Based on a 99-line program, the Morris Worm managed to do what today we can only hope is impossible—take down the Internet. Attacking only Sun and VAX BSD-based systems, in less than a day the Internet Worm attacked popular system services and infested over 5000 of the best-connected machines in the country.

Sendmail provided one of the potential entry points for the worm. To quote Eric Allman, "The trap door resulted from two distinct 'features' that, although innocent by themselves, were deadly when combined (kind of like binary nerve gas)." The remote attacker took advantage of sendmail installations that were compiled with the `DEBUG` flag and the ability of sendmail to deliver messages to a system process rather than a user. Specifically, the attacking program would connect to the server, and provide a null sender and a subject line that would include the necessary keyboard commands to remove the preceding mail headers and insert the code to start a command interpreter. The body of the message contained the code necessary to compile and start the worm process again.

Although apparently not intended to be malicious, the worm itself contained bugs. The intended operation for the worm was to infect quietly and maintain a single harmless process running on each infected system. Unfortunately, the worm did not prevent itself from reinfecting an already infected machine. As a result, each infected machine started more and more worm processes, resulting in a rapid degradation of system services and eventual failure. For a complete history on the worm, the infestation, and the resulting network disaster, read Don Seely's "A Tour of the Worm" at `http://world.std.com/~franl/worm.html`.

NOTE

In reading the chronology of Don Seely's account of the worm, take notice of the length of time it took for sendmail to be patched after the exploit was discovered. Open Source has its benefits.

Recent Exploits

After weathering the Internet Worm, sendmail remained relatively quiet until the Internet (and thus email) became popular in the 90s. Over the years, numerous exploits have been found, and all have quickly been solved with an update. To give you an idea of what you're facing, here are a few of the bugs that have surfaced over the years.

Input Validation Bugs

Sendmail is often called from the command line to process and send email. To do so, it must be run SUID root. Unfortunately, numerous implementations of the server have suffered from poor input bounds checking, allowing local users to execute code as root on a number of operating systems. Several of the bugs are referenced here:

- **Linux**. (CVE: CVE-2001-0653) `http://online.securityfocus.com/advisories/3517` `http://online.securityfocus.com/advisories/3513`
- **IRIX**. (CVE: CAN-2001-0714 and CAN-2001-0715) `http://online.securityfocus.com/advisories/3666`
- **NetBSD**. `http://online.securityfocus.com/advisories/3548`

The Vacation Exploit

Although not directly related to a problem with sendmail, the Unix vacation utility, used almost exclusively with the sendmail server, triggered an inappropriate exploit through the MTA. "Vacation" was used to send an autoreply ("I'm on vacation!") to those who emailed your account. Rather than providing a sender address to sendmail within the body of its outgoing message, it used the command line to provide the address. The trouble with this approach is that vacation didn't check to see whether the command-line address truly *was* an email address. Malicious users could instead provide command-line arguments that would force sendmail to read an alternative configuration file and ultimately execute arbitrary code. A description of this exploit can be found at `http://www.insecure.org/sploits/vacation_program_hole.html` (CVE: CVE-1999-0057).

Unsafe Signal Handling

Used in a theoretical exploit, signal handling in sendmail could potentially lead to a race condition and effectively allow local users to execute arbitrary code as root, or cause a locally based DOS attack. Because this is not a remotely exploitable attack (and has never been seen implemented as an actual exploit), it should be of little concern to those running a dedicated mail server. Additionally, sendmail 8.12 eliminates the possibility of the attack taking place by removing the SUID sendmail requirement. To learn more about this potential exploit, read `http://online.securityfocus.com/advisories/3328` (CVE: CAN-2001-1349).

Sendmail Exploit Resources

If you're interested in trying a few exploits on your Linux boxes (Linux distributions ship with a number of different sendmail versions), take a look at the following:

- **Phreak.org.** `http://www.phreak.org/archives/exploits/unix/sendmail-exploits/`—A code collection of sendmail exploits, cataloged by version number.
- **PacketStormSecurity.nl.** `http://packetstormsecurity.nl/unix-exploits/sendmail-exploits/`—Dozens of sendmail exploits and exploit descriptions.
- **Hacker Internet Security Services.** `http://www.hacker.com.br/exploits.php?id=3051`—Exploits for the most recent versions of sendmail on the Linux platform.

As you can see, "stuff happens," but there are no reported OS X sendmail exploits at this time. Your primary concern should be getting sendmail set up *safely* with no chances of attack due to misconfiguration. In addition, you should learn how to update sendmail in case vulnerabilities do become an issue in the future. These topics will be the focus of the next several pages of the chapter. You must pay close attention to three areas, in particular:

- **File/Path Ownership and Permissions**. Sendmail is picky (for good reason), about where you put your files and who has access to them.
- **Relay and Access control**. Who can use your server, and when. Sendmail has a number of options to determine whether and when mail should be accepted and processed.
- **Local Users Access control**. If you plan to run your server on a computer where users have access (`ssh`/`ftp`/etc) to their accounts, you should limit their ability to intentionally (or unintentionally) compromise system security.

Activating Sendmail on Mac OS X

Assuming you want to test the version of sendmail that came with your computer, you're about five minutes away from having a running sendmail on your system. First, however, you need to make a decision based on how you're going to be using your computer. Mac OS X is an operating system designed for *Mac* users. The `admin` group is often shared among multiple users, often with disregard for the role that those users play in the actual operation of the machine. Administrative users can write to the root level (`/`) of the drive, which is typical of the "Mac" way of doing things.

TIP

If you're planning to run sendmail as a full-time MTA, we recommend updating to the latest release, which you'll learn about later in this chapter.

Breaking the Mac Mold or the Sendmail Security Model

Sendmail, by default, has extremely strict permission requirements for the directory where it is installed:

- Files that are group writable or are located in group-writable directories will not be read.
- Files cannot be written to directories that are group writable.
- `.forward` files that are links to other files will not be processed.

The root level of your Mac OS X file system is group writable, which immediately breaks the first rule. To adhere to the sendmail security model, you need to "break" the longstanding Mac tradition of being able to install applications and folders anywhere you want. The root level of the system must be off-limits for changes to anyone except the root user.

NOTE

Most software installation packages (MindVise, InstallerMaker, and so on) automatically authenticate as root and install software without needing a root login. Admin users, however, will not be able to manually add items at the root level.

CAUTION

If you're serious about running an MTA on your Mac OS X computer, you should think about running a dedicated server, not sharing a computer with general users.

Many sendmail attacks have been *local* exploits, allowing local users to gain root access. To be honest, if you're running a sendmail server *and* using it as a general use computer, you're asking for trouble. This is *not* a recommended Maximum Mac OS X Security practice.

Testing the Sendmail Path Permissions

To determine the current state of sendmail permissions at any time, open the Terminal and use the command `/usr/sbin/sendmail -v -d44.4 -bv postmaster`. This runs a test of all sendmail file permissions and reports on the results. (Only the relevant output is shown here).

```
# /usr/sbin/sendmail -v -d44.4 -bv postmaster
safefile(/etc/mail/sendmail.cf, uid=0, gid=20, flags=6000, mode=400):
safedirpath(/etc/mail, uid=0, gid=20, flags=6000, level=0, offset=0):
        [dir /] mode 41775 WARNING
safedirpath(/private/etc, uid=0, gid=20, flags=6000, level=1, offset=1):
        [dir /private/etc] OK
        [dir /etc/mail] OK
        [uid 0, nlink 1, stat 100644, mode 400]         OK
safefile(/etc/mail/local-host-names, uid=0, gid=20, flags=6580, mode=400):
safedirpath(/etc/mail, uid=0, gid=20, flags=6580, level=0, offset=0):
        [dir /] mode 41775 FATAL
        [dir /etc/mail] Group writable directory
/etc/mail/sendmail.cf: line 93: fileclass: cannot open '/etc/mail/local-host-
➥names': Group writable directory
safefile(/etc/mail/relay-domains, uid=0, gid=20, flags=6580, mode=400):
safedirpath(/etc/mail, uid=0, gid=20, flags=6580, level=0, offset=0):
        [dir /] mode 41775 FATAL
        [dir /etc/mail] Group writable directory
safefile(/etc/mail/service.switch, uid=0, gid=20, flags=6480, mode=400):
safedirpath(/etc/mail, uid=0, gid=20, flags=6580, level=0, offset=0):
        [dir /] mode 41775 FATAL
        [dir /etc/mail] Group writable directory
        No such file or directory
safefile(/etc/mail/service.switch, uid=0, gid=20, flags=6480, mode=400):
safedirpath(/etc/mail, uid=0, gid=20, flags=6580, level=0, offset=0):
        [dir /] mode 41775 FATAL
        [dir /etc/mail] Group writable directory
        No such file or directory
safedirpath(/var/spool/mqueue, uid=0, gid=20, flags=4, level=0, offset=0):
        [dir /] mode 41775 WARNING
safedirpath(/private/var, uid=0, gid=20, flags=4, level=1, offset=1):
        [dir /private/var] OK
        [dir /var/spool/mqueue] OK
```

The group-writable directories are flagged in the output, and, as you can see, many of these errors are *fatal,* meaning sendmail won't even run. This problem can be eliminated by either of two methods: removing the group write permissions or telling sendmail to ignore them.

Fixing Sendmail Path Permission

To remove group write permissions from your directory, open a Terminal window and type the following three commands:

```
sudo chmod g-w /
sudo chmod g-w /etc
sudo chmod g-w /etc/mail
```

Assuming you follow Apple's updates, your system directory permissions are at Apple's whim. Several sections in this book discuss how to counteract the effects of the Apple updates. It's the price we pay for automated updates and Apple's watchful eye. Table 13.2 contains the preferred sendmail directory and file modes.

TABLE 13.2 Sendmail Directory and File Permissions

Directory	Permission Mode	Owner
/	755	root
/var	755	root
/var/spool	755	root
/var/spool/mqueue	700	root
/etc	755	root
/etc/mail	755	root
/etc/mail/*	644	root

If you'd prefer to "slightly" break the sendmail model, you can limit the extent to which sendmail enforces its security checks by employing the `DontBlameSendmail` configuration option. This configuration directive forces sendmail to drop one or more of its security policies to make for a more "forgiving" installation.

Open the `/etc/mail/sendmail.cf` file in your favorite text editor, then search for the line that reads

```
#O DontBlameSendmail=safe
```

Replace the text with

```
O DontBlameSendmail=GroupWritableDirPathSafe
```

As the name may lead you to believe, this option makes sendmail consider directories with group write attributes set as "safe." Your sendmail installation is now operable and ready to be started.

In a recent OS update, a second configuration file `submit.cf` was added for a second instance of Sendmail that handles local message submissions. In order to use Sendmail locally, you will need to make the same changes to this file that you've made to `sendmail.cf`.

TIP

If you're interested in loosening the sendmail file permission reins even more, you can get a complete list of the `DontBlameSendmail` options at `http://www.sendmail.org/tips/DontBlameSendmail.html`. Keep in mind that the less strict the file permissions, the more likely it is that a local exploit could take place.

Removing NetInfo Dependence

By default, Mac OS X's sendmail distribution attempts to read its configuration from NetInfo. This can lead to hours of frustration as you try to determine why the configuration changes you're making in the `/etc/mail/sendmail.cf` file are simply being ignored. To fix the problem, execute these two commands (as root) to tell sendmail to pay attention to the *correct* config file:

```
# niutil -create . /locations/sendmail
# niutil -createprop . /locations/sendmail sendmail.cf /etc/mail/sendmail.cf
```

Be absolutely certain that you've completed this step before proceeding; otherwise future examples within the chapter may not work as documented.

Setting Your Server Name

I'm making the assumption that you already have DNS support for your mail server and a static IP address for its use. At the very least, you should have an A record registered, and very probably an MX record. For more information on mail servers and DNS settings, check out `http://www.graphicpower.com/techarticles/mailsvr.stm`.

For whatever names you want your system to receive email, you must edit the file `/etc/mail/local-host-names` with the hostnames that identify your mail server. For example, my machine has both the names `poisontooth.com` and `shadesofinsanity.com`. For sendmail to recognize both of these as valid names, I've added them both to my `local-host-names` file:

```
# more /etc/mail/local-host-names
poisontooth.com
shadesofinsanity.com
```

Be sure to create and save this file before continuing with the setup. As with `sendmail.cf`, this should be owned by root and have the permission mode `644`.

Activating the Sendmail Daemon

Apple includes a script for starting sendmail in the `/System/Library/StartupItems/Sendmail` directory on *both* the Mac OS X Client and Server operating system distributions. The startup script looks for a corresponding MAILSERVER line in the /etc/hostconfig. You need to be logged in as root to make changes to this file.

Edit /etc/hostconfig, and look for this line:

```
MAILSERVER=-NO-
```

To activate sendmail, change -NO- to -YES-:

```
MAILSERVER=-YES-
```

Save the file, and you're ready to go.

NOTE

If you're a Mac OS X Server user, you should make sure that the Apple Mail Service is disabled, either through the Server Admin utility or by editing the /private/etc/watchdog.conf file.

Apple's Mail Service is started in watchdog.conf by this line:

```
mailservice:respawn:/usr/sbin/MailService -n
```

To run sendmail, be sure to set this line to

```
mailservice:off:/usr/sbin/MailService -n
```

Attempting to run both servers at the same time may result in your untimely insanity.

The next time you reboot your computer, sendmail will start. Alternatively, you can start sendmail immediately with sudo /usr/sbin/sendmail -bd -q1h. The two options used when starting sendmail, -bd and -q1h, tell the MTA to operate as a background daemon and set the queue processing interval to 1 hour. Table 13.3 contains a few of the sendmail switches that can be used to fine-tune the control of the MTA.

TABLE 13.3 Sendmail Runtime Options

Command-Line switch	Description
-bd	Run as a daemon on port 25.
-bD	Run as a daemon in the foreground. Useful for testing and debugging.
-bp	Show messages in the sendmail queue.
-d<#>	Set sendmail debugging level to the given number. For more information on debugging levels, visit http://www.unet.univie.ac.at/aix/aixbman/commadmn/ml_debug.htm
-C<*filename*>	Use an alternate configuration file (for testing). Sendmail will not run as root when an alternative config file is in use.
-q<#*s*|*m*|*h*|*d*|*w*>	Set the interval at which stored queue items will be processed. Use one or more numbers, followed by s,m,h,d,w for second, minute, hour, day, or week values.

TABLE 13.3 Continued

Command-Line switch	Description
`-qI<substring>`	Process only items whose queue ID contains the given substring.
`-qR<substring>`	Process only items whose recipient line (To:) contains the given substring.
`-qS<substring>`	Process only items whose sender line (From:) contains the given substring.
`-X <logfile>`	Log all activity through sendmail to the named log file.

This is only a partial list of switches that may be of use during initial testing and deployment of sendmail. For a complete list of options, you'll need to look at the Sendmail Installation and Operation Guide (`http://www.sendmail.org/~ca/email/doc8.10/op.html`)—not even the man pages list all the possible settings.

Protecting Sendmail

After sendmail is installed and operational, your next step is customizing the configuration to suit your needs. The central sendmail config file is located at `/etc/mail/sendmail.cf`. Sendmail is unique in that you can edit either the main configuration file (as we did with the `DontBlameSendmail` option earlier), but more frequently you'll make your first changes to a macro file (`.mc`), which is then run through the `m4` macro processor to generate the more complex `/etc/mail/sendmail.cf` file.

If this seems confusing, don't worry—it is. The `sendmail.cf` file is extremely difficult to configure by hand. To counteract the complexity, sendmail has built macros (called "Features") that can generate many of the complex settings for you. You edit the macro-based configuration file, process it with `m4`, and voila: The final `sendmail.cf` file is generated.

NOTE

You'll need to be logged in as root or use `sudo` to make changes and generate the sendmail configuration file.

Apple has included the basic Darwin (Mac OS X) sendmail macro configuration in the file `/usr/share/sendmail/conf/cf/generic-darwin.mc`. You should *not* make any changes to this file. Instead, create a copy (`sendmail.mc`) and use it to add your changes.

To begin, let's take a look at how to generate the basic configuration that came with your computer. You can follow these steps to reset sendmail to its "fresh-install" state:

1. First, copy the Darwin macro file someplace safe for editing: `cp /usr/share/sendmail/conf/cf/generic-darwin.mc /tmp/sendmail.mc`.

2. Next, run the `m4` macro processor on the file: `m4 /usr/share/sendmail/conf/m4/cf.m4 /tmp/sendmail.mc > /etc/mail/sendmail.cf.`
3. The `sendmail.cf` is regenerated.

If you make any mistakes or find that sendmail is no longer starting, this is a quick way to get the system back to a state that you can deal with.

> **CAUTION**
>
> Each time you regenerate your `sendmail.cf` file, whether to add a configuration option or reset it to the default state, you *must* edit the file to add the `DontBlameSendmail` option discussed earlier, unless you chose to modify directory permissions in lieu of relaxing the sendmail security restrictions.

Now let's look at how you can protect your newly active server. As I mentioned earlier, you are not susceptible to many of the earlier attacks that plagued sendmail, so your primary focus should be on protecting the server from unauthorized use, such as relaying or being used to deliver SPAM to your users.

You're in luck—partially. The sendmail distribution that ships with Mac OS X is already configured to block relay requests. However, you still need to tell the server what it should *allow*. Setting the domains allowed for relaying is a matter of creating and editing the file `/etc/mail/relay-domains`.

The `relay-domains` file can contain individual hosts or domains for which your server will relay messages. For example, if I want my server to accept messages from the domains `poisontooth.com`, `shadesofinsanity.com`, and `vujevich.com`, I'd add each of these to the `/etc/mail/relay-domains` file:

```
# more /etc/mail/relay-domains
poisontooth.com
shadesofinsanity.com
vujevich.com
```

You can also add individual hostnames or IP addresses to the `relay-domains` file if you prefer to restrict access to specific machines.

After making updates to your relay list, you *must* restart sendmail (by rebooting or sending a HUP signal with `kill`) for the changes to take effect.

Sendmail Features

For the simple level of relay control we've seen so far, you won't need to generate a new `sendmail.cf` file. Many more relay "features" can fine tune the relay conditions for your server, and these *will* require you to edit your `sendmail.mc` file and regenerate `sendmail.cf`. Table 13.4 contains a list of available features and their use.

NOTE

To use any of the following features you should first create a copy of `/usr/share/sendmail/conf/cf/generic-darwin.mc` for editing—such as `/tmp/sendmail.mc`.

All new features will then be added as new lines to `/tmp/sendmail.mc`, which will be used to generate `/etc/mail/sendmail.cf` when you type `m4 /usr/share/sendmail/conf/m4/cf.`
`➥m4 /tmp/sendmail.mc > /etc/mail/sendmail.cf`.

Sendmail must be restarted after adding features.

TABLE 13.4 Sendmail Relay Features

Feature	Description
`FEATURE('relay_hosts_only')`	Matches only specific hosts in the `relay-domains` file, rather than domains.
`FEATURE('relay_entire_domain')`	Relays for your entire local domain.
`FEATURE('access_db')`	Uses a hash database `/etc/mail/access` for controlling relay options. We'll examine this in detail later in this chapter.
`FEATURE('blacklist_recipients')`	Uses the `/etc/mail/access` database for controlling mail *recipients* as well as senders.
`FEATURE('dnsbl')`	Enables real-time blacklisting service for incoming messages. We'll also look at this in detail shortly.
`FEATURE('accept_unqualified_senders')`	Loosens the restriction of having to have a domain name as part of a sender address. Allows simple usernames (such as "jray") to be used.
`FEATURE('accept_unresolvable_domains')`	Instructs sendmail to accept messages from domain names that cannot be resolved with DNS lookups. Not a good idea.
`FEATURE('relay_based_on_MX')`	Allows relaying for any domain that has an MX record that points to your mail server.
`FEATURE('relay_local_from')`	Relays messages that "appear" to come from your domain. Because this is easily spoofed, it doesn't provide very good protection.
`FEATURE('promiscuous_relay')`	Relays everything. A very *very* bad idea.
`FEATURE('smrsh')`	Limit users' program access from `.forward` files.

NOTE

For more information on sendmail relaying, read the official documentation at `http://www.sendmail.org/tips/relaying.html`.

Sendmail's Access Database

One of the more powerful relaying options is the sendmail `access_db` feature. This gives you control over the messages that move through your system down to the email address level. You can reject domains, hosts, and email addresses, all from a single location. Enable the access database by adding the following lines to your `sendmail.mc` file, generating the `sendmail.cf` file, and restarting sendmail:

```
FEATURE('access_db')
FEATURE('blacklist_recipients')
```

The first of the two lines enables the access control database, whereas the second (optional) line allows entries into the database that will block outgoing messages to specific recipients.

The access database is built from a simple text file that consists of lines containing a hostname, domain, IP address, or email address and an action that should be taken when the element is matched. Table 13.5 shows the five available actions.

TABLE 13.5 Access Database Actions

Action	Result
`OK`	Accept mail regardless of any other rules or access control blocks.
`RELAY`	Accept email to or from the named domain.
`REJECT`	Reject email to or from the named address. An error message is returned to the client.
`DISCARD`	Silently reject email to or from the named address.
`ERROR:<### Message>`	Identical to `REJECT`, but allows a custom error message to be sent.

For example, consider the following access database file (`/etc/mail/access.txt`):

```
annoying@badplacestuff.com      ERROR: "500 You won't spam us again."
evilandgood.com                 ERROR: "500 Your domain is a known spam source."
nicepeople.evilandgood.com      OK
poisontooth.com                 RELAY
10.0.1.250                      RELAY
```

- **Line 1**. Mail to or from `annoying@badplacestuff.com` is rejected.
- **Line 2**. Sets up the same rejection behavior for any messages coming from the `evilandgood.com` domain.
- **Line 3**. Overrides the line 2 rejection for the host `nicepeople.evilandgood.com`.
- **Line 4**. Relay messages to/from `poisontooth.com`.
- **Line 5**. Relay messages from the host 10.0.1.250.

Set up your own rules in a temporary text file, such as `/etc/mail/access.txt`. This file will then be processed with the `makemap hash` command to generate the binary hash file that sendmail uses internally:

```
# makemap hash /etc/mail/access < /etc/mail/access.txt
```

The access database should be owned by root and writable only by root. As with most everything, you need to restart sendmail after updating the access database.

Real-Time Blacklisting

Another useful feature of sendmail is the ability to use real-time DNS blacklisting (RBL) services to block messages from known spam and open-relay sources. After blacklisting is enabled, each incoming connection is checked against a dynamic online database (on mail-abuse.org) to determine whether it is from a known open relay or spammer. If a match is found, the message is rejected. The list of relays and spam sources is kept up to date by user submissions, so it is always growing and evolving.

To activate this feature for your server, add the line

```
FEATURE('dnsbl')
```

to your `sendmail.mc` file, then use `m4` to regenerate the main configuration file, as discussed earlier.

To test for blacklisted addresses, a standard DNS lookup is performed on a specially constructed version of a hostname. For example, if you want to check the IP address 140.254.85.225 to see whether it is blacklisted, you would look up the special address `225.85.254.140.blackholes.mail-abuse.org`. As you can probably tell, this is nothing but the IP address reversed with `.blackholes.mail-abuse.org` added to the end. If a lookup on the address *fails*, it is not blacklisted:

```
%nslookup
Default Server:  carrot3.poisontooth.com
Address:  10.0.1.250

> 225.85.254.140.blackholes.mail-abuse.org
Server:  carrot3.poisontooth.com
Address:  10.0.1.250

*** carrot3.poisontooth.com can't find 225.85.254.140.blackholes.mail-abuse.org
```

To see an example of a "successful" (or blacklisted) lookup, use the IP address 127.0.0.2—or `2.0.0.127.blackholes.mail-abuse.org`. This address, reserved for testing, should show return a valid DNS lookup:

```
%nslookup
Default Server:  carrot3.poisontooth.com
Address:  10.0.1.250

> 2.0.0.127.blackholes.mail-abuse.org
Server:  carrot3.poisontooth.com
Address:  10.0.1.250

Name:     2.0.0.127.blackholes.mail-abuse.org
Server:  carrot3.poisontooth.com
Address:  127.0.0.2
```

For more information on the RBL system, visit `http://mail-abuse.org/rbl/usage.html`. Unfortunately, commercial licenses to the mail-abuse.org service *do* cost money. Noncommercial use is free, but you must register your mail server with mail-abuse.org before you can successfully query the DNS.

Other RBL services are available that you can use at no charge if you don't want to use the built-in mail-abuse.org settings. To use an alternative RBL server, simply specify a second parameter to the features, such as:

```
FEATURE('dnsbl','spamguard.leadmon.net')
```

Searching for `RBL` or `RBL DNS` is the easiest way to find the "latest and greatest" blacklisting servers that are currently active. Here are a few to try for starters:

- relays.osirusoft.com
- spamguard.leadmon.net
- spam.dnsrbl.net
- korea.services.net
- sbl.spamhaus.org
- spamsites.relays.osirusoft.com

Restricted Shell

If you're running an "open" system with user shell accounts, you should consider restricting what they can do with their `.forward` files, which can be created inside a user's home directory. The `.forward` file is typically used to forward messages to another account, or invoke another program, providing incoming email contents as standard input. These files should nominally be set to mode `600`; looser restrictions cause sendmail to ignore them.

The `.forward` file consists of a line of destinations, separated by commas. While usually the file contains a single external email address for forwarding (such as `johnray@mac.com`), the destinations can be local accounts, email addresses, files, or piped utilities. An example for my account (`jray`), might look like this:

```
\jray, "| /usr/bin/vacation jray"
```

In this example, the first destination, `\jray`, causes a copy of the incoming message to be delivered to my local account. The `\` indicates that this is an end address and no aliasing should take place (to help eliminate the chance of infinite mail loops). The second destination `"| /usr/bin/vacation jray"` pipes the incoming message to the `vacation` utility with the command-line parameter `jray`. Commands (in this case, `vacation`) are executed SUID the owner of the `.forward` files.

The trouble with `.forward` is that it provides a means for a user to execute a potentially untrusted program with arbitrary input. Even though the sendmail application may be secure, the called application may include a vulnerability that could be inadvertently (or intentionally) be exploited.

To limit what a user can execute, you should consider adding `FEATURE(smrsh)` to your `sendmail.mc` file and regenerating the `.cf` file. This feature activates the Sendmail Restricted Shell which limits what can be executed through the `.forward` file or `aliases` file to the programs contained, or linked, within the directory `/usr/adm/sm.bin`. The `smrsh` utility even rejects potentially dangerous characters such as redirects if they are included in the string to execute.

For example, if you wanted to provide users access to `vacation` and *only* `vacation`, you could do the following as root:

```
# mkdir -p /usr/adm/sm.bin
# chmod 600 /usr/adm/sm.bin
# ln -s /usr/bin/vacation /usr/adm/sm.bin/vacation
```

The first two lines create and set permissions for the `/usr/adm/sm.bin` directory. (The directory should be owned by root and writable only by root.) The third line creates a symbolic link from `/usr/bin/vacation` to `/usr/adm/sm.bin/vacation`, allowing it to be executed from `.forward` or your `aliases` file.

You should never link a shell or interpreter such as Perl into the `sm.bin` directory. This provides an open (and inviting) door for intrusion.

TIP

Even if you aren't using `.forward` files, you may still want to use the `smrsh` feature, because it provides the same restrictions for your `aliases` database. Although your `aliases` file should be writable only by root, if it were compromised, only the `/usr/adm/sm.bin` utilities could be invoked through it.

Sendmail Options

Now that you've tasted the feature macros that you can add to your `sendmail.mc` file, let's take a look at configuration options that can be added directly to `/etc/mail/sendmail.cf`. Unlike the macro-based features, you don't need to regenerate the configuration file each time you add an option. However, keep in mind that if you edit your `.mc` file later and regenerate `sendmail.cf`, you'll need to add the options to the file again. Table 13.6 contains a number of options for additional access and security control. Options are added, one to a line, preceded by `O`:

```
O <Option Name>=<Option Value>
```

TABLE 13.6 Sendmail Options

Option	Description
`AliasFile =` *`<alias path and filename>`*	Sets a location for the sendmail alias file. Mac OS X defaults to the Netinfo `/aliases` directory, rather than a local file.
`AllowBogusHELO`	No value needed. If specified, this option will allow non-RFC 1123 HELO/EHLO values to be sent.
`ConnectionRateThrottle =` *`<incoming connection limit>`*	Applies a limit to the number of incoming connections within a one-second time period.
`MaxDaemonChildren =` *`<child limit>`*	Sets a limit to the number of child processes that can be running simultaneously.
`MaxMessageSize =` *`<message size limit>`*	Sets an upper limit, in bytes, for incoming messages.
`MinFreeBlocks =` *`<free filesystem blocks>`*	Refuses to queue messages if the file system free space (in blocks) drops below this limit. Use `du` to display the free space on your mounted volumes.
`PrivacyOptions =` *`<option1, option2, ...>`*	Sets how sendmail adheres to the SMTP protocol. Options include `public`, `needmailhelo`, `needexpnhelo`, `noexpn`, `needvrfyhelo`, `novrfy`, `restrictmailq`, `restrictqrun`, `noreceipts`, `goaway`, and `authwarnings`, and will be discussed shortly.
`QueueDirectory =` *`<directory>`*	Directory to use as the mail queue.
`QueueLA =` *`<load average>`*	Sets the load average at which messages will be accepted, but sendmail will no longer try to deliver them.
`RecipientFactor =` *`<factor>`*	This number is added to the message priority (higher numbers are lower priority) for each recipient of the message. The more recipients, the lower the priority. Defaults to 30000.

TABLE 13.6 Continued

Option	Description
`RefuseLA = <load average>`	Limits incoming connections based on the server's load average. Use `uptime` to view your computer's load averages.
`RetryFactor = <factor>`	Priority factor added to each message as it is processed and reprocessed. Defaults to 90000.
`SafeFileEnvironment = <directory path>`	Limits sendmail's capability to deliver to anything but standard files in a specific location. Sendmail aliases and users with `.forward` files are forced to write any files to this directory.
`StatusFile = <file path>`	Path and filename of a file that is to store mail server statistics. This is a fixed-size log, and can be viewed at any time with `mailstats`.
`UnsafeGroupWrites`	When active, "include" files (as are often used in the alias file), and `.forward` files are considered "unsafe" and may not be used to write files or reference other programs.

Privacy Options

The `PrivacyOptions` option controls how strictly your sendmail server follows the SMTP protocol by enabling/disabling features in the SMTP protocol. For example, removing support for some functions (`EXPN`, `VRFY`) is a wise idea. It prevents remote attackers from verifying that an account name exists, or expanding an alias list to show the destinations. To use these two privacy options in the `/etc/mail/sendmail.cf` file, one would add the following line:

```
O PrivacyOptions=noexpn,novrfy
```

The complete list of privacy options is shown in Table 13.7.

TABLE 13.7 Available Privacy Options

Privacy Options	Description
`public`	Open access, no restrictions.
`needmailhelo`	Requires that the `HELO`/`EHLO` command be sent before `MAIL`.
`needexpnhelo`	Requires that the `HELO`/`EHLO` command be sent before `EXPN`.
`noexpn`	Disables the `EXPN` command entirely. This prevents alias lists from being expanded.
`needvrfyhelo`	Requires that the `HELO`/`EHLO` command be sent before `VRFY`.
`novrfy`	Disables the `VRFY` command, eliminating the opportunity for a remote user to verify that an account exists.
`restrictmailq`	Restricts the `mailq` queue-listing command to the owner or group of `/var/spool/mqueue` (root).
`restrictqrun`	Restricts the queue runs to the owner of `/var/spool/mqueue` (root).

TABLE 13.7 Continued

Privacy Options	Description
`noreceipts`	Disables return receipt acknowledgement.
`goaway`	Activates all privacy options except for `restrictmailq` and `restrictqrun`.
`authwarnings`	Adds `X-Authentication-Warning` headers to messages.

NOTE

By default, Mac OS X comes with the `authwarnings` option set. If you are customizing the base configuration file, you should either comment out the existing `PrivacyOptions` line and add your own, or add your options to the existing line.

Safe File Environment

Users and administrators can employ the `.forward` and `aliases` files to perform a number of tasks, including forwarding messages to other accounts, piping them to other utilities, and writing to files—such as mail archives. By allowing files to be created anywhere on the file system, sendmail opens itself to being capable of overwriting existing files, directories, and `/dev` device files. The `SafeFileEnvironment` option creates a `chroot` environment where files can be written and does not allow access outside the directory. By living with the inconvenience of only being able to write to a specific directory you can effectively shut sendmail off from being able to write to the rest of your system.

The `SafeFileEnvironment` is specified as an option and a directory, such as `/archive`:

```
O SafeFileEnvironment = /archive
```

You must, of course, also create the directory that sendmail is using as its Safe File Environment. You should also modify `.forward` files and the `aliases` database to use the correct path for any files they may write.

NOTE

In many cases, you may not need to update your alias/forward file paths (although it's still a good idea), because sendmail sets the base of any files being written to that of the `SafeFileEnvironment`. For an installation with `/archive` set, the two paths `/archive/mailinglists/logs` and `/mailinglists/logs` will be equivalent; both will write files to `/archive/mailinglists/logs`.

Aliases and Common Sense

A topic mentioned repeatedly throughout the sendmail configuration features and options is the aliases database. An alias is similar to a `.forward` file in functionality, except it applies to the entire mail server, not just a single account.

Aliases are more of an operational issue than one of security, so we've saved them until last. By default, Mac OS X stores sendmail aliases in the Netinfo `/aliases` directory, accessible through the NetInfo Manager or the `nicl` command-line utility. Although convenient from the Mac-user perspective, most sendmail installations on other systems use the file `/etc/mail/aliases` to store alias information. This file is easier to edit and more convenient for maintenance than the NetInfo directory. To activate the `/etc/mail/aliases` file on your system, edit `/etc/mail/sendmail.cf`, looking for the following line:

```
#O AliasFile=/etc/mail/aliases
```

Uncomment the line, so that it reads as follows:

```
O AliasFile=/etc/mail/aliases
```

Then save the configuration file. After restarting sendmail, you can start using `/etc/mail/aliases` for storing aliases. This file should be owned and writable by root. Opening it to editing by anyone else means risking your system's security. The `aliases` file itself contains the raw data defining account aliases—it is *not* the file that sendmail uses directly. The actual aliases database is stored in `/etc/mail/aliases.db` and you create it by running the `newaliases` command as root each time you make changes to the raw data in `/etc/mail/aliases`.

So, what *does* the alias database do, and how does it relate to security? As mentioned earlier, the alias database is similar to a `.forward` file. It takes incoming messages and directs them to a specific account mailbox, email address, utility, or file. As such, it has the same security risks as a `.forward` file, but encompasses the entire system, rather than a specific user account. By default, Mac OS X includes the following aliases in NetInfo:

administrator	root
dumper	root
MAILER-AGENT	postmaster
MAILER-DAEMON	postmaster
manager	root
nobody	root
postmaster	root

The alias (administrator, MAILER-AGENT, and so on) is paired with a destination—in the case of the default aliases, either root or postmaster. Because postmaster itself is aliased to root, the destination of all the aliases is the root account mailbox.

Within the NetInfo naming conventions the aliases are the Netinfo directory "names," and the aliases are the "members", as shown in Figure 13.1.

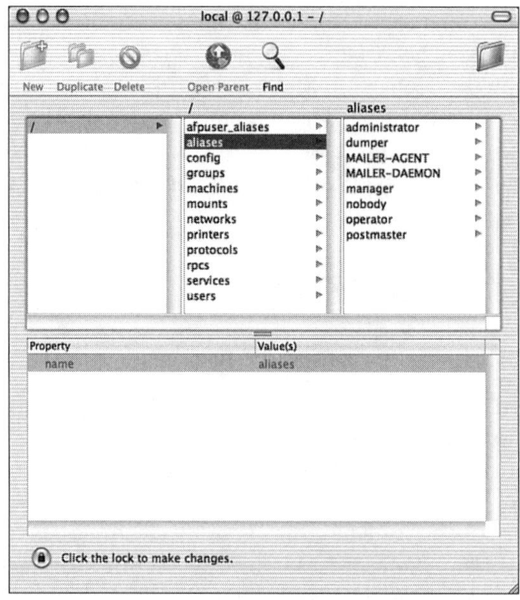

FIGURE 13.1 NetInfo stores the sendmail aliases in the `/aliases` directory.

The `aliases` file follows a similar structure of alias names and destination members: separated by a colon (:), one alias definition per line:

```
<alias name>:    <destination,destination,...>
```

The Netinfo aliases can be rewritten to a standard `/etc/mail/aliases` file like this:

```
administrator:        root
dumper:            root
MAILER-AGENT:        postmaster
MAILER-DAEMON:        postmaster
manager:        root
nobody:            root
postmaster:        root
```

Besides just aliasing a single name to an account (or another alias), you can also add *multiple* destinations to a given alias name, and these destinations don't *have* to be accounts. Alias destinations can be any of the following:

- **Full qualified email addresses**. Besides just local accounts, you can use full email addresses, such as `myaccount@anotheraddress.com`, to forward the mail to another server.

- **File Names**. A file in which to store the contents of the incoming message, useful for archiving incoming messages.
- **Included Destinations**. For creating a simple mailing list that works by redirecting incoming messages to a list of recipients, you can add a special "include" destination by prefixing a fully qualified path to the list of destinations (usually just a list of email addresses) with the text `:include:`. For example, to include a list of email addresses in the file `/etc/mail/mylittlelist` as destinations, I'd use `:include:/etc/mail/mylittlelist` as one of the destinations for my alias.
- **Programs**. Like a `.forward` file, an alias can also use a program as a destination. This is often used for "auto-responders" that deliver help or other information when a message is sent to a given email address.

Because of the capabilities of the `aliases` file (and Netinfo `/aliases`), you should always make sure you know *exactly* what is contained in your system aliases. Often people inherit mail servers with extremely complex alias definitions, some of which may be security risks. Keep in mind that the `SafeFileEnvironment` option and `smrsh` feature both affect the `aliases` database, so activating these options will help protect your aliases from being used for something nefarious.

Updating Your Sendmail Installation

Mac OS X originally shipped with sendmail 8.10.2. Unfortunately, at the same time, the sendmail distribution was progressing through the 8.12.x series. Apple rectified this situation with Mac OS X 10.2 (Jaguar), but the fact remains: Apple's distribution has always lagged the official sendmail release. To keep your system as secure as possible, you should pay close attention to the `http://www.sendmail.org` notices and update your installation manually, if necessary.

CAUTION

Keep in mind that Apple's security updates will likely overwrite your customized sendmail installation, so you should always review the Installer receipts (`/Library/Receipts`) and keep a copy of your configuration files backed up. Alternatively, because Apple's installation uses the standard sendmail file layout, you may wish to create a custom installation layout to avoid having your files overwritten.

If a new version of sendmail becomes available, you can quickly install it on top of the Apple-supplied binary by downloading the latest source distribution (8.12.6 at the time of this writing) and following these instructions.

First unarchive and enter the distribution directory:

```
# tar zxf sendmail.8.12.6.tar.gz
# cd sendmail-8.12.6/
```

CAUTION

It is strongly recommended that you review the PGP signature of the sendmail code as described in the CERT advisory (`http://www.cert.org/advisories/CA-2002-28.html`), MacGPG (`http://macgpg.sourceforge.net/`), or PGP (`http://www.pgp.com/`). In October 2002, a Trojan horse–infected sendmail was widely distributed, forcing users to take additional steps to verify the integrity of their downloads.

Next, use `sh Build` to compile the daemon. Sendmail already "knows" about Darwin/Mac OS X, so the compile should progress smoothly:

```
# sh Build
Making all in:
/Users/jray/Desktop/sendmail-8.12.6/libsm
Configuration: pfx=, os=Darwin, rel=6.1, rbase=6, rroot=6.1,
➥arch=PowerMacintosh, sfx=, variant=optimized
Using M4=/usr/bin/gm4
Creating /Users/jray/Desktop/sendmail-8.12.6/obj.Darwin.6.1.PowerMacintosh/libsm
➥using /Users/jray/Desktop/sendmail-8.12.6/devtools/OS/Darwin
Making dependencies in sendmail-8.12.6/obj.Darwin.6.1.PowerMacintosh/libsm
cp /dev/null sm_os.h
...
```

Finally, type `make install` to install the binaries:

```
# make install
install -c -o root -g wheel -m 444 sendmail.0 /usr/share/man/cat8/sendmail.8
install -c -o root -g wheel -m 444 sendmail.8 /usr/share/man/man8/sendmail.8
install -c -o root -g wheel -m 444 aliases.0 /usr/share/man/cat5/aliases.5
install -c -o root -g wheel -m 444 aliases.5 /usr/share/man/man5/aliases.5
install -c -o root -g wheel -m 444 mailq.0 /usr/share/man/cat1/mailq.1
install -c -o root -g wheel -m 444 mailq.1 /usr/share/man/man1/mailq.1
install -c -o root -g wheel -m 444 newaliases.0 /usr/share/man/cat1/newaliases.1
install -c -o root -g wheel -m 444 newaliases.1 /usr/share/man/man1/newaliases.1
```

You can check your new sendmail installation by typing `sendmail -d` from the command line. You'll need to type `Control-C` to break out:

```
# sendmail -d
Version 8.12.6
```

```
Compiled with: DNSMAP LOG MAP_REGEX MATCHGECOS MIME7TO8 MIME8TO7
               NAMED_BIND NETINET NETINFO NETUNIX NEWDB NIS PIPELINING SCANF
               USERDB XDEBUG
```

Sendmail Resources

Unfortunately, sendmail is a *large* application that requires years to master. If you need to create complex configurations, you should invest in a book dedicated to the topic of managing sendmail servers. Here are a few resources that can help you get started:

- *Sendmail*, by Bryan Costales and Eric Allman, published by O'Reilly. This is the definitive guide to sendmail. Written by Eric Allman, the original sendmail programmer, this book contains every feature, tip, and trick necessary to tweak sendmail for any configuration.
- *Sendmail: Theory and Practice*, by Paul A. Vixie and Frederick M. Avolio. Covers the history and architecture of mail servers, as well as sendmail setup. Useful for gaining a perspective on sendmail and its place as an Internet server.
- `http://www.sendmail.org`. The home of your sendmail server software. Updates, FAQs, and documentation can be found here.
- `http://www.sendmail.net`. Discussion and articles on the implementation and maintenance of sendmail.
- `http://www.sendmail.org/%7Eca/email/misc.html`. Claus ABmann's email software documentation, tips, and links.

Postfix as an Alternative

Sendmail is a monster of an MTA. Rarely is it necessary for an organization to use sendmail for the advanced (and remarkably obscure) features. More frequently one would be better off installing an alternative server, such as Postfix (`http://www.postfix.org/`). To quote the author:

> Postfix attempts to be fast, easy to administer, and secure, while at the same time being sendmail compatible enough to not upset existing users. Thus, the outside has a sendmail-ish flavor, but the inside is completely different.

Many people are hesitant to move away from mainstream software such as sendmail, but Postfix has gained a following as one of the easiest and most stable Unix MTAs available. Better yet, it installs as a drop-in sendmail replacement, meaning that any other software or scripts that rely on sendmail (such as CGI scripts) will continue to function without additional modifications.

Postfix supports Mac OS X, integrates with the `Netinfo:/aliases` map, and is much easier to configure than sendmail. If you don't mind a few minutes compiling, you can be rid of sendmail for good.

Of course, Postfix isn't without fault. Before you start the installation, it's a good idea to take a look at the list (the *short* list) of exploits for Postfix.

Recent Postfix Exploits

As with sendmail, two kinds of exploits can potentially affect Postfix: local and remote attacks. Strangely enough, there are two reported Postfix exploits, one local and one remote. Unlike sendmail, the known Postfix exploits are minor in the severity and occur only in extreme conditions.

Logfile DOS Attack

Versions of Postfix prior to 0.0.19991231pl11-2 could potentially be targets of a DOS attack aimed at filling drive space. Early versions of Postfix kept extensive SMTP debugging logs. Attackers could create and drop connections in an attempt to overflow the log and disrupt server operations. There are no known occurrences of this attack taking place. For more information visit `http://online.securityfocus.com/advisories/3722`. Because we will be installing a more recent version of Postfix, this will not be an issue with our installation. (CVE: CVE-2001-0894)

`sudo` MTA Invocation

On some Linux systems, an error existed in the `sudo` package which could be exploited by local users. Attempting to invoke `sudo` would result in an error message being generated and Postfix being started SUID root to deliver the message without the proper environment settings. This does not affect Mac OS X, and anyway, it was easily fixed by removing or upgrading `sudo`. More information is available at `http://online.securityfocus.com/advisories/3799` (CVE: CVE-2001-0279).

Although Postfix is obviously a less widely used MTA than sendmail, the lack of serious problems is still very telling. Over time, as with any software, new exploits will be found, but, if peace of mind is of any concern to you, I recommend following through with the replacement of sendmail.

Installing Postfix

Postfix installation under Mac OS X is verging on trivial. The Postfix software includes several scripts for everything from backing up your sendmail installation to adding the necessary users to Netinfo. This is an excellent example of the open source community's embracing of Mac OS X.

Preparing the System

First, download the latest version Postfix from `ftp://postfix.webweaver.net/official/postfix-1.1.8.tar.gz`. Be sure that you find the "correct" latest version—Postfix seems to have changed numbering sequences recently. At the time of this writing, 1.1.8 was the most recent.

Unarchive the software and `cd` into the software installation directory:

```
% tar zxf postfix-1.1.8.tar.gz
% cd postfix-1.1.8/
```

Next, you'll need to back up your existing sendmail installation in case you want or need to go back to the original software. The `auxiliary/MacOSX` directory contains a script called `backup-sendmail-binaries`, which, as its name suggests, does just that. You'll want to either `su` to root or use `sudo` to execute the rest of the installation:

```
# cd auxiliary/MacOSX
# ./backup-sendmail-binaries
```

NOTE

If you'd like to back up the sendmail binaries by hand, the files you want to copy are `/usr/sbin/sendmail`, `/usr/bin/newaliases`, and `/usr/bin/mailq`.

Now, it's time to add the users and groups necessary to run Postfix. There are two groups (`postfix` and `maildrop`) and a user account (`postfix`) that must be created before you install Postfix. The script `niscript` (also located in the `auxiliary/MacOSX` directory) will do it all for you.

```
# ./niscript
This script massages your netinfo database.  This can severely break
your system. If your netinfo database breaks, you get to keep the parts.

No Warranty. Really.

This script tries to create two groups (if they do not already exist):
- postfix
- maildrop
and tries to create a user (if it does not already exist)
- postfix
which is member of group postfix.

Will create postfix as gid 88
Will create maildrop as gid 89
Will create postfix as uid 88
```

NOTE

The postfix and maildrop UID and GIDs are not hardcoded to 88 and 89 as shown in the example. The script automatically chooses unused numbers for you.

Finally, cd back into the main source distribution directory and compile the software with a simple make:

```
# cd ../..
# make
make -f Makefile.in MAKELEVEL= Makefiles
set -e; for i in src/util src/global src/dns src/master src/postfix
➥src/smtpstone src/sendmail src/error src/pickup src/cleanup src/smtpd
➥src/local src/lmtp src/trivial-rewrite src/qmgr src/smtp src/bounce
➥src/pipe src/showq src/postalias src/postcat src/postconf src/postdrop
➥src/postkick src/postlock src/postlog src/postmap src/postqueue
➥src/postsuper src/nqmgr src/qmqpd src/spawn src/flush src/virtual; do \
 (set -e; echo "[$i]"; cd $i; rm -f Makefile; \
 make -f Makefile.in Makefile MAKELEVEL=) || exit 1; \
done;
[src/util]
...
cc  -g -O -I. -I../../include -DRHAPSODY5 -I.. -c unknown.c
cc  -g -O -I. -I../../include -DRHAPSODY5 -I.. -o virtual virtual.o
➥mailbox.o recipient.o deliver_attr.o maildir.o unknown.
➥o ../../lib/libmaster.a ../../lib/libglobal.a ../../lib/libutil.a
➥   -flat_namespace
cp virtual ../../libexec
```

Basic Setup

After Postfix has successfully compiled, the next step is to run the install script. It prompts you for various settings (for most, the default answer will suffice). Type make install to run the install script (the output of which is summarized for the sake of brevity):

```
# make install

Please specify the prefix for installed file names. This is useful
if you are building ready-to-install packages for distribution to
other machines.
install_root: [/]
```

```
Please specify a directory for scratch files while installing
Postfix. You must have write permission in this directory.
tempdir: [/Users/jray/Desktop/book code/postfix-1.1.8] /tmp

Please specify the destination directory for installed Postfix
configuration files.
config_directory: [/etc/postfix]

Please specify the destination directory for installed Postfix
daemon programs. This directory should not be in the command search
path of any users.
daemon_directory: [/usr/libexec/postfix]

Please specify the destination directory for installed Postfix
administrative commands. This directory should be in the command
search path of adminstrative users.
command_directory: [/usr/sbin]

Please specify the destination directory for Postfix queues.
queue_directory: [/var/spool/postfix]

Please specify the full destination pathname for the installed
Postfix sendmail command. This is the Sendmail-compatible mail
posting interface.
sendmail_path: [/usr/sbin/sendmail]

Please specify the full destination pathname for the installed
Postfix newaliases command. This is the Sendmail-compatible command
to build alias databases for the Postfix local delivery agent.
newaliases_path: [/usr/bin/newaliases]

Please specify the full destination pathname for the installed
Postfix mailq command. This is the Sendmail-compatible mail queue
listing command.
mailq_path: [/usr/bin/mailq]

Please specify the owner of the Postfix queue. Specify an account
with numerical user ID and group ID values that are not used by
any other accounts on the system.
mail_owner: [postfix]
```

```
Please specify the group for mail submission and for queue management
commands. Specify a group name with a numerical group ID that is
not shared with other accounts, not even with the Postfix mail_owner
account. You can no longer specify "no" here.
setgid_group: [postdrop] maildrop

Please specify the destination directory for the Postfix on-line
manual pages. You can no longer specify "no" here.
manpage_directory: [/usr/local/man]

Please specify the destination directory for the Postfix sample
configuration files.
sample_directory: [/etc/postfix]

Please specify the destination directory for the Postfix README
files. Specify "no" if you do not want to install these files.
readme_directory: [no] /etc/postfix/readme
...

    Warning: you still need to edit myorigin/mydestination/mynetworks
    parameter settings in /etc/postfix/main.cf.

    See also http://www.postfix.org/faq.html for information about
    dialup sites or about sites inside a firewalled network.

    BTW: Check your /etc/aliases file and be sure to set up aliases
    that send mail for root and postmaster to a real person, then
    run /usr/bin/newaliases.
```

After the install has completed, you should create an archive of the Postfix installation. This will enable you to swap Postfix/sendmail at will by using the included Postfix scripts. Change back into the `auxiliary/MacOSX` directory and run the `backup-postfix-binaries`.

```
# ./backup-postfix-binaries
```

Finally, activate the Postfix installation by using the `activate-postfix` script:

```
# ./activate-postfix
```

This surprisingly useful script automatically does everything you need to finish setting up the installation. The `/System/Library/StartupItems/Sendmail` startup item is automatically disabled while a `/System/Library/StartupItems/Postfix` item is created. You can reverse this process by using the script `activate-sendmail`.

Basic Host Settings

When you reboot your Mac OS X computer, Postfix starts. (You can also start it at any time by typing `/usr/sbin/postfix start`.) Unfortunately, you need to make a few more settings before the software will run successfully.

Almost all the Postfix configuration you'll perform is done in the `/etc/postfix/main.cf`. All options in `main.cf` consist of lines in the form:

```
<setting>=<value>[,<value>]
```

where *<setting>* is one of the Postfix directives, and *<value>* is a simple setting (such as a hostname, timeout value, etc), a path to a hash file, such as `hash:/etc/aliases.db`, or, in the case of Mac OS X, a NetInfo path, such as `netinfo:/aliases`. In some cases, lists of values can be used, separated by commas.

WHAT IS A HASH FILE?

A hash file is a binary lookup table that holds key and value pairs. To create a hash file, use either the `postmap` or `postalias` commands. Alias files, for example, contain *<key>* and *<value>* fields, separated by a colon (:) and whitespace, such as this example `/etc/aliases` file:

```
postmaster: root
operator: jray
admin: jray
```

All other hash files simply contain *<key>* and *<value>* fields separated by whitespace. The `postalias` command works exclusively on alias files, whereas `postmap` is used to generate all other hashes.

To use the Postfix utilities to generate hash files from the corresponding text file, type either `postmap <text file>` or `postalias <alias text file>`. Within a few seconds, a binary hash is created in the same location as the original file, with the extension `.db`.

Edit the `/etc/postfix/main.cf` file now. To get up and running quickly, you need to tell Postfix what your server's hostname and domain are by using the `mydomain` and `myhostname` directives.

Look for the `myhostname` and `mydomain` lines, both of which are initially commented out with the # character. Uncomment both of the lines and change them to accurately reflect the state of your server and network. For example, my server is `mail.poisontooth.com` on the domain `poisontooth.com`. Thus, my `mail.cf` file reads:

```
myhostname = mail.poisontooth.com
mydomain = poisontooth.com
```

NOTE

After assignment, these setting variables (`myhostname`, `mydomain`, `etc`) can by referenced with a dollar sign (`$`) in other configuration directives.

Your Postfix server should now be ready to run. To verify the configuration, run `/usr/sbin/postfix check`. This checks for errors in your setup. Start the server itself by rebooting or typing `/usr/sbin/postfix start` as root.

```
# /usr/sbin/postfix start
postfix/postfix-script: starting the Postfix mail system
```

Verify that Postfix is running by Telneting to port 25 on your server computer. Use the `QUIT` SMTP command to exit:

```
# telnet localhost 25
Trying 127.0.0.1...
Connected to localhost.poisontooth.com.
Escape character is '^]'.
220 client1.poisontooth.com ESMTP Postfix
QUIT
```

Assuming your system responds similarly, everything has gone according to plan and you're ready to fine-tune the Postfix system. For simple setups, this may be as far as you need to go. Postfix automatically configures itself to relay only for those machines on the same class subnet to which you're connected. All others are denied.

Protecting Postfix

When you changed the `myhostname` and `mydomain` directives a moment ago, you edited two out of hundreds of configuration options available for use in the `/etc/postfix/main.cf` file. Thankfully, the Postfix installation includes a number of sample configuration files with documentation inside the `/etc/postfix` directory. These files are *not* meant to be used as drop-in replacements for the standard `main.cf` file; they simply document and provide options that you can use *in* `main.cf`. For example, the `sample-aliases.cf` contains the instructions you need to add an alias map to Postfix. Table 13.8 contains a number of settings you may find useful.

TABLE 13.8 Common Postfix `main.cf` settings

Setting	Description
`myhostname =` *`<Postfix server name>`*	Sets *unqualified* hostname for the machine running the mail server.
`mydomain =` *`<Postfix server domain>`*	The domain of the Postfix server.
`inet_interfaces =` *`<all|hostname|ip,...>`*	A list of the network interfaces on which Postfix will be active. By default it works on all active interfaces.
`mydestination =` *`<domain name, ...>`*	A list of domain names and hostnames for which Postfix will accept email. By default, Postfix accepts email for `$myhostname` and `$myhostname.localhost`. If your server accepts email for the entire domain, you should add `$mydomain` and `$myhostname.$mydomain`.

TABLE 13.8 Continued

<table>
<tr><th>Setting</th><th>Description</th></tr>
<tr><td>mynetworks_style = <class|subnet|host></td><td>Sets how Postfix determines what portion of the local network it should trust for relaying. By default, the local subnet is trusted. To trust clients in the same class, use the class setting. Finally, to trust only the local computer, use host.</td></tr>
<tr><td>mynetworks = <network/netmask,...></td><td>Used in lieu of mynetwork_style, mynetworks sets a list of network addresses that should be considered local clients. Specified in the format network/netmask, such as 10.0.1.1/24. This can also be set to a hash file, or any of the supported Postfix table lookup methods, including a Netinfo path.</td></tr>
<tr><td>relay_domains = <host|domain|file></td><td>A list of domains for which Postfix will relay mail. The list can consist of host or domain names, files containing host names, or lookup tables (such as hash tables or Netinfo paths). These are in addition to the mydestination and mynetworks settings.</td></tr>
<tr><td>local_recipient_maps = <user lookup tables></td><td>A list of lookup tables for usernames that will be accepted as local for the mail server. By default, this is set to the local user accounts and any alias lookup tables that exist.</td></tr>
<tr><td>alias_maps = <alias lookup tables></td><td>One or more lookup tables that contain the alias lists for the database. You may want to consider using hash:/etc/aliases, netinfo:/aliases—which corresponds to the defaults for sendmail. Remember, postalias is used to regenerate the alias hash file.</td></tr>
<tr><td>home_mailbox = <mail box path></td><td>The path to the local mailbox files. Mac OS X users should use the default /var/mail.</td></tr>
<tr><td>smtpd_banner = $myhostname <banner text></td><td>Sets banner text to be displayed when a host connects. RFC requirements state that the hostname must come at the start of the banner ($myhostname).</td></tr>
<tr><td>local_destination_ concurrency_limit = <limit integer></td><td>A limit on the number of local simultaneous deliveries that can be made to a single user. The default is 2.</td></tr>
<tr><td>default_destination_ concurrency_limit = <limit integer></td><td>The number of simultaneous connections that Postfix will make to deliver mail. The default is 10. Keeping this number low can help protect against inappropriate use of your server if it is compromised. It is unlikely that your server will ever need to make 10 simultaneous connections to a single domain at a time.</td></tr>
<tr><td>disable_vrfy_command = <yes|no></td><td>Disables the VRFY SMTP command, which can be used by spammers to verify that an account exists on the server.</td></tr>
<tr><td>smtpd_recipient_limit = <limit integer></td><td>The maximum number of recipients that will be accepted per message. Keeping this limit low makes your server unusable for mass spam.</td></tr>
<tr><td>smtpd_timeout = <timeout s|m|h|d|w></td><td>The timeout period to wait for a response from an SMTP client (in seconds, minutes, hours, days, or weeks).</td></tr>
<tr><td>strict_rfc821_ envelopes = <yes|no></td><td>Sets a requirement for RFC821-compliant messages. If set to "yes," MAIL FROM and RCPT TO addresses must be specified within <>.</td></tr>
<tr><td>smtpd_helo_required = <yes|no></td><td>Determines whether postfix will require the HELO or EHLO SMTP greeting at the start of a connection.</td></tr>
</table>

TABLE 13.8 Continued

Setting	Description
`smtpd_client_ restrictions = < restrictions>`	Used to fine-tune the restrictions on the postfix clients and can handle everything from real-time blacklisting to access control lists.
`smtpd_helo_ restrictions = <restrictions>`	Used to fine-tune the restrictions on what machines are permitted within a HELO or EHLO greeting.
`smtpd_sender_ restrictions = <restrictions>`	Used to fine-tune the restrictions on what machines are permitted within a MAIL FROM address.
`smtpd_recipient_ restrictions = <restrictions>`	Used to fine-tune the restrictions on what machines are permitted within a RCPT TO address.

Using `smtpd restrictions`

Because the `smtp_restrictions` directives are a bit more complex than what can be described in a table column, we'll provide more detailed coverage now. If you remember the sendmail configuration, the `FEATURE(access_db)` and `FEATURE(dnsbl)` macros were used to set up a relay control list and blacklisting. In Postfix, these features (and several others) are activated by `smtp restrictions`, but rather than simply being compared against the mail sender these access controls can be applied against clients, HELO/EHLO headers, and MAIL FROM/RCPT TO addresses.

Four different types of restrictions are considered here: client, helo, sender, and recipient (as defined in Table 13.8). They all share some common restriction options, so the rather than list them separately, Table 13.9 combines them.

TABLE 13.9 Common Options for Setting the `smtpd` Restrictions

Restriction	Description	Use In
`reject_unknown_client`	Reject the client if the hostname is unknown.	`client, helo, sender, recipient`
`reject_invalid_hostname`	Reject the connection if the HELO/ELHO hostname is invalid.	`helo, sender, recipient`
`reject_unknown_hostname`	Reject the connection if the HELO/ELHO hostname does not have a matching DNS A or MX record.	`helo, sender, recipient`
`reject_unknown_ sender_domain`	Reject if the HELO/ELHO sender does not have a matching DNS A or MX record.	`sender`
`reject_non_fqdn_sender`	Reject sender addresses that are not fully qualified.	`recipient, sender`

TABLE 13.9 Continued

Restriction	Description	Use In
`reject_non_fqdn _recipient`	Reject recipient addresses that are not fully qualified.	`recipient`
`check_client_access` *<lookup table>:<path>*	Restricts based on a lookup table that consists of key and value pairs where the key is a hostname, domain, or address, and the value is REJECT or OK.	`client`, `recipient`
`check_helo_access` *<lookup table>:<path>*	Restricts based on a lookup table that consists of key and value pairs where the key is a hostname, domain, or address, and the value is REJECT or OK.	`helo`, `recipient`
`check_sender_access` *<lookup table>:<path>*	Restricts based on a lookup table that consists of key and value pairs where the key is a hostname, domain, or address, and the value is REJECT or OK.	`sender`, `recipient`
`check_recipient_access` *<lookup table>:<path>*	Restricts based on a lookup table that consists of key and value pairs where the key is a hostname, domain, or address, and the value is REJECT or OK.	`recipient`
`reject_maps_rbl`	Rejects the connection, message, or so on, based on blacklisting DNS.	`client`, `helo`, `sender`, `recipient`

You may want to check out the `sample-smtpd.cf` file that came with Postfix. This is a list of the more common (and useful) restrictions, but several more are documented in the sample file. Out of the box, Postfix is easier to work with than sendmail, but there are still hundreds of potential settings—beyond what can easily be documented in a single chapter.

Postfix Resources

For more information about Postfix and its operation and configuration, look into these resources:

- *Postfix*, by Richard Blum, Sams Publishing. The only printed reference specifically for Postfix, this book covers the use and configuration of the Postfix MTA in an easy-to-follow format.
- `http://www.postfix.net`. The Postfix homepage provides links to the latest software release, FAQs, and supporting documentation.

- `http://www.deja.com/group/mailing.postfix.users`. An archive of the Postfix mailing list. (For information on subscribing to the list itself, see the Postfix home page.)
- `http://www.bsdtoday.com/2000/September/Features274.html`. A BSD Today article on Postfix compilation, setup, and configuration.

As the popularity of the MTA increases, additional resources will likely become available, but for now, the selection is quite limited.

Delivering Mail—UW IMAP

An MTA is only half of a mail server. Unless the server is also the client computer, or you plan to use local mail clients such as pine or elm, you need to provide delivery services for clients to access the stored mail spools. To handle delivery for messages received by the SMTP system, you can install the University of Washington's `imapd` (UW IMAP) software. This server can deliver to both POP and IMAP clients, and is simple to compile and install on Mac OS X.

Recent Exploits

Because your system doesn't come with UW IMAP installed, you need to install a version. Obviously you'll install the latest version, which (equally obviously) won't have any exploits at the time you download and install it. That, however, doesn't mean that its past has been squeaky clean; in fact, a number of exploits have affected the software in the past.

`AUTHENTICATE` buffer overflow

The UW IMAP server has been subject to a number of buffer overflow problems. One of the most notable was the `AUTHENTICATE` command overflow. Used during the login process, IMAP's `AUTHENTICATE` command is used to specify the authentication method that the IMAP client uses. When the buffer for `AUTHENTICATE` suffers a specific overrun, it allows remote attackers to send arbitrary machine code to the server, which would then be executed. Previously, a similar exploit had been found that functioned in much the same way, but was accessed through the `LOGIN` IMAP function.

These exploits are extremely serious because the server process executes with root permissions, and the "injected" exploit code runs as part of the already active process, making it difficult to detect. One positive note is that the existing exploit code is (as expected) x86-centric. This isn't saying that the exploit isn't possible on the PPC architecture, but rather that it would need to be reworked to affect an early IMAP server running on Mac OS X. For more information, visit `http://www.yale.edu/its/security/archive/unix-sysadmins-security/9807/msg00008.html`.

Other Buffer Overflows

The last reported remote root exploit for UW IMAP was in the late 90s. Unfortunately, since that time, several other buffer overflows have been reported to (or by) the authors, as late as mid-2001. These are not root exploits, yet still pose a risk of allowing remote users to execute code on the affected server. For more information, see `http://online.securityfocus.com/archive/1/190251`.

IMAP and POP Protocol Exploits

Unfortunately, even with a perfectly healthy UW IMAP, your mail server is *far* from secure. As you've learned repeatedly throughout the book, *many* common TCP/IP protocols are insecure and open for sniffing. Web, FTP, and Mail protocols make up a large portion of the Internet's traffic. None of these, in their default states, offer any sort of protection from a network sniffer.

For example, POP-based email is the most popular form of mail delivery online. Yet the exchange of username and password isn't protected at all:

```
% telnet mail.mac.com 110
Trying 204.179.120.64...
Connected to mail.mac.com.
Escape character is '^]'.
+OK Netscape Messaging Multiplexor ready
USER johnray
+OK password required for user johnray
PASS Gringle121
+OK Maildrop ready
```

In this sample POP connection with `mail.mac.com`, I connect to port 110, provide my username and password in clear text, and I'm logged in. Similarly, IMAP servers also support cleartext passwords:

```
% telnet mail.mac.com 143
Trying 204.179.120.64...
Connected to mail.mac.com.
Escape character is '^]'.
* OK Netscape Messaging Multiplexor ready
00001 login johnray Gringle121
00001 OK User logged in
```

Sniffing this information on `mac.com` compromises my email. Sniffing a username and password on your server's email potentially compromises your account—and presumably *you* have root privileges.

One might think, "Eh, so what?" Who is going to sit around all day and watch network traffic waiting to see a username and a password? The answer is *no one*.

Instead, they'll use one of dozens (or perhaps dozens of dozens) of available network sniffers that are programmed with basic knowledge of common protocols and can simply watch for username/password pairs and record them to a file. One such software package, available for Mac OS X, is ettercap (`http://ettercap.sourceforge.net/`). You'll learn more about this in Chapter 7, "Eavesdropping and Snooping for Information: Sniffers and Scanners." For now, understand that the basic mail protocols are not secure. Not without some additional help.

SSL and UW IMAP

To eliminate some of the threat of sniffing account passwords directly from IMAP and POP traffic, you can create the SSL-wrapped equivalents of these services by using OpenSSL. SSL (Secure Sockets Layer) protects against sniffing by encrypting all traffic moving across the network. Developed by Netscape for use on the Web, SSL has been adopted as an industry standard for encrypting a number of protocols—in this case, IMAP and POP. For an easy-to-understand introduction to SSL, visit `http://developer.netscape.com/docs/manuals/security/sslin/contents.htm`.

Outlook, Entourage, and Mac OS X's Mail application all support SSL-encrypted mail traffic natively—just check an SSL check box. You can find this option by clicking the Options button in the Account Information tab within account preferences in Mac OS X's Mail, as seen in Figure 13.2.

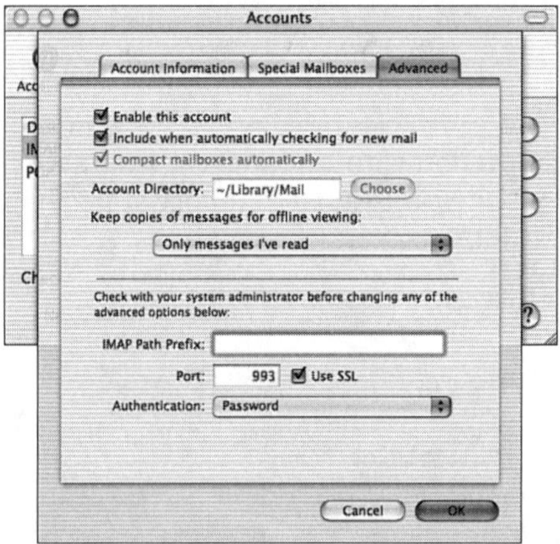

FIGURE 13.2 SSL is supported natively in Mac OS X's Mail.app.

The SSL-enabled versions of IMAP and POP are referred to as IMAPS and POPS, and operate by using TCP from ports 993 and 995, respectively. Conveniently, these services (and their nonencrypted counterparts) are already listed in Mac OS X's `/etc/services` file, so you're ready to configure and install UW IMAP.

Compiling and Installing

Installation and setup of your IMAPS/POPS server is fast and painless. Fetch the latest version of UW IMAP from the University of Washington's FTP site, `ftp://ftp.cac.washington.edu/imap/`.

Uncompress and unarchive the `imap.tar.gz` file, then `cd` into the source directory:

```
$ tar zxf imap-2002.DEV.SNAP-0205.tar.gz
$ cd imap-2002.DEV.SNAP-0205032002
```

Before compiling, you need to make a few important changes to the source code. Unfortunately, UW IMAP is not very "user-friendly" for setting up, so you need to do all configuration by editing the `src/osdep/unix/env_unix.c` file. This isn't difficult, but is atypical for most modern Unix software distributions.

Open the `env_unix.c` file in your favorite text editor now.

Look for the line reading

```
static char *mailsubdir = NIL;  /* mail subdirectory name */
```

and change it to

```
static char *mailsubdir = "Library/Mail/Mailboxes";  /* mail subdir name */
```

This sets the IMAP server to use your account's standard `Mailboxes` directory for storing IMAP mailboxes.

Now it's compile time. Make sure that you're within the root level of the UW IMAP distribution. Because you want to compile for Mac OS X with SSL support built in, you need to provide two options to the `make` command: `osx` and `SSLTYPE=unix`:

```
% make osx SSLTYPE=unix
Applying an process to sources...
tools/an "ln -s" src/c-client c-client
tools/an "ln -s" src/ansilib c-client
tools/an "ln -s" src/charset c-client
tools/an "ln -s" src/osdep/unix c-client
tools/an "ln -s" src/mtest mtest
tools/an "ln -s" src/ipopd ipopd
tools/an "ln -s" src/imapd imapd
ln -s tools/an .
make build EXTRACFLAGS='' EXTRALDFLAGS='' EXTRADRIVERS='mbox'
➥EXTRAAUTHENTICATORS='' PASSWDTYPE=std SSLTYPE=unix EXTRASPECIALS='' BUILDTYPE=osx
...
```

Following the compile, the server binaries will be stored in `imapd/imapd` and `popd/ipop3d`. You should copy these to `/usr/local/libexec`:

```
# cp popd/ipop3d /usr/local/libexec
# cp imapd/imapd /usr/local/libexec
```

WU IMAP is now installed, but you still need to make a few more configuration changes for the `inetd/xinetd`.

Launching Through `inetd/xinetd`

Chapter 11 provided detailed information on setting up services to run under `inetd` and `xinetd`. Because you have an entire chapter dedicated to this, we won't be providing the complete instructions. Table 13.10 contains the parameters you need for setting up the services with either of these Internet daemons.

TABLE 13.10 Parameters for Configuring `inetd` or `xinetd`

Service Name	Socket Type	Protocol	wait / nowait	User	Server Process	Arguments
imaps	stream	tcp	nowait	root	/usr/libexec/tcpd	/usr/local/libexec/imapd
pops	stream	tcp	nowait	root	/usr/libexec/tcpd	/usr/local/libexec/ipop3d

NOTE

This assumes that you'll also want to use TCP Wrappers with the IMAPS and POPS services, which isn't necessary under `xinetd`. Keep in mind that you need to add similar entries for IMAPS/POP if you want to run cleartext versions of the services.

In addition, there is no need to provide access to both IMAPS and POPS unless required by your users. If you don't need one or the other, don't add it.

Creating a Certificate

The IMAPS and POPS services require two certificates be installed: `imapd.pem` and `ipop3d.pem`. We're going to look at creating self-signed certificates. Production servers should consider purchasing certificates from a qualified CA.

For the IMAPS server, issue the following command at a shell prompt:

```
# openssl req -new -x509 -nodes -out imapd.pem -keyout imapd.pem -days 3650
```

This creates a new self-signed certificate named `imapd.pem` with a 10-year expiration within the current directory. You should also create a `ipop3d.pem` certificate if adding support for POPS. Both of these certificates must then be copied or moved to `/System/Library/OpenSSL/certs` or `/usr/local/ssl/certs` if you're using a fresh install of OpenSSL.

```
# cp *.pem /System/Library/OpenSSL/certs
```

If you haven't created a certificate with `openssl` before, the following is a sample of the questions you will be asked during setup. For your mail server, the critical piece of information is the Common Name. This value should be set to the hostname to which users will connect when using their email clients. In this example, I've chosen to use the IP address `10.0.1.101`. If I were using this certificate with real clients, they would need to connect to the mail server based on this IP address.

```
Generating a 1024 bit RSA private key
.........++++++
...................................................................++++++
writing new private key to 'imapd.pem'
-----
You are about to be asked to enter information that will be incorporated
into your certificate request.
What you are about to enter is what is called a Distinguished Name or a DN.
There are quite a few fields but you can leave some blank.
For some fields there will be a default value.
If you enter '.', the field will be left blank.
-----
Country Name (2 letter code) [AU]:US
State or Province Name (full name) [Some-State]:OH
Locality Name (eg, city) []:Dublin
Organization Name (eg, company) [Internet Widgits Pty Ltd]:Poisontooth
Organizational Unit Name (eg, section) []:
Common Name (eg, YOUR name) []:10.0.1.101
Email Address []:
```

After you've created the certificates and configured the Internet daemon entries, you can restart `inetd/xinetd` to start using UW IMAP (`kill -HUP` *<process ID>*). The server should be ready for use.

Be sure that you configure your email clients to use SSL or they won't be able to connect (unless you've also added support for straight `imap` and `pop`).

Summary

This concludes this brief look at mail servers. Although we've tried to pack as much information into a single chapter as possible, this is not meant to be a replacement for books dedicated to setting up and configuring sendmail. Security requirements differ from server to server. Some users may need nothing more than one or two autoresponders; others may run email servers with hundreds of accounts. Who has access to your machine and what they're using it for makes a big difference in how you approach MTA security.

No matter *how* you choose to configure your server, keep in mind that many security holes come from permission problems. Sendmail, no matter how carefully configured, becomes a security nightmare without the proper file and directory permissions. (As a rule of thumb, make sure that no MTA configuration files are group writable.) If you've been meticulous while setting up your server, you're already well on your way to a secure mail server.

14

Remote Access: Secure Shell, VNC, Timbuktu, Apple Remote Desktop

IN THIS CHAPTER

- What Is SSH?
- SSH Vulnerabilities
- Vulnerabilities in telnet and rlogin
- Activating SSH
- Advanced SSH Features
- GUI Access Methods

Remote access is a way of using your machine without being at the console. OS X ships with services that allow remote access—such as `telnet`, `rlogin` and `ftp`—disabled. Unlike many other flavors of Unix. OS X in its default state is more secure as a result. However, as connectivity becomes more important to you, you may be interested in being able to remotely access your OS X machine. This chapter examines how to do this as securely as possible.

What Is SSH?

SSH, also known as secure shell, is a protocol for secure remote login, file transfer, and tunneling. It can be used as a secure replacement for the more familiar telnet and rlogin protocols without any noticeable difference to the user. For file transfers, SSH can be used as a secure replacement for `rcp` and `ftp`. Finally, SSH can be used to tunnel traffic over an encrypted channel. In other words, SSH can be used to transport otherwise insecure traffic more securely. For example, it can be used to encrypt the username and password data transmitted by `ftp`.

SSH is a more secure protocol than the traditional protocols because it encrypts traffic. The other protocols transmit data in cleartext, which, as you know, can then be captured by packet sniffers.

There are two versions of the SSH protocol: SSH1 and SSH2. As you might have guessed, SSH1 is the original version, and SSH2 is a more recent development. The SSH2 protocol is the version currently being developed, although fixes are occasionally released for SSH1 because it is still in use. It seems like it's a good idea to keep both around: When critical bugs are discovered in one, a typical fallback is to recommend switching it off and using only the other, until the bugs are repaired.

The SSH protocol was first developed by Tatu Ylonen in 1995. In that same year he also founded SSH Communications Security, and currently serves as its president and CEO. SSH Communications Security offers commercial and free versions of their SSH server and client products. The company originally sold products through another company called Data Fellows, which is now F-Secure. F-Secure has marketing rights for SSH and also sells SSH servers and clients. Both companies currently work on further developing SSH2.

There is also an SSH Open Source project called OpenSSH. This is the SSH distribution that Apple includes with Mac OS X. OpenSSH shares a common history with OpenBSD, which is the BSD variant most concerned with security above all else. It is also based upon Tatu Ylonen's early SSH code. OpenSSH provides support for both SSH1 and SSH2 protocols. There is usually little noticeable difference between using an SSH server from one of the companies and using the OpenSSH package.

Because the OpenSSH package is the package included with Mac OS X, it is the package on which we will concentrate our discussion. The package supports these encryption algorithms: DES, 3DES, Blowfish, CAST-128, Arcfour, AES, RSA, and DSA.

NOTE

If you are interested in the underlying specifics of the SSH protocol, check the Internet drafts of the Secure Shell (secsh) Working Group of the IETF at `http://www.ietf.org/ids.by.wg/secsh.html`. A good one to start with is the draft on the overall architecture of the SSH protocol.

SSH Vulnerabilities

Although more secure than traditional protocols, SSH is not without vulnerabilities. The various SSH packages have some vulnerabilities in common and some that are unique to the distribution. We will look at only some of the vulnerabilities that have affected OpenSSH since the introduction of Mac OS X. For more details on OpenSSH security, see OpenSSH's security page at `http://www.openssh.com/security.html`.

- Zlib Compression Library Heap Vulnerability (CVE-2002-0059, CA-2002-07, Bugtraq ID 4267)

  A bug in the decompression algorithm of the `zlib` compression library (version 1.1.3 and earlier) can cause problems with dynamically allocated memory. An attacker can take advantage of this vulnerability in programs that link to or use the `zlib` compression library. Potential impacts include denial of service, information leakage, or execution of arbitrary code with permissions of the vulnerable program. So far there are no reports of this vulnerability being exploited.

This vulnerability is not an OpenSSH-specific vulnerability, but because OpenSSH can be affected, it is included here. Because this vulnerability appears in programs that link to or use the `zlib` compression library, it affects many programs and many operating systems. The solution is to get a patch from your vendor or download the latest version of `zlib` from `http://www.zlib.org/`. Then, where possible, recompile any programs that use the `zlib` compression library. However, depending on how they use the `zlib` compression library, you might not able to fix the problem yourself.

Mac OS X is reportedly not affected by this exploit. However, if you look for `libz` on a Mac OS X system, you will see files that contain 1.1.3 in the name. We assume that Apple has taken care of this problem without changing any filenames. The `libz` included with Mac OS X 10.2 is definitely different than that included with Mac OS X 10.1 and earlier. You can try to update `libz` yourself. If you succeed, you can then try to update OpenSSH. Other packages mentioned in this chapter that can be affected by this vulnerability include TightVNC and VNCThing.

- Trojan Horse OpenSSH Distributions (CA-2002-24, BugTraq ID 5374, CAN-1999-0661)

  Although a Trojan horse distribution of a package is not a vulnerability inherent in a software package itself, Trojan horse versions of software do exist, even for security software. From July 30–August 1, 2002, Trojan horse versions of OpenSSH 3.2.2p1, 3.4p1, and 3.4 were distributed on the OpenBSD FTP server and may have propagated to other FTP servers via the mirroring process.

  The Trojan horse versions execute code when the software is compiled. The software connects to a fixed remote server on 6667/tcp, and opens a shell running as the user who compiled OpenSSH.

- Challenge Response Handling Vulnerabilities (CAN-2002-0639, CAN-2002-0640, CA-2002-18, BugTraq ID 5093)

  Versions of OpenSSH between 2.9.3 and 3.3 have two vulnerabilities involving the challenge-response authentication. One is an integer overflow in the number of responses received during the challenge-response authentication. The other vulnerability is a buffer overflow in the challenge-response authentication. Either vulnerability can be used for a denial of service attack, or for the execution of arbitrary code with the privileges of OpenSSH. These vulnerabilities are fixed in OpenSSH 3.4, and the Mac OS X 10.1 July 2002 Security

Update includes OpenSSH 3.4. More information on the vulnerability is also available at `http://bvlive01.iss.net/issEn/delivery/xforce/alertdetail.jsp?oid=20584`.

- Off-by-one Error Allows Execution of Arbitrary Code with the Privileges of OpenSSH (CVE-2002-0083, BugTraq ID 4241)

  Versions of OpenSSH between 2.0 and 3.0.2 contain an off-by-one error in the channel code. Exploiting this vulnerability can result in the execution of arbitrary code with the privileges of OpenSSH. This vulnerability is fixed in OpenSSH 3.1, and the Mac OS X 10.1 April 2002 Security Update includes OpenSSH 3.1p1. More information on the vulnerability is also available at `http://www.openbsd.org/advisories/ssh_channelalloc.txt`.

- UseLogin Allows the Execution of Arbitrary Code with the Privileges of OpenSSH (CVE-2001-0872, VU# 157447, BugTraq ID 3614)

  In some versions of OpenSSH, if the user turns on the `UseLogin` directive, which uses `login` to handle interactive sessions, a user can pass environment variables to `login`. An intruder can exploit this vulnerability to execute commands with the privileges of OpenSSH, which usually has `root` privileges. This vulnerability is fixed in OpenSSH 3.0.2, and the Mac OS X 10.1.3 update includes OpenSSH 3.0.2p1.

- Timing Analysis (CAN-2001-1382, VU# 596827)

  Monitoring delays between keystrokes during an interactive SSH session can simplify brute-force attacks against passwords. During the interactive SSH sessions, user keystrokes and system responses are transmitted as packets with an echo. However, if a user types a password during the interactive session, the password is transmitted without an echo. An intruder can detect the lack of echo and analyze delays between the keystrokes to simplify a brute-force attack against the password. Exploiting the vulnerability does not necessarily result in a compromised password. OpenSSH 2.5.0 has fixes for this. Mac OS X's first update includes OpenSSH 2.30p1, which has this vulnerability. However, the Mac OS X Web Sharing Update 1.0 addresses this issue by including OpenSSH 2.9p2.

- SSH CRC32 Attack Detection Code Can Lead to Execution of Arbitrary Code with the Privileges of the SSH Daemon (CVE-2001-0144, VU# 945216, BugTraq ID 2347)

  The SSH1 CRC32 attack detection code contains a remote integer buffer overflow that can allow the execution of arbitrary code with the privileges of the SSH daemon, usually root. OpenSSH 2.3.0 contains a fix for this vulnerability.

The first Mac OS X update includes OpenSSH 2.3.0p1, which is not vulnerable. More information on the vulnerability is also available at `http://razor.bindview.com/publish/advisories/adv_ssh1crc.html`.

Vulnerabilities in telnet and rlogin

SSH can replace a number of protocols. Included here is some information on vulnerabilities for two of the most popular protocols it is used to replace: telnet and rlogin.

telnet

telnet's single largest vulnerability is in its specification, but as a demonstration of the additional insecurity that can be found, even in an application that never tried to be secure in the first place, we've included a listing of some recent telnet vulnerabilities, as well as NCSA Telnet vulnerabilities, since 1991. These telnet vulnerabilities turn out to be typical Unix application vulnerabilities, and problems of this type are common in most Unix network applications: vulnerabilities that can allow arbitrary execution of code as the process owner and a vulnerability that can lead to denial of service.

Although these vulnerabilities are serious, the most serious vulnerability that telnet has is its inherent cleartext nature. The telnet protocol transmits everything, including usernames and passwords, in cleartext. The best solution to this vulnerability is to not enable telnet, and not use it as a client. If you are curious about seeing what telnet traffic looks like, install Etherpeek, IPNetMonitor, or Snort, or use the built-in `tcpdump` program, or any other similar package on a machine, do a bit of telnetting around, and see how much you can see with the sniffers. You can find these programs at `http://www.wildpackets.com/products/etherpeek_mac`, `http://www.sustworks.com/site/prod_ipm_download.html`, `http://sourceforge.net/projects/snort/`, and under `man tcpdump` in the `man` pages. The telnet protocol RFC is available at `http://www.ietf.org/rfc/rfc0854.txt`.

telnet vulnerabilities include the following:

- Buffer Overflow in BSD Derived Versions of `telnetd` (CVE-2001-0554, CA-2001-21)

  A buffer overflow in BSD derived versions of `telnetd` can result in either crashing the system, or in the arbitrary execution of code with the privileges of `telnetd`, usually `root`. More information can also be found at `ftp://ftp.FreeBSD.org/pub/FreeBSD/CERT/advisories/FreeBSD-SA-01:49.telnetd.v1.1.asc`.

Mac OS X was affected by this vulnerability, but it was fixed with the release of Mac OS X 10.1.

- Denial of Service Vulnerability (BugTraq ID 1955)

  The TERMCAP telnet variable in client-server negotiations can cause telnetd to search the file system for files containing termcap entries. Because this is done before authentication, an attacker can cause many telnetd processes to be started, thereby exhausting system resources.

  This was found to be a vulnerability in many versions of FreeBSD, but patches fixed the problem. However, there were no reports of the vulnerability having been exploited.

- Environment Variable Format String Vulnerability (CVE-2000-0733, IN-2000-09, BugTraq ID 1572)

  With the way telnetd sets the _RLD environment variable, an intruder can supply data to telnetd such that it can be executed with the privileges of telnetd, usually root.

  The exploit was used to add accounts with root privileges; install root kits containing replacements for various commands, including telnetd; install packet sniffers; and/or install irc proxy programs.

  This vulnerability was discovered in various versions of IRIX. Patches were made available to fix the problem.

- Mac/PC NCSA Telnet Vulnerability (CVE-1999-1090, CA-1991-15)

  This vulnerability does not exploit anything inherent to telnet itself. The default configuration for NCSA Telnet for the PC and Macintosh enables FTP with no password setting. This can result in an intruder gaining read/write access to a system, including its system files.

  The temporary solution to this problem was either to specifically disable FTP or to enable password protection. NCSA later changed that default. In a later release, NCSA changed how the configuration for the program was set—from having the settings in an external text file called config.tel to setting them in a graphical interface. Support for NCSA Telnet was discontinued with version 2.6, which was released in October 1994.

rlogin

Like telnet, vulnerabilities involving rlogin include typical vulnerabilities: buffer overflows from which `root` access can be gained.

Although such vulnerabilities are serious, the most serious vulnerability with rlogin, like telnet, is that it transmits everything, including usernames and passwords, in cleartext. As with telnet, the best solution to this vulnerability is to not enable `rlogind`.

NOTE

Believe it or not, rlogin was an attempt at a secure protocol. It was developed at a time when Unix machines were owned by companies, and personal Unix machines were rare. Security-conscious system administrators did not want to incur security problems on either their own machines or someone else's. They never created an account for a "bad" user. Therefore, someone connecting to a system via `rlogin` was assumed to be a trustworthy user coming from another Unix system.

The rlogin RFC, available at `http://www.ietf.org/rfc/rfc1282.txt`, contains a cautionary tale on the security problems that spoofing a trusted host might incur. However, the RFC does not express any concern about rlogin's transmission of data in cleartext. Obviously, the author never envisioned a world with so many untrustable Unix hosts and users.

Vulnerabilities involving rlogin include:

- Buffer Overflow in System V–Derived `login` (CVE-2001-0797, CA-2001-34, BugTraq ID 3681)

  A buffer overflow occurs in System V–derived versions of `login` when they handle environment variables. The vulnerability can be exploited to execute arbitrary code with the privileges of `login`. When `login` is called by applications that use it for authentication, its privileges are elevated to those of the application. For `telnetd`, `rlogind`, and `sshd`, if it is so configured, the privileges are that of `root`. As a result of the `login` buffer overflow, an intruder can gain `root` access to a system.

  Vendors have made patches available to fix the problem.

- Buffer Overflow Vulnerability (CVE-1999-0046, CA-1997-06, BugTraq ID 242)

  The handling of the `TERM` variable in some implementations of `rlogin` can cause a buffer overflow, which can result in the arbitrary execution of code as `root`.

  This vulnerability was discovered in many versions of Unix. Vendors made patches available to fix the problem.

Activating SSH

If you want to be able to connect to your machine via the command line, and do it securely, using SSH is the best security precaution available to you today. If you are just interested in connecting from your OS X machine to another machine running an SSH server, then you do not need to activate the SSH server on your machine. However, if you want to be able to access your Macintosh remotely, you need to turn on the SSH server. To activate the SSH server, check the Remote Login box under the Services tab of the Sharing pane.

The SSH server starts from `/System/Library/StartupItems/` and also has a control in `/etc/hostconfig`.

Basic Configuration

There are two basic configuration files for SSH: `/etc/sshd_config` and `/etc/ssh_config`. The first file is the configuration file for the SSH server itself, `sshd`. The second file is the configuration file for the client, `ssh`. You can also use command-line options at startup for configuring `sshd`. Command-line options override settings in `/etc/sshd_config`.

/etc/sshd_config

The default configuration file for `sshd`, `/etc/sshd_config`, is shown here. Because `sshd` processes run for each incoming connection, it is easiest to make changes to your `sshd` from the console. A brief explanation for the sections is included.

```
#       $OpenBSD: sshd_config,v 1.56 2002/06/20 23:37:12 markus Exp $

# This is the sshd server system-wide configuration file.  See
# sshd_config(5) for more information.

# This sshd was compiled with PATH=/usr/bin:/bin:/usr/sbin:/sbin

# The strategy used for options in the default sshd_config shipped with
# OpenSSH is to specify options with their default value where
# possible, but leave them commented.  Uncommented options change a
# default value.

#Port 22
#Protocol 2,1
#ListenAddress 0.0.0.0
#ListenAddress ::

# HostKey for protocol version 1
#HostKey /etc/ssh_host_key
# HostKeys for protocol version 2
#HostKey /etc/ssh_host_rsa_key
#HostKey /etc/ssh_host_dsa_key
```

```
# Lifetime and size of ephemeral version 1 server key
#KeyRegenerationInterval 3600
#ServerKeyBits 768
```

This section of the configuration file sets some general configuration settings. By default, `sshd` runs on port `22`. The protocol option enables you to specify which SSH protocols `sshd` should support. The default is `2,1`. By default, `sshd` listens on all local addresses. However, there can be multiple `ListenAddress` statements, where you can specify settings for each interface.

```
# Logging
#obsoletes QuietMode and FascistLogging
#SyslogFacility AUTH
#LogLevel INFO
```

This section controls the facility code and level of logging that `sshd` does.

```
# Authentication:

#LoginGraceTime 600
#PermitRootLogin yes
#StrictModes yes

#RSAAuthentication yes
#PubkeyAuthentication yes
#AuthorizedKeysFile     .ssh/authorized_keys

# rhosts authentication should not be used
#RhostsAuthentication no
# Don't read the user's ~/.rhosts and ~/.shosts files
#IgnoreRhosts yes
# For this to work you will also need host keys in /etc/ssh_known_hosts
#RhostsRSAAuthentication no
# similar for protocol version 2
#HostbasedAuthentication no
# Change to yes if you don't trust ~/.ssh/known_hosts for
# RhostsRSAAuthentication and HostbasedAuthentication
#IgnoreUserKnownHosts no

# To disable tunneled clear text passwords, change to no here!
#PasswordAuthentication yes
#PermitEmptyPasswords no
```

```
# Change to no to disable s/key passwords
#ChallengeResponseAuthentication yes

# Kerberos options
#KerberosAuthentication no
#KerberosOrLocalPasswd yes
#KerberosTicketCleanup yes

#AFSTokenPassing no

# Kerberos TGT Passing only works with the AFS kaserver
#KerberosTgtPassing no

# Set this to 'yes' to enable PAM keyboard-interactive authentication
# Warning: enabling this may bypass the setting of 'PasswordAuthentication'
#PAMAuthenticationViaKbdInt yes
```

This section addresses various authentication issues. By default, `PermitRootLogin` is set to `yes`. This is typically a poor choice in networked Unix installations. It's usually better to require administrative users to log in as themselves and then `su` to `root`, rather than allowing direct login as `root`. This forces slightly better tracking of who's doing what. Possible values for this directive are `yes`, `without-password`, `forced-commands-only`, or `no`. The `without-password` value disables password authentication for `root`. The `forced-commands-only` option permits `root` to log in with public key authentication, but only if the command has been specified on a key in the `authorized_keys` file with the `command=...` option. This option can be useful for doing remote backups on a system where `root` is not normally permitted to log in. If the only commands that `root` is allowed to execute are commands that can't compromise security (be very careful when making this assessment!), then the `without-password` option may be acceptable in this case.

This section also provides some settings for a user's session. By default, `~/.rhosts` and `~/.shosts` are ignored for `RhostsAuthentication`, `RhostsRSAAuthentication`, or `HostbasedAuthentication`. The `/etc/hosts.equiv` files and `/etc/shosts.equiv` are still used. The `~/.rhosts` and `~/.shosts` files allow users to specify trusted hosts. Typically, the `/etc/hosts.equiv` and `/etc/shosts.equiv` files specify systemwide trusted hosts. In Mac OS X, it might be necessary to create these maps in the NetInfo database instead.

This section also specifies what authentication methods are allowed. The `RhostsRSAAuthentication` and `RSAAuthentication` are protocol 1 directives. Public key authentication is allowed by default for protocol 2. By default, `PasswordAuthentication` is set to `yes`. If you only want to permit public key authentication, set this option to `no`.

```
#X11Forwarding no
#X11DisplayOffset 10
#X11UseLocalhost yes
#PrintMotd yes
#PrintLastLog yes
#KeepAlive yes
#UseLogin no
#UsePrivilegeSeparation yes
#Compression yes
```

In this section you can also set whether to allow X11 forwarding, the printing of the message of the day, when the user last logged in, and whether the server sends TCP keepalive messages. Having the server send TCP keepalive messages prevents a connection from hanging if the network goes down or the client crashes.

```
#MaxStartups 10
# no default banner path
#Banner /some/path
#VerifyReverseMapping no
```

This section includes options for more general settings for `sshd`. The `MaxStartups` option enables you to specify the maximum number of concurrent unauthenticated connections to `sshd`. When specified as a set of three colon-separated numbers, this option specifies a random early drop as `start:rate:full`. The point at which random early dropoff starts is when the number of unauthenticated connections reaches `start`. When the number of unauthenticated connections reaches `full`, all the connections are refused. The `sshd` refuses connections with a probability of `rate`/100 if the number of connections is `start`. The probability increases linearly to 100% as the number of unauthenticated connections reaches `full`. The `VerifyReverseMapping` directive specifies whether `sshd` should verify the remote hostname for an IP address by checking that the resolved hostname maps back to the same IP address.

```
Subsystem       sftp    /usr/libexec/sftp-server
```

The default configuration file ends with the preceding line. This option activates the `sftp` server. It is on by default. In earlier versions of Mac OS X, this option was commented out, and therefore off by default. If you don't think you will have a need for the `sftp` functionality, you can turn it off here.

Some additional interesting directives are noted in Table 14.1. Be sure to read the man page for more details.

TABLE 14.1 Select Additional Options for `/etc/sshd_config`

Option	Function
`AllowGroups`	Takes a list of group name patterns, separated by spaces. If specified, login is allowed only for users whose primary group or supplementary group list matches one of the patterns. By default, login is allowed for all groups.
`AllowUsers`	Takes a list of username patterns, separated by spaces. If specified, login is allowed only for usernames that match one of the patterns. By default, login is allowed for all users.
`Ciphers`	Specifies the ciphers allowed for protocol version 2. Multiple ciphers must be comma separated. The default is `aes128-cbc,3des-cbc,blowfish-cbc,cast128cbc,arcfour, aes192-cbc,aes256-cbc`.
`ClientAliveInterval`	Sets a timeout interval in seconds, after which if no data has been received from the client, `sshd` sends a message through the encrypted channel to request a response from the client. The default is `0`, indicating that these messages will not be sent to the client. Protocol version 2 option only.
`ClientAliveCountMax`	Sets the number of client alive queries that may be sent without `sshd` receiving any messages back from the client before `sshd` gets suspicious. If this threshold is reached while client alive messages are being sent, `sshd` disconnects the client, terminating the session. The default value is `3`.
`DenyGroups`	Takes a list of group name patterns, separated by spaces. Login is disallowed for users whose primary group or supplementary group list matches one of the patterns. By default, login is allowed for all groups.
`DenyUsers`	Takes a list of username patterns, separated by spaces. Login is disallowed for usernames that match one of the patterns. By default, login is allowed for all users.
`MACs`	Specifies the available MAC (message authentication code) algorithms. The MAC algorithm is used in protocol version 2 for data integrity protection. Multiple algorithms must be comma separated. The default is `hmac-md5,hmac-sha1,hmac-ripemd160,hmac-sha1-96,hmac-md5-96`
`PidFile`	Specifies the file that contains the process identifier of `sshd`.
`PubkeyAuthentication`	Specifies whether public key authentication is allowed. Argument must be `yes` or `no`. Default is `yes`. Protocol version 2 option only.
`UsePrivilegeSeparation`	Specifies whether `sshd` separates privileges by creating an unprivileged child process to deal with incoming network traffic. After successful authentication, another process will be created that has the privilege of the authenticated user. The goal of privilege separation is to prevent privilege escalation by containing any corruption within the unprivileged processes. The default is `yes`.
`VerifyReverseMapping`	Specifies whether `sshd` should try to verify the remote hostname by checking that the resolved hostname for the remote IP address maps back to the very same IP address. The default is `no`.

TABLE 14.1 Continued

Option	Function
X11DisplayOffset	Specifies the first display number available for sshd's X11 forwarding. This prevents sshd from interfering with real X11 servers. The default is 10.
X11Forwarding	Specifies whether X11 forwarding is permitted. The default is no. Note that disabling X11 forwarding does not improve security in any way; users can always install their own forwarders. X11 forwarding is automatically disabled if UseLogin is enabled.
X11UseLocalhost	Specifies whether sshd should bind the X11 forwarding server to the loopback address or to the wildcard address. By default, sshd binds the forwarding server to the loopback address and sets the hostname part of the DISPLAY environment variable to localhost. This prevents remote hosts from connecting to the proxy display. However, some older X11 clients may not function with this configuration. X11UseLocalhost may be set to no to specify that the forwarding server should be bound to the wildcard address. The argument must be yes or no. The default is yes.
XAuthLocation	Specifies the full pathname of the xauth program. The default is /usr/X11R6/bin/xauth.

sshd **Command-Line Options**

By default sshd does not start with any commnd-line options, but you can edit the startup file to control which options will be used for your installation. Command-line options override settings in /etc/sshd_config. If you choose to have sshd start with certain command-line options, edit /System/Library/StartupItems/SSH/SSH accordingly and restart sshd. Table 14.2 provides a listing of possible runtime options. See the man page for more details.

TABLE 14.2 Command-Line Options for sshd

Option	Function
-b <bits>	Specifies the number of bits in the ephemeral protocol version 1 server key (default 768).
-d	Debug mode. The server sends verbose debug output to the system log, and does not put itself in the background. The server also does not fork and only processes one connection.
-e	Sends output to standard error instead of /var/log/system.log.
-f <configuration_file>	Specifies the name of the configuration file. Default is /etc/sshd_config. sshd refuses to start if there is no configuration file.
-g <login_grace_time>	Gives the grace time for clients to authenticate themselves.
-h <host_key_file>	Specifies a file from which a host key is read. This option must be given if sshd is not run as root (because the normal host key files are normally not readable by anyone but root).

TABLE 14.2 Continued

Option	Function
`-i`	Runs `sshd` from `inetd`. `sshd` is normally not run from `inetd` because it needs to generate the server key before it can respond to the client, and this may take tens of seconds. Clients would have to wait too long if the key was regenerated every time. However, with small key sizes (for example, 512) using `sshd` from `inetd` may be feasible.
`-k <key_gen_time>`	Specifies how often the ephemeral protocol version 1 server key is regenerated. A value of `0` indicates that the key will never be regenerated. Default is 3600 seconds or 1 hour.
`-o <option>`	Can be used to give options in the format used in the configuration file. Useful for specifying options for which there is no separate command-line flag.
`-p <port>`	Specifies the port on which the server listens for connections. Multiple port options are permitted. Ports specified in the configuration file are ignored when a command-line port is specified. Default is `22`.
`-q`	Quiet mode. Sends no output to `/var/log/system.log`.
`-t`	Test mode. Checks only the validity of the configuration file and the sanity of the keys. Useful for updating `sshd` reliably because configuration options may change.
`-u <len>`	Specifies the size of the field in the `utmp` structure that holds the remote hostname. If the resolved hostname is longer than `<len>`, the dotted decimal value is used instead.
`-D`	`sshd` does not detach and does not become a daemon. Allows for easy monitoring of `sshd`.
`-4`	Forces `sshd` to use IPv4 addresses only.
`-6`	Forces `sshd` to use IPv6 addresses only.

/etc/ssh_config

`/etc/ssh_config`, the default systemwide configuration file for the client, `ssh`, is shown following. The configuration file is divided into host sections. Because parameters are determined on a first-match-wins basis, more host-specific values should be given at the beginning of the file, with general values at the end of the file. Users can also configure the `ssh` client to suit their needs by creating a `~/.ssh/config file`. Specifying `Host` as `*` sets parameters for all hosts.

```
#       $OpenBSD: ssh_config,v 1.15 2002/06/20 20:03:34 stevesk Exp $

# This is the ssh client system-wide configuration file.  See
# ssh_config(5) for more information.  This file provides defaults for
# users, and the values can be changed in per-user configuration files
# or on the command line.
```

```
# Configuration data is parsed as follows:
#  1. command line options
#  2. user-specific file
#  3. system-wide file
# Any configuration value is only changed the first time it is set.
# Thus, host-specific definitions should be at the beginning of the
# configuration file, and defaults at the end.

# Site-wide defaults for various options

# Host *
#   ForwardAgent no
#   ForwardX11 no
#   RhostsAuthentication no
#   RhostsRSAAuthentication no
#   RSAAuthentication yes
#   PasswordAuthentication yes
#   BatchMode no
#   CheckHostIP yes
#   StrictHostKeyChecking ask
#   IdentityFile ~/.ssh/identity
#   IdentityFile ~/.ssh/id_rsa
#   IdentityFile ~/.ssh/id_dsa
#   Port 22
#   Protocol 2,1
#   Cipher 3des
#   Ciphers aes128-cbc,3des-cbc,blowfish-cbc,cast128-cbc,arcfour,aes192-cbc,aes
256-cbc
#   EscapeChar ~
```

The default `/etc/ssh_config` file lists some options that you may want to set. Table 14.3 includes a description of some of the options shown in this file, along with other selected options. For more details, be sure to read the man pages for `ssh` and `ssh_config`.

CAUTION

Options that you can set in a systemwide `/etc/ssh_config` include `LocalForward` and `RemoteForward`. We discourage setting up any tunnels in a systemwide configuration. If an intruder does gain access to your machine, your systemwide forwarding settings make it that much easier for an intruder to access other machines.

TABLE 14.3 Select Options for `/etc/ssh_config` or `~/.ssh/config`

Option	Function
`Host`	Restricts the following declarations (up to the next Host keyword) to be for only those hosts that match one of the patterns given after the keyword. The host is the hostname argument given on the command line (that is, the name is not converted to a canonicalized host name before matching).
`BatchMode`	If set to yes, disables passphrase/password querying. Useful in scripts and other batch jobs where no user is present to supply the password. The argument must be `yes` or `no`. Default is `no`.
`BindAddress`	Specifies the interface from which to transmit on machines with multiple interfaces or aliased addresses. Option does not work if `UsePrivilegedPort` is set to `yes`.
`CheckHostIP`	If set to `yes`, `ssh` also checks the host IP address in the `known_hosts` file. This allows `ssh` to detect whether a host key changed because of DNS spoofing. If set to `no`, the check is not executed. Default is `yes`.
`Cipher`	Specifies the cipher to use for encrypting the session in protocol version 1. `blowfish`, `3des`, and `des` are supported, although `des` is supported in the `ssh` client only for interoperability with legacy protocol 1 implementations that do not support the `3des` cipher. Its use is strongly discouraged because of cryptographic weaknesses. Default is `3des`.
`Ciphers`	Specifies the ciphers allowed for protocol version 2 in order of preference. Multiple ciphers must be comma separated. The default is `aes128-cbc,3des-cbc,blowfish-cbc,cast128-cbc,arcfour,aes192-cbc,aes256-cbc`.
`ClearAllForwardings`	Specifies that all local, remote, and dynamic port forwardings specified in the configuration files or on the command line be cleared. Primarily useful when used from the `ssh` command line to clear port forwardings set in configuration files, and is automatically set by `scp` and `sftp`. Argument must be `yes` or `no`. Default is `no`.
`ForwardX11`	Specifies whether X11 connections will be automatically redirected over the secure channel and `DISPLAY` set on the remote machine. Argument must be `yes` or `no`. Default is `no`.
`GlobalKnownHostsFile`	Specifies a file to use for the global host key database instead of `/etc/ssh_known_hosts`.
`HostKeyAlgorithms`	Specifies, in order of preference, the protocol version 2 host key algorithms that the client should use. Default is `ssh-rsa,ssh-dss`.
`HostKeyAlias`	Specifies an alias that should be used instead of the real hostname when looking up or saving the host key in the host key database files. Useful for tunneling `ssh` connections or for multiple servers running on a single host.
`HostName`	Specifies the real hostname to log in to. This can be used to specify nicknames or abbreviations for hosts. Default is the name given on the command line.

TABLE 14.3 Continued

Option	Function
IdentityFile	Specifies a file from which the user's RSA or DSA authentication identity is read. Defaults are $HOME/.ssh/identity for protocol version 1, and $HOME/.ssh/id_rsa and $HOME/.ssh/id_dsa for protocol version 2.
LocalForward	Specifies that a TCP/IP port on the local machine be forwarded over the secure channel to the specified host and port from the remote machine. Only the superuser can forward privileged ports.
MACs	Specifies the MAC (message authentication code) algorithms in order of preference. The MAC algorithm is used in protocol version 2 for data integrity protection. Multiple algorithms must be comma separated. Default is hmac-md5,hmac-sha1,hmac-ripemd160,hmac-sha1-96,hmac-md5-96.
NumberOfPasswordPrompts	Specifies the number of password prompts before giving up. Argument must be an integer. Default is 3.
Port	Specifies the port number to connect to on the remote host. Default is 22.
PreferredAuthentications	Specifies the order in which the client should try protocol 2 authentication methods. Default is hostbased,publickey,keyboard-interactive,password.
Protocol	Specifies the protocol versions ssh should support, in order of preference. The possible values are 1 and 2. The default is 2,1. In other words, ssh tries version 2 and falls back to version 1 if version 2 is not available.
PubkeyAuthentication	Specifies whether to try public key authentication. Argument must be yes or no. Default is yes. Protocol version 2 option only.
RemoteForward	Specifies that a TCP/IP port on the remote machine be forwarded over the secure channel to the specified host and port from the local machine. Only the superuser can forward privileged ports.
StrictHostKeyChecking	Argument must be yes, no, or ask. Default is ask. If set to yes, ssh never automatically adds host keys to the $HOME/.ssh/known_hosts file, and refuses to connect to hosts whose host key has changed. This provides maximum protection against Trojan horse attacks, but can be annoying when the /etc/ssh_known_hosts file is poorly maintained, or connections to new hosts are frequently made. Forces the user to manually add all new hosts. If set to no, ssh automatically adds new host keys to the user-known hosts files. If set to ask, new host keys are added to the user-known host files only after the user has confirmed that that is what he really wants to do, and ssh refuses to connect to hosts whose host key has changed. The host keys of known hosts are verified automatically in all cases.

TABLE 14.3 Continued

Option	Function
UsePrivilegedPort	Specifies whether to use a privileged port for outgoing connections. Argument must be yes or no. Default is no.
User	Specifies as what user to log in. This can be useful when a different user name is used on different machines. This saves the trouble of having to remember to give the username on the command line.
UserKnownHostsFile	Specifies a file to use for the user host key database instead of $HOME/.ssh/known_hosts.

Use

SSH provides for secure encrypted traffic transmission across a network. Most SSH software, including that provided by Apple, includes both the encrypted transmission facility and rudimentary tools for making use of that functionality. These tools include the ability to use the encryption to provide secure terminal services and file transfer support. The user can add other functionality as needed by making use of just the secure transport portion of the software to encrypt the traffic between otherwise insecure external software packages.

A common use for the SSH package is for making remote terminal connections. Although you can set a number of options to `ssh` in a user configuration file, you will probably find yourself using `ssh` with command-line options initially. This is actually the easiest way to start using `ssh`. After you have been using `ssh` with command-line options for a while, you will get a feel for what options, if any, you may want to specify in either `~/.ssh/config` or `/etc/ssh_config`.

To use the `ssh` client, you can run either `ssh` or `slogin`. If you are accustomed to using `rlogin` on a system, then `slogin` will be the natural choice for you. Otherwise, you probably won't have any preferences.

The most commonly used syntax for `ssh` is

```
ssh -l <username> <remote_host>
ssh <username>@<remote_host>
```

If you are logging in to a remote host for the first time, you will be asked if you want to accept the host's key:

```
[localhost:~] joray% slogin -l jray primal.ag.ohio-state.edu
The authenticity of host 'primal.ag.ohio-state.edu (140.254.85.2)'
can't be established.
RSA key fingerprint is b3:60:d8:e3:1d:59:bc:2c:2d:9e:c3:83:9a:84:c3:a1.
Are you sure you want to continue connecting (yes/no)? yes
```

```
Warning: Permanently added 'primal.ag.ohio-state.edu,140.254.85.2' (RSA)
 to the list of known hosts.
jray@primal.ag.ohio-state.edu's password:
Welcome to Darwin!
[primal:~] jray%
```

Table 14.4 provides a listing of select command-line options to ssh. Be sure to read the man page for more details.

TABLE 14.4 Select Command-Line Options to ssh

Option	Function
-b <bind_address>	Specifies the interface to transmit from on machines with multiple interfaces or aliased addresses.
-c blowfish|3des|des	Selects the cipher to use for encrypting the session. Default is 3des. des is supported only for compatibility with legacy protocol 1 servers.
-c <cipher_spec>	Additionally, for SSH2, a comma-separated list of ciphers.
-f	Requests ssh to go to background just before command execution. Useful if ssh is going to ask for passwords or passphrases, but the user wants it in the background. Implies -n.
-g	Allows remote hosts to connect to local forwarded ports.
-i <identity_file>	Selects a file from which the identity (private key) for RSA or DSA authentication is read. Defaults are $HOME/.ssh/identity for protocol version 1, and $HOME/.ssh/id_rsa and $HOME/.ssh/id_dsa for protocol version 2. Identity files may also be specified on a per-host basis in the configuration file.
-l <login_name>	Specifies the user as which to log in on the remote machine. This may also be specified on a per-host basis in the configuration file.
-m <mac_spec>	Specifies a comma-separated list of MAC (message authentication code) algorithms in order of preference for protocol version 2.
-n	Redirects stdin from /dev/null (actually, prevents reading from stdin). This must be used when ssh is run in the background.
-N	Does not execute a remote command. This is useful for just forwarding ports (SSH2 only).
-o <option>	Can be used to give options in the format used in the configuration file. Useful for specifying options for which there is no separate command-line flag.
-p <port>	Specifies the port to connect to on the remote host. This can be specified on a per-host basis in the configuration file.
-P	Uses a nonprivileged port for outgoing connections. This can be used if a firewall does not permit connections from privileged ports.

TABLE 14.4 Continued

Option	Function
`-v`	Verbose mode. Causes `ssh` to print debugging messages about its progress.
`-x`	Disables `X11` forwarding.
`-X`	Enables `X11` forwarding. This can also be specified on a per-host basis in a configuration file.
`-F <configfile>`	Specifies an alternative per-user configuration file. If a configuration file is given on the command line, the systemwide configuration file (`/etc/ssh_config`) is ignored. Default per-user configuration file is `$HOME/.ssh/config`.
`-L <port>:<host>:<hostport>`	Specifies that the given port on the local (client) host is to be forwarded to the given host and port on the remote side. Port forwardings can also be specified in the configuration file. *Only root can forward privileged ports.*
`-R <port>:<host>:<hostport>`	Specifies that the given port on the remote (server) host is to be forwarded to the given host and port on the local side. Port forwardings can also be specified in the configuration file. *Privileged ports can be forwarded only when you are logging in as root on the remote machine.*
`-1`	Forces SSH1 protocol only.
`-2`	Forces SSH2 protocol only.
`-4`	Forces `ssh` to use IPv4 addresses only.
`-6`	Forces `ssh` to use IPv6 addresses only.

Clients

From other Unix machines with an SSH server installed you should be able to use `ssh` or `slogin` to connect to your Mac OS X machine remotely. But you don't need a Unix machine to connect to your Mac OS X machine. Windows and traditional Mac OS clients are also available. A brief description of each client's features is included. At this time, not all the features will necessarily have meaning, but they will by the end of the chapter.

Windows

A number of Windows SSH clients are available. Among the available clients are

- **Tera Term Pro with TTSSH**. Tera Term is a free terminal emulation program available at `http://hp.vector.co.jp/authors/VA002416/teraterm.html`. A free extension DLL called TTSSH is available for Tera Term at `http://www.zip.com.au/~roca/ttssh.html`. With the extension, Tera Term can be used as an SSH client. It supports only the SSH1 protocol. Additionally, it can handle public key authentication, tunneling, and X11 forwarding.

- **PuTTY**. PuTTY is a free telnet and SSH client available at `http://www.chiark.greenend.org.uk/~sgtatham/putty/`. PuTTY supports both the SSH1 and SSH2 protocols, with SSH1 being the default protocol. It also supports public key authentication, tunneling, and X11 forwarding. Additionally, it includes `scp` (PSCP) and `sftp` (PSFTP) clients.
- **F-Secure SSH**. F-Secure SSH is a commercial SSH client. It is available for Windows 95/98/ME/NT 4.0/2000/XP. It supports both the SSH1 and SSH2 protocols. It also supports public key authentication, tunneling, and X11 forwarding. Additionally, it includes a built-in `-sftp` client and command-line `-ssh` tools. For more product information, see `http://www.f-secure.com/`.
- **SSH Secure Shell**. SSH Communications Security has both a commercial and free SSH client for Windows 95/98/ME/NT 4.0/2000/XP. It supports both the SSH1 and SSH2 protocols. It also supports public key authentication, tunneling, and X11 forwarding. Additionally, it includes a built-in `sftp` client. For more product information, see `http://www.ssh.com/`. To download the freely available client, go to `ftp://ftp.ssh.com/pub/ssh/` and select the latest Windows client.
- **SecureCRT**. SecureCRT is a commercial SSH client available from `http://www.vandyke.com/products/securecrt/`. It supports both the SSH1 and SSH2 protocols. It also supports public key authentication, tunneling, X11 forwarding, and `sftp`.

Macintosh 8/9

A few SSH clients are available for the traditional Mac OS. The clients that work in the traditional Mac OS probably also work in Mac OS X's Classic mode. As a matter of fact, to tunnel connections in Classic mode, you need one of these clients with tunneling capabilities. Available clients include

- **NiftyTelnet 1.1 SSH r3**. NiftyTelnet 1.1 SSH r3 is a free telnet and SSH client available at `http://www.lysator.liu.se/~jonasw/freeware/niftyssh/`. It supports only the SSH1 protocol. It also supports public key authentication and has a built-in `scp` function.
- **MacSSH**. MacSSH is a free SSH, telnet, and various other protocols client available at `http://www.macssh.com/`. For SSH, it supports only the SSH2 protocol. Additionally, it supports public key authentication, tunneling, and X11 forwarding.
- **MacSFTP**. MacSFTP is a shareware `sftp` client available at `http://www.macssh.com/`. You can download a 15-day trial. If you decide you like it, the shareware cost is $25. It has an interface similar to Fetch's.

- **F-Secure SSH**. F-Secure SSH is a commercial SSH client. It supports both the SSH1 and SSH2 protocols. Additionally, it supports public key authentication, tunneling, and X11 forwarding. For more product information, see `http://www.f-secure.com/`.

Mac OS X

Mac OS X, of course, has the command-line `-ssh` tools available. However, if you are new to the command line, you may also be wondering whether any SSH GUI tools are available. You should also check whether your favorite FTP client includes or will include SFTP support. Available clients include

- **JellyfiSSH**. JellyfiSSH is a freeware product available from `http://www.arenasoftware.com/grepsoft/`. It provides a GUI login interface and bookmarking capabilities. After you enter your login information, it brings up a terminal window to the remote host. If you are comfortable with using `slogin` or `ssh` to log in to a remote host, this application may not be useful to you. If you like the basic GUI login interface of the clients for traditional Mac OS, this application may be useful to you. If you want to learn how to use the `ssh` command-line client, this application might be useful for you because you can see how the command was issued.
- **Fugu**. Fugu is a freeware product available from `http://rsug.itd.umich.edu/software/fugu/`. It is an `ssh` tunneling/`scp`/`sftp` client.
- **MacSFTP**. MacSFTP also works in OS X. It is a shareware `sftp` client available at `http://www.macssh.com/`. You can download a 15-day trial. If you decide you like it, the shareware cost is $25. It has an interface similar to Fetch's.
- **RBrowser**. RBrowser is an application available from `http://www.rbrowser.com/`. It provides a finder interface to `ssh`, `scp`, and `sftp`, and also supports tunneling. If you do not like the command line at all, this may be the application for you. The `sftp` feature works by dragging files from one "finder" to the other. This is a shareware product with two levels of licensing—a basic level that covers `ftp` and `sftp` features and a professional level that includes `ftp`, `sftp`, Unix, `ssh`, and `ssh` tunneling. Demo licenses are also available.
- **F-Secure SSH.** As of this writing, F-Secure is working on a client for OS X. However, it is not yet available. Because it is supposed to be similar to the F-Secure SSH 2.4 client, it is expected to be able to do tunneling. Check `http://www.f-secure.com/` for more information.

Advanced SSH Features

In addition to allowing you to log in remotely to another machine running an SSH server, SSH can be used for tunneling connections from one machine to another, securely transferring files, and public key authentication. Table 14.5 lists the primary tools in the SSH suite and their function.

TABLE 14.5 Primary Utilities in OpenSSH

Utility	Description
`sshd`	SSH server.
`ssh`	SSH client.
`sftp`	An interactive secure file transfer program.
`scp`	A copy program for copying files between hosts.
`sftp-server`	SFTP server subsystem started automatically by `sshd`.
`ssh-keygen`	A utility that generates keys for public key authentication.
`ssh-agent`	Authentication agent that manages keys for public key authentication users so that they don't have to enter a passphrase when logging in to another machine. It starts at the beginning of an X11 session or `login` session, and windows and programs start as its children.
`ssh-add`	Utility that adds keys to the `ssh-agent`.

Tunnel Encryption

As you saw in Chapter 12, "FTP Security," one of the features of the SSH protocol is its ability to tunnel connections. In other words, you can set up an encrypted channel between machines and use the encrypted channel to send an otherwise insecure protocol. In Chapter 12, you saw in great detail how to restrict access to the FTP server and to tunnel a connection to the server. Services that you might also be interested in tunneling include POP, IMAP, and X11. Recall that X11 forwarding is off by default in the `/etc/sshd_config` file.

To summarize what was discussed in that chapter, first restrict access to the server that is to be tunneled. This is done by adding a line to the `/etc/hosts.allow` file that restricts access to the machine with the server. For example, as you saw earlier for an FTP server, this can be done as

```
in.ftpd: <machine-IP> 127.0.0.1 localhost: allow
in.ftpd: deny
```

if you are only using the `/etc/hosts.allow` file, or as

```
in.ftpd: <machine-IP> 127.0.0.1 localhost
```

if you are using the traditional `/etc/hosts.allow` and `/etc/hosts.deny` files.

Alternatively, if you are using the access restriction capabilities of xinetd, you could add a line to the /etc/xinetd.d/ftp file like

```
only_from       = <machine-IP> 127.0.0.1 localhost
```

Next, use an SSH client to set up a tunnel. For Windows, traditional Mac OS, or Mac OS X Classic mode, this is a matter of using an SSH client to enter the local port to use on your machine, the name of the server, and the port number to use on the server. From a Unix machine, such as the native Mac OS X side of your Macintosh, use ssh with a port forwarding option. The following example sets up a tunnel without requiring that you have a terminal connection:

```
% slogin 192.168.1.17 -l sage -N -L 2121:192.168.1.17:21
sage@192.168.1.17's password:
```

In the preceding statement, a tunnel is set up between the local machine and the remote host 192.168.1.17 for user sage. The remote host can be specified as a host-name or an IP address. The tunnel is created between the local host at port 2121 and the remote host at port 21. The -N option enables you to set up a tunnel without initiating a terminal session. Please note that only root can forward ports under 1024. So if you wanted to use a port number under 1024 on the local machine, you would have to have root privileges.

After the port forwarding is set up in the SSH client, then use the regular client for the service, providing it with the appropriate local port to use and localhost or 127.0.0.1 as the host.

An FTP session over this encrypted channel would look like this:

```
% ftp localhost 2121
Connected to localhost.biosci.ohio-state.edu.
220 192.168.1.17 FTP server (lukemftpd 1.1) ready.
Name (localhost:joray): sage
331 Password required for sage.
Password:
230-
    Welcome to Darwin!
230 User sage logged in.
Remote system type is UNIX.
Using binary mode to transfer files.
ftp> cd printing
250 CWD command successful.
ftp> passive
Passive mode on.
ftp> get test-1.tiff
```

```
local: test-1.tiff remote: test-1.tiff
227 Entering Passive Mode (192,168,1,17,192,9)
150 Opening BINARY mode data connection for 'test-1.tiff' (431888 bytes).
226 Transfer complete.
431888 bytes received in 0.516 seconds (837284 bytes/s)
ftp> quit
221-
    Data traffic for this session was 431888 bytes in 1 file.
    Total traffic for this session was 432551 bytes in 1 transfer.
221 Thank you for using the FTP service on 192.168.1.17.
```

In short, the basic procedure to follow for tunneling a given protocol is as follows:

1. Optionally restrict access by setting up the server to accept connections from only the server machine. Depending on your circumstances, you may have to have this restriction anyway.
2. Set up an SSH client with port and server information.
3. Set up the client for the service being tunneled with the local port number to use and `localhost` or `127.0.0.1` as the host.
4. Use the client for the tunneled service as you ordinarily would.

A notable exception to this basic procedure is the procedure for tunneling X11 connections. The SSH server on the remote machine whose display you want to have displayed to your local machine should have X11 forwarding enabled. From your local machine, simply connect with the `ssh` or `slogin` command with the `-X` option, which tunnels an X11 connection. Because SSH takes care of handling everything else to make it work, you don't have to worry about details such as setting the `DISPLAY` environment variable. However, if this doesn't quite work for you, it may also be necessary for the remote host to add a line to `/etc/hosts.allow` to enable your IP address to have access to the `sshdfwd-X11` service.

Figure 14.1 shows remotely running X11 applications being displayed to an OS X machine via SSH tunneling.

Secure File Transfer

As you also saw in Chapter 12, the OpenSSH package also includes two utilities for transferring files: `scp` (secure copy) and `sftp` (secure FTP). Table 14.6 provides documentation on the options available to `scp`. Table 14.7 provides documentation on options available to the command line in `sftp` as well as commands available interactively.

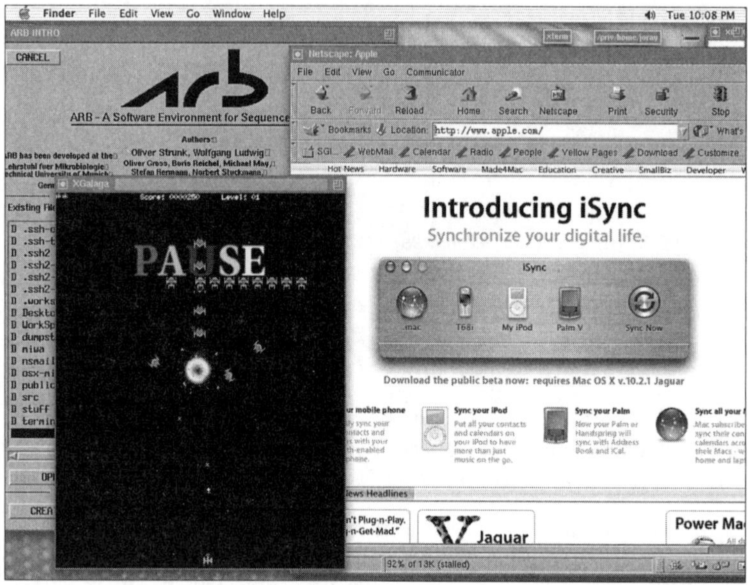

FIGURE 14.1 Remotely running X11 applications are being displayed on an OS X machine via SSH tunneling.

The basic syntax for scp is

```
scp <from> <to>
```

The <*from*> or <*to*> can be specified as a remote host and file, expanding the basic syntax to:

```
scp [[<username>@]<remote_host>:]<pathtofile> [[<username>@]<remote_host>:]
➥<pathtofile>
```

The <*remote_host*> can be a name or IP address. Here is sample output from copying a file on the remote host, ~sage/terminal/term-display-1.tiff, to the current directory on the local machine:

```
% scp sage@192.168.1.17:terminal/term-display-1.tiff ./
sage@192.168.1.17's password:
term-display-1.tiff  100% |*********************************|   900 KB   00:01
```

While the transfer occurs, the percentage and amount transferred increases over time. You cannot use scp to copy files from your OS X machine unless you have activated the SSH server.

TABLE 14.6 Options for `scp`

Option	Function
`-c <cipher>`	Selects the cipher to use for encrypting the data transfer. Option is passed directly to `ssh`.
`-i <identity_file>`	Selects the file from which the identity (private key) for RSA authentication is read. Option is passed directly to `ssh`.
`-p`	Preserves modification times, access times, and modes from the original file.
`-r`	Recursively copies entire directories.
`-v`	Verbose mode. Causes `scp` and `ssh` to print debugging messages about their progress.
`-B`	Selects batch mode, which prevents passwords or passphrases from being requested.
`-q`	Disables the progress meter.
`-C`	Enables compression. Passes the `-C` flag to `ssh` to enable compression.
`-F <ssh_config>`	Specifies an alternative per-user configuration file for `ssh`. Option is passed directly to `ssh`.
`-P <port>`	Specifies the port to connect to on the remote host.
`-S <program>`	Specifies `<program>` as the program to use for the encrypted connection. The program must understand `ssh` options.
`-o <ssh_option>`	Passes options to `ssh` in the format used in the `ssh` configuration file. This is useful for specifying options for which there is no separate `scp` command-line flag. For example, forcing the use of protocol version 1 is specified using `scp -o Protocol=1`.
`-4`	Forces `scp` to use IPv4 addresses only.
`-6`	Forces `scp` to use IPv6 addresses only.

The `sftp` command can also be used to securely transfer files. Its basic syntax, shown following, initiates an interactive session that works much like regular `ftp`:

```
sftp [<usesrname>@]<remote_host>
```

Here is sample output from an interactive `sftp` session:

```
% sftp sage@192.168.1.17
Connecting to 192.168.1.17...
sage@192.168.1.17's password:
sftp> get terminal/term-display-2.tiff
Fetching /Users/sage/terminal/term-display-2.tiff to term-display-2.tiff
sftp> quit
```

In this example, `sftp` is used to transfer a file on the remote host, `~sage/terminal/term-display-2.tiff`, to the current directory on the local machine. As with `scp`, you cannot use `sftp` to transfer files from your OS X machine unless you have activated the SSH.

TABLE 14.7 Documentation for `sftp`

Option	Function
`-b <batchfile>`	Batch mode. Reads a series of commands from an input `batchfile` instead of `stdin`.
`-o <ssh_option>`	Passes options to `ssh` in the format used in the `ssh` configuration file. Useful for specifying options for which there is no separate `sftp` command-line flag. For example, to specify an alternate port, use `sftp -oPort=24`.
`-s <subsystem> | <sftp_server>`	Specifies the SSH2 subsystem or the path for an `sftp` server on the remote host. A path is useful for using `sftp` over protocol version 1, or when the remote `sshd` does not have an `sftp` subsystem configured.
`-v`	Raises logging level. Option is also passed to `ssh`.
`-B <buffer_size>`	Specifies the size of the buffer that `sftp` uses when transferring files. Larger buffers require fewer round trips at the cost of higher memory consumption. Default is 32768 bytes.
`-C`	Enables compression (via `ssh`'s `-C` flag).
`-F <ssh_config>`	Specifies an alternative per-user configuration file for `ssh`. Option is passed directly to `ssh`.
`-P <sftp_server path>`	Connects directly to a local `sftp-server` (rather than via `ssh`). May be useful in debugging the client and server.
`-R <num_requests>`	Specifies how many requests may be outstanding at any one time. Increasing this may slightly improve file transfer speed but increases memory usage. Default is `16` outstanding requests.
`-S <program>`	Specifies `<program>` as the program to use for the encrypted connection. The program must understand `ssh` options.
`-1`	Specifies the use of protocol version 1.
Interactive Commands	
`bye`	Quits `sftp`.
`cd <path>`	Changes remote directory to `<path>`.
`lcd <path>`	Changes local directory to `<path>`.
`chgrp <grp> <path>`	Changes group of file `<path>` to `<grp>`.
`chmod <mode> <path>`	Changes permissions of file `<path>` to `<mode>`.
`chown <owner> <path>`	Changes owner of file `<path>` to `<owner>`.
`exit`	Quits `sftp`.
`get [<flags>] <remote-path> [<local-path>]`	Retrieves the `<remote-path>` and stores it on the local machine. If the local path name is not specified, it is given the same name it has on the remote machine. If the `-P` flag is specified, then the file's full permission and access time are copied, too.
`help`	Displays help text.
`lls [<ls-options> [<path>]]`	Displays local directory listing of either `<path>` or current directory if `<path>` is not specified.

TABLE 14.7 Continued

Option	Function
Interactive Commands	
`lmkdir <path>`	Creates local directory specified by `<path>`.
`ln <oldpath> <newpath>`	Creates a symbolic link from `<oldpath>` to `<newpath>`.
`lpwd`	Prints local working directory.
`ls [<path>]`	Displays remote directory listing of either `<path>` or current directory if `<path>` is not specified.
`lumask <umask>`	Sets local umask to `<umask>`.
`mkdir <path>`	Creates remote directory specified by `<path>`.
`put [<flags>] <local-path> [<remote-path>]`	Uploads `<local-path>` and stores it on the remote machine. If the remote pathname is not specified, it is given the same name it has on the local machine. If the `-P` flag is specified, then the file's full permission and access time are copied, too.
`pwd`	Displays remote working directory.
`quit`	Quits `sftp`.
`rename <oldpath> <newpath>`	Renames remote file from `<oldpath>` to `<newpath>`.
`rmdir <path>`	Removes remote directory specified by `<path>`.
`rm <path>`	Deletes remote file specified by `<path>`.
`symlink <oldpath> <newpath>`	Creates a symbolic link from `<oldpath>` to `<newpath>`.
`! <command>`	Executes command in local shell.
`!`	Escapes to local shell.
`?`	Synonym for help.

Public Key Authentication

In addition to the standard method of user authentication—a username and password—SSH provides another method: public key authentication. With the traditional authentication method, the remote host stores a username and password pair for a user. With public key authentication, the user creates a key pair on a given host. The key pair consists of a private key and a public key that is protected with a passphrase. Then the user transfers the public key to the remote host to which she would like to connect. So the remote host stores a set of public keys for machines on which you have generated a key pair and transferred a copy of your public key. Furthermore, you protect your keys with a passphrase, rather than a password.

The procedure for enabling public key authentication is similar for both SSH1 and SSH2. Table 14.8 provides documentation on options for `ssh-keygen`, the utility that generates key pairs. Table 14.9 provides descriptions for files used in public key authentication. To enable public key authentication, do the following:

1. Generate a key pair on the host from which you want to access another host. (For example, call the host from which you want to connect the local host, and the host to which you want to connect the remote host.) Use a good passphrase to protect your key. It is recommended that a good passphrase be 10–30 characters long, and not simple sentences or otherwise easily guessable. Include a mix of uppercase, lowercase, numeric, and nonalphanumeric characters.

2. Transfer the public key of the key pair generated on the local host to the remote host. The public key is public, so you can use any method necessary to transfer it to the remote host.

3. Add the public key you just transferred to the file on the remote host that stores public keys.

4. Test logging into the remote host. You should now be prompted for the passphrase that you used to generate your key pair, because the private key of the local host is paired with its public key that was transferred to the remote host.

TABLE 14.8 Options for `ssh-keygen`

Option	Function
`-b <bits>`	Specifies the number of bits in the key to create. Minimum is 512 bits. Default is 1024 bits.
`-c`	Requests the changing of the comment in the private and public key files. This operation is supported for only RSA1 keys.
`-e`	Reads a private or public OpenSSH key file and prints the key in a SECSH Public Key File Format to `stdout`. This option exports keys that can be used by several commercial SSH implementations.
`-f <filename>`	Specifies the filename of the key file.
`-i`	Reads an unencrypted private (or public) key file in SSH2-compatible format and prints an OpenSSH compatible private (or public) key to `stdout`. `ssh-keygen` also reads the -SECSH Public Key File Format. This option imports keys from several commercial SSH implementations.
`-l`	Shows fingerprint of specified public key file. Private RSA1 keys are also supported. For RSA and DSA keys, `ssh-keygen` tries to find the matching public key file and prints its fingerprint.
`-p`	Requests that the passphrase of a private key file be changed rather than that a new private key be created.
`-q`	Quiet mode. Silences `ssh-keygen`.
`-y`	Reads a private OpenSSH format file and prints an OpenSSH public key to `stdout`.
`-t <type>`	Specifies the type of the key to create. The possible values are `rsa1` for protocol version 1 and `rsa` or `dsa` for protocol version 2.

TABLE 14.8 Continued

Option	Function
`-B`	Show the `bubblebabble` digest of the specified private or public key file.
`-C <comment>`	Provides the new comment.
`-D <reader>`	Downloads the `RSA` public key stored in the smartcard in reader.
`-N <new_passphrase>`	Provides the new passphrase, `<new_passphrase>`.
`-P <passphrase>`	Provides the (old) passphrase, `<passphrase>`.

TABLE 14.9 Files Used in Public Key Authentication

File	Description
`$HOME/.ssh/identity`	Contains the user's protocol version 1 `RSA` authentication identity. This file should not be readable by anyone but the user. It is possible to specify a passphrase when generating the key; that passphrase will be used to encrypt the private part of this file with `3DES` encryption. File is not automatically accessed by `ssh-keygen`, but is offered as the default file for the private key. `ssh` reads this file when a login attempt is made.
`$HOME/.ssh/identity.pub`	Contains the protocol version 1 `RSA` public key for authentication. The contents of this file should be added to `$HOME/.ssh/authorized_keys` on all machines where the user wishes to log in using RSA authentication. There is no need to keep the contents of this file secret.
`$HOME/.ssh/id_dsa`	Contains the user's protocol version 2 DSA authentication identity. This file should not be readable by anyone but the user. It is possible to specify a passphrase when generating the key; that passphrase will be used to encrypt the private part of this file with `3DES` encryption. This file is not automatically accessed by `ssh-keygen`, but it is offered as the default file for the private key. `ssh` reads this file when a login attempt is made.
`$HOME/.ssh/id_dsa.pub`	Contains the protocol version 2 `DSA` public key for authentication. The contents of this file should be added to `$HOME/.ssh/authorized_keys` on all machines where the user wants to log in using public key authentication. There is no need to keep the contents of this file secret.
`$HOME/.ssh/id_rsa`	Contains the user's protocol version 2 `RSA` authentication identity. This file should not be readable by anyone but the user. It is possible to specify a passphrase when generating the key; that passphrase will be used to encrypt the private part of this file with `3DES` encryption. This file is not automatically accessed by `ssh-keygen`, but it is offered as the default file for the private key. `ssh` reads this file when a login attempt is made.
`$HOME/.ssh/id_rsa.pub`	Contains the protocol version 2 `RSA` public key for authentication. The contents of this file should be added to `$HOME/.ssh/authorized_keys` on all machines where the user wants to log in using public key authentication. There is no need to keep the contents of this file secret.

Not only are there differences in public key authentication between SSH1 and SSH2, but there are differences between SSH packages as well. The keys for SSH1 and SSH2 generated by OpenSSH differ from the ones made by SSH Communications Security's SSH servers, which are the other variety you are most likely to encounter. Be sure to thoroughly read the `ssh-keygen`, `ssh`, and `sshd` man pages for the SSH servers you have to connect to, because the information you need to know for connecting via public key authentication will most likely be spread among those man pages. The keys look a bit different for the different protocols, and can look quite different between the SSH packages. Fortunately, OpenSSH's `ssh-keygen` can import and export keys.

To give you an idea of how the various public keys look, some sample public keys are shown here. The samples were made using the defaults, except for this first key, which does not have a default for the algorithm. This key is a sample SSH2 public key generated in OpenSSH with the DSA algorithm option (`ssh-keygen -t dsa`), stored as `~/.ssh/id_dsa.pub`:


```
ssh-dss AAAAB3NzaC1kc3MAAACBALzT9RbceziStHPmMiHmg78hXUgcMP14sJZ/7MH/p2NX
/fB0cmbULPNgEN8jrs8w9N73J7yUFHSPR/LVfBj+UwkIzwjyXUW/z/VmCs25IDF/UBn1OQK5
PCi16rF0F+Cx0hMN4R3AaFAetXBdLqoom5x4Yo9gdspPqhhB44QnT43JAAAAFQDWTkKDJ2m4
SApHZ/qRnRpMN5whTQAAAIAVADOsHpnUdUOFKjIgxZ0Hwh7IaMQ2ofGt/6PmbmNG/8zXRdxm
u/JrBzieWHq6sSRSkWDSDIjuEuTkZyJ4wx3KsLmhIrtlBw3NCcsJT2GfGQ9gEBm8fkUpeQyK
AQcirbx4Hw93iMFC3g9A8cwqmA4DalKSX3un7cweNU32Irhq+gAAAIAz+lDSjqjFzuTV4vJ/
P83nH2uwb62/iCSIB9cL32hrOm234imaAceu8pN9qqEAPr9AilCWa+lqGvgcdyDK0vZTvKQn
k6KOU3TJfDyMR7i/gzW4P4TA/
```


This is a sample SSH1 public key generated in OpenSSH with the RSA algorithm (`ssh-keygen -t rsa`), stored as `~.ssh/identity.pub`:


```
1024 35 155721298510659584179944539389589685520184296531692648011618717 8
47931275273178693642653436228988381482922069944869579300829219135525658 1
25248351354000991356228685632047778649000628072666080837001969287828694 1
83286791348827043363003985437592043458504034267132999021632074427678357 6
664388358911747235081029563 87 miwa@Sage-Rays-Computer.local.
```


This key is a sample SSH2 public key generated in SSH Communications Security's SSH server with the DSA algorithm (`ssh-keygen2 -t dsa`), stored in `~/.ssh2/id_dsa_1024_a.pub`:


```
---- BEGIN SSH2 PUBLIC KEY ----
Subject: miwa
Comment: "1024-bit dsa, miwa@Rosalyn, Thu May 16 2002 23:33:30 -0500"
AAAAB3NzaC1kc3MAAACBAIxEJgV24AtDzKyFzMAD5agu/YHOZnhUma12zVX31Ov5Xj9hU/
0VB/FdxtctLKbUMRra5b9azzHFsdJl/f1VqoQ8feEfFZ/4nTcSVbL5f5KydmSe0Mmyq4vq
IqSC4jyDjIHMUcDfj2Z/kRhF9o6VxCdCUd5OvkpZmEfWqLNR9oPlAAAAFQD02rAsEPS2uU
```

```
VTAa/pHqKhcrC6mwAAAIB3UDIDjP9TOJNaap34/9o0qW1o7agFMXcJftlUgZEtUfc5v/jX
MplQiL77CggJU+rdv9WQbyefaFjWLQAibV5M71kt2mdkYVtuQzbmBTDW9v8YP1/QMnnjOK
v8xRmrsplC/lv9/rmzS0gI1Hfbbuq60zW/ULdg6c61y7HyZ/Qf5AAAAIArWb/PIWRhMxLR
aY9VZvFZOYjOxcIR66aoybkneODPaAwZsW5yq1q2XEpxxza4q2yTyZ7drTYLCUBbXwG4Cu
RVv3CMTiXQ47AXlKYPECVT0I4bTZyY60GuLI4TUsyHLk5HFF0Ctt/6OB8WEHOn6LGDNNoN
DF4M7MlGbyOVNZnGCw==
---- END SSH2 PUBLIC KEY ----
```

This is a sample SSH2 public key generated in SSH Communications Security's SSH server with the RSA algorithm (`ssh-keygen2 -t rsa`), stored in `~/.ssh2/id_rsa_1024_a.pub`:

```
---- BEGIN SSH2 PUBLIC KEY ----
Subject: miwa
Comment: "1024-bit rsa, miwa@Rosalyn, Sun Sep 08 2002 23:00:14 -0500"
AAAAB3NzaC1yc2EAAAADAQABAAAAgQDenNONzW2v+TB/ZeRHZvKRWJk24Lk7LsA4+uWsYL
5L+bNoPYV0oKD3UMYddEacM47gcSd2e1E511Wlx/+X0MjrvPqEIlqw9owkjwOukm38iISz
qypT4uvawOW9GcKE7c5KH8BD9tfhvCkwZE+oAsJk3jfTBRSdOdxhvhF87RgbcQ==
---- END SSH2 PUBLIC KEY ----
```

This is a sample SSH1 public key generated in SSH Communications Security's SSH server with the RSA algorithm (`ssh-keygen1`), stored in `~/.ssh/identity.pub`:

```
1024 35 150523262886747450533481402006467053649597280355648477085483985
712083176768664660899834191983286561976032166628443720186802736469866695
561784637378345179225111133633075841684444147236898954804613540972039555
146309834605363142493240937409415470774407489421467610336509326725169133
155150617149168536905710250843163 miwa@Rosalyn
```

After you have transferred your public key to the remote host, you have to let the remote host know that you want to allow public key authentication from your local host. How this is done depends on the SSH server. For OpenSSH, authorized public keys for SSH1 and SSH2 keys are stored in `~/.ssh/authorized_keys`. Each line of a basic `authorized_keys` file contains a public key. Blank lines and lines starting with # are ignored. However, limitations can be further placed on an authorized public key if you use the options listed in Table 14.10. The following is a sample `~/.ssh/authorized_keys` file:

```
1024 35 1557212985106595841799445393895896855201842965316926480116187178
479312752731786936426534362289883814829220699448695793008292191355256581
252483513540009913562286856320477786490006280726660808370019692878286941
832867913488270433630039854375920434585040342671329990216320744276783576
66438835891174723508102956387 miwa@Sage-Rays-Computer.local.
```

```
ssh-dss AAAAB3NzaC1kc3MAAACBALPMiCqdPDGxcyB1IwPrPXk3oEqvpxR62EsspxGKGGbO
M6mf60i1hwTvjZzDhUSR7ViGeCopKtjJIqn2ljgeLbhFsQUX2UyJ6A1cFVuef0x6GVAsybqb
tJc8JBh41U+iSXJKppEY5BI+REMydpBXJf2qT/8yZeq3NPjiOiMb6TyjAAAAFQDYvvV4WQK1
Zu23q/7iLKg5j/zi5wAAAIBR7vgrQpjKW2cprIUJsnenTm4hnBrEO7NMUomjgezrY23iZdIS
QlU1ESMgx9W9nnZstd2vjeqHDSmmcD2p/aGqhl3N1WlYk8zgFYYJilPwRxVm77Np/vXz/MQp
ygJE7ToXGvfHqVmdBpUyakyfx6DveWhFPis1Ab8N1RCPWm6PMwAAAIAytHjAAMYscqX2tl4i
cw3oOku3HIvoHBCx9D6Q9LjCqt7DqqgMN2e5vuvNz0hzqBaBDJsjNA/A4bI88ZrgLhfJM/Nh
s2xkcb7AYeHEtuGKVbsbB0EjsECtLRHydfmk3wDQjUVT92HsodFvsIl4Je7seWUuiAEe0V1x
fF7XrXuwNQ== miwa@hobbes
```

For an SSH Communications Security SSH1 server, the authorized public keys are also stored in `~/.ssh/authorized_keys`. An SSH2 server by SSH Communications Security, however, stores references to files that contain authorized public keys in `~/.ssh2/authorization`. Here is a sample `~/.ssh/authorization` file:

```
Key hobbes.pub
Key ryoohki.pub
```

As an example, suppose you want to allow public key authentication from a machine running an SSH Communications Security SSH2 server. First, generate a key pair on the remote SSH2 machine by using `ssh-keygen2`.

Then transfer the public key of the key pair to your Mac OS X machine by whatever method you choose.

In this case, because you want to allow public key authentication from a machine running a non-OpenSSH SSH server, you have to convert the public key file that was transferred to something compatible with your OpenSSH server. The `ssh-keygen` utility can convert between SSH formats. Run a command of the following form:

```
ssh-keygen -i -f <transferred_public_key> > <converted_transferred_public_key>
```

The preceding statement imports the transferred public key file and directs the converted output to a file specified by *<converted_transferred_public_key>*. We recommend including the name of the remote host in your filename to make things easier for you. OpenSSH's `ssh-keygen` can also export its keys to the IETF SECSH format.

Then add that file to the `~/.ssh/authorized_keys` file, the file that contains your public keys from machines authorized to connect via public key authentication. This can be done in whatever way you feel most comfortable. Issuing the following statement does this quite neatly:

```
cat <converted_transferred_public_key> >> .ssh/authorized_keys
```

Now that the public key from the non-OpenSSH machine has been transferred and converted to a format used by OpenSSH, you can log in to your Mac OS X machine from the remote host via pubic key authentication.

Logging in to a machine running a non-OpenSSH SSH server from your OS X machine is similar. First generate the key pair on your OS X machine by using `ssh-keygen`. Then convert the public key file to the IETF SECSH format by running a command of the form:

```
ssh-keygen -e -f <public_key> > <converted_public_key>
```

Transfer the converted public key file to the remote host by whatever method you choose. Then add a reference to the form's `~/.ssh2/authorization` file:

```
Key <public_key_filename>
```

Now that the public key generated on your OS X machine has been transferred to the remote host running a non-OpenSSH SSH server, and a reference to it has been added to the `~/.ssh2/authorization` file, you can log in to the remote host via public key authentication.

The details provided here address logging in via public key authentication between the major different SSH servers using the SSH2 protocol. Because the SSH1 protocol is not under active development, we are not discussing the details involved there. However, if you need to connect to an SSH1 server via public key authentication, it is easier than what needs to be done for the SSH2 protocol. You do not have to convert the key formats. On the non-OpenSSH machine, the file that contains the public keys is `~/.ssh/authorized_keys`, and you add public keys themselves to the file, rather than references to the public key files.

If you don't like the command line, you might try Gideon Softworks' `SSH Helper`, available at `http://www.gideonsoftworks.com/`. It is a freely available package.

TABLE 14.10 Options for `~/.ssh/authorized_keys`

Option	Function
`from="pattern-list"`	Specifies that in addition to RSA authentication, the canonical name of the remote host must be present in the comma-separated list of patterns.
`command="command"`	Specifies that the command is executed whenever this key is used for authentication. The command supplied by the user (if any) is ignored. This option might be useful to restrict certain RSA keys to perform just a specific operation, such as a key that permits remote backups but nothing else.
`environment="NAME=value"`	Specifies that the string is to be added to the environment when logging in using this key. Environment variables set this way override other default environment values. Multiple options of this type are permitted. This option is automatically disabled if `UseLogin` is enabled.
`no-port-forwarding`	Forbids `TCP/IP` forwarding when this key is used for authentication. This might be used, for example, in connection with the command option.

TABLE 14.10 Continued

Option	Function
`no-X11-forwarding`	Forbids `X11` forwarding when this key is used for authentication.
`no-agent-forwarding`	Forbids authentication agent forwarding when this key is used for authentication.
`no-pty`	Prevents `tty` allocation.
`permitopen="host:port"`	Limits local `ssh -L` port forwarding to connect to only the specified `host` and `port`.

A Butler to Hold Your Wallet: `ssh-agent`

The SSH suite of applications is wonderful for protecting your communications, but although entering a passphrase instead of a password for logins through `ssh` is only a minor inconvenience, repeating it over and over to copy files with `scp` can be a real annoyance. Thankfully, the designers thought of this, and have created an auxiliary application that enables you to authenticate yourself once to it, and it can then use the stored private keys and the passphrases associated with your SSH identities (SSH key pairs generated by `ssh-keygen` and authorized on another host) to authenticate to remote hosts for you automatically. Essentially, this software acts as your agent and responds for you, whenever a remote host asks for your passphrase. This eliminates any need for you to respond to passphrase queries from remote hosts for which the agent knows a proper response, and can drastically decrease the effort involved in using the SSH applications.

If you're dealing with SSH on a daily basis, using `ssh-agent` is almost certainly the way you'll want to use the SSH software; it will make your life much easier. The process for using the agent is simple as well, and can be summarized as follows:

1. Start the `ssh-agent`.
2. Set up your environment so that SSH applications can find the agent.
3. Add identities to the agent.
4. Use SSH applications (`slogin`, `scp`, etc.), and never get asked for your passphrase.

However, although the difference in practice is significant, the difference in print is subtle. Previously in this chapter you've learned how to perform all the steps necessary to work through SSH, but for the sake of clarity with respect to what `ssh-agent` can actually do for you, we'll recap from the position of a user who's never used SSH to authenticate to remote hosts. In the examples that follow, we've left the prompt intact so that you can tell in which machine and directory we're working. The input/output fragments that follow were collected as a single stream of actions by our test user `miwa`, and we've split them up to intersperse some comments on what he's doing. If you follow along, by the end of this section you'll have set up a user with two independent SSH identities that can be used to authenticate against both `ssh.com` and `openssh.org` type `sshd` servers.

1. Look first at what files `miwa` has in his `~/.ssh` directory.

   ```
   [Sage-Rays-Computer:~] miwa% ls -l .ssh
   ls: .ssh: No such file or directory
   ```

2. We're starting with a clean slate—we've deleted `miwa`'s `~/.ssh` directory so that it's as if he's never used the SSH software before.

   ```
   [Sage-Rays-Computer:~] miwa% ssh-keygen -t rsa -b 1024
   Generating public/private rsa key pair.
   Enter file in which to save the key (/Users/miwa//.ssh/id_rsa):
   Created directory '/Users/miwa//.ssh'.
   Enter passphrase (empty for no passphrase):
   Enter same passphrase again:
   Your identification has been saved in /Users/miwa//.ssh/id_rsa.
   Your public key has been saved in /Users/miwa//.ssh/id_rsa.pub.
   The key fingerprint is:
   f4:ab:15:d4:47:54:5b:4b:d4:79:be:e6:f7:f3:ca:6d
   ➥miwa@Sage-Rays-Computer.local.
   ```

3. To use SSH applications, `miwa` needs keys. Create his default key as an RSA key of 1024 bits. The "`//`" in the path to his key file is an artifact of the way the software determines paths, and will collapse safely to a single `/`. Enter a passphrase for `miwa`, but notice that it's not echoed to the screen.

   ```
    [Sage-Rays-Computer:~] miwa% ls -l .ssh
   total 16
   -rw-------  1 miwa  staff  951 Feb 17 13:43 id_rsa
   -rw-r--r--  1 miwa  staff  240 Feb 17 13:43 id_rsa.pub
   ```

4. In his `~/.ssh` directory, there are now two files, containing the private and public key pair for his default identity.

   ```
   [Sage-Rays-Computer:~] miwa% slogin ryoko.biosci.ohio-state.edu
   miwa@ryoko.biosci.ohio-state.edu's password:
   Last login: Mon Feb 17 2003 13:51:04 -0500 from cvl232015.columb
   You have mail.
   ryoko miwa 1 >ls -l .ssh2
   .ssh2: No such file or directory
   ```

```
ryoko miwa 2 >mkdir .ssh2
ryoko miwa 3 >exit
Connection to ryoko.biosci.ohio-state.edu closed.
```

5. `miwa` logs into `ryoko.biosci.ohio-state.edu`, using his password for the system. `ryoko` is a Sun Enterprise Server running `ssh.com`'s version of the SSH software. It doesn't keep its key files in the same place as does our Macintosh's `openssh.org` version. `miwa` creates the required `~/.ssh2` directory in his home directory on `ryoko` and then logs off the machine. For the best security, we recommend disabling passworded logins from the network entirely, and accepting only passphrases, but this requires physical access to both machines for at least a little while, or some other way of transferring a public key without being able to log in to the remote machine via the network.

```
[Sage-Rays-Computer:~] miwa% cd .ssh
[Sage-Rays-Computer:~/.ssh] miwa% ls -l
total 24
-rw-------  1 miwa  staff  951 Feb 17 13:43 id_rsa
-rw-r--r--  1 miwa  staff  240 Feb 17 13:43 id_rsa.pub
-rw-r--r--  1 miwa  staff  633 Feb 17 13:45 known_hosts
[Sage-Rays-Computer:~/.ssh] miwa% ssh-keygen -e -f id_rsa
---- BEGIN SSH2 PUBLIC KEY ----
Comment: "1024-bit RSA, converted from OpenSSH by
➥miwa@Sage-Rays-Computer.local."
AAAAB3NzaC1yc2EAAAABIwAAAIEAttgqNkpzwf991Siz3EpJsPTt2cHt3aecCqc542+rIw
8P3PdmQP78+uFHiFMEQMr5/NcoxPxDWS1QGb06iihYt3j8QoxTbRD/b7b9mdHHDzJekCH2
jSonnVCh+XUsCAG8KeZ64VZuLEbXOf9VRlBZC2T7MWt6woMgVJvvKqyJVuk=
---- END SSH2 PUBLIC KEY ----
```

6. `miwa` needs to get the public key for the identity he wants to use on `ryoko` into a form that `ryoko`'s `sshd` can understand. Pleasantly, `ssh-keygen` cannot only generate keys, but it can also translate them into the standard format that `ssh.com`'s server version wants. A `known_hosts` file has appeared in `miwa`'s `.ssh` directory along with his `id_rsa` identity files. In this file is recorded the public host key for `ryoko`.

```
[Sage-Rays-Computer:~/.ssh] miwa% ssh-keygen -e -f id_rsa > home_rsa.ietf
[Sage-Rays-Computer:~/.ssh] miwa% ls -l
total 32
-rw-r--r--  1 miwa  staff  347 Feb 17 13:57 home_rsa.ietf
-rw-------  1 miwa  staff  951 Feb 17 13:43 id_rsa
-rw-r--r--  1 miwa  staff  240 Feb 17 13:43 id_rsa.pub
-rw-r--r--  1 miwa  staff  633 Feb 17 13:45 known_hosts
```

7. Using `ssh-keygen`, `miwa` writes out an IETF formatted version of the public key for his `id.rsa` key, and puts it in his `.ssh` directory. Because the SSH implementation on Mac OS X won't use this key for anything, he could actually store it just about anywhere, but this seems like as good and safe a place as any.

```
[Sage-Rays-Computer:~/.ssh] miwa% scp ./home_rsa.ietf
➥miwa@ryoko.biosci.ohio-state.edu:.ssh2/home_rsa.ietf
miwa@ryoko.biosci.ohio-state.edu's password:
scp: warning: Executing scp1 compatibility.
home_rsa.ietf        100% |****************************|   347       00:00
```

8. `miwa` copies the key to `ryoko` by using `scp`. Because it's a public key, it wouldn't be a problem even if he had to copy it over a protocol where data is visible. If passworded logins are blocked, this key transfer needs to be done in some other fashion, such as transporting it on removable media.

```
[Sage-Rays-Computer:~/.ssh] miwa% slogin ryoko.biosci.ohio-state.edu
miwa@ryoko.biosci.ohio-state.edu's password:
Last login: Mon Feb 17 2003 13:53:54 -0500 from cvl232015.columb
You have mail.
ryoko miwa 1 >ls -l .ssh2
total 2
-rw-r--r--   1 miwa     class        347 Feb 17 14:01 home_rsa.ietf
ryoko miwa 2 >cd .ssh2
ryoko .ssh2 3 >cat >> authorization
Key home_rsa.ietf
^D
```

9. An `authorization` file must be created on `ryoko`, listing the key `miwa` just transferred as valid for logins. `miwa` just `cat`s the line in append mode onto his `authorization` file. The file doesn't exist, so it'll get created, but if it did exist, this Key line would simply be added as new data at the end of the file. The `cat` command is terminated with a `Control-D` on a line by itself.

```
ryoko .ssh2 4 >ls -l
total 4
-rw-r--r--   1 miwa     class         18 Feb 17 14:02 authorization
-rw-r--r--   1 miwa     class        347 Feb 17 14:01 home_rsa.ietf
ryoko .ssh2 5 >chmod 600 authorization home_rsa.ietf
ryoko .ssh2 6 >ls -l
total 4
-rw-------   1 miwa     class         18 Feb 17 14:02 authorization
-rw-------   1 miwa     class        347 Feb 17 14:01 home_rsa.ietf
ryoko .ssh2 7 >cat authorization
```

```
Key home_rsa.ietf
ryoko .ssh2 8 >exit
Connection to ryoko.biosci.ohio-state.edu closed.
```

10. The authorization file now exists, and contains the data expected. Even though it's a public key and theoretically can't be usefully abused, `miwa` `chmod`s both files in his `.sshd` directory so that only he can read them, just to be sure.

```
[Sage-Rays-Computer:~/.ssh] miwa% slogin ryoko.biosci.ohio-state.edu
Enter passphrase for key '/Users/miwa//.ssh/id_rsa':
Last login: Mon Feb 17 2003 14:05:00 -0500 from cvl232015.columb
You have mail.
ryoko miwa 1 >exit
Connection to ryoko.biosci.ohio-state.edu closed.
```

11. Back on Sage's computer, `miwa` can now `slogin` to `ryoko`, and be asked for a passphrase rather than his considerably weaker password.

```
[Sage-Rays-Computer:~/.ssh] miwa% ssh-keygen -t rsa -b 1024
Generating public/private rsa key pair.
Enter file in which to save the key (/Users/miwa//.ssh/id_rsa):
➥/Users/miwa//.ssh/internal_rsa
Enter passphrase (empty for no passphrase):
Enter same passphrase again:
Your identification has been saved in /Users/miwa//.ssh/internal_rsa.
Your public key has been saved in /Users/miwa//.ssh/internal_rsa.pub.
The key fingerprint is:
62:47:b5:71:2b:23:08:ee:87:e2:cc:7d:0b:ce:4d:44
➥miwa@Sage-Rays-Computer.local.
```

12. For some reason, `miwa` wants another, separate identity for use on his internal (private) network. Perhaps it's because he's going to allow (against our good advice) other users to log in to his account and use it for connecting to other machines on the internal network. By using a separate identity, and giving out the passphrase only to his internal identity, he can mitigate the danger in this scheme and protect his external identity. Here, `miwa`'s chosen to create it into the nondefault file `internal_rsa`, again as a 1024-bit RSA key.

```
[Sage-Rays-Computer:~/.ssh] miwa% ls -l
total 48
-rw-r--r--  1 miwa  staff  347 Feb 17 13:57 home_rsa.ietf
-rw-------  1 miwa  staff  951 Feb 17 13:43 id_rsa
-rw-r--r--  1 miwa  staff  240 Feb 17 13:43 id_rsa.pub
-rw-------  1 miwa  staff  951 Feb 17 14:11 internal_rsa
```

```
-rw-r--r--  1 miwa  staff  240 Feb 17 14:11 internal_rsa.pub
-rw-r--r--  1 miwa  staff  633 Feb 17 13:45 known_hosts
```

13. Now there are files in `~miwa/.ssh/` for both his default `id_rsa` identity and his `internal_rsa` identity. `miwa` needs to transfer the public key from the `internal_rsa` key pair to any of the private, internal-network hosts he wants to be able to access via passphrase. In this case, `192.168.1.200`, otherwise known as `creampuf`, will be used as an example.

```
[Sage-Rays-Computer:~/.ssh] miwa% slogin 192.168.1.200
The authenticity of host '192.168.1.200 (192.168.1.200)'
➥can't be established.
RSA key fingerprint is f3:62:16:8e:25:7f:75:ab:4c:cd:99:5d:39:bc:3c:b7.
Are you sure you want to continue connecting (yes/no)? yes
Warning: Permanently added '192.168.1.200' (RSA)
➥to the list of known hosts.
miwa@192.168.1.200's password:
Welcome to Darwin!
[creampuf:~] miwa% ls -l .ssh
ls: .ssh: No such file or directory
[creampuf:~] miwa% mkdir .ssh
[creampuf:~] miwa% touch .ssh/authorized_keys
[creampuf:~] miwa% chmod 600 .ssh/authorized_keys
[creampuf:~] miwa% exit
Connection to 192.168.1.200 closed.
```

14. Again, `miwa` hasn't logged in to this host before, so creating the directory to contain SSH keys is necessary. This time it's a Mac OS X machine, so it uses the `openssh.org` way of specifying authorized remote users, that being a single `authorized_keys` file of (concatenated) authorized keys. `miwa` creates the file, and sets its permissions to owner read/write only.

```
[Sage-Rays-Computer:~/.ssh] miwa% ls -l
total 48
-rw-r--r--  1 miwa  staff  347 Feb 17 13:57 home_rsa.ietf
-rw-------  1 miwa  staff  951 Feb 17 13:43 id_rsa
-rw-r--r--  1 miwa  staff  240 Feb 17 13:43 id_rsa.pub
-rw-------  1 miwa  staff  951 Feb 17 14:11 internal_rsa
-rw-r--r--  1 miwa  staff  240 Feb 17 14:11 internal_rsa.pub
-rw-r--r--  1 miwa  staff  856 Feb 17 14:13 known_hosts
```

15. Back on Sage's computer, the known_hosts file has grown because it's accumulated the host key from 192.168.1.200 now as well.

```
[Sage-Rays-Computer:~/.ssh] miwa% scp internal_rsa.pub ➥
miwa@192.168.1.200:.ssh/miwa_sage_rsa.pub
miwa@192.168.1.200's password:
internal_rsa.pub     100% |****************************|   240       00:00
[Sage-Rays-Computer:~/.ssh] miwa% !slo
slogin 192.168.1.200
miwa@192.168.1.200's password:
Welcome to Darwin!
[creampuf:~] miwa% cd .ssh
[creampuf:~/.ssh] miwa% ls -l
total 8
-rw-------  1 miwa  staff    0 Feb 17 14:17 authorized_keys
-rw-r--r--  1 miwa  staff  240 Feb 17 14:19 miwa_sage_rsa.pub
[creampuf:~/.ssh] miwa% cat miwa_sage_rsa.pub >> authorized_keys
[creampuf:~/.ssh] miwa% cat authorized_keys
ssh-rsa AAAAB3NzaC1yc2EAAAABIwAAAIEAr0JLpso1q7HrZ9EGiK8Gk4lvvxnV2GHAQ
➥CACC4Pdf76NheY3df6+sAmDBhgJ/N8DGorYCmMpd5TdnZkSK+61V3LAtqGno1nFnmNgTy
➥n8HDXm99hJJk0GGnXKi3s74RBqQEcQu3LQtlfJfQW3j51gC9c6XyVANRi53UlorxbADvc
➥= miwa@Sage-Rays-Computer.local.
[creampuf:~/.ssh] miwa% chmod 600 miwa_sage_rsa.pub
[creampuf:~/.ssh] miwa% exit
Connection to 192.168.1.200 closed.
```

16. miwa transfers his public key from his internal_rsa key pair to 192.168.1.200, and saves it as miwa_sage_rsa.pub in his .ssh directory on 192.168.1.200. It's good to come up with a standardized naming scheme for keys that gives you some idea of what user the key was for, and from what host it will allow them access. In this case, because miwa might be allowing other users to log in to his account, he might eventually have many other users' public keys stored in his authorized_keys files in his various accounts around the internal network. Keeping a copy of each of them named in terms of who it allows access, and from which machine, enables him to sort through his authorized_keys file and delete entries if it becomes necessary to limit access in the future.

    After he's transferred his internal_rsa public key to creampuf, he logs in to creampuf (again using his password) and cats the key (in append mode) onto the end of his ~/.ssh/authorized_keys file. He also chmods it to owner read/write only—again, just to be safe.

```
[Sage-Rays-Computer:~/.ssh] miwa% cd ~
[Sage-Rays-Computer:~] miwa% slogin 192.168.1.200
miwa@192.168.1.200's password:
^C
```

17. Back on Sage's machine, `miwa` tests his setup and lands at a `password` prompt. That wasn't the expected behavior. Everything was copied over properly, so maybe it's something about `slogin` that `miwa` doesn't yet understand—maybe it's not smart enough to pick the correct identity credentials from the ones he's created, and it's trying to authenticate to the internal server with his default ID? Reading the `man` page, he discovers that you can specify an ID explicitly, and he tries that option.

```
[Sage-Rays-Computer:~] miwa% slogin 192.168.1.200 -i internal_rsa
Warning: Identity file internal_rsa does not exist.
miwa@192.168.1.200's password:
^C
```

Again, not the desired response, but this time it's a complaint that the identity doesn't exist. Perhaps `slogin`'s not smart enough to look in the default location for anything other than the default identity as well?

```
[Sage-Rays-Computer:~] miwa% slogin 192.168.1.200 -i .ssh/internal_rsa
miwa@192.168.1.200's password:
Welcome to Darwin!
[creampuf:~] miwa% tail -3 /var/log/system.log
Feb 17 14:29:45 creampuf sshd[571]: Could not reverse map
address 192.168.1.17.
Feb 17 14:29:45 creampuf sshd[571]: Authentication refused: bad ownership
or modes for directory /Users/miwa
Feb 17 14:29:53 creampuf sshd[571]: Accepted password for miwa
from 192.168.1.17 port 49182 ssh2
```

Although it doesn't show up in print, there was actually a fairly long pause after `miwa` issued this `slogin` command before it brought up the `password` prompt. Clearly it knows about the ID; it didn't complain about the specification this time, so maybe something's wrong with the server on the remote host. A quick look at the diagnostics from `sshd` in `system.log` reveals the problem. There's something about the permissions of `miwa`'s home directory that `sshd` doesn't like, and it's therefore refusing to allow passphrased access.

```
[creampuf:~] miwa% ls -ld /Users/miwa/
drwxrwxr-x  28 miwa  staff  952 Feb 17 14:17 /Users/miwa/
```

The problem is that miwa has been sloppy with security, and has left his home directory with write access for the staff group. This would enable a malicious user who is a member of group staff to potentially edit or overwrite files in miwa's directory. Because this could allow her to modify miwa's ~/.ssh/authorized_keys file without permission, sshd recognizes this as a security hole, and disables use of that file for authorization.

```
[creampuf:~] miwa% chmod 755 .
[creampuf:~] ls -ld /Users/miwa/
drwxr-xr-x  28 miwa  staff  952 Feb 17 14:17 /Users/miwa/
[creampuf:~] miwa% exit
Connection to 192.168.1.200 closed.
```

18. miwa changes the permissions on his home directory to disallow write access for anyone except himself, and logs out to try again.

```
[Sage-Rays-Computer:~] miwa% slogin 192.168.1.200 -i .ssh/internal_rsa
Enter passphrase for key '.ssh/internal_rsa':
Welcome to Darwin!
```

19. Success! miwa can now log in to either ryoko.biosci.ohio-state.edu, or to 192.168.1.200, and each uses an independent ID with independent passphrases. This brings us to the conclusion of the recap, and to where miwa uses ssh-agent to make his life easier by removing the need for him to constantly type passphrases to use SSH tools.

```
[Sage-Rays-Computer:~] miwa% ssh-agent
setenv SSH_AUTH_SOCK /tmp/ssh-QjvPgj3h/agent.607;
setenv SSH_AGENT_PID 608;
echo Agent pid 608;
```

20. When run, ssh-agent prints out some information regarding how it can be contacted, and forks itself into the background. At that point, it's your agent, ready and willing to answer passphrase requests for you, but it doesn't yet have copies of any of your credentials, and none of the software that needs access to your credentials knows how to find it. The information that it prints out (by default) is csh-syntax commands that will set up a shell so that SSH tools run in that shell can find the agent.

    To use the information, simply copy the lines that ssh-agent prints, and execute them as commands at the command-line prompt.

```
[Sage-Rays-Computer:~] miwa% setenv SSH_AUTH_SOCK /tmp/ssh-
➥QjvPgj3h/agent.607;
[Sage-Rays-Computer:~] miwa% setenv SSH_AGENT_PID 608;
```

21. `miwa` runs the two `setenv` commands, and ignores the `echo`. The output of `ssh-agent` is designed so that you can wrap it into a script that calls it, and executes its suggested shell commands automatically. The `echo` is only there so that you get diagnostic output to your terminal if you use it in this fashion.

    Next, `miwa` must supply the credentials that he wants the agent to provide in response to queries from SSH programs. This is accomplished with the `ssh-add` command.

    ```
    [Sage-Rays-Computer:~] miwa% ssh-add
    Enter passphrase for /Users/miwa//.ssh/id_rsa:
    Identity added: /Users/miwa//.ssh/id_rsa (/Users/miwa//.ssh/id_rsa)
    [Sage-Rays-Computer:~] miwa% ssh-add .ssh/internal_rsa
    Enter passphrase for .ssh/internal_rsa:
    Identity added: .ssh/internal_rsa (.ssh/internal_rsa)
    ```

22. `miwa` uses `ssh-add` to add his default identity, and then to add his `internal_rsa` identity. Both identities require that he supply the passphrase, just as if he were logging in to the remote systems that accept these identities by using `slogin`.

    ```
    [Sage-Rays-Computer:~] miwa% ssh-add -L
    ssh-rsa
    AAAAB3NzaC1yc2EAAAABIwAAAIEAttgqNkpzwf991Siz3EpJsPTt2cHt3aecCqc542+rIw8P3PdmQ
    ➥P78+uFHiFMEQMr5/NcoxPxDWS1QGb06iihYt3j8QoxTbRD/b7b9mdHHDzJekCH2jSonnVCh+XUsC
    ➥AG8KeZ64VZuLEbXOf9VRlBZC2T7MWt6woMgVJvvKqyJVuk= /Users/miwa//.ssh/id_rsa
    ssh-rsa
    AAAAB3NzaC1yc2EAAAABIwAAAIEAr0JLpso1q7HrZ9EGiK8Gk4lvvxnV2GHAQCACC4Pdf76NheY3d
    ➥f6+sAmDBhgJ/N8DGorYCmMpd5TdnZkSK+61V3LAtqGno1nFnmNgTyn8HDXm99hJJk0GGnXKi3s74
    ➥RBqQEcQu3LQtlfJfQW3j51gC9c6XyVANRi53ULorxbADvc= .ssh/internal_rsa
    ```

23. Just for good measure, `miwa` checks the credentials that `ssh-agent` is holding for him, and then goes on to test whether `slogin` now works without requiring him to supply his passphrase:

    ```
    [Sage-Rays-Computer:~] miwa% slogin ryoko.biosci.ohio-state.edu
    Last login: Mon Feb 17 2003 14:09:49 -0500 from cvl232015.columb
    ```

```
You have mail.
ryoko miwa 1 >exit
Connection to ryoko.biosci.ohio-state.edu closed.
[Sage-Rays-Computer:~] miwa% slogin 192.168.1.200
Welcome to Darwin!
[creampuf:~] miwa% exit
Connection to 192.168.1.200 closed.
```

The end demonstration is almost anticlimactic, but it's what `miwa` *doesn't* do here that's significant. It looks as if there's no authentication, as though `ryoko` and `creampuf` simply allowed him to `slogin` in, without bothering to check his credentials. This isn't the case. His ID was validated, but it was `ssh-agent` acting as his assistant that answered the query and responded with the appropriate credentials. `ssh-agent` will continue to do so for any SSH commands that are run in this terminal, or for any other terminal that has had the environment variables set so that SSH commands run in it, and can find the `ssh-agent` to talk to it.

Table 14.11 provides a listing of options for `ssh-agent`. Table 14.12 provides a listing of options for `ssh-add`.

CAUTION

It should be noted that using `ssh-agent` in this fashion is, as they say, putting all your eggs in one basket. If a malicious user could find a way to co-opt the use of your `ssh-agent`, he could spoof connections because you and your `ssh-agent` would happily provide your credentials to verify his false claim. Properly configured file permissions for keys in your `.ssh` directory will go a long way toward minimizing this problem. However, if a cracker has actually managed to break into your account, he can access your key files with your permissions, and a running `ssh-agent` that you've started will have no way to tell you apart. Should this happen, using `ssh-agent` does materially weaken your security.

If you use SSH only in a mode where the remote systems require you to enter your passphrase directly out of your brain, a cracker who has broken one of your accounts is no closer to cracking your others. If you use `ssh-agent` to hold all your credentials, and the cracker happens along while you've a running copy of `ssh-agent` that's serving credentials for you, the cracker will have full access to your accounts on machines for which `ssh-agent` holds credentials.

TABLE 14.11 Options for `ssh-agent`

Option	Function
`-a <bind_address>`	Binds the agent to the Unix-domain socket `<bind_address>`. The default is `/tmp/ssh-XXXXXXXX/agent.<ppid>`.
`-c`	Generates C-shell commands on `stdout`. This is the default if `SHELL` looks like it's a `csh` style of shell.

TABLE 14.11 Continued

Option	Function
`-s`	Generates Bourne shell commands on `stdout`. This is the default if `SHELL` does not look like it's a `csh` style of shell.
`-k`	Kills the current agent (given by the `SSH_AGENT_PID` environment variable).
`-d`	Debug mode. When this option is specified, `ssh-agent` does not fork.

TABLE 14.12 Options for `ssh-add`

Option	Function
`-l`	Lists fingerprints of all identities currently represented by the agent.
`-L`	Lists public key parameters of all identities currently represented by the agent.
`-d`	Deletes the identity from the agent.
`-D`	Deletes all identities from the agent.
`-x`	Locks the agent with a password.
`-X`	Unlocks the agent.
`-t <life>`	Sets a maximum lifetime when adding identities to an agent. The lifetime may be specified in seconds or in a time format specified in `sshd(8)`.

A Better-Looking, More Helpful Butler: `SSH Agent` (the GUI Version)

If you're comfortable with the risks that using `ssh-agent` brings, then there's a quite useful GUI tool that you might want to consider using. It, the Mac OS X Keychain, and some `Terminal.app` features all working together can make for wonderfully convenient secure remote connections. Xander Schrijen is actively developing a quite useful front end to the `ssh-agent` command-line utility, and endowing it with some nice auxiliary functions. `SSH Agent` acts sort of like a meta-agent for `ssh-agent`. It provides a GUI front end for the features of `ssh-agent`, and further can be configured to use your login credentials to store your passphrases in the OS X Keychain, thereby allowing for `ssh-agent` functionality without you needing to do anything but successfully log in. To try out `SSH Agent`, download it from `http://www.phil.uu.nl/~xges/ssh/` and follow the Quick-Start installation instructions. At this time, this means performing the following steps:

Download the software from `http://www.phil.uu.nl/~xges/ssh/`.

Mount the disk image and copy the `SSH Agent` application to some convenient place on your drive. If you'd like it to be available to all your users, putting it in `/Applications/` would be appropriate. Eject the disk image when you're done.

Run the `SSH Agent` application and open the Preferences panel.

In the `Startup` tab, shown in Figure 14.2, check the `Make Agent Global` setting.

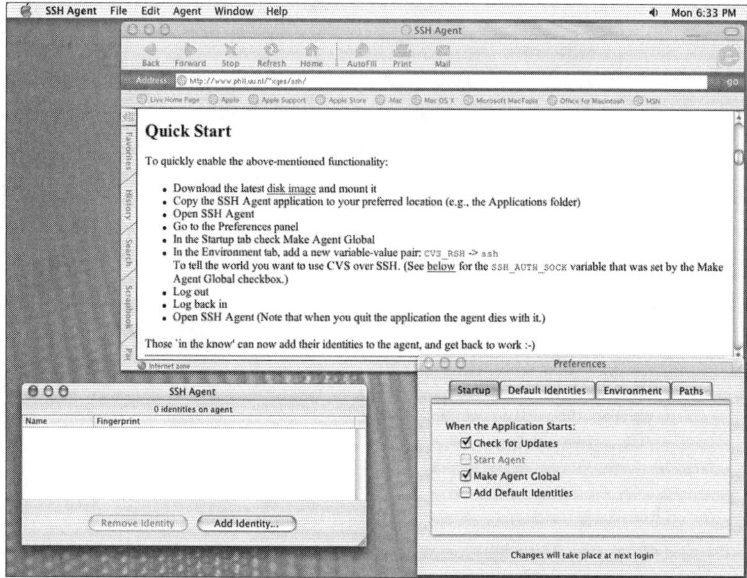

FIGURE 14.2 Setting the `SSH Agent` application to serve credentials globally.

In the `Environment` tab, use the `Add Variable` button to add a variable named `CVS_RSH` and set its value to `ssh`.

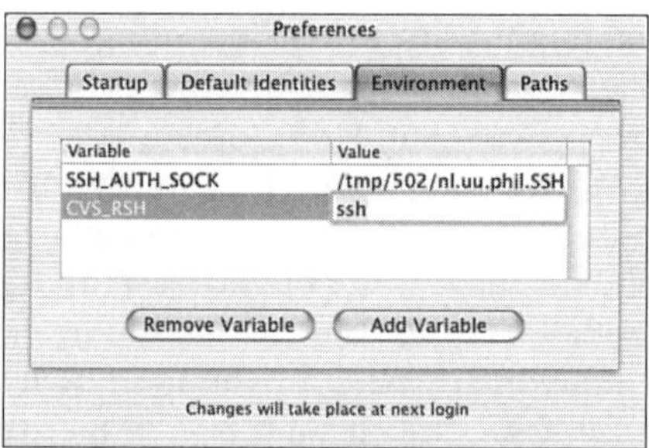

FIGURE 14.3 Setting Environment variables through `SSH Agent`.

Log out, log back in, and restart `SSH Agent`. Open the Preferences panel again, and go to the Default Identities pane. Initially, it will appear as shown in Figure 14.4. Click on the Add Identity button and the dialog shown in Figure 14.5 appears. The IDs shown in this dialog should be familiar from the recap of `miwa`'s SSH key generation earlier in this section. Select the private key from the key pair for any identity you want to use by default. In this example, we're adding both IDs that `miwa` created earlier.

FIGURE 14.4 Like `ssh-agent`, out of the box, `SSH Agent` knows no identities.

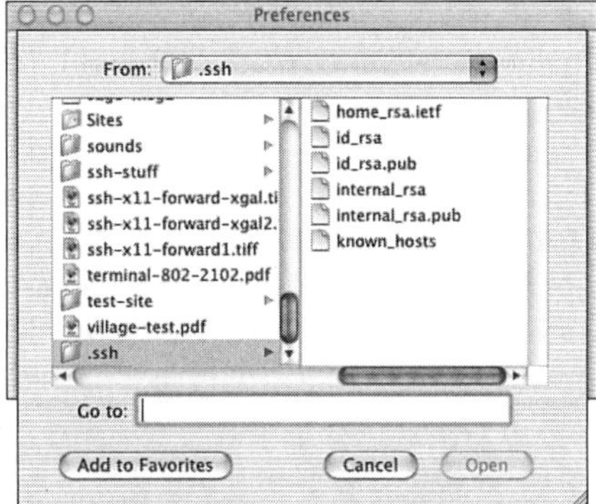

FIGURE 14.5 Clicking the Add Identity button enables you to select among any SSH identities that you've previously created. There's also a New Identity function under the File menu where you can create key pairs in `SSH Agent` de novo. Here, you need to select the private keys of each key pair you wish to use.

After you've selected the identities to add, the IDs appear in the Default Identities tab, as shown in Figure 14.6.

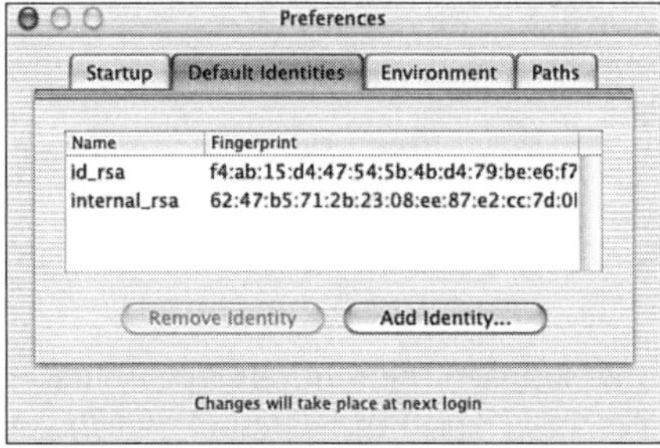

FIGURE 14.6 The Default Identity pane after some IDs have been added.

Go back to the Startup pane and select Add Default Identities, as shown in Figure 14.7, and then quit `SSH Agent` again.

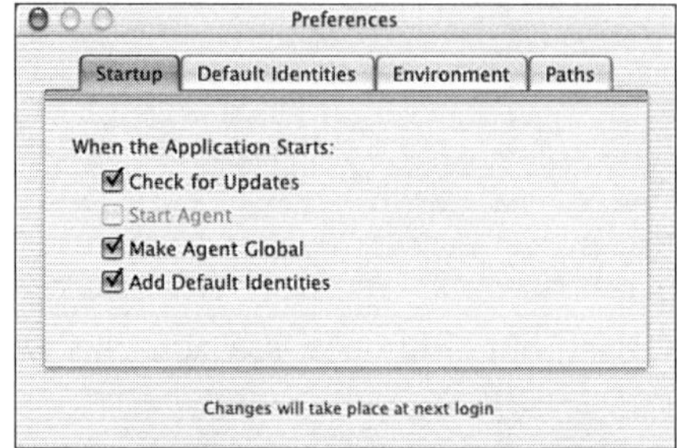

FIGURE 14.7 Setting the final preference that you need to configure before you can start making use of `SSH Agent`.

When you start `SSH Agent` again, you'll see a dialog as shown in Figure 14.8, where `SSH Agent` is asking you for the passphrase for an ID. Pay attention to the path shown for the identity, as `SSH Agent` will ask you for the passphrase for each identity you've configured it to load by default. Figure 14.9 shows what `SSH Agent` looks like after you've successfully supplied the requested passphrases.

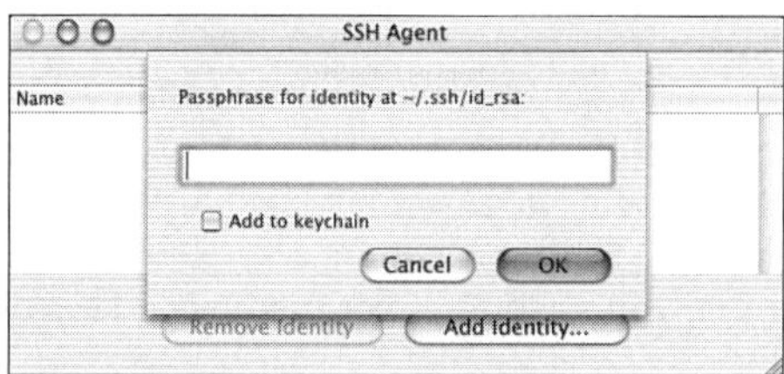

FIGURE 14.8 `SSH Agent` prompts for the passphrases for each identity you've asked it to hold for you.

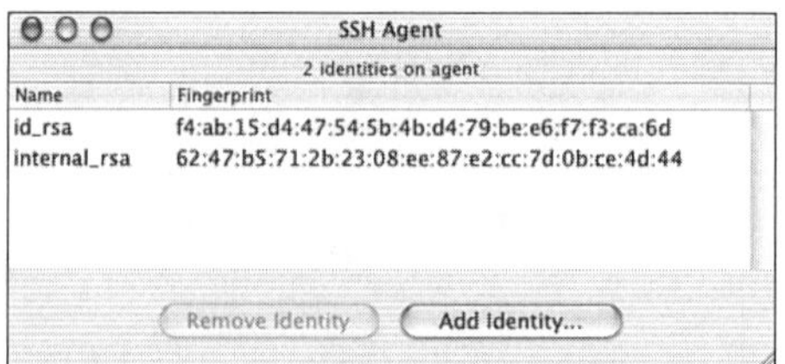

FIGURE 14.9 After you've supplied the requested passphrases, `SSH Agent` shows the loaded identities. From this window (which you can bring up from the Agent menu if the window is closed), you can also load additional nondefault identities selectively and as needed.

Now, if you start a terminal you can use the credentials held by `SSH Agent`, and you don't even need to execute the `setenv` commands as you needed to for the command-line `ssh-agent`. Figure 14.10 shows our `miwa` user making use of these IDs in a terminal.

If you'd like to avoid even the work of having to enter the passphrases once at the startup of `SSH Agent`, you can select the Add to Keychain option seen in Figure 14.8, and the passphrases you enter for your identities will be saved in your Keychain. If you do this, your default identities will be loaded automatically when you start `SSH Agent`, and you won't need to enter the passphrases for them again.

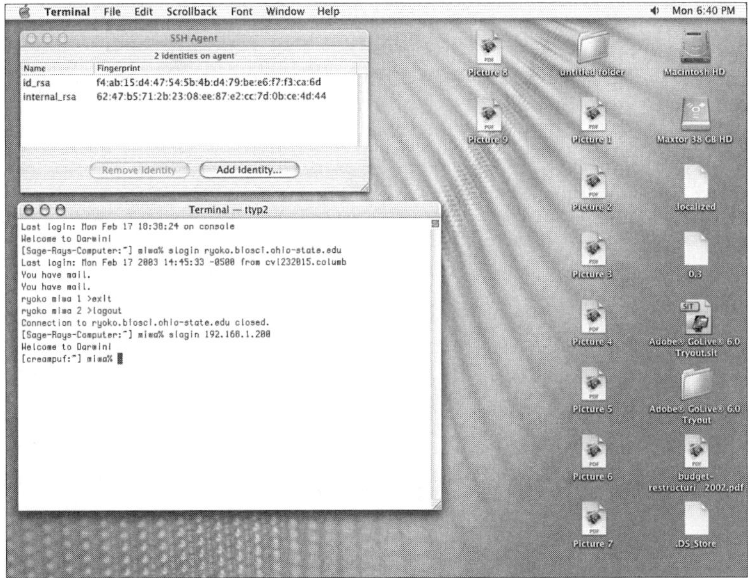

FIGURE 14.10 Now `SSH Agent` can provide you with the conveniences of `ssh-agent`, without you needing to set environment variables. This is nice, but the good part is still to come.

Combining this capability with some of the capabilities of `Terminal.app` is where the big payoff in ease of use comes in. `Terminal.app` has an infrequently used function under the File menu listed as New Command. This function enables you to execute a command and open a terminal window containing the executing results of that command. Figure 14.11 shows it being used to set up an `slogin` session to `192.168.1.200`.

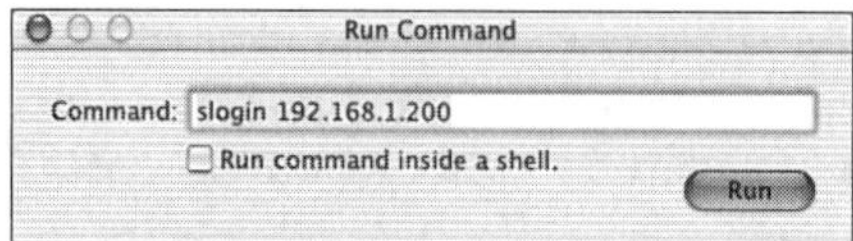

FIGURE 14.11 Setting up a terminal session to run a command. Usually, you would just run the command in a terminal session yourself, but this use is special.

Not surprisingly, the result of running the command in a shell is a connection to `creampuf` (`192.168.1.200`). The neat thing is that you can now use another little-used feature of `Terminal.app` to save this terminal. Select the Save As item under `Terminal.app`'s File menu. This brings up a dialog like the one shown in Figure 14.12. In this dialog, provide a useful name that will help you remember where these terminal settings take you. Also, remember to set the save location to some place that you'll actually find useful.

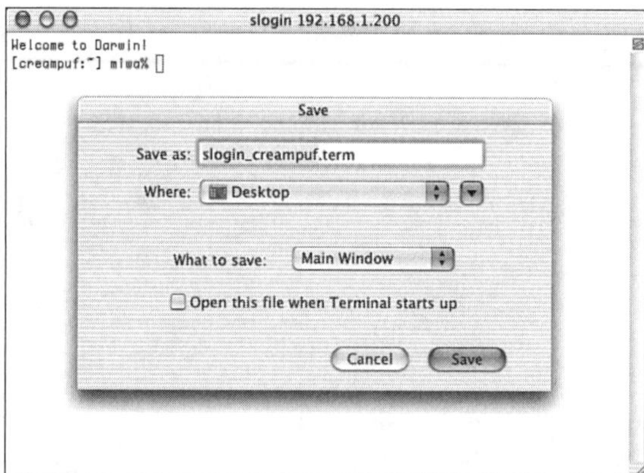

FIGURE 14.12 Saving a `Terminal.app` terminal session. This isn't saving the contents—it's saving what the terminal is doing.

And finally the nifty part. Figure 14.13 shows what `miwa`'s done with his `SSH Agent`-supplied identities, and with saved `Terminal.app` terminal sessions. The two icons shown in the dock, one of which is labeled `slogin_ryoko.term`, is a saved terminal file for one of `miwa`'s IDs. The icon next to it is another saved `.term` file that `miwa` created for his `creampuf` ID. He's applied interesting icons to each, to make them a bit more distinctive than the default little white rectangle icons they come with. Clicking on either launches a terminal session, using the command `miwa` set for it from the `New Command` menu item. That command queries the running `SSH Agent`, gets the appropriate passphrase for `miwa` as necessary, and the connection to the remote server will be made with no further interaction needed on `miwa`'s part.

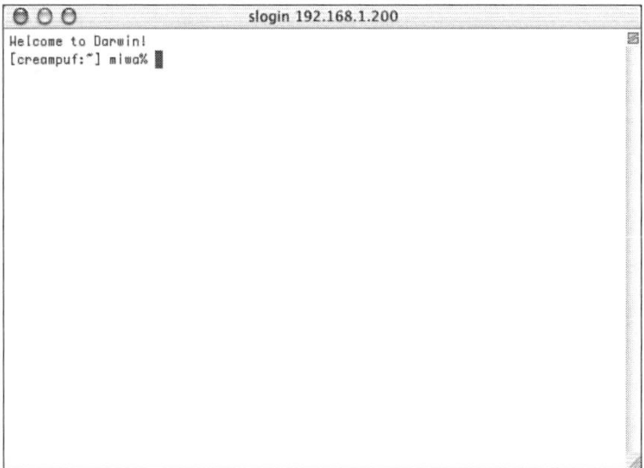

FIGURE 14.13 Saved `.term` files enable you to rerun their saved commands—in this case, saved `slogin` commands, which `SSH Agent` allows to create secure connections with no further authentication required.

Single-click, secure, encrypted connections to remote servers. What could be slicker than that?

GUI Access Methods

In addition to remote terminal access, slick or otherwise, you may also be interested in what GUI access methods may be available. This section takes a brief look at VNC, Timbuktu, and Apple Remote Desktop.

VNC

AT&T Laboratories Cambridge has developed a platform-independent remote display protocol called VNC, Virtual Network Computing. The display protocol enables you to display a desktop running on a remote host on your local machine. A VNC server runs on the remote host, and a VNC client runs on the local machine. For more information on VNC, visit `http://www.realvnc.com/` and `http://www.uk.research.att.com/vnc/`. The AT&T VNC team now distributes the latest version of its software at the RealVNC site as source and for some selected platforms, but the AT&T site still has older versions and versions for platforms not available at the RealVNC site. A VNC server and client are available directly from AT&T for traditional Mac OS. Additionally there are links to ports to Mac OS X, and source code is available. For Mac OS X a number of VNC viewers are available, and a VNC server for X11 has been ported to OS X. Additionally, a couple servers that display the aqua interface are available. Regularly check AT&T's site at `http://www.uk.research.att.com/vnc/contribs.html`, and also `http://sourceforge.net/`, and `http://www.versiontracker.com/` for information on such projects.

Vulnerabilities

The primary vulnerability with the VNC protocol is that it is a cleartext protocol. A password is required when a VNC viewer connects to a VNC server, and this password is encrypted, but the following graphical data is not. It is recommended that if you are going to use it, use it over SSH.

In addition to the flaw in the protocol itself, a few vulnerabilities in VNC software have been discovered so far. They include the following:

- **Weak Authentication Process** (VU# 303080, BugTraq ID 2275)

  VNC's authentication process can allow an intruder eavesdropping on the network traffic to gain access to a desktop and its system. The weakness is in the challenge and response system between the server and client. The recommended solution is to tunnel VNC connections over SSH.

- **WinVNC Server Buffer Overflow** (CAN-2001-0168, VU# 598581, BugTraq ID 2306)

  A vulnerability exists in WinVNC server's handling of HTTP requests that can result in an attacker's being able to execute arbitrary code with the privilege of the WinVNC server process. The vulnerability exists in WinVNC Server 3.3.3r7 and earlier. Upgrade to the latest version or apply a patch that is available on CERT's site.

- **WinVNC Weak Registry Permissions** Permissions (CVE-2000-1164, VU# 197477, BugTraq ID 1961)

  A default WinVNC installation creates a Registry key that contains connection password, IP address, and query restrictions with full access granted to Administrator and System accounts. An attacker could modify the registry to allow unauthenticated access to the service. The recommended solution is to remove the Everybody and Standard Users permissions from the registry key.

VNC on Mac OS X

The following sections list some of the Mac OS X ports that are currently available:

Servers

- `Xvnc`. Information on `Xvnc`, a VNC server for serving X11 applications from MacOS X, is available at `http://www.cdc.noaa.gov/~jsw/macosx_xvnc/`. Ultimately, versions of `Xvnc` for Mac OS X are distributed via the `fink` system, which is available at `http://fink.sourceforge.net/`.

  To install this port of the server, first install `fink`. Then install the `xfree86-base` package. Finally, install either the `vnc` or the `tightvnc` package. The `tightvnc` package is a port of TightVNC, a version of VNC that is optimized for slower network connections, among other things. For more information, see `http://www.tightvnc.com/`.

- `OSXVnc`. `OSXVnc` is an Aqua VNC server, available from `http://prdownloads.sourceforge.net/osxvnc/`. For information on OSXVnc, check Redstone Software's site at `http://www.redstonesoftware.com/osxvnc/`.
- `Share My Desktop`. `Share My Desktop` is another Aqua VNC server, available from `http://www.bombich.com/software/smd.html`.

VNC Viewers Various VNC viewers are available for Mac OS X. Some of the viewers are also available for older versions of Mac OS. Among them are

- Chicken of the VNC, available from `http://www.geekspiff.com/software/cotvnc`. This is a Mac OS X application.
- VNCDimension, available from `http://www.mdimension.com/cgi-bin/WebObjects/mDimension.woa`. This is a Mac OS X application.
- VNCThing, available from `http://webthing.net/vncthing/`. This runs on Mac OS 8.1 and later.
- VNCViewer, available from `http://homepage.mac.com/kedoin/VNC/VNCViewer/`. This is a Mac OS X application.
- VNCViewer, available from `http://www.geocities.com/tim_senecal/vnc.html`. This site has a carbon version, a noncarbon version, and even one for 68k Macs.

Sample Usage

After VNC is installed, you start `Xvnc`, the server, on the remote host whose desktop you want to access, and you run a VNC viewer, the client, on the local machine. Typically, `Xvnc` is started by `vncserver`. If you are using `Xvnc` for Mac OS X, try `vncserver` with the `-depth` and `-geometry` options to set bit depth and screen resolution suitable to your monitor.

As you may recall from the section on VNC vulnerabilities, it is recommended that VNC be run over SSH. When you log in to the remote host and run `vncserver`, it will return a display number. The VNC protocol uses port `59XX`, where `XX` is the display number. Here is a sample of starting `Xvnc`:

```
Rosalyn joray 66 > vncserver


New 'X' desktop is Rosalyn:1
```

```
Starting applications specified in /net/rosalyn/home2/joray/.vnc/xstartup
Log file is /net/rosalyn/home2/joray/.vnc/Rosalyn:1.log
```

The first time you run vncserver, you will be asked to create a password.

In the preceding example, 1 is the display number, making the port that you use on the remote host 5901. To create the tunnel, use the -L option in ssh:

```
% slogin rosalyn -L 5902:rosalyn:5901
joray@rosalyn's password:
```

In this example, the display number on the local machine is 2. You then tell a VNC viewer to use the local display number 2 by connecting to localhost at display 2. Figure 14.14 shows the remote host specified in Chicken of the VNC, and Figure 14.15 shows the resulting remote X desktop that is displayed. The remote desktop is running Netscape and an xterm. For some VNC viewers, you may have to use localhost:<display number> as the syntax or localhost:<port number>.For more information on using VNC, see the AT&T and RealVNC sites.

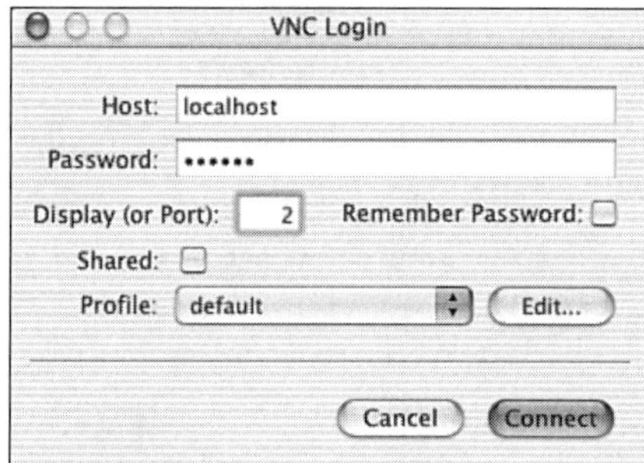

FIGURE 14.14 Connecting to a remote VNC server serving an X desktop over SSH in Chicken of the VNC.

To share your OS X desktop, the procedure is very similar to sharing an X desktop. Use an application such as OSXVnc or Share My Desktop to serve your OS X desktop. When you start one of the applications, you can specify the port to use and set up a VNC password. Share My Desktop does not seem to remember passwords between uses. Then from the client machine, set up an SSH tunnel, as was done in the example involving an X desktop, and connect to the VNC server in a VNC viewer by specifying the host as localhost and listing the appropriate display or port. Figure 14.16 shows an Aqua desktop running Internet Explorer being displayed in a VNC viewer on a Mac OS X machine, and Figure 14.17 shows the same Aqua desktop being displayed in a VNC viewer on a Mac OS 9 machine.

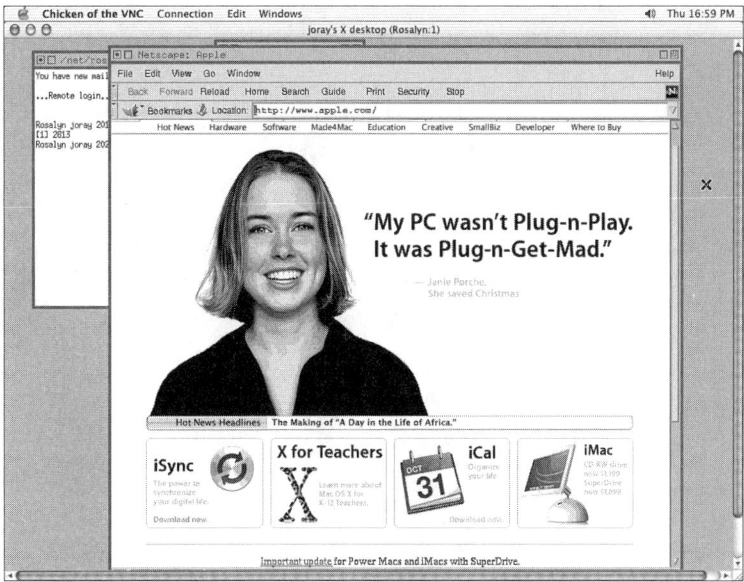

FIGURE 14.15 Displaying a VNC served X desktop in Mac OS X using Chicken of the VNC.

FIGURE 14.16 Using Chicken of the VNC over SSH to connect to an Aqua desktop served by Share My Desktop.

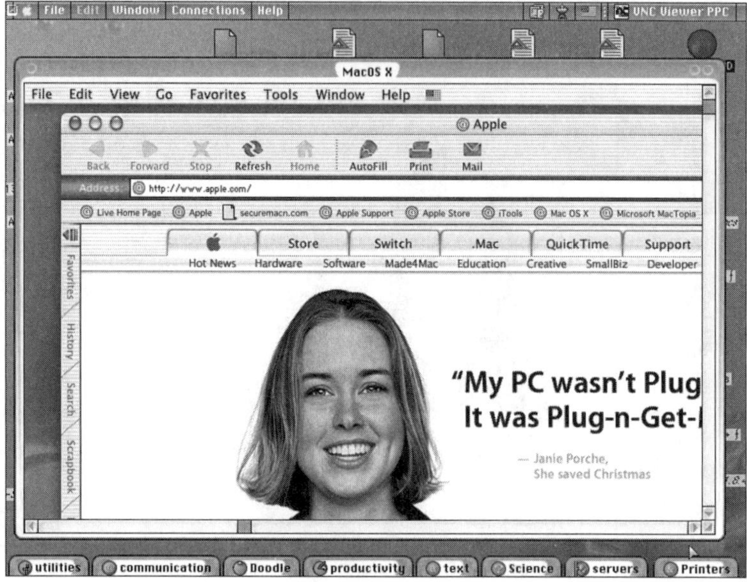

FIGURE 14.17 Using a VNC Viewer PPC over SSH to connect to an Aqua desktop served by Share My Desktop.

Timbuktu

Timbuktu is a commercial application that allows you to view, among other things, a remote desktop and transfer files. It supports the Windows and Mac OS platforms. For more information on the Timbuktu product and to download a trial version, visit `http://www.netopia.com/`.

Vulnerabilities

Only one vulnerability in Timbuktu has been issued an advisory so far. There have been discussions of older versions of Timbuktu for NT transmitting passwords in cleartext, but no advisory was issued. A preview version of Timbuktu for Mac OS X placed the Timbuktu control icon in the upper left portion of the login screen. Its `About Timbuktu` menu gave full access to the Apple menu and System Preferences. That hole has since been fixed. If you are interested in security issues regarding Timbuktu, the best place to check is SecurityFocus's Web site, `http://www.securityfocus.com/`, in that Netopia, the company that produces Timbuktu, watches reports submitted to SecurityFocus's BugTraq mailing list.

- Timbuktu Pro 6.0.1 and Older Denial of Service Vulnerability (CAN-2002-0135, BugTraq ID 3918). If a large number of connections are made to Timbuktu, the server no longer accepts connections. No patches have been issued at this time to fix the problem. It is not known if Timbuktu Pro 6.0.2 fixes the problem.

Sample Usage

Timbuktu must be installed on the remote host and the local host. Timbuktu has various levels of access, including `Public Visitor`, `Ask Permission`, and an authorized user. Create a user and password for each user who should be granted authorized access to the system. For Mac OS 8/9 you can allow incoming access via `AppleTalk`, `TCP/IP`, and `Direct Dial`. Incoming access via AppleTalk is not an option in the Mac OS X version.

Older versions of Timbuktu run as a UDP service on port 407. By version 5.2.x, the default protocol for Timbuktu became TCP, listening on port 407. However, the current versions still listen for connections on UDP port 407 for backward compatibility. You can change the default TCP port by following the instructions available on Netopia's site at `http://www.netopia.com/en-us/support/howtodocs/mac/tcpport.html`.

Unfortunately, Timbuktu does not allow connections to `localhost`, making straightforward tunneling over SSH not an option. In other words, Timbuktu can't be forwarded via a tunnel on the client computer. Instead, a tunnel has to be set up on a third computer, and Timbuktu connections can be tunneled through it. The latest version, 6.0.2, advertises a new layer of security with the scrambling of the guest-to-host stream.

Figure 14.18 shows a Mac OS 9 desktop running Netscape being displayed on a Mac OS X machine.

FIGURE 14.18 A Mac OS 9 desktop being displayed on a Mac OS X machine using Timbuktu.

Apple Remote Desktop

`Apple Remote Desktop` is another commercial application that enables you to view or control a desktop. It is a UDP application that runs on port 3283. Unlike `Timbuktu`, it supports only the Macintosh platform. `Apple Remote Desktop` works on a system of administrative machines and client machines. The administrative machine can observe, control, or lock a desktop or send its desktop to a client for viewing. Additionally, an administrative machine can gather reports involving hardware, software, and so forth on the client machine, copy files, open files, and sleep or wake a client. Some models may give you trouble with sleeping and waking. Make sure the client is capable of choosing to wake for network administrative access. You might find this application especially suitable in a computer lab setting.

Vulnerabilities

No advisories or other comments have thus far been issued regarding vulnerabilities in Apple Remote Desktop.

Sample Usage

At this time, the versions of Apple Remote Desktop in use by both the administrative and client machines must be the same. To use software, set up the client machines to be administered. Specifically, set up administrative users for the client, and decide what permission each administrative user has. On Mac OS X clients, you select the appropriate permissions for each real user on the machine who should be allowed such access. You might find it helpful to set up a user whose specific purpose is to allow Apple Remote Desktop access. In traditional Mac OS, you create administrative user accounts within the Apple Remote Desktop application. After the clients are set up, then on the administrative machine create a list or lists of clients to be administered and perform whatever administration needs to be done. Figure 14.19 shows the computer named Tangerine Star being observed. It is currently running Netscape. Figure 14.20 shows a sample of a System Information Report. The items picked to be included in this report include ethernet address, open transport version, IP address, amount of free space, amount of built-in memory, and bus clock speed.

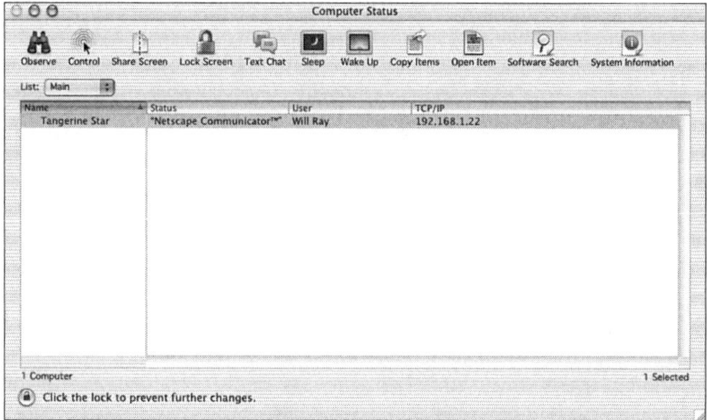

FIGURE 14.19 Apple Remote Desktop on the administrative machine shows that Netscape is currently running on client Tangerine Star.

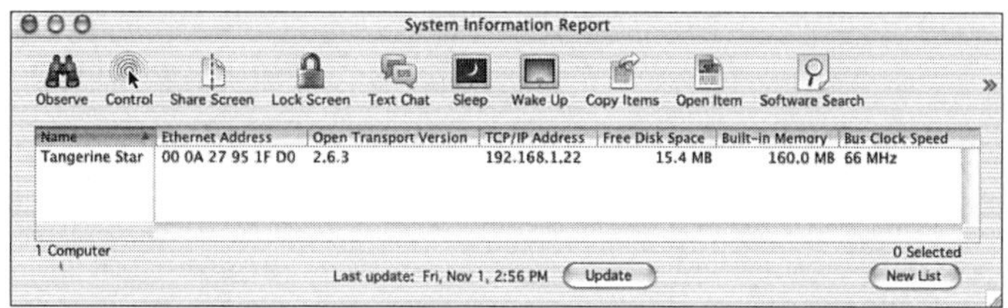

FIGURE 14.20 A sample System Information Report for client Tangerine Star.

Summary

If you need to access your OS X machine from a remote terminal, we recommend that you do not enable either `telnet` or `rlogin`. Instead, activate the SSH server. With SSH you have secure terminal access, secure file transfer capabilities, and the ability to tunnel otherwise insecure protocols over a secure channel.

If you must have remote desktop access to the machine, tunnel the connections over SSH where possible. If it is not possible to tunnel the connection, then reserve such use only for machines on a private network.

15

Web Server Security

IN THIS CHAPTER

- Introducing Apache
- SSL-Protected Apache
- Additional Resources

Mac OS X, both Server and Client, ship with the world's most popular (and arguably powerful) Web server: Apache. Unfortunately, neither distribution of the operating system provides configuration control beyond the most cursory setup. In cases where a static Web site is being served, you likely don't need anything beyond the simple on/off OS X controls; but as soon as you venture into the realm of serving dynamic information or providing Intranet services, you'll need to learn the ins and outs of your Web server software. This chapter introduces you to the Apache security model, SSL support, and provides the information you need to take your server far beyond what is possible with Apple's included pushbutton controls.

Introducing Apache

The Apache Web server is the posterchild of the Open Source movement. Having won over both academic and enterprise users, it now accounts for over 55% of the Web sites on the Internet, almost double those that run on Microsoft's often-exploited IIS system (`http://www.netcraft.net/survey/`). Apple has worked closely with the Apache Software Group to ensure that Apache works correctly on Mac OS X and is easy to both compile and update.

NOTE

Like other software we've discussed in this book, Apple does not always include the latest Apache distribution with OS X. Although upgrading manually isn't difficult, you must pay close attention to Apple's automatic security updates; these updates often include changes to Apache and its components, replacing any custom installation you may have performed.

At the time of this writing, the Apache Web server was in its initial 2.0 release, but had not yet been adopted by Apache for Mac OS X Client or Server. In addition to new features and extensibility, 2.0 brings robust Windows support, which will undoubtedly increase its popularity even more.

Recent Exploits

I've had the pleasure of recently being part of a conversation that started with the words, "If Apache was as popular a server as Windows, you'd see it being attacked as well." As mentioned previously, Apache is *more* popular than IIS, and has had its share of attacks over the past few years. The difference, however, is that Apache's problems have paled in comparison to IIS's, in terms of both frequency and severity, as well as how they're addressed by the server administrators. Good Unix administrators have learned to keep track of system updates and apply them as needed. In today's "install-Windows-2000-and-you're-an-instant-administrator" IT climate, too many NT/2000/XP systems go unpatched, are compromised, and remain online in a "hacked" state doing who-knows-what.

Here is a brief history of Apache exploits, starting with the initial Mac OS X release version, up to October of 2002:

Use of `mod_rewrite` can reveal arbitrary file contents (Apache 1.3.12)
The Apache `mod_rewrite` module is used to redirect page requests to another location, which it does by rewriting the request on the fly. It can be used to seamlessly transition between different servers, and even includes a proxy function for mapping remote Web servers "onto" your local server. The exploit took effect when `mod_rewrite` mapped a request onto a file whose name contained a regular expression. Examples and more information are available from `http://archives.neohapsis.com/archives/bugtraq/2000-09/0352.html` and `http://cve.mitre.org/cgi-bin/cvename.cgi?name=CVE-2000-0913`. This bug was corrected in Apache 1.3.14.

Bug in `mod_vhost_alias` provides access to CGI source code (1.3.12)
A bug in Apache's virtual host module allowed remote attackers to view the contents of CGIs, rather than execute them, if the `cgi-bin` directory was located at the document root of the server. Corrected in Apache 1.3.14. More information can be found at `http://cve.mitre.org/cgi-bin/cvename.cgi?name=CAN-2000-1204`.

Malformed URL displays directory contents (Apache 1.3.14)
Inappropriate URL handling by `mod_negotiation`, `mod_dir`, and `mod_autoindex` allowed attackers to create URLs with a large number of slash (`/`) characters (as in thousands) and potentially reveal directory listings rather than the appropriate index file. An example exploit script written in Perl can be found at `http://online.securityfocus.com/archive/1/193081`. More information on the bug is located at `http://cve.mitre.org/cgi-bin/cvename.cgi?name=CAN-2001-0925`.

Multiviews bug (Apache 1.3.20)

The Apache Multiviews feature enables the Apache server to intelligently respond to a request for a resource that, as named, is not present. When the Multiviews option is set, the server will attempt to respond to a request for a file that isn't present by matching the base file name against others in the directory, and will serve the best match to the client. In Apache 1.3.20, if the resource was called with the query string `M=D` appended to it, a directory listing would be returned instead. Although basic file permissions were not overridden, this did reveal file information that otherwise would be hidden and resulted in pages that should not have been easily seen. This error was fixed in Apache 1.3.22. See `http://cve.mitre.org/cgi-bin/cvename.cgi?name=CAN-2001-0731` for more information.

Denial of service attack against Apache (1.3.24)

A serious bug, this DoS attack resulted from a mishandling of chunked encoding by the Web server. In some systems, it posed no more of a threat than simply using additional system resources. On others—namely Windows and 64-bit platforms—the bug was found to enable the remote attacker to execute arbitrary code on the server. This is one of the most serious Apache bugs to surface since its inception. The problem affected almost all platforms, and all versions of Apache, including the early 2.0 releases. It was corrected in Apache 1.3.26. The original CERT warning can be found at `http://www.cert.org/advisories/CA-2002-17.html`, and additional resources are available from `http://cve.mitre.org/cgi-bin/cvename.cgi?name=CAN-2002-0392`.

Shared memory DoS exploit (1.3.26)

The Apache "scoreboard" provides shared stats for all the active Apache processes running. It also suffered from a serious security hole that enabled any user with the Apache processes' user ID (that is, any scripts running from the server) to send a SIGUSR1 signal to any local process as root. The implications of this depend on the system being attacked, but range from a simple DoS attack to taking down the entire machine. The default action for SIGUSR1 is to terminate the target process unless the signal is handled internally. This error has been fixed in Apache 1.3.27. More information and links can be found at `http://archives.neohapsis.com/archives/vulnwatch/2002-q4/0012.html` and `http://cve.mitre.org/cgi-bin/cvename.cgi?name=CAN-2002-0839`.

NOTE

Two well-known Mac OS X–specific Apache exploits also existed that could be used to reveal sensitive information. The first is related to the lack of case sensitivity in the default Mac OS X file system—HFS+. Unless Apache is serving from a UFS formatted file system, it incorrectly assumes that HFS+ is case sensitive. As a result, one could create a directory named `myprivateinformation` that was blocked to everyone but a select few. As long as the resource was accessed exactly as it was defined, the block worked. Unfortunately, however, if you attempted to access the resource using a different case variation, such as

MYprivateINFORMATION, the block would not be applied, and the information would be served. To get around this, Apple created the mod_hfs_apple Apache module, which correctly deals with case sensitivity between requests. This module is installed by default on your system, but if you recompile and reinstall Apache, you should also reinstall mod_hfs_apple.

The second Mac OS X–specific security problem deals with the .DS_Store files created by the operating system to hold file-specific information. These metadata files could originally be requested in a URL, potentially revealing sensitive system information (names, types, permissions, and so on). Apple has since corrected the problem in Mac OS X 10.1.

Apache Configuration

Apache is a *very* large piece of software that has hundreds of configuration options and possible setups. A number of books have been written about Apache. This section looks at the most common attributes that can be configured and how they affect your system. It is not meant to be a complete reference to Apache. Version 2.0 of Apache is available from http://www.apache.org, but it is not yet distributed with Mac OS X and lacks support for many popular modules including PHP (which you'll learn about in the next chapter). The current shipping version, 1.3.27, is discussed here.

Apple has done an excellent job of making the Apache Web server configuration manageable for machines with large numbers of personal Web sites. Instead of a single monolithic configuration, like the standard Linux or Windows installation, the server can be configured on two different levels:

- **Systemwide configuration** (path: /etc/httpd/httpd.conf). This is the master configuration file. It contains information about the system as a whole: what directories are accessible, what plug-ins are in use, and so on. Changes to the Web server as a whole are included here.
- **User-directory configuration** (path: /etc/httpd/users/<*username*>.conf). When the Mac OS X Users System Preference panel creates a new account, it automatically adds a basic configuration file for that user within the /etc/httpd/users directory. This mini configuration file determines the security for the Web pages within a user's Sites folder.

By splitting up the configuration, the administrator can quickly adjust Web permissions on a given account. To edit the user or system configuration, you must either log in (or su) as root, or use sudo.

NOTE

Although the user configuration files are stored based on the user's name, they have no real connection to the actual user other than containing the path to a personal `Sites` folder. These files can contain any Apache configuration option, including those that affect other users. The division by username is for ease of editing only.

Apache approaches configuration in a very object-oriented manner. The configuration files are XML-like, but not compliant, so don't attempt to edit them by using the `plist` editor. Apache calls each configuration option a directive. There are two types of configuration directives:

- **Global**. Global directives affect the entire server—everything from setting a name for the Web server to loading and activating modules.
- **Container-based**. An Apache container is one of a number of objects that can hold Web pages. For example, a directory is a container, a virtual host is a container, and an aliased location is also a container. If you don't know what these are, don't worry, we'll get there. For now, just realize that each container can be configured to limit who has access to what it contains, and what pages within it can do.

Before you look at the security-related "container" directives, it's a good idea to first become familiar with the global directives you're likely to encounter while editing `/etc/httpd/httpd.conf`. The goal of this chapter is to give you a well-rounded knowledge of Apache configuration, rather than just dump a series of commands on you and leave you to your own resources.

Global Options

The global options can fall anywhere within the server configuration file. If you're running a heavy-traffic Web site you'll definitely want to change the defaults. By default, Apache starts only one server and keeps a maximum of five running at any given time. These numbers do not allow the server to quickly adapt to increased server load.

Table 15.1 documents the most important configuration directives contained in the `/etc/httpd/httpd.conf` file. They are listed in the order that you're likely to encounter them in the `httpd.conf` file.

NOTE

Several of the Apache directives refer to the number of server processes that should be started. These processes are subprocesses of the parent Apache process. When you use `apachectl` to control the server, you are controlling *all* the Apache processes.

TABLE 15.1 Global Apache Directives

Directive	Description
`ServerType <standalone|inetd>`	The Server type determines how Apache starts. Standalone servers are the default. Inetd-based servers use the `inetd` process to activate a server only when it is accessed. This is inefficient and not recommended for all but the lowest-traffic systems.
`ServerRoot` *`<path>`*	The base path of the Apache binary files.
`PidFile` *`<path/filename>`*	The path (and filename) of the file that should store Apache's process ID.
`Timeout` *`<seconds>`*	The number of seconds that Apache will wait for a response from a remote client. After the time period expires, the connection will be closed.
`KeepAlive` *`<On|Off>`*	Allow more than one request per connection. This is the default behavior of HTTP/1.1 browsers. Shutting this off might result in a higher server load and longer page load times for clients.
`MaxKeepAliveRequests <#>`	The maximum number of requests that can be made on a single connection.
`KeepAliveTimeout` *`<seconds>`*	The number of seconds to wait between requests on a single connection.
`MinSpareServers <#>`	Apache automatically regulates the number of running servers to keep up with incoming requests. This is the minimum number of servers kept running at any given time.
`MaxSpareServers <#>`	The maximum number of servers that will be kept running when there is no load. This is not a limit on the total number of server processes to start; it limits the number of unused processes that will be kept running to adapt to changes in load.
`StartServers <#>`	The number of servers to start when Apache is first launched.
`MaxClients <#>`	The `MaxClients` directive sets an upper limit on the number of servers that can be started at a given time. Keeping this number low can help prevent denial of service attacks from eating up all system resources. A heavy-volume server should rarely need more than 100.
`MaxRequestsPerChild <#>`	Some systems have memory leaks. A memory leak is a portion of the system software in which memory usage slowly grows in size. Apache recognizes that memory leaks might exist and automatically kills a server after it has processed a given number of requests, freeing up any memory it was using. The server process is then restarted, fresh and ready to go.
`LoadModule` *`<modulename>`* *`<modulepath>`*	Loads an Apache module. Many modules will be installed automatically, so you rarely need to adjust anything.
`AddModule` *`<modulename.c>`*	Activates a loaded module.
`Port <#>`	The port number that the Apache server will use. The standard HTTP port is 80.
`User` *`<username>`*	The user ID under which Apache will run. Apache has the full access permissions of this user, so never, ever, EVER, set this to the `root` account. Mac OS X has the user www configured for the purpose of running Apache.

TABLE 15.1 Continued

Directive	Description
`Group` *<groupname>*	The group ID under which Apache will run. Like the `User` directive, this should never be set to a privileged account. If it is, any broken Web applications could compromise your entire computer. You should use the www group for this purpose on Mac OS X.
`ServerAdmin` *<Email Address>*	The e-mail address of the Web server operator.
`ServerName` *<Server Name>*	If your server has several different hostnames assigned, use the `ServerName` directive to set the one that will be returned to the client browser. This cannot be an arbitrary name; it *must* exist!
`DocumentRoot` *<path to html files>*	This defines the path to the main server HTML files. The Mac OS X default is `/Library/WebServer/Documents`.
`UserDir` *<name of user's website directory>*	The personal Web site directory within each user's home directory. As you already know, OS X uses `Sites`; the default used in most Apache installs is `public_html`. Removing this directive renders individual users unable to create Web sites.
`DirectoryIndex` *<Default HTML file>*	When a URL is specified by only a directory name, the Web server attempts to display a default HTML file with this name.
`AccessFileName` *<Access Filename>*	The name of a file that, if encountered in a directory, will be read for additional configuration directives for that directory. Typically used to password-protect a directory. The default name is `.htaccess`.
`DefaultType`	The default MIME type for outgoing documents. The `text/html` type should be used to serve HTML files.
`HostnameLookups` *<On|Off>*	If activated, Apache stores the full hostname of each computer accessing the server rather than its IP address. This is *not* recommended for servers with more than a trivial load. Hostname lookups can greatly slow down response time and overall server performance.
`TypesConfig` *<mime-type configuration file>*	The path to a file that contains a list of MIME types and file extensions that should be served with that MIME type. For example, the type `text/html` is applied to files with the `.html` extension. The default MIME types are located at `/private/etc/httpd/mime.types`.
`LogLevel` *<level>*	One of eight different error log levels: `debug`, `info`, `notice`, `warn`, `error`, `crit`, `alert`, or `emerg`.
`LogFormat` *<Log Format> <short name>*	Defines a custom log format and assigns it to a name. Discussed shortly.
`CustomLog` *<Log filename><short name>*	Sets a log filename and assigns it to one of the `LogFormat` types.
`Alias` *<URL path> <server pathname>*	Creates a URL that aliases to a different directory on the server.
`ScriptAlias` *<URL path> <server pathname>*	Creates a URL that aliases to a directory containing CGI applications on the server.

TABLE 15.1 Continued

Directive	Description
`Redirect` *<old URL> <new URL>*	Redirects (transfers) a client from one URL to another. Can be used to transfer between URLs on the same server, or to transfer a client accessing a local Web page to a remote site.
`AddType` *<MIME-type> <extension(s)>*	Adds a MIME-type without editing the `mime.types` file.
`AddHandler server-parsed` *<file extension>*	Activates server-side `includes` for files with the specified extension. The default SSI extension is `.shtml`.
`AddHandler send-as-is` *<file extension>*	When activated, files with the defined extension are sent directly to the remote client as is.
`AddHandler imap-file` *<file extension>*	Sets the extension for server-side imagemap features. All modern Web browsers use client-side image maps, but if you need compatibility with Netscape 1.0 browsers, you need to use server-side maps.
`ErrorHandler` *<error number> <Error Handler>*	Sets an error handler from any one of the standard HTML error messages. This will be discussed in greater detail shortly.
`Include` *<directory>*	Reads multiple configuration files from a directory. This is set to `/etc/httpd/users`.

This is only a partial list of commonly used directives; for a complete list, visit Apache's Web site. To get a handle on configuration, let's take a look at a few different directives in use. These commands, because of their global nature, can be used anywhere within the `/etc/httpd/httpd.conf` configuration file.

Logs

Apache on Mac OS X stores its log files in the directory `/var/log/httpd`. By default, there are two logs: `access_log` and `error_log`.

The `access_log` file contains a record of what remote computers have accessed Apache, what they asked for, and when they did it. Logging is, obviously, one of the best ways to keep track of inappropriate access to your computer. For example:

```
65.24.76.109 - - [08/Nov/2002:11:49:07 -0500]
  "GET /scripts/..%c1%1c../winnt/system32/cmd.exe?/c+dir HTTP/1.0" 404 295
65.24.76.109 - - [08/Nov/2002:11:49:10 -0500]
  "GET /scripts/..%c0%2f../winnt/system32/cmd.exe?/c+dir HTTP/1.0" 404 295
65.24.76.109 - - [08/Nov/2002:11:49:13 -0500]
  "GET /scripts/..%c0%af../winnt/system32/cmd.exe?/c+dir HTTP/1.0" 404 295
65.24.76.109 - - [08/Nov/2002:11:49:16 -0500]
  "GET /scripts/..%c1%9c../winnt/system32/cmd.exe?/c+dir HTTP/1.0" 404 295
```

This log excerpt shows four requests for a `cmd.exe` file on the Web server. This is a standard Windows IIS attack. Five fields are stored with each log entry:

- **Remote Client**. The machine accessing the Apache Web server. In these examples, that client is `65.24.76.109`.
- **Date and Time**. A time and date stamp for when the request was made.
- **Request String**. The actual request that the remote machine made. Most requests begin with `GET` and are followed by the resource to retrieve, then the version of the HTTP protocol with which to retrieve it.
- **Response Code**. Identifies how the remote server responded to the request. The code 200 shows that the request was successfully served. A 404, on the other hand, indicates that the request couldn't be satisfied because the resource wasn't found. The response codes for HTTP 1.1 are available from `http://www.w3.org/Protocols/rfc2616/rfc2616-sec6.html`.
- **Response Size**. The number of bytes sent to the remote client to satisfy the request.

NOTE

There are actually seven fields in this log format. The second and third fields contain a `-` that indicates a value could not be determined. It is unlikely you'll see values here.

Apache knows this style of access log as the common log format. Use of the `LogFormat` directive makes log formats completely customizable. The common format is defined as

```
LogFormat "%h %l %u %t \"%r\" %>s %b" common
```

Each of the `%h` elements denotes an element to be stored in the log file. The `\"` is an escaped quote, meaning that a quote will also be stored in that location. You can build a log format by using any of the following:

- `%h`. Hostname of the requesting computer.
- `%a`. IP address of the remote computer.
- `%r`. Request string.
- `%t`. Time of request.
- `%T`. Amount of time taken to serve the request.
- `%b`. Bytes sent.

- `%U`. URL path requested.
- `%P`. Process ID of the child that served the request.
- `%>s`. The last status reported by the server.
- `%{Referer}i`. The referring URL (the URL that contained the link to current page).
- `%{User-Agent}i`. The string identifies the remote browser.

TIP

This is only a partial listing. You can find a complete list of the Apache Log elements at `http://httpd.apache.org/docs/mod/mod_log_config.html#logformat`.

You define a log format by using the `LogFormat` line, a string containing the format elements, and a name for the file. For example, to define a log called `mylog` that stores only the hostname of the remote client for each request, you would use

```
LogFormat "%h" mylog
```

Except for custom solutions, you'll be best served by one of Apache's default log formats. Although the `common` log *is* common, it probably isn't the best thing for doing extensive reporting. A better choice is Apache's `combined` log format. The `combined` log format includes `referer` and `user-agent` strings with each request. Most Web analysis packages use the combined log style.

To activate a log format, use the `CustomLog` directive, followed by the pathname for the log and the log name. To activate the `combined` log format, use it within the `/etc/httpd/httpd.conf` file:

```
CustomLog "/private/var/log/httpd/access_log" combined
```

Log files are an important part of any Web server. They can provide important data on the popular pages of the server, errors that have occurred, and how much traffic your system is getting.

NOTE

The `error_log` is not shown here because it should contain only startup and shutdown messages. If a security violation or configuration error occurs, it is recorded to this file. In addition, programmers can find detailed information about program errors written to this location.

Container Options

The second type of Apache directives are container based. These directives control how Apache serves a certain group of files. Files are chosen based on pattern, location (URL), or directory, and are denoted by a start and end tag in the Apache configuration file. For example, the `/etc/httpd/users/` configuration files define a container consisting of each user's `Sites` directory. This is the configuration file created for my `jray` user account (in my case, that file would be `/etc/httpd/httpd.conf`):

```
<Directory "/Users/jray/Sites/">
    Options Indexes MultiViews
    AllowOverride None
    Order allow,deny
    Allow from all
</Directory>
```

In this example, the directory `/Users/jray/Sites` is the container. Web pages within this container can use the `Indexes` and `Multiviews` options. The `AllowOverride`, `Order`, and `Allow` directives control who has access to the files within this container. This will be explained in more detail shortly.

Besides a directory container, other constructs can also be added to the configuration file(s):

- **Directory**. Creates a directory-based container. All files within the named directory are part of the container.
- **DirectoryMatch**. Like Directory, but uses a regular expression to match directory names. Check out "So What's A $#!%% Regular Expression, Anyway?!" for a nice introduction to writing and understanding regular expressions: `http://www.devshed.com/Server_Side/Administration/RegExp/page1.html`.
- **Files**. Groups files based on their names. All files matching the specified name are included in the container. The filename should be given exactly, or you should use the `?` and `*` wildcards to match a single unknown character or any number of unknown characters.
- **FilesMatch**. Similar to Files, but matches filenames based on a regular expression rather than an exact name.
- **Location**. The Location container is similar to Directory, but matches Web content based on a URL, rather than a full-server directory.
- **LocationMatch**. If you've been following along, you'll probably guess correctly that LocationMatch is the same as Location, but matches the URL based on a regular expression.

- **VirtualHost**. The VirtualHost container defines a virtual server within the main server. For external clients, the virtual host appears identical to any other Web server. To you, the system administrator, it is a directory on your server that gets its very own domain name. You'll see how this can be set up shortly.

Within the container objects, the administrator can add a number of directives to control access to the contents, or whatever special features are available in that location. Table 15.2 includes the container directives you'll encounter most often.

TABLE 15.2 Apache Container Directives

Directive	Description
`Options` *<Option List>*	Sets the special abilities of the server container. There are eight possible options; each can be preceded by an optional + or - to add or remove it.
`AllowOverride` *<All>*|*<None>*|*<Directive Type>*	Chooses the server-defined directives that a local `.htaccess` file can override. The `.htaccess` file is used to apply directives outside of the main Apache server configuration and can be edited by any user with access to the directory. For that reason, it is important to allow only trusted users to override options. `None` disables all overrides; `All` allows all server directives to be overridden, or specifies a combination of `AuthConfig`, `FileInfo`, `Indexes`, `Limit`, or `Options` to allow these directive types to be overridden.
`Order` *<Deny|Allow>*, *<Deny|Allow>*|`mutual-failure`	Controls the order in which security controls are evaluated, whether or not the list of allowed hosts (`Allow`) or denied hosts (`Deny`) is checked first.
`Allow from` *<allowed networks*|`all`>	A list of IP addresses, networks and subnets, or domain names that can be *allowed* access to the resource.
`Deny from` *<allowed networks*|`all`>	A list of IP addresses, networks and subnets, or domain names that should be *denied* access to the resource.
`AuthType <Basic|Digest>`	Attaches HTTP authorization password protection to a directory.
`AuthName` *<text string>*	Identifies the password-protected resource to the end user.
`AuthUserFile` *<userfile path>*	Sets a path to the userfile being used for basic authentication.
`AuthDigestFile` *<digest userfile path>*	Sets a path to the MD5 Digest password file used with Digest authentication.
`AuthGroupFile` *<groupfile path>*	Sets the path to a file containing group definitions for use with authentication.
`Require user|group|valid-user` *<user/group list>*	Allows only listed users, groups, or any valid user to access a directory. The users and groups are *not* Mac OS X users unless you're using `mod_auth_apple`, discussed shortly. They are created with the `htpasswd` command.

TABLE 15.2 Continued

Directive	Description
`ErrorDocument` *`<Error ID><Document Path>`*	Used to substitute a custom-error page in place of the default Apache pages. Use the standard HTTPD error codes (such as 404) and a path to the HTML page to display when the error occurs within the given resource.
`ServerAdmin`	The email address of the administrator of a virtual host.
`DocumentRoot`	The root-level directory for a virtual host.
`ServerName`	The fully qualified domain name for a virtual host, such as `www.poisontooth.com`.

Now let's see how these directives can be used to refine and secure your Apache Web server.

> **NOTE**
>
> Mac OS X ships with very restrictive settings for the Apache server already in place. It is unlikely that you'll have any problems if you work with the default settings. This chapter assumes that you want to customize your environment to deal with multiple users and multiple Web sites.

Defining Directory Options

The options that you permit to be used in a directory are critical to your server's security. For example, you don't want to enable every user to execute CGI applications that haven't been approved. Used with a "container" object (such as a directory), the `Options` directive will help you "lock down" areas of your server.

In short, the `Options` directive lets you choose what *can* happen in a given directory. Available `Options` directives are described in Table 15.3.

TABLE 15.3 `Options` Values

Option	Effect
`ExecCGI`	Enables CGI execution.
`FollowSymLinks`	Follows symbolic links in the directory.
`Includes`	Enables server-side `includes`.
`IncludeNOEXEC`	Enables server-side `includes` without allowing application execution.
`Indexes`	Displays a directory listing if an index document doesn't exist.
`MultiViews`	Uses content negotiation to activates multiple views.
`SymLinksIfOwnerMatch`	Follows symbolic links only if the owner of the link matches the owner of the linked directory.
`All`	Enables all options (except for `MultiViews`, which must be named explicitly). This is the default.
`None`	Disables all options.

In general, you should enable as *few* of the `Options` directives as is possible. Providing access to CGIs and Server Side `Includes` enables users to execute arbitrary code on your server with the user ID of the Web server (`www` on Mac OS X). Unless you truly trust your users and their code, you should never provide `ExecCGI` or `Includes` options for general users.

Another potentially bad option is `FollowSymLinks`. This option allows the Web server to process symbolic links in the directory as if the files were actually located *in* the given directory. Private files, for example, could be "linked" into a Web directory and viewed online, even if they were outside the normal "Web space."

Finally, the `Indexes` option provides a directory listing if a directory name is specified and no `index.html` file is present. If you aren't comfortable with users browsing your file system, this should not be active.

Options are specified within a container object and you can give them a + or - prefix to add or remove them. The + and - really come in handy only to add or remove privileges from nested resources. For example, assume you want to provide `Indexes` and `Includes` on the default Web location `/Library/WebServer/Documents`:

```
<Directory /Library/WebServer/Documents>
Options Indexes Includes
</Directory>
```

Suppose, however, another directory, `/Library/WebServer/Documents/PDFFiles`, exists inside the Documents directory and you *do not* want `Indexes` activated for it, but *do* want `ExecCGI` enabled. In this case, you could modify the `Options` that you inherit from the main directory by adding the following:

```
<Directory /Library/WebServer/Documents/PDFFiles>
Options -Indexes +ExecCGI
</Directory>
```

If you specify options without +/-, you'll override any inherited options from the parent directories. If you're comfortable with this, there's no reason why you can't do it. Inherited options are cleaner, but can lead to difficult-to-read configuration files.

`AllowOverride` and `.htaccess`

Apache directives are usually specified within the main `/etc/httpd/httpd.conf` file or any of the `httpd.conf` included files (such as the `/etc/httpd/users` directory). Constantly having to edit the server configuration files can be a bit of a pain, so Apache provides a means of creating an "on-the-fly" directory configuration by placing a file named `.htaccess` within the directory you want to change.

NOTE

You can change the .htaccess filename to anything you'd like by using the AccessFileName *<htaccess file name>* global Apache directive, but .htaccess is the default and standard.

An .htaccess file can contain the same sort of "container" configuration directives as in the main httpd config files and is read each time the Web server accesses a directory containing the .htaccess file. You can create configuration changes in the file without needing to restart the server! This flexibility, however, makes it possible for users to place .htaccess files in their Web directories with contents such as

```
Options +ExecCGI
```

This would enable the user to execute CGIs without the system administrator even knowing about it. To guard against this happening, you can use the AllowOverride *<directive-type(s)>* directive to choose exactly what can be overridden in the .htaccess file. There are eight possible override types, documented in Table 15.4.

TABLE 15.4 The AllowOverride Directive Types

Directive Type	Purpose
All	Allow all directive types to be overridden by .htaccess.
None	Don't allow *any* directives to be overridden in .htaccess.
AuthConfig	Allow all authentication directives to be used within .htaccess.
FileInfo	Provide access to directives controlling document types to the .htaccess file.
Indexes	Allow .htaccess to control directory indexing attributes.
Limit	Let .htaccess provide control over host access with Allow, Deny, and Order.
Options	Allow .htaccess to change the options specified by the Options directive.

For example, if you want to enable any site under the /Users directory to create its own password-protected directories by creating .htaccess files with the appropriate authentication options (which we'll learn next), you can add this to /etc/httpd/httpd.conf:

```
<Directory /Users/*>
    Options None
    AllowOverride AuthConfig
</Directory>
```

In this example, all Options are disabled, but users are enabled to override AuthConfig directives, and thus password-protect their own resources.

NOTE

The AuthConfig directives are those directives that deal with setting up Apache authentication. Prefixed with Auth, these include AuthGroupFile, AuthName, AuthType, AuthUserFile, and Require, which we'll cover directly.

Basic Password Protection: htpasswd

Password-protecting a directory is extremely simple. For example, suppose a user wants to password-protect his entire public Web site for development purposes. The first step is to set up a username and password file that will contain the login information for those who are allowed to access the resource. This is accomplished with htpasswd. There are two steps to the process: First, create a new password file with a single user; second, add additional usernames/passwords to it.

To create a new file, use the syntax `htpasswd -c <password pathname> <initial username>`. For example:

```
% htpasswd -c /Users/jray/.htpasswd jray
New password: ******
Re-type new password: ******
Adding password for user jray
```

A new password file (/Users/jray/.htpasswd) is created, and the initial user jray is added.

Subsequent users can be added to the existing file with `htpasswd -b <password pathname> <username> <password>`:

```
% htpasswd -b /Users/jray/.htpasswd testuser testpass
Adding password for user testuser
```

The password file .htpasswd now has two entries: the initial jray user and now testuser.

Next, create a directory container that encompasses the files that need to be protected. Because this example is protecting a personal Web site, the container already exists as a <username>.conf file in /etc/httpd/users:

```
<Directory "/Users/jray/Sites/">
    Options Indexes MultiViews ExecCGI
    AllowOverride None
    Order allow,deny
    Allow from all
</Directory>
```

NOTE

This example file has been modified slightly since the initial Mac OS X installation. The `options` directive includes `ExecCGI` to allow CGI development to take place.

To this directory container, add `AuthType`, `AuthName`, `AuthUserFile`, and `Require` directives. You must be `root` or using `sudo` to edit the file:

```
<Directory "/Users/jray/Sites/">
    AuthType Basic
    AuthName "Development"
    AuthUserFile /Users/jray/.htpasswd
    Require valid-user
    Options Indexes MultiViews ExecCGI
    AllowOverride None
    Order allow,deny
    Allow from all
</Directory>
```

The `AuthUserFile` is set to the name of the password file created with `htpasswd`, whereas the `Require valid-user` directive allows *any* user in the password file to gain access to the protected resource. The `AuthName` directive provides a simple label describing the resource that will appear when a user connects. To activate the authentication, use `sudo /usr/sbin/apachectl restart`:

```
% sudo /usr/sbin/apachectl restart
/usr/sbin/apachectl restart: httpd restarted
```

Attempting to access the `/Users/jray/Sites` directory (`~jray`) now opens an HTTP authentication dialog, as shown in Figure 15.1.

In some cases, your access control might become complex enough that you'll want to group your users together to simplify granting access to resources. This is easily accomplished with the `AuthGroupFile` directive. Group files consist of group records: a single line with the group name, followed by a colon (:), and a space-separated list of the users who should be in the group. For example, assume I've defined the users "jray," "agroves", "robyn," and "jackd" in my `.htpasswd` file and I want to group "jray," "agroves," and "robyn" into a group called "admin." I'd create a new group file name (such as `/Users/jray/.htgroup`) with the contents:

```
admin: jray robyn agroves
```

FIGURE 15.1 The directory is protected with basic authentication.

The group file is plaintext, so creating it doesn't require a special tool (beyond your favorite editor). Now, to provide access to my `/Users/jray/Sites` directory to everyone in the admin group, I'd change my `/etc/httpd/users/jray.conf` file to read as follows:

```
<Directory "/Users/jray/Sites/">
    AuthType Basic
    AuthName "Development"
    AuthUserFile /Users/jray/.htpasswd
    AuthGroupFile /Users/jray/.htgroup
    Require group admin
    Options Indexes MultiViews ExecCGI
    AllowOverride None
    Order allow,deny
    Allow from all
</Directory>
```

The `AuthGroupFile` directive names the location of the group definitions (in this case `/Users/jray/.htgroup`), whereas the `Requires` directive has now been modified with the `group` clause to force authentication against the users in the group `admin`.

Unfortunately, Basic authentication is just that—basic. It is easily sniffable because the username and password are transmitted as plaintext across the network. The name and password are transmitted with *each* request to a given resource, so potential attackers have a large window of opportunity to scan network traffic for the password.

TIP

Digital Cow Software (`http://dcs.digicow.net:8000/`) has created a System Preference panel called Weblock, which provides a GUI for password-protecting Apache-served directories and managing user and group files. If you find yourself repetitively setting up authentication directives, you might want to take a look at this software.

MD5 Digest Password Protection: `htdigest`

To partially eliminate the problem with plaintext passwords, Apache also supports MD5 Digest authentication. Defined in `http://www.faqs.org/rfcs/rfc2617.html`, digest authentication does not (at any time) send the cleartext password over the network, but a "digested" version instead. This, however, does not provide a complete security solution in that many early browsers do not support MD5 Digest authentication. Additionally, the digested password *is* capable of being sniffed, and attackers could potentially use the digested form of the password to gain access to the protected resources. The only *real* solution for Web site security is SSL, which we'll be getting to shortly.

To activate MD5 Digest authentication for a resource, we'll use the `htdigest` command-line utility and the `AuthUserFile`, `AuthName`, `AuthDigestFile`, and `AuthType Digest` directives to provide protection.

First, we'll use `htdigest -c <password pathname> <realm> <username>` to create a new MD5 Digest password file. The arguments are self-explanatory, except the *realm*, which you can set to the same value as `AuthName`—or, for this example, "Development":

```
% htdigest -c /Users/jray/.htdigest Development jray
Adding password for jray in realm Development.
New password: *****
Re-type new password: *****
```

The password file `/Users/jray/.htdigest` is created with the initial user `jray`. Adding additional users requires that you drop the `-c` option from the `htdigest` command: `htdigest <password pathname> <realm> <username>`.

After creating the password file, use the same techniques described in the previous section, "Basic Password Protection: `htpasswd`," to protect the resources, substituting `AuthDigestFile` for `AuthUserFile` and setting `AuthType` to `Digest`. For example, to protect the contents of my personal `Sites` directory, I'd change my `/etc/httpd/users/jray.conf` file to read as follows:

```
<Directory "/Users/jray/Sites/">
    AuthType Digest
    AuthName "Development"
```

```
    AuthDigestFile /Users/jray/.htdigest
    Require valid-user
    Options Indexes MultiViews ExecCGI
    AllowOverride None
    Order allow,deny
    Allow from all
</Directory>
```

The Require directive functions identically to what you've already seen in Basic authentication. You can Require individual users, groups, or any valid user.

Authenticating Against User Accounts with mod_auth_apple

Using the basic and MD5 authentication mechanisms is fine in many cases, but you may find yourself wanting to protect resources based on actual user accounts on your computer. Although it's simple enough to create a password file for each user, these passwords will not be updated as users update their Mac OS X passwords. In some cases (such as running a Web server with users that access their sites through WebDAV) managing all the necessary password files can truly become a hassle. The best solution would be to provide an authentication mechanism by which resources could be protected by actual system accounts and system passwords. This is entirely possible courtesy of Apple's mod_auth_apple Apache module.

Included with Mac OS X Server by default, Mac OS X client users can download and install mod_auth_apple with very little trouble. There are two components to the install: First, a missing header file Security/checkpw.h must be copied from the Darwin CVS repository or mirror, then the source code for mod_auth_apple can be downloaded and installed.

The header file can be downloaded directly from Apple at http://developer.apple.com/darwin/projects/darwin/darwinserver/, but you'll need to register before downloading. Alternatively, download the header from http://www.opendarwin.org/cgi-bin/cvsweb.cgi/src/Security/checkpw/. After downloading, make a new directory /usr/include/Security, and copy the header file to the new location:

```
# curl -O "http://www.opendarwin.org/cgi-bin/cvsweb.cgi/~checkout~/
➥src/Security/checkpw/checkpw.h?rev=1.1.1.2&content-type=text/plain"
# mkdir /usr/include/Security
# mv checkpw.h /usr/include/Security/
```

Next, download the latest mod_auth_apple package from http://developer.apple.com/darwin/projects/darwin/darwinserver/, unarchive it, then enter the source distribution directory:

```
# tar zxf mod_auth_apple-XS-10.2.tgz
# cd mod_auth_apple
```

Be sure to check the Apple README file for installation instructions; they may change between versions. The instructions shown here are "modified" from Apple's directions so that the software configures automatically. Use `make` followed by `apxs -i -a mod_auth_apple.so` to compile and install the module:

```
# make
/usr/sbin/apxs -c  -Wc,"-traditional-cpp -Wno-four-char-constants
-F/System/Library/PrivateFrameworks -DUSE_CHKUSRNAMPASSWD" -Wl,"-bundle_loader
/usr/sbin/httpd -framework Security" -o mod_auth_apple.so mod_auth_apple.c
gcc -DDARWIN -DUSE_HSREGEX -DUSE_EXPAT -I../lib/expat-lite -g -Os -pipe
-DHARD_SERVER_LIMIT=2048 -DEAPI -DSHARED_MODULE -I/usr/include/httpd -traditional
-cpp -Wno-four-char-constants -F/System/Library/PrivateFrameworks
-DUSE_CHKUSRNAMPASSWD  -c mod_auth_apple.c
...
# apxs -i -a mod_auth_apple.so
[activating module 'apple_auth' in /private/etc/httpd/httpd.conf]
cp mod_auth_apple.so /usr/libexec/httpd/mod_auth_apple.so
chmod 755 /usr/libexec/httpd/mod_auth_apple.so
cp /private/etc/httpd/httpd.conf /private/etc/httpd/httpd.conf.bak
cp /private/etc/httpd/httpd.conf.new /private/etc/httpd/httpd.conf
rm /private/etc/httpd/httpd.conf.new
```

The `mod_auth_apple` module is now compiled and installed. Using it is identical to the examples we've already seen for Basic and Digest authentication, except no password file is needed. For example, to protect a resource so that only my account (jray) can access it, I would add directives like this to the appropriate place in `/etc/httpd/httpd.conf`, or to a separate `.htaccess` file in the directory I want to protect:

```
AuthType Basic
Authname "Whatever"
Require user jray
```

To verify against any account on the machine, one would replace `Require user jray` with `Require valid-user`. Alternatively, to validate against a group, `Require group` *<groupname>* could be employed.

Unfortunately, this *is* Basic authentication—passwords are not encrypted, and the slightly-more-secure digest mode is not even available. The only truly secure way to use `mod_auth_apple` is to encrypt the entire authentication sequence by using HTTPS and `mod_ssl`. This will be your next stop in setting up a secure Web server.

Apple added a new module (`mod_auth_digest_apple`) to the Darwin project that is capable of handling digest authentication. You can now download and install it using the same procedure you used with `mod_auth_apple`.

Restricting Access by Network

To create more stringent control over the users who can access a given resource, use `Allow` and `Deny` to set up networks that should or shouldn't have access to portions of your Web site. This is extremely useful for setting up intranet sites that should be accessible only by a given subnet. For example, assume that you want to restrict access to a resource from everyone except the subnet `192.168.0.x` (having the netmask 255.255.255.0). The following rules define the access permissions:

```
Allow from 192.168.0.0/255.255.255.0
Deny from all
```

Because there isn't an ordering specified, what really happens with these rules is ambiguous. Is a connection from 192.168.0.100 allowed because of the `allow` statement? Or denied because all the connections are denied?

To solve the problem, insert the `Order` directive:

```
Order Deny,Allow
Allow from 192.168.0.0/255.255.255.0
Deny from all
```

With this ordering, an incoming connection is first compared to the deny list. Because `all` access is denied by default, *any* address matches this rule. However, the `Allow` directive is used for the final evaluation of the connection and allows any connection from the network `192.168.0.0` with the subnet `255.255.255.0`.

The `Allow` and `Deny` directives can also be used based on domain name, FQDN, or a partial IP address. One can, for example, provide write rules such as

```
Deny from evildomain.com johnsmachine.badpeopleplace.net 10.0.1
```

Here, requests from the machine `johnsmachine.badpeopleplace.net` would be denied, as would requests from *any* host in `evildomain.com` (`john.evildomain.com`, `www.evildomain.com`, and so on), and any host with an IP address that starts `10.0.1`.

To add one additional option to the mix, one can use the `mutual-failure` ordering option. The rarely used setting ensures that *both* the `Allow` and `Deny` directives must evaluate to `true` for the resource to be displayed. For example, assume that you have a corporate intranet that should be visible to everyone on your local domain (`mycorporation.com`), except some guest workstations in the lobby (`guest1.mycorporation.com` and `guest2.mycorporation.com`). In this case, you would use `Order mutual-failure` with the following `Allow` and `Deny` directives:

```
Order mutual-failure
Allow from mycorporation.com
Deny from guest1.mycorporation.com guest2.mycorporation.com
```

Using different orderings and different Allow/Deny lists, you can lock down a Web site to only those people who should have access, or disable troublesome hosts that misuse the site.

TIP

As with any change to the Apache configuration file, you must use `/usr/sbin/apachectl` to restart the server.

An alternative to restarting is to add an `.htaccess` file to the directory you want to protect. This file can contain any of the standard directory container directives and will be read automatically when Apache attempts to read any file from the directory.

Choosing Between Multiple Access Controls: `Satisfy`

When using authentication directives and the `Allow` directives, you may run into a situation where you want only one or the other to be true, but not both. For example, suppose you've protected a directory with the following:

```
<Directory "/Users/jray/Sites/">
    AuthType Digest
    AuthName "Development"
    AuthDigestFile /Users/jray/.htdigest
    Require valid-user
    Order Deny,Allow
    Allow from 192.168.0.0/255.255.255.0
    Deny from all
</Directory>
```

In this example configuration, my directory is protected so that a request *must* come from the 192.168.0.0/255.255.255.0 subnet *and* have a valid username and password given. Suppose, however, one wanted to deny access to everyone except the 192.168.0.0 subnet *or* anyone who enters a valid username and password. If any of security controls are satisfied, the Apache should provide access to the user, rather than enforcing all the controls.

This change is quite simple: Add the `Satisfy any/all` directive. `Satisify all`, the default, requires that both the user authentication and `Allow` limits be satisfied. `Satisfy any`, on the other hand, allows access to the resource if *either* of the limits is satisfied. Thus, the configuration becomes

```
<Directory "/Users/jray/Sites/">
    AuthType Digest
    AuthName "Development"
    AuthDigestFile /Users/jray/.htdigest
```

```
    Require valid-user
    Order Deny,Allow
    Allow from 192.168.0.0/255.255.255.0
    Deny from all
    Satisfy any
</Directory>
```

Disabling Rendezvous Advertising in Apache

Starting in Mac OS X 10.2.4, Apple included a special `mod_rendezvous_apple` module that advertises your main Web site *and* individual users' `Sites` directories via Rendezvous to compatible browsers such as Safari and Chimera.

Although not a security risk per se (the sites are available via HTTP, after all), this might not be a desired behavior on your network. You can disable the Rendezvous support by commenting out the following lines in your `/etc/httpd/httpd.conf` file:

```
LoadModule rendezvous_apple_module libexec/httpd/mod_rendezvous_apple.so
AddModule mod_rendezvous_apple.c
```

Presumably Apple will add an interface to this at some time in the future, but for now, it seems a bit inappropriate for *all* machines to be advertising their services to the network unbeknownst to the machine's operator.

SSL-Protected Apache

Try as we might, protecting Apache directories based on a username and password does not give you *true* security by any stretch of the imagination. Even if a directory's contents are protected with an authentication mechanism, the data is still transferred over the network unencrypted. A sniffer can easily pick up the contents of a Web page regardless of whether a user entered a password to access the page.

To secure your private information, encryption must be taken to the level of the HTTP—that is, *all* web traffic must be protected. This is accomplished by using SSL and `https`—the SSL-protected version of the HTTP. Apache support for SSL is added through the use of the `mod_ssl` module. Be aware that this adds an additional layer of complexity to Apache, and the potential for even more security holes.

For example, since the introduction of Mac OS X, the following `mod_ssl` exploits have surfaced:

```
http://archives.neohapsis.com/archives/bugtraq/2002-02/0313.html
http://cve.mitre.org/cgi-bin/cvename.cgi?name=CAN-2002-0653
```

Both exploits involve buffer overflows that enable users to potentially execute arbitrary code on the server. Although there's nothing you can do to avoid problems like this (other than shutting your computer off and curling up in a corner), it does serve as yet another poignant reminder that system security is highly dependent on keeping installed components up to date and being aware of the critical errors as they are discovered.

Compiling Apache with `mod_ssl` Support

To build Apache with SSL support, you need a few components before you can get started. Unlike most Apache modules, the `mod_ssl` software must be compiled at the same time as the Apache source code. In addition, you need to download the OpenSSL software that `mod_ssl` uses for security. Later in the chapter you'll see how to enable the `mod_ssl` module included with Mac OS X 10.2. Enabling the module, although faster than recompiling, is not as clean as using the certificate management tools in the full Apache distribution, and isn't likely to be as up to date. If you do decide to just enable the existing `mod_ssl`, feel free to skip ahead in the chapter to "Activating the Included `mod_ssl`."

First, download the latest Apache source from `http://www.apache.org/`, the most current version of `mod_ssl` from `http://www.modssl.org`, and the Darwin-patched OpenSSL distribution from `http://www.openssl.org`. Place them in a common build directory:

```
% mkdir apachebuild
% cd apachebuild/
% curl -O ftp://www.modssl.org/source/mod_ssl-2.8.10-1.3.27.tar.gz
% curl -O http://www.apache.org/dist/httpd/apache_1.3.27.tar.gz
% curl -O ftp://ftp.openssl.org/source/openssl-0.9.6g.tar.gz
```

Now, decompress and untar (`tar zxf <filename>`) each of the archives:

```
% tar zxf apache_1.3.27.tar.gz
% tar zxf mod_ssl-2.8.10-1.3.27.tar.gz
% tar zxf openssl-0.9.6g.tar.gz
```

All done! Let's move on.

Preparing `mod_ssl`

The next step is to prepare `mod_ssl`—this can be skipped if you are simply upgrading Apache and have no desire to add SSL support. Use the command `./configure --with-apache=<path to apache source distribution>` from within the `mod_ssl` distribution directory, substituting the appropriate name of your Apache distribution:

```
# ./configure —with-apache=../apache_1.3.27
Configuring mod_ssl/2.8.10 for Apache/1.3.27
 + Apache location: ../apache_1.3.27 (Version 1.3.27)
 + Auxiliary patch tool: ./etc/patch/patch (local)
 + Applying packages to Apache source tree:
   o Extended API (EAPI)
   o Distribution Documents
   o SSL Module Source
   o SSL Support
   o SSL Configuration Additions
   o SSL Module Documentation
   o Addons
Done: source extension and patches successfully applied.
```

The `mod_ssl` configuration will include several additional instructions on how to finish the Apache installation. *Do not* follow them or your compiled Apache server will be missing some important functions.

Preparing OpenSSL

Now it's time to set up the OpenSSL system—again, skip this step if you have no intention of running an SSL-enabled server.

> **NOTE**
>
> If you already have a fresh install of OpenSSL on your system, there's no need to recompile. Just be sure to set the `SSL_BASE` to the appropriate location in the next step ("Building Apache").

Compiling might take quite a while, depending on your system speed. You might want to start this process, then walk away for a few minutes. To configure OpenSSL for compilation, enter the distribution directory and type `./Config`:

```
% ./Config
Operating system: ppc-apple-darwin
Configuring for darwin-ppc-cc
Configuring for darwin-ppc-cc
IsWindows=0
...
```

After the software has been configured, use `make` to compile OpenSSL:

```
% make
+ rm -f libcrypto.0.dylib
+ rm -f libcrypto.dylib
```

```
+ rm -f libcrypto.0.9.6.dylib
+ rm -f libssl.0.dylib
+ rm -f libssl.dylib
+ rm -f libssl.0.9.6.dylib
making all in crypto...
```

Finally, it's time to compile and install Apache.

Building Apache

Building Apache is straightforward. Apple has worked with the Apache group to incorporate information about the Mac OS X (Darwin) operating system into the source code distribution. What this means to *you* is that Apache, when compiled and installed, will correctly integrate itself with the Mac OS X operating system.

To configure Apache for installation, first move into the source distribution directory. If you are compiling with SSL support, you must set the `SSL_BASE` environment variable to point to the directory containing the OpenSSL source distribution:

```
% setenv SSL_BASE=../openssl-0.9.6g
```

Next, use `./configure --enable-module=all --enable-shared=max` to set up the distribution for the Mac OS X environment:

```
% ./configure --enable-module=all --enable-shared=max
Configuring for Apache, Version 1.3.27
 + using installation path layout: Darwin (config.layout)
Creating Makefile
Creating Configuration.apaci in src
Creating Makefile in src
 + configured for Darwin platform
 + setting C compiler to gcc
 + setting C pre-processor to gcc -E -traditional-cpp
 + checking for system header files
 + adding selected modules
    o rewrite_module uses ConfigStart/End
      enabling DBM support for mod_rewrite
    o dbm_auth_module uses ConfigStart/End
    o db_auth_module uses ConfigStart/End
      using Berkeley-DB/1.x for mod_auth_db (-lc)
    o ssl_module uses ConfigStart/End
      + SSL interface: mod_ssl/2.8.10
      + SSL interface build type: DSO
      + SSL interface compatibility: enabled
      + SSL interface experimental code: disabled
```

```
+ SSL interface conservative code: disabled
+ SSL interface vendor extensions: disabled
+ SSL interface plugin: Configured DBM (-ldbm)
+ SSL library path: /Users/jray/apachebuild/openssl-0.9.6g
+ SSL library version: OpenSSL 0.9.6b 9 Jul 2001
+ SSL library type: source tree only (stand-alone)
```

If an error occurs, make sure that you have correctly set the `SSL_BASE` and typed the command-line options exactly as they appear here.

Now, one tiny correction needs to be made to the SSL module `Makefile`. From within the main Apache source distribution, go into `src/modules/ssl/`. Open the file `Makefile` in your favorite text editor and look for the line that reads

```
SSL_LIBS= -ldbm -lssl -lcrypto -L/usr/lib -lgcc
```

Change it to

```
SSL_LIBS= -lssl -lcrypto -L/usr/lib -lgcc
```

If you fail to follow these steps, the compilation process will complain of a missing library.

Finally, compile your new version of Apache by typing `make` from within the root level of the Apache source directory:

```
% make
===> src
===> src/regex
sh ./mkh  -p regcomp.c >regcomp.ih
...
```

The compile should finish in roughly three minutes on a base 1GHz G4. When the compile finishes, Apache displays a success message with the following instructions:

```
+--------------------------------------------------------------------+
| Before you install the package you now should prepare the SSL       |
| certificate system by running the 'make certificate' command.       |
| For different situations the following variants are provided:      |
|                                                                     |
| % make certificate TYPE=dummy    (dummy self-signed Snake Oil cert) |
| % make certificate TYPE=test     (test cert signed by Snake Oil CA) |
| % make certificate TYPE=custom   (custom cert signed by own CA)     |
| % make certificate TYPE=existing (existing cert)                    |
|        CRT=/path/to/your.crt [KEY=/path/to/your.key]                |
|                                                                     |
```

```
| Use TYPE=dummy    when you're a  vendor package maintainer,         |
| the TYPE=test     when you're an admin but want to do tests only,   |
| the TYPE=custom   when you're an admin willing to run a real server |
| and TYPE=existing when you're an admin who upgrades a server.       |
| (The default is TYPE=test)                                          |
|                                                                     |
| Additionally add ALGO=RSA (default) or ALGO=DSA to select           |
| the signature algorithm used for the generated certificate.        |
|                                                                     |
| Use 'make certificate VIEW=1' to display the generated data.        |
|                                                                     |
| Thanks for using Apache & mod_ssl.       Ralf S. Engelschall        |
|                                          rse@engelschall.com        |
|                                          www.engelschall.com        |
+---------------------------------------------------------------------+
```

You now have the most recent version of Apache, and it is ready to start handling secure Web traffic! All that remains is a few more minutes of setting up a basic certificate. If you are not using SSL, you can type `sudo make install` to start using the new version of Apache immediately.

Creating a Certificate and Installing

Secure Web servers rely on a CA (Certificate Authority) signed certificate to prove their identity and open a secure connection with a client. Unfortunately, obtaining a certificate isn't as simple as going to a Web site and buying one. An official certificate can be issued only by a CA, and only after you generate and send a CSR (Certificate Signing Request) to it. Luckily, for the purposes of testing SSL-enabled Apache, you can sign your own certificate. This will create a secure server, but most Web browsers will display a dialog box when accessing a server that isn't signed by a known CA. For the purposes of this chapter, we'll assume that you want to get up and running quickly, and that you'll want to use a VeriSign or other CA signed certificate later on.

Assuming that you're in the top level of the Apache distribution directory, type `make certificate TYPE=test`. This will take you through the steps of setting up a certificate, allowing you to automatically sign it with a fictional CA so that it can be used immediately, and then creating a CSR file so that you can send in a request for a real certificate in the future. During the certification creation, you are asked a series of questions related to your business or organization. Of all the questions, it is most important to correctly answer the Common Name prompt. This is your Web server's hostname (for example, `www.poisontooth.com`). Any questions you are unsure of can be left with their default values:

```
% make certificate TYPE=test
SSL Certificate Generation Utility (mkcert.sh)
Copyright (c) 1998-2000 Ralf S. Engelschall, All Rights Reserved.

Generating test certificate signed by Snake Oil CA [TEST]
WARNING: Do not use this for real-life/production systems
______________________________________________________________________

STEP 0: Decide the signature algorithm used for certificate
The generated X.509 CA certificate can contain either
RSA or DSA based ingredients. Select the one you want to use.
Signature Algorithm ((R)SA or (D)SA) [R]:
______________________________________________________________________

STEP 1: Generating RSA private key (1024 bit) [server.key]
2529186 semi-random bytes loaded
Generating RSA private key, 1024 bit long modulus
..........................++++++
......++++++
e is 65537 (0x10001)
______________________________________________________________________

STEP 2: Generating X.509 certificate signing request [server.csr]
Using configuration from .mkcert.cfg
You are about to be asked to enter information that will be incorporated
into your certificate request.
What you are about to enter is what is called a Distinguished Name or a DN.
There are quite a few fields but you can leave some blank
For some fields there will be a default value,
If you enter '.', the field will be left blank.
-----
1. Country Name             (2 letter code) [XY]:US
2. State or Province Name   (full name)     [Snake Desert]:Ohio
3. Locality Name            (eg, city)      [Snake Town]:Dublin
4. Organization Name        (eg, company)   [Snake Oil, Ltd]:PoisonTooth, Ent.
5. Organizational Unit Name (eg, section)   [Webserver Team]:
6. Common Name            (eg, FQDN)      [www.snakeoil.dom]:www.poisontooth.com
7. Email Address        (eg, name@FQDN) [www@snakeoil.dom]:jray@poisontooth.com
8. Certificate Validity     (days)          [365]:
______________________________________________________________________
```

```
STEP 3: Generating X.509 certificate signed by Snake Oil CA [server.crt]
Certificate Version (1 or 3) [3]:
Signature ok
subject=/C=US/ST=Ohio/L=Dublin/O=PoisonTooth, Ent./OU=Webserver Team/
CN=www.poisontooth.com/Email=jray@poisontooth.com
Getting CA Private Key
Verify: matching certificate & key modulus
read RSA key
Verify: matching certificate signature
../conf/ssl.crt/server.crt: OK
______________________________________________________________________

STEP 4: Enrypting RSA private key with a pass phrase for security [server.key]
The contents of the server.key file (the generated private key) has to be
kept secret. So we strongly recommend you encrypt the server.key file
with a Triple-DES cipher and a Pass Phrase.
Encrypt the private key now? [Y/n]: n
Warning, you're using an unencrypted RSA private key.
Please notice this fact and proceed at your own risk.
______________________________________________________________________

RESULT: Server Certification Files

o  conf/ssl.key/server.key
   The PEM-encoded RSA private key file which you configure
   with the 'SSLCertificateKeyFile' directive (automatically done
   when you install via APACI). KEEP THIS FILE PRIVATE!

o  conf/ssl.crt/server.crt
   The PEM-encoded X.509 certificate file which you configure
   with the 'SSLCertificateFile' directive (automatically done
   when you install via APACI).

o  conf/ssl.csr/server.csr
   The PEM-encoded X.509 certificate signing request file which
   you can send to an official Certificate Authority (CA)
   to request a real server certificate (signed by this CA instead
   of our demonstration-only Snake Oil CA), which later can replace
   the conf/ssl.crt/server.crt file.

WARNING: Do not use this for real-life/production systems
```

In this example, there is only one nonintuitive response: the use of encryption for the server key (`Encrypt the private key now? [Y/n]: n`). If the server key *is* encrypted, you have to manually enter a password to unlock the key each time the server is started, or write a script to supply the password to the server. When the key is left unencrypted, the assumption is made that your server protection is sufficient to keep the file safe from prying eyes. The Apache server and certificate are ready to install. Type `sudo make install` to prepare the software:

```
% sudo make install
===> [mktree: Creating Apache installation tree]
./src/helpers/mkdir.sh /usr/bin
./src/helpers/mkdir.sh /usr/sbin
...
+--------------------------------------------------------+
| You now have successfully built and installed the      |
| Apache 1.3 HTTP server. To verify that Apache actually |
| works correctly you now should first check the         |
| (initially created or preserved) configuration files   |
|                                                        |
|   /etc/httpd/httpd.conf
|                                                        |
| and then you should be able to immediately fire up     |
| Apache the first time by running:                      |
|                                                        |
|   /usr/sbin/apachectl start
|                                                        |
| Or when you want to run it with SSL enabled use:       |
|                                                        |
|   /usr/sbin/apachectl startssl
|                                                        |
| Thanks for using Apache.       The Apache Group        |
|                                http://www.apache.org/  |
+--------------------------------------------------------+
```

Unfortunately, the installation of the newly compiled Apache needs a modified version of the configuration file, so you still need to make two final changes before you're done. Open the file `/etc/httpd/httpd.conf.default` and add the following line to the bottom of the file:

```
Include /private/etc/httpd/users
```

Next, search for the directive

```
UserDir public_html
```

and change it to

```
UserDir Sites
```

Save the configuration file and copy it to take the place of `/etc/httpd/httpd.conf`. *Now* you're ready to go. Stop the existing Apache server (`apachectl stop`) and start the new SSL-enabled server with `apachectl startssl`.

```
% sudo /usr/sbin/apachectl stop
/usr/sbin/apachectl stop: httpd stopped
# /usr/sbin/apachectl startssl
Processing config directory: /private/etc/httpd/users
 Processing config file: /private/etc/httpd/users/jray.conf
 Processing config file: /private/etc/httpd/users/robyn.conf
 Processing config file: /private/etc/httpd/users/test.conf
 Processing config file: /private/etc/httpd/users/test2.conf
/usr/sbin/apachectl startssl: httpd started
```

To configure Mac OS X to automatically start Apache in SSL mode each time it boots, edit the file `/System/Library/StartupItems/Apache/Apache` and change the line

```
apachectl start
```

to read

```
apachectl startssl
```

That wasn't so bad, was it? Your Mac OS X machine is now a full- fledged secure Web server. To test it, open a Web browser and point to a URL on the machine, prefacing the URL with `https://` rather than the usual `http://`. Your browser might display a message about the certificate and signing authority not being recognized and ask you if you want to accept it, as shown in Figure 15.2.

You can expect to see these messages until you send in a certificate-signing request to a recognized CA. Upon loading the now-secure the page, you'll notice the small "lock" icon in the status bar of your browser window, indicating the traffic is secure.

USING CERTIFYING AUTHORITIES

When you created your server certificate, you also created a CSR that can be sent to a CA to generate a real certificate. The certificate signing request file is stored in `/etc/httpd/ssl.csr/server.csr`. This file can be sent to a CA, such as

VeriSign: `http://digitalid.verisign.com/server/apacheNotice.htm`

Thawte: `http://www.thawte.com/html/RETAIL/ssl/index.html`

After processing your request, the CA will return a new digitally signed certificate file. Replace the existing */etc/httpd/ssl.crt/server.crt* certificate with the CA signed certificate, and your server will be official.

FIGURE 15.2 Until you have a certificate issued by a real Certificate Authority, you'll see warnings when accessing a page.

Reinstalling `mod_hfs_apple` Support

Any time you recompile Apache manually, you should add `mod_hfs_apple` support back into the system; otherwise you put yourself at risk for the case-sensitivity exploit discussed earlier in the chapter. To reinstall `mod_hfs_apple`, download the source distribution from Apple's Darwin repository at `http://www.opensource.apple.com/projects/darwin/6.0/projects.html` or from `http://www.opendarwin.org/cgi-bin/cvsweb.cgi/src/apache_mod_hfs_apple/`.

The distribution consists of a Makefile and a source file—which you install much the same way as you did the `mod_auth_apple`. Unarchive and enter the module distribution. As always, the installation needs to take place as root, or use `sudo` for the final step:

```
# tar zxf apache_mod_hfs_apple-3.tar.gz
# cd apache_mod_hfs_apple-3
```

Next, edit the `Makefile` line. Look for the section reading

```
all build $(MODULE): $(MODULE_SRC) $(OTHER_SRC)
        ln -sf $(SRCROOT)$(SRCPATH)/Makefile $(OBJROOT)/Makefile
        ln -sf $(SRCROOT)$(SRCPATH)/mod_hfs_apple.c $(OBJROOT)/mod_hfs_apple.c
```

Comment out the two `ln` link lines:

```
all build $(MODULE): $(MODULE_SRC) $(OTHER_SRC)
        #ln -sf $(SRCROOT)$(SRCPATH)/Makefile $(OBJROOT)/Makefile
        #ln -sf $(SRCROOT)$(SRCPATH)/mod_hfs_apple.c $(OBJROOT)/mod_hfs_apple.c
```

While you're still in the file, look for the line commented-out that looks like

```
# /usr/sbin/apxs -i -a -n hfs_apple $(MODULE)
```

Uncomment it so that it reads:

```
/usr/sbin/apxs -i -a -n hfs_apple $(MODULE)
```

You're now ready to compile and install using `make DSTROOT=. OBJROOT=.` and `make install DSTROOT=. OBJROOT=.`, respectively:

```
# make DSTROOT=. OBJROOT=.
#ln -sf /Makefile ./Makefile
#ln -sf /mod_hfs_apple.c ./mod_hfs_apple.c
cd . ; /usr/sbin/apxs -c -S LDFLAGS_SHLIB="-bundle -bundle_loader
...
# make install DSTROOT=. OBJROOT=.
Installing product...
/bin/mkdir -p ./usr/libexec/httpd
/bin/cp ./mod_hfs_apple.so ./usr/libexec/httpd
/bin/chmod 755 ./usr/libexec/httpd/mod_hfs_apple.so
/usr/bin/strip -x ./usr/libexec/httpd/mod_hfs_apple.so
/usr/sbin/apxs -i -a -n hfs_apple mod_hfs_apple.so
[activating module `hfs_apple' in /private/etc/httpd/httpd.conf]
cp mod_hfs_apple.so /usr/libexec/httpd/mod_hfs_apple.so
chmod 755 /usr/libexec/httpd/mod_hfs_apple.so
cp /private/etc/httpd/httpd.conf /private/etc/httpd/httpd.conf.bak
cp /private/etc/httpd/httpd.conf.new /private/etc/httpd/httpd.conf
rm /private/etc/httpd/httpd.conf.new
```

The `mod_hfs_apple` module is now compiled and installed, and your server is again protected from case-sensitivity issues.

Activating the Included `mod_ssl`

If you'd rather just use the Apple-supplied version of `mod_ssl` with Apache, you can avoid the entire compile process and simply activate the existing module by changing a few lines in `/etc/httpd/httpd.conf`. The benefit to this approach is time savings coupled with the ability to blame Apple if exploits are found for the version they've provided. (That's sarcasm, folks! It's *your* responsibility to keep track of security issues, especially for components such as `mod_ssl`, which Apple doesn't formally support on the Mac OS X client.)

There are three steps to this process:

1. Create a Certificate-Signing Request. This request is usually sent to a CA, where it is signed, and a server certificate is returned.
2. Create and use a CA to sign the request. You'll be signing the request yourself, rather than using a third party (which should be done on a production server).
3. Configure Apache for SSL. Because SSL support wasn't built into Apache, you need to do a bit of editing by hand to make the server work as expected.

Creating the Certificate-Signing Request

You'll be using OpenSSL for most of the remainder of the chapter to create private keys, signing requests, and act as the CA. This will be similar to creating the OpenSSL-enabled mail server in Chapter 13, "Mail Server Security," but we'll go through the process, step-by-step, so you know what to expect.

First, create and enter a new directory that you'll use for the entire process:

```
% mkdir ssltmp
% cd ssltmp
```

You'll need some random data to seed the encryption. There are a number of ways to generate pseudo-random data for this purpose. One of the easiest is to use `/dev/random`. Create a file with random data by typing `head /dev/random > random.seed`.

```
% head /dev/random > random.seed
```

Next, use `openssl genrsa -des3 -rand random.seed -out server.key 1024` to generate a 1024-bit RSA key.

```
% openssl genrsa -des3 -rand random.seed -out server.key 1024
1890 semi-random bytes loaded
Generating RSA private key, 1024 bit long modulus
.++++++
.......++++++
e is 65537 (0x10001)
Enter PEM pass phrase: *****
Verifying password - Enter PEM pass phrase: *****
```

During this process, you'll be asked for a passphrase. This phrase is used to protect the server.key, which is, itself, the private key for your server. If this is confusing, see Chapter 5, "Picking Locks: Password Attacks," for more information on encryption and public/private key systems.

Now, to create the certificate signing request, use the command `openssl req -new -key server.key -out server.csr`. When prompted, enter the passphrase you used when creating the server key. The other critical piece of information is the Common Name, which, in this case, refers to your server's fully qualified domain name—in this example, `www.poisontooth.com`.

```
% openssl req -new -key server.key -out server.csr
Using configuration from /System/Library/OpenSSL/openssl.cnf
Enter PEM pass phrase: *****
You are about to be asked to enter information that will be incorporated
into your certificate request.
What you are about to enter is what is called a Distinguished Name or a DN.
There are quite a few fields, but you can leave some blank
For some fields there will be a default value.
If you enter '.', the field will be left blank.
-----
Country Name (2 letter code) [AU]:US
State or Province Name (full name) [Some-State]:Ohio
Locality Name (eg, city) []:Columbus
Organization Name (eg, company) [Internet Widgits Pty Ltd]:PoisonTooth Ent.
Organizational Unit Name (eg, section) []:Development
Common Name (eg, YOUR name) []:www.poisontooth.com
Email Address []:jray@macosxunleashed.com

Please enter the following 'extra' attributes
to be sent with your certificate request
A challenge password []:
An optional company name []:
```

You've now created the file `server.csr`, which contains your certificate-signing request. In a production server environment, you'd send this file to a "real" Certificate Authority, then receive back a signed server certificate (`server.crt` in the examples throughout this chapter), which you could install in Apache and go. If you *are* creating a production server, you'll want to proceed with getting the real `.crt` file and skip the next step, which allows you to sign your own certificate.

Signing the CSR

To sign the request that you just generated, you need to create a CA key (using the same process required to generate the `server.key` file) and then use that key to create a self-signed CA certificate. This certificate, when completed, will be used to sign your original request. You're becoming your own Certificate Authority—which, while inappropriate for production servers, is fine for a test environment.

First, create the CA keyfile using `openssl genrsa -des3 -rand random.seed -out ca.key`. As you did previously, choose a passphrase you can remember, and it *shouldn't* be the same one that you used earlier:

```
% openssl genrsa -des3 -rand random.seed -out ca.key
1890 semi-random bytes loaded
Generating RSA private key, 512 bit long modulus
....++++++++++++
........++++++++++++
e is 65537 (0x10001)
Enter PEM pass phrase:
Verifying password - Enter PEM pass phrase:
```

Next, create the CA certificate with `openssl req -new -x509 -days 100 -key ca.key -out ca.crt`. You may want to change the `days` attribute to increase the length of time the certificate will be valid if you plan to use it for signing requests in the future.

```
% openssl req -new -x509 -days 1000 -key ca.key -out ca.crt
Using configuration from /System/Library/OpenSSL/openssl.cnf
Enter PEM pass phrase: ******
You are about to be asked to enter information that will be incorporated
into your certificate request.
What you are about to enter is what is called a Distinguished Name or a DN.
There are quite a few fields but you can leave some blank
For some fields there will be a default value,
If you enter '.', the field will be left blank.
-----
Country Name (2 letter code) [AU]:US
State or Province Name (full name) [Some-State]:Ohio
Locality Name (eg, city) []:Columbus
Organization Name (eg, company) [Internet Widgits Pty Ltd]:PoisonTooth Ent.
Organizational Unit Name (eg, section) []:IT Department
Common Name (eg, YOUR name) []:John Ray
Email Address []:jray@macosxunleashed.com
```

Now it's time to sign the `server.csr` file by using the CA certificate and key. To do this, you need to download the utility `sign.sh` included in the `mod_ssl` package. The easiest way to do this is grab it from the Open Darwin CVS: `http://www.opendarwin.org/cgi-bin/cvsweb.cgi/src/apache_mod_ssl/mod_ssl/pkg.contrib/sign.sh`. After downloading, make sure to give execute permissions to the script (`chmod +x sign.sh`). Finally, use `sign.sh server.csr` to create your `server.crt` file:

```
% ./sign.sh server.csr
CA signing: server.csr -> server.crt:
```

```
Using configuration from ca.config
Enter PEM pass phrase: *****
Check that the request matches the signature
Signature ok
The Subjects Distinguished Name is as follows
countryName           :PRINTABLE:'US'
stateOrProvinceName   :PRINTABLE:'Ohio'
localityName          :PRINTABLE:'Columbus'
organizationName      :PRINTABLE:'PoisonTooth Ent.'
organizationalUnitName:PRINTABLE:'Development'
commonName            :PRINTABLE:'www.poisontooth.com'
emailAddress          :IA5STRING:'jray@macosxunleashed.com'
Certificate is to be certified until Oct 31 03:42:41 2003 GMT (365 days)
Sign the certificate? [y/n]:y


1 out of 1 certificate requests certified, commit? [y/n]y
Write out database with 1 new entries
Data Base Updated
CA verifying: server.crt <-> CA cert
server.crt: OK
```

NOTE

Because this certificate is being signed for a test server, you may want to bump the 365-day limit up by editing the `sign.sh` file and changing the `default_days` attribute to something else.

The server certificate is now signed and ready for use. When using `mod_ssl`, Apache will require your initial passphrase to start and access the `server.key` file. There are two ways to solve this problem. On a production server, Apache's startup should be modified so that the password is supplied to it (via script or another mechanism); otherwise the server process will hang while it waits for the input. The alternative approach, which we'll use here, is to create an unencrypted version of `server.key`:

```
% cp server.key server.key.original
% openssl rsa -in server.key.original -out server.key
read RSA key
Enter PEM pass phrase: *****
writing RSA key
```

Finally, create the directories /etc/httpd/ssl.crt, /etc/httpd/ssl.csr, /etc/httpd/ssl.key, into which you'll copy the files server.crt, server.csr, and server.key. You'll need to use sudo or be logged in as root to do this:

```
% sudo -s
# mkdir /etc/httpd/ssl.crt
# mkdir /etc/httpd/ssl.key
# mkdir /etc/httpd/ssl.csr
# cp server.crt /etc/httpd/ssl.crt
# cp server.csr /etc/httpd/ssl.csr
# cp server.key /etc/httpd/ssl.key
```

The directory structure isn't of importance. The names used in this example are based on those of the default Apache mod_ssl distribution. Of the files you've moved, only the .crt and .key files are actually used by Apache. The server.csr file, however, might be useful to keep around if you want to submit it to a real Certificate Authority later.

You can get rid of ca.crt and ca.key files, unless you want to use them for signing additional requests. The CA certificate and key could potentially be misused by a third party to impersonate you. They are your personal identifiers and should not be made publicly accessible or left unprotected on the server.

Preparing Apache

The final step in activating mod_ssl is to edit /etc/httpd/httpd.conf to include the appropriate directives to load mod_ssl and the server certificate you just created. Open /etc/httpd/httpd.conf now.

> **NOTE**
>
> Adding SSL support is going to require adding quite a few new lines to your httpd.conf file. These lines are shown here with the official Apache comments preceding them. If you don't want to do as much typing, leave out the configuration lines that begin with #.

First, uncomment the mod_ssl lines in the file, changing

```
#LoadModule ssl_module         libexec/httpd/libssl.so
#AddModule mod_ssl.c
```

to

```
LoadModule ssl_module         libexec/httpd/libssl.so
AddModule mod_ssl.c
```

Now, you're going to (more or less) rebuild the SSL-enabled config file that comes with Apache if you compile in SSL support by hand. Apache must be told to listen on port 443 (`https`) in addition to port 80. Locate the line `Port 80` in your config file and add the following immediately after it:

```
##
##  SSL Support
##
##  When we also provide SSL we have to listen to the
##  standard HTTP port (see above) and to the HTTPS port
##
<IfDefine SSL>
Listen 80
Listen 443
</IfDefine>
```

Next, move to the bottom of the configuration file and insert the following directives. The comments aren't critical, so you can feel free to skip them if you'd like:

```
##
##  SSL Global Context
##
##  All SSL configuration in this context applies to both
##  the main server and all SSL-enabled virtual hosts.
##

#
#   Some MIME-types for downloading Certificates and CRLs
#
<IfDefine SSL>
AddType application/x-x509-ca-cert .crt
AddType application/x-pkcs7-crl    .crl
</IfDefine>

<IfModule mod_ssl.c>

#   Pass Phrase Dialog:
#   Configure the pass phrase gathering process.
#   The filtering dialog program ('builtin' is an internal
#   terminal dialog) has to provide the pass phrase on stdout.
SSLPassPhraseDialog  builtin
```

```
#   Inter-Process Session Cache:
#   Configure the SSL Session Cache: First the mechanism
#   to use and second the expiring timeout (in seconds).
SSLSessionCache        dbm:/var/log/httpd/ssl_scache
SSLSessionCacheTimeout  300

#   Semaphore:
#   Configure the path to the mutual exclusion semaphore the
#   SSL engine uses internally for inter-process synchronization.
SSLMutex  file:/var/log/httpd/ssl_mutex

#   Pseudo Random Number Generator (PRNG):
#   Configure one or more sources to seed the PRNG of the
#   SSL library. The seed data should be of good random quality.
#   WARNING! On some platforms /dev/random blocks if not enough entropy
#   is available. This means you then cannot use the /dev/random device
#   because it would lead to very long connection times (as long as
#   it requires to make more entropy available). But usually those
#   platforms additionally provide a /dev/urandom device that doesn't
#   block. So, if available, use this one instead. Read the mod_ssl User
#   Manual for more details.
SSLRandomSeed startup builtin
SSLRandomSeed connect builtin

#   Logging:
#   The home of the dedicated SSL protocol logfile. Errors are
#   additionally duplicated in the general error log file. Put
#   this somewhere where it cannot be used for symlink attacks on
#   a real server (that is, somewhere where only root can write).
#   Log levels are (ascending order: higher ones include lower ones):
#   none, error, warn, info, trace, debug.
SSLLog      /var/log/httpd/ssl_engine_log
SSLLogLevel info

</IfModule>
```

NOTE

The paths used for SSLSessionCache and SSLMutex are different from the Apache defaults. In this example, they're configured to the same values Apple uses for Mac OS X Server. You can change them to something more logical, such as `/var/db` or `/var/run`, if you'd like.

As a final step, you need to "turn on" the SSL Engine for your Web server. You can do this either for a given virtual host or for the entire server. This example uses a virtual host entry for `/Library/WebServer/Documents` (which *is* the main server). The advantage of this approach is that the SSL-protected accesses can be logged and dealt with separately, rather than combined with the main site logs and rules. Add the following to the bottom of your `/etc/httpd/httpd.conf` file. Again, comments aren't necessary; they're provided to reflect the defaults in the Apache SSL installation. Be sure to change the `ServerName` and `ServerAdmin` directives to match your particular installation:

```
<IfDefine SSL>

##
## SSL Virtual Host Context
##
<VirtualHost _default_:443>
#General setup for the virtual host
DocumentRoot "/Library/WebServer/Documents"
ServerName www.poisontooth.com
ServerAdmin jray@macosxunleashed.com
ErrorLog /var/log/httpd/ssl_error_log
TransferLog /var/log/httpd/ssl_access_log

#   SSL Engine Switch:
#   Enable/Disable SSL for this virtual host.
SSLEngine on

#   SSL Cipher Suite:
#   List the ciphers that the client is permitted to negotiate.
#   See the mod_ssl documentation for a complete list.
SSLCipherSuite ALL:!ADH:!EXPORT56:RC4+RSA:+HIGH:+MEDIUM:+LOW:+SSLv2:+EXP:+eNULL

#   Server Certificate:
#   Point SSLCertificateFile at a PEM encoded certificate.  If
#   the certificate is encrypted, then you will be prompted for a
#   pass phrase.  Note that a kill -HUP will prompt again. A test
#   certificate can be generated with 'make certificate' under
#   built time. Keep in mind that if you've both a RSA and a DSA
#   certificate you can configure both in parallel (to also allow
#   the use of DSA ciphers, etc.)
SSLCertificateFile /etc/httpd/ssl.crt/server.crt
```

```
#   Server Private Key:
#   If the key is not combined with the certificate, use this
#   directive to point at the key file.  Keep in mind that if
#   you've both a RSA and a DSA private key you can configure
#   both in parallel (to also allow the use of DSA ciphers, etc.)
SSLCertificateKeyFile /etc/httpd/ssl.key/server.key

#   SSL Engine Options:
#   Set various options for the SSL engine.
#   o FakeBasicAuth:
#     Translate the client X.509 into a Basic Authorization.  This means that
#     the standard Auth/DBMAuth methods can be used for access control.  The
#     user name is the 'one line' version of the client's X.509 certificate.
#     Note that no password is obtained from the user. Every entry in the user
#     file needs this password: 'xxj31ZMTZzkVA'.
#   o ExportCertData:
#     This exports two additional environment variables: SSL_CLIENT_CERT and
#     SSL_SERVER_CERT. These contain the PEM-encoded certificates of the
#     server (always existing) and the client (only existing when client
#     authentication is used). This can be used to import the certificates
#     into CGI scripts.
#   o StdEnvVars:
#     This exports the standard SSL/TLS related 'SSL_*' environment variables.
#     Per default this exportation is switched off for performance reasons,
#     because the extraction step is an expensive operation and is usually
#     useless for serving static content. So one usually enables the
#     exportation for CGI and SSI requests only.
#   o CompatEnvVars:
#     This exports obsolete environment variables for backward compatibility
#     to Apache-SSL 1.x, mod_ssl 2.0.x, Sioux 1.0 and Stronghold 2.x. Use this
#     to provide compatibility to existing CGI scripts.
#   o StrictRequire:
#     This denies access when "SSLRequireSSL" or "SSLRequire" applied even
#     under a "Satisfy any" situation, i.e. when it applies access is denied
#     and no other module can change it.
#   o OptRenegotiate:
#     This enables optimized SSL connection renegotiation handling when SSL
#     directives are used in per-directory context.
#SSLOptions +FakeBasicAuth +ExportCertData +CompatEnvVars +StrictRequire
<Files ~ "\.(cgi|shtml|phtml|php3?)$">
    SSLOptions +StdEnvVars
</Files>
```

```
<Directory "/Library/Webserver/CGI-Executables">
    SSLOptions +StdEnvVars
</Directory>

#   SSL Protocol Adjustments:
#   The safe and default but still SSL/TLS standard compliant shutdown
#   approach is that mod_ssl sends the close notify alert but doesn't wait for
#   the close notify alert from client. When you need a different shutdown
#   approach you can use one of the following variables:
#   o ssl-unclean-shutdown:
#     This forces an unclean shutdown when the connection is closed, i.e. no
#     SSL close notify alert is send or allowed to received.  This violates
#     the SSL/TLS standard but is needed for some brain-dead browsers. Use
#     this when you receive I/O errors because of the standard approach where
#     mod_ssl sends the close notify alert.
#   o ssl-accurate-shutdown:
#     This forces an accurate shutdown when the connection is closed, i.e. a
#     SSL close notify alert is send and mod_ssl waits for the close notify
#     alert of the client. This is 100% SSL/TLS standard compliant, but in
#     practice often causes hanging connections with brain-dead browsers. Use
#     this only for browsers where you know that their SSL implementation
#     works correctly.
#   Notice: Most problems of broken clients are also related to the HTTP
#   keep-alive facility, so you usually additionally want to disable
#   keep-alive for those clients, too. Use variable "nokeepalive" for this.
#   Similarly, one has to force some clients to use HTTP/1.0 to work around
#   their broken HTTP/1.1 implementation. Use variables "downgrade-1.0" and
#   "force-response-1.0" for this.
SetEnvIf User-Agent ".*MSIE.*" \
         nokeepalive ssl-unclean-shutdown \
         downgrade-1.0 force-response-1.0

#   Per-Server Logging:
#   The home of a custom SSL log file. Use this when you want a
#   compact non-error SSL logfile on a virtual host basis.
CustomLog /var/log/httpd/ssl_request_log \
          "%t %h %{SSL_PROTOCOL}x %{SSL_CIPHER}x \"%r\" %b"

</VirtualHost>
</IfDefine>
```

If you'd rather just SSL-enable your entire server, you can leave out the `<VirtualHost>` tags and the `DocumentRoot`, `ServerName`, `ServerAdmin`, and `ErrorLog` directives. This uses the default setting for your Web server, but enables `mod_ssl` globally, rather than for a virtual host.

WHAT IS A VIRTUAL HOST?

A virtual host is a unique container object, in that it can define an entirely separate Web space unrelated to the main Apache Web site or user sites. For example, the three domains `poisontooth.com`, `vujevich.com`, and `shadesofinsanity.com` are all being served from a single computer. To the end user, these appear to be different and unique hosts. To Apache, however, they're just different directories on the same hard drive.

There are two types of virtual hosts: name-based and IP-based.

Name-based virtual hosts rely on the HTTP/1.1 to work. A single IP address is used on the server, but there are multiple DNS entries for that single address. When connecting to the server, the client browser sends a request for a Web page, along with the name of the server from which it should come. Apache uses that information to serve the correct page. This works for all but the oldest 2.0 revision browsers.

IP-based virtual hosts relyon Apache's capability to listen to multiple IP addresses simultaneously. Each domain name is assigned to a different IP address. Apache can differentiate between the different incoming addresses and serve the appropriate documents for each. This works on *any* browser, but is costly in terms of the IP addresses that it consumes.

There are only two differences in the Apache configuration of name-based and IP-based virtual hosts. Name-based hosts must include the `NameVirtualHost` directive, whereas IP-based hosts need to use `Listen` to inform Apache of all the available addresses. Let's take a look at two different ways to configure the virtual hosts `www.mycompany.com` and `www.yourcompany.com`. First, using named-based hosting:

Assume that both `mycompany` and `yourcompany` domain names point to the IP address `192.168.0.100`. To configure name-based virtual hosts, you could add the following directives to the end of the `/etc/httpd/httpd.conf` file:

```
NameVirtualHost 192.168.0.100

<VirtualHost 192.168.0.100>
        ServerName www.mycompany.com
        DocumentRoot /Users/jray/mycompany
        ServerAdmin president@mycompany.com
</VirtualHost>

<VirtualHost 192.168.0.100>
        ServerName www.yourcompany.com
        DocumentRoot /Users/jray/yourcompany
        ServerAdmin president@yourcompany.com
</VirtualHost>
```

The NameVirtualHost sets up the IP address on which Apache expects multiple domain name requests to come in. The two VirtualHost directives define the basic properties of the two sites: what their real domain names are, where the HTML documents are loaded, and the email address for the person who runs the site.

Creating this same setup using IP-based hosts doesn't require much additional effort. For this sample configuration, assume that www.mycompany.com has the address 192.168.0.100 and www.yourcompany.com uses 192.168.0.101. The configuration becomes

```
Listen 192.168.0.100
Listen 192.168.0.101
<VirtualHost 192.168.0.100>
        ServerName www.mycompany.com
        DocumentRoot /Users/jray/mycompany
        ServerAdmin president@mycompany.com
</VirtualHost>
<VirtualHost 192.168.0.101>
        ServerName www.yourcompany.com
        DocumentRoot /Users/jray/yourcompany
        ServerAdmin president@yourcompany.com
</VirtualHost>
```

This time, the Listen directive is used to tell Apache to watch for incoming Web connections on both the available IP addresses. The VirtualHost containers remain the same, except they now use different IP addresses for the two different sites.

Starting your SSL Server

To start your SSL-enabled Apache, you should use the command `sudo http -DSSL`. This defines the runtime SSL variable, which, in turn, enables the SSL configuration we've created in `/etc/httpd/httpd.conf`. If you use the standard `/usr/sbin/apachectl start` command, SSL support will be turned off.

If you've read through this entire section, you may have noticed that when you install an SSL-enabled Apache by hand, you can use `/usr/sbin/apachectl startssl` to start Apache with SSL support. Unfortunately, the version of `apachectl` that Apple is currently distributing with Mac OS X does *not* support this feature.

To be sure that Apache starts with SSL support, you can open the `/usr/sbin/apachectl` script and change the line that reads

```
HTTPD=/usr/sbin/httpd
```

to

```
HTTPD="/usr/sbin/httpd -DSSL"
```

Your system can now start and stop your `mod_ssl` Apache as it normally does.

mod_ssl Configuration Directives

No matter how you choose to enable mod_ssl on your system, you're going to end up seeing some unfamiliar SSL-related directives in your Apache configuration file. The best reference for what these do is the source: http://www.modssl.org/docs/. For your convenience, a summary of the directives used in the configuration we just created is provided in Table 15.5.

TABLE 15.5 mod_ssl Configuration Directives

Directive	Purpose
SSLPassPhraseDialog builtin|exec:<*path to executable*>	Choose how the server's private key will be decrypted. The builtin method prompts the user when Apache is starting. Because we removed the password from our key, no password is required. Alternatively exec can be used to provide a program that is executed to provide the passphrase.
SSLMutex none|file: <*file path*>|sem	Determines how the SSL engine will create mutually exclusive locks for operations in the Apache server processes. Mac OS X users should use the file method.
SSLRandomSeed server| connect builtin|file: <*file path*>|exec:<*path to executable*>	Determines how random numbers are seeded at server startup (server) or when a connection (connect) is created. Mac OS X users can use the builtin method or file:/dev/random.
SSLSessionCache none| dbm:<*file path*>	Creates an optional SSL session cache file. Mac OS X users can use a dbm database file to store the cache.
SSLSessionCacheTimeout <*seconds*>	The length of time in seconds before an SSL session expires in the cache.
SSLEngine on|off	Turns SSL on for the server or a configured virtual host.
SSLProtocol +/- <*protocol*>..	Chooses the SSL protocols the server is to use. Valid options are All, SSLv2, TLSv1. Protocols can be prefixed with + or - to add or subtract them from the list.
SSLCipherSuite <*Cipher list*>	Chooses the ciphers that the client computer is allowed to use during the SSL handshake. See http://www.modssl.org for a full list of the available options.
SSLCertificateFile <*filename*>	Specifies the path to the site certificate file—/etc/httpd/ssl.crt/server.crt for our examples.
SSLCertificateKeyFile <*filename*>	Sets the path of the private key file—/etc/httpd/ssl.key/server.key.
SSLLog <*log file pathname*>	Logfile dedicated to logging SSL protocol errors and exceptions.
SSLLogLevel none|error| warn|info|trace|debug	Determines the amount of information that will be logged to the SSLLog file—listed in order of increasing verbosity.
SSLOptions +/- <*option*>SSL	Sets SSL runtime options. Please set the comments in the Apache options earlier in the chapter or visit http://www.modssl.org for a full list and description of options.
SSLRequireSSL	When applied to a directory or virtual host, non-SSL access will be prohibited to that resource.

Additional Resources

Like so many other things, Apache and `mod_ssl` are not *little* topics. To help supplement the information in this chapter, I suggest checking out these additional resources:

- `http://httpd.apache.org/`. The Apache Project homepage. The best location for learning Apache directives and their uses.
- `http://www.apacheweek.com/features/security-13`. ApacheWeek's security vulnerability list for Apache 1.3.
- `http://www.linuxplanet.com/linuxplanet/tutorials/1527/1/`. "Security and Apache: An Essential Primer." As its name says, this is an excellent overview of Apache security.
- `http://www.bignosebird.com/apache/a11.shtml`. "The Common Sense Guide to Apache Security."
- `http://stein.cshl.org/~lstein/talks/perl_conference/apache_security/`. "Apache Security from A-Z." A presentation on Apache security, covering everything from firewalls to SSL.
- `http://www.intersectalliance.com/projects/ApacheConfig/index.html`. "Apache Security Configuration Document." A detailed document on installing and protecting Apache.
- *Maximum Apache Security*, Sams Publishing, 067232380x.

Summary

Apache is a complex piece of software that provides a number of mechanisms for controlling access to its resources. Unfortunately, the Web is not a safe place, and any information served from your default Mac OS X Web server is still capable of being intercepted by third parties. To overcome this, one must use SSL encryption and the Apache `mod_ssl` module.

This chapter introduced you to the Apache authentication directives `Limit`, `Satisfy`, and `Option`, as well as the steps necessary to create a `mod_ssl` secured server either from scratch, or using Apple's included software.

16

File Sharing Security

IN THIS CHAPTER

- Apple Filing Protocol
- WebDAV
- Sharing Files with Samba
- Common Unix Printing System
- Other Resources

Mac OS X can share files and resources with other machines through a variety of mechanisms, such as AppleShare, Samba, and CUPS. Resource sharing opens a system to misuse: Servers such as CUPS and AppleShare open your computer's file system and peripherals to the world. Apple has provided very few controls over the Mac OS X file and resource sharing, leaving advanced setup and security to those willing to dig beyond the interface.

Apple Filing Protocol

The Apple Filing Protocol (implemented as "AppleShare") provides the bread and butter of Mac OS X file sharing. Sharing between client computers or between clients and Mac OS X Server almost certainly takes place with AFP.

AFP Security History

Traditionally, AFP has been relatively low on the radar of attackers. Running over ethernet and LocalTalk cables, it was easily sniffable, but did not use TCP/IP as a transport, making sniffing a somewhat specialized activity. In the mid/late 90s, Apple introduced AppleShare IP, which enabled AFP to run over TCP/IP, and thus the Internet—opening it to all the problems of any other Internet protocol.

As you'll see demonstrated shortly, a huge failing in AFP is content encryption. With the data stream passed as cleartext, AFP becomes extremely susceptible to content injection and other hijacking attacks. In a security-conscious environment, AppleShare should *never* be used to securely transfer data unless it is either tunneled through SSH or via IPSec.

As of early 2003, there are no known local or remote exploits for the `AppleFileServer` daemon in Mac OS X.

Authentication

AFP provides an extensible user authentication architecture, and includes several default UAMs (User Authentication Mechanisms), listed in Table 16.1. Additional modules can be installed in `/Library/Filesystems/AppleShare/Authentication`, but must be present on all machines involved in a connection.

Mac OS X *does* warn the user when making an insecure connection. But, by default, it will very happily send your username and password in cleartext. This very likely means sending your system account password unsecured.

NOTE

I say *"very likely"* because it is certainly possible to have a system login dissimilar from an AppleShare username. This isn't the default behavior for Mac OS X-based servers, but isn't uncommon.

TABLE 16.1 Default UAMs for Mac OS X

UAM String	Name	AFP Client Description
`No User Authent`	No user authentication	Guest
`Cleartxt Passwrd`	Cleartext (unencrypted) password	Cleartext Password
`Randnum Exchange`	Random Number Exchange	???
`2-Way Randnum`	Two-Way Random Number Exchange	Two-Way Encrypted Password
`DHCAST128`	Diffie-Hellman Exchange	Encrypted Password Transport
`DHX2`	Diffie-Hellman Exchange 2	Encrypted Password Transport v2
`Client Krb v2`	Kerberos	Kerberos Authentication v4/v5

Apple documents the inner workings of the UAMs at `http://developer.apple.com/techpubs/macosx/Networking/AFP/Chapter_1/AFP_Login.html`.

What UAM will be used is determined by a request from the AFP client, but is ultimately enforced by the server. If the server does not support a given UAM, the other options are attempted. To view the UAM that will be used for your connection, click the Options button on the server login screen after making the initial connection in the Finder. For example, in Figure 16.1, Two-Way Encrypted Password Transport is being used.

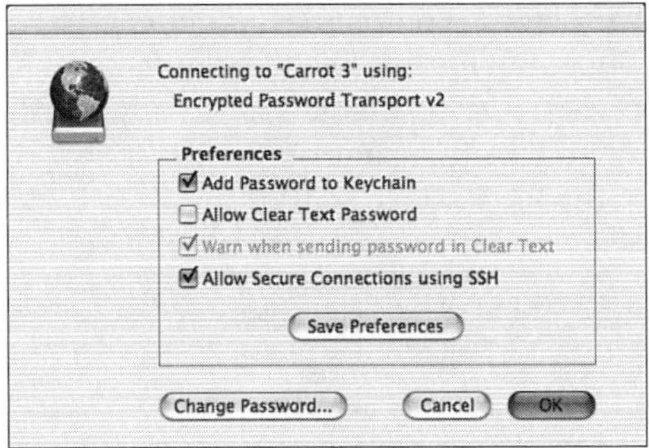

FIGURE 16.1 View the UAM being used for the login.

Also included on the connection screen are preferences for password handling:

- **Add Password to Keychain**. Store the connection password in the Keychain for quick future access to the resource.
- **Allow Clear Text Password**. Allow passwords to be transmitted without any encryption.
- **Warn When Sending Password in Clear Text**. This should *always* be checked. Mac OS X will display a warning dialog if the login will use an unencrypted password.
- **Allow Secure Connections Using SSH**. Enable content encryption (if supported by the remote server). This will be covered directly.

Be absolutely certain that, at the least, the cleartext warning is enabled, or, at best, cleartext is disabled altogether. Click the Save Preferences button to store the settings.

Mounting with `mount_afp`

To force the use of a specific UAM, use the command-line `mount_afp` utility along with an AFP URL formatted like `mount_afp afp://<username>[;AUTH=<UAM string>][:<password>]@]<hostname>[:<port>]/<volume name>`

You can use any of the UAM strings in Table 16.1, but you must URL-encode them. For these particular strings, all you really need to do is make sure that spaces are replaced with `%20`.

Content Encryption

Although the initial password conversation with an AppleShare server can be performed securely, there is no encryption of the subsequent network traffic. If an attacker wants data, AppleShare transfers will play right into their hands. For example, Figure 16.2 displays the output of the sniffer ettercap (see Chapter 7, "Eavesdropping and Snooping for Information: Sniffers and Scanners," for details) as I open a file named `fixperm.pl` over a basic Mac OS X AppleShare connection. The display of the transmitted data (the pane on the left side of the window) clearly shows the contents of the file while in transit.

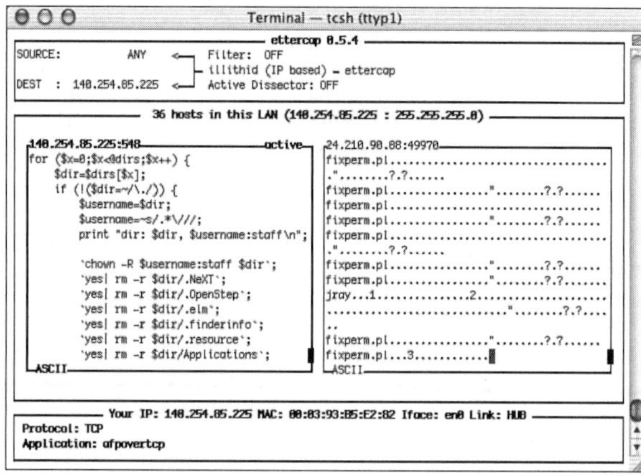

FIGURE 16.2 Appleshare transfers—clear as can be.

Starting in Mac OS X 10.2, AppleShare connections can be automatically tunneled via SSL, providing full encryption of the traffic. Unfortunately, this feature is "reserved" for Mac OS X Server users; client users have no more control over AppleShare serving than the simple Start/Stop button, shown in Figure 16.3.

You toggle SSL tunneling on by setting the NetInfo property `/config/AppleFileServer/ssh_tunnel` equal to 1.

Unfortunately, this is a bit of a problem with using the Apple encryption: The tunneling is *very* poorly documented, and offers no assurances that it is working. In the course of writing this chapter, I worked with four Mac OS X Server machines, and a number of clients. In almost every case, SSH-tunneled connections were *not* created, despite the dialog box saying that a secure connection was being established. The data copied over the connection was still easily sniffable with ettercap (see Chapter 7).

Using SSH directly, however, you can create a tunnel that works *regardless* of whether the point-and-click solution is functioning. SSH is covered in depth in Chapter 14, "Remote Access: Secure Shell, VNC, Timbuktu, Apple Remote Desktop," but creating a tunnel is easy enough to discuss directly here.

To manually tunnel AFP via SSH, use the following syntax:

```
ssh <username>@<afp server> -L 10548:127.0.0.1:548
```

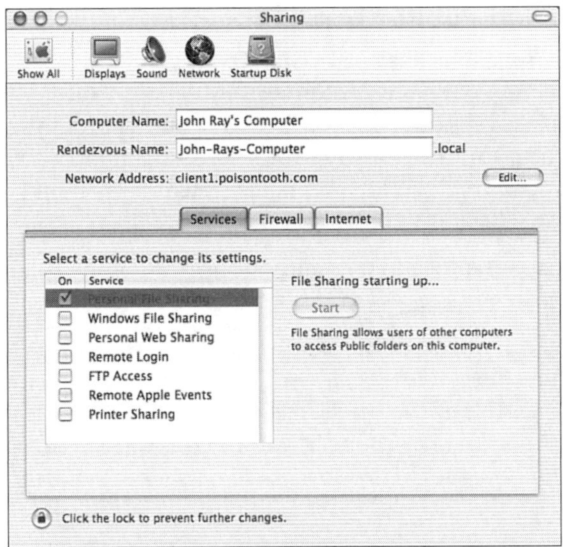

FIGURE 16.3 Start and stop file sharing: easy, friendly, and insecure.

Assuming the remote AFP server is running SSH and you have a username and password for the server, this will tunnel AppleShare traffic from port 548 on the server to port 10548 on your local machine.

You can subsequently connect to `afp://127.0.0.1:10548` from the Finder and securely access your files.

TIP

You may want to add `sleep` *`<seconds>`* to the end of the `ssh` command to provide a "login window" during which you can create the secure connection. Otherwise you'll remain at a command prompt on the remote server—which represents a potential risk.

This trick will work with SSL-enabled AppleShare servers (such as Mac OS X), but is not an out-of-the box solution for Windows NT or third-party Windows 2000 Server add-ons.

If you need a secure tunnel, this is an effective solution—and one that is verifiably secure, unlike the current Apple interface to SSH tunneling.

TIP

The software product "Vapor" (`http://www.afp548.com/Software/Vapor/index.html`) can be used to create SSH tunnels without using the command line—if typing isn't your bag.

Guest Access and Public Shares

If you enabled Personal File Sharing in Mac OS X, you've just allowed anyone with network access to your computer to connect. By default, Mac OS X will accept guest connections and allow mounting, browsing, and storing files to your system. Yes, guest access provides unrestricted file writes to your computer—while this isn't a security risk in and of itself, an attacker could potentially fill up your entire drive without needing to "hack" your system.

To remove guest access altogether, modify the NetInfo property `/config/AppleFileServer/guest_access` to equal `0` (the default is `1`).

Alternatively, you can get rid of the `Drop Box` folder in each user's `Public` directory. A drop box is nothing but a folder with write and execute permission for the "dropees" (`chmod 733 <folder>`). To remove the `Public` directory share altogether, just delete the value for the NetInfo `sharedDir` property within each user's NetInfo account path. For example, my account name is `jray`, so I would delete the value for `/users/jray/sharedDir`.

NOTE

Don't just *change* the `sharedDir` property, *delete* it! Otherwise the file server will attempt to share whatever value you've provided.

TIP

Not covered here is access logging. By default, Apple has disabled *all* logging of the AFP server. This is discussed in depth in Chapter 19, "Logs and User Activity Accounting."

Service Advertisement via SLP

A somewhat annoying feature of Mac OS X is its insistence on registering the servers that are running on your computer with SLP (Service Location Protocol, `http://www.faqs.org/rfcs/rfc2608.html`). In Mac OS X server, this includes advertisements for the remote admin server, Web server, AppleShare server, and so on. The client restricts itself to AFP servers only.

Services are registered in the file `/private/var/slp.regfile`—each on a single line:

```
# initial reg file automatically generated
afp://10.0.1.250/?NAME=File%20Server&ZONE=,en,10800,afp
scopes=DEFAULT

radminx://10.0.1.250,en,10800,radminx
scopes=DEFAULT
```

```
servermgr://10.0.1.250?NAME=File%20Server,en,10800,servermgr
scopes=DEFAULT

http://10.0.1.250:80,en,10800,http
scopes=DEFAULT
```

In early versions of Mac OS X, service lines would often be repeated. When a machine received a new IP address (via DHCP, for example), the service would be reregistered and subsequently appear multiple times when browsed remotely. Although solved around Mac OS X 10.1, this remains one of the most frequently asked questions from readers of *Mac OS X Unleashed*, and a very simple way that a user can throw a Mac OS X network into disarray. Manually forcing multiple registrations of phantom services can make the Finder's network browser almost useless by flooding it with duplicate server names and making browsing a guessing game. The `slp.regfile` can be safely removed if it becomes corrupted; it will be rebuilt automatically the next time your machine reboots.

To block SLP, you'll need to manually firewall TCP port 427 on your computer. Apple automatically *opens* port 427 if file sharing is turned on and the firewall is activated, so be sure that you don't end up with conflicting rules.

WebDAV

WebDAV (Web Distributed Authoring and Versioning) is another popular form of file sharing built into Mac OS X. Apple's .Mac service provides iDisk access via WebDAV, and the Mac OS X Apache distribution includes `mod_dav`, enabling your machine to serve other Linux, Windows, and Mac clients.

WebDAV is unique in that it doesn't introduce another protocol or server process to your machine. Instead, it piggybacks on HTTP, using the Apache server process and all its access controls to manage who can access what. See RFC 2518 for more information `http://asg.web.cmu.edu/rfc/rfc2518.html`.

WebDAV Security History

As far as security goes, consider this statement, taken from the `mod_dav` FAQ:

> Apache and `mod_dav` are quite secure. There has not been a single reported exploit of the code in the past three years (when it was first released). You can misconfigure your Apache/`mod_dav` system (in fact, SuSE Linux released an RPM like this and had to issue a security advisory and upgrade). But given that you take the precautions listed in the installation document, Apache and `mod_dav` are quite secure.

Although there are no known exploits of mod_dav, there are several potential problems:

- Improper file permissions can lead to files being modified that shouldn't be. mod_dav runs with the Apache server permissions, meaning files/directories that can be written to by the www user or group can be modified through WebDAV.
- Users can store arbitrarily large files on the server, eating up disk space.
- Large recursive requests can be sent to the server, using up resources and potentially resulting in a DoS attack.

Although you can deal with the first two issues with basic system administration skills, the third may require fine-tuning the mod_dav DAVDepthInfinity and LimitXMLRequestBody directives, discussed shortly.

Starting WebDAV

To enable WebDAV, edit the file /etc/httpd/httpd.conf. You need to do this as root to make changes.

Look for the (noncontiguous) lines

```
#LoadModule dav_module        libexec/httpd/libdav.so
#AddModule mod_dav.c
```

Remove the comments from both lines, so that they read

```
LoadModule dav_module           libexec/httpd/libdav.so
AddModule mod_dav.c
```

NOTE

Normally we would recommend that software be installed from scratch, but because the mod_dav code has remained largely static for the past two years this seems unnecessary. Apache 2.0 incorporates mod_dav in the base distribution, so this won't even be a consideration when Apple makes the migration to the new server in the future.

If you would like to download and compile mod_dav by hand, it is available from http://www.webdav.org/mod_dav/.

The mod_dav module adds several special directives to the Apache configuration that you'll need to use to set up your WebDAV shares. These are listed in Table 16.2.

TABLE 16.2 mod_dav Directives

Directive	Purpose
DAVLockDB <Path and Lock base name>	Required. The path and base file name (such as /var/tmp/moddavlock) that will be used for mod_dav lock files. This is a global directive that should be used once in the /etc/httpd/httpd.conf file.
DAVMinTimeout *<seconds>*	Optional. The minimum lifetime of a file lock in seconds. May be used within an Apache container or globally in httpd.conf.
DAV On	Required. Used in an Apache container, this directive enables WebDAV support within that container. The standard Apache access directives are still needed to control security for the resource.
DAVDepthInfinity <on|off>	Optional. If off (the default), mod_dav will not allow infinite depth commands to be processed. This will prevent remote machines from collecting (recursively) information about every resource under the WebDAV share, potentially using a great deal of server resources and possibly creating a denial of service condition. Can be used either globally or in an Apache container.
LimitXMLRequestBody <byte limit>	Optional. Sets a limit on the size of the XML request that the client can send. All WebDAV functions are encoded in XML, and mod_dav will attempt to parse the requests in RAM—again leading to a resource usage problem and potential DoS condition. The default is 1,000,000 bytes.

Each WebDAV operation is sent as an HTTP function to the remote server along with an XML body containing the details of that request. If you've used HTTP, you're probably already familiar with GET and POST methods of sending and retrieving information from a server. WebDAV introduces several others that are needed for the additional file sharing features it offers:

- PROPFIND. Return information about a given resource (file) or a collection of files (directory).
- PROPPATCH. Change information about a specified resource or collection (such as author).
- MKCOL. Create a new collection (directory).
- COPY. Create a duplicate of an existing resource.
- DELETE. Remove an existing resource.
- MOVE. Move a resource from one location to another.
- LOCK. Lock a resource or collection.
- UNLOCK. Unlock a resource or collection.

Obviously, you can't have *every* user issuing these commands to the server, so it must be protected against unauthorized access. This is performed with Apache's <Limit> directive. One simply needs to limit the dangerous functions to the appropriate users.

Because Apache security is discussed in depth in Chapter 15, "Web Server Security," we won't repeat it here. A sample configuration that shares the `/Library/Webserver/Documents` directory to a user with an account on the Mac OS X machine is shown in Listing 16.1. This assumes that the `mod_auth_apple` module (also discussed in Chapter 15) is present and active.

LISTING 16.1 Sharing `/Library/Webserver/Documents` via WebDAV

```
DAVLockDB /var/tmp/moddavlock
DAVDepthInfinity off
<Directory "/Library/WebServer/Documents">
    DAV On
    AuthType Basic
    AuthName "Webserver documents"
    <Limit DELETE PROPPATCH MKCOL COPY MOVE LOCK UNLOCK>
        require valid-user
    </Limit>
</Directory>
```

CAUTION

Because WebDAV works over HTTP, it suffers from the same authentication and privacy issues as Apache. If you want to use an encrypted login, for example, you need digest passwords. If you want completely encrypted transfers, you need `mod_ssl` up and running—and you'll also need to provide secure (`https:`) connection URLs to the clients.

Sharing Files with Samba

Samba, used by Apple to implement Windows-compatible file sharing, is another complex server product, approaching Apache in terms of options. Although we'll do our best to cover the basic settings and security directives you need to run an effective server, it would be worth your while to buy a dedicated text for advanced file sharing environments. Sams *Teach Yourself Samba in 24 Hours* (ISBN: 0672316099) and the Samba Web site are great sources for information (`http://www.samba.org`).

NOTE

Apple has done an admirable job of keeping Samba up to date, but if you need to update Samba, it compiles easily, without any tweaks. Download the latest Samba source from `http://www.samba.org/`, and `configure`, `make`, then `make install`.

Samba Security History

As you can imagine, a project that required Microsoft's proprietary protocols to be reverse-engineered has experienced a few rocky points during its development. At the time of this writing, Apple was shipping version 2.2.3a, which is several versions behind the latest release. Luckily, Samba compiles and installs cleanly on Mac OS X, so if you'd like to build the latest version, you can download the source from `http://us1.samba.org/samba/ftp/`. The 2.2.3a version suffers from one (known) potential exploit:

- **DoS and Root Exploit** (CVE: CAN-2002-1318). The 2.2.3a-2.2.6 releases contain a buffer overflow that can be exploited to cause a denial of service attack and potentially execute arbitrary code on the server. There are no known exploits of this condition, but it is corrected in the 2.2.7 release.

Previous exploits include the following:

- **SymLink Attack** (CVE: CAN-2001-0406). Versions of Samba prior to 2.2.0 suffered from a bug that allowed local users to overwrite arbitrary files by querying the printer queue or using `smbclient`. This error was corrected in the 2.2.0 release.
- **SWAT DoS** (CVE: CAN-2000-0939). SWAT suffered from a potential denial of service attack that would force the process to be restarted when requested with a URL formatted as `localhost:901?somethingthatdoesntexist`. This is recognized as an `inetd` problem that is simply made easier to exploit via SWAT.
- **Remote File Overwrite** (CVE: CVE-2001-1162). In versions of Samba prior to 2.2.0a, remote attackers could overwrite local files by providing Unix path characters within a NETBIOS name, such as `..`. These were subsequently substituted for `%m` anywhere it occurred in the `smb.conf` file.

Activating Samba

To turn on Samba, open the Sharing System Preferences panel, highlight the Services tab, then either click the check box in front of the Windows File Serving line or highlight it and click the Start button. The sharing panel updates and shows the path that can be used to map the drive on a Windows-based computer, as demonstrated in Figure 16.4.

Like AppleShare file sharing in OS X, the built-in Samba configuration is limited to sharing each user's home directory—and, by default, none of the user accounts are enabled for login. Enable login from Windows by opening the Accounts System Preferences panel, selecting the user to have Samba access, then clicking the Edit User button. Your screen will look similar to Figure 16.5.

FIGURE 16.4 Start the Samba daemon by using the Sharing preference panel.

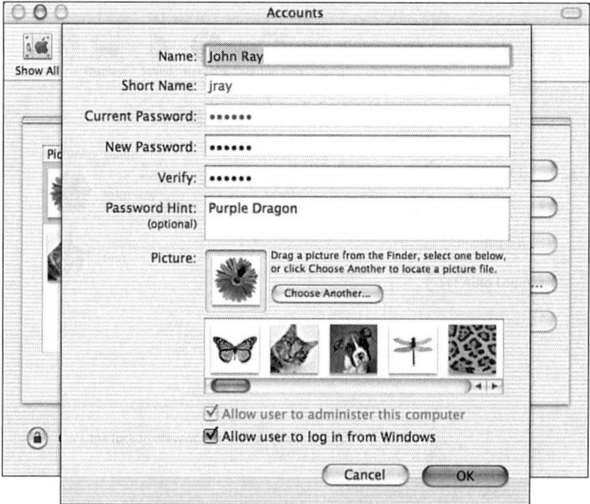

FIGURE 16.5 Edit the user accounts that should be able to access your computer from Windows.

If necessary, enter the current user password, press Enter, then click the Allow User to Log In from Windows check box. The configured user should now be able to access his or her home directory with the SMB/CIFS path format:

```
\\<hostname or IP address>\<username>
```

NOTE

Windows login is enabled and disabled by adding `;LocalWindowsHash;` to the NetInfo key `authentication_authority` in each user's NetInfo directory.

The first time Windows access is enabled through the Accounts panel, a Windows password hash file is created in the directory `/private/var/db/samba/hash`. Subsequent checking and unchecking of the Allow User to Log In from Windows check box will simply toggle the NetInfo authentication settings.

Apple has included a GUI means of setting one's workgroup and WINS server by using the Directory Access utility (Path: `/Applications/Utilities/Directory Access`). Open the utility, then authenticate by using the lock button in the lower right corner.

Next, highlight the SMB service and click the Configure button. Mac OS X prompts for a workgroup name and WINS server, which are subsequently added to the `/etc/smb.conf` file.

Activating SWAT

Although Samba can be activated and used with Apple's default configuration, you'll be missing 99% of the functionality. Samba offers many advanced features that can only be accessed when you manually edit the setup. The Samba setup is contained in the very readable file `/etc/smb.conf`. Configuration is handled entirely through a Web-based GUI called SWAT.

CAUTION

Samba is *intended* to be configured with SWAT. Although you can manually edit `/etc/smb.conf`, it is not recommended and can quickly lead to an invalid setup.

If the file does become corrupted, return to the original Mac OS X Samba configuration by copying the file `/etc/smb.conf.template` over `/etc/smb.conf`.

SWAT is included with your system, but is not ready for use. SWAT requires additional setup that enables it to activate when a Web browser accesses port 901 on your computer. To start, be sure that you have the 10.2 Developer Tools installed.

CAUTION

If you attempt to use SWAT without the Developer Tools, it will *almost* run, but will generate seemingly unintelligible error messages.

Open your `/etc/services` file and add the following line:

```
swat        901/tcp # SWAT
```

Assuming you're running `xinetd`, create a new file `/etc/xinetd.d/swat` with the following contents:

```
service swat
{
        disable         = no
        socket_type     = stream
        wait            = no
        user            = root
        server          = /usr/sbin/swat
        groups          = yes
        flags           = REUSE
}
```

If you're using `inetd`, add the following line to the end of `/etc/inetd.conf`:

```
swat stream tcp nowait root /usr/libexec/tcpd /usr/sbin/swat
```

This tells the `inetd` (Internet Daemon) to start `/usr/sbin/swat` when it gets a request for the SWAT service. It also employs TCP Wrappers to protect against unauthorized incoming requests.

SWAT is ready to run. Either reboot Mac OS X to enable SWAT access on port 901, or use `kill -HUP` to reload settings for the `inetd` or `xinetd` processes. (You'll need to use `sudo` to do this.)

To configure Samba, start a Web browser and point it at port 901 of the Samba server (`http://localhost:901`). SWAT will prompt for an administrative username and password; use the `root` account to have access to all features.

The top of the SWAT display, shown in Figure 16.6, includes seven buttons to control the server's operation:

- **Home**. Provides links to Samba documentation and supplemental material.
- **Globals**. Settings that affect the entire server, such as its name and security model.
- **Shares**. Shared file resources. If you used the sample configuration file that came with the Apache distribution, there should be a single home directory share already configured.
- **Printers**. Shared printers. To share a printer, it must first be set up so that it can be accessed from the `lpr` command in Unix.

- **Status**. Monitor and view the status of the server. If logged in as `root`, you can restart or stop the server process.
- **View**. View a copy of the text configuration file.
- **Password**. Set and edit Samba user passwords.

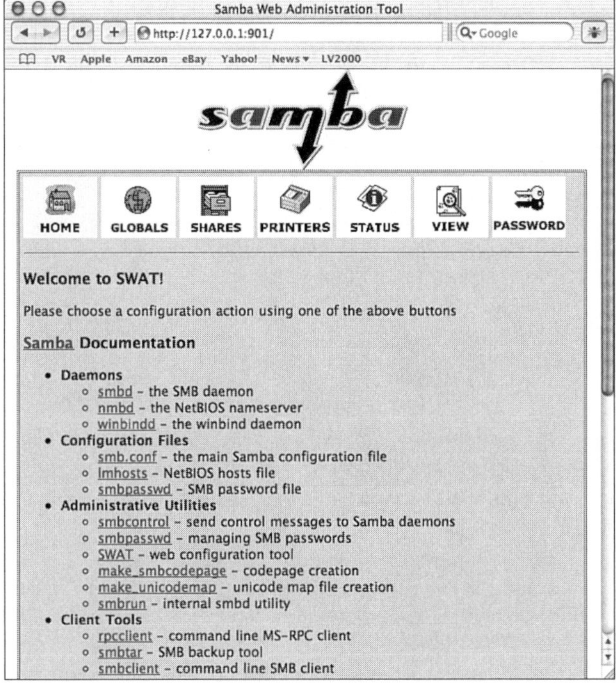

FIGURE 16.6 SWAT opens with a page providing easy access to Samba documentation.

Security configuration is scattered throughout these seven pages, so we'll cover what is appropriate for basic setup and security as well as the configuration directives contained in the default `/etc/smb.conf` file.

TIP

You can also handle security through the Mac OS X firewall by restricting access to TCP/UDP ports 137-139 (Samba), and TCP 901 (SWAT). Since SWAT runs as root and controls file sharing for your whole system, you should, at the very least, limit access through `xinet/TCP Wrappers`.

Globals

The Globals Variables page is the starting point for setting up your Samba server. Many people jump the gun and immediately start setting up file shares. Failure to properly configure the global options might make it impossible to mount or browse shared resources.

Three buttons can save server settings (Commit Changes), reset changes (Reset Values), or access advanced options (Advanced View). Choosing Advanced View shows additional options, a number of which are listed in Table 16.3. If you don't see the setting you're looking for in default view, move to the Advanced mode.

TABLE 16.3 Globals Options and Their Purpose

Option	Purpose
`coding_system`	Defines the how Japanese characters from the client computer are mapped to the Unix file system. It is unlikely that you will ever need to change the default Mac OS X setting.
`client_code_page`	Specifies the code page that Samba clients will use to access the server. It is unlikely that you will ever need to change the default Mac OS X setting.
`workgroup`	Sets the workgroup or domain to which the server belongs. Set this to the same value as the workgroup/domain of local Windows clients; otherwise, they will not be able to browse the server.
`netbios_name`	The Windows (NetBIOS) name of the server.
`netbios_aliases`	A list of additional NetBIOS names to which the Samba server will respond. (Advanced)
`password_level`	The number of case changes that will be checked between the client login and the server password. Because client operating systems might transmit passwords in uppercase, they have to be altered to authenticate with the server. (Advanced)
`username_level`	The same as the password level, but alters the username in a similar manner. For example, if I have a Mac OS X username of `jray` and a Windows login of `JRAY`, I have to set this value to `4` for it to be successfully permuted into the lowercase version. (Advanced)
`server_string`	The text used to identify the server.
`interfaces`	The network interfaces that Samba will broadcast over. For example, Mac OS X's primary interface is `en0`. By default, all active interfaces will be used. To limit the interfaces, enter the interface names to use, or the network address followed by a subnet mask (that is, `192.168.0.0/255.255.255.0`).
`security`	The type of security model to use. `User` security bases access upon a user login. `Share` password protects individual shared resources. Domain and server security passes authentication duties to other NT or Samba servers, respectively. You'll probably want user or share-level security.
`encrypt_passwords`	Sets encrypted password negotiation with the client. If you are using Windows 98 or later, set this to `Yes`. Encrypted passwords also require the use of the `smbpasswd` file, which is configured through the SWAT Password page. The Mac OS X default is `Yes`.

TABLE 16.3 Continued

Option	Purpose
`update_encrypted`	Used when migrating from an unencrypted password on an existing server to a local encrypted `smbpasswd` file. This shouldn't be needed unless you are using an advanced configuration.
`guest_account`	The local user that should be used for guest access and resource browsing. Mac OS X should use `unknown`.
`hosts_allow`	A list of hostnames, IP addresses, IP addresses and subnet masks (`192.168.0.0/255.255.255.0`), or partial addresses (`192.168.0.`) that can access the server. The `except` keyword can create an exception to a rule. For example, `192.168.0.0/255.255.255.0` except `192.168.0.5` would allow any host in the `192.168.0.0` subnet, except `192.168.0.5`, to access the server. If left blank, all remote hosts can access the server.
`hosts_deny`	Like `hosts allow`, but used to list servers that should not have access to the server. Configured by the same method as `allow`.
`log_file`	The logfile in which to store server accesses. The `%m` in the default path appends the name of the remote machine to the logfile name.
`max_log_size`	The maximum size in kilobytes that a logfile should be allowed to reach before rolling over.
`os_level`	A number used to determine the ranking of Samba when a master browser is being elected on a Windows network. If Samba is the only server on the network, use the default `20`. If NT 4.0 or 2000 machines are on the network, and you'd like Samba to be the master browser, set this to a value greater than `32`.
`domain_logon`	Accept domain logins. This allows Windows clients to recognize the Samba server as a PDC (Primary Domain Controller). (Advanced)
`preferred_master`	If set to `yes`, the Samba server will attempt to force an election for master browser. Do not use on networks with multiple servers that want to be masters.
`local_master`	Enables Samba to try to become the master browser for the local area network. If set to `no`, it will not attempt to assume this role.
`domain_master`	Enables Samba's `nmbd` component to become a domain master browser that collects browse lists from remote subnets.
`dns_proxy`	Attempts to resolve WINS queries through DNS if they cannot be resolved from locally registered machines.
`wins_server`	A remote WINS server that Samba should query to service NetBIOS name requests.
`wins_support`	Enables Samba's WINS service. Only a single machine should act as a WINS server on a given subnet.

The default settings should be sufficient for most small networks, with the exception of the base and security options.

Samba security is set both globally for the server and for each individual share. What follows are the global settings you may want to consider changing to either alter the type or improve the quality of security on your machine.

Security Levels

Before creating a share, you need to decide what security model to use for the server—set with the `security` directive. By default, Mac OS X's Samba implementation uses the `user` security level.

- **User level**. The easiest security model to manage is user level, which requires Windows users to log in to their computers with the same username and password that they set up on the Mac OS X machine. When using user-level access, Windows users are mapped directly to Samba users. The Mac OS X file permissions apply directly to the permissions of the connected user. Assume, for example, the Mac OS X user `jray` has read/write permissions to the folder `/Stuff`, which is also set to be a Samba share. If `jray` logs in to a Windows computer using the same username as on Mac OS X, he will be able to access the `Stuff` share and have read/write access. The SWAT Password page or `smbpasswd` utility (covered shortly) can be used to map Unix users to the passwords that they will use on the remote Windows client if it doesn't match their default OS X password.
- **Share level**. In the case of `share` security, a single password is needed to access the share for *all* users. The Mac OS X user that is used to access the data depends on the share configuration and the password that is given when mounting the share. This can be a bit confusing because unlike Windows, where you *can* set a password for a share, Samba still requires a password *and* username for `share` security, but the username is determined dynamically based on the share configuration. If a share is set with a `username` directive, whichever username whose password matches what the client supplies when connecting is then used to access the data. If a `username` is not supplied, then the `guest_account` password is used as the share password.

  To simplify share-level security, create a new Mac OS X user with Allow User to Log In from Windows permissions. Then set the `username` option for the share equal to the Mac OS X username.
- **Server/Domain level**. Server-level security can be used if you need to integrate with an existing Windows server. When using `server` or `domain` security, the Samba process attempts to authenticate usernames and passwords against an existing SMB server or an NT Domain, respectively. The `password_server` directive is used to set the queried server. The `encrypt_passwords` must be set to `yes`.

NOTE

Samba has rudimentary support for acting as a PDC. It does not support operating as a BDC. For a simple tutorial on setting up Samba as a PDC, visit http://hr.uoregon.edu/davidrl/samba/.

Limiting Access

The `hosts_allow` and `hosts_deny` directives should be used, if possible, to limit Samba access to only the client or client subnet that will be accessing your server. If you have multiple network connections, be sure that the `interfaces` setting is applied to *only* the interfaces that should provide SMB service. If, for example, you're using the Mac OS X Internet sharing feature, you may not want to enable Samba on the broadband interface.

Encrypted Passwords

To negotiate encrypted password transmission with the connecting client, set `encrypt_passwords` to `yes`. Clients earlier than Windows 98 do not support encrypted passwords, so if you have any *early* Windows machines connecting, this should be set to `no`. The Mac OS X default is `yes`.

Password and Username Mangling

The `username_level` and `password_level` directives control the number of case permutations between a true password/username and the user-supplied information that can take place and still be considered a match. A `username_level` of 1, for example, would allow one permutation —matching "`Jray`" to "`jray`"— while `2` could match "`JrAy`" to "`jray`", and so on. Setting these to *zero* forces an exact password match and is recommended. Higher values increase the possibility of an attacker being able to access your system with what would normally be an incorrect password.

Shares

The Share Parameters page sets up file shares that can be mounted on networked Windows-based computers. To create a new share, type a share name in the Create Share field, and then click the Create Share button. To edit an existing share, choose its name from the pop-up list, and then click Choose Share—or click Delete Share to remove it completely. With the default Mac OS X Samba configuration file, there should be a single `homes` share already available. The `homes` share is unique because it is equivalent to each user sharing his home directory with himself.

Like the Globals Variables page, there is an Advanced button to show all possible configuration features for file sharing. Table 16.4 lists the sharing- and security-related options.

TABLE 16.4 File-Sharing Options and Values

Option	Purpose
`comment`	A comment to help identify the shared resource.
`path`	The pathname of the directory to share. Be aware that in user-level security, you must make sure that the corresponding Mac OS X user accounts have access to this directory. When using share-level security, a single-user account is used—usually either the `guest_account` or an account specified with `username`.
`guest_account`	The account used to access the share if the remote client is logged in as a guest. The default is `nobody`, but, if set to another username, the guest user will have the read/write permissions of that local user account. If you want to use share-level access control, you can set this value to the account whose permissions should be used when accessing the share.
`force_user`	If entered, the `force_user` username will be used for all accesses (read/write) to the file share, regardless of the username used to log in. (Advanced)
`force_group`	Similar to `force_user` but forces a group rather than a user. (Advanced)
`read_only`	When set to `Yes`, users cannot write to the share, regardless of the Mac OS X file permissions.
`create_mask`	A set of permissions that newly created files will have. By default, the mask is set to 0744. (Advanced)
`inherit_permissions`	When set to `yes`, new directories will inherit the Unix permission bits from the parent (enclosing) directory.
`guest_ok`	If set to `yes`, guests can log in to the server without a password.
`hosts_allow`	A list of hostnames, IP addresses, IP addresses and subnet masks (`192.168.0.0/255.255.255.0`), or partial addresses (`192.168.0.`) that can access the share. The `except` keyword can create an exception to a rule. For example, `192.168.0.0/255.255.255.0 except 192.168.0.5` would allow any host in the `192.168.0.0` subnet, except `192.168.0.5`, to access the server. If left blank, all remote hosts can access the server.
`hosts_deny`	Like `hosts_allow`, but used to list servers that should not have access to the server. Configure using the same method as `allow`.
`max_connections`	Restricts the number of simultaneous users who can access the share. (Advanced)
`browseable`	When set to `yes`, the share shows up in the Windows network browser. If `No`, the share still exists, but remote users cannot see its name.
`available`	If set to `yes`, the share is made available over the network. Setting to `no` disables access to the share.
`username`	A comma-separated list of usernames whose passwords are to be used for login validation. If a username is prefixed with a +, the username is interpreted as a group name and is expanded to all the users within the group. (Advanced)
`valid_users`	A list of usernames that will be allowed to access the share. If a username is prefixed with +, it will be processed as a group name.

TABLE 16.4 Continued

Option	Purpose
veto_files	A /-separated list of file/directory names that will be invisible and inaccessible via a mounted share. The wildcards * (any character string) and ? (any single character) can be used as within the names. For example, /*.html/*.tmp/tmp????.txt. This feature can be used to stop the spread of viruses by denying access to certain types of Windows files, such as .eml, .vbs, .dll and other files commonly created by virus-infected clients. (Advanced)
hide_files	Like veto_files, but files are only hidden; they still remain accessible to the client. (Advanced)
hide_unreadable	When set to yes, files that are unreadable to a given user are hidden. (Advanced)
invalid_users	The opposite of the valid_users directive, useful within the homes share. (Advanced)

Users and Permissions

As with the global settings, share access can be limited by IP with the hosts_allow and hosts_deny directives. Restricting a volume to a specific user is performed with the valid_users and invalid_users options, both of which can also accept a group name prefixed with a + to simplify user management.

Users who are sharing directories that need to maintain file ownership different from the logged-in Samba user may find the force_user and force_group directives useful. These can be employed to force all file accesses to be from a named user and group (such as www). In cases where overlapping file sharing is taking place, such as via WebDAV and Samba, this can greatly ease the difficulty of maintaining compatible permissions.

To alter the umask for files that are created via Samba, use the create_mask directive with a standard Mac OS X umask setting. If you want to provide read (no write) access to files regardless of the actual file permissions, set the read_only attribute equal to yes.

Disabling and Hiding Shares and Files

To temporarily disable an active share, set the available directory to no. You can hide active shares from direct Network Neighborhood browsing by setting browseable to no. This does not keep users from accessing the share, but they need to know the share name to connect.

CAUTION

Disabling browseability is not an acceptable form of security. The browseable attribute is useful for setting up temporary administrative shares or other shares that don't necessarily need to be advertised to your general user base.

You can hide the files contained within a share based on simple name patterns with DOS-style `*` and `?` wildcards that you set by using the `hide_files` directive. Hidden files remain accessible by name, but appear (to Windows) as if they have the hidden attribute set. To easily hide any file that a user can't read, set `hide_unreadable` equal to `yes`.

To make files both hidden *and* inaccessible, use `veto_files`, which blocks any user interaction with files matching the supplied pattern.

Printers

Samba can act as a full print server for a Windows network. The one small catch is that your printers must first be accessible via `lpr` at the command line.

To create a new shared printer, enter a name (for the Windows network) in the Create Printer field, and then click the Create Printer button. You can select an existing printer from the pop-up menu and edit it by clicking Choose Printer, or remove it from the Samba configuration by clicking Delete Printer.

From Samba's perspective, there is very little difference between a shared printer and a file share. The same directives used to configure and secure shared files can also be applied to a printer. The common printer-specific directives are shown in Table 16.5.

TABLE 16.5 Printer-Sharing Options

Option	Purpose
`path`	A directory where print spool files will be saved before printing. The directory must be configured to be world-writable and have the sticky bit set.
`printable`	Allows authenticated clients to write to the print spool directory.
`printer name`	The CUPS name for the printer. You must switch to Advanced View to see this option. To view a list of the CUPS-recognized printers on your system, type `lpstat -p`. Any available printer can be shared.
`postscript`	Forces print jobs to be interpreted as PostScript.

Status

The SWAT Status page provides a quick overview of the server's current conditions, including active connections, shares, and files. The administrator can use this screen to restart the server or disable any active connections.

Each of the visible buttons effects a change on the server:

- **Auto Refresh**. Sets the SWAT status page to auto refresh based on the Refresh Interval field. This is useful for monitoring server activity.
- **Stop/Start/Restart smbd**. Stops, starts, or restarts `smbd`—the Samba SMB file/print server. All active connections are terminated.

- **Stop/Start/Restart nmbd**. Stops, starts, or restarts `nmbd`—the Samba NetBIOS name server. Does not affect active connections.
- **Kill**. The Kill button appears to the right of every listed connection. Clicking the button immediately terminates the link.

TIP

Samba (`smbd`) must be restarted for changes to the configuration to take effect.

View

View offers a glimpse at the configuration file behind SWAT's GUI. Sometimes it's easier to scan through a text file to locate a problem than to work with the Web interface. There are two modes in the View page. The Normal view shows the minimum configuration file needed to implement your settings.

Switching to the Full view displays all the settings, including default options, for the Samba configuration. Each option is explicitly listed, regardless of its necessity.

Samba Passwords

Any user who has Windows access enabled through the Allow User to Log In from Windows option already has a Windows password enabled and stored in a private hash file found in `/private/var/db/samba/hash/`. As long as she is satisfied with using the same password on both Mac OS X and Windows, there are no changes you need to make.

If a user wants to use a different password to access Samba from a Windows computer, she can use the SWAT password settings to add a new password entry in the `/private/var/db/samba/smbpasswd` file.

The SWAT Password page is used to set up Samba passwords for existing Mac OS X users, or change remote user passwords if using domain-level security and a remote host for user authentication.

The Server Password portion of the screen configures local users and passwords. Be aware that these options *do not* affect the actual Mac OS X usernames and passwords, but must be based on valid local usernames. If you've enabled a Mac OS X user so that he can log into his account from Windows, you've effectively already used this feature. There is no need to set a new password unless you want a Windows login password that is different from your Mac OS X password.

The following options are found in the Server Password page:

- **User Name**. The Mac OS X username to add to the Samba password database file. Only required for Mac OS X users where the Allow User to Log In from Windows option has not been selected.
- **New Password**. The Samba password to set for that user.
- **Re-type New Password**. The same as the New Password option; used to verify typing.
- **Change Password**. Changes the password for a given user.
- **Add New User**. Adds the new username/password mapping to the Samba password database.
- **Delete User**. Deletes the named user from the Samba password database. This does not affect the Mac OS X user.
- **Disable User**. Disables a user's ability to access Samba. Again, Mac OS X does not alter its user account whatsoever.
- **Enable User**. Enables a disabled user account.

If Samba is using domain-level security, another server (such as a Windows primary domain controller) is the source for all authentication information. To change a user's password on the remote server, use the Client/Server Password Management features of the Password screen:

- **User Name**. The remote user to change.
- **Old Password**. The user's existing password.
- **New Password**. The new password to set on the remote server.
- **Re-type New Password**. The same as the New Password option; used to verify typing.
- **Remote Machine**. The remote server that contains the username/password mappings.

Click the Change Password button to send the password changes to the remote server.

An alternative to SWAT password management is to use the `smbpasswd` command-line utility.

smbpasswd

The smbpasswd command is used to alter user information in the /private/var/db/samba/smbpasswd file. This can be used to set up Samba user account passwords from the command line or shell scripts.

By default, the smbpasswd command changes the Samba password for the currently logged in Mac OS X user:

```
% smbpasswd
Old SMB password:
New SMB password:
Retype new SMB password:
Password changed for user jray
```

As an administrative user, you can perform several additional functions with the command. The complete syntax for the smbpasswd is smbpasswd *<options>* *<username>* *<password>*. Table 16.6 shows the available options.

TABLE 16.6 smbpasswd Options

Option	Purpose
-a	Adds a new username to the local smbpasswd file.
-d	Disables the named user.
-e	Enables the named user.
-D <0-10>	Sets a debug level between 0 and 10 to control the verbosity of error reporting.
-n	Sets a user's password to null.
-r *<remote host>*	Sets the remote host to send password changes.
-j *<domain name>*	Joins a domain.
-U *<username>*	The username to send to the remote host when using -r.
-h	Displays a command summary.
-s	Silent output. Accept all input from standard input. This is useful for scripting smbpasswd.

smbstatus

The smbstatus utility provides information about the active connections and users. This is equivalent to the Status page within the SWAT management tool. For example:

```
% /usr/local/samba/bin/smbstatus

Samba version 2.2.3a
```

```
Service      uid      gid      pid     machine
----------------------------------------------
Programs  jray jray  12746   brushedtooth (192.168.0.107) Sun Sep 1 03:46:41 2002
MyMP3s    jray jray  12746   brushedtooth (192.168.0.107) Sun Sep 1 22:21:32 2002

No locked files
```

The available `smbstatus` options are shown in Table 16.7.

TABLE 16.7 `smbstatus` Options

Option	Purpose
`-b`	Summary of connected users.
`-d`	Detailed connection listing. This is the default mode.
`-L`	Lists locked files only.
`-p`	Lists the `smbd` process IDs and exits.
`-S`	Lists connected shares only.
`-s <config file>`	Chooses the `smb.conf` file to use.
`-s <username>`	Displays only information relevant to a given username.

Common Unix Printing System

Starting in Mac OS X 10.2, Apple has built the CUPS (Common Unix Printing System) into the operating system. CUPS uses the IPP (Internet Printing Protocol) to access and provide access to printers across TCP/IP networks. IPP uses HTTP 1.1 as its transport protocol (See RFC 2568 for details: `http://www.ietf.org/rfc/rfc2568.txt`) and, in fact, is configured very much like the Apache server in Chapter 15, "Web Server Security." Basic printer management is handled either through the Mac OS X Print Center, or via the CUPS internal Web server, accessible by pointing your browser to `http://127.0.0.1:631`.

In Mac OS X, CUPS is simply referred to within Mac OS X as "Printer Sharing," and like the other services that we've seen, is activated by clicking the Printer Sharing button within the Sharing System Preferences panel, as shown in Figure 16.7.

As you've seen with other Mac OS X servers, clicking a little button sometimes has implications greater than what the user expects. Who, for example, are you sharing the printer *to*? We'll get to this, and information on how you can fine-tune printer access, shortly. First, the dirt on CUPS.

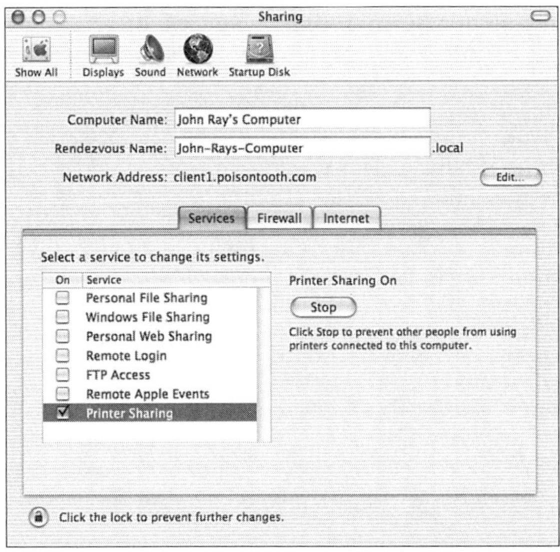

FIGURE 16.7 Printer sharing—sounds great.... Now what did I just do?

CUPS Security History

Like any Internet-connected service, CUPS is prone to remote exploits. Because of its resource-sharing nature, denial of service attacks are what you are most likely to encounter if you use the service. The following five potential attack points are taken from the CUPS security reference (`http://127.0.0.1:631/ssr.html`):

1. Establishing multiple connections to the server until the server will accept no more.
2. Repeatedly opening and closing connections to the server as fast as possible.
3. Flooding the network with broadcast packets on port 631.
4. Sending partial IPP requests; specifically, sending part of an attribute value and then stopping transmission.
5. Sending large/long print jobs to printers, preventing other users from printing.

Unfortunately, no mechanisms in place within CUPS or IPP can stop these attacks. The `MaxClients` (and related) directives can help stave off unreasonable numbers of connections, whereas `MaxRequestSize` can be used to keep abnormally large requests from being sent to the CUPS server.

Since the introduction of Mac OS X 10.2, there have been several vulnerabilities in the Apple CUPS distribution and a number of operating system updates to fix them.

In Mac OS X 10.2.2, a DoS attack via Web Administration (CVE: CAN-2002-1267) was corrected. The Apple-supplied version of CUPS shipped with port 631 open to machines other than localhost. This resulted in a potential for remote users to access the port and caused a denial of service condition.

The subsequent release of Mac OS X 10.2.3 included a patched version of CUPS that addressed a collection of vulnerabilities submitted as a collection in mid-October 2002.

- Integer Overflows (CAN-2002-1383)
- Race Condition (CAN-2002-1366)
- Add Printers with UDP Packets (CAN-2002-1367)
- Negative Length `memcpy()` calls (CAN-2002-1368)
- Integer Overflows in `pdftops` and `Xfilter` (CAN-2002-1384)
- Unsafe `strncat()` call (CAN-2002-1369)
- Root Certificate Design Flaws (CAN-2002-1370)
- Zero Width Images (CAN-2002-1371)
- Unchecked File and Socket Operations (CAN-2002-1372)

These vulnerabilities enable an attacker to crash the CUPS daemon by providing a negative content length in the HTTP headers:

```
% telnet 127.0.0.1 631
POST /printers HTTP/1.1
Host: localhost
Authorization: Basic AAA
Content-Length: -1
```

Other attacks allow remote users to add printers by sending properly formatted UDP packets, execute arbitrary code, and gain root privileges. These issues were promptly fixed in CUPS 1.1.18, and included in Apple's 10.2.3 distribution. Users of earlier versions were advised to update CUPS or disable it completely. The original report of these exploits, along with examples, is provided at `http://marc.theaimsgroup.com/?l=bugtraq&m=104032149026670&w=2`.

CUPS Configuration Files

Apple's Printer Sharing controls do nothing more than toggle a few directives within the CUPS settings and restart the server process. The Mac OS X CUPS configuration files are stored in the `/etc/cups` directory. You need to be concerned with three primary config files:

- `classes.conf`. Contains settings and access information for "classes" of printers. A class can be considered a collection of multiple printers that will be managed as a unit. Imagine a class as a directory, whereas individual printers are like files. Like the directory and file controls in Apache, you can restrict access to classes and printers.
- `cupsd.conf`. The main CUPS setting file. This file is modified by the Apple GUI to enable/disable printer sharing.
- `printers.conf`. Settings for the individual printers—connection information, limits, and so forth.

Printers and classes are defined virtually identically to Apache containers. Please refer to Chapter 15 if you find this confusing.

A printer, as defined in `/etc/cups/printers.conf`, for example, looks like this:

```
<DefaultPrinter MyPrinter>
Info 10.0.1.200
DeviceURI lpd://10.0.1.200
State Idle
Accepting Yes
JobSheets none none
QuotaPeriod 0
PageLimit 0
KLimit 0
</Printer>
```

`MyPrinter` is defined, along with attributes for quotas, active status, and so on.

The `/etc/cups/classes.conf` file is very similar:

```
<Class OurPrinters>
Info test
State Idle
Accepting Yes
JobSheets none none
Printer MyPrinter
Printer YourPrinter
```

```
QuotaPeriod 0
PageLimit 0
KLimit 0
</Class>
```

The class `OurPrinters` looks exactly like a printer, with the addition of the `Printer` directives, which add the printers `MyPrinter` and `YourPrinter` to the class. Like a printer, a class of printers can also have access control mechanisms to limit usage.

Access Control Directives

Provide access control for a named printer or class by using a `Location` container (sounding more and more like Apache, isn't it?). Unlike Apache, Location containers are used to refer to a printer or class, not a URL. A Location is defined and configured within the `/etc/cups/cupsd.conf` file.

Table 16.8 lists the defined CUPS Location values.

TABLE 16.8 CUPS Location List

Location	Descriptions
/	All operations on any resources.
/admin	Administrative operations.
/classes	All printer classes.
/classes/<*class name*>	The named printer class.
/jobs	All jobs.
/jobs/<*job id*>	The named job ID.
/printers	All configured printers.
/printers/<*printer name*>	The named printer.
/printers/<*printer name*>.ppd	The PPD for the named printer.

For example, to set up a location that can be used to control access to the printer `MyPrinter`, one would use

```
<Location /printers/MyPrinter>
</Location>
```

Within the location, use the directives in Table 16.9 to protect the printers, printer classes, or any of the CUPS locations. Some directives apply globally to the server, rather than a single location.

TABLE 16.9 Directives to Limit Access to the CUPS Locations

<table>
<tr><th>Directive</th><th>Description</th></tr>
<tr><td>Allow from <<i>source</i>></td><td>Allow access to the resource by the named source. The source may be expressed as All, None, a domain name, an IP address, an IP address/subnet mask, or @LOCAL for the local subnet.</td></tr>
<tr><td>Deny from <<i>source</i>></td><td>The opposite of Allow from, this directive denies access to the source.</td></tr>
<tr><td>Order <allow,deny|deny,allow></td><td>The order in which Allow and Deny directives are processed—whether browsing is assumed to be allowed or denied by default.</td></tr>
<tr><td>AuthClass anonymous|user|system|group</td><td>Sets the level of authentication required to access the location. Anonymous allows anyone to access the resource, user requires a valid username and password, system requires username and password of a member of the sys group, whereas group requires that authentication of a valid user of the group be set by AuthGroupName.</td></tr>
<tr><td>AuthGroupName <<i>group</i>></td><td>The user group to use with AuthClass.</td></tr>
<tr><td>AuthType None|Basic|Digest|BasicDigest</td><td>Choose the type of authentication required for the resource. These are identical to Apache directives, because IPP is based on HTTP.</td></tr>
<tr><td>Require user|group|valid-user <users or groups></td><td>Sets the required authentication. If user or group are specified, a list of space-separated users or groups must be provided to use for authentication. Alternatively, the valid-user option will authenticate against any valid user.</td></tr>
<tr><td>BrowseAllow from <<i>source</i>></td><td>(Global) Like the Allow directive, this directive is used to determine what machines CUPS will respond to for printer browsing. The Mac OS X default (when print sharing is active) is @LOCAL.</td></tr>
<tr><td>BrowseDeny from <<i>source</i>></td><td>(Global) The opposite of BrowseAllow, denies access to printer browsing for the named source(s).</td></tr>
<tr><td>BrowseOrder <allow,deny|deny,allow></td><td>(Global) The order in which BrowseAllow and BrowseDeny directives are processed—whether browsing is allowed or denied by default.</td></tr>
<tr><td>Browsing On|Off</td><td>(Global) Turns printer browsing on and off.</td></tr>
<tr><td>AccessLog <<i>path</i>></td><td>(Global) Path to store the CUPS access log.</td></tr>
<tr><td>ErrorLog <<i>path</i>></td><td>(Global) Path to store the CUPS error log.</td></tr>
<tr><td>PageLog <<i>path</i>></td><td>(Global) Path to store the CUPS page log.</td></tr>
<tr><td>LogLevel debug2|debug|info|warn|error|none</td><td>(Global) Level of information stored in the error log, listed here from greatest detail to least.</td></tr>
<tr><td>MaxLogSize <<i>bytes</i>|<i>megabytes</i> m></td><td>The maximum size of a logfile before it is automatically rotated.</td></tr>
<tr><td>MaxClients <<i>number</i>></td><td>(Global) Maximum number of clients allowed to connect to the server.</td></tr>
<tr><td>MaxClientsPerHost <<i>number</i>></td><td>(Global) The maximum number of clients allowed to connect from a single host.</td></tr>
</table>

TABLE 16.9 Continued

Directive	Description
`MaxJobs <number>`	(Global) Maximum number of jobs to keep in memory at a given time. Jobs over this limit are rejected. 0 disables the setting.
`MaxJobsPerPrinter <number>`	(Global) Maximum number of jobs that can be allowed on a printer or class of printers at a time. 0 disables the setting.
`MaxJobsPerUser <number>`	(Global) Sets the limit on active jobs from a single user. 0 disables the setting.
`MaxRequestSize <bytes|megabytes m>`	The maximum size of a request (print file) that can be sent to CUPS. 0 disables the setting.
`Klimit <size in k>`	(Printer/Class) Sets the job size (in k) for a specific printer or class.
`PageLimit <number>`	(Printer/Class) Sets the maximum number of job pages for a printer or class.
`QuotaPeriod <time in seconds>`	(Printer/Class) Amount of time before a quota resets.
`Accepting <yes|no>`	(Printer/Class) Choose whether the printer or class is accepting jobs.

The complete list of CUPS security (and general) directives can be found at `http://www.cups.org/sam.html`.

TIP

The CUPS Web administrative interface (`http://127.0.0.1:631`) can, by default, be accessed by any local user. Assuming there are multiple users on the CUPS machine, you should limit access to the `/admin` location to prevent undesired changes.

Digest Authentication and `lppasswd`

When using digest authentication, you must manually add users to the CUPS `passwd.md5` file by using the command-line tool `lppasswd`. The `lppasswd` syntax is simply `lppasswd [-a] [-g <groupname>] [-x] [username]`.

The most common use of the command for an administrator is `lppasswd` followed by `-a` and a username. Doing so adds a username to the MD5 password file. If the `-g` flag is used with a group name, the user is added as a member of the named group. If no group is specified, the default system group is used. For example:

```
# lppasswd -a jray
Enter password:
Enter password again:
```

If specified without a username, `lppasswd` changes the MD5 password of the user executing the command.

To delete an existing user from the file, use `-x` *<username>* as the arguments to `lppasswd`.

NOTE

`lppasswd` does not have any effect on the Mac OS X users or passwords—only the CUPS `passwd.md5` file.

Other Resources

For additional information on WebDAV, CUPS, Samba, and AFP, you might want to review these resources:

- Apple Filing Protocol 3.1, `http://developer.apple.com/techpubs/macosx/Networking/AFP/index.html`.
- "WebDAV and Apache (PDF)," Greg Stein, `http://www.webdav.org/papers/ApacheCon-2002-US-TH01.pdf`.
- "`mod_dav` FAQ," `http://www.webdav.org/mod_dav/faq/`.
- "Unofficial Samba HOWTO," David Lechnyr, `http://hr.uoregon.edu/davidrl/samba/`.
- "How to Configure Samba 2.2 as a Primary Domain Controller," `http://us1.samba.org/samba/ftp/docs/htmldocs/Samba-PDC-HOWTO.html`.
- "Implementing CIFS," Christopher Hertel, `http://www.ubiqx.org/cifs/`.
- "Samba Troubleshooting," Paul Green, `ftp://ftp.stratus.com/pub/vos/customers/samba/`.
- "Sam's Teach Yourself Samba in 24 Hours: Troubleshooting Techniques," `http://us3.samba.org/samba/ftp/docs/Samba24Hc13.pdf`.
- "Linux Networking: Exploring Samba," William Wong, `http://www.linuxplanet.com/linuxplanet/tutorials/2047/5/`.
- "CUPS Software Security Report," `http://www.cups.org/ssr.html`.
- "Internet Printing Protocol," `http://www.pwg.org/ipp/`.
- "Mac OS X Printing," `http://developer.apple.com/printing/index.html`.

Summary

This chapter covered the Mac OS X daemons used to share resources between other computers. Although Apple has done a great job of "hiding" software such as CUPS and making it easy to use, they've also made a number of decisions that may expose more of your computer than you'd like. This chapter covers the security features of Samba, WebDAV, AppleShare, and CUPS so that you can take advantage of the software without risking remote users taking advantage of you.

PART IV

Prevention, Detection, and Reaction to Attacks: Health Care and Checkups for Your Machine

IN THIS PART

17

Blocking Network Access: Firewalls

IN THIS CHAPTER

- Firewalling
- Built-In GUI Mac OS X Firewall Tools
- Built-In Command-Line Mac OS X Firewall Tools
- Firewall Hardware
- Firewall Resources

A majority of this text (Chapters 7–16) have dealt with network services and attacks. It stands to reason that a solution should exist for dealing with controlling network access *in general*—and it does, in the form of a firewall. A firewall is a device or piece of software that blocks network packets before they can reach server daemons. Rather than managing access for individual processes, a firewall provides a central point for controlling network traffic across the board.

Firewalling

Firewalls have become a necessity for modern networks. Hundreds of pieces of software are released each year that, when installed, provide remote access to your machine, and, as such, are a security risk to the network. Much of this software is marketed to individuals as simple "helpful" applications, but to the network administrator, they can be a nightmare.

Software products such as Kazaa, GNUtella, and so on are popular for downloading music and movies, but they also open file servers that deliver the contents of their computers to outside clients. Dozens of variations of these applications exist, and, on a large decentralized network, it is virtually impossible to keep them from being installed. Even if user application policies are put in place, should a remote exploit be discovered that affects the operating system of all machines on the network, the only recourse for the network administrator may be to wait (patiently?) for a patch.

A solution to both these potential problems is a firewall. A firewall blocks specific network traffic before the critical services on a machine can process it. There are three general types of firewalls:

- **Personal firewall**. A personal firewall is configured on each network workstation. It blocks traffic at that station and does not affect any other machines on the network. This is useful for users who must live on a network without a network firewall and understand the risks of leaving their system open.
- **Network firewall**. A network firewall protects a large number of computers (an entire network) by blocking traffic at the main network feed. It is a dedicated piece of hardware with two (at least) network cards that is usually placed immediately after a network's router. Traffic comes in on one interface, is compared against the firewall rules, and, if appropriate, passes out the second interface—and vice versa. Mac OS X is capable of running a NAT-based system that provides similar functionality, but is not yet capable of acting as a true network firewall. For those in need of non-NAT-based solutions, instructions for creating a transparent bridging firewall in Linux are provided at the end of this chapter.
- **Proxy firewall**. A proxy is typically a special piece of software that runs on an Internet-connected server and is accessed by a network of non-Internet-accessible machines. The proxy receives incoming requests for resources ("Hey, could you fetch me the current `versiontracker.com` page?") and, if the request is deemed appropriate, returns the resource as if it *were* the remote server. Proxies have their uses, but the focus for this chapter will be on personal and network firewalls and how they work with Mac OS X.

Of these firewall types, home users will be most interested in personal firewalls, whereas individuals dealing with enterprise or even SOHO (Small Office/Home Office) networks may want to consider a network firewall of some sort.

I've heard (and even read in earlier Maximum Security books) the comment that managing a firewall is more trouble than it's worth. Although that was perhaps a somewhat valid point in the mid-1990s, this is hardly the case today. A firewall can exist on a network and not block anything until it is needed. You aren't forced to selectively open ports for internal services as they are required. Rather, a firewall can remain in an open state and be closed only in response to attacks or unpatched operating system vulnerabilities. Firewalls are useful tools that should be kept at the ready anywhere the potential for network attack is possible and the resources are available.

CAUTION

Before going any further, it's important to point out what a firewall isn't:

A firewall *isn't* an end to network attacks. Services that are passed through the firewall are still open to exploit, and the firewall itself may even become the target of a DoS attack.

A firewall *isn't* a solution for securing network traffic. Information that is sent unencrypted is still just as susceptible to eavesdropping as on an unprotected network.

A firewall *isn't* an intrusion detection device (although they are often combined). A firewall blocks what you tell it to—nothing more, nothing less. If your rules do not cover the threats your machine or network faces, only you are to blame.

A firewall *isn't* a reason to entirely forget about internal network security. A single disgruntled employee can be more of a threat to your network than any outside attacker.

A firewall *isn't* an instant solution to network attacks. Firewall configuration often takes weeks to complete and requires that an administrator fully understand his or her network topology and active services.

Built-In GUI Mac OS X Firewall Tools

Starting in 10.2, Apple has provided the means necessary to configure the BSD firewall built into Mac OS X as well as deliver NAT services to an entire network, effectively creating a networkwide firewall. These tools, developed with the lowest common denominator in mind, are easy to use, but lack many of the features afforded their command-line equivalents. After seeing what's possible through the GUI, we'll take a closer look at what can be done at a command prompt.

Apple's Firewall Tool

Apple has done a nice job of making a basic Mac OS X firewall simple for even the most novice users to configure. Using the Services tab of the Sharing panel in System Preferences, shown in Figure 17.1, users turn on and off network services on their computer such as file sharing, Web sharing, and so on.

In doing this, one is also setting up a simple firewall configuration that, when active, will protect everything *except* the active network services. For example, in Figure 17.1, three services are active. To firewall anything else that might be running on the machine, just click the Firewall tab, shown in Figure 17.2.

The default firewall settings are picked up from the active services. Clicking the Start button blocks all traffic to the ports that aren't listed. You cannot "uncheck" an active network service; you must first disable it at the Services tab.

FIGURE 17.1 The Sharing pane provides control over active network services.

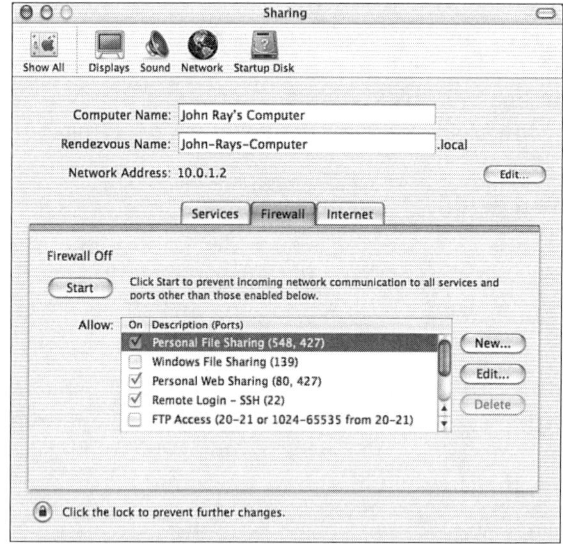

FIGURE 17.2 The firewall picks up settings from the Sharing pane.

By default, there are seven services' ports that you can choose to leave open when the firewall is started (file sharing, FTP, printer sharing, and so on). You can add to these by clicking the New button to the right of the list. Choose a port name (several popular services are included by default, such as Retrospect, ICQ, and so on). Choosing Other will let you type your own service description, as shown in Figure 17.3. The description is arbitrary and used only to help you identify the settings.

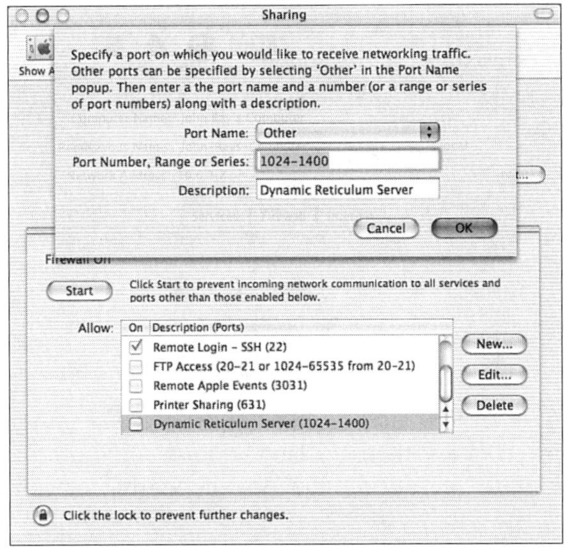

FIGURE 17.3 Add your own open service ports.

TIP

If you have a trusted user base and specialized network services, you might want to generate a customized firewall configuration file that includes more than base Apple services. Do this by editing the XML file `/Library/Preferences/com.apple.sharing.firewall.plist`. The format (XML obviously) is simple to understand: Each service is defined along with the ports that it uses. Changes in this file are reflected in Apple's firewall GUI.

After entering a description, provide a port number (for example, 1024), a range of ports (for example, 1024–1400), or a list of port numbers (for example, 1024, 1025, 1026).

NOTE

Notice that the Apple firewall does not provide protocol-specific settings such as TCP/UDP ports. Only TCP ports will be blocked if you use the Apple GUI. You'll need the command line to provide additional control.

Click OK to save the settings. You need to stop and start the firewall to enable your changes.

Network Address Translation

NAT on a Mac OS X machine can serve as a network firewall for an entire LAN of any sort of client computers (Mac, Windows, Linux, and so forth). The computer serving as the gateway will provide outgoing Internet access to the LAN side, whereas incoming connections will be rejected.

WHAT IS NAT?

NAT, or Network Address Translation, provides network access to multiple machines on a private subnet through a single public network address—this is frequently referred to as "IP Masquerading." NAT enables networks to increase in size without using valuable (and sometimes costly) public IP addresses. For more information on this technology, read RFC 1631: `http://www.cis.ohio-state.edu/cgi-bin/rfc/rfc1631.html`.

To use this feature, you need multiple network interfaces in your computer—usually two ethernet adapters or an ethernet adapter and an AirPort card. Your Internet source should be connected and active. Open the Sharing panel in System Preferences, then click the Internet tab and then the Start button to begin sharing the connection, as shown in Figure 17.4.

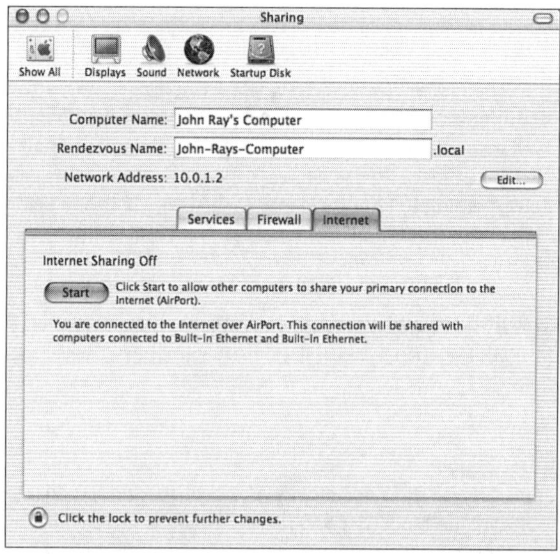

FIGURE 17.4 Click Start to activate NAT service.

LAN-side computers should be connected to the network interface indicated in the Sharing panel. If, for example, you are sharing through an ethernet card, you need to connect a switch or hub to the ethernet port on your computer, then connect the additional client machines to the switch.

NOTE

A quick refresher: Be sure to wire from your computer to a *normal* switch/hub port, *not* an uplink port. You'd be amazed how often this mistake is made when wiring computers to switches.

Mac OS X provides DHCP service to the LAN, eliminating the need for manual configuration of the client computers. At the time of this writing, Internet Sharing could not be automatically enabled at startup. To do this, you need to script it manually.

CAUTION

The Internet Sharing feature in the shipping version of 10.2 suffers from a somewhat serious issue: DHCP is served on both Internet and LAN interfaces, which could easily conflict with other DHCP servers on a network. This feature has been strictly forbidden on some networks. See `http://www.net.princeton.edu/mac/internet-sharing-x/` for a warning published by Princeton University.

Built-In Command-Line Mac OS X Firewall Tools

As with many of the Mac OS X GUI system tools (Web, FTP, Windows Sharing, and so forth) the Firewall and Internet Sharing functions are nothing more than a GUI on top of BSD command-line utilities—`ipfw` and `natd`, respectively.

You can gain far better control over your system by using the command-line tools directly. Firewall functions can be built into scripts, or used with intrusion detection tools such as Snort and Guardian (see Chapter 18, "Alarm Systems: Intrusion Detection") to dynamically protect against attacks as they occur. Although the GUI tools are probably enough for most users, they lack the flexibility that many high-end users and network administrators require.

IP Firewall Tool: `ipfw`

The `ipfw` tool is used to create, modify, and remove firewall rules from the built-in Mac OS X firewall. The first step is to list the active firewall rules with `ipfw list` (you will need to be `root` or use `sudo` to access `ipfw`). By default, your Mac already has a single rule, even if you aren't blocking traffic:

```
# ipfw list
65535 allow ip from any to any
```

Each line starts with an arbitrary number between 1 and 65535, followed by the rule. Packets are matched against rules in the order of the line numbers. When a match is found, that rule is interpreted, and the proper action is carried out (the packet is dropped, accepted, and so on). In most cases, no further matching is carried out. For the default rule (`65535`), IP packets from any machine to any machine are allowed.

Try configuring a firewall by using Apple's GUI, allowing Remote Login (SSH, port 22) and denying all others. Then use `ipfw list` to display the results:

```
# ipfw list
02000 allow ip from any to any via lo*
02010 deny ip from 127.0.0.0/8 to any in
02020 deny ip from any to 127.0.0.0/8 in
02030 deny ip from 224.0.0.0/3 to any in
02040 deny tcp from any to 224.0.0.0/3 in
02050 allow tcp from any to any out
02060 allow tcp from any to any established
02070 allow tcp from any to any 22 in
12190 deny tcp from any to any
65535 allow ip from any to any
```

NOTE

Although you can certainly use the GUI and command-line tools simultaneously, you should choose one or the other when creating custom configurations. Firewall rulesets usually start by flushing any existing ruleset. If you attempt to write your own scripts *and* use Apple's, you may find that one is being replaced by the other, depending on the startup order.

A number of rules are added automatically to the firewall in addition to the rule for allowing Remote Login. This is a line-by-line breakdown:

- **02000**. Allow any IP packets to/from any destination to be passed by the loop-back interface (`lo`).
- **02010**. Disallow any packets purporting to be from 127.0.0.0/8 (loopback).
- **02020**. Disallow any incoming IP packets to 127.0.0.0/8 (loopback).
- **02030**. Deny incoming TCP packets from 224.0.0.0/3 (multicast).
- **02040**. Deny incoming TCP packets to 224.0.0.0/3 (multicast).
- **02050**. Allow any TCP packet to be sent to any outside machine.

- **02060**. Allow any TCP packets to pass as long as they are part of an established connection.
- **02070**. Allow any incoming TCP packets to port 22 (SSH).
- **12190**. Deny all other TCP packets.
- **65535**. Allow all other IP packets.

The brunt of the firewall's work is performed by the rule in 12190, which disallows all TCP packets from anywhere to anywhere. The rest of the rules are simply exceptions that "poke holes" in the firewall for various services. Apple's ruleset explicitly denies values that should not be seen on your interface (lines 02010-02040). Typically firewalls include rules to deny incoming packets from all IANA (`http://www.iana.org/`)–reserved addresses (see RFC 3330: `http://www.potaroo.net/ietf/rfc/rfc3330.txt`), and you may wish to add these addresses to your firewall.

Firewall rules are typically composed of two things: packet matching criteria (source, destination, protocol, interface, and so on) and an action (allow, drop, and so on). For example, if I wanted to set up a firewall ruleset to allow incoming requests for my personal Web server from the subnet 192.168.0.0/16, I could add a rule like this:

```
ipfw add allow tcp from 192.168.0.0/16 to any 80
```

Any Web traffic (port 80) from the subnet 192.168.0.0/16 would immediately be allowed to pass through the firewall.

As was mentioned earlier, the ordering of the rules makes a difference in how they are interpreted. If you're starting with a blank slate, adding the previous rule has no purpose as there is already the default rule to allow all packets to pass (`65535`). It is at this point that you must make the decision about how your firewall will be configured moving forward: Will you start with an entirely open system and close it off as the need arises, or will you begin with a closed system and open it as necessary? Assuming you choose to keep the system closed and open specific ports when appropriate, you'll need a set of rules very similar to what Apple provides to start the firewall correctly: The loopback interface *must* be left open, for example. If you take the opposite approach, rules can be added at will, because *everything* starts out open.

Typically, rules are stored in a file and read by `ipfw` all at once. This eliminates the need to invoke the command repeatedly. A perfectly legitimate script to accomplish the previously defined task of opening only port 80 for the 192.168.0.0/16 subnet looks like this:

```
flush
add allow ip from any to any via lo
```

```
add allow tcp from 192.168.0.0/16 to any 80
add deny ip from any to any
```

These rules can be stored sequentially in a file (such as `/etc/firewall.rules`), then loaded with `ipfw /etc/firewall.rules`.

```
# ipfw /etc/firewall.rules
Are you sure? [yn] y

Flushed all rules.
00100 allow log ip from any to any via lo0
00200 allow tcp from 192.168.0.0/16 to any 80
00300 deny ip from any to any
```

The most common use of `ipfw` that you'll encounter is adding a new rule. The syntax for this is `add [Rule number 1-65535]` <*action*> `[log [logamount` <*number*>`]` <*protocol*> `from` <*source*> `to` <*destination*> `[interface spec]`.

Rule numbers are optional and, if not assigned manually, will be automatically added in increments of 100, starting at 00100.

Actions choose what to do with a packet that matches. Common actions include:

- `allow`. Allow the packet to pass, stop processing rules.
- `deny`. Discard the packet, stop processing rules. No response is returned to the remote device.
- `unreach` <*code*>. Discard the packet and attempt to send an ICMP response (0-254) to the remote device and stop processing rules.
- `reset`. Discard the packet, send a TCP reset notice, and stop processing rules.

Immediately following an action is the optional keyword `log`. If specified, any matches to the rule are logged via `syslogd` with a facility of `LOG_SECURITY`. If you intend to use logging, however, you must first enable it in the kernel by typing `/usr/sbin/sysctl -w net.inet.ip.fw.verbose=1` (as root):

```
# /usr/sbin/sysctl -w net.inet.ip.fw.verbose=1
net.inet.ip.fw.verbose: 0 -> 1
```

NOTE

Logging must be enabled each time your computer restarts. If you intend to build a firewall script that runs at bootup, you should activate logging at the same time.

Logs should only be written to help debug firewall problems, or to document network violations. Logging *all* traffic, for example, is extremely hard on your system's resources and may result in dropped packets.

To limit logs to only a certain number of entries per rule, add `logamount` *<number>* after the `log` keyword. This limits the total number of messages a rule can generate. Setting the number to zero removes the limit.

Protocols can be given as a number or name (see `/etc/protocols` for a list of IP protocols by number): `tcp`, `udp`, `icmp`, and `ip` (all) are commonly used and constitute most traffic on a TCP/IP network.

The source and destination of a rule can be given in the form of *<address/mask>* (for example, 192.168.0.0/16), as a hostname, or if you use the shortcuts `me` or `any` to match the firewall box's address or any address. The `not` keyword can be included in front of a source or destination to match anything *except* that address. To further narrow down a match, one can add a port, port list (#,#,#), port range (#-#), port and mask pair (#:#), or service name (`http`, `ssh`, and so on—see `/etc/services` for details).

Finally, an interface can be specified in the rule to differentiate between multiple active network cards or the direction that traffic is flowing. The following is a list of commonly used interface specifications:

- **in**. Match only incoming packets.
- **out**. Match only outgoing packets.
- **via *<interface>***. Match packets going through the named interface.
- **recv *<interface>***. Match packets received by the named interface.
- **xmit *<interface>***. Match packets transmitted by the named interface.

For example, the rule to allow Web connections from the `192.168.0.0/16` subnet could be applied to *only* connections coming through `en1` (the second ethernet interface—often an AirPort card) if you were to modify it to read `add allow tcp from 192.168.0.0/16 to any 80 via en1`.

As your firewall works, you can view what it has done (aside from logging) by checking the counter values for each rule. For each rule, internal counters are maintained for the number of packets that have matched the rule, the number of bytes matched, and a timestamp of the last match. You can view these counters by adding the switches `-a` and `-t` (counters and timestamp respectively) to `ipfw list`:

```
# ipfw -t -a list
00100 4215 555183 Mon Dec 30 23:07:55 2002 allow log ip from any to any via lo0
00200    0      0                          allow tcp from 192.168.0.0/16 to any 80
00300  109  24884 Mon Dec 30 23:07:34 2002 deny ip from any to any
65535    0      0                          allow ip from any to any
```

Rules can be referred to by the rule number for deleting rules or resetting rule counters. To delete a firewall rule, use `ipfw delete` *<rule number>*. You can reset a counter with `ipfw reset` *<rule number>*. Depending on whether you've configured a packet logging limit, you may need to reset the log counter after the maximum count is reached; this action can be performed with `ipfw resetlog` *<rule number>*.

For more information on `ipfw`, read the man page and consult the resource list at the end of this chapter. Misconfiguring a firewall can cause problems with your computer and your network, so it isn't a task to take lightly. Remotely configuring a firewall isn't advised as one can very easily block his/her own access and lose control of the firewall.

NOTE

The `ipfw` man pages describe traffic-shaping facilities of the firewall that are currently unavailable in the shipping `ipfw` configuration. Traffic-shaping enables an administrator to control the network bandwidth available to a given process. Thankfully, a third-party tool, Carrafix (`http://www.carrafix.com/`) brings this feature to Mac OS X with an easy-to-use GUI.

Third-Party Firewall Tools

Firewall configuration can be extremely complex, depending on your network. Although `ipfw` can be used directly, there are a number of third-party firewall tools that can make setting up a firewall easier, and even include prewritten rules for blocking a known network attack. Check out these tools for a more convenient way to set up your firewall.

- **BrickHouse**, `http://personalpages.tds.net/~brian_hill/brickhouse.html`.
- **Firewalk X**, `http://www.pliris-soft.com/products/firewalkx/index.html`.
- **Impasse**, `http://glu.com/products/impasse/`.
- **sunShield**, `http://homepage.mac.com/opalliere/Menu3.html`.
- **Norton Personal Firewall**, `http://www.symantec.com/sabu/nis/npf_mac/`.
- **NetBarrier**, `http://www.intego.com/netbarrier/home.html`.

Internet Sharing Through NAT: `natd`

Sharing your network connection to an entire LAN via NAT is an effective way to provide network access to multiple machines without allowing incoming network access. Apple enables you to do this, but their single-button solution falls short in several areas—most notably in the ability to forward incoming connections to LAN-side computers. This, for example, allows an administrator to create internal Web servers, mail servers, and so forth that, although behind the NAT firewall, are still accessible from the Internet.

Let's walk through the steps necessary to create Internet Sharing by hand. To do this, assume that there are two interfaces being used: `en0`, with a live Internet connection, and `en1`, an interface that will feed the internal network.

To start, create a basic configuration file (`/etc/natd.conf`) for the `natd` daemon:

```
interface en0
same_ports yes
use_sockets yes
unregistered_only yes
```

If you do not have a static Internet connection, you should also add the line `dynamic yes` to the file as well; this enables the process to adapt to changes on the Internet-connected interface.

The `same_ports` and `use_sockets` directives increase the reliability of connections by attempting to maintain a specific port number for outgoing connections and allocating sockets for direct file transfers. The setting `unregistered_only` forces the server to alter only packets coming from private addresses (which is exactly what should be appearing on the LAN side of the connection).

If you would like to log packets that are blocked at the NAT device, add the line `log_denied no`.

Next, configure your internal interface (assumed `en1`) with a private address, such as `10.0.1.1`. Your internal network will be based on this address and will use it as the gateway to the rest of the Internet.

Now, start the `natd` process by using the `/etc/natd.conf` configuration file (this must be performed as `root`):

```
# /usr/sbin/natd -f /etc/natd.conf
```

Before you can begin using NAT, IP forwarding must be enabled in the kernel:

```
# sysctl -w net.inet.ip.forwarding=1
```

To start forwarding at bootup, change the `IPFORWARDING=-NO-` line in `/etc/hostconfig` to read `IPFORWARDING=-YES-`.

Finally, using `ipfw`, add a `divert` rule that will route packets from the internal network to the external interface (`en0`):

```
# ipfw add divert natd ip from any to any via en0
```

Internal computers based on this configuration should be set with the following network configuration

- **IP Address**: `10.0.1.x` (any node other than `10.0.1.1`)
- **Subnet Mask**: `255.255.254.0`
- **Router**: `10.0.1.1`
- **DNS**: *<same as ISP-assigned DNS>*

TIP

If desired, you can enable a caching name server on your NAT router by changing the line `DNSSERVER=-NO-` in `/etc/hostconfig` to read `DNSSERVER=-YES-`. This, however, starts an additional network service that, if inappropriately configured, will be exposed on the Internet side of your connection.

To run publicly accessible services on a NAT-based network, incoming connections must be mapped from the single addressable network address (`en0`) to any of the computers connected via `en1`. The `natd` syntax for this operation is `natd -n` *<Internet interface>* `-redirect_port` *<protocol> <internal address:port> <external port>*. For example, to redirect incoming TCP connections on port 80 of the Internet-connected side of the NAT machine to a public Web server on the LAN address of `10.0.1.100`, one would issue the following command:

```
natd -n en0 -redirect_port tcp 10.0.1.100:80 80
```

Like the firewall configuration, you can easily add the `natd` setup to a script that runs at startup. See Chapter 11, "Introduction to Mac OS X Network Services," for examples of startup scripts.

Firewall Hardware

Configuring your Mac to perform Internet Sharing or setting up firewall software to block your machines isn't difficult, but it isn't necessarily the appropriate solution for everyone—especially those that do not want to dedicate a Mac to maintaining a network connection.

Consumer Firewall Appliances

A number of consumer solutions are virtually plug, play, and forget. Usually sold under a "broadband router" moniker, these devices typically perform NAT, serve DHCP, and are configured through a Web interface, as shown in Figure 17.5. Many can create VPN connections via IPSec, easily forward incoming connections to internal IP addresses, and are available in wired, wireless, or both configurations. Starting at around $50 for an ethernet-based model, they're affordable and eliminate the necessity for custom configuration on your individual Mac.

NOTE

Firewall appliances are *not* to be considered the equivalent of a professional firewall. They work well for most personal and SOHO applications, but are not suited to handling networks with a real assigned subnet. In fact, being based on NAT, these appliances may be against the network policies set up by your service provider.

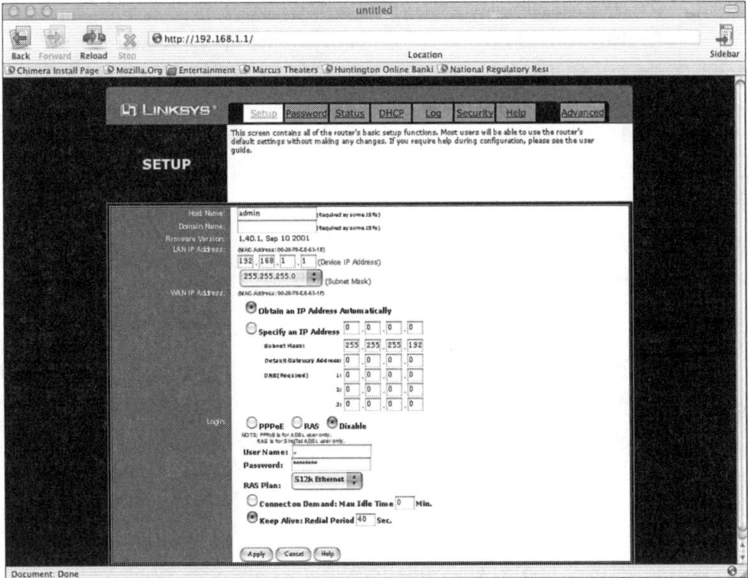

FIGURE 17.5 Firewall appliances are easy to set up and don't require custom computer configuration.

Table 17.1 contains a list of popular firewall appliances that can be used with your network.

TABLE 17.1 Popular Internet Sharing Devices

Manufacturer	Product	URL
Apple	AirPort Extreme	`http://www.apple.com/airport/`
Belkin	4-Port Cable/DSL Gateway Router (F5D5230-4)	`http://www.belkin.com/`
Belkin	Wireless Cable/DSL Gateway Router (F5D6230-3)	`http://www.belkin.com/`

TABLE 17.1 Continued

Manufacturer	Product	URL
Buffalo Technology	AirStation (WBR-B11)	`http://www.buffalotech.com/wireless/products/wbr-b11/index.php`
DLink	AirPlus (DI-614+)	`http://www.dlink.com/products/digitalHome/wireless/11b+/di614+/`
DLink	Express Ethernetwork (DI-604)	`http://www.dlink.com/products/broadband/di604/`
LinkSys	Etherfast Router (BEFSR41)	`http://www.linksys.com/Products/product.asp?grid=23&prid=20`
LinkSys	Wireless Access Point Router (BEFW11S4)	`http://www.linksys.com/Products/product.asp?grid=23&prid=415`
NetGear	Cable/DSL ProSafe (FM114P)	`http://www.netgear.com/products/prod_details.asp?prodID=138`
NetGear	Cable/DSL Web Safe Router (RP114)	`http://www.netgear.com/products/details/RP114.asp`

Although this list is accurate at the time of writing, the market for these devices is growing daily. New models with bigger and better features will always be "just around the corner." Most of these devices range from $50 (wired) to $150 (wireless), with the exception of Apple's AirPort Extreme, which tops out at $250 for the high-end model. The AirPort Extreme, however, provides dial-in support (including AOL) if necessary, and, with two ethernet ports, USB printer sharing, 802.11g support, and 50-user capacity, can serve as an ethernet/wireless bridge.

CAUTION

A common misconception is that hardware devices are *not* exploitable. Although it is unlikely that an attacker will compromise your Internet appliance and, say, set up a pirate software server, they provide a single point of failure at which a network can be attacked.

The LinkSys BEFSR41 (prior to firmware 1.42.7), for example, could be crashed if its Web interface is accessed with a request formatted like this: `http://192.168.1.1/Gozila.cgi?` (CVE: `CAN-2002-1236`).

The only fix for exploits such as this is to download a firmware patch from the manufacturer. Although these errors are far less common than exploits found in OS components, they are real, and do require that you pay attention to the updates for your particular router.

Broadband routers typically provide a means of mapping incoming connection ports to IP addresses within the internal private network, or setting a DMZ (demilitarized zone) machine that, for all intents and purposes, sits outside the protection of the firewall and receives all incoming traffic. Keep in mind that doing this will expose internal machines to the same risks (on the passed ports) that they would experience if they were connected to the Internet directly. A firewall is effective only when it is used to block potentially dangerous traffic.

Commercial Firewalls

Commercial firewalls differ from the "lighter" SOHO fare by providing support for larger numbers of computers, integrating features such as VPN and intrusion detection, and, most importantly, providing protection for a subnet of nonprivate addresses.

Broadband routers typically work by taking a single incoming connection with one nonprivate IP address, and making that connection available to an internal subnet (NAT). The trouble with this arrangement is that you cannot, for example, run two Web servers on the internal subnet and have them be visible from the outside world (unless one of the servers was not using the standard port 80). For commercial applications where the vast majority of the network must be addressable from the Internet, NAT devices fall short.

CAUTION

Some service providers prohibit the use of NAT devices because they serve as a cloak for the internal network. An attacker can sit behind a NAT-based router and wage war, but the attacks themselves can be traced back to only the publicly visible IP address of the router. On a network with hundreds of machines, the attacker can stay virtually anonymous.

Commercial firewalls connect between an incoming network feed (such as a router), and the devices that feed the LAN side of the connection (usually a switch). Firewalls of this nature function as a bridge, passing traffic from one side of the firewall to the other, and vice versa, transparently "bridging" the internal and external networks. While handling the traffic flow, a firewall can also perform packet inspection, dropping packets that fail to match the network policies for the LAN. As `ipfw` can be configured to block packets directly at your OS X machine, a commercial firewall can block the packets before they even *reach* a machine.

Commercial firewall solutions cost in the $1000+ range, and often come with dedicated software and monitoring utilities. Many offer service-specific packet filtering, allowing administrators to block inappropriate Web and email content before it reaches internal servers or clients. These devices are appropriate for any network that requires a single point for controlling service access, as well as those that require security for an entire Internet-addressable subnet. To locate a firewall appropriate for your network, you may want to check out these manufacturers:

- **WatchGuard**—`http://www.watchguard.com/`
- **Novell**—`http://www.novell.com/products/bordermanager/`
- **SAGE Inc.** —`http://www.thirdpig.com/`
- **SonicWALL**—`http://www.sonicwall.com/solution/index.asp`
- **Trustix**—`http://www.trustix.com/`

- **KarlNet**—`http://www.karlnet.com/`
- **Cisco**—`http://www.cisco.com/`
- **BorderWare**—`http://www.borderware.com/`
- **NetScreen**—`http://www.netscreen.com/main.html`
- **Actane**—`http://www.actane.com/controll.htm`
- **Sun Microsystems**—`http://www.sun.com/servers/entry/checkpoint/`

CAUTION

Commercial firewalls usually come preconfigured with well-known factory passwords. Administrators in a hurry to protect their networks sometimes forget to change the passwords, giving attackers an easy target to one of the most critical components of a network infrastructure.

A Cheap and Effective Solution

Because you're already involved with a Unix operating system (Mac OS X), you might want to consider building your own firewall with Linux. This provides a cost-effective solution that can operate as a transparent bridge (like a commercial system), but requires some command-line configuration to work.

NOTE

No, creating a bridging firewall in Mac OS X is not currently possible. A proxy ARP-based solution may be doable, but can easily wreak havoc on a network if not configured correctly.

Linux provides an extremely easy-to-implement solution that can be put into place for the cost of a cheap Pentium and two ethernet cards.

Besides, why would you want to dedicate a perfectly good Mac to the role of a has-been PC?

To create a transparent Linux firewall, you'll need

- **A PC that can be dedicated to firewalling**. A 400MHz PII w/ 128MB RAM can easily handle a network of 300+ workstations while running active intrusion detection—so nothing extravagant is required.
- **A Linux distribution with the bridging code included in the kernel**. 2.4 or later should suffice. The RedHat 8.x distribution is easy to install and should work nicely for most people. The latest patches to the kernel bridging code can be downloaded from `http://bridge.sourceforge.net/download.html`.
- **Two network cards**. Two network cards rated for the speed and media type used on your LAN. A safe option is the Intel EtherExpress Pro.

First, set up the PC and install the Linux distribution. Do not choose to set up a firewall at this time. Allow the installer to configure the network cards so that each is visible on your network. Use `chconfig` or `ntsysv` to disable all unnecessary network services. Be sure that `iptables` *is* enabled and that `ipchains` is not.

You should take the time to determine which physical port is recognized as `eth0` and which is `eth1`. This might require pinging the interfaces from outside devices, then disconnecting the wires to see when the packets are dropped.

Next, download and install the kernel bridging utilities from `http://bridge.sourceforge.net/download.html`, unarchive, and enter the source distribution directory:

```
# curl -O http://bridge.sourceforge.net/bridge-utils/bridge-utils-0.9.6.tar.gz
# tar zxf bridge-utils-0.9.6.tar.gz
# cd bridge-utils
```

Configure, compile, and install the software with `./configure`, `make`, and `make install`:

```
# ./configure
checking for gcc... gcc
checking for C compiler default output... a.out
checking whether the C compiler works... yes
checking whether we are cross compiling... no
checking for suffix of executables...
checking for suffix of object files... o
checking whether we are using the GNU C compiler... yes
checking whether gcc accepts -g... yes
checking for a BSD-compatible install... /usr/bin/install -c
checking for ranlib... ranlib
checking how to run the C preprocessor... gcc -E
checking for ANSI C header files... yes
...
# make
for x in libbridge brctl doc; do (cd $x && make ); done
make[1]: Entering directory `/home/jray/bridge-utils/libbridge'
gcc -Wall -g -I/usr/src/linux/include -c libbridge_compat.c
gcc -Wall -g -I/usr/src/linux/include  -c libbridge_devif.c
gcc -Wall -g -I/usr/src/linux/include  -c libbridge_if.c
gcc -Wall -g -I/usr/src/linux/include  -c libbridge_init.c
gcc -Wall -g -I/usr/src/linux/include  -c libbridge_misc.c
...
# make install
for x in libbridge brctl doc; do (cd $x && make install ); done
make[1]: Entering directory `/home/jray/bridge-utils/libbridge'
```

```
mkdir -p /usr/local/include
install -m 644 libbridge.h /usr/local/include
mkdir -p /usr/local/lib
install -m 644 libbridge.a /usr/local/lib
make[1]: Leaving directory `/home/jray/bridge-utils/libbridge'
make[1]: Entering directory `/home/jray/bridge-utils/brctl'
mkdir -p /usr/local/sbin
/usr/bin/install -c -m 755 brctl brctld /usr/local/sbin
make[1]: Leaving directory `/home/jray/bridge-utils/brctl'
make[1]: Entering directory `/home/jray/bridge-utils/doc'
mkdir -p /usr/local/man/man8
install -m 644 brctl.8 /usr/local/man/man8
make[1]: Leaving directory `/home/jray/bridge-utils/doc'
```

Finally, install the script (`bigwall.sh`) shown in Listing 17.1 on the Linux computer. The location is not important, but you will need to edit this file to add rules to the firewall.

LISTING 17.1 Linux Firewall Startup Script (`bigwall.sh`)

```
#!/bin/sh

# Used for bridge
BR="/usr/local/sbin/brctl"
IFCONFIG="/sbin/ifconfig"
LAN_IP="0.0.0.0"
WAN_IP="0.0.0.0"
FIREWALL_IP="0.0.0.0"
FIREWALL_MASK="255.255.255.0"
FIREWALL_GW="0.0.0.0"

# Only used for firewall
IPTABLES="/sbin/iptables"
LAN_SUBNET="10.0.1.0/255.255.255.0"
ROUTE="/sbin/route"

$BR addbr firewall
$BR addif firewall eth0
$BR addif firewall eth1
$IFCONFIG eth0 $WAN_IP promisc
$IFCONFIG eth1 $LAN_IP promisc
$IFCONFIG firewall $FIREWALL_IP netmask $FIREWALL_MASK promisc up
$ROUTE add -net $LAN_IP gw $FIREWALL_GW dev firewall

```

LISTING 17.1 Continued

```
25 # Flush and delete user chains
26 $IPTABLES -F
27 $IPTABLES -X
28
29 # The KEEP_STATE chain keeps established connections (from the inside)
30 $IPTABLES -N KEEP_STATE
31 $IPTABLES -F KEEP_STATE
32 $IPTABLES -A KEEP_STATE -m state --state INVALID -j DROP
33 $IPTABLES -A KEEP_STATE -m state --state RELATED,ESTABLISHED -j ACCEPT
34
35 # Accept packets from the firewall's gateway
36 $IPTABLES -A FORWARD -s $FIREWALL_GW -i eth0 -d 0/0 -j ACCEPT
37
38 # Log spoofed packets (source is internal LAN but external interface)
39 $IPTABLES -A FORWARD -s $LAN_SUBNET -i eth0 -d 0/0
➥ -j LOG --log-level DEBUG --log-prefix "Spoof attempt: "
40
41 # Add traffic blocks here
42 ###########################
43 #
44 #
45 #
46 #
47
48 # Keep established connections
49 $IPTABLES -A FORWARD -j KEEP_STATE
50
51 # Allow all outgoing traffic
52 $IPTABLES -A FORWARD -s $LAN_SUBNET -j ACCEPT
53
54 # Drop everything else
55 $IPTABLES -A FORWARD -m limit --limit 20/minute --limit-burst 10
➥ -j LOG --log-level DEBUG --log-prefix "FORWARD packet died: "
56 $IPTABLES -A FORWARD -j DROP
```

Minimal configuration consists of setting the `LAN_SUBNET` value in line 14. This should be set to the IP/mask of the network that the firewall will be protecting. The firewall itself has *no* IP address and cannot be accessed from the outside world. To provide access, assign an IP, netmask, and gateway using the variables `FIREWALL_IP`, `FIREWALL_MASK`, and `FIREWALL_GW` in lines 8, 9, and 10, respectively.

By default, the firewall will allow all outgoing packets and incoming packets that are associated with an internally originated connection to pass. All other packets (incoming traffic) are blocked and logged. The interface `eth0` should be plugged into the "Internet" side of connection; this enables the rule in line 39 to log spoof attempts by checking for incoming IP addresses that match the local subnet's addresses—something that *should* be impossible.

To control the firewall, you'll need to add rules of your own by using Linux's `iptables` syntax. Rules should be added into the script starting at line 42. For example, to pass incoming Web connections (port 80) to the internal machines 10.0.1.25 and 10.0.1.36, you could add

```
$IPTABLES -A FORWARD -p tcp -s 0/0 -d 10.0.1.25 --dport 80 -j ACCEPT
$IPTABLES -A FORWARD -p tcp -s 0/0 -d 10.0.1.36 --dport 80 -j ACCEPT
```

To enable incoming SSH access (port 22) for the entire `10.0.1.0/24` subnet, you could add

```
$IPTABLES -A FORWARD -p tcp -s 0/0 -d 10.0.1.0/24 --dport 22 -j ACCEPT
```

The script can be built to hold as many rules as you like. Obviously, if you need a configuration more complex than simply allowing or blocking a few ports, you'll want to read up on the Linux `iptables` documentation. The `iptables` man page is a good place to start, followed by the Iptables tutorial, located at `http://people.unix-fu.org/andreasson/iptables-tutorial/iptables-tutorial.html`.

To start the firewall, simply run `bigwall.sh` from the shell:

```
# ./bigwall.sh
```

Running the firewall script (`./bigwall.sh`) creates a virtual network interface called `firewall`; this interface serves to bridge the `eth0` and `eth1` traffic. Iptables rules are applied to the virtual interface and strip blocked packets from the bridge before they reach the outgoing network interface. Running `ifconfig` should show all three interfaces as up and active:

```
# /sbin/ifconfig
eth0      Link encap:Ethernet  HWaddr 00:02:B3:9A:3E:16
          UP BROADCAST RUNNING PROMISC MULTICAST  MTU:1500  Metric:1
          RX packets:168352531 errors:0 dropped:0 overruns:0 frame:0
          TX packets:152420826 errors:0 dropped:0 overruns:0 carrier:0
          collisions:0 txqueuelen:100
          RX bytes:510956821 (487.2 Mb)  TX bytes:3484029491 (3322.6 Mb)
          Interrupt:12 Base address:0x1000
```

```
eth1      Link encap:Ethernet  HWaddr 00:02:B3:9A:59:BF
          UP BROADCAST RUNNING PROMISC MULTICAST  MTU:1500  Metric:1
          RX packets:150615474 errors:0 dropped:0 overruns:0 frame:1268544
          TX packets:164704397 errors:0 dropped:0 overruns:0 carrier:0
          collisions:0 txqueuelen:100
          RX bytes:3337027408 (3182.4 Mb)  TX bytes:4102786752 (3912.7 Mb)
          Interrupt:11 Base address:0xc000

firewall  Link encap:Ethernet  HWaddr 00:02:B3:9A:3E:16
          inet addr:164.107.48.6  Bcast:164.107.255.255  Mask:255.255.254.0
          UP BROADCAST RUNNING PROMISC MULTICAST  MTU:1500  Metric:1
          RX packets:317481071 errors:0 dropped:0 overruns:0 frame:0
          TX packets:3851572 errors:0 dropped:0 overruns:0 carrier:0
          collisions:0 txqueuelen:0
          RX bytes:3013262010 (2873.6 Mb)  TX bytes:924730826 (881.8 Mb)
```

After verifying that the firewall starts correctly, you can place it between your incoming network feed and LAN. There is likely to be a 5–10 second pause while port speeds are negotiated, after which normal network connections will resume. The script `bigwall.sh` can be added to one of the `/etc/rc.d/init.d` scripts (such as `network`) to automatically start at boot, if desired.

TIP

The Linux firewall can be used with intrusion detection software such as Snort and Guardian (see Chapter 18) to provide networkwide protection that can recognize and react to attacks as they occur.

Firewall Resources

The purpose of this chapter is to introduce the reader to firewalls and the built-in Mac OS X tools. Because firewall configuration varies from network to network, your ruleset may require only a handful of entries, whereas another may encompass hundreds. Additional information on firewalls and building firewall rulesets can be found in the following resources:

- "BSD Firewalls: IPFW," O'Reilly ONLamp.com, `http://www.onlamp.com/pub/a/bsd/2001/04/25/FreeBSD_Basics.html?page=1`.
- "BSD Firewalls: IPFW Rulesets," O'Reilly ONLamp.com, `http://www.onlamp.com/pub/a/bsd/2001/05/09/FreeBSD_Basics.html`.

- "IPFW Logging," O'Reilly ONLamp.com, `http://www.onlamp.com/pub/a/bsd/2001/06/21/FreeBSD_Basics.html`.
- "Setting Up Firewall Rules on Mac OS X 10.2," D. Cote, `http://www3.sympatico.ca/dccote/firewall.html`.
- *Building Linux and OpenBSD Firewalls*, Wes Sonnenreich and Tom Yates, ISBN 0471353663.
- "Protecting Your Private Network Using FreeBSD," Peter Brezny, `http://www.bsdtoday.com/2000/December/Features359.html`.
- "IPFW How To," `http://www.defcon1.org/html/NATD-config/firewall-setup/ipfw-1.html`.
- "Security," *FreeBSD Handbook*, Gary Palmer and Alex Nash, `http://www.freebsd.org/doc/en_US.ISO8859-1/books/handbook/firewalls.html`.

Summary

Firewalls block network traffic before they can be passed up the TCP/IP stack and used by active processes and daemons on your system. The Mac OS X built-in firewall GUI and command-line tool `ipfw` can be used to create a personal firewall for your workstation. Alternatively, Internet Sharing via `natd` can provide protection to an entire network by using IP masquerading (NAT) connections behind a single Mac OS X machine.

In some cases, setting up a Mac OS X firewall may not be the appropriate solution for your network. Consumer and commercial firewall solutions exist that don't require any configuration of your Mac. For those wanting an enterprise-worthy solution without a high cost of ownership, Linux can be used to create a transparent bridging firewall for the price of an old PC and two network cards.

18

Alarm Systems: Intrusion Detection

IN THIS CHAPTER

- What Is Intrusion Detection?
- Psionic PortSentry
- Snort
- IDS Resources

Throughout this book, we've dealt with the problem of attackers on a per-application basis. If someone is attempting to exploit a hole in Apache or sendmail, the solution has been to find a fix, or upgrade. Unfortunately, most attackers attempt to exploit multiple services and will simply move on to other daemons after finding one impenetrable. All the while, you, the administrator, remain oblivious to the fact that anything is even afoot. This chapter attempts to change that, providing the details you need to detect and react to attacks as they occur.

What Is Intrusion Detection?

It's midnight on a Monday. A quick look at the logs (covered in Chapter 19, "Logs and User Activity Accounting") on your Mac OS X computer shows the following lines occurring within the span of 15 minutes:

```
SHELLCODE x86 inc ebx NOOP
ICMP Destination Unreachable (Host Unreachable)
NETBIOS NT NULL session [arachnids 204]
➥[cve CVE-2000-0347] [bugtraq 1163]
ICMP Destination Unreachable (Undefined Code!)
ICMP Destination Unreachable (Port Unreachable)
SNMP public access udp [cve CAN-2002-0013]
➥[cve CAN-2002-0012]
WEB-IIS fpcount access [bugtraq 2252]
WEB-CGI calendar access
Portscan detected from 200.188.186.79: 21 targets 21
➥ports in 8 seconds
Portscan detected from 213.76.191.40: 6 targets 6 ports
➥in 2 seconds
```

```
Portscan detected from 213.76.191.40: 21 targets 21 ports in 7 seconds
Portscan detected from 202.103.185.8: 6 targets 6 ports in 1 seconds
Portscan detected from 202.103.185.8: 20 targets 21 ports in 9 seconds
Portscan detected from 212.58.240.37: 1 targets 21 ports in 3 seconds
WEB-FRONTPAGE shtml.dll access [arachnids 292]
```

What's happening? Is this the launch of a massive attack on your network? Possibly, but not necessarily. In fact, the previous lines *were* taken from my machine logs at midnight on a Monday, but they are typical of what one might see on a low-traffic public network.

While your computer goes about its business every day, it is being subjected to poking and prodding by external machines. Even though many of these attacks have little meaning on Mac OS X, the ability to log and react to them can mean increased protection for your entire network—even those legacy Windows machines you keep around for solitaire.

Intrusion Detection Systems (IDSs) enable you to detect and react to attacks as they are occurring—and before they take down your systems. By recognizing *how* various attacks are constructed, intrusion detection software can classify the attack type, risk, and, if necessary, dynamically build firewall rules to block any further communications with the attacker.

THIS SOUNDS TOO GOOD TO BE TRUE—WHY AREN'T IDSS USED INSTEAD OF TRADITIONAL FIREWALLS?

Intrusion Detection is *not* an exact process; it relies on matching known attack signatures against incoming activity—the equivalent of criminal profiling. Unfortunately, signatures can match both malicious and *benign* activity, resulting in false positives. Running an effective IDS requires tweaking and fine-tuning to minimize the number of false alerts.

IDS development is still in its infancy, but is proving to be a promising new area of network technology development. Whereas commercial systems sell for thousands of dollars, we'll take a look at a few different Open Source solutions for Mac OS X that can be deployed on your network for free.

Psionic PortSentry

One of the most common precursors to a network attack is a portscan. Portscans (discussed in Chapter 20, "Disaster Planning and Recovery") test remote sites for open ports, and can be used to identify potential vulnerabilities and even use the responses to determine the remote operating system. Attackers typically scan entire subnets, locate potential targets, then mount a real attack using known service exploits. PortSentry detects many types of stealth portscans, and can be used to provide quick and dirty protection on individual systems or a firewall. This provides very basic intrusion detection, is extremely simple to set up and configure, and provides an excellent starting point for exploring intrusion detection options on your Mac OS X system.

NOTE

At the time of this writing, PortSentry 2.0 was in beta testing, and requires a few tweaks in compilation/configuration to work correctly on Mac OS X. I highly recommend reading the `README.install` file included in the source distribution because it is likely that there will be differences between the instructions provided here and the latest version available.

Installing PortSentry

To start, download PortSentry 2.0 from Psionic (shortly to be owned by Cisco Systems) at `http://www.macosxunleashed.com/downloads`. Be sure to download the 2.0 version; PortSentry 1.0 installs and works on Mac OS X, but does not support stealth scan detection on our favorite platform. As stealth scans are the bread and butter of attackers, their detection is critical for any semblance of security. Unarchive and enter the source distribution directory after downloading the archive.

```
% curl -O "http://www.macosxunleashed.com/downloads/portsentry-2.0b1.tar.gz"
% tar zxf portsentry-2.0b1.tar.gz
% cd portsentry-2.0b1
```

Next, attempt to compile the software by typing `make bsd`. At this point in the current distribution, the compile will fail with errors detecting a nonexistent `ip_ether.h` header file. Assuming the errors are still present, edit `portsentry.h`, looking for these lines:

```
#ifdef BSD
        #include <netinet/in_systm.h>
        #include <netinet/ip_ether.h>
#endif
```

Comment out the line `#include <netinet/ip_ether.h>` by adding the prefix `//` :

```
#ifdef BSD
        #include <netinet/in_systm.h>
//      #include <netinet/ip_ether.h>
#endif
```

Now, try the compile process (`make bsd`) once again:

```
% make bsd
SYSTYPE=bsd
```

```
Making
cc -O -Wall -DBSD44 -o ./portsentry ./portsentry.c \
        ./portsentry_io.c ./portsentry_util.c -lpcap
```

Finally, type `make install` (as root) or `sudo make install` to install the software in `/usr/local/psionic/portsentry2`:

```
# make install
Creating psionic directory /usr/local/psionic
Setting directory permissions
Creating portsentry directory /usr/local/psionic/portsentry2
Setting directory permissions
chmod 700 /usr/local/psionic/portsentry2
Copying files
cp ./portsentry.conf /usr/local/psionic/portsentry2
cp ./portsentry.ignore /usr/local/psionic/portsentry2
cp ./portsentry /usr/local/psionic/portsentry2
Setting permissions
chmod 600 /usr/local/psionic/portsentry2/portsentry.ignore
chmod 600 /usr/local/psionic/portsentry2/portsentry.conf
chmod 700 /usr/local/psionic/portsentry2/portsentry

Edit /usr/local/psionic/portsentry2/portsentry.conf and change
your settings if you haven't already. (route, etc)
```

Configuring PortSentry

To finish the PortSentry setup, you must configure it to recognize your network interface and the ports that you want to monitor for scans. Currently PortSentry is limited to monitoring only specific ports; by the time you read this, it should be capable of monitoring a port range (a feature available in the 1.0 release).

Open the config file, `/usr/local/psionic/portsentry2/portsentry.conf`, now. We'll work our way through the file starting at the top.

First, set the network interface that will be monitored and the IP address of the interface by using the `INTERFACE` and `INTERFACE_ADDRESS` options, respectively. By default, the `INTERFACE` is set to `auto`, which automatically detects your primary interface. If you have multiple active interfaces, you can choose which PortSentry will monitor by specifying them in a comma separated list, such as `en0, en1`. The `INTERFACE_ADDRESS` should be set to the IP address of your active network interface:

```
###########################
# Interface Configurations#
###########################
```

```
# You can set the interface to monitor with this option. Examples include
# "eth0", "ep0", etc. You do not need to put in the dev directory path.
# If you leave this as "auto" PortSentry will attempt to monitor the
# primary interface automatically. Most people should leave this alone
# unless you have a multi-homed system (firewall, etc.) and want to monitor
# a particular interface only.
INTERFACE="auto"

# This MUST BE SET to the address of the interface being monitored on
# your system. It is NOT determined automatically in this version of
# PortSentry.
INTERFACE_ADDRESS="10.0.1.101"
```

Next, provide a list of ports to monitor with the TCP_PORTS and UDP_PORTS directives. In the current software, there is a low limit on the number of ports that the Mac OS X libpcap packet filter can handle, so you'll probably need to remove some of the monitored ports from the default values included in the file.

```
#######################
# Port Configurations #
#######################
#
#
# Some example port configs for stealth modes
#
# We like to always keep some ports at the "low" end of the spectrum.
# This will detect a sequential port sweep really quickly and usually
# these ports are not in use (i.e. tcpmux port 1)
#
# Use these if you just want to be aware (default):
TCP_PORTS="1,11,15,79,111,119,143,515,540,635,666,1080,
           1524,2000,6667,12345,12346"
UDP_PORTS="1,7,9,69,161,162,513,635,2049,27444"
```

Although the port list is arbitrary, the monitor is most effective if the ports are those of commonly exploited services, or ports left open by such things as Trojan horses. They should *not* overlap any services that are running and actively serving information on your computer (such as port 80 if you're running a Web server).

Next, if desired, you can change the location of the ignore, history, and blocked files. These three files are used by PortSentry to determine what hosts should never be blocked, where a history (log) of portscans should be stored, and finally, where a list of the currently blocked hosts should be stored. By default, these files are stored in

/usr/local/psionic/portsentry2/portsentry.ignore, /usr/local/psionic/portsentry2/portsentry.history, and /usr/local/psionic/portsentry2/portsentry.blocked, respectively.

```
######################
# Configuration Files#
######################
#
# Hosts to ignore
IGNORE_FILE="/usr/local/psionic/portsentry2/portsentry.ignore"
# Hosts that have been denied (running history)
HISTORY_FILE="/usr/local/psionic/portsentry2/portsentry.history"
# Hosts that have been denied this session only (temporary until next restart)
BLOCKED_FILE="/usr/local/psionic/portsentry2/portsentry.blocked"
```

PortSentry, like other software, such as Apache, won't log hostnames for attacking machines—just IP addresses. This is standard practice because name resolution can drastically slow things down, potentially resulting in a DoS attack on PortSentry itself. If you want to enable name resolution, change RESOLVE_HOST="0" to RESOLVE_HOST="1".

```
##############################
# Misc. Configuration Options#
##############################
#
# DNS Name resolution - Setting this to "1" will turn on DNS lookups
# for attacking hosts. Setting it to "0" (or any other value) will shut
# it off. Turning on this value can slow down PortSentry if a lot of attacks
# are coming in concurrently while it waits for the DNS resolution to return.
# This option can can also alert an attacker to PortSentry's presence if they
# see DNS queries come to a nameserver they control after they initiate an
# attack. The default is to keep this off.
RESOLVE_HOST = "0"
```

The most powerful aspect of an intrusion detection system is the ability to react to attacks rather than simply log them. PortSentry can react to scans by logging, blocking them with TCP Wrappers, running an arbitrary command, or using the Mac OS X firewall to stop the attacking traffic. Firewall rules are more strict than TCP Wrappers; they are capable of blocking all traffic from a remote system and don't require the server process to execute through xinetd/inetd, nor do they support TCP Wrappers.

When processing an attack, three variables are made available for passing to external commands:

- `$TARGET$`. The address of the computer that is attacking.
- `$PORT$`. The port that triggered the attack response.
- `$MODE$`. The type (UDP or TCP) of scan.

The first step in setting up your defense is choosing how PortSentry will respond to TCP and UDP scans, which you do by setting `BLOCK_UDP` or `BLOCK_TCP` to a value between 0 and 2. You can choose to simply log the scans (0), block them (1), or run an external command of your choice (2). For our purposes, we'll be blocking hosts that perform scans.

```
##################
# Ignore Options #
##################
# These options allow you to enable automatic response
# options for UDP/TCP. This is useful if you just want
# warnings for connections, but don't want to react for
# a particular protocol (i.e. you want to block TCP, but
# not UDP). To prevent a possible Denial of service attack
# against stealth scan detection for TCP, you may
# want to disable blocking, but leave the warning enabled.
# We personally would wait for this to become a problem before
# doing though as most attackers really + command
# in case of a scan to have a pager script or such execute
# but not drop the route. This may be useful for some admins
# who want to block TCP, but only want pager/e-mail warnings
# on UDP, etc.#
#
# 0 = Do not block UDP/TCP scans.
# 1 = Block UDP/TCP scans.
# 2 = Run external command only (KILL_RUN_CMD)

BLOCK_UDP="1"
BLOCK_TCP="1"
```

Next, set the `KILL_ROUTE` variable to the `ipfw` command to execute upon an attack. There are a few dozen preset `KILL_ROUTE` options already entered in the file. Be sure to use the one for FreeBSD: `/sbin/ipfw add 1 deny all from $TARGET$/32 to any`. This will force all traffic from the remote host to be blocked.

NOTE

If you'd like to be a bit more lenient on the attacker, you can, instead, choose to block only traffic to the port that triggered the attack. To do this, change the `KILL_ROUTE` to `/sbin/ipfw add 1 deny $MODE$ from $TARGET$/32 to any $PORT$`.

```
###################
# Dropping Routes:#
###################
# This command is used to drop the route or add the host into
# a local filter table.
#
# The gateway (XXX.XXX.XXX.XXX) should ideally be a dead host on
# the *local* subnet. On some hosts you can also point this at
# localhost (127.0.0.1) and get the same effect. NOTE THAT
# XXX.XXX.XXX.XXX WILL *NOT* WORK. YOU NEED TO CHANGE IT!!
#
# ALL KILL ROUTE OPTIONS ARE COMMENTED OUT INITIALLY. Make sure you
# uncomment the correct line for your OS. If your OS is not listed
# here and you have a route drop command that works then please
# mail it to us so we can include it. ONLY ONE KILL_ROUTE OPTION
# CAN BE USED AT A TIME SO DON'T UNCOMMENT MULTIPLE LINES.
#
# NOTE: The route commands are the least optimal way of blocking
# and do not provide complete protection against UDP attacks and
# will still generate alarms for both UDP and stealth scans. We
# always recommend you use a packet filter because they are made
# for this purpose.
#

# For those of you running FreeBSD (and compatible systems) you can
# use their built-in firewalling as well.
#
KILL_ROUTE="/sbin/ipfw add 1 deny all from $TARGET$/32 to any"
```

Next, if you want to add the blocked hosts to your TCP Wrappers file, configure the `KILL_HOSTS_DENY` line with what should be added to the `/etc/hosts.deny` TCP Wrapper file. The default value should be fine and will result in the line `ALL:` *`<ip address>`* being added to the wrapper file to deny access to all services.

```
###############
# TCP Wrappers#
###############
# This text will be dropped into the hosts.deny file for wrappers
# to use. There are two formats for TCP wrappers:
#
# Format One: Old Style - The default when extended host processing
# options are not enabled.
#
KILL_HOSTS_DENY="ALL: $TARGET$"
```

We're close to wrapping things up! If you choose to run an arbitrary command in response to a scan (to send an email or perform some other action), you can set that command by using the `KILL_RUN_CMD` option, and choose whether it should run before it is blocked by the firewall or after by setting `KILL_RUN_CMD_FIRST` to 1 or 0, respectively.

```
###################
# External Command#
###################
# This is a command that is run when a host connects, it can be whatever
# you want it to be (pager, etc.). This command is executed before the
# route is dropped or after depending on the KILL_RUN_CMD_FIRST option below#
#
# WE NEVER RECOMMEND YOU PUT IN RETALIATORY ACTIONS AGAINST THE HOST SCANNING
# YOU!
#
# TCP/IP is an *unauthenticated protocol* and people can make scans appear out
# of thin air. Do you really want to counter-attack an innocent third party?
# That could happen if you aren't careful.
#
# The KILL_RUN_CMD_FIRST value should be set to "1" to force the command
# to run *before* the blocking occurs and should be set to "0" to make the
# command run *after* the blocking has occurred.
#
#KILL_RUN_CMD_FIRST = "0"
#
#
#KILL_RUN_CMD="/some/path/here/script $TARGET$ $PORT$ $MODE$"
```

Finally, choose the number of connects that constitute a "connect." A value of 0, the default, reacts immediately, even if a single port is scanned. If you find that you're blocking too many hosts, you may wish to raise this value.

```
#####################
# Scan trigger value#
#####################
# Enter in the number of port connects you will allow before an
# alarm is given. The default is 0 which will react immediately.
# A value of 1 or 2 will reduce false alarms. Anything higher is
# probably not necessary. This value must always be specified, but
# generally can be left at 0.
#
SCAN_TRIGGER="0"
```

Setting Up the PortSentry Ignored Hosts

Before starting PortSentry, you should edit the `/usr/local/psionic/portsentry2/portsentry.ignore` file to include the IP addresses and subnets that should *never* trigger an attack. Be sure to leave the default values in the example file because they will prevent your machine from detecting an attack from itself.

Addresses should be added to the file in the form `<IP address>/<mask>`. For example, a Class C subnet of 192.168.1.xxx could be entered as `192.168.1.0/24`. Individual hosts can simply be entered as the IP address with no mask; a 32-bit subnet mask will be assumed.

Starting and Testing PortSentry

To start PostSentry, simply start the daemon from the command line as root:

```
# /usr/local/psionic/portsentry2/portsentry
```

You should be able to check `/var/log/system.log` and verify that the PortSentry process has indeed started:

```
Nov  7 01:33:56 portsentry[2408]: Monitoring interface en1 and
➥address: 10.0.1.101
Nov  7 01:33:56 portsentry[2408]: Initializing PortSentry BPF filters.
Nov  7 01:33:56 portsentry[2408]: Monitoring TCP ports:
➥1,11,15,79,111,119,143,515,540,635,666,1080,1524,2000,6667,12345,12346
Nov  7 01:33:56 portsentry[2408]: Monitoring UDP ports:
➥ 1,7,9,69,161,162,513,635,2049,27444
Nov  7 01:33:56 portsentry[2408]: PortSentry is initialized and monitoring.
```

To verify that PortSentry is working, log into another machine and use a portscanner (or simply attempt to Telnet into a monitored port) to "attack" the protected computer. Monitor your `/var/log/system.log` file to verify that the scan is detected and blocked:

```
Nov  7 01:38:38 portsentry[951]: attackalert: TCP SYN scan from
➥ host 10.0.1.250/10.0.1.250 to TCP port: 1 from TCP port: 50427
Nov  7 01:38:38 portsentry[951]: attackalert:
➥  Host 10.0.1.250 has been blocked via wrappers with string: "ALL: 10.0.1.250"
```

In this example, a scan is initiated from the host 10.0.1.250 to the PortSentry monitored machine. The scan is detected as soon as it hits port 1, is blocked, and subsequent scans are blocked. Remember that a history of scans is stored in `/usr/local/psionic/portsentry2/portsentry.history`, while the details are logged with `syslog`. For more information on `ipfw` and how to manually add or remove blocks, see Chapter 17, "Blocking Network Access."

Your computer is now running an "entry-level" intrusion detection system, capable of recognizing and transparently dealing with potential attackers scanning your system.

To start PortSentry at boot-time, create a new folder named `Portsentry` in `/Library/StartupItems`. Add two files: `StartupParameters.plist` and `Portsentry` into the folder `StartupParameters.plist`:

```
{
  Description     = "Portsentry Portscan Detection";
  Provides        = ("PSDetection");
  Requires        = ("Resolver");
  OrderPreference = "Last";
  Messages =
  {
    start = "Starting Portsentry";
  };
}
```

and `Portsentry`:

```
#!/bin/sh
##
# Start Portsentry
##

. /etc/rc.common

if [ "${PORTSENTRY:=-NO-}" = "-YES-" ]; then
    ConsoleMessage "Starting Portsentry Portscan Detection"

   cd /usr/local/psionic/portsentry2
   ./portsentry &
fi
```

Finally, add the line `PORTSENTRY=-YES-` to `/etc/hostconfig` to turn the automatic startup on.

Snort

Although PortSentry can provide a good tip-off that something "inappropriate" is about to happen to your computer, it cannot detect targeted attacks to services that are actually open and running on your system, nor can it identify attempted attacks that aren't preceded by a portscan. For simple setups that just want to keep tabs on who might be tweaking the system, PortSentry is a useful tool. Administrators who are responsible for the health of an entire network, however, should consider installing Snort.

Snort is a modular IDS that takes detection far beyond portscan detection and provides attack recognition by analyzing incoming packet payloads in real time. Most attacks are based on automated scripts that repeatedly issue the same exploit commands, or have very obvious "signatures" that can be used for detection. An attempted Nimda attack on a Windows IIS system (`http://www.cert.org/advisories/CA-2001-26.html`), for example, will show up in your Apache log files as follows:

```
65.24.217.121 - - [17/Nov/2001:15:07:02 -0500]
"GET /scripts/root.exe?/c+dir HTTP/1.0" 404 274
65.24.217.121 - - [17/Nov/2001:15:07:03 -0500]
"GET /MSADC/root.exe?/c+dir HTTP/1.0" 404 272
65.24.217.121 - - [17/Nov/2001:15:07:03 -0500]
"GET /c/winnt/system32/cmd.exe?/c+dir HTTP/1.0" 404 282
65.24.217.121 - - [17/Nov/2001:15:07:03 -0500]
"GET /d/winnt/system32/cmd.exe?/c+dir HTTP/1.0" 404 282
65.24.217.121 - - [17/Nov/2001:15:07:03 -0500]
"GET /scripts/..%255c../winnt/system32/cmd.exe?/c+dir HTTP/1.0" 404 296
65.24.217.121 - - [17/Nov/2001:15:07:03 -0500]
"GET /_vti_bin/..%255c../..%255c../..%255c../winnt/system32/
cmd.exe?/c+dir HTTP/1.0" 404 313
65.24.217.121 - - [17/Nov/2001:15:07:04 -0500]
"GET /_mem_bin/..%255c../..%255c../..%255c../winnt/system32/
cmd.exe?/c+dir HTTP/1.0" 404 313
...
```

Each attack is identical, and, given access to the actual contents of network traffic, it is easily recognizable. Snort makes it possible to recognize such exploits by writing rules that compare incoming packets to known attacks, and, if a match is detected, react appropriately. To sweeten the deal, Snort comes with rules for matching hundreds of known attacks out of the box.

SNORT USAGE AND DEPLOYMENT

At this point, you might be wondering, what does Nimda have to do with my Mac OS X system? Nothing: It won't harm your Apache installation other than force it to process unnecessary requests. Snort, however, is often deployed in conjunction with a firewall system to protect all computers on a network, not just a single platform. Someone needs to protect Windows users from themselves, don't they?

When Snort is used in the capacity of "network protector," it is usually placed either topologically in the same "space" as a firewall or on a firewall box itself. Today's computer networks, by and large, are switched networks. Rather than broadcasting traffic to all nodes on a network, a switch maintains an internal per-port ARP cache, and can match individual packets to the correct destination ports. The result is that each switch port "sees" only traffic that is destined for the devices connected to it. To be effective, the Snort monitor must be placed at the level of the network feed—before the first switch—where it can monitor all traffic to and from the network. From this vantage point, Snort can detect attacks destined for any machine on the local network, and respond by remotely triggering firewall blocks with SSH (Chapter 14, "Remote Access: Secure Shell, VNC, Timbuktu, Apple Remote Desktop"), or alerting the network administrator.

The easiest way to modify an existing network to include a Snort monitor is to take the incoming feed (usually from a router) to a hub. (Hubs, unlike switches, replicate network packets on each port.) One port on the hub can then, in turn, be used to feed the switch arrays for the rest of the network, while another port can be used with the Snort monitor, as shown in Figure 18.1.

The "best possible" scenario places a second IDS inside the firewall so that a comparison can be made between the "inside" and "outside" alerts to verify that the firewall is operating correctly.

Installing Snort

To compile and install Snort on Mac OS X, download the latest source (1.9.0 at the time of this writing) from `http://www.snort.org/`, unarchive, and enter the distribution directory.

```
% curl -O http://www.snort.org/dl/snort-1.9.0.tar.gz
% tar zxf snort-1.9.0.tar.gz
% cd snort-1.9.0
```

Next, use `configure` to prepare the source for compilation. Be sure to set the `--mandir` flag to store the Snort man pages in the standard Mac OS X location. This example also includes MySQL support with the `--with-mysql` flag. This will enable Snort to log alerts to a MySQL database, which can be used for reporting and traffic analysis. If you do not have MySQL on your system, you can download a precompiled version from `http://www.aaronfaby.com/mysql.php` or compile the source code from `http://www.mysql.com/`. Snort is fully functional without MySQL support, but a number of reporting packages require its presence.

```
% ./configure --mandir=/usr/share/man --with-mysql
creating cache ./config.cache
checking for a BSD compatible install... /usr/bin/install -c
checking whether build environment is sane... yes
checking whether make sets ${MAKE}... yes
checking for working aclocal... found
```

```
checking for working autoconf... found
checking for working automake... found
...
creating templates/Makefile
creating src/win32/Makefile
creating config.h
```

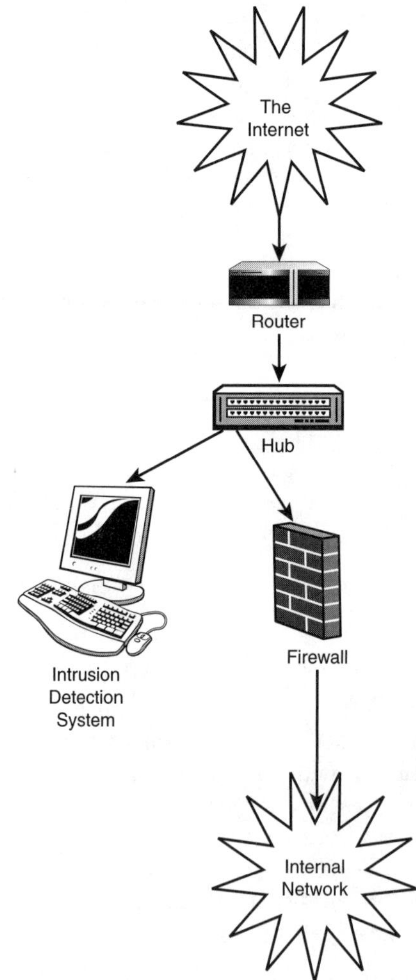

FIGURE 18.1 A network IDS should be placed so that it can monitor all network traffic.

After configure has completed, compile the source with make:

```
% make
make  all-recursive
Making all in src
Making all in win32
make[3]: Nothing to be done for 'all'.
Making all in output-plugins
gcc -DHAVE_CONFIG_H -I. -I. -I../.. -I../.. -I../../src -I/sw/include
-I../../src/output-plugins -I../../src/detection-plugins
-I../../src/preprocessors  -I/usr/local/include/mysql
-DENABLE_MYSQL  -g -O2 -Wall -c spo_SnmpTrap.c
```

Finally, install the software with make install (as root, or using make install prefixed with sudo):

```
# make install
/bin/sh ./mkinstalldirs /usr/share/man/man8
 /usr/bin/install -c -m 644 ./snort.8 /usr/share/man/man8/snort.8
...
```

You need to complete two more steps by hand before Snort can be used: copying the rule files to a common location and creating a directory for logging. From within the Snort distribution, issue the following commands (remember, root access is assumed):

```
# mkdir -p /usr/local/etc/snort/rules
# cp rules/* /usr/local/etc/snort/rules
# cp etc/* /usr/local/etc/snort
# chmod -R 600 /usr/local/etc/snort
# mkdir /var/log/snort
```

Before starting Snort for the first time, open /usr/local/etc/snort/snort.conf. You need to change the RULE_PATH to reflect the location of the rule files in relation to the snort.conf file. Search for the following line:

```
var RULE_PATH ../rules
```

Change it to

```
var RULE_PATH rules
```

Running Snort

After getting the basic configuration in place, you can start Snort for the first time. You'll need to make tweaks later for your IDS to be truly effective, but for now you can test to verify that the installation is correct, and even detect an attack or two.

Start Snort by typing `/usr/local/bin/snort -c /usr/local/etc/snort/snort.conf`. If everything has gone according to plan, you should see something like this:

```
# /usr/local/bin/snort -c/usr/local/etc/snort/snort.conf
Initializing Output Plugins!
Log directory = /var/log/snort

Initializing Network Interface en1

        --== Initializing Snort ==--
Decoding Ethernet on interface en1
Initializing Preprocessors!
Initializing Plug-ins!
Parsing Rules file /etc/snort/snort.conf

+++++++++++++++++++++++++++++++++++++++++++++++++++
Initializing rule chains...
No arguments to frag2 directive, setting defaults to:
    Fragment timeout: 60 seconds
    Fragment memory cap: 4194304 bytes
    Fragment min_ttl:   0
    Fragment ttl_limit: 5
    Fragment Problems: 0
Stream4 config:
    Stateful inspection: ACTIVE
    Session statistics: INACTIVE
    Session timeout: 30 seconds
    Session memory cap: 8388608 bytes
    State alerts: INACTIVE
    Evasion alerts: INACTIVE
    Scan alerts: ACTIVE
    Log Flushed Streams: INACTIVE
    MinTTL: 1
    TTL Limit: 5
    Async Link: 0
No arguments to stream4_reassemble, setting defaults:
     Reassemble client: ACTIVE
     Reassemble server: INACTIVE
```

```
     Reassemble ports: 21 23 25 53 80 143 110 111 513
     Reassembly alerts: ACTIVE
     Reassembly method: FAVOR_OLD
http_decode arguments:
    Unicode decoding
    IIS alternate Unicode decoding
    IIS double encoding vuln
    Flip backslash to slash
    Include additional whitespace separators
    Ports to decode http on: 80
rpc_decode arguments:
    Ports to decode RPC on: 111 32771
telnet_decode arguments:
    Ports to decode telnet on: 21 23 25 119
Conversation Config:
   KeepStats: 0
   Conv Count: 32000
   Timeout   : 60
   Alert Odd?: 0
   Allowed IP Protocols:  All

Portscan2 config:
    log: /var/log/snort/scan.log
    scanners_max: 3200
    targets_max: 5000
    target_limit: 5
    port_limit: 20
    timeout: 60
1273 Snort rules read...
1273 Option Chains linked into 133 Chain Headers
0 Dynamic rules
+++++++++++++++++++++++++++++++++++++++++++++++++++

Rule application order: ->activation->dynamic->alert->pass->log

        --== Initialization Complete ==--

-*> Snort! <*-
Version 1.9.0 (Build 209)
By Martin Roesch (roesch@sourcefire.com, www.snort.org)
```

Checking Snort Logs

To verify that Snort is truly functioning, try running a portscan or other “attack” from another machine. For example, try an `nmap` stealth scan against Snort: `nmap -sS` *`<your Snort machine>`*.

After `nmap` completes its run, you can check the Snort logs to see exactly what has been detected. By default, Snort stores its log files in `/var/log/snort`. Here you'll find several log files:

- `alert`. Security alerts generated by Snort. All logged intrusion attempts are stored here along with the information detailing the issue. For example, an `nmap` stealth scan is detected and logged as follows:

```
[**] [1:469:1] ICMP PING NMAP [**]
[Classification: Attempted Information Leak] [Priority: 2]
11/16-00:38:32.765794 10.0.1.1 -> 10.0.1.101
ICMP TTL:58 TOS:0x0 ID:41250 IpLen:20 DgmLen:28
Type:8  Code:0  ID:11693   Seq:0  ECHO
[Xref => arachnids 162]
[**] [117:1:1] (spp_portscan2)
Portscan detected from 10.0.1.1: 1 targets 21 ports in 1 seconds [**]
11/16-00:38:33.515666 10.0.1.1:61880 -> 10.0.1.101:1112
TCP TTL:59 TOS:0x0 ID:3927 IpLen:20 DgmLen:40
******S* Seq: 0x374170C6  Ack: 0x0  Win: 0x1000  TcpLen: 20
```

- `scan.log`. A detailed log of portscans, including the source and destination ports.

```
11/16-00:38:33.515666  TCP src: 10.0.1.1 dst: 10.0.1.101
   sport: 61880 dport: 111
   tgts: 1 ports: 21 flags: ******S* event_id: 0
11/16-00:38:33.525192  TCP src: 10.0.1.1 dst: 10.0.1.101
   sport: 61880 dport: 933
   tgts: 1 ports: 22 flags: ******S* event_id: 4
11/16-00:38:33.557660  TCP src: 10.0.1.1 dst: 10.0.1.101
   sport: 61880 dport: 700
   tgts: 1 ports: 23 flags: ******S* event_id: 4
11/16-00:38:33.567283  TCP src: 10.0.1.1 dst: 10.0.1.101
   sport: 61880 dport: 679
   tgts: 1 ports: 24 flags: ******S* event_id: 4
11/16-00:38:33.599891  TCP src: 10.0.1.1 dst: 10.0.1.101
   sport: 61880 dport: 580
   tgts: 1 ports: 25 flags: ******S* event_id: 4
```

- *<trigger ip>*. Directories are created for machines triggering attacks. For each triggered alert a separate log file is generated in the directory containing the attack details.

Snort generates two types of information: alerts and logs. An alert is a notification of a triggering event, whereas a log is the capture of the data that generated the alert.

Interpreting Snort alerts/logs does not require an in-depth knowledge of the TCP/IP suite, but can be overwhelming to the first-time user. Information includes the alert type, how it has been classified (severity) by the rule's authors, and a description of the packet that matched the rule. In many cases, a cross-reference is given to an online resource to look up further information about the attack type. In the portscan example shown previously, the cross-reference is to `archNIDS 162`. Table 18.1 contains the online references that you'll see in the output.

TABLE 18.1 Online Alert References

Reference System	URL
Bugtraq	`http://www.securityfocus.com/bid/`*<reference>*
CVE	`http://cve.mitre.org/cgi-bin/cvename.cgi?name=`*<reference>*
`arachNIDS`	`http://www.whitehats.com/info/IDS`*<reference>*
McAfee	`http://vil.nai.com/vil/dispVirus.asp?virus_k=`*<reference>*
<url>	`http://`*<url>*

For example, to look up the referenced `arachNIDS 162` alert, one would use `http://www.whitehats.com/info/IDS162`, which tells us:

> This event indicates that a ping request was sent to your network. This is usually used as a test to check whether a host is responsive. However, it can be misused to map your network. Nmap 2.36BETA (or earlier) versions probably generated this particular ping.

To better understand the additional information provided in the alerts, read the Snort rule design guide (`http://www.snort.org/docs/writing_rules/chap2.html#tth_sEc2.3`). It describes the packet header fields (TTL, TOS, and so on) that can be used for comparison against network traffic—the same fields you'll see logged with the alerts.

A number of other logging options are available—such as logging to `syslog` or MySQL, or disabling logging altogether—we'll get to those shortly.

Snort Startup Options

The Snort CLI syntax is simply `snort` *<options> <BPF Filter>* (See `tcpdump` in Chapter 7, "Eavesdropping and Snooping for Information: Sniffers and Scanners," for more information on BPF filters). When Snort is started without any command-line switches (such as -c/usr/local/etc/snort/snort.conf), it attempts to read its configuration from the file ~/.snortrc from your home directory. For our purposes, using -c to choose a systemwide config file works best. In addition to this switch, a number of additional startup options can, in some cases, alter Snort's fundamental operation. Table 18.2 shows many of the common Snort startup flags and their purpose.

TABLE 18.2 Snort Startup Options

Command-Line Switch	Purpose
-c <*Snort config*>	Set the configuration file Snort will use.
-v	Run as a network packet sniffer, outputting packet headers to STDOUT.
-d	Output application data (packet contents).
-e	Output data link headers.
-w	Output management and control frames.
-u <*user*>	Set the user ID under which Snort runs.
-g <*group*>	Set the group ID under which Snort will run.
-s	Log alerts to the syslog daemon (/var/log/system.log on your Mac OS X machine). This is overridden by the settings in the config file.
-v	Verbose output.
-D	Run as a background daemon. This is the mode you'll be using if you want to use Snort as an IDS for your network.
-b	Log packets in tcpdump mode. See Chapter 7 for more information on tcpdump.
-hn <*network/mask*>	Identify your local network to Snort.
-A [fast|full|console|none]	Set the alert logging mode. The fast mode logs a single line to the alert file for each alert, whereas full (the default) logs the full packet headers, console outputs the alerts to /dev/console, and none logs nothing.
-i <*interface*>	Listen on the named network interface.

For the example IDS, all that's needed to start Snort is /usr/local/bin/snort -D -c /usr/local/etc/snort/snort.conf. In some cases, running in fast log mode (-A fast) may be necessary if Snort can't keep up your network traffic. Unfortunately, some Snort reporting software may require the full format to operate correctly.

To start Snort at boot-time, create a new folder named Snort in /Library/StartupItems. Into this folder, add two files, StartupParameters.plist and Snort, with the following contents:

```
StartupParameters.plist:

{
  Description     = "Snort IDS";
  Provides        = ("IDS");
  Requires        = ("Resolver");
  OrderPreference = "None";
  Messages =
  {
    start = "Starting Snort IDS";
  };
}
```

and `Snort`:

```
#!/bin/sh
##
# Start Snort IDS
##

. /etc/rc.common

if [ "${SNORT:=-NO-}" = "-YES-" ]; then
    ConsoleMessage "Starting Snort IDS"

   cd /usr/local/bin
   ./snort -D -c /usr/local/etc/snort/snort.conf
fi
```

Finally, add the line `SNORT=-YES-` to `/etc/hostconfig` to turn the automatic startup on.

Snort Configuration Files

Although it's easy to set up and start using, Snort's true effectiveness comes with time and patience. In it's default setup, Snort detects everything that seems even the slightest bit "shady" on your network. Although it's interesting to watch for a short while, you'll quickly reach the (correct) conclusion that Snort is giving you information overload, and that you're being alerted to thousands of false positives. The reason for this is twofold. First, some perfectly legitimate traffic matches attack signatures. For example, Snort will happily detect and report on attempts to alter files through FrontPage serve extensions, even if the access is legitimate. Secondly, many Snort rules provide informational alerts and are not meant to signal the start of a network attack. There are rules included to alert you to network traffic containing pornography and other "inappropriate" material. These can help you enforce network policies (see Chapter 2, "Thinking Secure: Security Philosophy and Physical Concerns," for details), but in most cases simply get in the way of monitoring for the "real" attackers.

GIMME GUI

If you want to avoid the do-it-yourself approach to Snort, you can download a packaged and GUI-fied version called HenWen from `http://home.attbi.com/~dreamless/henwen.html`.

HenWen provides a precompiled Snort distribution and a point-and-click interface for configuration. HenWen lacks many of the fine-tuning features of running Snort from the command line, but provides value-added features, such as displaying pop-up messages as alerts occur.

snort.conf

The main Snort config file (`/usr/local/etc/snort/snort.conf`) controls the what/where/how of alerts. It is the most complicated of the Snort configuration files, so we'll walk through it step by step. You should use only the options that are appropriate for your network—don't start enabling options just because they're available. Unnecessary comments are removed for brevity.

First, configure the internal variable `HOME_NET` for your local network. This can be used in rules to ignore packets from trusted local computers, decreasing your chances of false positives. Variables are set in the Snort file using the syntax `var <variable name> <value>`. `HOME_NET` can be set to a network and mask (`var HOME_NET <network>/<mask>`, any address `var HOME_NET any`, or automatically to the network local to the interface on which Snort is running on—`var HOME_NET $eth0 ADDRESS`. In this example, it has been set to `10.0.1.0/24`, my internal network.

```
####################################################
# Step #1: Set the network variables:
#
# You must change the following variables to reflect
# your local network. The variable is currently
# set up for an RFC 1918 address space.
#
var HOME_NET 10.0.1.0/24
```

Like the internal network, you can also set up the addresses that constitute the "outside" world with the `EXTERNAL_NET` variable. In general, you can leave this as `any`, or, to exclude your local network machines, use the `!` character to negate the given address. For example, `!10.0.1.0/24` matches anything *except* the addresses on the `10.0.1.0/24` subnet.

```
# Set up the external network addresses as well.
# A good start may be "any"

var EXTERNAL_NET any
```

Use the DNS_SERVERS, SMTP_SERVERS, SQL_SERVERS, TELNET_SERVERS, and AIM_SERVERS variables to differentiate between the different types of servers running on your network. By default, these variables are set to the same value as HOME_NET, meaning that all IPs in your local network are covered. To set them for specific machines, list the machines' IP addresses surrounded by brackets and separated by commas—such as in [10.0.1.5,10.0.1.100]—without *any* spaces.

```
# Configure your server lists.  This allows snort to only look for attacks
# to systems that have a service up.  Why look for HTTP attacks if you are
# not running a web server?  This allows quick filtering based on IP addresses
# These configurations MUST follow the same configuration scheme as defined
# above for $HOME_NET.

# List of DNS servers on your network
var DNS_SERVERS $HOME_NET

# List of SMTP servers on your network
var SMTP_SERVERS $HOME_NET

# List of web servers on your network
var HTTP_SERVERS $HOME_NET

# List of sql servers on your network
var SQL_SERVERS $HOME_NET

# List of telnet servers on your network
var TELNET_SERVERS $HOME_NET

# AIM servers.  AOL has a habit of adding new AIM servers, so instead of
# modifying the signatures when they do, we add them to this list of
# servers.
var AIM_SERVERS [64.12.24.0/24,64.12.25.0/24,64.12.26.14/24,64.12.28.0/24,64.12.
29.0/24,64.12.161.0/24,64.12.163.0/24,205.188.5.0/24,205.188.9.0/24]
```

Set the ports that Snort will monitor for attacks by using the variables HTTP_PORTS, SHELLCODE_PORTS, ORACLE_PORTS, and AIM_SERVERS. Ports can be specified as either a single number or a port range if the upper and lower limits of the range are separated by a :. Individual port lists are *not* allowed, although the ! as a negation operator can be used to choose any port *but* a named value.

```
# Configure your service ports.  This allows snort to look for attacks
# destined to a specific application only on the ports that application
# runs on.  For example, if you run a web server on port 8081, set your
```

```
# HTTP_PORTS variable like this:
#
# var HTTP_PORTS 8081
#
# Port lists must either be continuous [eg 80:8080], or a single port [eg 80].
# We will adding support for a real list of ports in the future.

# Ports you run web servers on
var HTTP_PORTS 80

# Ports you want to look for SHELLCODE on
var SHELLCODE_PORTS !80

# Ports you do oracle attacks on
var ORACLE_PORTS 1521
```

WAIT—WHAT ABOUT SSH PORTS, MY MYSQL SERVERS, AND SO ON?

There are many (*many*) other port list values and server lists that you might feel apply to your network. Unfortunately, these values are just variables; they do not have any effect internally on Snort. It is up to the Snort rules (we're getting there!) to use the variables appropriately when sensing attacks. You can add additional variables—such as `MYSQL_SERVERS`—but you need to create your own rule files to use them. These examples apply to only the included rule files, not every possibility that could exist.

Set the `RULE_PATH` variable to the path of the `rules` directory. For the example installation, `rules` is a directory at the same level as the `snort.conf` file, so you can use a simple relative path (`rules`) as the setting.

```
# Path to your rules files (this can be a relative path)
var RULE_PATH rules
```

Although Snort's primary value comes from its expandable rule base, a number of preprocessor modules and detection plug-ins make up the program and work at a lower level to detect packet modifications, such as IP fragmentation attacks and portscans, and to normalize packet contents for detection by the Snort ruleset. You should not need to change the default values for these settings. The preprocessor documentation is provided in Table 18.3 for your reference. Please refer to `snort.conf` for additional information on their use and logged values.

SNORT

Some of the preprocessor modules are commented out because they are either experimental or perform the same functions as other modules. You do not, for example, want to enable both the `portscan` and `portscan2` modules.

```
####################################################
# Step #2: Configure preprocessors
#
# General configuration for preprocessors is of
# the form
# preprocessor <name_of_processor>: <configuration_options>
```

TABLE 18.3 Snort Modules

Preprocessor	Enabled?	Description
`frag2`	yes	This preprocessor performs IP defragmentation. This plug-in also detects people launching fragmentation attacks (usually DoS) against hosts. No arguments loads the default configuration of the preprocessor, which is a 60-second timeout and a 4MB fragment buffer.
`stream4`	yes	Use in concert with the `-z [all|est]` command-line switch to defeat Stick/Snot attacks against TCP rules. Also performs full TCP stream reassembly, stateful inspection of TCP streams, and so on. Can statefully detect various portscan types, fingerprinting, ECN, and so on.
`http_decode`	yes	`http_decode` normalizes HTTP requests from remote machines by converting any `%XX` character substitutions to their ASCII equivalents. This is very useful for doing things such as defeating hostile attackers trying to stealth themselves from IDSs by mixing these substitutions in with the request. Specify the port numbers you want it to analyze as arguments.
`rpc_decode`	yes	RPC may be sent in alternate encodings in addition to the usual 4-byte encoding that is used by default. This preprocessor normalizes RPC traffic in much the same way as the `http_decode` preprocessor. This plug-in takes the ports numbers on which RPC services are running as arguments.
`bo`	yes	Detects Back Orifice traffic on the network. This preprocessor uses the Back Orifice "encryption" algorithm to search for traffic conforming to the Back Orifice protocol (not BO2K). This preprocessor can take two arguments. The first is `-nobrute`, which turns off the plug-in's brute forcing routine (brute forces the key space of the protocol to find BO traffic). The second argument that can be passed to the routine is a number to use as the default key to decrypt the traffic. The default value is 31337 (just like BO). Be aware that turning on the brute forcing option runs the risk of impacting the overall performance of Snort, so you've been warned...
`telnet_decode`	yes	This preprocessor "normalizes" Telnet negotiation strings from Telnet and FTP traffic. It works in much the same way as the `http_decode` preprocessor, searching for traffic that breaks up the normal data stream of a protocol and replacing it with a normalized representation of that traffic so that the "content" pattern-matching keyword can work without requiring modifications. This preprocessor requires no arguments.

TABLE 18.3 Continued

Preprocessor	Enabled?	Description
portscan	no	portscan preprocessor by Patrick Mullen <p_mullen@linuxrc.net>. This preprocessor detects UDP packets or TCP SYN packets going to four different ports in less than three seconds. "Stealth" TCP packets are always detected, regardless of these settings.
portscan-ignorehosts	no	Use portscan-ignorehosts to ignore TCP, SYN, and UDP "scans" from specific networks or hosts to reduce false alerts. It is typical to see many false alerts from DNS servers, so you may want to add your DNS servers here. You can add multiple hosts/networks in a whitespace-delimited list.
arpspoof	no	Experimental ARP detection code from Jeff Nathan, detects ARP attacks, unicast ARP requests, and specific ARP mapping monitoring. To make use of this preprocessor you must specify the IP and hardware address of hosts on the same layer 2 segment as you. Specify one host IP MAC combo per line. Also takes a -unicast option to turn on unicast ARP request detection.
asn1_decode	yes	This is an experimental preprocessor. This preprocessor detects abuses of the ASN.1 protocol on which higher-level protocols (such as SSL, SNMP, x.509, and so on) rely.
fnord	no	This is an experimental preprocessor. This preprocessor watches traffic for polymorphic NOP-type sleds to defeat tools such as ADMutate.
conversation	yes	This preprocessor tracks conversations for TCP, UDP, and ICMP traffic. It is a prerequisite for running portscan2.
portscan2	yes	Detect portscans in a new and exciting way.
perfmonitor	no	Provides performance stats for Snort.

Next, you can choose how Snort logs alerts. By default, it uses the `/var/log/snort` directory that you've already seen. However, there are a few other options that you might want to use instead.

The first option is to output to a `syslog` daemon. `Syslog` handles almost all the critical logging for your computer. (See Chapter 19 for more information on configuring `syslog`). Use the `output alert_syslog` *`<syslog facilities>`* to enable syslog logging:

```
###################################################################
# Step #3: Configure output plugins
#
# Uncomment and configure the output plugins you decide to use.
# General configuration for output plugins is of the form:
#
# output <name_of_plugin>: <configuration_options>
#
```

```
# alert_syslog: log alerts to syslog
# ----------------------------------
# Use one or more syslog facilities as arguments
#
# output alert_syslog: LOG_AUTH LOG_ALERT
```

Another option is to dump logged packets in `tcpdump`'s binary format by using the directive `output log_tcpdump: <log file name>`. For more information on `tcpdump`, see Chapter 7.

```
# log_tcpdump: log packets in binary tcpdump format
# -------------------------------------------------
# The only argument is the output file name.
#
# output log_tcpdump: tcpdump.log
```

One of the more interesting and useful log methods is logging to a database server, such as MySQL. To use a database output option, you must have built support into Snort when it was being compiled. (The sample compilation of Snort provided in this chapter included MySQL support.) Information can be output to the database by the Snort `alert` or `log` facilities. As mentioned earlier, an alert is the notification of a Snort event, whereas a log is a logging of the packet that generated the event. This is a particularly annoying and confusing area of Snort configuration because what one would expect isn't necessarily reality. The most important thing to remember is that not all alerts are subsequently logged. To capture all data, use the `alert` facility with MySQL. Using `log` will work, but does not capture events such as portscans, which do not use the Snort log facility.

Before you can use Snort with MySQL, you must first configure a MySQL database to hold the information. Assuming you have a MySQL installation, create a new empty database (such as `snortdb`) and a username and password that can access that database.

Next, load the database schema contained in the `contrib/create_mysql` file in the Snort source distribution with the syntax: `mysql -u<username> -p<password> -h <host with MySQL database server> <snort database name> < <path to create_mysql>`. You do not need to include the `-h <host..>` switch unless your MySQL server is on another machine:

```
$ mysql -ujray -pnopasshere snortdb < /Users/jray/snort/contrib/create_mysql
```

Finally, use `output database: alert, mysql, user=<mysql username> password=<mysql password> dbname=<snort database> host=<mysql hostname>` to turn on logging in Snort:

```
# database: log to a variety of databases
# ---------------------------------------
```

```
# See the README.database file for more information about configuring
# and using this plugin.
#
output database: alert, mysql, user=jray password=nopasshere dbname=snortdb
host=localhost
```

The full documentation on the Snort database scheme can be found at `http://www.andrew.cmu.edu/~rdanyliw/snort/snortdb/snortdb.html`.

Next, the `snort.conf` file includes two additional configuration files that define how attacks are classified and how references are provided to the different attack types. The contents of these files, which we'll see shortly, (`/usr/local/etc/snort/classification.config` and `/usr/local/etc/snort/reference.config`) could be included in the main configuration file, but are left separate for ease of management.

```
#
# Include classification & priority settings
#
include classification.config
#
# Include reference systems
#
include reference.config
```

Finally, Snort includes the rule files necessary to fingerprint the hundreds of possible attacks against your system. Each rule file is included from `/etc/snort/rules` and provides protection against specific types of attacks (for example, `ftp.rules` protects against FTP attacks, and so on). A number of rule files are commented out, such as `policy.rules` and `virus.rules`, that will need to be updated for your particular network setting; otherwise you may end up logging information that is of no value to your particular situation. We'll take a look at the anatomy of a rule file directly.

```
###################################################################
# Step #4: Customize your rule set
#
# Up to date snort rules are available at http://www.snort.org
#
# The snort web site has documentation about how to write your own
# custom snort rules.
#
# The rules included with this distribution generate alerts based on
# on suspicious activity. Depending on your network environment, your
# security policies, and what you consider to be suspicious, some of
# these rules may either generate false positives or may be detecting
```

```
# activity you consider to be acceptable; therefore, you are
# encouraged to comment out rules that are not applicable in your
# environment.
#
# Note that using all of the rules at the same time may lead to
# serious packet loss on slower machines. YMMV, use with caution,
# standard disclaimers apply. :)
#
# The following individuals contributed many of rules in this
# distribution.
#
# Credits:
#   Ron Gula <rgula@securitywizards.com> of Network Security Wizards
#   Max Vision <vision@whitehats.com>
#   Martin Markgraf <martin@mail.du.gtn.com>
#   Fyodor Yarochkin <fygrave@tigerteam.net>
#   Nick Rogness <nick@rapidnet.com>
#   Jim Forster <jforster@rapidnet.com>
#   Scott McIntyre <scott@whoi.edu>
#   Tom Vandepoel <Tom.Vandepoel@ubizen.com>
#   Brian Caswell <bmc@snort.org>
#   Zeno <admin@cgisecurity.com>
#   Ryan Russell <ryan@securityfocus.com>
#
#==========================================
# Include all relevant rulesets here
#
# shellcode, policy, info, backdoor, and virus rulesets are
# disabled by default.  These require tuning and maintance.
# Please read the included specific file for more information.
#==========================================

include $RULE_PATH/bad-traffic.rules
include $RULE_PATH/exploit.rules
include $RULE_PATH/scan.rules
include $RULE_PATH/finger.rules
include $RULE_PATH/ftp.rules
include $RULE_PATH/telnet.rules
include $RULE_PATH/rpc.rules
include $RULE_PATH/rservices.rules
include $RULE_PATH/dos.rules
include $RULE_PATH/ddos.rules
```

```
include $RULE_PATH/dns.rules
include $RULE_PATH/tftp.rules

include $RULE_PATH/web-cgi.rules
include $RULE_PATH/web-coldfusion.rules
include $RULE_PATH/web-iis.rules
include $RULE_PATH/web-frontpage.rules
include $RULE_PATH/web-misc.rules
include $RULE_PATH/web-client.rules
include $RULE_PATH/web-php.rules

include $RULE_PATH/sql.rules
include $RULE_PATH/x11.rules
include $RULE_PATH/icmp.rules
include $RULE_PATH/netbios.rules
include $RULE_PATH/misc.rules
include $RULE_PATH/attack-responses.rules
include $RULE_PATH/oracle.rules
include $RULE_PATH/mysql.rules
include $RULE_PATH/snmp.rules

include $RULE_PATH/smtp.rules
include $RULE_PATH/imap.rules
include $RULE_PATH/pop3.rules

include $RULE_PATH/nntp.rules
include $RULE_PATH/other-ids.rules
# include $RULE_PATH/web-attacks.rules
# include $RULE_PATH/backdoor.rules
# include $RULE_PATH/shellcode.rules
# include $RULE_PATH/policy.rules
# include $RULE_PATH/porn.rules
# include $RULE_PATH/info.rules
# include $RULE_PATH/icmp-info.rules
# include $RULE_PATH/virus.rules
# include $RULE_PATH/chat.rules
# include $RULE_PATH/multimedia.rules
# include $RULE_PATH/p2p.rules
include $RULE_PATH/experimental.rules
include $RULE_PATH/local.rules
```

Alert Classification and Priority

Each alert that is generated is given a classification and priority based on information in the rule that triggered the alert. For example, the stealth portscan triggered the following alert:

```
[**] [1:469:1] ICMP PING NMAP [**]
[Classification: Attempted Information Leak] [Priority: 2]
```

Here the classification is "Attempted Information Leak" with a priority of 2. Classifications and priorities are generated so that administrators and reporting software can better react to a given event; Snort does not handle them internally.

The classifications/priorities for the Snort rules included in the source distribution you've installed are stored in the file `/usr/local/etc/snort/classification.config`. Each line of the file consists of a shortname (single word) for the classification, a description, and a priority.

For example, the "Attempted Information Leak" alert was classified and prioritized by the following line:

```
config classification: attempted-recon,Attempted Information Leak,2
```

The rule that triggered the event classified it as `attempted-recon`. This was subsequently expanded to `Attempted Information Leak` and prioritized to level `2` by the `classification.config` line. In some cases, you may see alerts that have a priority level that does not match the assigned value in the classifications file. Priorities can be overridden by any rule if the rule explicitly states a priority level for the attack. Again, these are relatively arbitrary values and are provided for your benefit, not to change Snort's functionality.

You can create your own classifications and priority levels by simply adding `config classification` lines to any of the Snort configuration files (although `classification.config` makes the most sense). Existing rules can be modified to use the new classifications (via the classification's shortname) or new rules can be created for your own specific class of attack signatures.

Alert References

In addition to containing a classification shortname (which subsequently maps to a classification description and priority), rules can also contain a reference field, which, in turn, maps to an online reference for a given exploit. Earlier in the chapter you saw the included mappings in Table 18.1. The file `/usr/local/etc/snort/reference.config` contains lines of the format `config reference` *`<reference system>`* *`<reference URL>`*. For example, the arachNIDS online reference is denoted as

```
config reference: arachNIDS http://www.whitehats.com/info/IDS
```

If you are generating an extensive network policy of do's and don'ts, you may want to write your own ruleset and online database of policies. Your rules could subsequently map to an online reference of the policy that was broken.

As with the classifications, this is a mechanism that is provided for the benefit of the administrator. References are not included with all rules, and, given the coverage of the included references, it is unlikely that you'll ever need to add any of your own. If you happen to write a new rule that matches a known attack, you can simply use the existing reference mappings, such as CVE, which we've attempted to use for exploit references throughout the book.

Snort rules

The Snort rule files contain the "guts" of what makes Snort, Snort. Each rule defines a pattern against which incoming network traffic is compared, and if a match is found, an alert is generated. Rules follow the basic structure:

```
<alert|log> <protocol> <source address/network> <source port> <direction>
<destination address/network> <destination port> (<pattern> <output options>
<classification options> )
```

Although most of these values are self-explanatory (and those that aren't will be examined shortly), the direction operator can be a bit confusing. It can be either `->`, indicating that the source is sending data to the destination, or `<>`, in which case the rule will match traffic for the listed networks/ports heading either to or from the source or destination.

For example, the Papa Worm detection signature (found in `rules/virus.rules`) looks like this (with line numbers added):

```
alert tcp any 110 -> any any (
      msg:"Virus - Possible Papa Worm";
      content: "filename=\"XPASS.XLS\"";
      nocase;
      reference:MCAFEE,10145;
      sid:745;
      classtype:misc-activity;
      rev:3;
)
```

NOTE

In most cases, rules are written on a single line. Here, the Papa Worm rule has been broken into multiple lines for clarity. Either format works fine in Snort.

Line 1 indicates that an `alert` will be generated if the rule matches. (Alternatively, `log` could be used to send the event information directly to the log facility.) The network traffic that is examined is TCP-based traffic from port 110 (POP3) on any server to any other machine on any network (that is, any POP3 client retrieving mail from a local or remote network). The variables, such as `HOME_NET`, `EXTERNAL_NET`, and so on, may be used directly in the rule definitions to eliminate the hardcoding of addresses if specific network information is to be used. Variables must be prefixed by `$` (for example, `$HOME_NET`) when used in a rule.

On line 2, the `msg` keyword provides the alert message that will be generated if there is a match—in this case `Virus - Possible Papa Worm`.

Line 3 defines what the rule is looking for. In this case, it's examining the `content` of the packet for `filename=XPASS.XLS`, a string that is common to all Papa Worm attacks.

Line 4 tells Snort that the preceding `content` match should not be casesensitive.

Line 5 consists of a `reference` followed by the reference name and ID and is used to include online attack reference information in the logs. For example, here the reference is `MCAFEE,10145` which, using the file `reference.config`, can be mapped to the online URL: `http://vil.nai.com/vil/content/v_10145`—an online description of the Papa Worm virus.

Line 6 defines a unique signature ID for the rule.

Line 7 classifies the rule as the shortname `misc-activity`. This is later expanded through the mappings in `classification.config` to the classification `Misc Activity` with a priority of `3`.

Line 8 denotes that this is the third revision of the rule.

Snort rules can be as complex or as simple as you want. Those experienced with the TCP/IP can match against packet headers, RPC traffic, and so on. A full guide to creating Snort rules is available at `http://www.snort.org/docs/writing_rules/chap2.html#tth_chAp2`. Documentation of existing rules can be found at `http://www.snort.org/snort-db/`.

CAUTION

Snort rules are not infallible. In fact, the Papa Worm definition given here does not monitor mail traffic over port 143—IMAP. Alerts are generated only if the content match is made over a POP3 connection. To match IMAP content, a second rule could be added that monitors port 143 traffic. Unfortunately, both rules would fail if the traffic is encrypted.

As a Snort user, your first priority should be finding the rules that apply to your network and disabling the rest. There are a number of `misc-activity` rules, such as the `icmp.rules`, that will invariably trigger alerts on an active (and healthy) network. Run

Snort on your network for a day or two, making note of the alerts that have accumulated and which warrant attention. Remove the rules that aren't being used, or are generating false positives. Alternatively, alter the source and destination parameters of the rules so that they are not generated by your own network traffic. I, for example, have replaced the source address (hardcoded to `any` in most rules) to `$EXTERNAL_NET` to help cut down on false positives.

TIP

Snort rules are not static; they are updated on a continuing basis to reflect the latest network vulnerabilities. Keep your rules up to date by downloading the latest versions from `http://www.snort.org/dl/rules/`.

Blocking Attacks with Guardian

Out of the box, Snort is capable of watching your network and reporting on what it sees. It does not, however (without an experimental plug-in), *do* anything about potential alerts. If you'd like to block hosts that have generated alerts, you can use the Guardian software, included in the Snort distribution. Written in Perl for Linux, Guardian watches the Snort `/var/log/snort/alerts` file and blocks hosts that have generated alerts. To use the software, you need to have Snort running in a stable and predictable manner, and you'll also have to make a few changes to the Guardian script.

Go to the `contrib` directory of your Snort distribution, look for the file `Guardian.tar.gz`, unarchive, and enter its directory:

```
# tar zxf Guardian.tar.gz
# cd Guardian
```

Next, edit the `Guardian.pl` file and search for the line that reads

```
system ("/sbin/ipchains -A input -s $source -i $interface -j DENY");
```

Change it to

```
system ("/sbin/ipfw add 1 deny all from $source/32 to any");
```

Next, search for

```
if (/inet addr:(\d+\.\d+\.\d+\.\d+)/) {
```

and modify it to read

```
if (/inet (\d+\.\d+\.\d+\.\d+)/) {
```

Save your changes, then open the `guardian.conf` file and set the variables so that they match your system configuration. In this example file, I'm using `en0` as my network interface and a `HostGatewayByte` of `1` (meaning that my gateway address is the same as my IP address, except the last octet is ".1"). Enter the remainder of the values exactly as shown. You'll see some references to `ipchains`—the Linux firewall software. Don't pay any attention to it.

```
# The machine's IP address that is visable to the internet
# If this is left undefined, then guardian will attempt to get the information
# from ifconfig, as long as it has an interface to use. This would be usefull
# for people on ppp links, or dhcp machines, or if you are lazy :)
# HostIpAddr

# Here we define the interface which we will use to guess the IP address, and
# block incoming offending packets. This is the only option that is required
# for guardian to run. If the rest are undefined, guardian will use the default.
Interface       en0

# The last octet of the ip address, which gives us the gateway address.
HostGatewayByte  1

# Guardian's log file
LogFile          /var/log/guardian.log

# Snort's alert file
AlertFile        /var/log/snort/alert

# The list of ip addresses to ignore
IgnoreFile       /usr/local/etc/guardian.ignore

# The path to ipchains
ipchainsPath      /sbin/ipfw
```

Next, create the Guardian logfile with `touch /var/log/guardian.log`. You can also create a list of hosts that will *never* be blocked (one IP address per line) in the file `/usr/local/etc/guardian.ignore`. It's a good idea to place your `servers/DNS/gateways/etc` in this list so they aren't inadvertently blocked by a false positive reading.

Finally, copy `Guardian.pl` and `guardian.conf` to logical locations on your drive, such as `/usr/local/bin` and `/usr/local/etc`, respectively:

```
# cp Guardian.pl /usr/local/bin
# cp guardian.conf /usr/local/etc
```

You can now start Guardian from the command line with `/usr/local/bin/Guardian.pl -c /usr/local/etc/guardian.conf`:

```
# /usr/local/bin/Guardian.pl -c /usr/local/etc/guardian.conf
Warning! HostIpAddr is undefined! Attempting to guess..
Got it.. your HostIpAddr is 10.0.1.101
My ip address and interface are: 10.0.1.101 en1
Loaded 0 addresses from /usr/local/etc/guardian.ignore
Becoming a daemon..
```

As attacks occur, they are logged to `/var/log/guardian.log` and automatically blocked by your Mac OS X firewall.

TIP

If you want to be alerted "visually" to an attack, you can modify `Guardian.pl` to include something along the lines of `` `osascript -e 'display dialog "Blocking $source"'`; `` directly after the `system` line you edited in the `Guardian.pl` file. This will cause an Applescript dialog to be displayed with the IP address of the host being blocked.

Snort Reporting

A number of Snort reporting tools are available for download and use on your system. These products use the Snort log files and Snort MySQL logs to generate reports on the attack signatures that are being matched, where they're coming from, and even to provide tools for tracking them. Because Snort has a number of output options, you must make sure that the reporting tool you're attempting to use supports the log style you've decided on.

One of the easiest report tools to use is Snort Report, a PHP Web-based tool that relies on the MySQL logging that was set up earlier. You can download Snort Report from `http://www.circuitsmaximus.com/download.html`. After downloading, unarchive and move the Snort Report directory to a Web-accessible directory on your PHP-enabled server, then enter the Snort Report distribution directory:

```
% curl -O http://www.circuitsmaximus.com/snortreport/snortreport-1.11.tar.gz
% tar zxf snortreport-1.11.tar.gz
% cd snortreport-1.11
```

Edit the file `srconf.php`. This contains the information necessary for Snort Report to find your MySQL database. Look for the lines that are similar to this:

```
// Put your Snort database login credentials in this section.
$server = "localhost";
```

```
$user = "jray";
$pass = "nopasshere";
$dbname = "snortdb";
```

and change them to match the hostname, username, password, and database that you used when configuring Snort itself.

Finally, assuming you don't have GD support compiled into PHP (the Mac OS X default), skip down a few lines and change

```
$haveGD = TRUE;
```

to

```
$haveGD = FALSE;
```

NOTE

If you *have* GD support, you can leave this line as-is to enable a few graphs of the traffic distribution on your system. These graphs are not important to the operation of Snort Report and add little additional value beyond a "gee-whiz" factor. If you *want* GD support and don't have it, download a GD-enabled PHP from `http://www.entrophy.ch`.

Snort Report should now be configured for use through your browser. Open Mozilla or Internet Explorer and open the URL to the `alerts.php` file inside the Snort Report directory. If everything has gone according to plan (and Snort has logged an alert or two), you should see something similar to that of Figure 18.2.

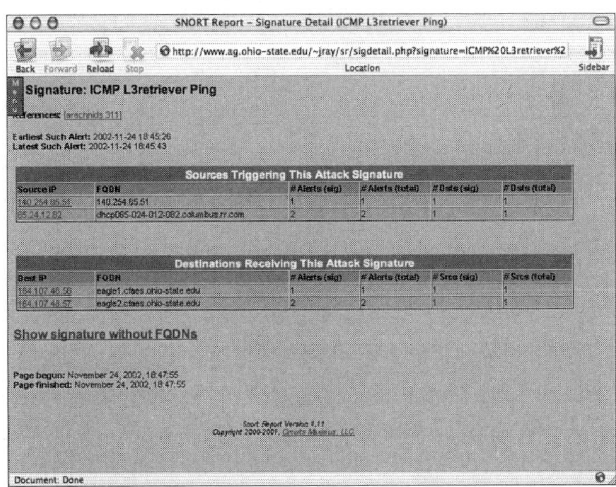

FIGURE 18.2 Snort Report provides easy-to-read access to your IDS logs.

As mentioned earlier, there are a number of Snort reporting packages—all sorts of shapes, sizes, and colors. If you find that Snort Report isn't performing as you had hoped, you may want to look into one of these other systems:

- **SnortSnarf.** `http://www.silicondefense.com/software/snortsnarf/index.htm`
- **ACID.** `http://www.cert.org/kb/acid/`
- **snort-rep.** `http://people.ee.ethz.ch/~dws/software/snort-rep/`

IDS Resources

As you can probably tell by now, intrusion detection is not simply a matter of "plug-it-in-and-your-headaches-go-away." It requires monitoring, fine-tuning, and a willingness to keep your software and rules current with the day's threats. Although you should have plenty to start with, there are a number of additional intrusion detection tools and resources that you may be interested in. I recommend the following reading to help you get a better feeling for what is available and where IDS products are headed:

- **Threat Management: The State of Intrusion Detection**, Steven J. Scott, `http://www.snort.org/docs/threatmanagement.pdf`
- **The Science of Intrusion Detection System Attack Identification**, Cisco Systems, `http://www.cisco.com/warp/public/cc/pd/sqsw/sqidsz/prodlit/idssa_wp.htm`
- **A Distributed Autonomous-Agent Network-Intrusion Detection and Response System**, Joseph Barrus, Neil C. Rowe, `http://www.cs.nps.navy.mil/people/faculty/rowe/barruspap.html`
- **Intrusion Detection: A Brief History and Overview**, Richard A. Kemmerer and Giovanni Vigna, `http://www.computer.org/computer/sp/articles/kem/`
- **Network Intrusion Detection Signatures**, Karen Frederick, `http://online.securityfocus.com/infocus/1524`
- **The Use of Intrusion Detection in Securing Information Assets**, Dr. David Dampier, Rayford B. Vaughn, Jr., `http://www.wmrc.com/businessbriefing/pdf/securesystems2002/publication/vaughn.pdf`
- **Stateful Intrusion Detection for High-Speed Networks**, Christopher Kruegel, Fredrik Valeur, Giovanni Vigna, Richard Kemmerer, `http://www.computer.org/proceedings/sp/1543/15430285abs.htm`

- **LaBrea**. Intrusion detection software that works by "appearing" to be an entire network of virtual machines, waiting for connection attempts, then mishandling the connections so that the attacker is stuck in the connection negotiation phase and is effectively knocked out.
  `http://www.hackbusters.net/LaBrea/`

Summary

Intrusion Detection is an up-and-coming technology that you can put into practice today on your Macintosh. Be it simply monitoring and reacting to portscans on your local computer or watching the traffic for your entire enterprise network, there are Open Source security tools that are up to the task. To effectively use an IDS, you must first understand that they are *not* perfect systems and can be tricked by both clever attackers *and* innocent users who just happen to transmit data that matches an attack signature. Although the chance of false positives and undetected attacks is always a possibility, intrusion detection systems can provide an early warning to larger attacks around the corner, and provide protection to all members of your network—even Windows users.

19

Logs and User Activity Accounting

IN THIS CHAPTER

- The Role of Logs
- User Logins and Accounting
- Automated Log Monitoring: LogSentry
- Common System Log Changes

Chapter 18, "Alarm Systems: Intrusion Detection," gave you the tools to monitor the health of your network and identify potential attacks. But no amount of packet analysis can tell you what is actually taking place on your computer. The key to monitoring your computer's health is managing and interpreting the logfiles that are generated. Logs are Mac OS X's means of providing feedback to you, the user. Logs are also the first target of any attacker attempting to gain access to your machine. Without logs, you may never even realize your computer has been compromised.

The Role of Logs

Almost every server process on your computer generates a logfile. What is logged, and when, is up to the software that is writing to the log. A centralized process, called `syslog`, manages the incoming log data from other applications and directs it to the system console, files, or remote `syslogd` servers. Many applications send data to `syslog`, some to `syslog` and local logfiles, others only to local files. Our first priority will be getting you familiarized with the primary Mac OS X logfiles as they are initially configured on your computer.

Tracking Activity

Apple designed Mac OS X so that an average user need never look at logs nor even know that they exist. At the same time, they provide the same (potentially unknowledgeable) users the ability to enable services such as SSH and FTP—both excellent entry points for attackers.

Assuming that "because it's a Mac, it's safe" is no longer wise. Logs are your window to check up on how your machine is working, who is logged in, what they've been doing, and when. They also provide a means of tracking the path of an intruder through a compromised system, and are often the first target of an attack. Disable a machine's capability to report your presence, and you're virtually invisible.

Assume an attacker gains SSH access to your computer through an exploit. Unless you have something of value on your system that he's after, his next step will be to use your computer to monitor and potentially exploit other machines, or even set up file trading services for his 3L1t3 friends. An intelligent attacker will lie low and draw as little attention to himself as possible.

Your computer, however, has logfiles that make it easy to identify an unknown presence. The file `/var/run/utmp` stores information about the currently logged-in user, whereas `/var/log/wtmp` tracks all user logins/logouts, shutdowns, reboots, and crashes.

For example, `last` uses `wtmp` to display a user login history:

```
% last
jray      ttyp1    dhcp024-210-090- Tue Nov 19 21:17   still logged in
jray      ttyp0    dhcp024-210-090- Sat Nov 16 23:44 - 01:26  (01:42)
jray      ttyp0    despair.ag.ohio- Fri Nov 15 15:11 - 17:19  (02:08)
ohioline  ttyp0    dhcp35-112.ag.oh Fri Nov 15 15:02 - 15:10  (00:08)
jray      ttyp1    postoffice.ag.oh Fri Nov 15 11:08 - 11:08  (00:00)
hlaufman  ttyp0    theotormon.ag.oh Fri Nov 15 08:09 - 11:17  (03:08)
jray      ttyp1    despair.ag.ohio- Thu Nov 14 15:23 - 17:03  (01:39)
jray      ttyp2    despair.ag.ohio- Fri Nov  8 16:01 - 17:00  (00:59)
...
hlaufman  ttyp1    theotormon.ag.oh Fri Nov  8 15:14 - 16:52  (01:37)
reboot    ~                         Thu Nov  7 09:50
shutdown  ~                         Thu Nov  7 09:49
hlaufman  ttyp1    theotormon.ag.oh Wed Nov  6 14:42 - 15:52  (01:10)
jray      ttyp1    despair.ag.ohio- Mon Nov  4 12:16 - 12:17  (00:00)
robyn     console  www              Mon Nov  4 11:57 - 11:59  (00:01)
jray      ttyp1    despair.ag.ohio- Mon Nov  4 11:20 - 12:00  (00:39)
hlaufman  ttyp0    theotormon.ag.oh Mon Nov  4 08:35 - 16:48  (08:12)
jray      console  www              Mon Nov  4 00:04 - 00:04  (00:00)
hlaufman  ttyp1    dhcp065-024-072- Sun Nov  3 18:54 - 20:38  (01:43)
jray      ttyp0    despair.ag.ohio- Fri Nov  1 09:29 - 14:24  (04:54)

wtmp begins Fri Nov  1 09:29
```

Someone who has gained login access to your computer would quite clearly show up in both `utmp` and `wtmp` as either an unknown account and/or an unknown remote hostname. Unfortunately, these files will be some of the first targets for someone who intends to commandeer your system.

Attackers have a number of options to cover their tracks. They can simply remove these accounting files and replace them with an empty copy:

```
% last

wtmp begins Tue Nov 19 21:31
```

Alternatively, they can copy an archived `wtmp/utmp` file over the originals and set the logs' immutable flags. The result is a user login history that *looks* normal to an overworked and unobservant administrator—but never updates.

A third and more devious approach is to not modify the logfiles, but to modify the output of the utilities that *display* the files. My username is `jray` on a number of systems. If I've gained access to a machine and created an account for myself (or gained access via someone else's account), I'd want to hide my logins when the administrator used reporting tools such as `last` to show account activity. Assuming I've gained access to the machine via a root exploit, I can simply replace the existing reporting commands with a modified "filtered" copy:

```
% last
ohioline  ttyp0    dhcp35-112.ag.oh Fri Nov 15 15:02 - 15:10  (00:08)
hlaufman  ttyp0    theotormon.ag.oh Fri Nov 15 08:09 - 11:17  (03:08)
hlaufman  ttyp1    theotormon.ag.oh Fri Nov  8 15:14 - 16:52  (01:37)
reboot    ~                         Thu Nov  7 09:50
shutdown  ~                         Thu Nov  7 09:49
hlaufman  ttyp1    theotormon.ag.oh Wed Nov  6 14:42 - 15:52  (01:10)
robyn     console  www              Mon Nov  4 11:57 - 11:59  (00:01)
hlaufman  ttyp0    theotormon.ag.oh Mon Nov  4 08:35 - 16:48  (08:12)
hlaufman  ttyp1    dhcp065-024-072- Sun Nov  3 18:54 - 20:38  (01:43)

wtmp begins Fri Nov  1 09:29
```

To generate this conveniently `jray`-free output, an attacker would first rename the `last` command: `/usr/bin/oldlast`. Next, a simple script could be installed in `/usr/bin/last` that performs the filter:

```
#!/usr/bin/perl

$last=`oldlast`;
$last=~s/jray.*?\n//g;
print $last;
```

Most modern rootkits include modified versions of commands such as `last`, `who`, `netstat`, and `ps` that will filter output to remove logins, processes, and connections, effectively allowing the attacker to remain invisible until other attacks are traced back to your computer.

With a number of methods for "beating" the system, how can logs be of any use in identifying attacks?

First, if an attacker takes the approach of removing, modifying, or locking a logfile, the output of your reporting functions *will* be noticeably different from that of a healthy system. If, however, you don't know what the logs should contain, you're in trouble. This is exactly what we aim to correct in this chapter.

Second, I have yet to see a rootkit or attacker who is thorough enough to completely hide its presence. Discrepancies between logs and reporting functions are often obvious, no matter how meticulous an attacker has been. The `ac` command, for example, outputs the total amount of time each user has been logged into your system and a systemwide total. A filter would obviously result in inaccurate system totals. Given enough insight into the operating system, it's certainly possible to modify or remove every single log of activity, but it's extremely unlikely that a vigilant admin would remain completely ignorant of all evidence of system compromise. Additionally, software such as Tripwire (`http://sourceforge.net/projects/tripwire/`) can be installed to report on any changes to your system files, identifying the altered reporting utilities immediately.

NOTE

Interestingly enough, I've seen a large number of Linux rootkits that, while modifying the output of `ls` and `find` to hide directories, do not remove the `locate` database or modify `locate` to hide files or directories. Searching for files that consist of periods and spaces quickly reveals the attacker's working directory.

Policy Violations

Not all nefarious actions on your computer system are the result of attack. Early in this book we discussed the necessity of creating a comprehensive security policy for your network and appropriate-use guidelines for computers on the network. Unfortunately, although it is possible to put constraints on individual accounts, it isn't feasible to micromanage a server with hundreds of users.

Web servers, for example, often provide FTP access to user accounts for uploading content. Unfortunately, many users are far from protective of their login information. Entire offices may share a single account, and passwords may be used at home or at work, and are rarely maintained in the possession of the original account holder.

A highly trafficked university Web server recently became a pirate software trading zone after a student who was entrusted to update a department's Web site passed the information out to his friends. Thankfully, a weekly audit of the FTP transfer logs (which aren't enabled by default in Mac OS X) revealed hundreds of megabytes in zip files moving to and from the server. The logs provided the time, date, account, and hostname—more than enough information to locate the machine and subsequently the student who had caused the trouble.

In this case, there wasn't an "attack," nor was there a software exploit, or any Apple Security update that could have solved the problem. Yet the incident is definitely a breach of security.

NOTE

For the record, if you're running a Web server with a large number of accounts, you may want to consider using WebDAV for file transfers. WebDAV does not require "real" user accounts for connections, and thus eliminates the potential for those accounts to be compromised and gain access to other parts of the server. Depending on your user needs, this isn't always a possibility.

Now consider that Mac OS X enables an inexperienced user to turn FTP access on, but doesn't provide any easy way for the same user to see the logs generated by the FTP server. In fact, the FTP server isn't even configured by default to log what files are transferred via FTP—it records only logins. If FTP was being misused on an out-of-the-box Mac OS X system by an inexperienced administrator, it would be virtually impossible to detect that anything was afoot.

Knowing what logs are on your computer and understanding what they contain and how to configure them is an important part of maintaining a secure system.

Mac OS X Logfile Locations

Mac OS X, like other Unix systems, uses `/var/log/` as its primary repository for logfiles. For some reason, however, Apple has also chosen to create `/Library/Logs` for a handful of other "Apple-specific" logfiles and `/Library/Receipts` for logs of installed software. This isn't really a problem—just somewhat unusual in that there isn't an obvious reason for the separation.

NOTE

Logfiles, by their nature, log things. In doing so, they use up drive space. It is common practice to use a separate partition for `/var/logs` (or reconfigure system processes to log to a different drive) so that an attacker can't fill up a volume with logfile entries, thus disrupting processes that are attempting to store critical data on the same drive.

So, what *is* stored on your system? Table 19.1 lists the common default Mac OS X logfiles, their location, and what they contain.

TABLE 19.1 Mac OS X Default Log Locations

Logfile	Description
/var/log/cups	The cups directory contains access_log, error_log, and page_log—providing information on access to the CUPS Web interface, errors encountered by the CUPS process, and a print job log, respectively. CUPS, incidentally, refers to the Common Unix Printing System—the printing "backbone" of Mac OS X.
/var/log/ftp.log	Logs login/logout information from the Mac OS X FTP server lukemftpd.
/var/log/httpd	The httpd directory contains a Web server access_log with each Apache request, and an error_log containing errors reported by the server process.
/var/log/lastlog	Similar to /var/log/wtmp, identifies the last time a user has logged in (binary logfile).
/var/log/lookupd.log	Typically, the location for errors from the Mac OS X lookupd process. lookupd, however, does not use this file in Mac OS X 10.2, and it should remain empty (unless configured otherwise in NetInfo) on your system. Instead, lookupd logs to syslog, which places lookupd messages in /var/log/netinfo.log.
/var/log/lpr.log	Logs print requests made via lpr.
/var/log/mail.log	Contains sendmail errors and message delivery logs.
/var/log/netinfo.log	Includes messages logged from the Mac OS X netinfo—the central repository for user/group/host information on your computer. Also contains error messages logged by lookupd.
/var/log/samba	The samba log directory contains the log.smbd and log.nmbd, which contain access and error messages from the Samba file server, and the Samba NetBIOS name server, respectively.
/var/log/secure.log	Logs authorization failures, such as failed FTP logins.
/var/log/system.log	Contains operating system notices, authorization failures, errors, and other logging goodness get stored in the main Mac OS X system.log.
/Library/Logs/DirectoryService	The Apple Directory service logs (DirectoryService.server.log and DirectoryService.error.log) log messages and errors related to Apple's directory service architecture—BSD files, NetInfo, LDAP, and so on.
/Library/Logs/CrashReporter	Consists of detailed logs containing application-specific crash information for use in troubleshooting software instability.
/Library/Logs/AppleFileService	AppleFileServiceAccess.log and AppleFileServiceError.log record logins and errors in the built-in Mac OS X Appleshare server. The Access log is not enabled by default.
/Library/Logs/Software Update.log	Logs all automatic updates performed via the Software Update preference panel.
/var/log/wtmp	Contains a history of user logins/logouts and system restarts. (Binary logfile)
/var/run/utmp	Stores the currently logged-in users.

Looking at this list you might be wondering, "Why are logs for multiple services showing up in a single logfile?" or "Why are multiple logfiles used for a single service?"

Earlier it was mentioned that many processes log their output via a centralized process called `syslog`. Messages that are sent to `syslog` can be stored in multiple locations and directed to different logfiles depending on their *level*—a 32-bit value that contains an encoded facility and level. As you add new Unix software to your computer (such as Snort, in the preceding chapter), you'll find that many applications can and do log via `syslog`—and the only real way to know *what* is going *where* is to understand how `syslog` works, and how you can configure it.

WHY ARE THERE LOGFILES WITH THE EXTENSION `.#.GZ` AND NO RECORDS OLDER THAN A WEEK?

Many of the Mac OS X logfiles are rotated on a daily, weekly, or monthly basis by the files `/etc/daily`, `/etc/weekly`, and `/etc/monthly`, respectively. To view the contents of a file that is rotated out of use, you need to unzip it (`gunzip` *`<filename>`*) first.

In some cases, you may want to disable the rotation altogether, or change it so that it operates at a different interval. You can do this by either commenting out or simply moving the appropriate portions of the daily, weekly, and monthly files. This code, for example, rotates the `/var/account/acct` file (in `/etc/daily`):

```
if [ -f /var/account/acct ] ; then
    if [ -x /usr/bin/gzip ]; then gzext=".gz"; else gzext=""; fi
    echo ""
    echo "Gathering accounting statistics:"
    cd /var/account
    if [ -f "acct.2${gzext}" ] ; then mv -f "acct.2${gzext}" "acct.3${gzext}" ;
fi
    if [ -f "acct.1${gzext}" ] ; then mv -f "acct.1${gzext}" "acct.2${gzext}" ;
fi
    if [ -f "acct.0${gzext}" ] ; then mv -f "acct.0${gzext}" "acct.1${gzext}" ;
fi
    cp -pf acct acct.0
    if [ -x /usr/bin/gzip ]; then gzip -9 acct.0; fi
    sa -s > /dev/null
fi
```

To change the rotation, simply move these lines to a script that is executed at a different interval, or comment them out.

Additionally, these same script files *remove* some of the logfiles after a certain number of days. This is *not* a good idea if you intend to maintain any historical data. You can disable the removal by editing the script files, looking for these lines, and commenting them out:

```
if [ -d /var/log/httpd ]; then
    echo ""
    echo -n "Cleaning web server log files:"
    cd /var/log/httpd && \
        find . -type f -name '*_log.*' -mtime +7 -exec rm -f -- {} \; >/dev/null
 2>&1;
fi
```

In this code fragment the `httpd` (Apache) logfiles that are older then seven days are found and removed.

NOTE

Some system messages aren't logged to *any* file, but to the system console device. The console can be viewed (along with other system files) through the Mac OS X application `Console` or the Logs tab of the `Apple System Profiler`.

Additionally, the `dmesg` command displays the contents of the system message buffer, which may contain useful messages held in memory.

Using Syslog

The Syslog daemon can be a bit confusing for users coming from other platforms, or migrating from earlier versions of the Macintosh. The first point to understand is that `syslogd` is *not* generating the messages that are showing up in your logfiles. It provides a logging system that other software can take advantage of, rather than that software having to write its own files—similar to Window's Event Viewer. Syslog can redirect incoming log information to remote `syslog` servers, the console, logged-in users, and, of course, files—providing far more flexibility to developers than if each had to develop logging functions independently. The second point is that `syslog`-generated files are often configured to be "message-centric" rather than "application-centric," meaning that logs contain a similar type of message (failed logins, perhaps) from multiple different daemons, rather than multiple messages from a single daemon.

NOTE

In centralizing the system's logging, `syslog` also presents a single point for disrupting critical log messages for attackers. As you'll see shortly, `syslog` could easily be configured to dump high-level messages to `/dev/null`.

Facilities and Levels

To configure `syslogd`, one first needs to understand the "vocabulary" of the logging system. There are four terms used by `syslog`, its documentation, and our discussion that you must understand before proceeding:

- **Facility**. An identifier for the portion of the system that is sending the log entry to `syslog`, such as the kernel, mail, or FTP processes.
- **Level**. A ranking of the importance of the incoming log message, from simply informational notifications to emergency warnings.
- **Selector**. A combination of one or more facilities and levels that are matched against log messages coming into `syslog`. If the selector matches the level and facility of the message, `syslog` executes an *action*.
- **Action**. A `syslog` action determines what happens to an incoming log message if it matches a selector in the configuration file. Actions can write to files and devices, forward the messages to remote log servers, and notify logged-in users.

Levels and facilities are *not* arbitrary values that the user determines. The `syslog` daemon defines them. Table 19.2 provides the documentation for the available Mac OS X facilities as defined in `/usr/include/sys/syslog.h`:

TABLE 19.2 `Syslog` Logging Facilities

User-Level Name	Direct Name	Logging Purpose
`kern`	`LOG_KERN`	Kernel messages
`user`	`LOG_USER`	User-level messages
`mail`	`LOG_MAIL`	Mail system
`daemon`	`LOG_DAEMON`	System daemons
`auth`	`LOG_AUTH`	Security/authorization messages
`syslog`	`LOG_SYSLOG`	Internal syslog messages
`lpr`	`LOG_LPR`	Line printer subsystem
`news`	`LOG_NEWS`	Network news subsystem
`uucp`	`LOG_UUCP`	UUCP subsystem
`cron`	`LOG_CRON`	Clock daemon
`authpriv`	`LOG_AUTHPRIV`	Security/authorization messages (private)
`ftp`	`LOG_FTP`	FTP daemon
`netinfo`	`LOG_NETINFO`	NetInfo daemon
`remoteauth`	`LOG_REMOTEAUTH`	Remote authentication/authorization
`mark`	`LOG_MARK`	Logs an info message every 20 minutes

What facility a daemon uses to log is determined not by `syslogd` but by the daemon itself. You should check the documentation of your applications to determine what facilities are used, and how, if desired, to change them.

Note that there are "user-level" facility names and "direct" facility names. You'll use the short "user-level" names when configuring `syslogd` actions for each facility, but will likely need to use the direct name (which maps to an internal constant) when configuring to what facility individual daemons are logging. (See Chapter 18's Snort `syslogd` configuration as an example.)

As there are different facilities, there are a number of predefined "levels" that can be sent to `syslog` with a log message. Levels indicate the nature of the incoming message, and are also defined within `/usr/include/sys/syslog.h`. Table 19.3 documents the `syslogd` priorities ranked from most to least serious.

TABLE 19.3 `Syslogd` Priorities

User-Level Name	Direct Name	Level Meaning
`emerg` or `panic`	`LOG_EMERG`	System is unusable.
`alert`	`LOG_ALERT`	Action must be taken immediately.
`crit`	`LOG_CRIT`	Critical conditions.
`err` or `error`	`LOG_ERR`	Error conditions.
`warn` or `warning`	`LOG_WARNING`	Warning conditions.
`notice`	`LOG_NOTICE`	Normal but significant condition.
`info`	`LOG_INFO`	Informational.
`debug`	`LOG_DEBUG`	Debug-level messages.
`none`	`INTERN_NOPRI`	No priority.

/etc/syslog.conf

The `syslogd` process is configured via `/etc/syslog.conf`—a simple text file that matches selectors (facilities and levels) with an action to perform.

A selector is written as `<facility>.<level>`, where the values are taken from Table 19.2 and 19.3. An asterisk (`*`) can be substituted for the facility and/or level to match any facility (except `mark`) or level.

NOTE

The level in a selector is the *base* level for a match. All levels equal to (or greater than) the base level are matched.

Actions can consist of any of the following:

- A path to a logfile (for example, `/var/log/ftp.log`).
- A remote syslog server specified with the syntax `@<hostname or ip>` (for example, @192.168.0.100).
- A device (for example, `/dev/console`).
- A comma-separated list of usernames (for notifying users logged in via terminal sessions) or an asterisk (`*`) to notify everyone.

For example, to log all messages logged to the `ftp` facility at the level of `error` or higher to the file `/var/log/ftperror.log`, one would use a line like:

```
ftp.error                       /var/log/ftperror.log
```

CAUTION

The selector and action must be separated by a *tab*. If spaces are used, the entry will not work.

If you want multiple selectors to log to the same file, you can use multiple `/etc/syslogd.conf` lines, or add multiple selectors to a single line by separating them with semicolons. For example, to log *all* authentication information to the console, one could write:

```
authpriv.*;remoteauth.*               /dev/console
```

The asterisk can also be applied to the facility in a selector to select *all* facilities at a particular level. This can be combined with the `none` level to exclude certain facilities from the selector. For example, to log all errors, *except* those coming from the mail facility:

```
*.err;mail.none                 /var/log/allerrorsexceptmail.log
```

A final "shortcut" is to write multiple facilities that share the same selector as a comma-separated list with only the last facility also containing a level, such as `ftp,mail,netinfo.error`, which is the same as writing `ftp.error;mail.error;netinfo.error`.

The Mac OS X default `syslogd.conf` file should look like this:

```
*.err;kern.*;auth.notice;authpriv,remoteauth.none;mail.crit
➥/dev/console
*.notice;*.info;authpriv,remoteauth,ftp.none;kern.debug;mail.crit
➥/var/log/system.log
```

```
# Send messages normally sent to the console also to the serial port.
# To stop messages from being sent out the serial port, comment out this line.
#*.err;kern.*;auth.notice;authpriv,remoteauth.none;mail.crit
➥/dev/tty.serial

# The authpriv log file should be restricted access; these
# messages shouldn't go to terminals or publically-readable
# files.
authpriv.*;remoteauth.crit                          /var/log/secure.log

lpr.info                                            /var/log/lpr.log
mail.*                                              /var/log/mail.log
ftp.*                                               /var/log/ftp.log
netinfo.err                                         /var/log/netinfo.log

*.emerg                                             *
```

As you can see, many of the Mac OS X logfiles covered earlier are created via `syslog`, and the `system.log` file and `console` contain selectors that will capture messages from all available facilities. This will result in some of the redundancy you'll find when viewing the logfiles.

NOTE

Any changes to `/etc/syslogd.conf` can be put into effect immediately by sending the `-HUP` signal to the `syslogd` process (`killall -HUP syslogd`).

TIP

Apple does *not* include the output of TCP Wrappers in any of the default Mac OS X logs. If you use TCP Wrappers (which log to the `syslog` facility), you may consider adding this line to `/etc/syslog.conf`:

```
syslog.err                     /var/log/secure.log
```

A Network `syslog` Server

Creating a centralized network log server can help get you keep an eye on all your systems without having to directly watch dozens of different machines and files. Any centralized server should not be directly Internet accessible, or it could easily be subjected to a DoS attack based on an overwhelming number of logging requests.

To start `syslogd` in "insecure" mode, you must modify `/System/Library/StartupItems/SystemLog` so that `syslogd` starts with the `-u` switch. In this mode, `syslogd` listens on UDP port 514. Edit the file `/System/Library/StartupItems/SystemLog/SystemLog` and change the line

```
syslogd
```

to read

```
syslogd -u
```

Client machines can then be configured to send log messages to the centralized server. The default Mac OS X `syslog.conf`, for example, could be rewritten to send its logs to a logserver at `192.168.0.100` like this:

```
*.err;kern.*;auth.notice;authpriv,remoteauth.none;mail.crit
➥/dev/console
*.notice;*.info;authpriv,remoteauth,ftp.none;kern.debug;mail.crit
➥@192.168.0.100

# Send messages normally sent to the console also to the serial port.
# To stop messages from being sent out the serial port, comment out this line.
#*.err;kern.*;auth.notice;authpriv,remoteauth.none;mail.crit
➥/dev/tty.serial

# The authpriv log file should be restricted access; these
# messages shouldn't go to terminals or publicly-readable
# files.
authpriv.*;remoteauth.crit      @192.168.0.100

lpr.info                        @192.168.0.100
mail.*                          @192.168.0.100
ftp.*                           @192.168.0.100
netinfo.err                     @192.168.0.100

*.emerg                                                     *
```

Thankfully, `syslog`-written logs contain the hostname of the machine generating the message. Logs follow the format:

```
<time stamp> <host generating message> <process name> <log message>
```

This enables an administrator to quickly `grep` through the contents of a combined logfile for a specific machine's messages.

Whether you choose to create a centralized server for a network or simply monitor the activity on your personal computer, a knowledge of `syslogd` will help make it easier. The remainder of this chapter will be dedicated to helping you decipher the contents of your Mac OS X logfiles and automate the process of tracking them.

NOTE

Unfortunately, knowing how to use `syslog` isn't going to help you read and analyze your logs. The messages that are written to the logging daemon are arbitrary—determined by the program that sends them. The facility and level are also arbitrary, which can lead to log messages that you don't necessarily feel are appropriately classified, but the author did.

User Logins and Accounting

If your Mac OS X computer is shared among multiple users, keeping track of their activity should be a reasonably important priority. Although it's possible to limit the applications a user can run in Mac OS X (see Chapter 13, "Mail Server Security," for details), how to track their activity on the BSD subsystem isn't as obvious.

As noted earlier, there are three binary logfiles that track users: logged-in users (`utmp`), user login/logout history (`wtmp`), and each user's last login (`lastlog`). This section of the chapter will document the utilities that read these files and introduce the idea of an accounting log, which will track exactly what each user does at the command line.

Current Users: `who` and `w`

To display information about the currently logged-in users, use the `w` or `who` commands. Each displays roughly the same information, gleaned from `/var/run/utmp`, but in a slightly different format.

Executing `who`, for example, provides an output of username, controlling terminal, date, and remote hostname:

```
# who -Hu
USER     LINE     WHEN         IDLE     FROM
jray     console  Nov 22 10:47 01:26
jray     ttyp1    Nov 22 11:21   .
jray     ttyp2    Nov 22 11:28   .
sally    ttyp3    Nov 22 11:29 00:43    (postoffice.ag.oh)
jray     ttyp4    Nov 22 11:27 00:43
sally    ttyp5    Nov 22 11:28 00:43    (www.ag.ohio-stat)
jray     ttyp6    Nov 22 11:35   .
```

NOTE

A terminal type of `console` indicates a login directly at the Mac OS X machine.

The syntax of `who` is `who <options> [filename]`. The options are defined in Table 19.4.

TABLE 19.4 `who` Command-Line Switches

Option	Description
`-m`	Displays information about only the active terminal.
`-T`	Prints a + or - after each username to indicate whether the terminal is writable (a la `write <username>` or `talk <username>`).
`-u`	Prints idle time for each user.
`-H`	Displays column headings.
`am I`	Returns the real username of the person invoking the command.
`filename`	If a filename is given on the commandline, `who` reads the results from that file, such as `/var/log/wtmp`, and displays the login/logout records for the stored user records.

Like `who`, the `w` command produces output on the actively logged-in users, but includes `uptime` stats and is also capable of sorting by idle time, displaying the IP (rather than hostname) of logged-in users, and filtering the output by a single user account. `w` also purports to display the current active process running in each terminal, but this does not currently function in Mac OS X. (Check a Linux system to see what the output *should* look like.)

For example:

```
# w -i
11:55AM  up 1 day,  1:09, 8 users, load averages: 0.00, 0.00, 0.00
USER     TTY FROM              LOGIN@  IDLE WHAT
jray     p7 dhcp024-210-090- 11:45AM     0 -
jray     p1 -                Fri11AM     5 -
jray     p6 -                Fri11AM     5 -
jray     p2 -                Fri11AM 23:42 -
sally    p3 postoffice.ag.oh Fri11AM 24:26 -
jray     p4 -                Fri11AM 24:26 -
sally    p5 www.ag.ohio-stat Fri11AM 24:26 -
jray     co -                Fri10AM 25:09 -
```

The syntax of `w` is simply `w <options> [username]`. Table 19.5 describes the basic command options.

TABLE 19.5 w Command-Line Switches

Option	Description
-h	Suppresses heading.
-i	Sorts the output by idle time.
-n	Shows numeric IP addresses.
username	Filters the results for the specified username.

Login/Logout History: last and lastlog

The command `last` displays accounting information from `/var/log/wtmp` about who has logged in and out of the system, along with date and time of reboots, crashes, and shutdowns.

For example:

```
% last
jray      ttyp1    dhcp024-210-090- Sat Nov 23 13:01   still logged in
ansci     ttyp3    dhcp35-112.ag.oh Fri Nov 22 14:16 - 15:13  (00:56)
ohioline  ttyp3    dhcp35-112.ag.oh Fri Nov 22 14:15 - 14:15  (00:00)
robyn     ttyp1    dhcp35-219.ag.oh Fri Nov 22 14:12 - 14:20  (00:08)
ansci     ttyp1    dhcp35-112.ag.oh Fri Nov 22 12:45 - 13:26  (00:40)
ansci     ttyp1    dhcp35-112.ag.oh Fri Nov 22 12:43 - 12:43  (00:00)
ohioline  ttyp1    dhcp35-112.ag.oh Fri Nov 22 12:23 - 12:31  (00:08)
robyn     ttyp1    dhcp35-219.ag.oh Fri Nov 22 11:39 - 11:56  (00:17)
joe       ttyp1                     Fri Nov 22 11:38 - 11:39  (00:00)
joe       ttyp1                     Fri Nov 22 11:38 - 11:38  (00:00)
jray      ttyp2    despair.ag.ohio- Fri Nov 22 11:36   still logged in
robyn     ttyp1    dhcp35-219.ag.oh Fri Nov 22 11:31 - 11:38  (00:06)
robyn     ttyp1    dhcp35-219.ag.oh Fri Nov 22 11:28 - 11:29  (00:00)
jray      ttyp0    despair.ag.ohio- Fri Nov 22 11:28   still logged in
robyn     ttyp0    dhcp35-219.ag.oh Fri Nov 22 11:25 - 11:26  (00:01)
jray      ttyp1    despair.ag.ohio- Thu Nov 21 15:11 - 15:39  (00:28)
ohioline  ttyp1    dhcp35-112.ag.oh Thu Nov 21 14:31 - 14:32  (00:01)
```

Because the `wtmp` can become very large on an active machine, `last` has a number of filtering options for narrowing your output down to a specific user or host. The `last` syntax is `last` *<options>* `[username]`. The command-line switches for these features are documented in Table 19.6.

TABLE 19.6 `last` Command-Line Switches

Option	Description
`-f <filename>`	Reads from an alternative file, rather than `/var/log/wtmp`.
`-n <number of lines>`	Limits the output to the specified number of lines.
`-t <tty filter>`	Filters the results for a specific TTY (for example, `-t console` would display all direct logins).
`-h <hostname or ip>`	Filters based on a hostname or IP address.
`username`	If given, only records matching the given `username` will be displayed.

A similar log to `wtmp` resides in `/var/log/lastlog`, which provides a record of the last time each system user has logged in to the machine. Unfortunately, Apple does not provide the corresponding `lastlog` utility to read this file with Mac OS X. Although the same information can be fetched by reading through the output of `last`, this provides an alternative source that isn't dependent on the `wmtp` for its output. If you want you use the `lastlog` file, a simple reader is provided at `http://www.macosxunleashed.com/downloads/lastlog.c`. The source, originally written for Solaris, has been slightly modified to run on Mac OS X.

The `lastlog` utility can be compiled (assuming Apple's Developer Tools are installed) with `gcc -o lastlog lastlog.c`. The resulting executable (`lastlog`) displays the entire contents of `/var/log/lastlog` or limits the output to a single user by using the syntax `lastlog [username]`:

```
% ./lastlog
User        TTY       Date
------------------------------------------
root        console   Sat Aug 17 02:22:17 2002
jray        ttyp6     Sat Nov 23 13:14:43 2002
test        console   Sun Sep 15 11:24:24 2002
```

Unfortunately, the user logs discussed so far, although they let you keep track of the who, when, and where of user activity, do not provide information about *what* the users are doing. For that, you'll need to enable user accounting on Mac OS X.

Tracking User Activity: `accton` and `acct`

If a user on your system causes a problem (such as attacking a remote system from a Mac OS X account), you can use `wtmp` to find out who was logged in at the same time of the attack, but on a system with hundreds of accounts there may be a few dozen simultaneous logins at the time of attack, or even if you identify the attacker you may be required to produce forensic evidence to back up your accusations.

System-level accounting can be activated via the `accton` command. By default, accounting is not provided as a startup option either through the Mac OS X interface or any of the `Library/StartupItems`. If you want to enable full-time accounting, you have to add it as a new startup item.

The `accton` command takes a single parameter: the pathname of the logfile to use. If the command is given *without* a filename, accounting is disabled. The default logfile location is `/var/account/acct`, which must be created before logging can be used:

```
# mkdir -p /var/account
# touch /var/account/acct
# chown -R root:admin /var/account
# chmod -R 660 /var/account
```

After setting up the directory and logfile, start accounting with `accton /var/account/acct`:

```
# accton /var/account/acct
```

Finally, you can perform reporting on the log by using `lastcomm`. For example, here is a brief excerpt of the accounting log:

```
Mail        -S    jray    __      201.25 secs Fri Nov 22 03:20 (22:15:28.00)
iTunes      -S    jray    __        2.84 secs Sat Nov 23 01:36 (0:00:08.97)
cddafs.uti  -S    root    __        0.02 secs Sat Nov 23 01:36 (0:00:00.14)
cddafs.uti  -S    root    __        0.00 secs Sat Nov 23 01:36 (0:00:00.00)
cddafs.uti  -S    root    __        0.03 secs Sat Nov 23 01:36 (0:00:00.47)
Terminal    -S    jray    __        3.16 secs Fri Nov 22 23:01 (3:34:24.00)
tcsh        -S    jray    ttyp1     0.09 secs Fri Nov 22 23:01 (3:34:16.00)
nslookup    -X    jray    ttyp1     0.02 secs Sat Nov 23 01:12 (0:24:56.00)
login       -SX   jray    ttyp1     0.97 secs Fri Nov 22 23:01 (3:34:16.00)
sh          -S    root    __        0.05 secs Fri Nov 22 03:15 (0:00:06.30)
rm          -S    root    __        0.00 secs Fri Nov 22 03:15 (0:00:00.00)
sh          -SF   root    __        0.00 secs Fri Nov 22 03:15 (0:00:04.83)
cat         -S    root    __        0.00 secs Fri Nov 22 03:15 (0:00:04.80)
sh          -SF   root    __        0.02 secs Fri Nov 22 03:15 (0:00:04.83)
cp          -S    root    __        0.00 secs Fri Nov 22 03:15 (0:00:00.00)
cat         -S    root    __        0.00 secs Fri Nov 22 03:15 (0:00:00.00)
```

Each line consists of the command executed, flags indicating the state of the process, the user, the controlling terminal, the CPU time used by the process, when the process was started, and, finally, the elapsed execution time of the process.

The process flags can be any combination of the following:

- **S**. The process was run as the super user.
- **F**. The process is the result of a fork.
- **D**. The process terminated and wrote a core file (usually indicating a crash).
- **X**. The process was terminated by a signal (such as is sent by the `kill` command).

The `lastcomm` utility syntax is `lastcomm [-f file] [command <command>] [user <user>] [terminal <terminal>]`. Table 19.7 describes these command-line options and their purposes.

TABLE 19.7 `lastcomm` Command-Line Switches

Option	Description
`-f <filename>`	Read from an alternative accounting logfile, rather than `/var/account/acct`.
`command <command>`	Filter the output for a specified command.
`user <user>`	Filter the output for a specified user.
`terminal <terminal>`	Filter the output for a specified terminal.

For example, to view a history of the use of `emacs` on my machine, I could type:

```
# lastcomm emacs
emacs     -S    root    ttyp2     0.67 secs Mon Nov 18 23:45 (0:00:27.25)
emacs     -S    root    ttyp2     0.67 secs Mon Nov 18 23:43 (0:00:25.91)
emacs     -     jray    ttyp2     0.62 secs Mon Nov 18 23:43 (0:00:15.86)
emacs     -     jray    ttyp2     0.53 secs Mon Nov 18 23:43 (0:00:02.66)
```

The accounting log will grow very quickly; it will contain entries for commands that are executed via `cron`, spawned by other processes, or run from the Mac OS X Finder. On a busy system, you could easily see hundreds of entries per minute.

Starting `accton` at Bootup

To start `accton` at boot-time, create a new folder named `Accounting` in `/Library/StartupItems`. Into this folder, add two files: `StartupParameters.plist` and `Accounting`, with the following contents:

`StartupParameters.plist:`

```
{
  Description     = "System Accounting";
  Provides        = ("Process Accounting");
```

```
    OrderPreference = "None";
    Messages =
    {
      start = "Starting Accounting";
    };
  }
```

Accounting:

```
#!/bin/sh
##
# Start Process Accounting
##

. /etc/rc.common

if [ "${ACCOUNTING:=-NO-}" = "-YES-" ]; then
    ConsoleMessage "Starting Accounting"
    /usr/sbin/accton /var/account/acct
fi
```

Finally, add the line `ACCOUNTING=-YES-` to `/etc/hostconfig` to turn the automatic startup on.

Automated Log Monitoring: LogSentry

The biggest problem with logging is information overload. How can one administrator be expected to monitor thousands and thousands of lines each day? Many people will quickly admit that they *do* check their logs, but only when they want to diagnose a problem that already exists. Logs, properly monitored, can provide an effective form of intrusion detection, enabling one to react to potential problems before they become disasters.

In the previous chapter, we looked at a portscan monitor, PortSentry, by Psionic software. In this chapter, we introduce another Psionic product, LogSentry. LogSentry is an extremely simple utility that performs a very important task: It watches your logfiles for you.

As you read through the available logs on your system, you'll notice that problems are typically denoted with words such as `denied` or `refused`. LogSentry contains a long list of "danger" words that can indicate an attack or unusual system activity. On a timed schedule, it checks your logfiles against the keyword list and generates a report of log information that you may want to investigate further. LogSentry doesn't have any problem with keeping track of its place when reading the file, nor does it mind logfile rotations. Best of all, it's easy to set up and adds next to no overhead to your system.

Installing LogSentry

To install LogSentry, first make sure that you have your logs configured appropriately and have a list of the files that you want to monitor. If you have installed additional software that you want to monitor, you may want to check through the logs it generates to look for keywords that indicate warnings you want reported.

Next, download LogSentry from Psionic at `http://www.macosxunleashed.com/downloads`. Unarchive and enter the distribution directory:

```
% curl -O http://www.macosxunleashed.com/downloads/logsentry-1.1.1.tar.gz
% tar zxf logsentry-1.1.1.tar.gz
% cd logcheck-1.1.1/
```

Now, a somewhat odd second step: Move the file `INSTALL` to a different filename. The compilation process attempts to use a file name `install`, but fails because of the lack of casesensitivity of the Mac OS X HFS+ filesystem.

```
% mv INSTALL INSTALL.readme
```

Create the directories where LogSentry will be installed: `/usr/local/etc/`, `/usr/local/bin`, and `/usr/local/etc/tmp`:

```
# mkdir -p /usr/local/etc/tmp
# mkdir /usr/local/bin
# chmod 600 /usr/local/etc/tmp
```

Finally, make and install the software with `make bsdos`.

```
# make bsdos
make install SYSTYPE=bsdos
Making generic
cc -O -o ./src/logtail ./src/logtail.c
./src/logtail.c: In function `main':
./src/logtail.c:51: warning: return type of `main' is not `int'
Creating temp directory /usr/local/etc/tmp
Setting temp directory permissions
chmod 700 /usr/local/etc/tmp
Copying files
cp ./systems/generic/logcheck.hacking /usr/local/etc
cp ./systems/generic/logcheck.violations /usr/local/etc
cp ./systems/generic/logcheck.violations.ignore /usr/local/etc
```

```
cp ./systems/generic/logcheck.ignore /usr/local/etc
cp ./systems/generic/logcheck.sh /usr/local/etc
cp ./src/logtail /usr/local/bin
Setting permissions
chmod 700 /usr/local/etc/logcheck.sh
chmod 700 /usr/local/bin/logtail
chmod 600 /usr/local/etc/logcheck.violations.ignore
chmod 600 /usr/local/etc/logcheck.violations
chmod 600 /usr/local/etc/logcheck.hacking
chmod 600 /usr/local/etc/logcheck.ignore
Done. Don't forget to set your crontab.
```

LogSentry is now installed and can be accessed via `/usr/local/etc/logcheck.sh`, but first you should customize the location where your logfiles are stored and where the resulting reports should be sent.

Configuring LogSentry

To do this, open the file `/usr/local/etc/logcheck.sh` in your favorite editor. First, configure where the outgoing report should be sent. The default value, `root`, can be changed to a remote email address. Search for the `SYSADMIN` line:

```
# Person to send log activity to.
SYSADMIN=root
```

and change it to reflect your email address:

```
# Person to send log activity to.
SYSADMIN=mynamehere@mycompany.com
```

NOTE

You *must* have sendmail configured properly for this to work. It does not need to run as a daemon, but must still have the appropriate directory permissions (or `DontBlameSendmail` flags) set to process outgoing mail.

Next, search for the BSDI logfile configuration section. In the out-of-the-box `logcheck.sh` file, it should look like this:

```
# BSDI 2.x
$LOGTAIL /var/log/messages > $TMPDIR/check.$$
$LOGTAIL /var/log/secure >> $TMPDIR/check.$$
$LOGTAIL /var/log/maillog >> $TMPDIR/check.$$
$LOGTAIL /var/log/ftp.log >> $TMPDIR/check.$$
```

```
# Un-comment out the line below if you are using BSDI 2.1
#$LOGTAIL /var/log/daemon.log >> $TMPDIR/check.$$
```

Unfortunately, these aren't the appropriate names for your Mac OS X files. Modify the lines to read as follows:

```
# BSDI 2.x
$LOGTAIL /var/log/system.log > $TMPDIR/check.$$
$LOGTAIL /var/log/secure.log >> $TMPDIR/check.$$
$LOGTAIL /var/log/mail.log >> $TMPDIR/check.$$
$LOGTAIL /var/log/ftp.log >> $TMPDIR/check.$$
```

NOTE

This example assumes that you haven't changed the Mac OS X `syslog` configuration. If you *have*, you should change the file to match your particular setup, including adding new lines to match additional logfiles.

For most users, setup is now complete. If, however, you'd like to customize the keywords to which LogSentry responds (or doesn't respond), four files in `/usr/local/etc/` can be changed:

- `logcheck.violations`. A list of "negative" keywords/strings that will be searched for and included in the LogSentry report.
- `logcheck.hacking`. A list of keywords/strings that could indicate a potential attack taking place. Matches against the hacking list will be flagged with the heading `ACTIVE SYSTEM ATTACK` in the output report.
- `logcheck.violations.ignore`. Strings that will be ignored, even if they match the `logcheck.violations` file.
- `logcheck.ignore`. Strings that will be ignored, regardless of whether they appear in either the `logcheck.violations` and `logcheck.hacking` files.

As soon as you are satisfied with your setup, run `logcheck.sh` for the first time by typing `/usr/local/etc/logcheck.sh`. If you have a reasonable amount of system activity, you should receive a log alert in your email. For example:

```
Security Violations
=-=-=-=-=-=-=-=-=-=
Nov 23 11:45:16 despair sshd[1025]:
    Failed password for jray from 24.210.90.88 port 49279 ssh2
Nov 23 17:54:10 despair su: jray to root on /dev/ttyp7
```

```
Nov 23 18:24:37 despair sendmail[1633]: gANNObux001633:
    SYSERR(root): hash map "access":
    unsafe map file /etc/mail/access.db: Permission denied
Nov 23 18:26:04 despair sendmail[1647]: gANNQ4ux001647:
    SYSERR(root): hash map "access":
    unsafe map file /etc/mail/access.db: Permission denied
Nov 23 18:26:45 despair sendmail[1672]: gANNQjux001672:
    SYSERR(root): hash map "access":
    unsafe map file /etc/mail/access.db: Permission denied

Unusual System Events
=-=-=-=-=-=-=-=-=-=-=
Nov 23 11:45:16 despair sshd[1025]:
    Failed password for jray from 24.210.90.88 port 49279 ssh2
Nov 23 11:45:18 despair sshd[1025]:
    Accepted password for jray from 24.210.90.88 port 49279 ssh2
Nov 23 11:46:11 despair sudo:
    jray : TTY=ttyp7 ; PWD=/Users/jray ; USER=root ; COMMAND=/bin/tcsh
Nov 23 17:25:50 despair sudo:
    jray : TTY=ttyp7 ; PWD=/Users/jray/logsentry/logcheck-1.1.1 ;
    USER=root; COMMAND=/bin/tcsh
Nov 23 17:54:10 despair su: jray to root on /dev/ttyp7
Nov 23 18:01:09 despair sudo:
    root : TTY=ttyp7 ; PWD=/Users/jray/logsentry/logcheck-1.1.1 ;
    USER=root; COMMAND=/bin/tcsh
Nov 23 18:24:37 despair sendmail[1633]: gANNObux001633:
    SYSERR(root): hash map "access":
    unsafe map file /etc/mail/access.db: Permission denied
    relay=localhost [127.0.0.1], reject=451 4.3.0
    Temporary system failure. Please try again later.
Nov 23 18:26:04 despair sendmail[1645]:
    starting daemon (8.12.2): queueing@01:00:00
Nov 23 18:26:04 despair sendmail[1647]: gANNQ4ux001647:
    SYSERR(root): hash map "access":
    unsafe map file /etc/mail/access.db: Permission denied
Nov 23 18:26:04 despair sendmail[1647]:
    ruleset=check_relay, arg1=localhost, arg2=127.0.0.1,
    relay=localhost [127.0.0.1], reject=451 4.3.0
    Temporary system failure. Please try again later.
```

As you can see, LogSentry does a great job of finding the entries that are worth looking at—and delivering them to your mailbox—without requiring any interaction with you (after you start the program).

Automating LogSentry

The author of LogSentry recommends running the `logcheck.sh` script every hour to keep LogSentry up to date on system activities. You can automate this by adding the following line to the `/etc/crontab` file:

```
00 * * * * root /bin/sh /usr/local/etc/logcheck.sh
```

Alternatively, you can create a `root` user cron job file with the contents

```
00 * * * * /bin/sh /usr/local/etc/logcheck.sh
```

and submit the file to the `cron` process with `crontab <filename>`.

Log-watching is a very monotonous and time-consuming process of being a system administrator. It's an often-overlooked task that *everyone* puts off. With LogSentry, it can be performed effortlessly.

> **TIP**
>
> An alternative logfile analysis program is swatch. Like LogSentry, swatch watches for potentially "bad" signs in your system logs. If you'd like to try something different, swatch is available at `http://www.oit.ucsb.edu/~eta/swatch/`.

Common System Log Changes

To finish up the chapter, we'll take a quick look at some of the common Mac OS X logs, and some improvements that can be made by changing the system defaults. These changes aren't necessary to run a secure system, but they do provide additional feedback on how your system is being used (or abused), which, in turn, make you less likely to be caught off guard in the future.

FTP Logs

On a default Mac OS X installation, the FTP process will simply log connections and login failures:

```
Nov 23 17:27:15 despair ftpd[1195]: connection from localhost to localhost
Nov 23 21:19:17 despair ftpd[1841]: connection from docs33-171.menta.net
    to despair.ag.ohio-state.edu
Nov 23 21:19:18 despair ftpd[1841]: ANONYMOUS FTP LOGIN
    REFUSED FROM docs33-171.menta.net
Nov 24 14:00:02 despair ftpd[2098]: connection from www.ag.ohio-state.edu
    to despair.ag.ohio-state.edu
Nov 24 14:00:07 despair ftpd[2098]: FTP LOGIN FROM www.ag.ohio-state.edu
    as jray (class: real, type: REAL)
```

This is of little use in determining who wrote those XBox ISO images to a directory that was accidentally left with world write permissions, or who has been eating up bandwidth by transferring personal files to and from the server for backups.

The default Mac OS X FTP server can be changed to log information about GETs and PUTs if you edit `/etc/xinetd.d/ftp` so that it passes *two* `-l` (log) switches to the daemon at startup:

```
service ftp
{
        disable = no
        socket_type     = stream
        wait            = no
        user            = root
        server          = /usr/libexec/ftpd
        server_args     = -l-l
        groups          = yes
        flags           = REUSE
}
```

Restarting `xinetd` (`killall -HUP xinetd`) (or starting and stopping the FTP service) puts the changes into effect.

With the additional logging function enabled, the logs will contain expanded information on the files being transferred:

```
Nov 23 23:51:01 www ftpd[23]: connection from
   27-pool1.ras14.ilchi-e.alerondial.net to www.ag.ohio-state.edu
Nov 23 23:51:02 www ftpd[23]: FTP LOGIN FROM
   27-pool1.ras14.ilchi-e.alerondial.net as gmg (class: real, type: REAL)
Nov 23 23:52:58 www ftpd[23]: get BUG.HTM = 545 bytes in 0.006 seconds
Nov 23 23:53:00 www ftpd[23]: get C_EDU.HTM = 15877 bytes in 0.027 seconds
Nov 23 23:53:05 www ftpd[23]: get C_FAIR.HTM = 20960 bytes in 0.033 seconds
Nov 23 23:53:52 www ftpd[23]: get Xpeople.htm = 79158 bytes in 3.618 seconds
Nov 23 23:53:54 www ftpd[23]: get XSTREET.HTM = 549 bytes in 0.017 seconds
Nov 23 23:55:53 www ftpd[23]: Data traffic: 191747 bytes in 23 files
Nov 23 23:55:53 www ftpd[23]: Total traffic: 199236 bytes in 24 transfers
Nov 24 00:52:24 www ftpd[24]: connection from
   27-pool1.ras14.ilchi-e.alerondial.net to www.ag.ohio-state.edu
Nov 24 00:52:25 www ftpd[24]: FTP LOGIN FROM
   27-pool1.ras14.ilchi-e.alerondial.net as gmg (class: real, type: REAL)
Nov 24 00:53:15 www ftpd[24]: put HOME.HTM = 1963 bytes in 0.978 seconds
Nov 24 00:53:17 www ftpd[24]: put LEFT.HTM = 1829 bytes in 0.778 seconds
Nov 24 00:53:20 www ftpd[24]: put RITE.HTM = 2311 bytes in 1.008 seconds
```

```
Nov 24 00:53:22 www ftpd[24]: put STyle.CSS = 2333 bytes in 0.948 seconds
Nov 24 00:53:24 www ftpd[24]: put TOP.HTM = 872 bytes in 0.689 seconds
Nov 24 00:53:29 www ftpd[24]: Data traffic: 9308 bytes in 5 files
Nov 24 00:53:29 www ftpd[24]: Total traffic: 16908 bytes in 7 transfers
```

Webserver Logs

The Mac OS X default Apache configuration uses the `common` log format. Although it is recognized by most log analysis software, the `common` format has been largely replaced by the `combined` log format, which contains the same information as the `common` format, but also includes fields for the referrer (what site linked to the page) and the user-agent (the browser type/version that accessed the page).

To switch to combined format, search for the definition of `CustomLog` in `/etc/httpd/httpd.conf` and change the last parameter of the line to read `combined`, like this:

```
#
# The location and format of the access logfile (Common Logfile Format).
# If you do not define any access logfiles within a <VirtualHost>
# container, they will be logged here. Contrariwise, if you *do*
# define per-<VirtualHost> access logfiles, transactions will be
# logged therein and *not* in this file.
#
CustomLog "/private/var/log/httpd/access_log" combined
```

Restart Apache (`/usr/sbin/apachectl restart`) to complete the switch.

TCP Wrappers

As mentioned earlier, if you're using TCP Wrappers to protect services in `/etc/inetd.conf`, you will *not* see connection attempts that are being denied. To log the messages from TCP Wrappers, you must add a line to `/etc/syslog.conf` that selects messages from the syslog facility and logs them to another log, such as `/var/log/secure.log`:

```
syslog.err                    /var/log/hum.log
```

After restarting `inetd`, the subsequent connections that are rejected by TCP Wrappers will be logged in `/var/log/secure.log`, like this:

```
Nov 23 17:42:54 despair ftpd[1234]:
   refused connect from soyokaze.biosci.ohio-state.edu
Nov 23 17:44:26 despair ftpd[1241]:
```

```
   refused connect from soyokaze.biosci.ohio-state.edu
Nov 23 17:46:39 despair ftpd[1247]:
   refused connect from soyokaze.biosci.ohio-state.edu
```

Obviously this is important information that would otherwise be missing from the system logs.

AppleShare

Logging of the Mac OS X AppleShare fileserver is limited to errors in the default configuration of Mac OS X. This can be quickly corrected if you toggle the `/config/AppleFileServer/activity_log` bit in the NetInfo database:

```
# nicl . -delete /config/AppleFileServer activity_log
# nicl . -create /config/AppleFileServer activity_log 1
```

After you start and stop File Sharing, the `/Library/Logs/AppleFileService/AppleFileServiceAccess.log` file will be created, and will log access to the server:

```
!!Log File Created On: 11/24/2002 15:24:55 327:0:0 GMT
**** - - [24/Nov/2002:15:24:55 -0500] "Mounted Volume Picasso" 0 0 0
**** - - [24/Nov/2002:15:24:55 -0500] "DiskArbStart -" 0 4355 0
IP 10.0.1.101 - - [24/Nov/2002:15:35:14 -0500] "Login John Ray" -5001 0 0
IP 10.0.1.101 - - [24/Nov/2002:15:35:15 -0500] "Login John Ray" 0 0 0
IP 10.0.1.101 - - [24/Nov/2002:15:35:30 -0500] "Create chimera-0.6.dmg" 0 0 0
IP 10.0.1.101 - - [24/Nov/2002:15:35:30 -0500] "OpenFork chimera-0.6.dmg" 0 0 0
IP 10.0.1.101 - - [24/Nov/2002:15:35:30 -0500] "OpenFork chimera-0.6.dmg" 0 0 0
IP 10.0.1.101 - - [24/Nov/2002:15:36:10 -0500] "OpenFork .VolumeIcon.icns" 0 0 0
IP 10.0.1.101 - - [24/Nov/2002:15:36:15 -0500] "OpenFork .DS_Store" 0 0 0
```

You can control the log's verbosity by altering the NetInfo key `/config/AppleFileServer/logging_attributes`. The default value of the `logging_attributes` key is

```
Login_ON,Logout_ON,CreateDir_ON,CreateFile_ON,OpenForkk_ON,Delete_ON
```

You can toggle each attribute to an OFF state by changing the `_ON` to `_OFF` in the attribute string, then writing the value back to NetInfo. Because each of these attributes is stored in a single string (that is, the list of attributes is a single value for `logging_attributes`), it's easiest to edit these from inside the NetInfo Manager, rather than to use `nicl`.

Samba Logging

Samba's default logging state records little more than logins and logouts to the Samba daemon (level 0). It is recommended that active Windows servers run at level 1 to collect a reasonable amount of information. Levels can be set to any value between 0 and 10, where values above 3 are not recommended for nondevelopers.

To set the log level for Samba, add `log_level=<level #>` to the global section of the `/etc/smb.conf` file:

```
# Global parameters
[global]
        log_level = 1
        coding system = utf8
        client code page = 437
        encrypt passwords = Yes
        os level = 255
        preferred master = True
...
```

Restart Windows File Sharing for the change to take effect.

Summary

Logging is a boring topic. It doesn't have the glitz and glamour of topics such as network intrusion detection, portscanning, or firewalling. It is, however, one of the only means for your computer to communicate with you. The `syslog` daemon serves as a central logging server, allowing processes to send their logs to a single location and place related types of information in the same file. Syslog can even be configured to accept incoming logs from all the computers on your network and allow you to monitor all your network logs from a single station. To help "liven up" monitoring logs, software such as Psionic's `LogSentry` can be installed to keep track of unusual and potentially problematic alerts as they occur.

No matter how an administrator approaches the task of logging, nor how mind numbing the topic of logging may seem, it is a critical part of maintaining a secure and healthy system.

20

Disaster Planning and Recovery

IN THIS CHAPTER

- What Is Disaster Recovery and Why Do You Need It?
- Creating a Disaster Recovery Plan
- Mac OS X Backup Software
- Synchronizing Files: `rsync`

Even when you've done everything possible to protect your computer's security, sometimes you must face the reality of recovering from a compromised system. Previously unknown exploits may be uncovered and used, or something as simple as a disk crash could creep up on you. Regardless of the cause, your Mac OS X will need to be returned to operable condition quickly. Creating a disaster recovery plan can greatly ease your mind should your system fail at any time.

What Is Disaster Recovery and Why Do You Need It?

Disaster recovery is the process of rebuilding your system to a known, working state after it has been compromised or otherwise rendered inoperable. This means being capable of dealing with everything from a failing network connection to a massive catastrophe. Many businesses involved in the World Trade Center disaster showed their resiliency by having critical services back online within hours of the tragedy.

Unfortunately, for many people, especially small organizations or businesses and educational institutions, disaster recovery is nothing more than a catchphrase that, when implemented, could cost thousands of dollars and never be needed. It is difficult to convince these underfunded and understaffed organizations that a failure, seemingly insignificant at the moment, could cost them more in the long run. The lack of a stable and secure Internet presence, for example, could easily cost a Web hosting service its clients, reputation, and business.

Types of Disaster Recovery

To understand disaster recovery, you must understand that a properly developed recovery plan addresses more than simply what to do if your computer is "hacked." Specifically, there must be provisions for the following:

- **Hardware Failure**. We will all die sometime (in the distant, distant future). Computers are not an exception.
- **Software Failure or Compromise**. Hard disk corruption or a hacker compromise places your system and network at risk.
- **Infrastructure Failure**. For Internet/intranet-based services, a computer that cannot communicate is useless.
- **Catastrophic Events**. Be prepared for fires, earthquakes, floods, UFO invasions, and other unforeseen events.

To get a better idea of what each of these provisions covers, let's take a more in-depth look at each of these topics.

NOTE

Disaster planning and recovery involves the steps you take if a problem occurs. Although not discussed here, it is assumed that you are already familiar with precautionary measures such as running Disk Utility to repair simple disk problems, or with packages such as Norton Utilities and Drive 10.

This chapter's focus is providing information on what can go wrong and how to plan for it.

Hardware Failure

Hardware failure is the one certainty of all computer systems. If you have a computer, especially one that runs constantly, it will eventually fail. This is an unavoidable fact. Although many computer components (power supplies) can easily be swapped for replacement units, you should be prepared at any given moment to replace any piece of mission-critical hardware you own. If your budget doesn't allow for this, you cannot have an effective recovery plan, and you shouldn't be running mission-critical services.

SCARY, ISN'T IT?

A Web development and hosting service (that shall remain nameless) once asked me to give an analysis of their server environment and offer suggestions for improvement. Upon touring the facility, I found that the three primary servers were running on entirely different hardware platforms, had no backup systems, and were even being used for development (while hosting commercial Web sites). I bluntly suggested creating at least a semblance of redundancy for their commercial users. I was assured that they would.

A few months later, I again toured the server space, to see the exact same setup with no changes. They had decided that the $3,000–$4,000 necessary to create a redundant Web server and backup system were more than they wanted to spend. Wondering how they could keep customers with this sort of setup, I read the contract for their hosting services, expecting to see exceptional prices. Instead, I found promises of "Nightly and Weekly Site and Database Backups." When I asked how they were providing this service, they just laughed and said they'd deal with it when they had to.

I left...and shortly thereafter, so did their customers.

Software Failure or Compromise

Although less demanding on the pocketbook than hardware failure, software corruption (be it unintentional or the result of malicious activity) is no less stressful for those who must deal with it. A machine that has been compromised poses a number of difficulties for the administrator.

First and foremost is data security: What has been compromised? The operating system? Applications? Can the existing data be saved? Because a still functional (albeit "cracked") machine is likely to have more recent files and data on it than a backup, the difficult determination of whether to "trust" a compromised machine must be made.

CAUTION

It is *very* rare that you can consider a compromised computer to be "trustable." Only when the exploit can be traced back to an individual service that does *not* provide a means of gaining shell access should you consider keeping the current Mac OS X installation without reformatting and reinstalling.

For example, there are quite a few CGI and PHP scripts that, when improperly installed, open themselves to exploit. These exploits often manifest themselves in the form of Web site defacing, but are well logged and contained within the directories with invalid permissions. The Web site would need to be restored, but the attack was verifiably contained to a specific area and wouldn't necessarily require you to reinstall the entire system.

On the other hand, if your Web site became defaced and there are no obvious entry points and no log of the incident, the entire server should be considered "untrustable" and reworked appropriately.

If a cracked machine is deemed "untrustable," as is often the case, how can it be restored to its original state? Backups are great, but do they include all the configuration files and settings necessary to make it "as it was"? Mac OS X is deceiving in that it puts a "Mac-like" face on the system. If you've backed up the `/Library/Webserver` directory, you have everything necessary to restore a Web server, right? Wrong. There is the hidden `/etc/httpd` directory with all your Web server settings, there are individual `Sites` directories that must be taken into consideration, as well as any additional Apache modules that have been installed (`/usr/libexec/httpd/`).

To successfully restore a computer, you must be able to account for everything that makes the system do its job. Every application, script, directory, `crontab` entry, and `/etc` file needed for operation must be documented, understood, and easily replaced.

Infrastructure Failure

A working computer is of little use if it cannot communicate with other computers, serve your network, or otherwise fulfill its obligations as a netizen. A failure of your computing infrastructure is often worse than failure of a single computer. Network failures, for example, can be difficult to diagnose and are likely to strike multiple computers simultaneously. The good news is that in many cases your ISP handles network setup, monitoring, and maintenance. Of course, your network is only one part of your computing infrastructure...a power failure can have equally disruptive results, and may even cause equipment failure.

SCARY, ISN'T IT? PART II

I enjoy using anecdotes to drive home a point. Not only do they show the book concepts in a real-world light, but they may also help open the eyes of those who haven't dealt directly with these issues (and their causes) before.

Infrastructure failures are usually the result of physical failure in wiring or supporting hardware. Sometimes, however, these failures are caused by people. For example, another "unnamed" small company who performed a variety of Internet services for clients decided that it wanted to rewire the phone system in the building. To save money, the company owners hired their friends to do the job. Everything went well until the electricians decided to strip out the old wiring as a favor. What they didn't realize was that one of the wires that they stripped out was the T1 line for the building.

To make matters worse, the line was cut flush with the conduit where it entered the building. The conduit itself was sealed in the building's concrete foundation. A split second with a pair of wire snips effectively shut the business down for four or five days, until the provider could completely restring the wiring.

Your computers are important, but without the necessary infrastructure, they're useless.

Catastrophic Events

Your hardware, software, and infrastructure can fail and, with some planning, be restored. But what if they fail *simultaneously* and *irreversibly*? This is a catastrophic failure.

Catastrophic failures can be the result of natural disasters, vandalism, or other uncontrollable events. In the case of catastrophic failure, there is no resurrection of your existing equipment. It is effectively gone, and you will eventually have to face the choice of shutting down your operations or picking up the pieces and moving on. If you have customers depending on your systems, they will likely take their business elsewhere unless given a feasible timeline within which you will redeploy their services. Administrators with a proper disaster recovery plan can often shift their entire operation to backup facilities in a matter of hours.

So, now that you're convinced that you never want to turn on a computer again, let alone deal with the responsibility of keeping it online, let's take a look at how you can develop a plan to make disaster recovery manageable and quite possible.

Creating a Disaster Recovery Plan

Planning for the unthinkable is not as difficult as it may seem. Computers and networks are not fickle creatures. They'll do what they're told until some event occurs that disrupts them. A disaster recovery plan is really just a matter of creating a list of standards and practices and adhering to it. If you fully understand your computing environment, what it is doing, and how it was created, you should be able to re-create the setup (or a portion of it) without going insane. Unfortunately, there is no way to gauge what is appropriate for any given person's situation, so the following rules may be a subset (or even a superset) of what you should lay down for your systems and network.

Standardization

Standardize, if possible, on a single hardware and software platform. Obviously, if you're reading this book, you probably want to standardize on the combination of Macintosh/Mac OS X.

In many ways, you have it *much* easier than your Windows counterparts. There is only a single source for Macintosh hardware (Apple), and an installation of Mac OS X (on, say, an external Firewire hard drive—your iPod, of course!) can be used to boot any of the existing compatible hardware. Reviving a server that is failing for hardware reasons, such as a dying network card or power supply, is often a matter of removing the drive from one machine and placing it in another. In the Windows world, unless you have identical hardware, trying a similar trick will likely play havoc with the computer as it busily tries to reconfigure itself for different motherboards, I/O controllers, video, and so on.

NOTE

Although standardizing on a platform will greatly improve the rate at which you can recover from a serious problem, it may introduce other issues. If an exploit is discovered that affects your platform of choice, it could be carried out against your entire network infrastructure. If support and equipment costs permit, implementing redundancy on multiple server platforms (Apache on Mac OS X *and* Apache on Linux, and so on) will help improve network resiliency.

Storage

Macintosh users, however, are still susceptible to hardware inconsistencies between models. The transition from SCSI to IDE has been a heartbreak for some, while a welcomed cost-saving measure for others. Apple's recent introduction of the Xserve, based on IDE drives, cements their belief that IDE technology is a viable alternative for server platforms. Those who believe otherwise are likely to stick with tower-based servers with build-to-order SCSI support.

NOTE

Visit `http://www.scsi-planet.com/vs/` for links to a number of SCSI versus IDE comparisons and evaluations.

Indecisiveness when choosing a storage standard often leads to "evaluating" a few standards (Firewire, IDE, SCSI) on different machines. Unfortunately, the end result of this approach is that none of the storage media is interchangeable. Set and maintain a storage standard for all your systems. Being able to swap media from a failing computer to one that is stable is a Macintosh advantage that system administrators should recognize and utilize.

Operating System

Okay, I've standardized on Mac OS X, now what? By saying you've standardized on Mac OS X, what does that mean? Mac OS X 10.0? 10.1? 10.1.5? Jaguar? Mac OS X Server? Mac OS X had been available for almost a year and half when this book started to be written. In that time, there have been over half a dozen releases, including two major updates, and the introduction of Mac OS X Server.

Although operating system standardization doesn't mean that you have to be running the latest version of Mac OS X, it does require that you run a standard release on each of your computers with the latest security patches, and that you can easily re-create the base system at a moment's notice. Create a patch CD that contains all the Apple system and security updates that have been released since the system version that you have on CD. Although usually installed with the Apple System Updater, you can download these packages directly from `http://www.info.apple.com/support/downloads.html` or use the Updater's Download Checked Items to Desktop Update menu option. Keeping all the updates (along with any specialized drivers you may need) in one place (such as on a CD or AppleShare server) will make reinstalling much less of a hassle.

TIP

You may want to consider joining one of Apple's Developer programs, `http://developer.apple.com/membership/descriptions.html`. Regardless of whether you actively develop for the Macintosh platform, the developer programs offer prerelease system software for testing, the latest (patched) versions of the system software on CD, and discounts on hardware and support services.

Utilize RAID and Journaling

Mac OS X supports two important technologies for maintaining data integrity: RAID and HFS+ Journaling. RAID provides a safety net for drive failures by writing information to two disks simultaneously. Journaling, on the other hand, stores a database of "change" information as data is written to a disk. If a power failure or crash corrupts the system, the database can be used to reconstruct the last "working" version of the data on the drive. Both these technologies are built into Mac OS X and are accessed in the Disk Utility application.

To activate RAID support, you must start with two identical disks in your computer. These disks will be combined into an array and appear to your system as a single drive. If you're planning to use the RAID array for your system installation, you must boot from your installation CD and run Disk Utility from the Installer menu.

Start the Disk Utility (/Applications/Utilities/Disk Utility) and click the RAID tab, as shown in Figure 20.1.

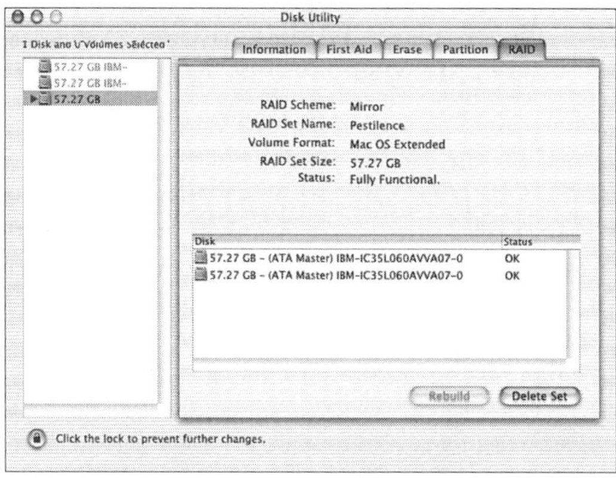

FIGURE 20.1 RAID support can increase the reliability of your system.

RAID support is available in one of two "flavors":

- **Mirroring (level 0).** Mirroring creates an exact duplicate of data on a second drive. If one disk fails, the second disk takes over. The disk can then be replaced without loss of information.
- **Striping (level 1).** Data is written in "stripes" on both disks. There is no data redundancy; the benefit lies in the speed at which data can be written and read because the drives can operate in parallel.

Drag the two disks to use in the array from the list on the left of the window into the "Disk" list on the right. Use the RAID Scheme pop-up menu to choose between mirroring and striping (mirroring provides the data security we're going for). Choose a name for the set. (This is the volume label of the disk that will appear on your desktop.) Finally, choose the file system type and click Create. After a few moments the RAID array is created and appears as a new single disk on the system. You can use this like any other disk, with the added benefit of data redundancy.

You enable journaling support from the command line in Mac OS X by using the syntax `diskutil enableJournal <mount path>`. For example, to enable Journal support on your root disk, you would type the following as root:

```
# diskutil enableJournal /
```

File System Layout

As was discussed in Chapter 1, "An Introduction to Mac OS X Security," you should do what you can to use a standardized Unix file system layout (third-party software is installed in `/usr/local`, partitions where possible, and so on). If necessary, you could reinstall Mac OS X on top of a properly configured file system and not replace any of the additional software you may have installed. The goal of disaster recovery is to restore your computer to a working state with as little trouble as possible. If that means spending a bit more time when you first set up your system, so be it.

TIP

As hinted at here, Mac OS X can be reinstalled on a partition without destroying the existing data. On a system that has failed or will no longer boot, you can rerun the Mac OS X Installer *without* erasing the destination drive. The operating system is installed, preserving user accounts and any additional software that was *not* part of the original system installation. If, however, you have upgraded versions of applications that are included on the CD (Apache, sendmail, and so on), these are replaced with what came on the CD.

Create a Division of Services

Although budget constraints may limit the extent to which you can divide the services you offer, you should still consider it a best-practices measure to be implemented whenever possible. If you run Mail, Web, and Appleshare services, it's in your best interest to keep them on separate machines. Small companies can often get away with keeping everything on a single server, but they risk losing everything should a single service fail or be compromised.

For example, storing your internal development and work files on your public Web server opens them to the possibility of being read, modified, or removed by external forces beyond your control. Keep in mind that no matter how many patches you've applied, and how well you've kept up with the security bulletins, software is rarely perfect. Something inevitably comes along with the potential of breaking even the most meticulously protected system. To lose your and your co-workers' documents or email, and perhaps expose private information simply because a previously unknown PHP bug is discovered is simply unacceptable.

SCARY, ISN'T IT? PART III

By keeping as few services running on a particular machine as possible, you greatly reduce the risk of any given service failing at any given time.

An example of the worst-case scenario occurred recently when a business was making a move from one building to another. Very little investment had been made in the company's server, and they had, in fact, made the mistake of placing all their eggs in one basket. The server being transported handled file serving, database, Web, and email. On the short trip from building to building, the jostling damaged the computer's drives. When it was plugged back in, it failed.

The first reaction was "We need to get a list of the customers so we can notify them that there is a problem." Unfortunately, the current customer list was in a database, stored where? On the failed server.

After much fumbling, written invoices were produced to gather the customer list. The next lament was, "I'm trying to email everyone, but it can't connect to the email server." Sadly, the DHCP server required to configure the internal network was also on the primary server—as was the mail server itself.

In the end, after configuring all the network settings by hand, email was sent from various personal accounts (Jotmail, AOL, and so on) to clients to inform them of what had happened. Think of the PR nightmare of explaining this scenario to *your* customers.

This is yet another example of poor planning, poor implementation, and poor recovery.

Division of services not only makes sense from the perspective of disaster recovery, but from the standpoint of service scalability, as well. Dedicated servers offer more scalability than a combination of services because they are not competing for resources. A file server, for example, makes a poor pairing companion with a Web server. Both can quickly become bound by the performance of the I/O systems—where they will be in perpetual competition. A combination file/DHCP server, however, *is* workable because the DHCP is *not* I/O bound (unless you have a very large network with extremely low lease times).

In addition to dividing services between machines, you should also consider making a division between internal and external services. Unnecessarily exposing internal network services (file server, intranet Web, and so on) to the Internet is an invitation for trouble. Internal services should, if possible, not have a viable route to the Internet, or should be firewalled at the very least.

Write Documentation

One of the most important disaster recovery precautions is creating appropriate system and infrastructure documentation. Although certainly less exciting than actually building your servers and network, documenting their components is just as important. How many people in your organization are familiar with your systems? How many could take over if something happened to *you*? Although the obvious solution is to cross-train employees, in reality, this is rarely completely possible. Employees specialize in different areas and it is a rare person who can simply serve as a "drop-in" replacement for another.

I've personally run into a situation where a network's administrator isn't present and the network goes offline. Although I understood the network, the problem was between the ISP and the building; diagnosis required an invasive test, initiated by the ISP. Unfortunately, the ISP required that trouble-tickets be created through a certain phone number (the administrator's cell phone) or that they be supplied with a personal password (of course, known only to the administrator). In this case, the network and computer systems were well documented, but a few pieces of information that normally wouldn't be needed were not available.

Specifically, you should keep tabs on the following:

- **Network Topology**. Networks aren't usually difficult to understand. For this reason, many people don't properly document their network wiring, switch configuration, and so on. Unfortunately, over time, networks tend to grow and evolve. When forced to re-create a network from scratch, it is often impossible to remember what goes where, and more importantly, why. Take the time to map your network properly. For some help, you may be interested in InterMapper (`http://www.intermapper.com/`) for mapping, autodevice discovery, and monitoring, or OmniGraffle (`http://www.omnigroup.com/applications/omnigraffle/`) for mapping only.
- **Service Providers**. Most people are not their own ISPs, nor their own power generators, nor telephone companies. These services are critical for communicating with your clients and users, keeping your services online, and providing a useful network environment for everyone. Create a list of contact information for reporting failures and monitoring service status. Make sure that this list is distributed among multiple support people outside your organization and that people understand when it should be used.
- **Hardware and Software Inventories**. For each server, you should keep a list of the software, services provided, and instructions on how the applications were installed and configured. Like networks, software configurations tend to change over time. Any modifications should be logged to the inventory at the time they are made, not after the fact.

- **Procedures**. Document routine procedures that may seem like common sense to you, but may not be known to others—such as creating backups and restoring, running disk maintenance software, performing network diagnostics, and so on. Obviously, these depend on the nature of your operation, but you should do everything possible to empower others to fix trouble should it occur. (Note: If you're concerned about job security because of documenting everything you do, consider what people might think if you don't document *anything*!)
- **Clients and Users**. Last but not least, document your clients and users—anyone who will need to know when there is a disruption in service. Unfortunately, in times of stress, end users are often the last to hear what is going on. You'll find that people are infinitely more understanding if they are kept informed of problems instead of having to discover them on their own.

When documenting your system, take the time to create print copies of all instructions. Commenting within configuration files is a good practice during routine system maintenance, but in the case of complete data loss, electronic documentation will be of little use. A copy of your printed documentation should also be stored offsite, guarding against catastrophic failure.

Of course, complete data loss should never happen, because of the final component of a well-rounded disaster recovery plan: backups.

Develop a Backup Schedule

The most important part of any disaster recovery plan is creating a backup schedule and following through on it. Backups should enable you to quickly restore a computer's settings without requiring a complete reinstall and setup. Additionally, a copy of all backups should be archived offsite; if an event occurs that can destroy your servers, it's a good bet that it will also take out your local backup systems. I recommend looking into an NAS (Network Attached Storage) unit for a remote backup solution that is simple to use and maintain. Quantum's SNAP server, for example, can be ordered in RAID configurations of hundreds of gigabytes. Hosting the NAS unit at a remote site or your ISP gives you the security of an offsite backup and (for the most part) worry-free operation.

Macintosh Backups

Running backups on Mac OS X is one of the more un-Mac-like tasks that can be undertaken on the operating system. The trouble stems from a difference between how the Mac has traditionally stored its files versus the standard Unix file system. The native Mac OS X file system, HFS+, stores many files as two separate forks: the resource fork and data fork. The resource fork stores menu and window definitions, icons, and other elements that can easily be changed even after a program is compiled. The data fork contains the "meat" of the file and is the only portion that can be read by most of the standard BSD command-line utilities. Copying a file with both data and resource forks by using `cp` effectively strips the resource fork from the file. In most cases the data fork cannot stand on its own, so the duplicate file is useless. Apple is slowly migrating to a bundle (basically folders of flat files) architecture, but until the entire system is migrated and third-party developers catch up, resource forks must still be taken into account.

Backup Strategies

The next section looks at the available built-in options for backing up and archiving information—both flat files and files with resource and data forks. But before deciding how you'll be performing your backups, however, you need to come up with a backup strategy. This, like so many other things we've discussed, is dependent on the services that a given computer is providing.

A Web server that is updated twice a year presents a very different backup scenario than a file server that changes every single day. In the case of the Web server, you'd be best off archiving the Web site after each update. With Mac OS X's built-in CD burning, you can simply copy the contents of the Web site(s) to the CD. A file server likely contains more than can fit on a single CD-ROM, and is in a constant state of flux. Here, a backup of only what has changed is more appropriate and will save you both time and backup media.

Backups generally fall into two categories: full and incremental. A full backup is an exact duplicate of everything within your file system (or a branch thereof, such as `/Users` or `/usr/local`). From a full backup you can quickly restore the state of all the backed up files as they existed at the time the backup was made. Full backups are time consuming (all files must be copied each time the backup is run) and cannot efficiently be used to store multiple versions of files over an extended period of time. If, for example, you want to have a copy of each day's updates to your fileserver for the period of a year, you would need to make 365 full copies of each of the files—this can quickly add up in terms of storage media. Full backups are usually reserved for mostly static information that can be copied and stored.

An incremental backup, on the other hand, is used to archive file systems that *aren't* static. You start with a single full backup, and then periodically back up the files that have changed since the full backup took place. Incremental backups can take place at multiple "levels," with each level backing up only the files that have changed since the preceding level was backed up.

For example, the BSD `dump` command creates backups at levels from `0` to `9`. A backup with a level of `0` is a full backup, and the subsequent levels can be assigned arbitrarily depending on how you want to structure your backup system. Many people work with a monthly, daily, weekly model. In this case, a full backup is made to start (level 0). On a monthly basis, the files that have changed since the last full backup are added (level 1). Weekly, the files that have changed since the last monthly backup are added (level 2). And, finally, daily, the files that have changed since the last weekly backup are added (level 3).

To restore the most recent set of files from an incremental backup, one would first restore the most recent 0 level dump (full), then the most recent level 1 dump (monthly), followed by the current level 2 dump (weekly), and finally the current day's level 3 dump. Following this model of daily/weekly/monthly incremental backups enables you to restore the file system to its exact state at the time the backup was performed for any given day. Of course you'll need to keep every single one of these backup sets to do that, but the amount of storage required to do this is significantly less than if a full backup were made every day. (The preceding statement is *usually* true. If *all* of the files change every day, there is no difference between an incremental backup and a full backup. This, however, is very, very unlikely.)

NOTE

When working with `dump`, the level numbers can be arbitrarily assigned between `1` and `9`—as long as you understand that higher numbered dumps back up whatever has changed since the next available lower dump. The assignment of level 1, 2, and 3 in this example could just as well been 2, 5, and 8. Only level `0` (full backup) has a specific purpose.

Other incremental backup tools, such as Retrospect, offer a more visual, user-friendly approach to incremental backups, so if this seems confusing, don't worry; it isn't the only option. The incremental backup "philosophy" is shared among many backup tools, but the verbiage of the documentation may vary between products.

WHAT BACKUP MEDIA SHOULD I USE?

Like so many other choices you make, there are advantages and drawbacks to the different types of backup media you use with your system.

Optical media, such as CD-ROMs, are inexpensive, durable, and easy to use. Unfortunately, they limit you to roughly 680MB per disc. With the base Mac OS X install itself occupying more than the capacity of a single CD, this can be a somewhat painful solution for doing complete system backups. CD carousels are one solution to the problem, but may not be priced within reach. DVD-R and DVD-RW offer greater storage capacities, but still well below that of today's hard drives.

Modern DAT systems are economical, have very large capacities, and are remarkably fast, but the potential for media failure is great. Tapes should be maintained in a temperature- and humidity-controlled environment. I've been witness to many failed restores because tapes were either mishandled in storage or left beside someone's CRT and inadvertently demagnetized. Tapes are the best high-capacity storage medium available, but must be cared for appropriately.

Disks, whether in the form of NAS (Network Attached Storage), Firewire drives, SCSI, and so on have only recently moved into the realm of being high enough in capacity and cheap enough in cost to be an effective backup medium. Although far more expensive than optical media or tapes, you can use disks effectively for periodic backups without spending thousands of dollars.

Choose what you can afford and what is needed to get the job done. You *must* have backups for effective disaster recovery—this is not a good place to skimp.

Mac OS X Backup Software

Your Mac OS X comes with software that *can* be used to back it up. Unfortunately, it does not include anything that could reasonably be considered an all-purpose backup tool. .Mac members can use the Backup software included with their accounts to back up documents and other account data, but this is hardly a comprehensive systemwide tool. The final topic of this chapter will take you through the available built-in applications, as well as some third-party applications you might want to look into.

ditto

The `ditto` command can be used to copy *any* Mac OS X directory structure from one location (or volume) to another. It can even be used to create complete booting copies of the operating system. It is *not* an incremental backup tool, but it can do what most standard Unix command-line tools can't: copy complete files, including their resource forks.

The `ditto` syntax is

```
ditto [<options>] <source> [<source>...] <destination>
```

Table 20.1 defines the `ditto` command-line options.

TABLE 20.1 `ditto` Command-Line Reference

Option	Description
`<source>`	Source path.
`<destination>`	Destination path. This is created if it doesn't already exist.
`-v`	Print a line of output for each directory copied.
`-V`	Print a line of output for each object copied (file, directory, and so on).
`-rsrc`	Copy resource forks for all files that have them.
`-arch [ppc|m86k|i386|hppa|sparc]`	When copying the files, remove information for system architectures other than what is specified. Because Mac OS X is available on only the PPC platform at this time, this of little use right now.
`-bom [Bill of Materials File]`	Restricts the objects being copied to those contained in a bill of materials (`.bom`) file. BOM files are stored with the `Contents/Resources` directory of Mac OS X package files.

If you'd like a GUI face on `ditto`, download Carbon Copy Cloner at `http://www.bombich.com/software/ccc.html`. Carbon Copy Cloner, shown in Figure 20.2, is shareware, and can be used to easily copy complete, bootable Mac OS X volumes.

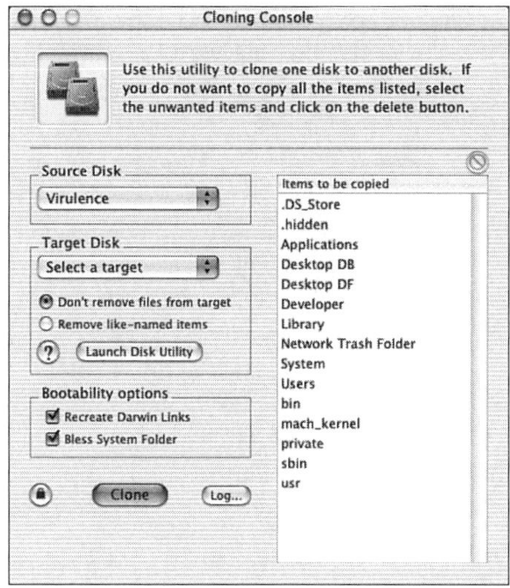

FIGURE 20.2 Carbon Copy Cloner adds a GUI to the `ditto` tool.

NOTE

Another command-line tool that can handle HFS+ is `hfspax` from Howard Oakley. It is a free download from `http://homepage.mac.com/howardoakley/FileSharing.html`.

Alternatively, an HFS+-aware version of tar can be found at `http://www.metaobject.com/Community.html#hfstar`.

dump/restore

The `dump` and `restore` commands work together to create an incremental backup system. Although typically used with tape drives (which are unsupported in Mac OS X's `dump/restore`), these commands can also be used to back up to disks, removable media, and remote tapes. Unfortunately, they do *not* support the HFS+ file system, so unless you've based your system on UFS, their usefulness to you may be quite limited. As you may guess from the names, `dump` creates the backup, and `restore` restores it.

The syntax for `dump` is simply

```
dump [-<options>] <filesystem>
```

As always, the complexity is in the details. Table 20.2 provides a reference for dump.

TABLE 20.2 Command-Line Reference for dump

Option	Description
<*filesystem*>	File system to back up. Should be specified as a device name on Mac OS X. The mount command displays mounted volumes.
u	Update the dumpdates (/etc/dumpdates) after each dump. This is required for dump to keep track of its backup status.
[0-9]	The level of the dump to perform. 0 is always a full dump, whereas 1–9 may be chosen for other levels when developing a backup strategy.
-f <*destination*>	The destination file to write to. The destination may be a normal file or a device such as a disk (/dev/diskxxx). You can also specify a remote device in the format username@hostname:device. The remote system must be configured to deal with these requests.
-b <*blocksize*>	The size (in k) of dump records written to the output device. This is constrained by the I/O system and is usually limited to 64KB.
-d <*density*>	The tape density in the bits per inch.
-s <*tape length*>	The length of the tape in feet.

Several of these options (b, d, s) are obviously related to backups that involve a tape device. Because Mac OS X doesn't support tapes at the command-line, these can be used only when backing up to remote tape drives, which, again, must be configured under Linux or another Unix flavor. If you do decide to use dump, read through the manpages; a number of more obscure options are not shown here.

After running a dump to a file, device, or remote tape, you can subsequently restore the contents by using the restore command. As with dump, the basic syntax is simple:

```
restore -i <options>
```

Obviously, options are required for telling restore *what* it is restoring. The most common command-line options are shown in Table 20.3

TABLE 20.3 Restore Options

Option	Description
-i	Run in interactive mode. We've provided this as part of the default syntax, but it *is* an option. If you're interested in other (noninteractive) methods of restoring files, please refer to the man pages.
-v	Output a line with each file's type and name as it is being restored.
-b <*blocksize*>	The size (in k) of the dump records in the backup file.
-f <*source backup set*>	The backup file created by dump. This may be a normal file, or a device such as a disk (/dev/diskxxx). You can also specify a remote device in the format username@hostname:device. The remote system must be configured to deal with these requests.
-s <*file number*>	If multiple dump files exist on a tape, chooses the file number to use. Files are numbered incrementally, starting at 1.

When running in interactive mode (`-i`), `restore` reads the backup file, then drops the user into to an interactive shell where they can pick and choose the files and directories that they want to restore.

Table 20.4 shows the interactive command reference for `restore`.

TABLE 20.4 Interactive `restore` Command Reference

Command	Description
`ls [`*<directory>*`]`	Lists the contents of the current or named directory.
`cd` *<directory>*	Changes to the named directory.
`pwd`	Displays the path of the current directory.
`add` *<file or directory>*	Adds a file or directory to the list of objects to restore. If a * is specified, all elements in the current directory are selected.
`delete` *<file or directory>*	Removes a file or directory from the list of objects to restore. This does *not* affect the data stored in the backup.
`extract`	Extracts the files that you've added to the restoration list. This is usually the final step in restoring files.
`help`	Displays a command reference.
`quit`	Exits the `restore` session. If you have added files to the restore list and not `extracted` them, the list will *not* be restored.

When using `restore`, remember that you're *not* working within your Mac OS X file system; you're viewing the contents of the `dump` file. What you see is what is available to restore, not what is currently on your system.

Again, unless you're in an all-Unix environment, `dump/restore` might not be appropriate for your system.

Retrospect 5.0

Dantz's Retrospect 5.0 for Mac OS X comes in a variety of different flavors, from a standalone "Retrospect Express" for a single computer to Retrospect Server, capable of backing up Windows and Mac OS 9/X clients and even sensing and archiving notebook computers as they connect to the network.

Retrospect is a full incremental backup solution that supports hundreds of storage devices, features built-in scheduling, and can automate offsite backups by storing information on FTP servers, as shown in Figure 20.3.

Whether you are running multiple Macintosh or Windows computers on a network or a single standalone computer, Retrospect is a wise investment. It provides a comprehensive cross-platform backup solution that behaves like a Macintosh application.

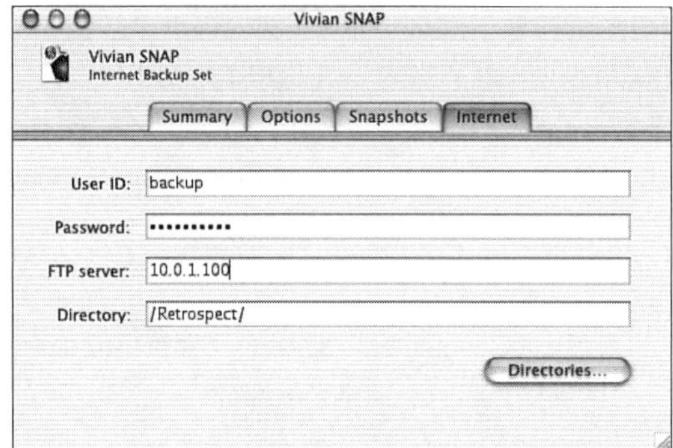

FIGURE 20.3 Retrospect can create offsite backups by archiving to remote FTP servers.

Disk Copy and `hdiutil`

The Disk Copy utility that comes with Mac OS X can create perfect disk images of a source volume. If you've downloaded `.dmg` or `.img` files before, you've worked with disk images. The entire contents of a partition can be copied to an image, giving you a complete archive of the partition at the time it was captured, including file ownerships and permissions. Because the image is stored in a single file, you can store multiple images on a single backup volume (such as a CD-ROM or Firewire Drive).

To create an image, start Disk Copy and choose New Image from Device (Option+Command+I) from the File menu. A device selector window appears, as shown in Figure 20.4. Expand the disk objects by clicking the disclosure arrow in front of each line. The disks display all available partitions. If only a single partition exists on the disk, you select it by choosing the disk itself; you cannot expand it in the list.

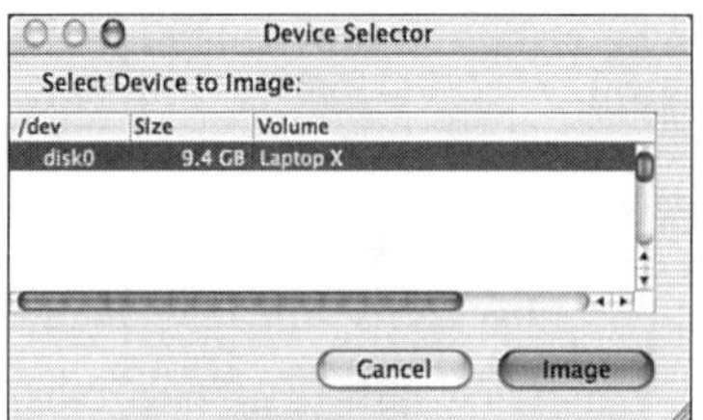

FIGURE 20.4 Disk Copy can create disk images from any readable partition.

Choose one of the disks or partitions and click the Image button. Mac OS X prompts you for image's destination, format (Read-only, Read/Write, Compressed), and whether or not it should be encrypted. If you're creating a backup, I recommend choosing a read-only format. The "compressed" format also results in a read-only image, but unless you're short on space, the length of time it takes to compress the image is rarely worth the space savings. Finally, don't bother with encryption unless you're storing a backup of sensitive information. Encrypting an image is also a time-consuming action, not necessary for most backups.

TIP

If you're not sure what partition you want to choose when making an image, you may want to use the `mount` command-line tool to show where the partitions are mounted. For example:

```
# mount
/dev/disk0s9 on / (local)
devfs on /dev (local)
fdesc on /dev (union)
<volfs> on /.vol (read-only)
/dev/disk0s10 on /Volumes/Laptop 9 (local)
```

Here you can see two disks: the main Mac OS X volume (mounted on /) corresponds to `disk0s9`, whereas my Mac OS 9 partition (Laptop 9) is `disk0s10`. Alternatively, use `disktool -l` to display slightly more detailed volume information.

To create an image from a folder within a partition, choose New Image from Folder or Volume from the File menu. You can then choose what data to image by using the standard Mac OS X file browser.

hdiutil

To create and manipulate disk images from the command line, you can use the `hdiutil` utility. `hdiutil` provides all the features of Disk Copy, accessible through a relatively simple syntax: `hdiutil <verb> [options]`. Available options are dependent on the verb. Several common verbs and options are shown in Table 20.5

TABLE 20.5 Common `hdiutil` Verbs and Options

Verb and Options	Use
`attach <imagename>`	Mount the named disk image.
`detach <device name> [-force]`	Unmount the disk image device. If the force option is used, the unmount is completed regardless of open files.
`create <imagename> <size spec> [options]`	Create a new disk image with the given image name and size. Size can easily be specified by using `-size <spec>` followed by a number and unit of measure (b/k/m/g/t/p/e), such as `-size 100g` for 100GB. Other options include `-volname <volume name>` to set a volume name, and `-fs <HFS+|HFS|MS-DOS|UFS>` to set a file system.
`resize <size spec> <imagename> [options]`	Resize an existing image. Options include `-imageonly` to resize the image file, not the partitions it contains, `-partitiononly` to resize the partitions, not the image, and `-growonly` or `-shrinkonly` to allow the image file to grow or shrink, respectively.

TABLE 20.5 Continued

Verb and Options	Use
`burn <imagename> [options]`	Burn the image to optical media. Use the options to control the burn process: `-testburn` tests the burn without actually writing, `-eject` ejects the CD after burning (`-noeject` does the opposite), `-verify` verifies the burn process (`-noverify` does the opposite), `-optimizeimage` optimizes the image for burning (`-nooptimizeimage`, again, does the opposite), `-speed <#>` sets the burn speed, `-erase` performs a quick erase on the media, and `-fullerase` erases the entire media.
`verify <imagename> [options]`	Verifies the checksum of an existing image.

`hdiutil` sports a large number of verbs and options, and I recommend reading the full man page to see all of them. Those provided in the preceding table are sufficient for most common tasks, such as imaging and burning CDs or DVDs of critical directories on your system. For example, the following sequence creates a new disk image, mounts it, copies the contents of my home directory to it, unmounts it, and, finally burns the image to a CD.

```
% hdiutil create -size 100m -fs HFS+ myimage
...............................................................................
Initialized /dev/rdisk2s2 as a 100 MB HFS Plus volume
/usr/bin/hdiutil: detach: "disk2s1" detached successfully.
/usr/bin/hdiutil: detach: "disk2s2" detached successfully.
/usr/bin/hdiutil: detach: "disk2" detached successfully.
created: myimage.dmg
% hdiutil attach myimage.dmg
/dev/disk2              Apple_partition_scheme
/dev/disk2s1            Apple_partition_map
/dev/disk2s2            Apple_HFS                         /Volumes/untitled
% ditto -rsrcFork /Users/jray /Volumes/untitled
% hdiutil detach /dev/disk2
hdiutil: detach: "disk2s1" detached successfully.
hdiutil: detach: "disk2s2" detached successfully.
hdiutil: detach: "disk2" detached successfully.
% hdiutil burn myimage.dmg
```

Synchronizing Files: `rsync`

Having a backup of critical files is the best way to avert disaster, but restoring a backup can be time consuming, and creating an exact mirror is often impractical on a day-to-day basis. In many cases, the best solution is to synchronize files between two or more machines as changes are made. Starting in Mac OS X 10.2, Apple has included rsync, an Open Source utility designed to make folder synchronization fast, scriptable, and painless.

NOTE

The version of rsync included in Mac OS X 10.2 does not include support for HFS+ resource forks, but a work-alike HFS+ compatible version is available for download through the Open Darwin Web site CVS, at http://www.opendarwin.org/cgi-bin/cvsweb.cgi/proj/rsync_hfs/.

Rsync can operate locally to synchronize files between directories on a single machine, or can work over a network. An especially nice feature of the software is its ability to use several different transport mechanisms for network transfers. The rsync utility, for example, can operate as a server and be used to host rsync-accessible directories on remote machines, but if setting up an additional dedicated server process isn't desirable, you don't have to. An alternative (and often overlooked) method of providing rsync access is through a remote shell such as SSH. If your Mac OS X machines are running SSH, they are ready to use rsync immediately—without any additional software or configuration.

Using rsync

The rsync syntax is simple: `rsync [options] <source> <destination>`. For example, to synchronize the contents of the folder /Users/jray/source with /Users/jray/destination, I would use the following:

```
% rsync -va source/ destination
rsync: building file list...
rsync: 6 files to consider.
./
Icon
apache_pb.gif
index.html
macosxlogo.gif
web_share.gif
wrote 25079 bytes  read 100 bytes  50358.00 bytes/sec
total size is 24711  speedup is 0.98
```

In this example, the -v (verbose) and -a (archive) options are included so that rsync displays files being copied and includes all attributes (permissions, owner, and so forth) of the original files. Running the command again produces slightly different output, because rsync doesn't need to recopy the files:

```
% rsync -va source/ destination
rsync: building file list...
rsync: 6 files to consider.
wrote 172 bytes  read 20 bytes  128.00 bytes/sec
total size is 24711  speedup is 128.70
```

Here, no files were copied because the directories are already in sync.

NOTE

Trailing slashes mean something to `rsync`. If a path is given with a trailing slash, it refers to the contents of the named directory. If the slash is excluded, it means the directory itself.

Although synchronizing local directories may be useful, the true power of `rsync` is revealed when it is used over a remote network connection. To do this, all that is needed is a running SSH daemon on the remote side, and an account with access to the directory you want to sync. If you've ever used `scp`, you'll recognize the syntax for an SSH-tunneled `rsync` immediately. For example, assume I want to synchronize the directory `/Users/jray/Tools` located on a remote server `www.poisontooth.com` with a local directory `Tools`—and, at the same time, compress the data as it is sent:

```
% rsync -vaze ssh  jray@www.poisontooth.com:/Users/jray/Tools/ Tools
jray@www.poisontooth.com's password: ******
receiving file list ... done
./
htdigsearch/
adduser
authuser.pl
backupdisdain.pl
cgiinput.pl
deluser
footer.html
htdigsearch/README.txt
htdigsearch/format.html
htdigsearch/long.html
htdigsearch/name.config
htdigsearch/nothing.html
htdigsearch/sample.conf
htdigsearch/search.php
htdigsearch/short.html
htdigsearch/syntax.html
indexsites.pl
johnclient.pl
```

```
johnscron
ptail.pm
runindex.pl
setupconfig.pl
ticker.tar
wrote 448 bytes  read 216031 bytes  18824.26 bytes/sec
total size is 1262138  speedup is 5.83
```

This example introduces the use of `-e ssh` to specify that `ssh` should be used as the remote shell through which `rsync` will connect and `-z`, which will compress data in real time to increase the transfer rate. There are a number of additional switches that can be used with `rsync` to change its behavior. Table 20.6 documents many of the useful options.

TABLE 20.6 Useful `rsync` Options

Option	Description
`-v`	Use verbose output.
`-a`	Recursively copy files, preserving as much information as possible.
`-c`	Calculate a checksum before sending and after receiving to verify file integrity.
`-b`	Create a backup of existing files. Any file that would be replaced is renamed with a ~ (tilde) extension.
`--suffix=`*`<string>`*	Set the string used as a suffix when using the -b option. By default, the suffix is ~.
`-u`	Skip any files that are already newer (have a more recent date stamp) at the destination.
`-n`	Perform a "dry run" of the operation, displaying what would be copied, but without making any changes.
`--existing`	Do not copy any files that don't already exist on the destination.
`--delete`	Delete files on the destination that are not in the source.
`--max-delete=<#>`	Set the maximum number of files that can be deleted (to avoid disaster).
`--delete-after`	Delete files only after they have been successfully transferred.
`--exclude=`*`<pattern>`*	Exclude files from the operation based on a pattern, such as `*.dmg`.
`--include=`*`<pattern>`*	Do not exclude files that match the given pattern (used in conjunction with `--exclude`).
`-z`	Compress transferred data.
`-p`	Transfer file permissions. Implied by `-a`.
`-o`	Transfer file ownership (must be root). Implied by `-a`.
`-g`	Transfer file group membership. Implied by `-a`.
`-t`	Transfer file modification times. Implied by `-a`.

Be certain to read through the `rsync` man page for additional information on command usage—the `include` and `exclude` options can be used to generate complex file selection rulesets beyond simple wildcards. Also, if you'd like to run a dedicated `rsync` server rather than using an SSH, you can view a tutorial on the setup of an `rsync` daemon at `http://www.macosxhints.com/article.php?story=20021023063424701`.

Other Options

Although Retrospect is "king" of Mac OS X backups, there are a number of other utilities that may or may not suit your needs. If you've reached this point and still don't see something you like, visit these product sites for a few more options:

- **FWB Backup Toolkit**. An incremental backup solution, lacking some of the features of Retrospect, but also lacking the price tag. `http://www.fwb.com/html/backup_toolkit.html`.
- **Tivoli Storage Manager Client**. A client for IBM's Tivoli enterprise backup system. Although not a backup solution on its own, it does help integrate Mac OS X into popular corporate backup systems. `http://www.ibmlink.ibm.com/usalets&parms=H_202-078`.
- **Synchronize! X/Synchronize! X Pro**. Award winning synchronization products that can be used to create scheduled bootable backups. `http://www.qdea.com`.
- **ChronoSync**. Synchronizes the contents of drives. Features rules for selecting files, full Applescript support, and the ability to sync across network volumes. `http://www.econtechnologies.com/`.
- **FoldersSynchronizer**. Quick and easy application to synchronize the contents of drives and folders. `http://www.softobe.com/products/flsy/pp.html`.
- **BackupScript**. A 100% Applescript-based backup solution. Although not nearly as robust as the other tools, the Applescript can be easily modified as you see fit. `http://www.railheaddesign.com/pages/software/backupscript/backupscript.html`.
- **Carbon Copy Cloner**. Carbon Copy Cloner, as mentioned earlier in the chapter, provides a GUI for the `ditto` command. Using CCC, you can create bootable mirror volumes of your Mac OS X computer. `http://www.bombich.com/software/ccc.html`.
- **Synk X**. Open source and written in Cocoa, Synk X provides synchronization services to Mac OS X and can keep multiple volumes up to date. Synk X provides powerful Applescripting features and intelligent change recognition, such as backing up files even if the only change is an altered permission setting. Download Synk X from `http://mypage.uniserve.ca/~rvoth/synk4_target.htm`.

Although half a dozen tools may seem quite a few to a Mac user (hey, we're used to a few *quality* applications!), the choices are still very limited. We are currently without an all-in-one incremental backup utility that can be executed and scripted from the command line. Although Retrospect is schedulable and quite flexible, it does not benefit from the BSD underpinnings of Mac OS X. In time, solutions for (and by) Unix administrators are likely to appear, but for now, Macintosh backup software is slowly trying to catch up with the radical changes between OS 9 and OS X.

Summary

Throughout this chapter—and we hope throughout the book—you've probably noticed that security has taken on a meaning beyond simply "locking down your network connection." Security is taking the necessary precautions to ensure that your computer keeps functioning as you expect. Likewise, the disaster recovery process is the act of restoring your system to that functional state.

It is our hope that in reading this book, you've learned how your computer can safely and effectively be used as an Internet server, how to protect your personal information and ensure that your private communications remain *private*, and finally, what you should know to keep your computer, your network, and your peace of mind from breaking down should the unthinkable happen.

Security is a rapidly changing and ever-evolving field. By the time you read this, there will be new software, new concerns, and new exploits racing through the Internet. By paying attention to security alerts and software updates, and by using a bit of common sense, you can maintain a secure and reliable Mac OS X.

Sincerely,

John Ray (`jray@macosxunleashed.com`)

William Ray (`wray@macosxunleashed.com`)

PART V
Appendixes

IN THIS PART

A

Glossary

`accton` Activates user accounting.

action (syslog) A `syslog` action determines what happens to an incoming log message if it matches a selector in the configuration file. Actions can write to files and devices, forward the messages to remote log servers, and notify logged-in users.

AFP Apple Filing Protocol. The protocol behind Mac OS X personal file sharing.

Apache An enterprise-class Open Source Web server that is usually documented in 1000+ page tomes. Included in Mac OS X as "Personal Web Sharing" and configured with an on/off button.

ARP Address resolution protocol. Used to map between ethernet MAC addresses and IP addresses.

`arp` Command-line tool for listing and manipulating (such as setting up a static ARP mapping) a Mac OS X computer's ARP cache.

ARP poisoning The act of creating invalid ARP table entries via ARP spoofing. Often for a man-in-the-middle attack.

`arpwatch` A third-party tool for monitoring and logging ARP advertisements on a network.

asymmetric In encryption, a system in which encryption and decryption are carried out with different but related keys. Public key encryption is asymmetric.

buffer overflow Also buffer overrun. A programming error in which data overwrites program code rather than fitting within the allocated storage space. Buffer overflows can sometimes be exploited to gain root access, crash processes, or cause other problems, depending on the process being exploited.

catastrophic events Fires, earthquakes, floods, UFO invasions, and other unforeseen events.

CERT Computer Emergency Response Team Coordination Center (`http://www.cert.org/`). Started by DARPA, CERT analyzes Internet security risks and provides protection information.

certifying authority A third-party organization that issues a digital certificate based on a CSR (certificate signing request).

certificate signing request A request that is sent to a CA (certifying authority) to generate a digital certificate.

cipher A character/symbol level transformation applied to a plaintext message with the intent to disguise the content.

ciphertext The enciphered version of a message or other information.

code A transformation applied to change a message from one symbol set to another. The transformation may be at the linguistic or character/symbol level, and is dictionary based.

container (Apache) A real or logical grouping of files and resources to which Apache directives (including security directives) can be applied.

cracker A dry, flat, and often salty bread-like food product. Or, a similarly tasteless person who would do your system harm.

cryptanalysis The science and practice of studying cryptographic systems to discover and exploit their weaknesses.

cryptography The practice of employing codes and ciphers.

cryptology The umbrella science encompassing both cryptography and cryptanalysis.

CUPS Common Unix Printing System. The Mac OS X printing system, starting in Mac OS X 10.2, is based on CUPS. CUPS provides a built-in Postscript rasterizer and provides access to previously Windows-only devices.

CVE Common Vulnerabilities and Exposures (`http://cve.mitre.org/`). A list of names for all publicly known vulnerabilities.

daemon Often called "services," daemons are the background processes that respond to requests made by other software on your system or remote (network) devices.

DDoS attack Distributed denial of service. A denial of service attack launched simultaneously from many (usually compromised) computers.

digital certificate A virtual "signature" that is included with messages/files and used to verify the authenticity of the transmitted data. The certificate is encrypted by a CA (certifying authority) and contains the owner's public key, along with location and contact information.

directive A configuration option.

disaster planning Preparing your computers and critical system components for possible failure.

disaster recovery Rebuilding system critical services in the event of an emergency.

`ditto` The Mac OS X command-line tool for copying files and folders while maintaining permissions, ownership, and resource forks.

DoS attack Denial of service. A DoS attack is any attack that causes access to a service to be disrupted—be it network services (such as a Web server), or local access to a machine.

`dump` A command-line incremental backup tool for UFS partitions. Not HFS+-compatible.

encipher Transform (algorithmically) from plaintext at the character/symbol level, with the intent to disguise the content.

encode Transform from plaintext into an alternate symbol set.

encryption The application of an algorithmic cipher that requires key-exchange for decoding (RFC-2828).

entropy In cryptology, the amount of randomness that is available in the symbol space used for an encryption key.

`ettercap` An Open Source packet sniffer capable of ARP poisoning, password harvesting, and content decryption (`http://ettercap.sourceforge.net`).

`facility` (syslog) An identifier for the portion of the system that is sending the log entry to `syslog`—such as the kernel, mail, or FTP processes.

firewall A device or piece of software used to block network access to a service, network, or device.

FQDN Fully qualified domain name. The full name for a computer, including host and domain, such as `www.poisontooth.com`.

Guardian Included with Snort, the Guardian script processes Snort output and can create firewall rules to block attacks as they occur.

hacker Someone who has been eating a cracker too quickly without a glass of water. Hackers prefer to devour crackers for breakfast with milk.

`hdiutil` A Mac OS X command-line tool for working with disk images. Analogous to the GUI Disk Copy tool.

`.htaccess` The default filename for the Apache configuration override file. Placed in any Web-accessable location, the `.htaccess` file will (if allowed) dynamically redefine the attributes for the enclosing container.

`htdigest` The Apache command-line tool for creating and modifying MD5 Digest password files.

ICMP Internet Control Message Protocol. A piece of the TCP/IP suite used to transmit error, control, and status messages between network devices.

IMAP Internet Message Access Protocol. A common means of accessing mail stored on a mail server—often used with cleartext passwords.

Infrastructure The network, electrical power, and other "outside the box" systems required for your computer to operate.

Intrusion Detection System (IDS) Enables you to detect and react to attacks as they occur—and before they take down your systems.

`ipfw` The BSD firewall tool. Used to add, delete, modify, and view the active firewall rules.

IPSec A protocol-enabling fully encrypted tunneling of information between two points on a network. Often used to implement Virtual Private Networks.

journaling file system A file system that maintains a log of changes between the current state and last-known working state. A journalled file system can automatically recover disk information in the event of a crash.

key A value that modifies the algorithmic behavior of a cipher such that it becomes a nondictionary-based transformation between plaintext and ciphertext symbol sets.

`last` Displays a list of the last user logins based on the `/var/log/wtmp` file.

`lastcomm` Displays user accounting data.

`lastlog` The `/var/log/lastlog` file stores a record of logins, but Mac OS X does not include a utility to read its contents.

level (syslog) A ranking of the importance of the incoming log message—from simply informational notifications to emergency warnings.

`/Library/Logs` The default location for Mac OS X–specific services such as AppleShare—and, for some reason, Samba.

`lppasswd` A CUPS command-line tool for editing the CUPS `passwd.md5` authentication file.

`LogSentry` A third-party product (`http://www.psionic.com/`) for monitoring logfiles and reacting to potential system problems.

`/Library/StartupItems` The default location of third-party service startup scripts.

malicious software Software that is designed to do or allow harm to your system. Usually not used for damaging software that is intentionally used by the end user for its damaging effect.

malware Malicious software.

man-in-the-middle attack Works by placing a computer in the "middle" of an established connection. Both ends of a connection must be "convinced" that they need to go through the attacking computer to speak to the other side.

message In cryptology, some piece of information that a user wishes to hide or exchange in a secure fashion.

mirroring (RAID level 1) Creates an exact duplicate of a volume by simultaneously writing the same information to another disk.

`mod_auth_apple` An Apache module that enables basic HTTP authentication to be made against the Mac OS X user database.

`mod_hfs_apple` An Apache module created to protect against attacks exploiting the Mac OS X case-insensitive HFS+ file system. This module should be installed and active on any Web server serving content from an non-UFS partition.

`mod_ssl` The Apache SSL (Secure Sockets Layer) module. Required for setting up a secure transport Web server. Included in an incomplete (but functional) form in Mac OS X.

MTA Message transfer agent. The server process charged with receiving and delivering incoming mail (that is, a mail server).

NAT Network address translation. A process by which a server can provide Internet access to a network via a single IP address. NAT has the useful side effect of being an effective firewall for the internal network.

`natd` The Mac OS X NAT daemon.

`netstat` Displays the status of network sockets on the host on which it is executed.

`nmap` The undisputed king of stealth network scans, NMAP is capable of OS fingerprinting and carrying out over 10 different network probes (`http://www.insecure.org`).

open relay A mail server that relays (sends) messages for any user, without authentication. Often used to send mass spam without the administrator's knowledge.

Ping of Death An IP packet constructed with a length greater than 65536 bytes (an illegal size) used to crash, disable, or otherwise disrupt systems running Windows 95, Mac OS 7.x, Windows NT, Linux, Netware, and a wide range of printers, routers, and other network devices.

plaintext The original, typically human-readable rendition of a piece of data.

POP Post office protocol. A common and (usually) insecure means of retrieving mail from a mail server.

PortSentry A third-party product (`http://www.psionic.com/`) for detecting and reacting to stealth/nonstealth port scans.

`Postfix` A drop-in replacement for the sendmail MTA. Known for its stability, ease of use, and security (`http://www.postfix.org`).

private key In asymmetric encryption, the member of a key pair that can (and must) be kept secret for the communication to be secure.

promiscuous mode A privileged operating mode in which a network card makes all (visible) traffic available to the host computer, rather than just broadcast and addressed traffic.

public key An encryption system that uses separate but related keys for encryption and decryption. Also, the publicly visible key that can be exchanged without fear of compromising the transmission when used in such a system.

RAID Redundant array of independent disks. A means of improving disk throughput and/or fault tolerance by combining multiple drives into a single logical volume.

RDDoS Reversed distributed denial of service attack. A distributed denial of service attack that is invoked against a third-party bystander by spoofing outgoing connections or attacks as though they came from the third party, and redirecting the traffic and wrath of the directly attacked machines against the innocent third party.

real-time blacklisting (RBL) The process of checking against known "bad" hosts—usually open relays and spammers on a mail server—and blocking access to the individuals in real time.

receipt A file (package) created by Mac OS X to log information about software installed with Apple's Installer.app. Receipt files are located in `/Library/Receipts`.

`restore` A command-line utility for loading `dump` backups.

rootkit A collection of tools used by an attacker to cover his or her tracks by deleting system logs and/or modifying system reporting utilities.

Samba The Open Source Windows-compatible CIFS/SMB file server. Samba works behind the scenes to implement the Mac OS X "Windows File Sharing."

scanning The act of probing a network to uncover its topology, hardware, and active services.

secret key In encryption, a key used in a symmetric algorithm, where the encryption key must be kept secret and secure for the encrypted data to remain secure.

selector (syslog) A combination of one or more facilities and levels that are matched against log messages coming into `syslog`. If the selector matches the level and facility of the message, syslog executes an *action*.

sendmail The MTA included in Mac OS X. Like Apache, sendmail is a very complicated piece of software that requires documentation beyond what is included here.

service See *daemon*.

session hijacking A means of gaining either total or partial control over an established TCP/IP connection. Session attacks rely on a trusted connection between two computers to be in place, and then works to either modify packets traveling between the machines or take the place of one of the two computers.

SLP Service locator protocol. The Mac OS X protocol for service discovery—replacing AppleTalk/Ethertalk for browsing.

`smbpasswd` A Samba command-line tool for creating user/password mappings for Samba logins.

`smrsh` The sendmail restricted shell—limits the commands that can be executed from a user's `.forward` file.

SMTP Simple mail transfer protocol. The protocol required to transmit messages to a mail server or to relay messages from point to point.

sniffing The act of "watching" network traffic while a network interface is in promiscuous mode—often with the goal of intercepting private information.

Snort A popular Open Source network intrusion detection system (`http://www.snort.org/`). Snort uses a rule-based architecture for detecting thousands of known network attacks in real time.

spoofing Providing false identity credentials for the purpose of carrying out a deceit. In some circles it's considered a requirement that this deceit be with the intent to obtain unauthorized access to a system or its resources; however, recent usage includes such situations as spoofing as a form of system defense.

steganalysis The study of ways to find or eliminate steganographic messages or signatures from works.

steganography Literally "secret writing." The science of developing and/or applying techniques for concealing one message within another. Used to either transmit the information secretly or make the information difficult to remove from the carrier without complete destruction of the carrier message.

striping (RAID level 0) Increases disk read and write speed by reading and writing to two volumes in parallel.

symmetric In encryption, a system that uses the same key for both encryption and decryption.

SYN flood A flood of packets that disrupt system services by forcing a server to allocate resources for a connection but then never complete the process.

SYN packet A packet used to initiate a TCP/IP connection.

`syslogd` The daemon responsible for providing a central logging repository. Capable of receiving log entries for remote systems, or sending log information *to* a remote `syslog` server.

TCP Transmission control protocol. The "TCP" in TCP/IP, TCP is a reliable protocol used by most Internet services (HTTP, SSH, and so on).

TCP/IP Transmission control protocol/Internet protocol. The network protocol suite that makes up Internet traffic.

tcpdump A command-line tool for logging TCP/IP packet headers. Useful for network diagnostics.

topology The "shape" of a computer network or communications system. On a modern network this is usually a bus, tree, or combination of the two.

Trojans Sometimes Trojan horses. Applications that claim to do one thing, while in fact doing something else—usually something malicious.

UAM User authentication mechanisms. Used for authenticating user connections to a machine. Additional modules can be installed in `/Library/Filesystems/AppleShare/Authentication`, but must be present on all machines involved in a connection.

UDP User datagram protocol. Part of the TCP/IP suite, UDP is an unreliable protocol used to transmit information without requiring an acknowledgement.

`utmp` Located at `/var/log/utmp`, this file tracks the currently logged-in users.

`/var/log` The default location for most Mac OS X BSD service logfiles.

viruses Viruses are microapplications that can embed themselves in documents or software in such a way that when the documents are opened or the software run, the microapplication also runs. When executed in this fashion, the virus replicates itself into other documents or applications. A key feature to note is that viruses are self-replicating, but require some action on the part of a user to become active and to propagate.

`WebDAV` Web distributed authoring and versioning. An HTTP-based file sharing protocol supported in most major operating systems.

`who`/`w` Displays a list of the currently logged-in users through the use of the `/var/log/utmp` file.

worms Worms are much like self-propagating viruses that do not require any human interaction to allow them to move from system to system or to replicate. Worms also do not require a "host" application in which to embed themselves, though they often propagate themselves by wrapping themselves in some document for the purpose of transmission.

`wtmp` Located at `/var/log/wtmp`, this file tracks logouts/logins/shutdowns/reboots.

B

Security Resources

Throughout the book we've discussed software, documents, and Web sites that will be useful for securing and maintaining your Macintosh system. This appendix provides quick access to some of the most useful resources available for Mac OS X administrators.

TABLE B.1 URLs for Software or Software Services

URL	Product
http://airsnort.shmoo.com/,	AirSnort (WEP decryption package)
http://www.amavis.org/	AMaViS—A mail virus scanner (a program that interfaces sendmail, Qmail, Postfix, and Exim with virus scanners, for Linux, Solaris, *BSD, AIX, and HP-UX)
http://www.apache.org/	Apache (Web server)
http://www.apple.com/remotedesktop/	Apple Remote Desktop (desktop sharing application for Mac OS X and traditional Mac OS)
http://www.securityfocus.com/data/tools/arpwatch.tar.Z	Arpwatch (Record ARP activity on your network)
http://personalpages.tds.net/~brian_hill/	BrickHouse (graphical interface for the built-in Mac OS X firewall)
http://www.bensoftware.com/	BTV Pro X (motion detection capture software)
http://www.macosxunleashed.com/article.php?sid=2	CGvirusscan 1.0 (virus scanner interface between CommuniGate Pro and Virex)
http://cotvnc.sourceforge.net/	Chicken of the VNC (a VNC viewer for Mac OS X)
http://clamav.elektrapro.com/	Clam AntiVirus (virus scanner for Unix)
http://www.stalker.com/cpro/default.html	CommuniGate Pro (email server for Mac OS)
http://ccitt5.net/archive/conflictd.tar.gz	conflictd (Spoofs "here I am" responses to Windows machine network initialization queries requesting the availability status for an IP address)
http://preciousgem.dnsalias.com:90/PreciousGem/Corundum/Corundum.html	Corundum (software to steganographically hide textual information in images—for Mac OS 8.5 or higher, including Mac OS X)
http://michel.arboi.free.fr/UKUSA/couic.html	Couic (connection cutting software)
http://www.cpan.org/	CPAN (Comprehensive Perl Archive Network—a source for everything relating to Perl)
http://www.wildpackets.com/products/etherpeek_mac	EtherPeek (network traffic and protocol analyzer for Macintosh)
http://ettercap.sourceforge.net/	Ettercap (multipurpose sniffer/interceptor/logger for switched LAN)
http://fink.sourceforge.net/	Fink (system that ports Unix software to Mac OS X)
http://www.gnu.org/	
http://www.fsf.org/	The GNU Project and the Free Software Foundation (home of such projects as gcc)
http://www.pliris-soft.com/products/firewalkx/index.html	Firewalk X (firewall software for Mac OS X)
http://freshmeat.net/	freshmeat.net (an opensource repository)
http://www.f-secure.com/	F-Secure SSH (SSH clients for Windows and Macintosh; SSH client and server for Unix)

TABLE B.1 Continued

URL	Product
http://rsug.itd.umich.edu/software/fugu/	Fugu (SFTP/SCP/SSH tunneling client for Mac OS X)
http://www.gideonsoftworks.com/gideon.html	Gideon (FTP/SFTP client for Mac OS X)
http://dreamless.home.attbi.com/	HenWen (Graphical interface to Snort)
http://www.metaobject.com/Community.html#hfstar	hfstar (a GNUtar derivative that supports HFS+)
http://pldaniels.com/inflex/	Inflex (email scanner that can be used to scan for viruses, for Linux, FreeBSD, Solaris)
http://www.sustworks.com/site/prod_ipm_download.html	IPNetMonitorX (network monitoring tools) IPNetTunerX (TCP/IP network performance optimizer) IPNetShareX (provides graphical access to Mac OS X's Network Address Translation (NAT))
http://www.arenasoftware.com/grepsoft/	JellyfiSSH (GUI interface to the `ssh` command for Mac OS X)
http://www.openwall.com/john/	John the Ripper (password cracking utility for Unix, DOS, Win32, BeOS, and OpenVMS)
http://www.iit.edu/~gawojar/ldap/	LDAP Browser/Editor (Java client for exploring LDAP servers)
http://www.nd.edu/~eds/search/ldap_search.shtml	University of Notre Dame's Public LDAP Directory Advanced Search
http://www.threenorth.com/LaBrea/	LaBrea (watches for incoming ARP requests that go unanswered and spoofs a response)
http://www.packetfactory.net/libnet/dist/deprecated/	libnet (network packet assembly/injection library—slightly out-of-date version for use with conflictd)
http://www.obdev.at/products/littlesnitch/index.html	Little Snitch (monitors for outgoing connection attempts and enables the user to allow or deny the connection)
http://www.macanalysis.com/	MacAnalysis (Comprehensive set of tools including intrusion detection (via SNORT) and vulnerability scanning)
http://macgpg.sourceforge.net/	Mac GNU Privacy Guard (GPG implementation for Mac OS X)
http://macscan.securemac.com/	MacScan ("Spyware" detector; locates stealth applications running on your system)
http://www.macssh.com/	MacSSH (SSH2 terminal for traditional MacOS) MacSFTP (SFTP client for traditional Mac OS and Mac OS X)
http://www.securemac.com/file-library/Malevolence.sit http://www.msec.net/	Malevolence (software for dumping an unshadowed version of the NetInfo password database for Mac OS X)
http://www.messagewall.org/	MessageWall (SMTP proxy that keeps out viruses, spam, and mail relaying, for Unix with an ANSI C compiler)

TABLE B.1 Continued

URL	Product
http://www.roaringpenguin.com/mimedefang/	MIMEDefang (email filter for Linux that can be used to filter viruses)
http://www.opensource.apple.com/cgi-bin/registered/cvs	CVS access to mod_auth_apple (Apache authentication module)
http://www.opensource.apple.com/cgi-bin/registered/cvs	CVS access to mod_hfs (Apache HFS+ case-sensitivity fix)
http://www.modssl.org/	_mod_ssl (SSL security for Apache)
http://www.lysator.liu.se/~jonasw/freeware/niftyssh/	NiftyTelnet 1.1 SSH r3 (SSH1 client with SCP capability for traditional Mac OS)
http://www.insecure.org/nmap/index.html	NMAP (THE network scanning tool)
http://www.symantec.com/nav/nav_mac/	Norton Anti-Virus
http://www.openantivirus.org/	Open AntiVirus Project (Java-based virus scanner)
http://www.openssh.org/	OpenSSH (SSH client and server for Unix)
http://prdownloads.sourceforge.net/osxvnc/	OSXvnc (an Aqua VNC server)
http://www.pgp.com/	PGP (commercial and free PGP software for multiple platforms)
http://www.pgpi.org/	PGP (free versions of PGP software for mulitple platforms)
http://www.pgpi.org/services/keys/keyservers/	International PGP's keyservers listing
http://www.openwall.com/passwdqc/	pam_passwdqc (PAM password strength checking module for Linux, FreeBSD, Solaris, and HP-UX)
http://www.puppysuite.com/	PuppySuite (hardware/software fingerprint biometric authentication solution for Mac OS X)
http://www.kernel.org/pub/linux/libs/pam/modules.html	Linux-PAM modules listing
http://www.postfix.org/	Postfix (drop-in replacement for the sendmail MTA)
http://www.chiark.greenend.org.uk/~sgtatham/putty/	PuTTY (SSH client for Windows)
http://personalpages.tds.net/~brian_hill/puzzlepalace.html	PuzzlePalace (encryption software for Mac OS X)
http://www.raeinternet.com/rav/ravforosx.html	RAV Anti-Virus for Mac OS X (virus scanner for CommuniGate Pro, SurgeMail, Courier, Postfix)
http://rsug.itd.umich.edu/software/radmind/	Radmind (integrity checking software for Solaris, Mac OS X, FreeBSD, OpenBSD, Linux, includes a GUI for Mac OS X)
http://www-stat.stanford.edu/~susan/surprise/Birthday.html	Random Birthday Applet
http://www.rbrowser.com/	RBrowser (FTP/SFTP/SCP/SSH tunneling client for Mac OS X)

TABLE B.1 Continued

URL	Product
http://www.opendarwin.org/cgi-bin/cvsweb.cgi/proj/rsync_hfs/	rsync_hfs (HFS+ aware version of rsync)
http://www.samba.org/	Samba Server (Windows-compatible CIFS/SMB server)
http://www.ssh.com/ ftp://ftp.ssh.com/pub/ssh/	SSH Secure Shell (SSH client for Windows; SSH client and server for Unix)
http://projekte.imd.net/	scan.sh 1.0b1 (mail filtering program for CommuniGate; no longer supported)
http://homepage.mac.com/cnorris/ScriptGUI/	ScriptGUI (software for running shell scripts in the Finder for Mac OS X)
http://www.gideonsoftworks.com/sshhelper.html	SSH Helper (GUI interface for configuring OpenSSH on Mac OS X)
http://www.vandyke.com/products/securecrt/	SecureCRT (SSH/SFTP/tunneling client for Windows)
http://www.bensoftware.com/	SecuritySpy (multicamera video surveillance software)
http://www.sendmail.org/	sendmail (mail transport agent)
http://sourceforge.net/projects/sendmail-milter/	Sendmail::Milter (Perl module for writing filters for milter, the mail filter API for sendmail)
http://www.bombich.com/software/smd.html	Share My Desktop (an Aqua VNC server)
http://www.phil.uu.nl/~xges/ssh/	SSH Agent (GUI for `ssh-agent`)
http://sourceforge.net/projects/snort/	Snort (Packet Sniffer/Logger)
http://www.sophos.com/	Sophos Anti-Virus
http://sourceforge.net/	SourceForge (an open source repository)
http://www.opensource.apple.com/projects/darwin/1.0/projects.html	Extra TCP Wrappers files for Mac OS X 10.1 and earlier
http://hp.vector.co.jp/authors/VA002416/teraterm.html	Tera Term Pro (Terminal emulator for Windows)
http://www.porcupine.org/forensics/tct.html	The Coroner's Toolkit (TCT) (collection of forensics analysis tools)
http://www.tightvnc.com/	TightVNC (an enhanced version of VNC; includes support for automatic SSH tunneling on Unix)
http://www.netopia.com/en-us/software/products/tb2/index.html http://www.netopia.com/en-us/support/howtodocs/mac/tcpport.html	Timbuktu (Remote desktop application for Macintosh and Windows)
http://tripwire.sourceforge.net/	Tripwire (integrity checking software)
http://www.zip.com.au/~roca/ttssh.html	TTSSH (an extension DLL for Tera Term Pro that allows Terra Term Pro to be used as an SSH1 client for Windows)

TABLE B.1 Continued

URL	Product
http://www.versiontracker.com/	Versiontracker (site that tracks the latest software updates for Mac OS X, traditional Mac OS, Windows, and Palm OS)
http://www.mcafeeb2b.com/products/virex/	Virex (antivirus software for Macintosh)
http://www.intego.com/virusbarrier/	Virus barrier (antivirus software for Macintosh)
http://www.realvnc.com/ http://www.uk.research.att.com/vnc/ http://www.uk.research.att.com/vnc/contribs.html	VNC (Virtual Network Computing—server and client software for multiple platforms)
http://www.mdimension.com/	VNCDimension (a VNC viewer for Mac OS X)
http://webthing.net/vncthing/	VNCThing (a VNC viewer for Mac OS 8.1 or later, including Mac OS X)
http://homepage.mac.com/kedoin/VNC/VNCViewer/	VNCViewer (a VNC viewer for Mac OS X)
http://www.geocities.com/tim_senecal/vnc.html	VNCViewer (a VNC viewer in a carbon, noncarbon, and 68k version)
http://www.wu-ftpd.org/	WU-FTPD (FTP server)
http://www.landfield.com/wu-ftpd/	WU-FTPD Resource Center
http://xamime.com/	Xamime (email filter that can establish an interface between a mail transport agent and virus scanners; for Linux, Solaris, or FreeBSD)
http://www.xinetd.org/	xinetd (a more secure replacement for inetd)
http://www.cdc.noaa.gov/~jsw/macosx_xvnc/	Xvnc (VNC server for serving X11 applications from Mac OS X)
http://www.zlib.org/	zlib compression library

TABLE B.2 URLs Relating to Physical Security Devices

Company	URL	Products Manufactured or Sold
123 Security Products	http://www.123securityproducts.com/	Security cameras, time lapse VCRs
ADT Security Services	http://www.adt.com/	Security services
Advanced Security Concepts	http://www.mediaprotection.com/	Media safes; electronic door locks
Air Magnet	http://www.airmagnet.com	Handhelds and laptops that can be used to manage wireless networks and identify security and interference issues
AnchorPad International	http://www.anchorpad.com/	Cable locks, plates, entrapments
Apple Computer, Inc.	http://www.apple.com/xserve/	Xserve (rack-optimized server)

TABLE B.2 Continued

Company	URL	Products Manufactured or Sold
BTV	`http://www.bensoftware.com/`	BTV Pro X (motion detection capture software); SecuritySpy (multicamera video surveillance software)
CCTV HQ Network	`http://www.cctvheadquarters.net/`	Fake security cameras, security camera systems
Champion Lockers	`http://www.championlockers.com/`	Lockers
Computer Security Systems, Inc.	`http://www.computersecurity.com/`	Cable locks, entrapments, plates, alarm systems, tracking systems, enclosures
Cutting Edge Products, Inc.	`http://www.cuttingedgeproductsinc.com/`	Fake security cameras
Federal Security Camera, Inc.	`http://fakecam.com/`	Fake security cameras
GoLocks.com	`http://www.golocks.com/`	Cable locks
Kensington Technology Group	`http://www.kensington.com/`	Cable locks; alarm unit
Kensington Technology Group	`http://www.kensington.com/html/1434.html`	Laptop security devices
Keyware	`http://www.keyware.com/`	Biometric building access system
Marathon Computer	`http://www.marathoncomputer.com/`	Rackmounts
Minatronics Corporation	`http://www.minatronics.com/`	Fiber optic alarm system
Penco Products	`http://www.pencoproducts.com/`	Lockers
Pentagon Defense Products	`http://www.pentagondefense.com/`	Fake security cameras
Polaris Industries	`http://www.polarisusa.com/`	Security cameras, multiplexors, time-lapse VCRs
PUPPY Suite for Mac OS X	`http://www.puppysuite.com/`	(Hardware/Software fingerprint biometric authentication solution for Mac OS X)
Republic Storage	`http://www.republicstorage.com/`	Lockers
Secure-It	`http://www.secure-it.com/`	Cable locks, entrapments, enclosures, tracking system, alarm system
Secureitall.com	`http://www.securitall.com/`	Alarm systems for home/business
Securityideas.com	`http://www.securityideas.com/`	Security cameras
SecurityKit.com	`http://www.securitykit.com/`	Cable locks
Security Tracking of Office Property (STOP)	`http://www.stoptheft.com/`	Tracking system
Secure Systems Services	`http://www.secureservices.com/`	Cable locks, entrapments
Targus	`http://www.targus.com/`	Alarm units
TrackIT	`http://www.trackitcorp.com/`	Alarm units

TABLE B.3 URLs for Reference Material and Additional Reading

URL	Article
http://www.3com.com/corpinfo/en_US/technology/tech_paper.jsp?DOC_ID=5298	3Com Technical Papers Layer 3 Switching: An Introduction
http://www.turnpoint.net/wireless/has.html	802.11b Homebrew Antenna Shootout—2/14/2
http://attila.stevens-tech.edu/~khockenb/crypt3.html	The Ambitious Amateur vs. crypt(3) or Pondering the Lifespan of Visible Passwords Against Brute-Force Attack
http://www.oreillynet.com/cs/weblog/view/wlg/448	Antenna on the Cheap (er, Chip)
http://www.2600.com/news/display/display.shtml?id=378	Appeal Heard in 2600/DECSS Case
http://www.counterpane.com/bfdobsoyl.html	The Blowfish Algorithm—One Year Later
http://www.securityfocus.com/news/925	BugBear—Nasty Email Virus
http://www.internetnews.com/bus-news/article.php/3_1138351	Can "Deep Linking" Lead to Deep Trouble?
http://www.fbi.gov/hq/lab/carnivore/carnivore.htm	Carnivore Diagnostic Tool (FBI communications-content scanning system)
http://csrc.nist.gov/nissc/2000/proceedings/papers/601.pdf	The Case for Beneficial Computer Viruses and Worms—A Student's Perspective
http://www.mcafee.com/aboutus/bus_dev/retail_users/newsletters/feb2002/classof2001.htm	The Class of 2001—Year in Review
http://www.securityfocus.com/news/1113	Clues, Vandalism, Litter Sendmail Trojan Trail
http://www.pff.org/encry.html	The Computer Revolution, Encryption and True Threats to National Security
http://www.cnn.com/2003/TECH/internet/01/25/internet.attack/index.html	Computer Worm Grounds Flights, Blocks ATMs
http://www.counterpane.com/bfsverlag.html	Description of a New Variable-Length Key, 64-Bit Block Cipher (Blowfish)
http://catless.ncl.ac.uk/Risks/13.06.html#subj3	"Desert Storm" Viral Myths
http://grc.com/dos/drdos.htm	Distributed Reflection Denial of Service
http://www.distributed.net/des/	distributed.net: Project DES
http://www.salon.com/tech/col/rose/1999/08/12/deep_links/	Don't Link or I'll Sue!
http://www.dontlink.com/	Don't Link to Us!
http://www.eff.org/descracker.html	EFF DES Cracker Project
http://www.sirbacon.org/edllibrary.htm	Edwin Durning Lawrence & His Bacon Library
http://www.privacyfoundation.org/resources/docbug.asp	FAQ: Document Web Bugs

TABLE B.3 Continued

URL	Article
http://www.rsasecurity.com/rsalabs/challenges/factoring/rsa155.html	Factorization of RSA-155
http://www.brainyquote.com/quotes/quotes/b/q118446.html	Famous Quotes: Benjamin Franklin (on security)
http://csrc.nist.gov/publications/fips/index.html	FIPS (Federal Information Processing Standards) Computer Security Resource Center
http://csrc.nist.gov/publications/fips/fips46-3/fips46-3.pdf	FIPS Publication 46-3 (Data Encryption Standard (DES))
http://csrc.nist.gov/publications/fips/fips186-2/fips186-2-change1.pdf	FIPS Publication 186-2 (Digital Signature Standard (DSS))
http://csrc.nist.gov/publications/fips/fips197/fips-197.pdf	FIPS Publication 197 (Announcing the Advanced Encryption Standard (AES))
http://www.cnn.com/2003/TECH/biztech/01/25/microsoft.security.ap/index.html	Gates Pledges Better Software Security
http://hepcvets.com/info/2002/mar/hepcvets512.pdf	Gene Repair in the New Age of Gene Therapy
http://www.bbsonline.org/Preprints/OldArchive/bbs.neuwelt.html	Gene Replacement Therapy in the Central Nervous System: Viral Vector Mediated Therapy of Global Neurodegenerative Disease
http://mitpress.mit.edu/e-books/HP/hyp000.htm	Hypnerotomachia Poliphili
http://www.iana.org/	IANA (Internet Assigned Numbers Authority)
http://www.ietf.org/	IETF (Internet Engineering Task Force)
http://www.scambusters.org/Scambusters55.html	Internet ScamBusters™ #55
http://sunland.gsfc.nasa.gov/info/guide/The_Internet_Worm.html	The Internet Worm
http://www.nwfusion.com/archive/1997/97-07-28____.html	InterNIC Domain Name Registry Rerouting
http://www.jjtc.com/pub/nfjidr99.pdf	An Introduction to Watermark Recovery from Images
http://info.astrian.net/jargon/terms/h/hacker_ethic.html	The Jargon Dictionary, "hacker ethic"
http://catb.org/jargon/	The Jargon File
http://jargon.watson-net.com/	The Jargon File (mirror)
http://www.catb.org/jargon/html/entry/Brooks's-Law.html	The Jargon File: Brooks's Law
http://catb.org/jargon/html/entry/cracker.html	The Jargon File: Cracker
http://www.catb.org/jargon/html/entry/hacker.html	The Jargon File: Hacker
http://www.catb.org/jargon/html/entry/hacker-ethic.html	The Jargon File: Hacker Ethic

TABLE B.3 Continued

URL	Article
http://www.catb.org/jargon/html/entry/leech.html	The Jargon File: Leech
http://www.catb.org/jargon/html/entry/patch.html	The Jargon File: Patch
http://www.catb.org/jargon/html/entry/sneakernet.html	The Jargon File: Sneakernet
http://www.catb.org/jargon/html/The-Story-of-Mel.html	The Jargon File: The Story of Mel
http://www.catb.org/jargon/html/entry/tiger-team.html	The Jargon File: Tiger Team
http://www.catb.org/jargon/html/entry/wizard.html	The Jargon File: Wizard
http://news.zdnet.co.uk/story/0,,t281-s2109785,00.html	MS .doc Bug Hibernates on Net
http://www.wired.com/news/print/0,1294,43389,00.html	MS May Have File-Trading Answer
http://www.cl.cam.ac.uk/ftp/users/rja14/tr500.pdf	The Memorability and Security of Passwords—Some Empirical Results
http://www.privacyfoundation.org/privacywatch/report.asp?id=39&action=0	Microsoft Word Documents That "Phone Home"
http://www.vmyths.com/hoax.cfm?id=123&page=3	NSA Printer Virus (1991)
http://www.nardware.co.uk/honeys/honey1/NardHoney1.htm	Nardware Honeypot Breach
http://psyber.letifer.org/downloads/priv/hacker_doc.pdf	A New Hacker Taxonomy
http://home.rica.net/alphae/419coal/	Nigeria—The 419 Coalition Website
http://www.cis.ohio-state.edu/cs/Services/rfc/	The Ohio State University's RFC Database
http://www.securityfocus.com/news/560	OpenSSH Trojaned!
http://ota.ahds.ac.uk/texts/1855.html	Oxford Text Archive, "The Gold Bug"
http://people.qualcomm.com/ggr/about_pgp.html	PGP, Phil Zimmerman, Life, the Universe and so on...
http://www.rsasecurity.com/rsalabs/pkcs/pkcs-1/	PKCS#1—RSA Cryptography Standard
http://www.securityfocus.com/news/2623	Program Hides Secret Messages in Executables
http://www.ietf.org/rfc/rfc0854.txt	RFC 854 (Telnet Protocol Specification)
http://www.ietf.org/rfc/rfc1282.txt	RFC 1282 (BSD Rlogin)
http://www.ietf.org/rfc/rfc1321.txt	RFC 1321 (MD5 Message-Digest Algorithm)
http://www.ietf.org/rfc/rfc2144.txt	RFC 2144 (CAST-128 Encryption Algorithm)
http://www.ietf.org/rfc/rfc2612.txt	RFC 2612 (CAST-256 Encryption Algorithm)

TABLE B.3 Continued

URL	Article
http://www.ietf.org/rfc/rfc2828.txt	RFC 2828 (Internet Security Glossary)
http://www.rfc-editor.org/rfc.html	RFC Editor RFC Database
http://www.cs.princeton.edu/sip/sdmi/riaaletter.html	RIAA/SDMI Letter, April 9, 2001
http://www.rsasecurity.com/rsalabs/faq/	RSA Laboratories' Frequently Asked Questions About Today's Cryptography, Version 4.1
http://www.moorecad.com/standardpascal/real_programmers.html	Real Programmers Don't Use Pascal
http://www.acm.org/classics/sep95/	Reflections on Trusting Trust
http://slashdot.org/features/01/05/03/2043244.shtml	The Rise of Steganography
http://www.cs.princeton.edu/sip/sdmi/sdmimessage.txt	SDMI Statement Read by Edward W. Felten at the Fourth International Information Hiding Workshop, in Pittsburgh, on April 26, 2001
http://www.ssh.com/tech/crypto/algorithms.cfm	SSH Communications Security's Cryptographic Algorithms site
http://filebox.vt.edu/users/sears/bloated.html	The Scary Secret Behind Bloated Word Documents
http://www.computerbytesman.com/privacy/wmp8dvd.htm	Serious Privacy Problems in Windows Media Player for Windows XP
http://www.studyworksonline.com/cda/content/explorations/0,,NAV2-76_SEP949,00.shtml	Studyworks! Online: The Birthday Problem (Hash collision statistics)
http://home.att.net/~mleary/pennl10.htm	Chapter 10: The Second Cryptographic Shakespeare
http://www.exploratorium.edu/ronh/secret/secret.html	The Secret Language
http://www.ietf.org/ids.by.wg/secsh.html	Secure Shell (secsh) Working Group of the IETF
http://www.trouble.org/survey/	Security Survey of Key Internet Hosts & Various Semi-Relevant Reflections
http://home.att.net/~tleary/sigs.htm	Shakspere's Signatures
http://www.snpp.com/episodeguide.html	The Simpsons Archive
http://www.spammimic.com/index.shtml	Spam Mimic (steganographic service that hides short text messages in email that looks like spam)
http://www.sans.org/rr/threats/spoofing.php	Spoofing: An Overview of Some the Current Spoofing Threats
http://www.ssh.com/support/cryptography/	SSH Communications Security's Cryptography A-Z
http://www.cs.princeton.edu/sip/sdmi/announcement.html	Statement Regarding the SDMI Challenge

TABLE B.3 Continued

URL	Article
`http://www.jjtc.com/stegdoc/steg1995.html`	Steganography
`http://www.jjtc.com/Steganography/`	Steganography & Digital Watermarking—Information Hiding
`http://grc.com/dos/grcdos.htm`	The Strange Tale of the Denial of Service Attacks Against GRC.COM
`http://www.mozilla.org/projects/security/pki/nss/draft-kaukonen-cipher-arcfour-03.txt`	A Stream Cipher Encryption Algorithm "Arcfour"
`http://www.sirbacon.org/links/evidence.htm`	Summary of Baconian Evidence for Shakespeare Authorship
`http://www.swiss.ai.mit.edu/6805/articles/computer-crime/schwartz-matrix-news.txt`	System Administration as a Criminal Activity or, the Strange Case of Randal Schwartz
`http://icbtollfree.com/pressetc/telephonyarticle10142002.html`	Telephony: Spelling Trouble
`http://www4.law.cornell.edu/uscode/17/`	US Code Collection: Title 17—Copyrights
`http://www4.law.cornell.edu/uscode/17/106.html`	US Code Collection: Title 17, Chapter 1, Section 106
`http://www4.law.cornell.edu/uscode/17/107.html`	US Code Collection: Title 17, Chapter 1, Section 107
`http://www4.law.cornell.edu/uscode/17/ch5.html`	US Code Collection: Title 17, Chapter 5
`http://www4.law.cornell.edu/uscode/17/1201.html`	US Code Collection: Title 17, Chapter 12, Section 1201
`http://www.snopes.com/business/consumer/cookie.htm`	Urban Legends Reference Pages: Business ((Costs a) Fortune Cookie)
`http://www.snopes.com/inboxer/children/shergold.htm`	Urban Legends Reference Pages: Inboxer Rebellion (Craig Shergold)
`http://vil.nai.com/vil/content/v_99728.htm`	W32/Bugbear@MM
`http://vil.nai.com/vil/content/v_99141.htm`	W32/SirCam@MM
`http://securityresponse.symantec.com/avcenter/venc/data/w97.melissa.a.html`	W97.Melissa.A
`http://www.cl.cam.ac.uk/~fapp2/watermarking/index.html`	Watermarking: Weaknesses of Existing Schemes
`http://www.cnn.com/2003/TECH/internet/02/05/virus.spread.reut/index.html`	Worm Spread Worldwide in 10 minutes
`http://www.kensington.com/html/1355.html`	Why Utilize the Kensington Security Slot in Your Designs?

TABLE B.4 URLs for Security Practices, Security Announcements, Vulnerabilities, and Ethics

URL	Content
`http://www.apple.com/support/security/security.html`	Apple Product Security
`http://www.info.apple.com/`	AppleCare Support
`http://www.auscert.org.au/`	AusCERT (Australian Computer Emergency Response Team)
`http://www.securityfocus.com/popups/forums/bugtraq/intro.shtml`	BugTraq
`http://www.cerias.purdue.edu/`	CERIAS (Center for Education and Research in Information Assurance and Security)
`http://www.cert.org/`	CERT™ Coordination Center
`http://www.cert.org/tech_tips/anonymous_ftp_config.html`	CERT™ Coordination Center's Anonymous FTP Configuration Guidelines
`http://www.ciac.org/ciac/`	CIAC (U.S. Department of Energy Computer Incident Advisory Capability)
`http://cve.mitre.org/`	Common Vulnerabilities and Exposures
`http://www.eff.org/`	Electronic Frontier Foundation
`http://www.ethics.org/`	Ethics Resource Center
`http://www.first.org/`	FIRST (Forum of Incident Response and Security Teams)
`http://isc.incidents.org/`	InternetStormCenter
`http://freaky.staticusers.net/security.shtml`	Freak's Macintosh Security Archive—Macintosh Security Issues, Exploits, and Insecurities (covers traditional Mac OS)
`http://www.macintoshsecurity.com/`	MacintoshSecurity.com
`http://www.macsecurity.org/`	MacSecurity.org
`http://vil.nai.com/vil/default.asp`	McAfee Virus Information Library
`http://www.nipc.gov/`	National Infrastructure Protection Center
`http://www.openssh.com/security.html`	OpenSSH's security announcements page
`http://www.packetstormsecurity.org/`	Packet Storm Security
`http://www.privacyfoundation.org/`	Privacy Foundation
`http://www.pff.org/`	The Progress & Freedom Foundation
`http://www.sans.org/`	SANS (SysAdmin, Audit, Network, Security) Institute
`http://www.securemac.com/`	SecureMac.com
`http://www.securityfocus.com/`	SecurityFocus Online
`http://www.symantec.com/avcenter/vinfodb.html`	Symantec Virus Information Database

TABLE B.5 Supplemental URLs for Some Vulnerabilties

URL	Vulnerability
FTP	
http://packetstormsecurity.nl/advisories/suid/001.txt	SUID Advisory for wu-ftpd
http://www.kb.cert.org/vuls/id/2558	File Transfer Protocol allows data connection hijacking via PASV mode race condition
http://www.attrition.org/security/advisory/misc/infowar/iw_sec_01.txt	FTP PASV "Pizza Thief" Exploit
OpenSSH	
http://bvlive01.iss.net/issEn/delivery/xforce/alertdetail.jsp?oid=20584	OpenSSH Remote Challenge Vulnerability
http://www.openbsd.org/advisories/ssh_channelalloc.txt	OpenSSH Security Advisory (adv.channelalloc)
http://razor.bindview.com/publish/advisories/adv_ssh1crc.html	Remote vulnerability in SSH daemon crc32 compensation attack detector
Telnet	
ftp://ftp.FreeBSD.org/pub/FreeBSD/CERT/advisories/FreeBSD-SA-01:49.telnetd.v1.1.asc	telnetd contains remote buffer overflow

C

Secure Web Development

IN THIS APPENDIX

- Web Development Risks
- Protecting Your Web Applications
- Adding and Using suEXEC
- Testing for Known CGI Vulnerabilities: Whisker
- Additional Resources

Developing applications for desktop use requires a knowledge of programming and the ability to write an airtight disclaimer to cover any mistakes you may have made that could affect the user's computer. Web (or server) development, however, poses a unique problem: Software is executed on *your* computer, not the users. Poorly written code can expose sensitive configuration information, task system resources, and bring an otherwise secure machine to its knees. This appendix presents basic development guidelines to help keep your dynamic server applications safe.

Web Development Risks

Web development differs from other development methods in that users' actions affect your computer, not theirs. Programming errors, either naive or malicious, can be made to provide intruders access to your system via the comfort of their Web browser. Many of the errors discussed in this book result from mishandling of user input. In the case of CGI applications, this is the primary focus of concern. If user input can be manipulated beyond the intentions of the developer, it can often be used in malicious ways.

Many Web developers consider Web pages to do nothing more than make a visual presentation: An interface is displayed, and users are given a few fields, switches, and toggles they can use to send information back to the server for processing. This, unfortunately, does not take into account the information contained within the page's HTML code. Consider, for example, the PHP code for a "system status" application shown in Listing C.1:

LISTING C.1 A "Harmless" System Status Application (`status.php`)

```
<?php
if ($action) {
$output='$action';
print "The result is:<br />";
print "<pre>$output</pre>";
} else {
?>
        <form action="<?php print $me; ?>" method="post">
        <select name="action">
                <option value="uptime">Uptime</option>
                <option value="who">Current Users</option>
        </select>
        <input type="submit">
        </form>
<?php
}
?>
```

This seemingly harmless (and potentially useful) tool allows users to view their computers' uptime or active users from a Web page, as shown in Figure C.1 and Figure C.2.

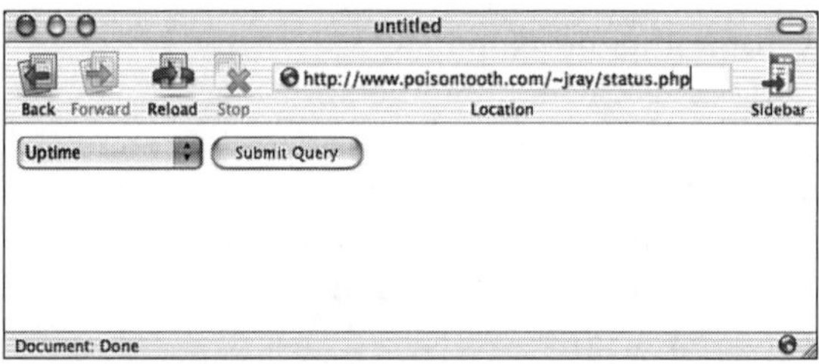

FIGURE C.1 Choose the information to display...

For average users, the page holds little risk beyond the obvious no-no of displaying valid usernames of the people currently logged in to the system. Enterprising individuals, however, may view the source code for the initial display screen (Figure C.1) and notice the lines:

```
<select name="action">
      <option value="uptime">Uptime</option>
      <option value="who">Current Users</option>
```

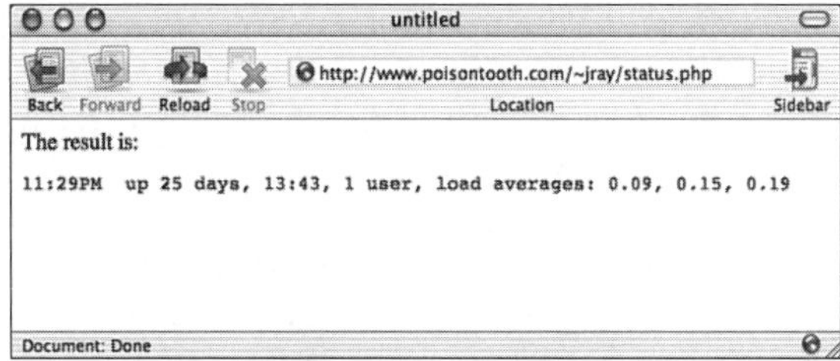

FIGURE C.2 ...and it is returned to the Web browser.

These lines contain the actual commands (`uptime` and `who`) that are used to generate the output. These commands are supplied to the application via the variable `action`. Although the interface to the application does not provide a means of choosing something other than `uptime` or `who`, this is easily circumvented by simply calling the Web application with an action specified in the URL. For example, `status.php?action=ls%20-alR%20/Users`, would execute the command `ls -alR /Users`—or a recursive list of all the user directories on the machine:

```
The result is:

total 10576
drwxrwxr-t   14 root      wheel        476 Oct 23 15:33 .
drwxrwxr-t   31 root      admin       1054 Nov 13 09:46 ..
-rw-rw-rw-    1 jray      unknown     6148 Oct  8 13:55 .DS_Store
-rw-r--r--    1 root      wheel          0 Jul 14 07:33 .localized
drwxrwxrwt    3 root      wheel        102 Jul 14 02:20 Shared
drwxr-xr-x   12 502       staff        408 Jun 27  2001 mysql
drwxr-xr-x   12 skonowal  admin        408 Sep 17  2001 skonowal

/Users/jray/:
 -rw-r--r--    1 root      staff        793 Sep 11 13:21 #Work.ics#
drwxr-xr-x  174 jray      staff       5916 Nov 19 21:39 .
drwxrwxr-t   14 root      wheel        476 Oct 23 15:33 ..
-rw-r--r--    1 jray      staff          3 Nov 14  2000 .CFUserTextEncoding
-rwxr-xr-x    1 jray      staff      12292 Oct 31 20:14 .DS_Store
-rw-r--r--    1 jray      staff       4727 Sep 12  2001 .DiskCopyLog
-rw-rw-rw-    1 jray      staff     153600 May  9  2001 .FBCIndex
drwxrwxrwx    3 jray      staff        102 May  9  2001 .FBCLockFolder
drwx------    3 jray      staff        102 Oct 14 15:34 .Trash
drwxr-xr-x    4 root      staff        136 Mar 27  2002 .cpan
drwxr-xr-x    3 root      staff        102 Oct 10 10:47 .emacs.d
-rw-------    1 jray      staff     129484 Nov 27 14:05 .mysql_history
drwxr-xr-x   17 jray      staff        578 Nov 22  2001 .ncftp
drwxr-xr-x    3 jray      staff        102 May 22  2001 .qt
```

Suddenly, the entire contents of the machine are accessible via the Web. Apache does a good job of providing access controls over what directories can be accessed and by whom, but in one fell swoop, all of Apache's access control is bypassed. Keep in mind that the Web application, although capable of executing arbitrary code on the server, has only the access privileges of the Apache process owner (www). Even so, the potential for damage is great. Executing the command `find / -exec "rm" "{}" ";"` would result in every single world-writable file and directory being removed from the attacked system. Directories such as `/tmp` and shared storage areas would be wiped clean—even entire drives that take advantage of Apple's Ignore Privileges on This Volume feature would be wiped out.

Obviously, this is an example of an extremely poorly designed Web application. Unfortunately, it isn't an uncommon development technique to make calls to the operating system to perform certain functions. User input, however, should *never* directly be used in a system shell call. By passing shell metacharacters to a shell command, a user can execute arbitrary code.

> **NOTE**
>
> A metacharacter is a character that is interpreted "differently" by a shell—not as part of a file name. The characters `&`, `;`, and `>` are examples of metacharacters. For more information on a given shell's metacharacters, read the associated man page (that is, `man tcsh`).

Consider another seemingly innocuous piece of PHP code shown in Listing C.2, `showfile.php`:

LISTING C.2 Another Disaster Waiting to Happen: `showfile.php`

```
<?php
$fp = popen ("cat /Users/jray/public_html/$filename", "r");
while (!feof($fp)) {
    $buffer .= fread($fp, 1024);
}
print "<pre>";
print $buffer;
print "</pre>";
?>
```

The `showfile.php` program performs (when working as intended) one simple task: It displays a named file in my HTML directory `/Users/jray/public_html` within the `<pre></pre>` tags. Unfortunately, there are a few problems with the code that may not necessarily be obvious at first glance.

First, although the full path is specified in the code (`/Users/jray/public_html/$filename`), a user can easily display any file by supplying a custom value for `filename` as a URL parameter. For example, consider `showfile.php?filename=../../jackd/secretfile`. This translates to the directory `/Users/jray/public_html/../../jackd/secretfile`, which is equivalent to `/Users/jackd/secretfile`—a location that was never intended to be accessible at all.

A second, less obvious problem also exists: the opportunity to execute arbitrary code, just as the first example offered. To do this, one can simply chain a command onto the end of the `$filename` variable. Multiple commands are separated in the shell by the ; character. To generate a listing of the root directory, for example, one could call the script using `showfile.php?filename=;%20ls%20-al%20/` (the `%20` is a URL-encoded space):

```
total 9409
drwxrwxr-t  31 root  admin       1054 Nov 13 09:46 .
drwxrwxr-t  31 root  admin       1054 Nov 13 09:46 ..
-rwxrwxr-x   1 jray  admin       6148 Oct 31 20:14 .DS_Store
d-wx-wx-wx   3 root  unknown      102 Oct  8 14:37 .Trashes
-r--r--r--   1 root  wheel        156 Jul 14 02:20 .hidden
dr--r--r--   2 root  wheel         96 Nov 13 09:46 .vol
drwxrwxr-x  28 root  admin        952 Oct 18 13:37 Applications
-rw-r--r--   1 root  admin      85504 Oct 31 16:31 Desktop DB
-rw-r--r--   1 root  admin     318114 Oct 29 11:48 Desktop DF
drwxrwxr-x  13 root  admin        442 Oct 10 12:27 Developer
drwxrwxrwx   3 root  unknown      102 Nov 13 09:46 File Transfer Folder
drwxrwxr-x  33 root  admin       1122 Oct 18 13:37 Library
drwxr-xr-x   6 root  wheel        204 Oct  8 17:24 Network
drwx---rwx   2 root  wheel         68 May 31  2001 Network Trash Folder
drwxr-xr-x   4 root  wheel        136 Oct 18 13:37 System
drwxrwxr-t  14 root  wheel        476 Oct 23 15:33 Users
drwxrwxrwt   2 root  wheel         68 Oct 31 20:14 Volumes
dr-xr-xr-x   1 root  wheel        512 Dec  1 14:57 automount
drwxr-xr-x  37 root  wheel       1258 Oct 15 09:53 bin
drwxrwxrwt   3 root  wheel        102 Oct 14 17:57 cores
dr-xr-xr-x   2 root  wheel        512 Nov 13 09:46 dev
lrwxrwxr-t   1 root  admin         11 Nov 13 09:46 etc -> private/etc
lrwxrwxr-t   1 root  admin          9 Nov 13 09:46 mach -> /mach.sym
-r--r--r--   1 root  admin     704492 Nov 13 09:46 mach.sym
-rw-r--r--   1 root  wheel    3678188 Sep  7 02:25 mach_kernel
drwxr-xr-x   6 root  wheel        204 Nov 13 09:46 private
drwxr-xr-x  60 root  wheel       2040 Oct  8 18:50 sbin
lrwxrwxr-t   1 root  admin         11 Nov 13 09:46 tmp -> private/tmp
drwxr-xr-x  11 root  wheel        374 Oct 10 12:27 usr
lrwxrwxr-t   1 root  admin         11 Nov 13 09:46 var -> private/var
```

As you can see, a piece of code that was actually designed for a specific purpose and hard coded for a given path is still easily exploited with nothing more than a simple understanding of how your computer parses input strings.

Protecting Your Web Applications

Protecting Web (and other server) applications requires developers to practice common-sense coding techniques. Although most programmers do not *intentionally* introduce bugs into their work, they are often pressured into turning out code faster than it can be appropriately error-checked. The result is often disastrous.

For example, a reasonably large commercial site ($20,000/day) that I was requested to audit was launched with a serious error that easily exposed credit card information to anyone with the slightest bit of Web savvy. The system provided a way for administrators to view invoices, including the billing information, simply by providing a username as an argument to an orphaned (unlinked) page on the site. Although this was a bad idea to start, it was made even worse by the fact that they forgot to protect their server so that it wouldn't display directory contents when a directory was requested rather than a specific page. Within hours of bringing a revised version of their site online, the files had been discovered by someone typing in the wrong URL. Luckily, the customer was kind enough to call and report the problem. (She had viewed another customer's credit card information.) If the page had been discovered by other less scrupulous individuals, it could have resulted in a serious compromise of customer information and a public relations nightmare for the company.

As scary as it may sound, the actual problems with this site were extremely small, but all it takes is one slipup to place your server and information at risk.

The following are steps you can take to avoid similar problems in your coding projects.

Understand the Security Requirements Appropriate for Your Site

Plan your development projects with the appropriate security precautions, rather than adding security as an afterthought. Sites that deal with sensitive information (such as patient records) should consider using `mod_ssl` for the all transactions, not just logins. Keep in mind that non-SSL-encrypted traffic is extremely easy to sniff. Be sure to plan for growth and future expansion. It isn't easy to retrofit an unprotected site with security features.

Place Administrative Functions on a Non-Internet-Exposed Server

Administrative functions such as accounting and reporting should not be housed on Internet-accessible servers. Although it's tempting to use a single server for *everything,* the preferred approach is to move all administrative functions (account editing, creation, auditing) to an internal (intranet) machine that does not have a direct connection to the Internet.

Do Not Use Internet-Accessible Database Back Ends

Database servers should *not* be made accessible via the Internet. Databases are the "holy grail" of the cracker: By cracking a database, an attacker can gain access to virtually all the sensitive information on the Web site. As an administrator, you should take every precaution to make your database servers inaccessible to anything except your Web server. Of course, the database server is still at risk if the Web server is compromised, but another potential entryway is eliminated.

Use the Security Features of Your Servers

There's no such thing as "overprotection." Apache provides a number of protection features to lock resources based on hostname, network, or HTTP AUTH. Using these controls to protect against unauthorized access of critical data provides a secondary level of protection that can be effective even if your Web applications can be compromised. Likewise, MySQL should be configured to accept usernames and logins only from trusted hosts.

Keep Your CGIs Contained

No matter how much your users complain, do everything you can to keep Web applications contained to a single location. Although it's tempting to enable `ExecCGI` for your entire server, this will inevitably lead to applications being installed without your knowledge and your server being exposed to the security holes they may bring.

Explicitly Code All Paths

When coding, use absolute paths (`/Users/jray/Sites/myfiles/myfile.txt`); relative paths (`myfiles/myfile.txt`) should be avoided. If an intruder can exploit the Web application or server process to change the current working directory, he or she may be able to overwrite or read from files that should not be accessible.

Do Not Trust User Input

As seen earlier in this appendix, user input should *never* be used directly when opening a file or pipe or providing arguments to an external process. If user input *is* accepted, it should be processed and stripped of potentially harmful characters before the Web application uses it internally. Languages such as PHP make this easy by providing functions such as `escapeshellcmd()` and `escapeshellarg()`, which escape and quote strings being used as arguments or shell commands. After they are escaped, the strings cannot be used to trick external processes into running arbitrary commands. Perl scripts can be started with `#!/usr/bin/perl -T` to turn on *tainting* checks, which prevent user input from being used directly in commands that affect files or programs outside your script.

Avoid Invoking the Shell or External Processes

You've already got enough to worry about with your own application without having to deal with the possibility of executing external applications. If possible, you should avoid using functions such as `system()`, `exec()`, and the Perl/PHP `` ` ` `` backticks. Unfortunately, sometimes this isn't feasible.

If user input is used in an external process that invokes the shell, one must be sure that the input doesn't contain shell metacharacters (;, `&`, `*`, `>`, and so on). To get around this, one must either verify all user input or execute code without invoking a shell. One can use the features of `system()` and `exec()` to execute commands without the shell. For example, rather than using `system("/usr/bin/find -name $filename")`, the code should be written as `system("/usr/bin/find","-name", "$filename")`. Without having to worry about metacharacters, one can safely pass user input as an argument to external programs.

Some external commands rely on the `$PATH` environment variable to be set. Like paths, you should explicitly set any needed environment variables directly in your code.

Use Stored Procedures

When—and *if*—possible, use stored procedures for handling sensitive data. Many database servers provide access to stored procedures. A stored procedure is a function that is programmed to run on the database server and return the results as a recordset to an application. Rather than using PHP (and therefore your Web server) to handle critical calculations and risk exposing the information necessary to complete the calculations to the outside world, you can keep the information on the database server, which can perform the actions internally, then provide the final results to the Web server application.

Perform Limit Testing on All Inputs

All input should be tested at its extremes (high, low, and limit values), as performing tests on the length limits of the input (exceeding or not meeting the required lengths). For example, if a number is expected to be between 0 and 5, input should be tested at 0, 5, values above 5, and values below zero. You should also verify what will happen when inappropriate values are provided (strings rather than numbers, and so on). To avoid buffer overflows, input length testing should also be performed.

(This is largely unneeded with scripting languages such as Perl and PHP where variables are dynamically defined.)

Verify "Authoritative" File Reads and Writes

When reading from files that contain "authoritative" data (critical information that the program requires to make decisions), one should *always* verify that the file is an actual file, not a symbolic link. It's best not to trust *any* input that isn't hard coded into the application.

Do Not Rely on Web Constructs for Security

HTML and HTTP were not designed for security. Although tags exist for storing information in hidden fields (`<input type="hidden">`) and hiding passwords (`<input type="password">`), these do nothing to actually protect the information they contain. The data in a hidden field can easily be replaced with arbitrary information, and neither input type offers any *real* protection beyond simple information hiding.

Likewise, the `GET` method of passing parameters via the URL should never be used for sending critical session information because the remote user can easily edit it. Most modern languages support automatic session management, eliminating the need to manually pass data.

Test and Retest

Finally, all code should undergo a formal code review and testing process before being deployed. Regardless of how late or overbudget the testing process places the project, it is absolutely critical to fully test your code before subjecting it to the masses.

Adding and Using suEXEC

A different approach to Web development security is to allow CGIs to run as a specific user, rather than with the permissions of the server process. This is typically performed with suEXEC, an addition to Apache that must be compiled into the daemon.

On a trusted server with trusted developers, suEXEC can be a godsend—no more setting special file or folder ownerships. On a system with inexperienced Web developers, however, it can open up an entirely different class of security issues. For example, rather than needing to be aware of the permissions for a single user (www in the case of Mac OS X), an administrator must be certain that anyone using suEXEC isn't opening up his or her account to attack. Files can be written and read from anywhere the suEXEC user or group has permissions.

Using suEXEC requires a complete recompile of Apache to install the necessary components. The compilation and installation process is detailed in Chapter 15, "Web Server Security," so only the configuration process is discussed here. To add suEXEC support to Apache, use the following options with the `./configure` command:

- `--suexec-docroot=/Library/WebServer/Documents`. The document root for Apache.
- `--suexec-userdir=Sites`. The directory that individual user accounts use to serve Web documents.
- `--suexec-safepath=/usr/local/bin`. The directories from which suEXEC will allow commands to be run. You may wish to add `/usr/bin` and `/bin` to this. Separate multiple paths with the : character.
- `--suexec-uidmin=500`. The minimum user ID that suEXEC will assume.
- `--suexec-gidmin=20`. The minimum group ID that suEXEC will assume (20 is the Staff group).
- `--suexec-caller=www`. The user that will be executing the suEXEC process (www on Mac OS X).
- `--suexec-umask=077`. Sets the file creation mask suEXEC will use.
- `--suexec-logfile=/var/log/suexec_log`. Logs suEXEC executions.

After installing, you should have a new binary: `/usr/sbin/suexec`. Removing this file disables suEXEC—there is no need to change anything directly within the `/etc/httpd/httpd.conf` file or enable or disable support.

Using suEXEC

Configuring suEXEC is simple: User accounts that have ExecCGI access enabled will automatically take advantage of suEXEC; virtual hosts can specify a username and password by using the `User` and `Group` directives. The `User` directive can be given either a username or a `#` character followed by a user ID to set the user under which suEXEC CGIs will run—such as `User jray` or `User #501`. Likewise, the `Group` directive should be used to set the group name or ID for CGI execution.

For the most part, suEXEC is "install and forget." Target CGIs that are executed through Apache will be "wrapped" by suEXEC and invoked with the permissions of the user account if accessed through a "~" user site, or the user and group set within a Virtual Host. CGIs will *not* be executed the unless following criteria are met:

- The user executing the wrapper is a valid user of the system.
- The executing user is the Apache user (that is, `www`).

- The program being executed is within an Apache-accessible directory and does not contain / or .. in its name.
- The CGI target user and groups are valid on the system.
- The minimum user and group ID requirements have been met.
- The target user and group are not the superuser or superuser group, respectively.
- The target program isn't writable, nor setuid or setgid.
- The owner of the target program is the same as the target user.
- The environment can successfully be cleaned with a known safe PATH.

Additional information on suEXEC is available from `http://httpd.apache.org/docs/suexec.html`. suEXEC should not be considered a solution to Web server security problems, but a tool to help enable developers to effectively create CGIs that operate outside the normal constraints of the www user.

NOTE

An alternative (albeit less integrated, but more customizable) solution is the CGIWrap utility. For more information, visit `http://sourceforge.net/projects/cgiwrap`.

Testing for Known CGI Vulnerabilities: Whisker

If you have the joy of monitoring an ad-hoc network of servers that could potentially be running Web services (that is, any university campus), you might want to employ some automated testing for known CGI vulnerabilities. A well-known Perl tool known as Whisker makes this possible. Whisker automatically crawls a given URL and tests located CGIs against a list of known vulnerability fingerprints. It also provides information about the server itself, including the Web root options and server response banners.

To install Whisker, download, unarchive, and enter the source distribution directory. Whisker can be downloaded from `http://www.wiretrip.net/`:

```
% curl -O http://www.wiretrip.net/rfp/bins/whisker/whisker-2.1.tar.gz
% tar zxf whisker-2.1.tar.gz
% cd whisker-2.1
```

Next, install the software (as root), using `perl install.pl`. The default installation values should be fine:

```
# perl install.pl
Whisker data files will be placed in the following directory:

        /usr/local/share/whisker/

If this is OK, then type 'Y', otherwise type 'N'.

Choice [y/n]: y
A whisker symlink will be made in the following directory:

        /usr/local/bin/

If this is OK, then type 'Y', otherwise type 'N'.

Choice [y/n]: y
Installing whisker.pl...done.
Copying CHANGES...done.
Copying html.plugin...done.
Copying LW.pm...done.
Copying main.test...done.
Copying newbie.help...done.
Copying README...done.
Making whisker symlink...done.


All done installing!

To run whisker, type:

        /usr/local/bin/whisker
```

After it is installed, Whisker can be invoked (in its simplest form) with `/usr/local/bin/whisker -h <url to check>`. For example, to check for potential vulnerabilities on the machine `fusion.poisontooth.com`, I'd type:

```
# /usr/local/bin/whisker -h http://fusion.poisontooth.com
-----------------------------------------------------------------------------
Title: Notice

Whisker scans for CGIs by checking to see if the server says a particular
URL exists.  However, just because a URL exists does not necessarily mean
it is vulnerable/exploitable--the vulnerability might be limited to only a
certain version of the CGI, and the server might not be using the
```

```
vulnerable version.  There is also the case where many scripts use the
same generic CGI name (like count.cgi); in this case, the exact CGI being
used may not be the same one that contains the vulnerability.

Thus, the actual vulnerability of the CGI must be verified in order to get
a true assessment of risk.  Whisker only helps in pointing out the problem
areas.  The next step after scanning with whisker is to review each found
CGI by reviewing the reference URLs or searching for the CGI name on
SecurityFocus.com or Google.com.

---------------------------------------------------------------------------
Beginning scan against http://fusion.poisontooth.com------------------------------
---------------------------------------------
Whisker is currently crawling the website; please be patient.---------------------
------------------------------------------------------
Title: Server banner
Id: 100
Severity: Informational

The server returned the following banner:
        Microsoft-IIS/4.0

---------------------------------------------------------------------------
Title: Alternate server type
Id: 103
Severity: Informational

Testing has determined that the server may not necessarily be an 'Microsoft-IIS'
server due to it not responding correctly to certain requests.  This means
that the admin may have changed the server banner to subvert attackers.
---------------------------------------------------------------------------
Title: Server OPTIONS results
Id: 109
Severity: Informational

The server responded to an OPTIONS query with the following public methods:
OPTIONS, TRACE, GET, HEAD, POST, PUT, DELETE

---------------------------------------------------------------------------
Title: ColdFusion installed
Id: 102
Severity: Informational
```

```
Allaire/Macromedia ColdFusion was found to be installed on the server.
ColdFusion has various security problems which are not possible to scan
for.  The following CVE entries indicate potential vulnerabilities which
may exist on the server:

1999-0760       2000-0050       2000-0051
2000-0297       2000-0334       2000-0410
2000-0862       2000-1049       2000-1051
2000-1050       2001-0179

----------------------------------------------------------------------------
Title: cfmlsyntaxcheck.cfm
Id: 502
Cve: 1999-0924
Found URL: /cfdocs/cfmlsyntaxcheck.cfm

No specific information is provided for this item.

References:
http://cve.mitre.org/cgi-bin/cvename.cgi?name=1999-0924

----------------------------------------------------------------------------
Title: index.cfm
Id: 505
Bid: 1314
Cve: 2000-0538
Found URL: /cfide/administrator/index.cfm

No specific information is provided for this item.

References:
http://online.securityfocus.com/bid/1314
http://cve.mitre.org/cgi-bin/cvename.cgi?name=2000-0538

----------------------------------------------------------------------------
Title: Notable directories found
Id: 101
Severity: Informational
Found URL: /cart/
```

```
Whisker scans for a list of 'notable' directories--that is, directories
which may contain interesting information and/or CGIs. The finding of a
directory does not immediately signal a problem; rather, you should go
back and review the contents of each found URL to determine if there is
any sensitive material in those directories.
...
```

Although most of the messages that are returned are classified as informational, those that represent a potential security risk are provided with CVE IDs for easy identification and correction. A default Mac OS X Apache installation should show only a few information messages and *no* exploitable conditions.

Whisker supports a number of command-line options to alter its behavior and performance. Table C.1 documents the available Whisker options.

TABLE C.1 Whisker Command-Line Options

Option	Description
`-h` *<URL to scan>*	Set the URL of the site to be scanned.
`-a` *<user:pass>*	Provide a username and password for use when Whisker encounters HTTP AUTH protected pages.
`-P` *<proxy server>*	Send requests via the named proxy server.
`-A` *<user:pass>*	Authenticate with a proxy server using the given username and password.
`-t` *<seconds>*	Specify a timeout (in seconds) for results to be returned to Whisker.
`-I` *<mode number>*	Enable Whisker's intrusion detection system evasion. Available modes are 1 URL encoding 2 /./ directory insertion 3 premature URL ending 4 long URL 5 fake parameter 6 TAB separation (not NT/IIS) 7 case sensitivity 8 Windows delimiter 9 session splicing (slow) 0 NULL method
`-S` *<string>*	Override the server banner to force Whisker to consider a specific server type—such as `apache`—regardless of how the server presents itself.
`-G`	Force all scans on all servers (regardless of the platform).
`-l` *<output file>*	Log the output to the named file.
`-q`	Quiet mode. Results are not sent to STDOUT.
`-d` *<level to crawl>*	Set the depth of the Web server "crawl" that will take place.

TABLE C.1 Continued

Option	Description
`-c` *<crawl options>*	Change Whisker's crawl log behavior. The available crawl options are
	`d` Do not crawl site.
	`p` Take URL parameters into account when crawling.
	`h` Use HEAD requests for potential speed increase.
	`l` Raise the URL buffer limit from 1,000 to 10,000.
	`a` Do not populate SPIDER directory array.
	`c` Add form target directories to CGIBIN directory array.
	`e` Do not add .asp or .php form targets to CGIBIN dir array.
`-T` *<tweak options>*	Tweak the Whisker output. Choose from these tweak options:
	`c` Track and handle cookies as a normal client would.
	`p` Include PHTML in generic PHP extensions.
	`l` Double-scan all mixed-case URLs as lowercase.
	`d` Suppress CGI disclaimer in output report.
	`i` Suppress all interactive questions.
	`r` Invert the `-r` parameter (as in, do *not* run those tests).
	`R` Turn off libwhisker retries feature.
	`0` Use HTTP/1.0.
	`3` Report all move (3xx) responses.
	`4` Report all authentication (401) responses.
	`5` Report all failure (500) responses.
	`f` Report all form targets.
	`C` Report all cookies given during scanning.
	`A` Report everything.
	`D` Print debug output to `STDERR`.
	`T` Dump TRACK hash to `track.log` in current directory when done.
	`H` HTML format output.

TIP

If invoked without any command-line arguments, Whisker provides a text-based "wizard" for configuring a scan. For those who don't like memorizing options, this is an easy way to set up a scan.

Although Whisker can help you identify potential Web application problems and basic Web server configuration issues, it cannot diagnose internal errors in your custom-built applications. It is a useful tool—but incapable of protecting you from yourself.

Additional Resources

As Web development changes, so do the security precautions necessary to protect against attack. The rules presented here should be considered best practices and are not a replacement for programming experience. For more information on secure Web development, you may want to read through the following online resources:

- "Best Practices for Secure Web Development," Razvan Peteanu, `http://www.securitymap.net/sdm/docs/secure-programming/Secure-Web-Development.pdf`.
- "The World Wide Web Security FAQ," `http://www.w3.org/Security/Faq/www-security-faq.html`.
- "Secure CGI/API Programming," Simson Garfinkel and Gene Spafford, `http://www.w3j.com/7/s3.garfinkel.wrap.html`.
- "Writing Secure CGI Scripts," `http://hoohoo.ncsa.uiuc.edu/cgi/security.html`.
- "Hacking the Web: A Security Guide," Anne Bilodeau, `http://www.webdeveloper.com/security/security_hacking_the_web.html`.
- "Web of Security," Paul Stone, `http://www.defenselink.mil/specials/websecurity/`.
- "CGI Security Compilation," `http://bau2.uibk.ac.at/matic/cgilist.htm`.
- "CGI Security: Avoiding Common Pitfalls," `http://paulisse.discusware.com/cgi-security/`.
- "Safe CGI Programming," Paul Phillips, `http://www.improving.org/paulp/cgi-security/safe-cgi.txt`.
- "Is Your Web Server Secure?" Wallace Keith Gardner, `http://www.gt.ed.net/keith/cgi/security.html`.

Index

Symbols

Numbers

A

B

C

D

E

F

G

H

I

J – K

L

M

N

O

Q – R

T

U

V

W

X

Y – Z

Other Related Titles

PHP and MySQL Web Development
Laura Thompson, Luke Welling
0-672-31784-2
$49.99 US/$77.99 CAN

mod_perl Developer's Cookbook
Geoffrey Young, Randy Kobes, Paul Lindner
0-672-32240-4
$39.99 US/$62.99 CAN

PHP Developer's Cookbook
Sterling Hughes, Andrei Zmievski
0-672-32325-7
$39.99 US/$62.99 CAN

Apache Administrator's Handbook
Rich Bowen
0-672-32274-9
$39.99 US/$62.99 CAN

Python Developer's Handbook
Andre Lessa
0-672-31994-2
$44.99 US/$67.95 CAN

Mac OS X Unleashed, Second Edition
John Ray, William Ray
0-672-32465-2
$49.99 US/$77.99 CAN

Maximum Windows 2000 Security
Anonymous
0-672-31965-9
$49.99 US/$77.99 CAN

www.samspublishing.com

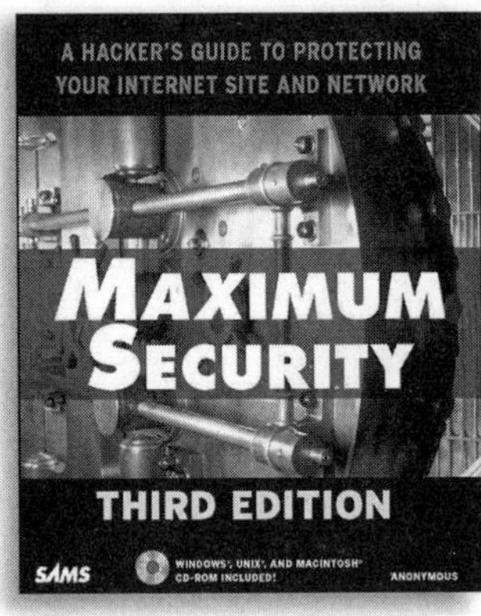

Maximum Security, Third Edition
Anonymous
0-672-31871-7
$49.99 US/$77.99 CAN

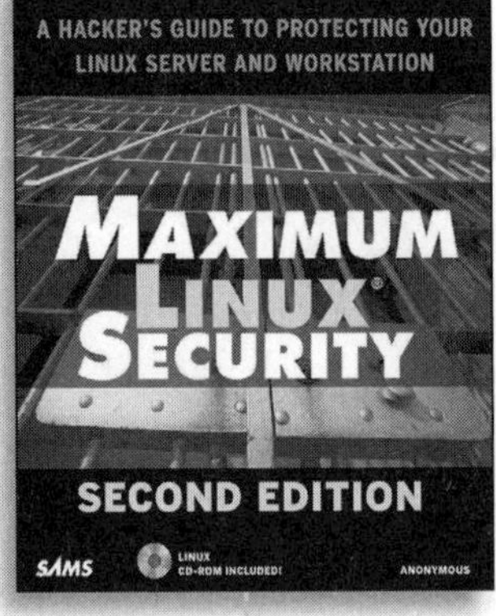

Maximum Linux Security, Second Edition
Anonymous
0-672-32134-3
$49.99 US/$77.99 CAN

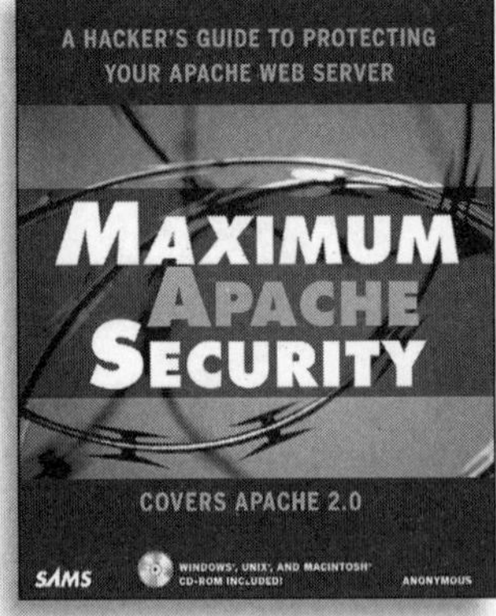

Maximum Apache Security
Anonymous
0-672-32380-x
$49.99 US/$77.99 CAN

All prices are subject to change.